Edited by
Marco Bussagli

ROME

ART & ARCHITECTURE

KÖNEMANN

Editorial Director:
Guido Ceriotti

Graphic Designer:
Gilberto Brun

Layout: Gilberto Brun
The captions were written by Robert Born in association with Delius
Publishing, Berlin and translated from German by Peter Barton in
association with Goodfellow & Egan
Translation from Italian: Janet Angelini, Paola Bortolotti, Jane Carroll,
Liz Clegg, Sharon Herson, Caroline Higgitt and Elizabeth Howard in
association with Goodfellow & Egan
Editing: Shayne Mitchell in association with Goodfellow & Egan
Typesetting: Goodfellow & Egan, Cambridge
Project Management: Jackie Dobbyne and Karen Baldwin
for Goodfellow & Egan Publishing Management, Cambridge
Project Coordination: Nadja Bremse
Assistant: Alex Morkramer
Production: Ursula Schümer
Printing and Binding: Mladinska knijga tiskarna, d.d., Ljubljana

Printed in Slovenia

ISBN 3-8290-2259-X

ROME

ART & ARCHITECTURE

Given the profusion of existent publications on Rome, it might seem superfluous to provide yet another weighty volume. However, the existing works fail to include a comprehensive panorama of the city's wonderful and incomparable artistic history, presented in a readable and attractive, yet scholarly, way.

Inevitably, writing about the art of Rome means writing about the art of the world. Rome is a unique and inimitable place, which has not only played the role of undisputed artistic catalyst, from the glories of the ancient city to the splendors of modern painting, but has been the crossroads between east and west, as well as between northern and southern Italy.

Throughout its long history, Rome has repeatedly occupied the position of artistic capital of Europe. The defining features of this extraordinary story, and the influences that determined its course, are understandable within the complete but concise picture that this book gives of the whole story, from its origins onwards, concluding with one of the most important periods, that of the School of Rome.

Written by leading scholars in their fields and painstakingly prepared over years, the book gives the reader an understanding of the process by which, through constant cultural, urban, and architectural development, the village of Romulus became successively the capital of an empire stretching across the whole Mediterranean area and beyond, the capital of the papacy, a medieval city state, the glory of the Renaissance, the cradle of the Baroque, and the birthplace of Neoclassicism. Without the art of Rome, Western civilization could not have flourished, given the fact that the city's entire history has been so closely interwoven with the history of the Western world and its artistic development.

Marco Bussagli

CONTENTS

The Fifteenth Century: the Early Renaissance

The Sixteenth Century: the Golden Age

The Rome of the Saints: the Baroque

The Eighteenth Century

The Nineteenth and Twentieth Centuries

The Development of the City of Rome

The Origins of the City

"No one could have succeeded better than Romulus, who, with divine foresight, made use of all the advantages offered by the sea, while at the same time avoiding its disadvantages by situating the city on the banks of a river which flows all year round and along an unchanging course into a broad estuary. This meant that the city's needs could be brought in and its surpluses exported by sea. At the same time, thanks to the river, it could procure all that was necessary for sustenance and for civil life not only from across the sea, but also from the hinterland. It seems, therefore, that Romulus foresaw that the city would one day be the center of the greatest of all empires".

This passage from Cicero, in *De republica* (II, 10), shows that the significance of Rome's topographical features was clearly understood by writers in ancient times, even if their descriptions of these features—and the moral stress they applied in interpreting them—can hardly be accepted today. Rome's location determined its fortunes from the very beginning, as archaeological discoveries made during recent decades have repeatedly demonstrated.

Imperial replica of a bust of Marcus Tullius Cicero. Rome, Capitoline Museums, Galleria dei Filosofi.

The Tiber Island is accessible by two bridges – the Pons Cestius, which connects it with the right bank, and the Pons Fabricius, Rome's oldest bridge. The Pons Fabricius, seen here on the right, was built in 62 BC by Lucius Fabricius, the official responsible for public roads.

The Forum Boarium

As far as the history of the earliest development of the city is concerned, the key area was the Forum Boarium (the Cattle Market). Here, just downstream from the Tiber Island, the conditions existed for major urban development. Anyone traveling from the coast of Etruria could cross the Tiber at this point and continue towards southern Latium and Campania. The Forum Boarium was also a suitable place for boats to unload after sailing up the Tiber from the sea or downstream from its upper reaches. The discovery of Bronze Age pottery in this area is proof that groups of pastoral people were living here at an early date. They had probably come from Sabine territory in search of winter pasture and the precious salt from the marshes around the mouth of the Tiber. Fragments of Greek pottery from the middle of the eighth century BC show that Greek traders were already visiting the area just at the time when, according to tradition, Rome was founded.

Roman road in Ostia Antica; this colony was probably founded in the final years of the fifth century BC and grew rapidly from the second century BC due to its important function as Rome's chief port.

The historical evidence is reflected in myth: the inscription recording the dedication by Hercules of the Ara Maxima (Great Altar) in the Forum Boarium describes Hercules' sojourn there with the herds of cattle he had captured from the monster Geryon, the theft of some of his cattle in turn by Cacus, and his strangling of Cacus. These legends illustrate the historical function of the Forum Boarium as a market place for both live-stock and salt, operating under the protection of the great hero. Control of so strategically and economically important a site would have been a decisive factor in the emergence of the city.

Rome as a Crossroads

As a frontier settlement at a crossroads between different cultures, contact between various groups of people was to be of great significance throughout Rome's history. Here too, reality was reflected in mythology. Rome's frontier status was portrayed as having developed out of an association on equal terms between Romans and Sabines, with the subsequent addition of other ethnic groups, beginning with the Etruscans. Rome stood on the edge of ancient Latium, whose physical and sacred center was the Alban Hills. The Tiber separated the territories of Latium and Etruria. The most perceptive ancient historians, including Claudius, who was emperor, historian, and antiquarian, were well aware of the significance of this contact between various peoples. In a discourse known in its original version from a bronze inscription in Lyons, Claudius referred to these contacts with peoples of other tribes, stressing that an openness to ethnic influences from outside was the reason behind Rome's power and success.

It is no coincidence, therefore, that the city's earliest roads seem to have converged on the river port and ford across the Tiber, in the area of the Forum Boarium. This is particularly true of the Via Salaria, the ancient route between Sabine territory and the mouth of the Tiber. Its name refers to its main function—the transport of that precious commodity, salt, into the interior. On the north bank of the Tiber, the road from the cities of southern Etruria, later known as the Via Aurelia, led to the Tiber crossing. Here the Pons Sublicius, the first bridge, was built out of wood and, according to tradition, by the fourth king of Rome, Ancus Marcius. Legend had it that this was the route taken by Tarquin the Elder (Tarquinius Priscus, traditionally 616–579 BC) when he traveled from his native Tarquinii in Etruria to seek fame and fortune, eventually becoming king of Rome.

On the south bank, two major roads from the south approached the valley which would later be occupied by the Circus Maximus. These were the future Via Latina and Via Appia, which linked Rome with the coastal plain and the inland plain of southern Latium and, beyond, with Campania. Other roads led in the direction of Veii and the port of Ostia.

The Temples of Fortune, Mater Matuta, Diana, and Ceres

The Forum Boarium, where so many important routes met, first began to be built during the sixth century BC, with the construction of a number of major temple complexes. It is possible to gain a clear picture of these temples, which were the nucleus of the future city, thanks to the excavations which have been carried out around the church of Sant'Omobono. Two temples discovered here, dedicated to the cults of Fortune (*Fortuna*) and of Mater Matuta (a goddess of growth), are attributable to the penultimate king of Rome, Servius Tullius (traditionally 578–535 BC). The earliest buildings on this site have been dated to between 580 and 570 BC, and thus to the reign of Servius Tullius, proving that the traditional date of the foundation of the temples was correct. The Ara Maxima must also have been created at around the same time. Alongside the monument, there was probably a temple containing a cult statue, perhaps made by the same sculptor who created the image of Jupiter on the Capitoline Hill, Vulca of Veii.

According to one plausible theory, Servius Tullius was also responsible for the magnificent temple to Diana on the Aventine Hill, inspired by the great sanctuary of Diana at Ephesus. Intended as a federal sanctuary for use by the Latins, it was therefore sited outside the *pomerium* of the city (the sacred boundary where soldiers had to lay aside their weapons). A few decades later, at the foot of the hill, close to the Circus Maximus, the Temple of Ceres, Liber Pater, and Libera (the gods of fertility) was erected, the focal point for the plebeians (*plebs*), who in the early years of the Republic were beginning their long struggle with the patricians for equal political rights.

By the start of the Republic, the centuries-long process of creating the city of Rome was already completed. Citizenship was barred to outsiders. The dominant class, the patricians, had closed ranks and had excluded large sections of the population from political rights, in particular the mass of more recent immigrants, who had coalesced into a large following under the patronage of the last king. Pushed out to the periphery of the city, this class was to be instrumental in the birth of the plebians. They chose to base themselves in the area of the Forum Boarium and the

Aventine Hill, an area of great importance economically but marginal in political terms.

The Forum and Comitium

Alongside this original nucleus, but away from the river and further inside the city, a second area had been developing, the Forum. This became, and remained, the political and religious center of the city. Around 600 BC, the Forum started to acquire the status of the administrative

Reconstruction of the Capitoline complex (J. Carlu, 1924). The appearance of the Capitol, one of the traditional seven hills of Rome, was essentially formed by the monumental structures erected by the Etruscan kings in the sixth century BC, such as the Temple of the Capitoline Triad (Jupiter, Juno, and Minerva). Paris, École Nationale Supérieure des Beaux Arts.

focus of the city. Archaeological discoveries have shown that the area was first paved during this period, which corresponds to what was traditionally the reign of Tarquin the Elder. It seems that the Velabrum, the valley lying between the Capitoline Hill and the Palatine, until then a marshy district used only for burials, was reclaimed through the construction of the Cloaca Maxima (the Great Drain). The works involved draining the Velabrum by an open watercourse

that crossed the valley of the Forum, which now could be used as the city's main square. Rows of shops, or *tabernae*, for the sale of foodstuffs, subsequently known as *tabernae veteres* (old) and *tabernae novae* (new), were probably built at this time on two sides of the square.

The earliest parts of the Comitium at the north end of the square, the area used for political and judicial activity, began to take shape. Archaeology has revealed that the lowest, and thus original, pavement of the Comitium is late seventh century BC and thus contemporary with the Forum Boarium. There is also a considerable amount of building work dating from just before the mid-sixth century. This included the erection of a cult *sacellum*, consisting of an altar dedicated to Vulcan and an inscribed stone, the celebrated *Lapis Niger* (Black Stone). This, the earliest known example of the Latin language, sets out rules governing sacrifices connected with the king's activities in the Comitium. The use of writing so early confirms that there was already a well-defined area intended specifically for the conduct of public judicial and religious affairs; it demonstrates that a concept of the state already existed.

The etymology of the word *comitium* is clear: "going together," in other words, an assembly. The word is traditionally linked with the meeting between Romulus and Titus Tatius at the end of hostilities following the seizure of the Sabine women, which was believed to have given rise to a new, wider community, uniting the two peoples. Once again, myth is used as a description of how a public space came into being.

Of key importance in the development of the Forum was the foundation by Tarquin the Elder of the great temple of Jupiter Optimus Maximus, Juno, and Minerva on the Capitoline Hill, which was to become the principal political sanctuary. Here, military ceremonies were carried out and international treaties kept. A defined urban territory was created in two closely-linked operations. The first was the designation of a central area to be used for civic, political, and judicial activity.

City Walls and Boundaries

The second was the delineation of concentric external boundaries: the symbolic city enclosure, the *pomerium*, the line marking the First Mile, separating civilian jurisdiction from military jurisdiction, and the territorial boundary. These physical boundaries were given sacred significance by cult sites marking them, such as the *mundus* (ritual pit) in the Forum, the initial fosse created by Romulus when he plowed the furrow indicating the *pomerium*, and a series of shrines along the First Mile and the territorial boundary (*ager Romanus antiquus*).

View of the Temple of Saturn. The original building of this Ionic temple on the Forum was erected at the beginning of the fifth century BC. Due to its significance as a symbol of the Golden Age, when Saturn reigned on the Capitol, this cultic structure was restored by Lucius Munatius Plancus in 42 BC, and again, following a fire, in AD 283.

The construction of the first city wall represented in physical form these symbolic boundaries which delineated the city. Archaeological investigation, confirming tradition, suggests that the first wall erected round the four hills dated from the sixth century BC and the time of Servius Tullius. It has been demonstrated that the so-called Republican walls built of square blocks of tufa from Grotta Oscura during the large-scale reconstruction that followed the capture of Veii in 396 BC by the Romans and the sack of Rome by the Gauls in 390 BC, replaced an earlier boundary made of local tufa blocks, which was on virtually the same line as the later wall. Recent excavations show that walls were built at this time around all the major cities of Latium. It is unlikely that Rome, indisputably the most important center of the region, would have been left without walls.

The length of these ancient Republican walls encircling the city is impressive: seven miles, enclosing an area of about 1,060 acres. The four urban districts created by the sixth-century wall had covered about 720 acres. (The discrepancy arises from the uninhabited districts within the walls and because large sectors of the city, such as the Aventine Hill and the Capitoline Hill, lay outside the *pomerium*, although not outside the enclosure wall.) It is obvious that a wall of this length could not be defended by a meager population, as is believed to have been the case at this time, and its strategic value would have been negated by lack of manpower. Moreover, the massive task of building the wall would have required adequate labor. This would certainly have been drawn from the city's own inhabitants who, according to ancient practice, were obliged to provide unpaid labor.

The Republic

In terms of building activity, the early years of the Republic show no sign of a break with the preceding period and seem instead to have been a phase of expansion. In addition to the new buildings connected with the emergence of the plebeians, such as the temples of Ceres and Mercury, others were being erected by the patrician class. These seem to have been concentrated in the Forum, such as the two large temples of Saturn, and of Castor and Pollux. All these cults were characterized by strong Hellenic influence. We know that there was direct Greek involvement: the two architects responsible for the Temple of Ceres, Damophilos and Gorgasos, were Greek, perhaps from the Greek colony of Syracuse in Sicily.

This phase of intense building activity was followed by a period of decline in construction, with only the construction of the Temple of Apollo (once again a Greek divinity) in the Campus Martius, between 433 and 431 BC. It was an age of political and social upheaval, marked by the struggle between patricians and plebeians, and by the continual military clashes with Sabelli peoples such as the Volsci, who lived in southern Latium. That there were also severe economic problems caused by successive famines which led to epidemics, is confirmed by archaeological evidence of a decline in international trade.

The Fourth Century: The Expansion of Rome

This period of crisis and of profound structural change continued until the beginning of the fourth century. The changes were linked to a number of events: the conquest of Veii (396 BC), after which Rome's territory was practically doubled in size; the resolution of the conflict between patricians and plebeians with the Licinian–Sextian laws (Lex Licinia Sextiae), which introduced political equality between the two classes; and, finally, the absorption of the Latins as a result of the war in Latium and the dissolution of the Latin League (338 BC). These events, and the consequent structural changes, were the springboard for the dynamic development of Rome which took place during the following period, and which within a few decades were to lead to the conquest of the entire Italian peninsula.

The sack of the city by the Gauls in 390 BC was an isolated event, without lasting consequences. Nevertheless, it had a profound effect on Roman collective memory and led to the last

The remaining three columns of the Temple of the Dioscuri on the Forum Romanum, built on a high podium. Constructed by the dictator Aulus Postumius Albinus to honor an oath, the temple was meant to serve as a memorial to the twins Castor and Pollux who, in an apparition, had prophesied a Roman victory over the Latins and their ally Tarquinius Superbus in the battle of Lacus Regillus in 499 BC.

great myth of the city: the belief that all its most ancient records had been destroyed during the capture of the city and that this was the explanation for the meager knowledge of the early history of Rome. Archaeological excavations have shown that the damage caused was less severe than previously believed. The episode was blamed for the chaotic urban development in the later centuries of the Republic. The most complete account of this redevelopment is found in Livy (V, 45; 2–5):

"The rebuilding of the city was carried out in a disorganized manner. The state provided the tiles and authorized the quarrying of stone and cutting of timber everywhere, provided there was a guarantee that construction work would be completed within the year. In the resulting haste, no care was taken to lay the streets along straight lines, because the construction was being carried out in an open space, without any account being taken of anyone's property boundaries. This is the reason why the ancient sewers, which previously ran across public land, now often pass beneath private houses, and therefore the city seems to be the result more of chaotic appropriation than of rational subdivision."

That Livy was describing the Rome of his own time is apparent from two other passages. Cicero, comparing Rome's confused urban development with the orderly example of the town of Capua, concluded (in *De lege agraria*, II, 96): "Rome is built on the tops of hills and in the bottom of valleys, almost suspended above the tiered storeys of its apartment blocks, with cramped streets and narrow alleys." Tacitus, referring to the Great Fire of AD 64, during Nero's reign, describes the state of the city (*Annals*, XV, 43):

"The part of the city spared by the Golden House [the Domus Aurea, Nero's new palace] was not rebuilt in a chaotic manner without any order, as had happened after the city was sacked

Terracotta head of the god Hermes. Fragment of an acroterion from the Portonaccio Temple in Veii, late sixth century BC. Rome, Museo Nazionale Etrusco di Villa Giulia.

Relief depicting a shop in which textiles and cushions are for sale. Rome, Museo Nazionale Romano in the Palazzo Massimo alle Terme.

in similar cases, such as Athens, the lack of organization confirms the uninterrupted continuity of urban development and consequently undermines the traditional account of the effects of the sack of Rome by the Gauls. Continuity is evident too in the city walls, which were almost entirely rebuilt during those years, along a course which, with very few exceptions, follows that of the original sixth-century walls. This suggests that after the crisis of the fifth century the city had recovered, in both economic and technological terms, to its earlier level.

The resources that the city was able to mobilize at this time suggest a city experiencing a period of strong economic and demographic expansion, as Rome certainly was at the beginning of the fourth century, following the conquest of Veii, which resulted in a more or less doubling of Rome's territory and of available resources in general (including people).

Social and Political Transformation

Over the following decades, with the definitive admission of the plebeians to political power, the centuries-long conflict between the two classes came to an end. This led to the formation of a broader ruling class, the patrician–plebeian nobility, with a growth in the size of the citizenship similar to that seen in the rest of Italy, which during those years was experiencing far-reaching changes in the social structure. The old patterns of traditional aristocratic society collapsed under the combined pressure of new economic practices—the use of money was just beginning in Rome, for example—and of the new social classes.

The repercussions of these great changes were also felt culturally. A marked homogeneity characterizes this period, particularly during the most active and creative years, that is between about 330 and 270 BC. Later, when the Republic encountered problems, this era was to be idealized.

The conditions that led to the conquest of the rest of Italy by Rome were also established during this period. First and foremost was population growth and the resulting internal tensions within the structure of the Roman state. Land hunger in the case of the Roman plebeians and the imperial ambitions of the ruling classes combined to set in motion the process of conquest of the whole peninsula. Following the dissolution of the Latin League in 338 BC, the number of colonies continued to grow, as did the allocation of individual land lots, which became steadily larger in area and ever more distant from Rome.

by the Gauls, but was given accurately measured districts, with wide streets; the height of buildings was meticulously specified, new squares were opened up, with porticos to protect the facades of the apartment houses... However, some are of the opinion that the previous arrangement of streets and houses in Rome had been more salubrious, because the narrowness of the streets and the height of the houses prevented the heat of the sun from penetrating."

Tacitus repeated, then, the legend that the chaotic urban development of Rome in the last centuries of the Republic was a consequence of the exceptional situation following the destruction of 390 BC. However, this explanation is unsatisfactory. As events after the Great Fire of AD 64 demonstrated, if Rome really had been razed to the point that property boundaries disappeared totally (in itself highly unlikely), the outcome would have been the opposite of disorganized. It seems clear that reconstruction was carried out in the early part of the fourth century BC, starting from scratch and in accordance with an appropriate master plan, for a number of reasons including the specific purpose of redefining property boundaries. We know that in similar situations in Latin colonies founded in those years (such as Norba), town plans on a regular grid pattern, like those for Greek colonies, were adopted.

The confused appearance of Rome in the late Republican era demonstrates the opposite. As

Public Space

Apart from the city walls, very little is known about the architecture of Rome during these years. Much was obliterated by subsequent building during the late Republican and the Imperial periods. The small amount of information available relates to public areas, in particular to the Forum. The Comitium, which had remained substantially unchanged from its archaic form, was altered for the first time in 338 BC, when the orators' platform was adorned with the *rostra*, or metal prows, of ships captured at the battle of Antium (Anzio) in 338 BC, resulting in the use of the name *rostra* for an orators' platform.

A second and more radical transformation took place in the middle of the third century BC, during the First Punic War, when a circular staircase, based on the Greek *ekklesiasterion* (seat of the assembly), was introduced. The model was subsequently copied in all Roman colonies.

In addition to these operations, the buildings around the Forum were renovated in 318 BC by the censor Gaius Maenius. The long sides of the square were remodeled, the old booths built mostly of wood were replaced by new, stone-built *tabernae* (shops and taverns). These had an upper story, with projecting balconies (called *maeniana* after their inventor). The premises of the money-changers (*argentarii*) were established here, testimony to the economic transformation of Roman society in those years. At the same time, the food market was relocated behind the Forum, further to the north, with a new type of building, the provision market (*macellum*). All this reveals a steady trend towards specialization in the use of public space, the consequence of increasingly complex social organization.

Similar transformations were occurring in other public spaces, such as the Forum Boarium, where the Temples of Fortune and Mater Matuta, and the Temple of Portunus (the deity protecting doors)

Obverse and reverse of a silver drachma (mid-third century BC). The reverse depicts the mythical founders of Rome, Romulus and Remus, being suckled by a she-wolf. Rome, Museo Nazionale Romano in the Palazzo Massimo alle Terme.

Fragment of a relief depicting money changers. In the course of the ambitious rebuilding of the Forum at the end of the fourth century BC the stalls of the money changers (*argentarii*) were erected on the longitudinal axis of the square. Rome, Museo Nazionale Romano in the Palazzo Massimo alle Terme.

were rebuilt in the new architectural style, entirely of stone. A vast area of the city, which stretched from the Palatine Hill to the Capitoline and the Quirinal Hills, was now undergoing change, with a large number of new buildings going up, particularly temples. These, mostly erected by victorious generals as thanks for victory, were the urban reflection of military conquests which by now were taking place all over the peninsula.

Private Building

With regard to private building, recent excavations on the northern slopes of the Palatine Hill have revealed the remains of a number of dwellings from the fourth century BC, built over archaic houses of the sixth century. These are of a considerable size, with ridge-roofed atriums.

houses of the wealthiest members of the aristocracy were still concentrated in this district, as were the palaces of the Imperial era.

In contrast to this category of housing, which became ever more grand and luxurious, were the dwellings in the crowded Quirinal, Esquiline, and Celio districts, built for the ordinary population, which was growing steadily. Unfortunately, almost nothing is known about these areas except from later descriptions, written in the age of Cicero, in the first century BC. These refer to a late stage in the urbanization process, when Rome had become the largest city in the ancient world.

The last two centuries of the Republic coincided, with the culmination of Rome's territorial conquests and with the period of most profound change in the social and economic structures of Italy. Wealth and political power became concentrated in the hands of a small

View of the Portunus Temple and the church of Santa Maria in Cosmedin. The antique building famous today as the Temple of Fortuna Virlis served as the cult site for the goddess of harbours and moorings. It was constructed on the former Forum Boarium to protect the nearby harbor on the Tiber, close to the Pons Aemilius (today the Ponte Rotto).

They must have belonged to members of the senatorial aristocracy, anxious to establish themselves in the most prestigious district, which, being close to the Forum, was also convenient for the conduct of political business. The excavations demonstrated that the most desired residential area remained unchanged from archaic times to the late Republican period, when the

aristocracy, while there was an ever growing urban population for the ruling classes to control. These new social classes were formed as a result of the impoverishment of the peasantry and the steady disappearance of small farms, replaced by large estates run with slave labor. The inexorable growth of the urban population led to the development of vast new housing

The sacred sites on the Largo Argentina are the most important group of Republican cult structures which survive in Rome. The oldest site in the Area Sacra was probably dedicated to the Italian goddess Feronia, whose cult was introduced into the city in 290 BC. The most recent building is the round temple for the Fortuna Huiusce Dieie (the Goddess of Everyday Luck), built in 102 BC.

districts, with speculative building of houses of several stories, which were regularly damaged by collapses or fire. At the same time, huge infrastructure schemes, from aqueducts to riverside warehouses, had to be undertaken, all essential for the survival of a population that was only partly engaged in the production of goods and services.

Monumental Rome: Temples and Porticos

As well as major infrastructure schemes, there was a growing number of impressive new public buildings, which were to turn Rome into a capital comparable to the great cities of the

The remains of the Basilica Julia on the Forum Romanum. This spacious building took up the entire area between the Temple of Saturn and the Temple of the Dioscuri.

OPPOSITE:
In the foreground are the three remaining columns of the Temple of Apollo which was situated in front of the Theater of Marcellus. Dedicated in 431 BC to the Greek god Apollo Medicus, the temple later came to be known as the Apollo Sosianus, in reference to Caius Sosius who rebuilt it in 34 BC

Begun by Caesar and completed by Augustus, the Theater of Marcellus was dedicated to Marcellus, Augustus' nephew and heir, in 13 bc, the year of his premature death.

Hellenic world. The new monumental quarter rising in the Campus Martius, in the loop of the Tiber river north of the Capitoline Hill, was ideal for the unhindered development of new urban planning schemes based on Hellenic models.

The area to the south of the Campus Martius, around the Circus Flaminius, was the starting point for triumphal processions, celebrating the military successes of the leading representatives of the senatorial aristocracy. It was here that, from the beginning of the second century BC, a series of temples and monumental porticos began to be built around the Circus, eventually forming an almost unbroken circle around it. It was not until later that a similar level of development took place in the central section of the Campus Martius, where the edifices designated for political and institutional activity, such as the census and elections, were concentrated. The most

imposing work was that created by Pompey the Great between 61 and 55 BC. The Pompey's theater and portico remained for years the most grandiose complex of buildings in the city.

Julius Caesar

Pompey's theatre and portico was rivaled by Julius Caesar's project, which in its final years assumed proportions that bordered on megalomania. The scheme envisaged the diversion of the Tiber river, removing altogether the great loop with Campus Martius on one side and the Vatican Hill on the other. In the middle of this level area of land was to have been an imposing temple of Mars, while on its east, at the foot of the Capitoline Hill, there was to be a theater of comparable magnificence. Caesar's violent death cut short his grandiose project before it was completed. The theater was eventually realized, but on a smaller scale, by Augustus, his successor (63 BC–AD 14) who called it the theater of Marcellus after his nephew.

The old public district of the city also saw radical change in this period. Archeological studies of the Forum have made it possible to partially reconstruct the transformations made to the square between the beginning of the second century BC and Augustus' era, at the end of the first century BC. The purpose of these changes was to adapt the Forum to its new function as the administrative and political center of a vast empire that extended throughout the Mediterranean.

The ancient Comitium, now totally inadequate for current needs, particularly those relating to judicial affairs, was gradually replaced by other buildings at various points in the Forum and was eventually demolished by Julius Caesar. Around the square rose the great basilicas (Porcia, Emilia, and Sempronia), public buildings for law courts, as well as for financial and banking activities. For the first time in its history the Forum took on a monumental appearance. The complex history of its development, however, meant that it lacked perfect architectural unity. Despite later changes introduced in the Imperial Age, it largely retained this appearance right to the end.

At the same time the Capitoline Hill was also acquiring a more monumental appearance. The real novelty in this area was, once again, provided by Julius Caesar's building schemes. These involved a complete reorganization, opening the way for the buildings that were to be erected in the Imperial era. The projects carried out in the old Forum were far from marginal. They included the demolition of the Comitium, with the rebuilding on a new site of the Curia (Senate House) and the Rostra, and the building of the imposing new Basilica Julia.

Marble portrait of Caesar. Vatican City,
Vatican Museums.

The Forum of Caesar

On an even larger scale was a new Forum, the Forum of Caesar, begun in 54 BC and completed in 46 BC. It became the model for future imperial fora. The characteristics of the new structure were revolutionary compared with the old Republican model. The ancient headquarters of the Senate, the Curia, was relocated and given a different orientation, the old Curia being turned into a mere appendage of the new Forum. With the addition of the Temple of Venus Genetrix (the Universal Mother), the new Forum assumed the character of a square designed for ceremonies. This is clearly illustrated by an episode narrated by the historian Suetonius, who describes Julius Caesar seated majestically like a priest in the center of the dais of the Temple of Venus Genetrix to receive the Senate and refusing to stand up before the venerable assembly, according to custom. The Senate's subordination to the new dynasty could not have been more clearly demonstrated.

Rome of the Emperors

It is generally felt that the urban development policies of Augustus were markedly different from those of Caesar, in that he eschewed grandiose schemes which were Hellenic in inspiration, with potentially monarchical connotations, and respected the republican tradition, if only in formal terms. Though this view is based on historical fact, it relates only to the period after the Augustinian principate was fully formalized. As a young man, Octavian, as he still was called (the Senate gave him the title "Augustus," meaning revered, in 26 BC), was closer to Caesar than might be imagined. During this time his building and urban development projects mirrored the marked oscillations that characterized his politics between 44 BC and 27 BC.

Augustus and Campus Martius

Again the key site is Campus Martius, the trial ground for experiments, which illustrates this continuity between Julius Caesar and Augustus. For example, members of the Triumvirate (the ruling group of three) continued Caesar's building works at the Saepta (a permanent enclosure used for voting in elections) and erected a temple dedicated to the Egyptian divinities Isis and Serapis, which had been part of Caesar's project.

After the conquest of Egypt in 30 BC, Octavian launched an ambitious program that was to affect the appearance of the Campus Martius right up to the end of the Imperial Age. This program included the construction of his own mausoleum (the Mausoleum of Augustus, probably inspired by the tomb of Alexander) and the Pantheon (later rebuilt as the existing Pantheon), dedicated to all the gods, a dynastic cult sanctuary based on the Hellenic model as its name indicates. Dedicated to the twelve heavenly divinities, the Pantheon also celebrated the dynasty, which was to be worshipped together alongside them like a god.

Urban Reorganization

During the middle period of his rule, Augustus devoted himself to a major reorganization of the city, the overall structure of which was to survive, essentially unaltered, until the end of the Empire. The ancient city of the age of Servius, which was divided into four districts, was radically transformed with a new division into fourteen districts, or regions (*regiones*), including eight in the area outside the walls. These in turn were divided into wards (*vici*). The scheme was begun in 12 BC when Augustus assumed the role of Pontifex Maximus (head of the college of priests and thus head of Roman religion) and was completed by 7 BC.

Control of the urban zone, despite being formally entrusted to senatorial magistrates, passed firmly into the hands of the emperor, through the encouragement of the cult of the *Lares compitales* (deities of crossroads) and of the *Genius* (spirit) of Augustus. The cult was supervised in each of the wards by special sacerdotal corporations of freedmen, who also served as the ward magistrates. By this means, the ancient cult of the Lares (guardians of crossings of all kinds, including thresholds and boundaries) was linked to the cult of the Emperor and his dynasty. In this way, political and social control of the urban populace was ensured through religion.

Also part of this scheme was a series of public works, executed partly by Augustus, partly by his successor Tiberius (AD 14–37), and partly by the surviving members of the senatorial aristocracy. Augustus' spiritual testament—the *Res Gestae*, or summary of his life, inscribed on two bronze plaques beside his Mausoleum— states that in the year 29 BC alone eighty-two temples were restored in Rome. This was the beginning of the "Rome of marble" which Augustus claimed to have left in place of the brick-built Rome he had found. The great quarries at Luni, the future Carrara marble quarries, were opened specifically for the creation of this Rome of marble.

Marble portrait of Octavianus Augustus. Rome, Capitoline Museums, Sala degli Imperatori.

Head of Mars Ultor, to which an upper body clad in armour was added in the sixteenth century. This head is thought to be an early second-century AD replica of a former cult image in the Augustinian Temple of Mars Ultor.

Temple of Mars Ultor (the "avenger"). Of the eight columns of Carrara marble on the sides of the temple, only three remain. The construction of the Forum and this temple are the result of a pledge made by Augustus before the battle of Philippi, in which Brutus and Cassius, two of Caesar's assassins, both met their ends.

Augustan Patronage

One of the most important building projects of the Augustan age was the Forum of Augustus. This was an extension of Caesar's plan to increase the size of the Republican square, with the Temple of Mars the Avenger (Mars Ultor), a reminder of the revenge carried out against the assassins of Julius Caesar at the battle of Philippi, at which they were defeated. The complex of buildings, as well as being used for trials and for the conduct of financial business, assumed the symbolic function of the focus of the emperor's military power. Military trophies were to be deposited here, starting with the standards of Crassus, from the Parthian war, testifying to the emperor's triumphs in all directions.

Members of Augustus' family were also responsible for a number of buildings, including the Theater of Marcellus, and the Porticos of Octavia and Livia, built with money from the emperor's private funds. Initially, victorious generals were also involved in the rebuilding of the city, with the construction or reconstruction of edifices in their name, including temples, porticos, and buildings for the presentation of spectacles. As well as Agrippa's building activity, there was also the Hall of Liberty (*Atrium Libertatis*, the office of the censors) of Asinius Pollio, the Theater of Balbus, and the amphitheater of T. Statilius Taurus, the first in Rome to be built of stone.

Tiberius, Caligula, and Claudius

Augustus' successors generally followed his example with regard to building schemes. Tiberius aimed, above all, at an efficient administration, devoting himself to the economic recovery of the state and disliking prestigious construction projects. His activity in the public sector was limited to the creation of the Temple of Augustus behind the Basilica Julia, in addition to a series of restoration projects, some of a utilitarian nature, such as the barracks of the Praetorian (imperial) Guard, the *Castra Praetoria*.

In the reign of Caligula (AD 37–41) the trend must have been completely the opposite, though it is difficult to assess his building achievement because of the *damnatio memoriae* (a decision by the Senate that the memory of a condemned man must not be perpetuated and that his name must be erased from inscriptions) made against Caligula, and the destruction of a large part of his works by his successors. It is clear, though, that he tried to construct a large amphitheater in the Campus Martius (demolished by Claudius) and that he undertook a large-scale project for an imposing residence on the north side of the Palatine Hill.

Of much greater importance—and much better preserved—are the projects undertaken by Claudius (AD 41–54). These particularly concerned schemes for the public benefit, such as the magnificent aqueducts of the New Anio and the Claudia, whose remains can still be seen in the Roman Campagna (the area around Rome). Claudius' traditional leanings are evident in operations such as the enlargement of the *pomerium*, which must have been linked to extensive urban development works,

Portrait of Claudius on a Roman coin. Tiberius Drusus Claudius (born 10 BC), was declared emperor by the Praetorian Guard after the murder of his nephew Caligula in AD 41. After marrying Agrippina and adopting the young Nero, Claudius died in AD 54, probably from poison administered by his wife.

particularly in the residential quarters, about which nothing is known.

Nero

A radical change in the city's urban development was brought about by the great fire of

The impressive remains of aqueducts built under Claudius are today still dominant elements in the landscape of the Roman Campagna.

Portrait of Nero, the last of the Julio-Claudian dynasty founded by Octavianus Augustus. Rome, Capitoline Museums, Sala degli Imperatori.

OPPOSITE:
The obverse of the coin shows a portrait of Nero, who was born in AD 37 and reigned as emperor from AD 54 to 68. In AD 64 a great fire destroyed much of Rome. Nero, whom the public suspected of deliberately starting the fire, used the event as an excuse to persecute Christians. He also exploited the situation to erect a villa complex of megalomaniac proportions: the famous Golden House. The reverse side depicts the helmeted goddess Roma seated on a captured throne; the figure of Victory rises from her right hand, while her left hand, resting on a shield, holds a short sword.

AD 64 in the time of Nero (ad 54–68), one of the most tragic, as well as the most famous, episodes in the history of Imperial Rome. Tacitus recorded that the fire completely destroyed three of the fourteen urban districts, or regions, and caused severe damage to another seven. Only four were left unscathed. Nero's construction projects included the great villa planned to rise from the city's ashes, the Domus Aurea (Golden House), and in particular his radical urban redevelopment scheme, the *nova urbs* (new city), started during the last few years of his life and continued by the subsequent Flavian emperors. A description of this project was recorded by Tacitus, who was an eyewitness to its last phase (*Annals*, XV, 42 ff.):

"Nero made use of the ruins of his fatherland to build for himself a palace, in which the greatest marvels are not so much the gold and precious stones, which by now had become common displays of luxury, but rather its meadows and lakes, its expanses of lonely woodland in one part, and open spaces and vistas in another. All this was the work of two architects and

engineers, Severus and Celer... Nero promised to hand [the new porticos in front of residential blocks in the city] over to the owners, after having had them built at his own expense and having had the squares cleared up. He also offered rewards, differentiated according to individuals' social class and financial means, and fixed a time limit within which the apartment blocks had to be complete in order to qualify for prizes. He arranged for the rubble to be dumped in the marshes around Ostia and ordered that ships bringing grain up the Tiber make the return journey loaded with rubble. He wanted buildings to be partly constructed not with timber but with stone from Gabii and Albano, because it resists fire. He placed guards on watch to ensure that water that had been illegally diverted by private individuals should be available more abundantly and in more places, to the benefit of all, and he arranged for fire-fighting equipment to be kept in public areas, and for each building to be contained within its own walls, with no party walls between buildings. All these measures, welcomed for their usefulness, also added ornament and dignity to the new city."

This description gives a clear idea of urban planning at the height of the Imperial era. Although Rome's eventful history means that little has been preserved of urban structures dating from after Nero, a good understanding of them can be gained from the excavated areas of the Roman port city of Ostia, at the mouth of the Tiber, which offer a reasonably precise image of the appearance of Imperial Rome.

Despite the precautions taken by planners in the age of Nero, disasters still occurred, from the fire that destroyed much of the Capitoline Hill in AD 69 to the one that razed the entire Campus Martius to the ground in the time of Titus, and yet another fire at the newly rebuilt Capitoline Hill, in AD 80. The Flavian emperors carried out extensive reconstruction work following these fires, but their main achievement was the creation of a vast complex of public works that was to completely alter Nero's layout of the city center.

The Flavian Emperors

The Flavian emperors were of relatively modest birth. Unlike the Julio-Claudian emperors before them, they had no aristocratic antecedents and wanted to be seen as the bringers of ancient Republican values. They were opposed to the sweeping Hellenization that had been the dominant trend during Nero's rule, along with its political and ideological corollaries such as the concept of the sacred nature of kingship. The fact that Republican

such as the Temple of Peace. In other words, there was a systematic process of restoration to the public realm of everything which had been privatized by Nero, who had taken over a large part of the city center for his own residence, a state of affairs targeted by a lampoonist: "Rome will become one house. Romans, emigrate to Veii—unless of course this house reaches Veii."

The Flavian emperors appear to have been active in the sphere of urban administration, which they largely remodeled, laying down the basis for a new imperial bureaucracy which was to become fully developed in the following century. Their concern for the public good—which was not without its demagogic aspect—was evident also in the completion of the rebuilding of

View of the excavations in Ostia Antica with imperial mosaics from the so-called Bacchus and Ariadne House in the foreground. Roman housing from the same era has not survived, but the remains of this residential complex convey a sense of the layout and fittings they must have had.

concepts were being reappraised and that Vespasian (AD 69–79), with his businesslike outlook, disliked the now customary deification of the deceased emperor, is confirmed in a number of anecdotes, in particular in the phrase which, according to Suetonius in his life of the emperor, Vespasian uttered on his deathbed: "Alas, I believe I am about to become a god!"

Given this context, it is easy to understand why Nero's megalomaniac schemes, especially the Golden House, were systematically eradicated. The Colosseum was built on the site of the ornamental lake in the grounds of the villa, while the nearby Baths of Titus are probably the successors to Nero's private baths, remodeled for public use. Likewise, the vast number of works of art that Nero had purloined from Greece were removed from the Golden House and displayed in newly built public buildings,

Portrait of Domitian (AD 81–96), the last Flavian on the imperial throne. After his murder by conspirators, a *damnatio memoriae* was declared against him.

Portrait of Trajan, emperor from AD 98 to 117. Born in Italica in Spain in AD 52, Marcus Ulpius Nerva Trajanus had a successful career in the army, winning the favour of the emperor Nerva, who made him governor of the province of Germania Superiore, adopted him, and made him co-ruler.

Rome, which had still not entirely recovered from the great fire in Nero's day. In AD 73 Vespasian and his son Titus (79–81) took the unusual step of together assuming an old role that had been long forgotten, the censorship, thereby demonstrating once again the allegiance they felt to Rome's republican tradition. At the same time, the *pomerium* was redefined and extended (it had already been extended by Claudius a few decades earlier). This can be seen as the starting point for the large-scale scheme for urban planning and administrative renewal already mentioned.

The third emperor of the Flavian dynasty, Domitian (81–96), must have carried out major building works but we know little about this because information was lost as a result of the *damnatio memoriae* declaration against him. We do know of the complete reconstruction of the Campus Martius and of the Capitoline Hill, made necessary by the disastrous fire of AD 80. In addition to restoring the Pantheon, the *Saepta*, and the Portico of Octavia, Domitian built the Stadium (the present-day Piazza Navona) and the nearby Odeon (small theater). These, a group of buildings designed for athletic contests and musical spectacles, were a clear display of renewed interest in Greek culture. Domitian also built a new Forum in the center of the city, the so-called Forum Transitorium (the passage-way forum). This was inaugurated by Nerva (96–98), Domitian's successor, and bears his name (the Forum of Nerva). It filled the gap between the Forum of Augustus and the Temple of Peace.

However, the most remarkable new building undertaken by Domitian was the magnificent residence on the Palatine Hill, so large and grand that it was to survive virtually unaltered right up to the end of the Roman Empire. Here too, Domitian's political ideals show a marked break from those of the first two Flavian emperors, displaying tendencies not unlike those of Nero's era. The new vision of power, linked to the enduring model of absolutist eastern monarchies, held the emperor to be a living "lord and god."

Trajan

The second century AD, from Trajan (98–117) to Septimius Severus (193–211), saw Rome's greatest demographic and urban expansion. The outstanding achievement of Trajan's rule was the creation of the largest and the most monumental public building in the city, the Forum of Trajan. In order to make room for it in an area that was by now crammed full, it was necessary to level the ridge of land that linked the Quirinal Hill and the Capitoline Hill, demolishing some ancient buildings such as Asinium Pollio's *Atrium Libertatis*. For the first time, the Fora were joined to the monumental district of the Campus Martius. At the same time the Forum of Caesar was completely rebuilt. This can be seen as the model for the new Forum of Trajan, reflecting the attitudes of the emperor, with his policy of military conquest.

There was also intense activity in the sphere of public works and private building. The architect responsible for the Forum of Trajan, Apollodorus of Damascus, also designed Trajan's Markets and the Baths of Trajan, which were erected on the Oppian Hill, obliterating what remained of the Golden House. The Baths of Trajan were the first example of the type of great Roman baths which is found virtually repeated, but on a slightly larger scale, in the Baths of Caracalla and of Diocletian. These buildings display the language of Roman architecture at its most highly developed, with the systematic use of huge brick structures with vaulted ceilings. It is a significant

Bust of the emperor Caracalla. Rome, Capitoline Museums, Sala degli Imperatori.

PREVIOUS PAGE:
Aerial view of the Piazza Navona which shows clearly how the shape of the ancient stadium of Domitian has inscribed itself into the cityscape.

The great exedra of the Markets of Trajan, which in antiquity housed traders' stalls, was built from designs by Apollodorus of Damascus; he had also drawn up the plan for the neighboring Forum of Trajan.

demonstration of how culturally unified the Empire had become that the engineer of these architectural works was an architect from the eastern part of the Hellenic world, Syria.

Hadrian

Building fever, particularly in the private sector, reached its peak with Hadrian and the Antonine emperors, The custom of stamping the names of the consuls for the year (the usual dating method) on bricks was started by Hadrian (117–38) in AD 123. Thanks to this practice, we know that the entire production of bricks had been restarted from scratch, a clear indication of the new trends that were under way. Major monumental works were still being undertaken, such as Hadrian's rebuilding of the Pantheon, with, until 1958, the largest dome ever constructed, and the immense Temple of Roma and Venus.

However, the spirit of the age is better reflected in the planned construction of whole districts of apartment houses of several stories, for example along the Via Lata (the present Via del Corso). A good idea of such residential quarters can be gained at Ostia, Rome's port.

Septimius Severus and Caracalla

Another fire in AD 191, during the rule of Commodus (180–92), was followed by yet more reconstruction, under Septimius Severus. This included the restoration of the Temple of Peace, the Portico of Octavia (its facade, visible today, dates from this time), and of the *Horrea Piperataria* (the spice market). The Palace of Domitian on the Palatine Hill was given a new wing and a great facade, the *Septizodium*,

facing the approach to the city from the Appian Way (Via Appia). According to the life of Septimius Severus in the *Historia Augusta* collection of biographies of emperors (24, 3), "when [Severus] had the *Septizodium* built, his sole aim was to display this monument in such a way as to be seen by those arriving from Africa." Septimius Severus was in fact born in Lepcis Magna in North Africa.

Of equal importance is the work carried out by Severus' successor, Caracalla (211–17). In addition to the famous Baths, the best preserved in Rome, Caracalla was responsible for the Temple of Serapis on the Quirinal Hill, probably the largest temple in the city. It housed the Dioscuri (Castor and Pollux standing by their horses) now on the Quirinal Hill, and the two river gods of the Nile and the Tiber, today at the top of Michelangelo's ramp to the Capitoline Hill.

An overall idea of the city in the early third century is provided by the large Marble Plan, a

Aerial view of the magnificent Thermal Baths of Caracalla. These were begun in AD 212 and, with the exception of the outer enclosure, which was added by the last Severan emperors Elagabalus (AD 218–22) and Alexander (AD 222–35), were completed during his reign. The baths were renovated during successive reigns by Aurelius, Diocletian and Theodoric.

Layout of the Baths of Diocletian (E. Paulin, 1880). This complex was built at the instigation of Augustus Maximianus Herculius between AD 298 and 316 and dedicated by Diocletian, co-regent and founder of the Tetrarchy. The huge scale of the structure marked the high point for this style of building in Rome. Part of the ancient complex has housed the Museo Nazionale Romano since 1899.

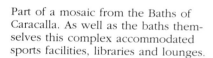

Part of a mosaic from the Baths of Caracalla. As well as the baths themselves this complex accommodated sports facilities, libraries and lounges.

large-scale map of Rome incised on a wall, fragments of which were discovered in the sixteenth century at the base of the still perfectly preserved wall to which it was originally fixed, between the Basilica of Maxentius and the facade of the church of Santi Cosma e Damiano. The plan, relating to the Severan restoration of the Temple of Peace, was in fact a copy of a large taxation map, probably kept in the same building. This building has been correctly identified as the headquarters of the City Prefect, the magistrate responsible for urban administration, whose importance would continue to increase.

The Third Century: Crisis and Recovery

The profound crisis which engulfed the Empire in the third century was accompanied by a sharp decline in building activity. A clear sign of this is the end of the practice of date-stamping bricks after Caracalla's reign, even though the last of the Severan emperors were still undertaking important works, particularly Elagabalus (218–22) and

Alexander Severus (222–35). The latter was responsible for, among other things, the last aqueduct to be built, the *Aqua Alexandrina*, and the rebuilding of the Baths of Nero in the Campus Martius.

During the following period, Aurelian (270–75) erected the Temple of the Sun in the Campus Martius. He was also responsible for what was probably the most important project of this period, the Aurelian Walls, the first new city wall since the Republic, a clear indication of the times and of the dangers now threatening the capital itself.

One sign of the recovery that took place towards the end of the third century under the Tetrarchy (rule of four whereby the Empire was divided into two, with two rulers in each) is the resumption of the custom of date-stamping bricks, which indicates renewed demand. Important schemes rose in the center of the city, again badly damaged by fire in AD 283, during the brief rule of Carus (282–83). All the buildings on the western side of the Forum, from the Basilica Julia to the Curia, were rebuilt, as was the Forum of Caesar. The most notable undertaking was the construction of the vast Baths of Diocletian at the edge of the Quirinal Hill. These, the largest baths ever built, were the work of the emperor of the western half of the empire, Maximian (286–305).

Maximian's son Maxentius (306–12) chose Rome as his capital and directed his efforts at restoring the remains of the city's ancient past, now in a state of decay. He rebuilt the Temple of Roma and Venus, which had been destroyed by fire, and built a magnificent new basilica, where the judicial business of the nearby urban prefecture was conducted. This basilica, like Maxentius' other buildings (for example, the new baths on the Quirinal), was subsequently named after Constantine (306–37), following the defeat of Maxentius in AD 312 at the battle of the Milvian Bridge.

Constantine

The battle of the Milvian Bridge seemed to mark the beginning of the final decline of the city's fortunes. Constantine's building activity in Rome was mostly associated with the establishment of numerous large Christian basilicas on the margins of the ancient urban center. In any case, his interest now lay, above all, in the new capital rising in the east, Constantinople. From this point, the city authorities, representing the old aristocracy (pagan and Christian), would apply their efforts almost exclusively to the conservation and restoration of the immense monumental heritage accumulated over the centuries, until, gradually losing their original functions, these great buildings were overtaken by fate and fell into ruin.

Filippo Coarelli

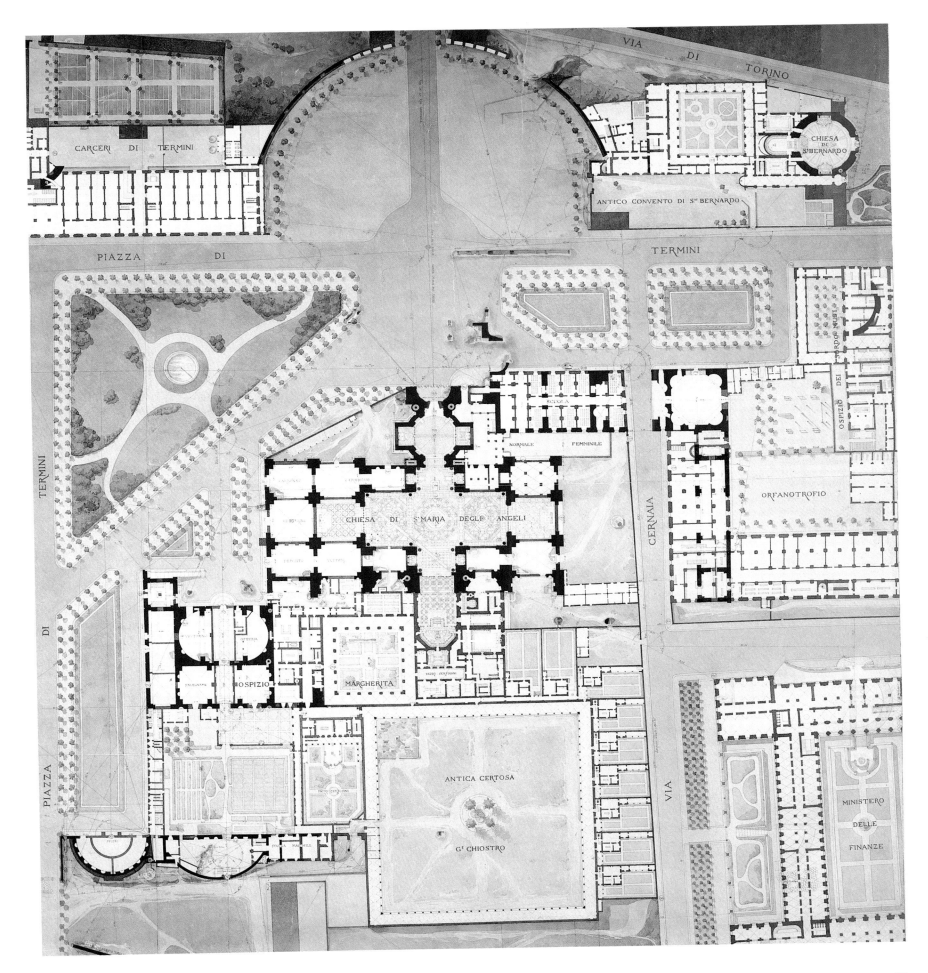

Roman Art and Architecture from its Beginnings to the Flavian Dynasty

Craftsmanship under the Kings and the Early Republic

Terracotta roof ornament in the shape of a woman's head from the end of the sixth century BC Rome, Museo Nazionale Etrusco di Villa Giulia.

Interior of the Tomba dei Capitelli in Cerveteri. On the ceiling sculptors have imitated certain features of monumental architecture, such as the beams running lengthways.

The mythical origins of Rome and its political and religious institutions were traditionally recorded by Roman historians through the legendary deeds of the seven kings, who ruled between 753 and 509 BC. The names of the kings of Rome were associated with various stages of the city's development, all equally important: Romulus with the foundation of Rome, Numa Pompilius with the codification of social and religious law, Tullius Hostilius and Ancus Marcus with the first military exploits in Latium, Tarquinius Priscus, Servius Tullius, and Tarquinius Superbus with Etruscan dominance over Rome.

Although it has been challenged in recent historiography, this ancient tradition has been reassessed and is now considered plausible in the light of important archaeological findings that appear to validate it. Thus Romulus himself—the most mysterious figure—as well as primitive Roman society have emerged from the mists of time. The remains of a fortification wall recently found on the northern slopes of the Palatine Hill can be traced back to the foundation of Rome and thus to the pomerium area (the sacred boundary of the city) of Romulus' city, as described in detail by Tacitus (*Annals*, XII, 24). In addition, a vase made of mixed materials bearing five scratched Greek letters found in a tomb at Osteria dell'Osa, twelve miles east of Rome, near the ancient town of Gabii, and dated to around 770 BC, is evidence of early links with the Greek world as well as proof of the tradition of Romulus and Remus which described them as educated in writing in Gabii.

The development of a specialized kind of craftsmanship was ascribed by Roman historians to the reign of Numa Pompilius. Numa divided artisans into craft guilds, just as he created laws to regulate Roman society while at the same time aiming at the integration of the Sabines and Latins (Plutarch, *Numa*, 17).

Among the artisans responsible for producing luxury items were potters and bronzemakers. Most important were those known as *tktones*, who included not only carpenters involved in the construction of buildings but also carvers of wood and of precious materials such as amber and bone. Unfortunately, due to their perishable nature, amber and bone objects are rare, but an outstanding discovery such as the wooden throne from Verucchio, near Rimini, decorated with exquisite inlay and dated to the

seventh century BC, gives an idea of the level of sophistication reached by this type of craft at this time.

Terracotta Roof Decoration

Numa's list of trades does not include the category of craftsmen who worked on all aspects of roofing and roof decoration, from large tiles to the ornamental elements, including lifesize figures, which decorated the ends and ridges of roofs. These elements imply a radically new concept of roofing, which would allow the realization of large architectural structures with features intended to be permanent. Aware of the significance of this concept, ancient historians linked the introduction of the art of roofing with the arrival in Italy of three *fictores* (literally makers) whose individual names describe their particular skill: Eucheir (The Skilled One), Eugrammos (The Good Designer), and Diopos (The Good Sighter), in reality names used to designate craftsmen able to carry out all aspects and stages of roofing, from the molding of the terracotta to its decoration and installation.

Cerveteri, Tomba dei Leoni Dipinti (Tomb of the Painted Lions), whose upper portion is clearly reminiscent of a hipped roof.

Here too the evidence in Roman literary tradition finds an extraordinary correspondence in the large number of Etruscan tombs which imitate in detail the architectural models by which they were inspired. It is clear that in the first half of the seventh century, monumental tombs reproduced in minute detail large huts with thatched roofing of straw and twigs (as in the Tomb of the Thatched Roof at Cerveteri). In the second half of the century, tombs began to include large chambers with trussed roofs—revealing the use of heavy clay roofs in buildings—designed for multiple burials (as in the Tomb of the Capitals and the Tomb of the Painted Lions at Cerveteri), according to what must by then have been a common feature of large houses.

Archaeological discoveries in Etruscan territory (Acquarossa near Viterbo and Murlo near Siena) and in Rome itself allow us to become better acquainted with the buildings which served as models for contemporary funerary architecture. These are large residential buildings—veritable palaces in terms of their structural complexity and wealth of decoration—which included all the symbols of royal power of the archaic period.

The Regia

Near the Forum in Rome are the remains of a building which always retained its ancient name of Regia (Royal Palace), in spite of the various functions and rebuildings it had over time. Originally this area was occupied by a cluster of huts. These were demolished in order to accommodate a larger building, the surviving scant traces of which seem to indicate at least three phases of rebuilding, all of a structure built around a large courtyard with at least three rooms opening on to the rear of the atrium, which had a wooden portico. Thanks to the literary sources, this area can be identified as the site chosen by Numa Pompilius, the second king of Rome, for his residence. It was later joined on the east, facing the Sacred Way (Via Sacra), by the private dwellings of his heirs.

The royal residence stood near other buildings associated with the king's roles and functions, such as the House of the Vestal Virgins (Atrium Vestae)—the official hearth whose cult reflected the tradition of the fire kept by the king's daughters—and the house of the chief priest (*rex sacrorum*), who in the republican age inherited some of the king's religious roles. This proximity seems to indicate that the small Regia was just part of a larger architectural structure comparable in both plan and function to the Etruscan palaces at Murlo and Acquarossa, where private living space was closely associated with spaces used for religious functions.

The wealth of these architectural complexes was emphasized by the use of elegant terracotta ornament, including lifesize statues and tiles used to protect the beams, in a similar fashion to contemporary religious architecture. What remains of the terracotta decoration from the second building phase of the Regia, dated to the second quarter of the sixth century BC, indicates that though it clearly belonged to this tradition further elements were added. One of the plaques shows a procession of cats and birds and a figure dressed in a short chiton wearing a bull mask, the Minotaur. This is connected with Theseus, the mythical hero who became king of Athens after slaying the Minotaur in Crete. On his journey home Theseus stopped on the island

Gold band from Pyrgi with an Etruscan inscription, which was also found on another band in Phoenician translation. It tells of King Thefarie Velianas, who ruled Cere with the help of the goddess Ishtar-Uni at the beginning of the fifth century BC, and his generous patronage of a famous place of worship on the coast. Rome, Museo Nazionale Etrusco di Villa Giulia.

of Delos, where he began the tradition of a type of dance called the dance of the crane (*ghranos*), symbolizing the difficult path he had followed to emerge successfully from the labyrinth, thanks to Ariadne's famous thread.

The plaque is important for understanding contemporary Roman aristocracy, as it provides evidence that the Greek myth was well known. Significantly, the myth of a famous Greek hero was being used to justify the right of the king (*rex*) resident in the Regia to royal power. The date of the tile corresponds to the traditional dates ascribed to Servius Tullius, one of the most controversial figures in early Roman history. The son of a slave, he had reached power thanks to the protection of the goddess Fortune, breaking the traditional rigid system of succession to the throne, until then in the hands of the aristocracy. Behind Servius Tullius and his politics emerge the signs of tyrannical power, found at the time also in many Etruscan cities such as Cerveteri, where the gold plates found at Pyrgi reveal the ascent to power of the tyrant Thefarie Velianas, under the protection of the goddess Uni, the Etruscan version of Aphrodite.

The Cattle Market

Servius Tullius' policy, which supported commerce at the expense of the aristocracy, was centered on the Cattle Market (Forum Boarium), an area which even before the foundation of the city was a natural trading site, a veritable sanctuary of business. The protector of the Cattle Market was Hercules, the demigod associated with commerce, in whose honor, according to tradition, Evander had dedicated an altar, the Great Altar (Ara Maxima), in gratitude for having defeated the giant Cacus.

The literary sources assign to Servius Tullius the monumental features of the area, two temples dedicated to Fortune and Mater Matuta (goddess of the dawn). This tradition was confirmed by archaeological excavations near the church of Sant'Omobono. The high quality of crafted features such as the terracotta figures of the Temple of Mater Matuta and their perfect insertion in the Greek Ionic style of the late archaic age reveal that Rome had by now reached the highest cultural and economic level.

New Temples

According to Roman historians, the period of Etruscan hegemony in Rome corresponded to a phase of great expansion of the city into Latium at the expense of the adjacent peoples. It is not surprising then that the kings of the Etruscan dynasty were considered responsible for important constructions which provided the city with public infrastructure and prestigious monumental features. During the reign of Servius Tullius, in the middle of the sixth century BC, the city walls—the so-called Servian Wall, which was considered essential to define and protect the urban area—were built as well as the Temple of Diana on the Aventine Hill, with which the king intended to replace, as a center of federal Latin worship, the temple of Diana at Nemi, which had been built by the cities of the Latin League under Tusculum after the destruction of the city of Alba Longa.

A more ambitious building campaign, which gave the city a new look, dates from Tarquinius Superbus, who promoted the construction of prestigious buildings such as the Temple of Jupiter Best and Greatest (Optimus Maximus), Capitolinus on the Capitoline Hill and the Circus Maximus, as well as public facilities such as the Great Drain (Cloaca Maxima). Roman historians, Livy in particular, mention the use of Etruscan workers on these projects, providing precious information on the mobility of artisans at this time. To Vulca, a sculptor from the city of Veii nearby, was attributed the terracotta decoration from the Temple of Jupiter Capitolinus which showed Jupiter seated holding his scepter and wearing a *tunica palmata*.

Vulca's artistic style can be more clearly perceived from the terracotta statues from the Portonaccio temple in Veii, his hometown, dated to the end of the sixth century BC. The group, which includes Apollo, Hercules slaying the Ceryneian hind, Hermes, and a woman carrying a child, perhaps Leto (Latona) holding her son Apollo, reveals in the asymmetries of Hercules' torso and in the deep folds of Apollo's garment an awareness of the devices necessary to correct the optical distortions which would result from viewing the work from below and from a distance. From a stylistic point of view, the sculptor of the Portonaccio temple—Vulca or his school—belongs to the Greek Ionic tradition, though a certain abundance, visible in the softly draping garments, is entirely original.

The expulsion from the city of Tarquinius Superbus in 509 BC and the resulting period of political instability affected building activity and the production of crafts in Rome. The production of luxury goods, always favored by the kings and their courts, decreased dramatically. Funeral goods in tombs—already greatly reduced by the mid-sixth century—were further reduced due to the sumptuary regulations in the laws of the Twelve Tables, resulting in a drastic reduction in the import of luxury items from the Greek and eastern worlds, so much so that such trade virtually ceased during the fifth century.

A bronze statue from the beginning of the fifth century bc showing the Capitoline Wolf which suckled Romulus and Remus.
The figures of the twins were added in the fifteenth century by Antonio Pollaiuolo. Rome, Capitoline Museums.

However, buildings closely linked to the new republican institutions assume particular importance. The period saw the development of the west side of the Forum, with the erection of the Temple of Saturn (497 BC), the Comitium (the place of elected political assembly), the Senate House, or Curia, and the Rostra (the orators' platforms).

Foreign workers were employed on some of these sites. On the Aventine Hill outside the pomerium, an area reserved for plebeians and foreigners, around 495 BC the large temple dedicated to Ceres, Liber, and Libera was built. These deities were preferred by the plebeians as an alternative to the three gods worshipped in the Capitoline Hill temples. The decoration of the temple was assigned to the Greek artists Damophilus and Gorgasus, perhaps from Taranto in the heel of Italy.

Sculpture

Evidence of the presence of foreign artisans in Rome in this period can also be found in the torso fragment from the Esquiline Hill, probably from a sculpture of a wounded warrior, where the design and use of color in the painted areas as well as the formal precision, especially in the drapery on the left shoulder, all are suggestive of a Greek sculptor.

According to Roman history, the earliest bronze sculpture dated from the early republican era. The earliest example is the statue dedicated to Ceres by the father of Spurius Cassius following the confiscation of his possessions, the destruction of his house, and his sentence to death for plotting tyranny (Pliny, *Natural History*, XXXIV, 15–16, Livy, *History of Rome*, II, 41, 10).

An example of bronzework from this era is the famous Capitoline Wolf, still today the symbol of Rome. The copy in the Capitoline Museums, the only one surviving, is probably the older of the two images of the wolf in republican Rome, one of which was kept on the Capitoline Hill. The other, with the wolf suckling the twins, was dedicated by the Ogulnii brothers in 295 BC with the revenues from the fines paid by usurers (*feneratores*) and was placed near the Ficus ruminalis (the fig tree associated with Romulus) in the Forum.

The Capitoline Wolf, whose twins Romulus and Remus were added by the sculptor Antonio Pollaiuolo in the late fifteenth century, has great expressive power. The wolf's stance, watchful and hostile, is effectively rendered in the sideways presentation of the body, with the head turned to the observer with half-open jaws. She is ready to protect her "offspring," whose presence is suggested by the emphasis given to her protruding teats. The wolf's body is thin, with the ribs in evidence. The detailed rendering of the hair on the back and neck, with symmetrical curls of hair, suggest a certain indulgence in decorativeness, characteristic of the few surviving Etruscan bronze artifacts of the early fifth century BC.

The Middle Years of the Republic

Though we have very few sources for the fifth century, a number of artifacts illustrates the artistic culture of the middle period of the republic, between the conquest of Veii in 396 BC and the end of the Second Punic War in 200 BC. This culture was expressed through the adaptation and development of motifs and themes borrowed from the great Greek heritage.

The Ficoroni Cista

Rome as a center of craft production is well documented by a piece of exceptional craftsmanship from Praeneste (modern Palestrina, east of Rome), the Ficoroni cista, a bronze vessel dated to about 340 BC, made in a Roman workshop by Novios Plautios on commission from a certain Dindia for his daughter Macolnia (Magulnia), according to an inscription on the base of the three figures which form the handle of the lid. The central section of the cista has a frieze with a scene from the story of the Argonauts, the torture of Amycus. With Athena and a small slave as onlookers, Amycus is tied to a tree by Polydeuces, who has just defeated him in a boxing match. A winged victory flies towards Polydeuces, holding the crown and ribbons for the winner. The rest of the frieze has scenes from the Argonauts' expedition to fetch the golden fleece at Colchis, with a view of their ship, the Argo.

The figures reveal the artist's indebtedness to the Greek painting style of the late classical age, especially the figures shown in perspective and the shadowing, masterfully rendered by hatching. The adoption of mythological themes—even complex and little-known ones found not just in the Ficoroni cista but also in a rich series of cistae and mirrors from Praeneste—reveals a close familiarity of the ruling Roman classes with Greek culture, made accessible through links with the Greek cities of southern Italy.

The Ficoroni cista (c. 340 BC), a cylindrical vessel originally used to store toilet articles and jewelry. Its ornamentation is impressive evidence of the way Greek motifs and themes were adopted and modified by Etruscan artists. Rome, Museo Nazionale Etrusco di Villa Giulia.

Painting

The close ties with Greek painting emerge from the scarce information available regarding one of the most important artists active in Rome in the early fourth century, Gaius Fabius Pictor (*pictor* meaning painter). A member of an ancient noble family and himself at the head of a major branch of the family, Gaius Fabius became known for his series of remarkable paintings in the Temple of Salus (the safety of the state), dedicated in 304–303 BC by the dictator Gaius Iunius Bubulcus, who had had Gaius Fabius elected consul during the war against the Samnites. Later, in 307 BC, Gaius Fabius was elected censor. The celebratory style of the temple—one of the first buildings to be dedicated directly by an individual victor, as opposed to collectively by the Roman people—suggests that the paintings must have illustrated the most important scenes of the battles, inspired by the *fabulae triumphales*, images displayed in the triumphal parade of the winning general to show his great deeds.

A fragment of wall painting from a tomb in the great Esquiline necropolis is an excellent example of the essential features of triumphal and celebratory painting. The fragment, illustrating a historical scene, seems to be in at least four registers. The top and bottom registers bear traces of the legs of a figure and part of a duel between two warriors. The middle registers, in better condition, depict meetings of two figures, wearing different garments. In one scene the figures stand before fortified city walls, in the other they are in the presence of a group of soldiers wearing capes. The inscriptions above their heads identify them as Marcus Fanios, on the left, and Quintus Fabios, on the right. The latter is portrayed wearing a toga as he hands Fannios a spear.

Sculpture

The celebration of individual glories, expressed, as could be seen in the case of Gaius Iunius Bubulcus, with a religious building, was also expressed in the erection of honorific bronze statues in the most prestigious public space, the Forum. The dedication of the first bronze equestrian statues, those of Lucius Furius Camillus and Gaius Menius, occurred immediately after their victory over the Latin League at Anzio in 338 BC (Livy, *History of Rome*, VIII, 13, 9). Gaius Menius was also responsible for the erection of the homonymous column—the first of a genre which was to include the well-known columns of Trajan and of Marcus Aurelius.

The only surviving portrait from the middle years of the republic is the so-called Capitoline Brutus in the Capitoline Museums. A sixteenth-century reconstruction joined the portrait head to a marble bust from the imperial age, though the slight forward tilt of the head and the downcast eyes seem designed to be seen from below, suggesting that the head may have originally belonged to an equestrian statue.

The intriguing identification of the portrait with Lucius Iunius Brutus, the hero who founded the Republic, suggested on the basis of the similarity of this portrait to that on the coins issued in 59 and 43 BC by a presumed direct descendant, Caesar's assassin, Marcus Iunius Brutus, remains to be proved. Nonetheless it is a powerfully expressive portrait. The taut features, determined gaze, and plainness of the pose, with tousled hair on the forehead and small irregular locks of beard effectively express the austerity (*gravitas*) considered by the Romans to be the ideal representation of the principal virtue of the early Romans who made Rome the capital of Italy. It is likely that the execution of the Capitoline Brutus, and of the other bronze honorific statues which are mentioned in the sources, is to be attributed to Greek or Campanian workshops, which resumed activity in Rome from the end of the fifth century BC after a long break (inferred from the decrease in imports of Greek pottery in the fifth century and the simultaneous interruption in the adoption of Greek religious cults).

This type of celebratory sculpture is not an exclusively Roman phenomenon. Rather, it seems to have been common in a large section of central and southern Italy, including remote areas such as the Samnium region, where the splendid sculpted head found near San Giovanni Lipioni, near Chieti, now in Paris, was found. This can be accounted for by the employment of Greek or Campanian artisans by the wealthy and powerful Italics, who were thus in a position to affect, along with the ideological messages they proposed, the formal choices within the established tradition of Greek portraiture.

From the Eastern Expansion to the Civil Wars

After winning the hard-fought war against Hannibal, which brought destruction to much of the Italian peninsula, Rome imposed on its powerful rival Carthage a heavy war indemnity and a peace treaty that guaranteed a decline in its political and commercial power, ensuring Roman control of most of the enormous and wealthy Iberian peninsula.

A few years after the important battle of Zama (202 BC), the Roman army was involved in a series of military incursions in the east against Philip V, king of Macedon, and Antiochus III, leaders, heads of the two Hellenistic kingdoms which had emerged from the collapse of Alexander the Great's empire. Victory in both wars, fought in 198–97 BC and 190 BC respectively, gave Rome a dominant position in the eastern Mediterranean, a role that the political structure of the Roman city-state in its legislative and executive functions could not support.

The great campaigns in the east marked the beginning of the personalization of politics, until then affected by the formation and opposition of numerous large patrician groups. Until the dramatic events of Marius' and Sulla's civil war, political life and foreign policy were molded by a handful of aristocratic families, among them the Aemilii, the Caecilii Metelli, the Fulvii, the Licinii, the Sempronii, and, especially, the Cornelii, whose major branch in those years was the Cornelii Scipiones.

The Tomb of the Scipios

In contrast to other cases, much is known of the deeds not only of the most outstanding exponents of the Cornelii Scipiones, but also of its minor members, thanks to the discovery of the family tomb, the Tomb of the Scipios, on a side road off the Via Appia, near Porta San Sebastiano. The oldest burial here seems to be that of Lucius Cornelius Scipio Barbatus, consul in 298 BC, a major figure of the last phase of the Samnite wars. The splendid sarcophagus, now in the Vatican Museums, is of the *ara* (altar) type, a form common in the Greek cities of southern Italy. The upper portion of the sarcophagus is decorated with a Doric frieze with triglyphs alternating with metopes filled with rosettes while the lid is embellished at the ends by two volutes which frame a cylindrical element ending with acanthus leaves.

Strong Greek influence is also evident in the style of the long elegiac verse inscription on the side. The elegies to the Scipios reflect the aristocratic values of the time, with exaltations of their great deeds and detailed lists of public offices held (which, of course, added to family glory).

The political significance of these texts lies in the juxtaposition of the traditional forms of aristocratic rule of the city and the attempt to centralize power into a few hands. This trend goes back to the first quarter of the second century BC and to Publius Cornelius Scipio, victor over Hannibal, who clashed with the conservative wing of the Senate, for which he was exiled. It is significant, however, that these absolutist tendencies were opposed not by a member of the senatorial aristocracy but by Cato the Elder,

The sarcophagus of Lucius Cornelius Scipionus Barbatus, consul in the year 298 BC, from his family tomb on the Via Appia. The eulogy on this altar-like sarcophagus was written in Saturnian verse. One of its phrases: "a courageous and wise man, whose appearance reflected his worth," is a translation of the Greek concept of *kalokagathia* (excellence), which attempted to combine ethical and aesthetic virtues. Rome, Vatican Museums.

who had been born into a peasant family in the village of Tusculum, far from the urban aristocracy. In other words, the senatorial aristocracy was unable to develop a new model to adapt to the changes in Roman society whilst at the same time safeguarding tradition.

What emerged was an idealization of the Roman people and their ruling class by citizens who had never been part of it. In this, the contribution of Romans from small villages who had worked their way up the social ladder is significant. The myth of the *mores maiorum* (the customs of the ancestors) and their deeds was eulogized by Cicero, Varro, Marius, and Asinius Pollio.

Eastern Influence

The first result of this new ideology was an increase in the influence of Hellenistic and eastern culture, which would eventually result in a hostile attitude towards artifacts of eastern Hellenistic origin, regarded as "Asiatic luxury" (*luxuria asiatica*). This antagonism affected the Scipios and the major writers of the second century BC—Pacuvius, Terence, Laelius, Lucilius, and the Greeks Polybius and Panetius. Here too there was a major contradiction: the Roman conquests in the east had brought enormous quantities of treasure and valuable objects which would be exhibited in triumph by victorious commanders. Livy, Plutarch, Strabo, and several other historians filled their histories with such episodes, lamenting the indiscriminate looting and mocking the conquerors' quite blatant ignorance of art.

Among the celebrated Greek works of art that reached Rome as booty, a unique example is the large bronze crater (bowl) in the Sala dei Trionfi di Mario in the Palazzo dei Conservatori (Capitoline Museums). The crater has a Greek inscription around the rim which identifies it as a gift from Mithridates VI, king of Pontus, to the members of a gymnastic association in an unspecified Greek city. This remarkable crater, found in Nero's imperial seaside villa at Anzio, must have belonged to the booty brought back to Rome by Sulla or Pompey, both of whom defeated Mithridates in battle.

Such works of art, gold, and precious objects were but a fraction of the enormous wealth which poured into Rome as a result of military conquest. Conquest also brought a considerable influx of slaves, who were employed on a large scale in all kinds of activities. This revolutionized the production system, which had been based essentially on revenues from small and medium-sized farms. The use of slaves had not been unknown in previous centuries. However,

Bronze crater given by Mithridates VI, the ruler of Pontus in Asia Minor, to members of a gymnasium; it later reached Rome with war booty. Triumphant processions, and the display of booty which went with them, had an important function in publicizing Oriental splendor in Republican times. Rome, Capitoline Museums.

from the early second century BC the phenomenon increased dramatically: Strabo recorded that the free port established in 166 BC in the island of Delos was a trade center where up to 10,000 slaves were sold every day.

Public Architecture

From the early third century, the most important area of the city, the Forum, became the focus for public building. The area appeared to have had a clutter of commercial buildings for the food trade (*tabernae*), possibly belonging to particular buildings known as *atria*. When the *tabernae lanienae* (butcher's shops) were moved behind the Forum and replaced with *tabernae argentariae* (currency exchanges), which were fitted with hanging balconies from which to watch the gladiators' games and processions on the square, the Forum assumed the political and religious role summed up in Varro's phrase *forensis dignitas* (the dignity of the Forum).

This aspect of the Forum was strengthened by the erection of the Macellum, a building that combined in one place trade in various types of food, and the civic basilicas, used as courtrooms and large public commercial halls. Compared to the earlier *atria publica*, whose functions they inherited, the basilicas that rose steadily around the Forum (the Basilica Porcia in 184 BC, the Basilica Fulvia in 179 BC, the Basilica Sempronia in 169 BC, the Basilica Paulli in 168 BC, and the Basilica Opimia in 121 BC) appear as structures with a particularly monumental character. Inside they were divided into several aisles separated by long rows of columns, with a high podium used as a tribunal at one end. The facade was preceded by a row of shops.

The erection of most public buildings in this period can be traced back to the initiative of the censors. The censors were almost always members of the great aristocratic families, whose building activities expanded on to the level land adjacent to the river port. Rome's tremendous economic expansion required the development of a new port to replace the one existing near the Cattle Market (Forum Boarium), which could not be expanded due to the topography in this spot. The erection of an area of docks and warehousing, the Emporium, was carried out in the district south of the Aventine Hill by Marcus Aemilius Lepidus, a builder, in 193 BC and completed in 179 BC, the year of his appointment as censor along with Marcus Fulvius Nobilior (and thus at the same time as the Porticus Aemilia).

Building the enormous structures of the port involved initially the construction of the embankment, over 1,600 feet long, and of the warehouses, the Porticus Aemilia. The censors of 174 BC were responsible for the stone cobbling of the Emporium and the piers. The Porticus Aemilia, part of which is still visible south of Via Marmorata, was a large building divided internally by 294 columns into fifty vaulted aisles, each slightly over twenty-six feet wide.

The Porticus Aemilia saw for the first time extensive employment of the use of concrete, a southern Italian (Campania) method already successfully used in the Temple of the Magna Mater on the Palatine Hill during the Second

Relief depicting a knife shop.
Rome, Museo della Civilitá Romana.

Depiction of work in a butcher's shop.
Rome, Museo della Civilitá Romana.

Punic War. As well as allowing the realization of daring architectural structures, this building technique had the great advantage of being economical and of not requiring highly specialized workmanship (as had been the case with older polygonal and square building structures). It was thus better suited for the employment of large numbers of slaves in all phases of construction, from the extraction of the raw material from quarries to the execution of building structures in large wooden molds.

Many other warehouses (*horrea*) were built behind the Porticus Aemilia, especially from the beginning of the age of the Gracchi (the late second century BC), when distribution of grain to the people began. The most important were the Horrea Galbana, built by order of Sergius Sulpicius Galba, consul in 108 BC, who had his own tomb built in front, breaking the tradition of the great family tombs and moving the focus of attention to the virtues of the individual. Of this tomb only the rectangular base remains, the center of which bears the funerary inscription framed within fasces, symbol of the consular rank held in life by the deceased.

Art and Propaganda: the *viri triumphales*

Along with the development of public buildings promoted by the censors, the second century BC saw a type of architecture of pure prestige which was intended to commemorate the deeds of *viri triumphali*, victorious men, outstanding figures in the history of the time. In the area outside the pomerium, that is, in the Circus Flaminius, Campus Martius, and the Cattle Market, were built both individual temples dedicated by victorious generals and large triumphal structures inspired by eastern imperial architecture, buildings which reflected contemporary political strife and also functioned as formidable instruments of propaganda.

Connected to the important naval victories of the First Punic War, at least two of the temples of the Forum Holitorium (the fruit and vegetable market) were built near the ancient port, whose position is still marked by the so-called Temple of Fortuna Virilis, dedicated to the patron god of the port, Portunus. This, erected around 300 BC, was transformed in the first century BC into the form visible today, with an Ionic colonnade. Though the individual religious buildings of the Forum Holitorium cannot always be identified, it has been suggested that the temple immediately north of the church of San Nicola in Carcere may be the Temple of Janus. South of the church, the ruins of a colonnaded structure with six Doric columns have

Exceptionally fine high relief of a saleswoman in an apothecary's store. Rome, Museo della Civilitá Romana.

51

The former harbor area of Rome had long been associated with the hero Hercules, and in the final two decades of the second century BC a temple dedicated to Hercules Victor was erected there. Hercules was also the patron divinity of the olive oil traders who had their businesses in the area, and for this reason Hercules was also known as Olivarius. The ambulatory of this centralized structure, which is today known as the Vesta Temple, is made up of twenty Corinthian columns of Pentelic marble set on a stepped base. The form of the temple, its material, and its artistic expression all serve to emphasize the essentially Greek character of the building. The design has been plausibly attributed to the architect Hermodoros of Salamina; he is known to have been working in Rome at that time.

been identified as belonging to the Temple of Spes (Hope), built in 254 BC to mark the naval victory over the Carthaginians off Palermo.

Slightly south of the Forum Holitorium, the Cattle Market was dominated by the figure of Hercules, whose deeds against the giant Cacus and his meeting with the earliest settlers on the Palatine under Evander, who had arrived there from Arcadia in Greece, were an integral part of the myth of Rome's origins. The cult of Hercules, the hero and civilizer, had been celebrated since the earliest history of Rome near the Ara Maxima.

The remains of an enormous altar found near the church of Santa Maria in Cosmedin suggest a monumental structure of the late republican period. Near the Ara Maxima were other religious buildings dedicated to Hercules, including the Temple of the Invincible Hercules (Hercules Victor), built by order of Scipio Aemilianus in 142 BC when he was appointed censor, and probably already voted for during the Third Punic War. Nothing survives of this temple but it is almost certain that it contained a series of paintings by the tragic poet Pacuvius, perhaps illustrating the conquest and destruction of Carthage.

The building that most influenced the area between the Campus Martius and the Forum Holitorium was the Circus Flaminius, built in 221 BC by the censor and tribune of the plebs Gaius Flaminius. It was from here, where the assemblies of the plebs were held, that the victory parades of triumphant generals began. It is therefore not by chance that during the second century BC the first triumphal porticos were built around it, some of which became well known for their remarkable decoration.

The Porticus Octavia was built on the north side of the Circus by the praetor Gnaeus Octavius to celebrate his naval triumph at the end of the third Macedonian war (171–168 BC). Nothing remains of this portico, which was renowned for its Corinthian capitals made entirely of bronze. It was replaced by a portico erected by Quintus Caecilius Metellus Macedonicus in 146 BC. We know—almost completely—the appearance the porticus acquired after its total refurbishment by Augustus between 33 and 23 BC, as a result of which it was dedicated to Augustus' sister, Octavia, and renamed the Porticus of Octavia.

Metellus Macedonicus' ambitious project involved an area already occupied by the Temple of Juno Regina, built by Marcus Aemilius Lepidus in 179 BC. Besides the reconstruction of the temple, the building works involved the erection of a temple dedicated to Jupiter Stator, for the first time constructed entirely of marble. In the Greek neo-Attic style, it was probably by the architect Hermodoros of Salamis. The two temples, in which the cult statues for worship were the work of the Greek sculptors Polycles and Dionysius, were framed by a large portico containing Lysippus' bronze composition taken from the sanctuary of Dion in Greece representing Alexander the Great surrounded by his companions who died in the battle of the Granicus in 334 BC.

Greek Artists in Rome

The great architectural triumphal complexes of this period were usually built by Greek architects and sculptors who employed skilled workers from their own areas, one of the many consequences of the changed political situation resulting from the Roman conquests. In some cases it is possible to trace the transfer of Greek workers to Rome and Italy to specific events. Around 145 BC Ptolemy VIII of Egypt sent into exile entire groups of scholars and artists associated with the Museum of Alexandria, whom he accused of supporting his brother and rival Ptolemy VI. As a result, he "peopled islands and cities with linguists, philosophers, mathematicians, musicians, painters, athletes, and all types of artisans. These men, reduced to poverty, ended up teaching what they knew and educating many illustrious men." (Athenaeus, *The Learned Banquet*, IV, 184c).

Sources record the presence in Rome as early as 164 BC of Demetrius the Topographer, almost certainly a landscape painter from the Alexandria Museum, as revealed by his familiarity with Ptolemy VI. From the first half of the second century BC, fine mosaics created with minute tesserae (*opus vermiculatum*) following designs from cartoons employed for the decoration of Egyptian royal palaces are found not only in Rome but also in other cities of ancient Italy such as Praeneste (modern Palestrina), Pompeii, and Priverno, where they were assembled by Egyptian craftsmen.

It was a large number of sculptors of Greek origin who probably produced many of the works of art which decorated the Forum and the buildings in the Campus Martius. Among the sculptures created in this period, those with honorific or commemorative functions were so abundant as to cause the severe reaction of the censors. Cato the Elder, faced with the proliferation of honorific statues, proudly declared that he was one of the few Romans not to possess one (Plutarch, Cato, 19). Among these celebratory statues of the second century BC, the bronze statue of a man known as the *Hellenistic Prince* in the Museo Nazionale Romano stands out as a remarkable example. This was found

Bronze statue, the so-called *Hellenistic Prince*. The heroic nudity of the figure and its posture, which clearly borrows from the famous statue of Alexander the Great holding a lance by Lysippus, shows how Hellenistic forms served as models for Roman art in the second century BC. Rome, Museo Nazionale Romano, Aula Ottagona.

on February 7, 1885 in a room, perhaps part of the Temple of Serapis, at the foot of the Quirinal Hill, together with the celebrated bronze *Seated Boxer*, in which the style of Lysippus has recently been recognized.

The *Hellenistic Prince* is an heroic male nude with a powerfully muscular body. His left arm raised, he leans on a spear. His weight is on his right leg, causing his left leg to flex in a resting position, opposite his right arm, which is bent behind his back. The decision to alter the vertical axis of the body and the position given to the arms and, in particular, to the head, which turns to the right, are reminiscent of the great formal expressions of the culmination of Hellenistic sculpture, notably the school of Pergamum.

The question of the man's identity is unresolved. The conventional name given to the sculpture reflects the hypothesis that it represents a mid-second century BC ruler. Demetrius I Soter of Syria, Attalus II of Pergamum, and, recently, Eumenes I of Pergamum have all been suggested. However, the rendition of the face, with deep-set eyes and a full mouth, seems removed from the idealized physiognomy typical of official Hellenistic portrait style and suggests instead the representation of an important Roman figure. Titus Quinctius Flaminius or Scipio Aemilianus are just two of the possible identifications.

The severe reaction of the more conservative elements of the Roman ruling class to the proliferation of statues erected by magistrates was caused, in all probability, by sculpture such as this, where clearly Hellenistic features seemed to threaten the principles of equality and fellowship still existing within the ruling class. As in the past, the acceptance of Greek cultural models did not occur without criticism. Rather, it proceeded by selecting those expressions best suited to the ideology produced by Roman society and to its social and political structure.

This filtering process resulted in the acceptance of an artistic style that, according to Pliny, caused a renaissance in the arts after nearly two centuries of decadence, a style which historians call neo-Attic. In reality, this style falls outside the development of Hellenistic art, of which it rejected the representation of space and variety of expression which had made the schools of Pergamum, Alexandria, and Rhodes famous. This explains the sense of cool detachment and artificiality that strike the modern observer of neo-Attic works of art, which range from large sculpture to small objects.

The renewal of decoration that took place in the second century BC in the center of Rome was in the neo-Attic style. In 164 BC, as part of the refurbishment of the eastern side of the Forum, Lucius Aemilius Paullus, censor at the time, decorated the basin of the Pool of Juturna (Lacus Juturnae) with marble statues of Castor and Pollux (the Dioscuri). The dedication on the sculpture was intended to commemorate the miraculous apparition of the heavenly twins watering their horses at the Spring of Juturna, when they announced Aemilius Paullus' victory at Pydna against Perseus, king of Macedon (they had appeared in the same way after the battle of Lake Regillus in 499 BC). The victorious outcome of that first battle had been celebrated, in 484 BC, with the building of the Temple of Castor and Pollux. In Lucius Aemilius Paullus' dedication, the wish to commemorate his own deeds publicly was a deliberate reference to ancient tradition. The best expression of these concepts could only be one inspired by neo-Attic sculptural models, in particular those in a severe style, popular at the time of the first apparition of Castor and Pollux in Rome.

Fragments of the statues of the Dioscuri are now in the Forum Antiquarium. They probably showed the twins standing beside their horses: the brothers' tall slim bodies can be clearly perceived from the one remaining horse's head. Both the structure and the style of the statues can be traced back to the austere period, to the point that some scholars have regarded this sculpture as a Greek original, from between 470 and 460 BC.

Recent analysis has revealed that anomalies in the rendering of the muscular torsos of the Dioscuri suggest a knowledge of successive phases of classical sculpture and of early Hellenistic sculpture, and must therefore be the result of a classicizing remake from the mid-second century BC, based on an original of the archaic period. This stylistic choice—intended to establish a further link between the two appearances of the Disoscuri in Rome—is well suited to the figure and the culture of Lucius Aemilius Paullus, the patron, who seems to have influenced the aristocracy's perception of Hellenistic cultural trends.

As opposed to the regal attitudes of the brothers Publius Cornelius Scipio and Lucius Cornelius Scipio, or the influence of a royal ideology on Titus Quinctius Flaminius, after the battle of Pydna ending the third Macedonian war, Lucius Aemilius Paullus revealed a strong preference for the Greek city-state, or *polis*, of the classical period and for its cultural and artistic production. He retained as personal booty only the great library from the royal palace at Pella, and he made a cultural pilgrimage to all the celebrated sites of Greece, above all Delphi and Olympia.

For these reasons, the second century BC saw in Rome numerous neo-Attic workshops, in

Bronze statue, the Seated Boxer, found on the Quirinal. Rome, Museo Nazionale Romano, Aula Ottagona.

particular those of Polycles and Timarchides of Athens, who moved between Greece and Rome. At the end of the second century BC, one such workshop was that of Scopas the Younger. Our knowledge of Scopas' work remains hazy due to confusion—already present in the sources—with another, better-known, sculptor also called Scopas, who worked in the fourth century BC. Scholars now attribute to Scopas the Younger the statues which according to Pliny decorated the cellae of the Temples of Mars and of Neptune, both built in the Circus Flaminius.

The reliefs of the so-called Ara of Domitius Ahenobarbus most probably belonged originally to the Temple of Neptune, as has been inferred from the base, decorated with the sculpture that Scopas the Younger had produced for the Temple of Neptune. Scenes include Neptune himself, Achilles, and Thetis. The reliefs, now in Paris (the Louvre) and Munich (the Glyptothek), differ greatly in material, subject, and style. They represent the *lustrum* (a purificatory ritual performed every five years by the censors) and a procession at sea. Taking into consideration the differences between the Munich and Paris reliefs, it has been suggested that originally all the reliefs had marine scenes, and that only at a later time was one of the reliefs replaced with that of the *lustrum* ceremony.

The links between the Temple of Neptune and Gnaeus Domitius Ahenobarbus are strong, since in 115 BC, at the height of his career, Gnaeus Domitius held the prestigious office of censor. The scene of Thetis and the sea deities handing weapons to Achilles alluded symbolically to the renewal in 122 BC of a military law ensuring the distribution of weapons directly to citizens by the state.

Another sculpture recently traced to the Temple of Neptune is one of the most famous statues found in Rome, the so-called *Mars* which became part of the Ludovisi collection in 1623 and was restored by Bernini. The thoughtful, melancholic figure may represent Achilles, not Mars, since Pliny mentions a statue of Achilles inside the "temple of Gnaeus Domitius in the Circus Flaminus" (*delubrum Cnaei Domitii in Circo Flaminio*).

Detail of the *Seated Boxer*, showing the scars characteristic of this sport, and illustrating the unsparing realism of this masterpiece. Rome, Museo Nazionale Romano, Aula Ottagona.

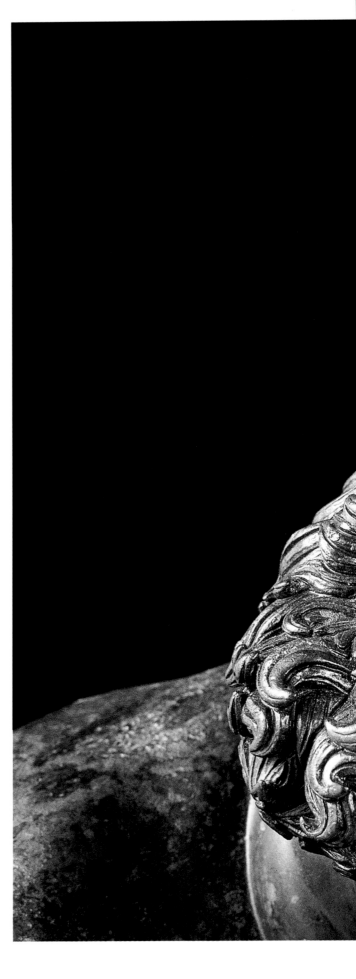

The so-called Ludovisi *Mars*, which, according to a new interpretation, may be seen as a representation of Achilles. Rome, Museo Nazionale Romano in the Palazzo Altemps.

From Sulla to Augustus: The End of the Republic

The final stages of the civil war between the senatorial faction of the *optimates* (the oligarchy) led by Sulla and the *populares*, Roman political leaders working through the people (*populus*) rather than the Senate, which were centered on Marius until his death in 86 BC, took place both in Praeneste, where Marius' son, Marius the Younger, who was consul in 82 BC, was besieged and defeated, and in Rome itself, where on November 1 the two armies clashed under the city walls in a terrible battle in which, according to the sources, over 50,000 men were killed.

The Temple of Jupiter Capitolinus

In 83 BC fire had destroyed the Temple of Jupiter Optimus Maximus on the Capitoline Hill, from time immemorial the symbol of Roman power. The lengthy and complex reconstruction of the temple again reveals how the great buildings of the city could be formidable instruments of propaganda in the hands of patrons and how their construction could hide political battles. Refurbishment probably began in 81 BC during the dictatorship of Sulla, under Quintus Lutatius Catulus. However, the real inspiration behind the project was Sulla, as Pliny informs us, since the new temple incorporated the large marble columns of the unfinished temple of Olympieion Zeus commissioned by Pisistratus, tyrant of Athens, which Sulla himself ordered to be brought to Rome. After Sulla's death in 78 BC, work advanced sluggishly, not just because of the economic difficulties of the state but also because of the determined opposition of the *populares*, who had regrouped around Julius Caesar and intended to remove the most obvious symbols of Sulla's dictatorship.

It was not until 69 BC that the new and magnificent Temple of Jupiter was inaugurated. Four more years were needed in order to see placed in its cella the new statue for worship of the god seated on the throne made of ivory and gold by the neo-Attic sculptor Apollonius, recalling Phidias' celebrated fifth-century BC Parthenon Athena and seated Zeus at Olympia, known through marble copies found in the Capitolia (temples of Jupiter, reproducing that in Rome) of Roman cities and colonies throughout Italy and the empire, the best-known of which is the Otricoli Jupiter.

A striking building from this period, due to its level of conservation and daring architectural features, is the Tabularium, the great structure used to store the official decrees of the state (*tabulae*), which enclosed like a giant architectural backdrop the west side of the Forum, joining the two summits of the Capitoline Hill, the Capitolium and the Arx (citadel).

The Basilica Aemilia

The civil war between the followers of Marius and Sulla which ended with Sulla's victory and dictatorship resulted in a period of political and cultural restoration, perfect ground for the ancient patrician families' exaltation of their history and for new ambitions to power through propagandistic artistic expression and large architectural projects. An example is the Basilica Aemilia (or Paulli), refurbished by Marcus Aemilius Lepidus, consul in 78 BC. Pliny's praising words inform us that during this restoration the basilica was given three rows of large Phrygian marble columns and decorated with a gallery of family portraits inserted in the center of shields hung on the baluster (*imagines clipeatae*), a type of decoration already employed in the celebratory buildings of Hellenistic kings.

To Marcus Aemilius Lepidus' restoration—or to that which followed under Julius Caesar—can be attributed the long frieze (about 300 by 240 feet) found in excavations of the basilica. This, of Pentelic (Greek) marble, illustrated episodes in the early, and legendary, history of Rome. The better-preserved one shows Tarpeia, the young daughter of the commander of the Capitoline Hill, treacherously opening the citadel to Titus Tatius, king of the Sabines, in exchange for what his soldiers wore on their left arms (she hoped for their gold armlets; they flung their shields on to her). From a formal point of view, it is possible to note the extent to which the frieze has assimilated historical illustrations of the type present on the Ara of Domitius Ahenobarbus. The narrative appears purposely didactic so as to minimize the interpretive effort required from the beholder. The original coloring of the figures, which strongly emphasized their features, would have helped in this.

The celebratory aspect of this frieze is fully appreciable if we keep in mind that the structure was considered a family glory. This form of political and family propaganda—by now almost a dynastic tradition—created the premises for the development of that value system that only a few decades later would be used by the Julio-Claudian family to justify, first through Julius Caesar, then through Octavian (later called Augustus), their ascent to power expressed in the form of a principate at the expense of the oligarchy idealized by Sulla.

The Otricoli Jupiter, a replica of the cult statue of Jupiter Capitolinus, made in the first half of the first century BC. Rome, Vatican Museums.

Pompey the Great

In such conditions, it is not surprising that the
struggle between the oligarchic factions should
have produced only a few figures capable of
inspiring widescread support through the un-
scrupulous use of huge wealth or the exploitation
of the glory of victorious military campaigns. This
trend culminated with the coalition of 60–53 BC,
known as the First Triumvirate, between a hugely
wealthy politician, Marcus Licinius Crassus, and
two generals who were descendants of famous
leaders, Pompey the Great, son of Pompeius
Strabo, the conqueror of Ascoli Piceno, during
the civil war, and Gaius Julius Caesar, nephew
on his father's side of the great Marius.

Julius Caesar's power echoed through the city
in a series of celebratory structures that surpassed any project previously commissioned by
returning triumphant generals *viri triumphales.*
In 61 BC, following victory in the east over the
pirates of Cilicia and Mitridates VI, king of
Pontus, Pompey was at the height of his fortune, enjoying the unconditional support of the
optimates and the people's trust.

It was now that a major architectural complex
was initiated which could include in one building spaces with various functions, such as
shows, leisure, and politics, a virtual "city of

Pompey" next to the city of the Romans. Once
again the choice of site was the Campus
Martius, within an area almost certainly already
belonging to Pompey, in which he commissioned a large residence surrounded by large
gardens, repeating the model found in the
Hellenistic capitals of Alexandria and
Pergamum, where the royal palace, buildings
for study or entertainment, and the most important public areas were all part of one complex.
The most innovative creation was the great
theater, decorated with enormous statues of
Apollo and the Muses, which reputedly could
seat—depending on the sources—between
17,000 and 40,000.

Until now, the strong opposition of the
Senate's conservative wing had always prevented the erection of permanent theaters in the
city, though for at least two centuries there had
been all major types of theatrical performances.
The aristocracy, through their spokesman
Cicero (*Pro Flacco*, 15–17), looked suspiciously
on a type of building associated with the demo-
cratic Greek city-state—so much so that it was
often confused with the site intended for meetings—for fear that it might be used for large
assemblies of people for subversive purposes.
In order to avoid this criticism, Pompey justified
the erection of the great structure by ensuring

that it was not just a theater but that its function was also that of a wide set of stairs leading up to the Temple of Venus Victrix. The fact that there was no opposition to Pompey's intentions goes to show that soon mere formalistic respect of republican principles and laws would be sufficient to justify a takeover of power.

Pompey's building was completed by a large portico, as Vitruvius recorded, a *porticus post scaenam* (a porticus beyond the stage), necessary to ensure the protection of the audience in bad weather. The decorative richness of the portico matched that of the theater. Paintings by famous artists such as Polygnotus and Pausanias were exhibited on easels under the portico while the central space was occupied by well-kept gardens shaded by plane trees and enlivened by ornamental fountains. To complete the structure, a series of square or semicircular exedras was built on the portico side opposite the theater, the largest of which was occasionally used for the meetings of the Senate until the death of Julius Caesar, who fell there under the blows of the conspirators in front of the statue of Pompey.

Julius Caesar

While Pompey's building activity was concentrated in the area used for large triumphal buildings, Julius Caesar wanted to leave his mark in the heart of the city, especially in the Forum area. Until now, construction there had been limited to the building of individual structures or the refurbishment of individual areas. The reorganization of the space of the area was unprecedented. In this sense, Julius Caesar's construction plans show clearly the new political structure taking shape following the forced peace after his victory over Pompey at Pharsalus in 48 BC. First, the Forum acquired a new square, between the Basilica Aemilia (Paulli) and the Capitoline Hill. This was the Forum of Caesar, the first in a number of imperial forums which were gradually added to the original republican Forum.

The new square, made in an area bought from private owners for large sums from 54 BC onwards, had a triple portico with two aisles. Along the long side—just as in the original Forum—were shops. On the short side was a large temple, richly decorated with columns and marble. From an architectural point of view, the complex did not differ greatly from the porticos built by the *viri triumphales*. The novelty was the deity worshipped in the square, Venus Genetrix (Universal Mother), a reminder of the family tradition which linked the origins of the Julian dynasty to Venus through Aeneas, a symbol of Rome's glorious beginning with Aeneas' flight from Troy in a night of fire, anguish, and death—and ending with the near total conquest of everything by one of Aeneas' descendants. The places that had seen the making of that history over the centuries were brought together definitively, since the passage between the old Forum and the new square was next to the new Senate House, established by Julius Caesar simultaneously with the demolition of its predecessor, the old Senate House, or Curia Hostilia, which had been restored by Sulla.

The Forum of Caesar included a large bronze equestrian statue, originally part of a monument to Alexander the Great, in which the figure of Alexander was replaced with one of Julius Caesar. Although with the building of the Forum of Caesar, Julius Caesar imposed on Rome the model of the Hellenistic sanctuary for the cult of deified rulers—later widely reproduced in the similar *Caesarea* built in the cities of the empire—his interest in the original republican Forum was undiminished. On the south side of the Forum, the space occupied by the Basilica Sempronia was chosen for the construction of the new Basilica Julia, while on the opposite side he financed nearly all the restoration of the Basilica Aemilia (Paulli), begun officially in 54 BC by Lucius Aemilius Paullus, showing respect for those families which, after contributing to the glory of Rome, maintained considerable political influence.

Nearly all the large projects commissioned by Julius Caesar were far from completion at the time of his assassination—the Forum of Caesar, the Basilica Julia, the Saepta Julia, or voting enclosure for the *comitia* (assemblies) in the Campus Martius. Only later, during Augustus' rule, did this last project reach completion, perhaps without respecting the original design.

Other urban planning projects dreamed up by Julius Caesar to change the appearance of Rome remained unfinished. They included diverting the course of the Tiber in order to join the Campus Martius with the Vatican, and surrounding the Capitoline Hill by large public buildings, following the building of a theater against its northern slopes.

The short period between Julius Caesar's victory over Pompey at the battle of Pharsalus in 48 BC and Octavian's over Mark Antony at Actium in 31 BC changed the way urban space was conceived for the practical purposes of the spaces designed to concentrate the symbols of power. The city of the individual who could become the

Remains of the temple built by Caesar to Venus Genetrix, the Matriarch of the Julian Dynasty.

ruler of the Romans coincided only minimally with the Rome of the *primus inter pares* (first among equals).

Images of an Oligarchy

Along with historical reliefs, portraits are a characteristic form of production of Roman art in this period. Several traditions contributed to its development: sculpture from the middle period of the republic, masterfully represented in the Capitoline Brutus, Greek Hellenistic portraiture, and, last but not least, the aristocratic tradition of the *ius imaginum*, a law which gave the right to possess and display in the atrium of the family house wax icons of family ancestors. The strict rules limiting access to the highest public offices were gradually being relaxed as this patrician privilege was extended to families, even of plebeian origin, whose members had held high offices (dictator, consul, praetor, or aedile), creating the basis for the *nobilitas* (nobility) of descent.

Such portraits of ancestors must have been reproduced in large quantities, even when they started to be of bronze or marble, since all descendants would possess some. Many surviving portraits are in fact much later replicas. Such *imagines maiorum* (portraits of the ancestors), small heads in the round, one-third lifesize and sometimes including the neck, can be seen in the House of the Menander at Pompeii and in the so-called *Barberini Man Wearing a Toga*, who holds two busts of ancestors.

Besides the shared search for realism, three consecutive stylistic trends can be distinguished in portraiture of the first century BC. The first trend, linked to the Hellenistic portrait tradition, is characterized by a rich plasticity and a search for expressiveness through an accentuation of physiognomic detail. The second trend is essentially veristic. The third trend is a synthesis of the first two, in which the style of Greek portraiture distances itself from an occasionally exaggerated plasticity in favor of a more sober and balanced composition.

The first style, in all probability traceable to the activity of Greek sculptors in Rome, is exemplified by the portrait of Aulus Postumius Albinus in the Vatican Museums, probably a copy of an original of the early first century BC, where the features are rendered with remarkable plasticity, with the clear intention of giving the character psychological depth.

The common veristic type portrait—for a long time considered one of the most characteristic expressions of Roman art—contains a detailed realism in the rendering of the facial features, with exaggerated attention to individual details and an obvious intention to impart a definite

character to the subject of the portrait. The anonymous portrait from Osimo near Ascoli Piceno (Roman Auximum) of an elderly man with a wrinkled face, thinning hair, and thin closed lips, is typical of this stylistic trend, which seems to have been popular for a brief period of time, from 90 BC to 32 BC, that is, between the age of Sulla and the Second Triumvirate.

Finally, the surviving copies of the portraits of Pompey the Great can be considered typical of the third style of the late republican age. In the statue of Pompey in Copenhagen, perhaps a copy of the statue by Pasiteles exhibited in Pompey's complex in the Campus Martius, the most important element is the smoothness of the face, only slightly marked by lines and framed by short tidy locks of hair, seeming to foreshadow the cool expressive composure of the Augustan age.

Private Luxury: Domestic Architecture

For the whole of the second century BC, the housing of the ruling class does not seem to have differed greatly from that of earlier periods. The refurbishment of ancient aristocratic houses on the northeastern slopes of the Palatine Hill following a fire around 200 BC included some substantial changes in the arrangement of the internal space. The new ground plan no longer comprised the typical atrium and garden but had instead two small atriums with *impluvia*, square basins to receive rain water, next to each other, leading to living and reception rooms. The first atrium was probably the vestibule used by the head of the family to receive his *clientes* (clients, or followers) during the daily ceremony of the *salutatio* (greeting). The larger, more secluded, atrium was probably the private area of the home, around which opened living rooms and bedrooms for the family.

The decoration of these rooms—though much less than that found in private homes elsewhere in Italy—reveals a certain elegance, well-suited to the high status of the owners. Reception rooms were generally paved with reddish floors made of fragments of terracotta *cocciopesto* or *signino* (from Segni, the place where this ancient technique, of Carthaginian origin, was mastered). They were often decorated with geometrical patterns made with white tesserae or were enlivened with randomly scattered colored stone fragments.

Despite this floor decoration, among the earliest of this type, the overall impression conveyed

Portrait of Aulus Postumius Albinus. Replica of an original from the first century BC The modeling of individual features shows the first attempts at psychological portraiture. Rome, Vatican Museums.

Portrait of an unknown man from Osimo. A superb example of verism, the accurate depiction of physiognomic features and a characteristic of Republican portraiture. Municipio di Osimo.

Portrait of Pompey the Great. The depiction of the hair standing up over the middle of his forehead – a motif referred to as anastolé – has been borrowed from portraits of Alexander the Great, and is a clear sign that Pompey was attempting to present himself as the new Alexander. Kopenhagen, Ny Carlsberg Glyptotek.

by these homes is of modesty, far from the pomp of the large public buildings and the flaunting of wealth visible in the more sumptuous houses in minor towns such as Pompeii, where at this time the House of the Faun, covering nearly over 30,000 square feet, was decorated with opulent mosaic and elegant wall decoration. Compared to Pompeii houses, Rome, paradoxically, seemed to prefer more sober and archaic styles.

Roman aristocrats were less interested in elegant house decoration and more concerned with the location of their residence, which had to be as close as possible to the Forum so as to be visible to all citizens. It is not by chance that the houses of Scipio Africanus Major and Scipio Africanus Minor, the most prominent figures in Rome at the beginning and end of the second century BC, were adjacent to the city's public area. Scipio Africanus Major, whose house was surrounded by modest shops, lived in an area of the Forum later occupied by the Basilica Sempronia and the Basilica Julia. Scipio Africanus Minor, probably murdered in his bed after a mysterious late-night political meeting,

was assigned a house near the Forum by the people for his political and military merits.

Official residences, houses similar in size and decoration to the House of the Faun in Pompeii, were used by individuals who held certain public offices. One such house was the *domus publica* (state-owned house) adjacent to the Regia in the Forum, with a terracotta-paste floor decorated with geometrical motifs and the remains of an exedra with two travertine columns. It was the home of the chief priest, the *pontifex maximus*, who at the beginning of the second century BC was assigned a state-owned home on the Sacred Way so as to be more easily accessible for consultation.

All the same, the Roman ruling class of the time was not made up of many austere Cato types. In fact, it was only Cato who in his speeches attacked the senatorial aristocracy, accusing it of dedicating exorbitant resources to private buildings and of indulging in the exhibition of luxuries in their homes. However, the context reveals that these residences were not in the city but in the country—not *domus* (houses) but *villae* (country villas), some of which, as Cato reminds us, had floors of Numidian marble, imported directly from rival Carthage.

Villas and Gardens

This period also saw a new phenomenon near Rome which was to enjoy great success during the late Republican Age and in the Imperial Age, the *hortus* (gardens). The model of the residential *hortus*—literally a cultivated and fenced field—was the parks of Hellenistic rulers and dignitaries (*pardeisoi*), particularly the gardens of the Carthaginian aristocracy. It is possible that these influenced Scipio Africanus Major, the first of the aristocrats to be remembered for his possession of *horti* of this type.

It was in such *horti* in the country, especially in residences in the most prestigious sites along the coast of Latium and Campania, outside the control of sumptuary laws to regulate private expenditure enforced in the city of Rome, that the aristocracy's exhibition of wealth reached its peak during the second and early first centuries BC. In these country residences or villas, often divided into two sections, one for the private residence of the owner (*pars urbana*), the other used for activities associated with agriculture or farming (*pars fructuaria*), architects strove to evoke through peristyles, exedrae, porticos, and triclinia the atmosphere of the great architectural complexes of Greece. They even reproduced whole sections of celebrated public buildings and their decoration, as Cicero claimed when he mentioned the presence of a *peripatos* (covered walk) and an academy in his splendid villa at Tusculum.

Pompeii, House of the Faun. Mosaic decoration showing a Nile landscape from the entrance to the Alexander Exedra. The themes and techniques used in the mosaics of this richly furnished house point to the work of Alexandrine craftsmen. Naples, Museo Archeologico Nazionale.

In the years around 100 BC, houses within Rome itself became larger and more luxurious. The periodical repetition of the laws regulating the amount of luxury were useless. Such laws limited the number of guests and parties, in an attempt to restrict the formation of increasingly larger assemblies of people at the host's disposal and to discourage social groupings that might influence public life.

Among the most splendid residences of the time are recorded those of Lucius Licinius

Pompeii, House of the Faun. Section from a mosaic showing ducks and fish. Naples, Museo Archeologico Nazionale.

Crassus and Marcus Aemilius Scaurus, both of whom, decorated the atriums of their houses with the marble columns used in the temporary theaters built during their magistracies. In the case of Crassus, in about 103 BC the large-scale refurbishment of the most important part of his residence was still the object of severe criticism, so much so that it earned Crassus the nickname of *Venus Palatina* (the Palatine Venus), probably because the back of the wide Corinthian atrium in which he received his clients reminded his rivals of the round temple of the Greek city of Cnidos which housed the famous Aphrodite (Venus) by Praxiteles. A few decades later, the house of Marcus Aemilius Scaurus, now acquired by Clodius Pulcher, Cicero's formidable opponent, was capable of hosting hundreds of visitors during the *salutatio*, showing it was worthy of a figure who in the building of his theater had shown a predilection for colossal architecture.

In the first century BC, the display of luxury in private spaces became common. Many of the best-known public figures were also remembered for the opulence of their residences. Lucullus' *horti*, for example, which became proverbially famous, were the destination of many visitors,

including Greek scholars who visited the library with its enormous collection of books. Almost certainly as sumptuous was the residence built for Pompey in the Campus Martius, later acquired by Mark Antony. Cicero himself, a new man (*homo novus*) whose assets were certainly not comparable with those of many Romans of noble and ancient lineage, was proud of owning a house on the slopes of the Palatine Hill which featured a peristyle—pompously referred to as a *palaestra*—and a covered walk (*xystus*).

During the period of the private political agreements such as that which resulted in the ratification of the First Triumvirate, aristocratic residences had to be capable of welcoming guests as well as featuring large rooms where important decisions were made, not just with regards to the family but also perhaps for all citizens.

It was precisely for this reason that Augustus strove to limit the opulence of private residences. He was the first to give up luxuries which might appear useless. One of the most symbolic acts of Augustus' architectural policy was the demolition of the opulent town house of the well-known Publius Vedius Pollio, which he inherited on Pollio's death. Augustus replaced it with a large public building, the Porticus of Livia, showing his preference for public magnificence (*publica magnificentia*) over private luxury (*luxuria privata*), in keeping with the best republican tradition.

Augustus: Images of a Consensus

Following the assassination of Julius Caesar on the Ides of March (March 15), 44 BC, and the death of his assassins at the battle of Philippi two years later, which officially marked the failure of the conspiracy, the struggle for succession lasted thirteen interminable years, years which saw the final destruction of the values of republican Rome.

Despite his youth and the fact that he was acting on the edge of legitimacy, the politically astute nineteen-year-old Octavian, great-nephew on his mother's side of Julius Caesar, was able to exploit the atmosphere of fear and confusion which followed Julius Caesar's death. With the support of clever propaganda, boosted by what Zanker has appropriately called "the power of images," the *divinus adulescens* (divine youth), as Cicero called him (*Philippics*, 5, 16, 42), managed to present the defeat of Mark Antony at the battle of Actium not as the final episode in a ruthless civil war but rather as part of a just war of Romans and of an upright

Italy against a corrupt and degenerate east. Once he had achieved total power, in 31 BC, Octavian's political style changed greatly and with it, images and architectural forms, now oriented towards a type of sophistication of impersonal and cool elegance perfectly suited to the balanced sobriety which Augustus imposed on himself and his entourage.

This change in Augustus' political persona and in the visual language he employed can be clearly seen by comparing three coins on which are depicted three honorific statues used by the Senate to commemorate Augustus' military victories, and the statues of Augustus found at Prima Porta and Via Labicana, which portray Augustus respectively in military and in religious dress. The three coins depict the equestrian gilt sculpture dedicated to Augustus in 43 BC, the honorific statue commemorating the victory over Sextus Pompey, son of Pompey the Great, at Naulochus in 36 BC, and the pillar topped with a statue of a naked Octavian, also celebrating the battle of Naulochus. The models of the three statues must be sought in the representations of Hellenistic kings; they belong to the demagogic and violent past of Julius Caesar's youthful successor.

In contrast, the new portrait created at the beginning of Augustus' principate, with harmonious proportions clearly inspired by Greek classical models, expresses a timeless, calm, and sublime beauty. It became the official image of Augustus, and was reproduced in every corner of the empire. Augustus' choice conferred an unmistakable character on official art—an elegant, almost hieratic, but ultimately cold style—condemning to decadence the Asiatic style of Hellenism.

If the Via Labicana statue portrayed Augustus in the role of officiating priest (*pontifex*), conveying the discreet and solemn image of the devout priest, the reliefs on the breastplate of the Prima Porta statue of Augustus, besides being a masterpiece of neo-Attic sculpture, contain elements of great importance for the ideology of Augustus' principate. In the center, framed by personifications of Germany and Pannonia, provinces that had been conquered by Tiberius, Augustus' stepson, between 12 and 8 BC, is Phraates IV, king of Parthia, in the act of giving back to a Roman general—probably Tiberius—the legionary standards captured by the Parthians from Crassus in 53 BC, as well as an image of the heavens, under which flies the chariot of the sun, preceded by Aurora (goddess of the dawn) and Phosphorus (the personification of the morning star). Below, Tellus (or Gaia, the Earth), Apollo on a griffin, and Diana on a doe complete the composition. The statue, which seems to have been executed around 8 BC to celebrate the military deeds of Tiberius, was probably intended to

Marble statue of Augustus carrying out a sacrifice in his role as Pontifex Maximus (High Priest). This piece was found in 1910 on the Via Labicana. Rome, Museo Nazionale Romano in the Palazzo Massimo alle Terme.

FOLLOWING PAGES:
Detail of the statue of Augustus from the Via Labicana showing the veiled head of Augustus. The motif of the *capite velato*, the veiled head, was taken from actual sacrificial practices and came to be a cipher for the piety of Rome's rulers, and an expression of their respect for gods and ancestors. Rome, Museo Nazionale Romano in the Palazzo Massimo alle Terme.

Statue of Augustus in armor from Livia's villa, Prima Porta. The imagery of the breastplate shows the return of the standard lost by Crassus in 53 BC in a battle against the Parthians. This important diplomatic success was skillfully given a pictorial rendering by Augustus in order to secure his dynastic aims. Rome, Vatican Museums.

71

support the claim of Tiberius as Augustus' successor in the principate.

The Mausoleum of Augustus

Between 32 and 28 BC Augustus commissioned the building of a family mausoleum on the north side of the Campus Martius, between the Tiber and the Via Flaminia. This was an enormous circular tomb over 280 feet across and nearly 130 feet high, consisting of two thick cylindrical masses faced with travertine and marble, separated by a sloped embankment planted with trees, on which probably stood a colossal statue of Augustus. The door to the tomb, on the south side, next to which were hung bronze plates containing Augustus' official autobiography, the *Res Gestae*, was flanked, following an Egyptian custom, by two obelisks (now in Piazza del Quirinale and in Piazza del Esquilino, in front of Santa Maria Maggiore). The structure, several stories high, was inspired by Hellenistic funerary architecture, with a tomb below and a funerary temple above.

The Mausoleum, whose official name, *tumulus Iuliorum* (tomb of the Julian dynasty), left no doubt as to the dynastic ambitions of the young Octavian, housed first of all the remains of Marcellus (his nephew), who died in 23 BC, then Agrippa (his son-in-law), Lucius and Gaius Caesar, Augustus himself, Drusus the Younger, Livia (his wife), and Tiberius. It is not certain whether Claudius was buried here. Apart from him, of the Julio–Claudian dynasty, only Julia, Augustus' daughter, and, later, Nero, were buried elsewhere.

The Palace of Augustus and Temple of Apollo

Augustus built his palace on the Palatine, the hill most closely linked with earliest Roman tradition, an area associated with Romulus and the god Apollo, whom Augustus had invoked for his victories, especially Actium. The palace consisted of two separate buildings, the so-called House of Livia, the living quarters, and the so-called House of Augustus, where Augustus received guests. The Temple of Apollo, begun immediately after the victory of Naulochus over Sextus Pompey in 36 BC, and dedicated on October 9, 28 BC, was included in the public space of the palace. The temple was built entirely of Carrara marble.

What survives of the Temple of Apollo is the concrete core, traces of the marble floor, and fragments of columns and Corinthian capitals—which, for its elaborate form was the favorite architectural style under Augustus. Also surviving

is part of the marble jamb of a door with a depiction of the tripod at the shrine of Apollo at Delphi, and fragments of complex scenes of the killing of the children of Niobe and of the expulsion of the Gauls from Delphi. The cult images of Apollo, Diana, and their mother Leto (Latona), Greek originals of the fourth century BC, masterpieces by Scopas the Elder, Timotheus, and Cephisodotos, are known to us only through Pliny. They are the first—and not isolated—case of the reuse of Greek statues as cult images in Roman temples. We know that it was decided to restore Timotheus' badly damaged Diana, choosing C. Avianius Evander, a Greek sculptor from Alexandria, rather than replacing it with a copy.

These statues are depicted in a relief on a marble votive base of the early imperial age now in Sorrento. In the center, on a pedestal next to a tripod is Apollo with the lute, or cithara, his mother Leto (Latona), and his sister Diana, who bears a torch as a *lucifera* (bearer of light). The Delphi Sibyl, crouched on the ground, points at the sibylline books. The statue thus portrayed Apollo in his role of peaceful singer.

The votive statue of Apollo vowed by Octavian before the battle of Actium, which stood outside the building, was perhaps a Greek original. Representing Apollo playing the cithara at an altar, it stressed the same peaceful aspect of Apollo and the sense of atonement which was typical of offerings. However, the depiction on the relief of the rostra (prows) of the Egyptian ships, evidently placed as decoration on the high pedestal of the statue, meant that the symbols of the victory over Mark Antony were prominent.

On each side of the Actium Apollo were the *armenta Myronis*, four sculptures of cows

Rome, House of Augustus on the Palatine Hill. View of murals from the end of the Second Pompeian Style (c. 30 BC) in the Room of the Masks. These pictures crown the sides of a perspectival depiction of fantastic architecture whose empty central section allows a view onto a painted landscape.

made by Myron, the fifth-century BC Greek sculptor who from the end of the second century BC onwards was regarded as the best sculptor of animal subjects (Propertius, *Poems*, II, 31).

The temple stood on a wide square enclosed by a portico, named after the Danaids, whose statues decorated it. The three famous herms, two in black marble, one in red, found during recent excavations in the surrounding area and now in the Palatine Antiquarium, may have belonged to the temple, as well as the splendid painted terracotta reliefs, some of which can be dated to about 30 BC. They show Perseus slaying Medusa and the dispute between Apollo and Hercules for the tripod at Delphi. The hieratic rigidity of the figures and, in the scene of the dispute between Apollo and Hercules, their heraldic position beside the tripod, are suggestive of a strong archaic character to the composition. On the other hand, the rendering of the bodies reveals strong dependence on early classical forms, following the new eclectic taste typical of the Augustan era.

As already mentioned, Augustus built his palace on a vast area northwest of the Temple of Apollo in the years immediately after the victory over Pompey at Naulochus, adding to the house he had acquired which had previously been owned by the great orator Quintus Hortensius Hortalus. The surviving structures consist of a series of square rooms of tufa, arranged in two rows. The smaller, more secluded, ones on the west side, with simple geometric mosaic floors, seem to have been living quarters while the rooms on the east side, on both sides of a large central room and with clear traces of mosaic (later removed), may have had an official function.

The first set of rooms includes two small rooms one next to the other, each splendidly decorated. They include a room with pine festoons hanging from thin pilasters and the so-called Room of the Masks, named after the masks depicted in frames halfway up the wall within a complex illusionistic architectural decor clearly inspired by theatrical backdrops. The center of each wall features an illusionistic painting of a rural santuary in a landscape.

The private area of the imperial residence of the House of Livia also has exquisite decoration, particularly the frescos of one of the rooms of the reception suite (the *Tablinum*), where the wall is conceived as a large theatrical backdrop on a low podium, preceded by Corinthian columns which divide the wall into three sections and support on top a lacunar framework. Each section has a painted door frame. The side doors, which are open, reveal architectural vistas in perspective while the central one, according to the prevailing neoclassical taste, has a mythological painting, a copy of a classical painting, perhaps by Nicias, of the heifer Io guarded by Argus with Mercury coming to rescue her. Two frames halfway up the wall contain little squares with sections showing genre images of Hellenistic subject matter.

More recent are the Farnesina paintings and stuccos now in the Museo Nazionale Romano in Palazzo Massimo, from a huge riverside villa which perhaps belonged to Augustus' son-in-law Agrippa. They bear the signature in Greek of a painter of Syrian origin, Seleucus.

Fresco portraying Apollo with a cithara taken from the area of the House of Augustus on the Palatine Hill. The quite deliberate linking of the emperor with the God of Purity was an important factor in defining the conception and the furnishings of his residence on the Palatine. Rome, Museo Palatino.

Livia's house on the Palatine. The part of the Augustinian residential complex reserved for Augustus' wife was decorated with murals from the late Second Style. This section shows a monochromatic yellow frieze with a garland.

Painting

The rich painting tradition discussed so far belongs to the Second Style, popular between 40 and 20 BC. Compared to older examples of the Second Style, the best of which are in the House of the Griffins, a wealthy private residence, innovative elements are introduced, in keeping with the eclectic taste which was characteristic of Augustan art. First, the central section of the wall appears entirely occupied by reproductions of well-known easel paintings of the Greek classical and Hellenistic periods, perhaps evidence of the habit of utilizing paintings in real scenes as well. The upper portion is often crowded with small genre paintings, still-lifes or landscapes. However, there are also more complex compositions, such as the attack of the man-eating Laestrygonians on Ulysses, represented in the panel originally in the uppermost wall section of a house in Via Graziosa on the Esquiline Hill, dated to around the mid-first century BC and associated with what Vitruvius called *Ulixis errationes per topia* ([depictions of] Ulysses' travels with landscapes).

In the Second Style, the walls are framed by illusionistic architectural elements that are not inspired by real architecture but instead are idealized and employed with great freedom of imagination. A series of detailed secondary decoration, often symbolic, and perfectly suited to the figurative language of official Augustan art, such as sphinxes, cornucopias, tripods, sacrificial objects, and floral elements, emerge—beyond all formal logic—out of columns and architraves. Vitruvius' assessment of this latter phase of the Second Style seems justified: with the great public and private architectural structures of the early first century BC in mind, Vitruvius considered such compositions veritable "monsters" (*monstra*) because they depicted "things that neither were nor could ever be."

A few years later, with the so-called Third Style, or ornamental style, which became popular in Rome from about 15 BC, the wall was conceived as a unity, not as a pretext for daring perspective games. Thus the already meager elements of the Second Style disappear completely, leaving room for floral themes, thin columnar frameworks, and slim candelabra placed to frame large monochrome surfaces, against which individual paintings by famous masters stood out.

Public Magnificence

In contrast with the emphasis on private luxury of the late republic, the grandiose public building projects which were completed by Augustus during his long reign resulted in the significant alteration of the appearance of entire urban districts. Besides seeing to the completion of some of Julius Caesar's unfinished projects, and the restoration of temples, Augustus can be said to have invaded the city with his buildings, laden with symbols of new power. According to Suetonius, in his life of Augustus (28, 3), Augustus boasted toward the end of his life that he had found Rome a city of brick and left it one of marble.

Augustus' building initiatives in the Forum brought a transformation of the ancient political heart of the city into a monumental square intended to celebrate the Julian-Claudian dynasty. In particular, the short eastern side accommodated the Temple of the Deified (Divus) Julius Caesar (29 BC), built on the spot where a marble column had marked the site of the cremation of Julius Caesar. A new tribune for orators was erected before the temple, the *rostra ad Divi Iulii*, which displayed the rostra from the battle of Actium, a companion to the tribune decorated with the rostra from the ships captured at Anzio in 338 BC—one of the most memorable battles of republican Rome—which Julius Caesar had had rebuilt at the opposite end of the Forum after the demolition of the structures on the Comitium.

Other works were also dictated by propagandistic and dynastic requirements. Thus the single arch on the south end of the Temple of Apollo which commemorated the victory over Sextus Pompey was replaced in 19 BC with a triple arch celebrating victory over Mark Antony.

If the entire east side of the Forum concentrated on the glorification of Augustus' family, the west side, with the original Senate House (the Curia), the original rostra, and the treasury of the Temple of Saturn appeared, by contrast, laden with symbols of the other foundation of Augustus' rule, the Senate. This dualism appeared again, in even more elegant forms, in the new architectural complex which Augustus built at ninety degrees to the Forum of Caesar, the Forum of Augustus.

The Forum of Augustus

The Forum of Augustus, which best displays all the themes of Augustan artistic propaganda, is dominated by the Temple of Mars the Avenger (Mars Ultor), vowed in 42 BC before the battle of Philippi but inaugurated only in 2 BC. The structure was financed *in privato solo*, that is, with the revenue derived from war booty alone. The new Forum turned out slightly smaller than planned because Augustus did not wish to expropriate the owners of adjacent properties. As a result the boundary wall is not straight. This imposing wall, of square blocks of peperino from Gabii and almost a hundred feet high, was a formidable barrier between the humble and dense Subura district and the religious atmosphere that pervaded the Forum, over 400 feet long and nearly as wide, resplendent with marble and full of allusions to the new ruler and his family. The side facing the Subura had two entrances, a single arch and a triple arch on each side of the temple, while stairs led from the Subura to the forum. At the bottom of the stairs in the northernmost entrance was the arch erected by Tiberius in honor of his son Drusus Minor. Outside the other entrance, the so-called Arch of Pantanus, stood the Arch of Germanicus, Tiberius' adoptive son and thus Augustus' great-nephew.

In the center of the Forum, which was paved with marble and was surrounded by Corinthian porticos of cipollino marble, on one level surmounted by a high attic decorated with caryatids and shields with the head of the ram-horned Jupiter Ammon, stood a bronze quadriga (chariot and four horses) with a statue of Augustus. The caryatids, symbolizing the conquered peoples, are an exact copy of those on the Erechtheum temple on the Acropolis in Athens. As ornament, they were not restricted to the Forum of Augustus, being employed generally at this time to confer classicism on entire architectural structures.

Behind each of the two colonnaded halls on the sides of the forum was a large exedra, a new feature in the design of the forums compared to the original Forum and the Forum of Caesar. The rear walls of the side porticos were divided by cipollino half-columns supporting a white marble architrave, framing niches with statues of figures identified by inscriptions, on the plinth, with the name and offices held by the individual portrayed (the *titulus*), and in a panel below, listing his most important deeds (the *elogium*, eulogy). In the large central niche in the left exedra were statues of Aeneas, Anchises, and Ascanius, a visual counterpart to the group in the right exedra of Romulus carrying the body of Acron, king of the men of Caenina, a well-known episode described in detail by Plutarch. On the side with the scene of Aeneas—founder of the Julio-Claudian dynasty and a classic example of filial duty—stood statues of Aeneas' descendants. On the side with Romulus—an example of military prowess and the legendary founder of Rome—stood statues of the *summi viri* (the Great Men) of the republic. The decorative program of the Forum of Augustus was thus a fusion of the Trojan and Romulus myths of the origins of Rome in order to celebrate the Julio-Claudian dynasty and the empire, as well as a providential end of the republic.

The area of the city which was most affected by Augustus' interventions and those of his family, in particular his son-in-law Agrippa, was the Campus Martius. Besides total reconstruction of the buildings surrounding the Circus Flaminius, a grandiose urban scheme was executed which profoundly changed the structure of the central area of the Campus Martius, until then an area beyond the pomerium still free of public buildings. Within a few decades, the Saepta Julia and the Diribitorium were completed (both begun by Julius Caesar), the Portico of the Argonauts, the Portico of Meleager, the original Pantheon, the Baths of Agrippa with the adjacent Stagnum—the vast artificial lake from which flowed the Euripus, the canal which flowed out into the Tiber—the Basilica of Neptune, and the Theater of Marcellus, all splendid buildings designed for the leisure activities of the Romans, and which had a strong ideological impact.

The Ara Pacis

The most important monument for the understanding of official Augustan art is the Ara Pacis (literally the altar of peace), an altar celebrating peace under Augustus which was decreed by the Senate on July 4, 13 BC to celebrate Augustus' return from Spain and dedicated on January 30, 9 BC. The altar, in 1938 placed inside a purpose-built building near the Mausoleum of Augustus, originally stood on the spot where the Via Flaminia entered the city. The altar itself, on which an annual sacrifice was performed, stood inside an open rectangular enclosure (thirty-eight by thirty-five feet) on a low podium. It was reached by a nine-step stairway and had two doors on the short sides, one facing Via Flaminia, the other the Campus Martius.

The external decoration of the enclosure is in two registers separated by a band decorated with a Greek meander motif. On the lower register are acanthus scrolls enlivened by small interspersed animals; in the upper register is a complex pictorial relief of sculptured panel paintings with the same separation, this time bands of vertical palmettes and lotus flowers. Two marble panels of allegorical or mythological scenes are placed one above the other on each side of the door. Next to the main door is the Lupercal, the cave where the wolf suckled Romulus and Remus, and Aeneas sacrificing the Laurentan sow and her thirty piglets.

The friezes beside the other door of the enclosure show the goddess Roma dressed as an Amazon sitting on a pile of armor and Tellus (Earth, alternatively identified as Italy, or Peace), depicted as a florid maternal figure

seated with two children in her lap and surrounded by fruit against a background of ears of wheat, poppies, and plants.

The long sides of the Ara Pacis depict the procession that may have taken place in 13 BC, with the hierarchy of priests (*ordo sacerdotum* and members of Augustus' family in a specific hierarchical order which probably reflected the order of succession conceived by Augustus around 10 BC.

All the symbolism of the reliefs of the enclosure wall associated Augustus with Peace (*Pax* in Latin), celebrating his transformation of Italy into a land of plenty as it prospered under the universal rule of Rome after the horrors of the civil wars. The association of the origins of Rome with Aeneas, the founder of the Julio-Claudian dynasty, and therefore with Augustus, is stressed. The rule of Augustus—as already suggested by the decorative scheme of the Forum of Augustus—signaled the end of the history of the Roman republic.

The altar proper has three steps on its sides, with five steps on the west to allow the priest celebrating access to the table. The decoration included a frieze with personifications (probably of conquered provinces) in the lower section and a frieze with a procession of Vestal Virgins and *victimaria* (priests' assistants) above. In the crowning *pulvinus* are tendrils and lion's heads.

From a stylistic perspective, the Ara Pacis is an eclectic work with a marked neoclassical element which emerges clearly in the long narrative frieze and the landscape relief, marked

The outer enclosure of the Ara Pacis Augustae dedicated in 9 BC. Reliefs belonging to the building which were found in the sixteenth and nineteenth centuries were restored on the occasion of the two-thousandth anniversary of Augustus' birth in 1938. In spite of being reconstructed out of the context of its original location, the complexity and brilliantly executed decoration of this altar make it one of the key monuments of Roman antiquity.

Rome, Ara Pacis Augustae. Relief showing the allegorical figure of Tellus, the Earth (or, variously, Italy or Peace), as a divine matriarch in classical dress. The great number of attributes in the composition serve to depict vividly a state of happiness brought about by peace.

by decisively Hellenistic taste. Genuine Roman style is fully apparent only in the small altar frieze. The same contraposition of allegorical and triumphal images was to recur in the triumphal arches, which gives clear illustration of what has been called the bipolar character of Roman art.

Decorative Arts

The best expression of the Augustan style is perhaps best found outside the official decorative programs, which heavily influenced the sculptors commissioned to execute them. It is in this period that toreutic relief metal work, that is, the art of working metal by engraving, embossing, and chiseling, started by late Hellenistic artists like Pasiteles, a native of Greek southern Italy, reached its peak.

Particularly plentiful is silverware, found throughout the empire, along with imitations of it in the typical fine red tableware pottery, the so-called *terra sigillata* that from the mid-first century BC replaced black pottery. A celebrated and remarkably fine example is the silver bell-shaped crater (vase) found in Hildesheim in Germany along with a further sixty pieces of exquisite workmanship, including every type of vessel of the late Hellenistic period and the early empire. The surface of the crater, embossed and finished off by chisel, is entirely covered with decoration. On the background of the base two griffins stand in heraldic contraposition while threadlike tendrils coil amongst plump putti who catch fish and shrimp with a trident. The images are derived from official sculpture and painting models, as revealed by a comparison with the acanthus frieze on the Ara Pacis or with the Farnesina stuccos and paintings, but fantasy and playfulness go beyond the formal rigor which permeates the works commissioned by Augustus' court.

The age of Augustus also saw the revival of glyptics, the art of carving or engraving gems, in which the portrait acquires great importance. This had already been employed in Hellenistic gems from the time of the Diadochi, the successors of Alexander the Great, and was resumed, not surprisingly, at the beginning of the imperial age of Rome, when this form of art particularly appealed to the emperor's family. The most famous gem engraver in Augustus' service was Dioscorides, who perhaps came from Cilicia, the maker of the seal which bore Augustus' image which was used by him and his successors to seal letters and documents (Suetonius, *Augustus*, 50).

The taste of this period—markedly neoclassical, refined, and elegant—found its perfect expression in glyptics. Besides the increasingly mass-produced imagery common to every artistic form of the time—putti, satyrs, maenads, and dancers—more intricate works were created such as portraits of the imperial family or historical and allegorical representations. Cameos were the preferred means of expression. In this context, the Augustus gems in Vienna and Paris deserve special mention.

The Heirs of Augustus

Julio-Claudian taste follows essentially the path traced during the Augustan age, marked by neo-Attic classicism though with an increased development of an authentic Roman style, fully apparent only in the small central altar reliefs of the model of official Augustan art, the Ara Pacis. Indeed, in a monument similar to the Ara Pacis, the so-called Base of the *Vicomagistri*, from the middle years of Tiberius' rule (AD 14–37), the abundant classical decoration of the cornices frames a scene which is enlivened by a spatial freedom previously unseen in Augustan art, obtained through a judicious arrangement of the figures, which have various poses and expressions. The individual figures, besides the conventionally rendered figures in the background, reflect the verist or "plebeian" tendency in Roman art, with a marked preference for static metallic forms, and with an intention to characterize individual portraits.

The relief, about sixteen feet long and three and a half feet high, was discovered in 1939 underneath the Palazzo della Cancelleria along with reliefs from the age of Domitian, to be discussed later. Formerly one side of the pedestal of an altar, it depicts a sacrificial procession with the figures that were associated with these ceremonies: *victimares*, *tibicines*, *liricines*, and *vicomagistri*, portrayed wearing togas. The *vicomagistri* were freedmen who guarded the *lares* (deity) and the *genius* (spirit) of Augustus, a cult started by Augustus himself in 7 BC. The first of a complex series of cults associated with Augustus, it was celebrated with sacrifices on the altars at the 265 *vici* (crossroads) of the city. The representation of the *vicomagistri* as togad figures, like the major magistrates of the city, shows pride in the position held, but also the disappearance of rank before the imperial majesty.

In contrast, sculptural fragments discovered near the church of Santa Maria in Via Lata can be traced back to a monument which was thought to be the Ara Pietatis Augustae (the Altar of Augustan Piety), though according to others it was the Ara Gentis Iuliae (the Altar of the Julio–Claudian House), authorized by the Senate in AD 22 and dedicated by Claudius in

AD 43. According to La Rocca, however, the fragments actually belong to an altar which was dedicated on the occasion of Claudius' *reditus* (return) from the northern provinces of the empire.

Essentially similar in structure to the Ara Pacis, it comprised an altar within an enclosure wall externally decorated with friezes illustrating scenes of sacrifices placed above a large panel decorated with acanthus and festoons with hanging plates. The narrative style—totally foreign to Augustan monuments—clearly emerges in the precise topographic location indicated by temples, and in the didactic representation of the key moments of the sacrificial ceremony. In the strictly stylistic sense, refined Augustan classicism appears here stiffened and simplified, revealing the employment of local sculptors, by now far removed from the sophisticated neo-Attic masters employed by Augustus.

The Auditorium of Maecenas

The building activity of the Julio-Claudian emperors, much less spectacular and intense than that of Augustus, continued in the direction already traced by Augustus. It was not until the rule of Nero, with the opportunity given by the great fire of AD 64, that an extensive and wide-ranging urban plan was created and carried out, changing the appearance of entire quarters of the city.

Besides the buildings commissioned by emperors or by high dignitaries of the imperial family, the period saw a proliferation of prestigious private residences, often surrounded by extensive gardens, mainly in the Aventine and Esquiline areas. Gaius Cilnius Maecenas, friend and adviser of Augustus, built a villa on the Esquiline Hill between 40 and 30 BC. Construction required covering an ancient necropolis with a thick layer of soil planted with trees and flowers, as well as building over the Servian Wall. At his death, Maecenas left his residence to Augustus, who used it when he was ill. It became Tiberius' residence in 23 BC when he returned from voluntary exile in Rhodes.

It was probably on that occasion that the paintings in the Third Style were made which decorate the walls of the only building remaining of the whole complex, the so-called Auditorium of Maecenas, probably a summer dining room or a nymphaeum. The frescos depict landscapes and gardens, according to contemporary taste, exemplified in the cycle of paintings in the Villa of Livia at Prima Porta.

Other gardens were developed on the Esquiline Hill near the gardens of Maecenas, belonging to the most prominent members of the Roman aristocracy, no longer interested in living near the center of power. The living quarters of these estates and their luxuriant gardens were richly decorated with statues, many of which were found at the end of the

Relief from the pedestal of the *Vicomagistri* depicting a procession. The eponymous *Vicomagistri* were responsible for the cults of domestic gods, patron divinities and the Augustinian spirits and are pictured here with veiled heads bearing statuettes of the various deities. In spite of their low social status as freed slaves, they are unusually shown as *togati*, a status reserved for the highest office bearers of the Empire.
Rome, Vatican Museums.

nineteenth century and are now in the Capitoline Museums. In particular, the Lamian Gardens Gallery there has statues from the Lamian Gardens, constructed probably by Lucius Aelius Lamia, consul in AD 3, and later acquired by Caligula. Besides sculpture of pure Hellenistic tradition such as the copies of the old fisherman and the old woman with a lamb, the splendid so-called Esquiline Venus, a statue of a seated girl, deserves attention. Dating from the first century BC, this represents a nude Venus in the act of tying a ribbon round her hair. It has been suggested that it may be a portrait of Cleopatra.

In the Uffizi in Florence are statues of the children of Niobe slain by Apollo and Diana, found near Piazza Vittorio Emanuele and originally probably in the Diaeta Apollinis (summer-house of Apollo), a building which may have been in the Lamian Gardens, as suggested by an inscription. This has recently been identified with a large complex found at the end of the nineteenth century between Piazza Dante and Via Emanuele Filiberto, now demolished.

The Basilica of Porta Maggiore

Another remarkable building, almost certainly originally part of a large *hortus* (garden), is the so-called underground basilica of Porta Maggiore, discovered in 1917. The area had belonged to Statilius Taurus, sentenced to death by Claudius in AD 53 on the charge of encouraging the diffusion of magic practices in Rome. The unusual structure, whose function—funerary basilica or neo-Pythagorean place of worship?—has been the subject of much debate, is a large underground room divided into three aisles articulated by six columns, with an apse at the end and a vaulted ceiling. There is a tiny vestibule at the other end. The complex underground structure was made by digging long trenches along the perimeter walls and pits corresponding to the six pillars. These cavities were then used as molds for concrete casts. The soil was subsequently removed.

The barrel-vaulted ceiling and apse are covered with miraculously intact complex stucco decoration, where cult scenes alternate with eschatological symbols and mythological allusions which are difficult to interpret, rendered in a refined style close to the Third Style. The nave vault is divided into three main sections depicting Castor or Pollux abducting one of the daughters of Leucippus, a winged genius seizing Ganymede, and the capture of the other daughter of Leucippus. Around are square panels containing mainly famous mythological couples: Iphigenia and Calchas, Hercules and Athena, Helen and Paris, Jason and Medea, Ulysses and Helen, Hercules and Hesione, and the zodiacal Taurus and Gemini.

The apse shows the scene of the poet Sappho's suicide from a cliff, in which she appears to be pushed by a putto and is about

to be caught by the sea-goddess Leucothea and by a triton in the presence of Apollo and Phaon. The scene suggests a symbology of salvation, beloved by the neo-Pythagoreans, who considered the act of diving into the sea the final moment of the human journey.

Nero's Golden House

During the Julio–Claudian age, all the great private gardens on the Esquiline Hill became imperial state property through bequests or expropriations. Eventually a huge park joined the other imperial properties on the Pincio and Quirinal Hills. The Domus Transitoria was built by Nero between AD 54 and 64 as the connection between the Palatine imperial residence—the Domus Tiberiana (expanded by Caligula towards the Forum)—and the residential complex on the Esquiline. Most of the Domus Transitoria was destroyed in the great fire of July 18, AD 64, which in six days almost completely destroyed the centre of the city (Tacitus, *Annals*, XV, 38-40), providing Nero with an excuse to rebuild the city according to strict building rules and Hellenistic town planning ideas. This would have made Rome a capital worthy of its title, with regular blocks of low stone buildings rather than wood.

The destroyed royal palace was replaced with another great imperial residence, the Golden House (Domus Aurea), the land for which was obtained through expropriation of most of the city center. "Rome has become just one house. Move to Veii—unless the house stretches to there!" lamented a well-known epigram, voicing the general discontent. The architects of the spectacular gigantic structure were Severus and Celer. Tacitus recognized their "ingenuity and boldness" (*ingenium et audacia*). The wall paintings were commissioned from a certain Fabullus, or Famulus, who used to paint for a few hours each day with great solemnity, always donning a toga, even on the scaffolding (Pliny, *Natural History*, XXXV, 120). The decoration of the Golden House suggests an exceptional artistic personality, who worked in the so-called Fourth Style, which originated in Rome in the mid-first century AD. Later Renaissance painters visited these places seeking inspiration.

The Greek sculptor Zenodorus was also commissioned to decorate the Golden House. The gigantic Colossus of Nero at the entrance of the Golden House, which portrayed the emperor as the sun-god, is his work. According to Pliny, Zenodorus could be considered one of the great artists of all times, capable of competing even with the masters of the first Hellenistic age, especially in the production of colossal metal statues. The Golden House was decorated with a huge number of statues looted by Nero from Greece and Asia Minor, among them the famous sculptures from Pergamum (of which only Roman copies survive), the *Dying Gaul* and the *Gaul Killing Himself and His Wife*.

The enormous complex of the Golden House, with pavilions and spa structures, porticos, nymphaeums, and small temples scattered through the park, looked more like a huge villa. It stretched from the Palatine and Velia Hills—where the great entrance with the Colossus of Nero was located—as far as the northern edges of the Oppian Hill, extending further east as far as the Caelian Hill—where the basement of the Temple of Divine (Divus) Claudius was transformed into a huge nymphaeum—then back to the Palatine.

The remains of the Golden House, principally on the Oppian Hill, comprise a conspicuous portion of a residential building (975 by 618 feet), which escaped destruction because it was later incorporated in the foundations of the Baths of Trajan, built after the fire of AD 104 and inaugurated on June 22, AD 109. In this wing of the palace, still on the Oppian Hill, remarkable differences have been noticed between the west side, with regular structures and decorated with high-quality paintings, and the east side, characterized by a much more articulated ground plan. These differences can probably be accounted for because the project was not unitary. The east side would have been added only later, though it is not easy to decide whether this was the Baths of Titus (*Domus Titi*), added by Titus (AD 79–81), second emperor of the Flavian dynasty, to Nero's residence, or whether it was part of the Golden House, added to the earlier Domus Transitoria. The older western side develops on a large rectangular square with colonnades on three sides, and a cryptoporticus on the north side built against the embankment. The most important rooms opened on to the south side of the square, among them a double hall with two alcoves on each side. It was evidently the private space of the imperial palace, which opened with large doors on to a portico overlooking the valley below.

The terrain was totally altered by work under Trajan, when the large openings were walled up. The original effects of architectural illusion must have been extraordinary, with light from well-planned openings and elegant fresco decoration, some of which survives.

These rooms are commonly known after their most notable decorative features—the Yellow Vaulted Room, the Owl Vaulted Room, the Black Vaulted Room. The lower portions of the walls were originally covered with marble revetments, removed in antiquity. The paintings, by the court painter Fabullus, are an extraordinary record of the Fourth Style—a florid style—in Rome (common in the houses in Pompeii rebuilt after the earthquake of AD 62). After the linear Third Style, decoration returned to complex architectural perspectives and elements, though in a world of pure illusion and fantasy where atmospheric, almost impressionistic, effects were conceived mainly for distant viewing.

On the east side of the Golden House, curved solutions prevailed, with rooms arranged around a large polygonal atrium, among them the famous so-called Golden Vault Room. Unfortunately this is in a poor state of conservation but we have a good idea of it thanks to Francesco d'Olanda's watercolor in the Codex Escurialensis, made around 1538. The complex vault appears to have been decorated with golden stucco framed squares depicting mythological scenes. It culminates with an unusual version of the abduction of Ganymede, with Jupiter carried off by the eagle along with the boy.

Another series of rooms radiated out from an octagonal space enclosed by walls with wide door openings, surmounted by a dome, which changes the space from octagonal to circular without the use of pendentives. The spatiality and illusionism pervading the Golden House represent a definitive turning point from Augustan classicism.

The same search for baroque painting effects in architecture and painting is also found in portraiture under Nero, in particular the portrait of Nero in the Museo Nazionale Romano, dating in all probability to the middle years of his

The murals of the Room of the Masks in the Golden House from the mature phase of the Fourth Style with their characteristic fantastic architectural forms. The high quality of their execution, a result of their state function in the imperial residence, marks them out from the Pompeian work of the same period.

reign. It is characterized by a psychological introspection recalling Hellenistic dynastic portraits, while the accurate rendering revealed in the soft treatment of the skin underlines the painterly quality of the sculpture, first seen in portraits of Claudius.

The Flavian Emperors: Vespasian, Titus, and Domitian

The ambitions of oriental-style charismatic monarchy embraced by Nero—who loved to call himself "the chosen one to be the vicar of the gods on earth" (Seneca, *On clemency*, I, 1, 2)—came to an end with his murder in AD 68. After a year of turbulence and war, emperors from the Flavian dynasty ruled for nearly thirty years (AD 69–96), seeking to introduce a more moral rule in opposition to the tyrannical style adopted by Nero, last of the Julio-Claudian dynasty, and reviving the traditional values expressed by Cato.

The Flavian emperors-Vespasian (AD 69–79), Titus (AD 79-81), and Domitian (AD 81–96)— ensured the return to the public domain of the vast areas acquired by Nero for his splendid private residence. The Baths of Titus were built on part of the site, perhaps as an adaptation of the private baths in the Golden House, while on the site that had been a lake in Nero's park a new, gigantic amphitheater was built, the Colosseum.

In the Temple-Forum of Peace, the great monumental square, at the time considered one of the wonders of the world, built by Vespasian between AD 71 and 75 to celebrate victory over the Jews (on the site of the Macellum, or Food Market, destroyed in a fire), were placed the statues which Nero had "taken by force and brought to Rome and exhibited in the rooms of his Golden House" (Pliny, *Natural History*, XXXIV, 84): Myron's cow, the sculptures of the Gauls from Pergamum, and works by Phidias, Leochares, Naukydes, and Polyclitus. Next to these masterpieces were exhibited spoils from the Temple in Jerusalem, such as the seven-branched candlestick (menorah) and the silver trumpets, which were depicted in the reliefs of the Arch of Titus.

The best-known period for public building and art under the Flavian emperors is that of Domitian. The great fire of AD 80 that destroyed the Campus Martius gave Domitian the opportunity to rebuild almost entirely this vast area of the city. Besides restoring the Theater of Marcellus, the Pantheon, the Baths of Agrippa,

the Saepta Iulia, and the Temple of Isis (or Iseum), Domitian built the Odeum and the Stadium (now Piazza Navona), two structures connected with the *certamen Capitolinum* he decreed in AD 86, and, to the east of the Saepta Iulia, the Porticus Divorum (Portico of the Gods), a colonnaded area with two small temples dedicated to Vespasian and Titus, erected on the site of the Villa Publica (State, or People's, Farm), where the two emperors had celebrated victory in Judea. With the erection of this portico and the round Temple of Minerva opposite it (known only from the huge marble plan of the city of Rome incised on a wall of a hall in the Temple of Peace), Domitian realized a dynastic cult sanctuary, on the lines of the Pantheon, which celebrated the glories of the Julio-Claudian dynasty.

A private cult sanctuary of the Flavian family was also built on the Quirinal Hill, where their family residence stood. Under the Caserma dei Corazzieri, on the present-day Via XX Settembre, were found the remains of a rich patrician house which the discovery of a water-pipe bearing the name of Titus Flavius Sabinus, Vespasian's brother, helped identify. Part of a nymphaeum reveals remarkable workmanship and extraordinary effect, as it is entirely covered with a glass paste mosaic in the Fourth Style depicting fantastic architectural structures and mythological scenes, including Hylas being pulled into the water by the waternymphs, surmounted by a semicircular niche decorated with mosaic. A concrete podium on the nymphaeum uphill may be part of the *aedes gentis Flaviae* (temple of the Flavian family), dedicated by Domitian to his deified family, which held the remains of his brother and father.

Domitian's Palace

The most impressive of Domitian's buildings were the new royal palace on the Palatine, the official imperial residence until the end of the empire, and the Forum of Nerva or Forum Transitorium (the passageway forum). In order to build the new palace on the Palatine, normally divided into a reception wing on the northwestern front (the Domus Flavia), a private wing in the center (the Domus Augustana), and a large stadium-shaped garden on the southeast, the architect Rabirius, in charge of the works, first had to level the southwestern side of the Palatine Hill, already occupied by republican and imperial buildings such as the House of the Griffins, the Aula of Isis, and part of Nero's Domus Transitoria. The work, begun in the early years of Domitian's reign, was completed in AD 92, as far as the palace proper is concerned.

Depiction of the Colosseum on a coin from the first century AD.

The brickstamps provide evidence that the stadium was completed only during the final years of Domitian's rule.

The palace, or Domus Flavia, is composed of a large square peristyle courtyard with a Numidian marble colonnade with an octagonal fountain and pool in the center and low walls arranged in a labyrinth pattern. A series of public audience halls lay around the courtyard: on the north, the so-called basilica and throne room and, perhaps, the *Lararium* (more likely the room for the praetorian guard, in charge of protecting the main entrance of the building); on the south a large dining room (*triclinium*) surmounted by an apse, with a nymphaeum with fountains on each side.

The throne room (Aula Regia)—the name given to the hall by eighteenth-century antiquarians—was a huge space a hundred feet high under a trussed roof covered with a caisson ceiling. The walls were articulated into various types of niches which held gigantic colored marble statues (those of Apollo and Hercules are now in Parma). At the back was an apse reserved to the emperor who on audience days could receive the *salutationes* of a large number of people.

The so-called basilica, recently identified with the emperor's council room, was divided into three aisles by a double row of columns, closed on the south end by a deep semicircular apse, and covered by a barrel vault.

The triclinium that overlooked the south side of the peristyle courtyard was in all probability the renowned and grandiose *Cenatio Iovis* (banquet hall of Jupiter), that is, the emperor's dining room. Its structure can be inferred from the brickmarks and the restoration under Hadrian. The marble floor is partly preserved and laid on to a hypocaust, having been restored under Maxentius.

The private quarters of the palace, the Domus Augustana, occupied two levels, to adapt to the slope of the hill. The entrance to this part of the palace is on the Circus Maximus side. The facade comprised a large exedra leading to a peristyle courtyard with a central fountain decorated with shield motifs, surrounded by a series of two-story rooms surmounted by dome or umbrella vaults.

Two flights of stairs permit access to the upper peristyle courtyard, which is placed on the same level as the official wing of the palace which featured a large pool with an island in the center.

Finally, the Stadium, or Hippodrome— gardens and a racetrack—was on the eastern side of the Domus Augustana, from the facade overlooking the Circus Maximus all the way up to the level of the second peristyle courtyard.

OPPOSITE AND FOLLOWING PAGES:
The construction of the amphitheater known today as the Colosseum was begun under Hadrian in an area formerly covered by an artificial lake in the park of the Golden House. The term Colosseum derives from the nearby colossal statue of Nero, which was reworked into a depiction of the god Sol after Nero's death. The building itself was dedicated in ad 80. by the emperor Titus. The exterior is a vertical series of three floors with arcades and a walled upper floor divided by pilasters. Each level was given its own order of columns: the succession of Tuscan, Ionic, and Corinthian orders in this building of Travertine stone became the model for a whole series of palace facades during the Renaissance. The division of internal seating into four areas (ima, media, summa cavea, and maenianum summum in ligneis) corresponded to a strict social hierarchy. According to the most recent calculations, this building had a capacity of up to 70 000 spectators. The highly functional design of the architecture meant that the arena could be quickly emptied by means of highly efficient exit routes.

Domitian's palace was a turning point in the history of Roman architecture, the first example of a dynastic palace. Whereas Nero's Golden House was still comparable to a large urban villa with pavilions freely arranged in space, the new palace was a compact and orderly structure capable of combining and sensibly separating the various rooms according to the many political and audience functions of an imperial residence. The articulation of the enormous complex over several levels allowed, moreover, the realization of those perspective illusions and views which are typical of architecture of the later Flavian period.

The Forum of Nerva

The same taste for baroque illusion pervading Domitian's palace can be found in another great work of the time, the Forum of Nerva, or Forum Transitorium, so called because it provided a link between the Forum of Augustus and the Temple of Peace. It is a good example of Domitian's town planning policy of integrating contrasting monuments into one complex, unifying the urban space.

Due to the limited space available, the new Forum, begun in AD 84 and inaugurated in AD 98 by Nerva (AD 96–98), was a long narrow structure (390 by 147 feet), with curved short sides and the mass of the Temple of Minerva in the background. An opening on the curved southwest side allowed access to the Argiletum, the street that led from the Forum to the Subura, and created lively perspective illusions. In the northwest corner of the square a clever system of curves and countercurves allowed the elimination of the dead corners that were created by the eastern exedra of the Forum of Augustus.

The solutions to make up for the lack of space inside the square were just as ingenious. The entire Temple of Minerva, except for its pronaos, stood outside the colonnaded area. The side columns were placed very close to the enclosure walls and connected to it by extremely short architraves.

The attic of the porticos was decorated with reliefs with divine figures and scenes of Minerva. The only section left above the two surviving Corinthian columns, the so-called *Colonnacce* (those ugly columns), shows various scenes of women's activities, including the myth of Arachne. The classicizing conception of the frieze stands in stark contrast with the chiaroscuro richness and baroque exuberance of the architectural decoration, revealing, in the use of the different formal expressions, the employment of artists from various workshops.

Statue of Hercules from the so-called Aula Regia, a conference room for imperial advisers in the Domus Flavia. This first imperial residence to combine both state and residential functions was laid out by the architect Rabirius at the end of the first century BC, during the reign of Domitian. Parma, Galleria Nazionale.

Further examples of sculpture from Domitian's era can help us understand the simultaneous presence of different artistic styles that make official urban art diverse and complex in character. Thus alongside the reliefs of the Arch of Titus, where the complex overlap of the levels, emphasized by the circular movement of the procession, expresses a spatial search unprecedented in Roman art, the reliefs that were discovered underneath the Palazzo della Cancelleria bear the cool and composed classicistic character of the Julio–Claudian age.

The Arch of Titus

The Arch of Titus—not mentioned in ancient literature, but identified thanks to the dedication on the eastern side of the attic—is still today an imposing sight at the highest point of the street at the end of the Forum. The single arch is a simple and solid structure in Pentelic marble, articulated with two half-columns of the Composite order on each side. Figures of the goddess Roma and of the genius of the Roman people decorate the keystones and flying victories on globes are in the spandrels of the arch. At the center of the vault, covered with elaborate caissons, a panel depicts the apotheosis of Titus, who rides an eagle which flies upwards.

On the architrave was a small frieze, now preserved only in the center of the eastern side, representing the triumphal procession celebrating Vespasian's and Titus' defeat of the Jews in AD 71. The inscription records that the Senate and the Roman People erected the arch to celebrate this victory. If the short figures carved in high relief in the small frieze belong to the style of the small frieze on the Ara Pacis, the two large panels on the inside of the arch depicting two episodes of the triumph over the Jews express a new artistic concept. The southern panel shows the initial moment of the ceremony, that is, the procession through the Triumphal Gate, shown in perspective from the right. Soldiers transport on stretchers the spoils from the Temple of Jerusalem, the silver trumpets and the menorah. The curved slabs probably bore painted inscriptions that listed the conquered cities and objects taken.

The panel on the north side shows the central episode of the triumph. Titus, accompanied by a Victory about to crown him, proceeds on his chariot drawn by four horses preceded by the lictors led by the goddess Roma and followed by allegorical figures of the Senate and the People of Rome, symbolized by a togad elder and a half-naked youth.

Through the prominence given to the figures and the crowding of objects above their heads,

Statue of Bacchus, originally placed in the niches of the Aula Regia of the Domus Flavia. These over-sized statues of gods and heroes were made from colored marble. Parma, Galleria Nazionale.

the two reliefs reveal a sense of spatial freedom skillfully rendered. The movement of the procession of the bottom panel thickens and becomes almost tangible thanks to the masterly arrangement of the figures above a line that is no longer horizontal but convex, nearly coming forward to meet the observer then disappearing, swallowed into the triumphal door.

Eclecticism and Innovation

In the art of the Flavian age, diverse stylistic levels, reflecting the traditions of different workshops, can be found within the same building or monument. This is the case with the reliefs from the tomb of the Haterii, at the third milestone on the ancient Via Labicana (now Via Casilina). Among the many fragments remaining of its rich architectural decoration are thin columns, pillars, parts of the entablature and the tympanum, fragments of inscriptions, friezes, and portraits. The owner of this tomb

has been identified as Quintus Haterius Tychicus, a builder. Because of his profession one of the reliefs depicts various monuments completed under Domitian: the Arch of Isis, erected in AD 80 at the entrance to the Temple of Isis, the Colosseum (still lacking the top story), an arch, perhaps the triumphal arch erected by Domitian, an *arcus in summa sacra via* (a gateway at the top of the Sacred Way), which can probably be identified with the monumental arch Domitian built on or near the site of the Porta Mugonia, the original gate to Romulus' city, and, finally, the Temple of Iupiter Custos, expanded around AD 90.

The other reliefs depict a scene of lamentation inside the house of the deceased and a complex scene with abundant funerary symbols. In the center stands the funerary structure, a four-column temple on top, and a high podium containing the crypt proper. On the left is lifting machinery, worked by slaves, culminating with a crane, on top of which two slaves arrange palm leaves and a basket containing the

View of the Arch of Titus on the Forum Romanum. This triumphal arch was erected by the Roman senate to commemorate the victorious campaign against the Jews by Vespasian and Titus in AD 71.

Relief from the tomb of the Haterii near Centocelle, depicting the deceased lying on a kline atop a temple. The crane, which is shown being operated by slaves, may well be a reference to the dead person's profession as builder. Rome, Vatican Museums.

eagle that, freed during the cremation, represented the apotheosis of the deceased. The upper portion of the composition ends with a scene depicting perhaps a deified deceased woman observing the ceremony of her apotheosis from the other world. The complex scene shows a peculiar podium supported by eagles and festoons, the deceased lying on a *kline*, an elderly woman near the altar, three putti, a candelabrum, and a curious monument containing a naked statue and surmounted with masks. The style of the reliefs is typical of plebeian art, with a proliferation of minute detail, deemed necessary for clear understanding of the episode narrated, and no regard for logical spatial relationships or proportions between the parts and figures.

The simultaneous presence of various styles in Flavian art can be found also in portraits. Alongside the veristic genre directly inspired by republican portraiture, exemplified in the portrait of Vespasian (Copenhagen, head no. 659a), was a neoclassical trend where the emperor's somewhat coarse and vulgar features are idealized. This is the case with the head in the Museo Nazionale Romano, possibly a posthumous portrait, based on models of AD 70, and with the statue of Titus wearing a toga, found near the Lateran. The Esquiline portrait of Domitian, which depicts the emperor in skewed perspective, is traceable to Hellenistic dynastic portraits, and can be ascribed to a Hellenizing baroque trend.

Fabrizio Pesando
Maria Paola Guidobaldi

BELOW:
Buildings of Domitian's reign, including the Arch of Isis and the Temple of Iupiter Custos, depicted on a relief from the tomb of the Haterii. Rome, Vatican Museums.

Roman Coins

Coins began to be cast or minted on a regular basis in Rome at the end of the fourth century BC. Their history is also the history of the images they bore. Since by their nature they circulated widely and at all levels of society, they were well suited as tools of propaganda.

During the first two centuries in which coins were minted they portrayed deities accompanied by generic symbols of power, or more or less explicit allusions to historical events. For example, the gold coin issued at the end of the third century BC known as the sesterce (*sestertius*) bore the head of Mars on the obverse and an eagle with a thunderbolt on the reverse. The silver coin known as a *Victoriatus* issued around 200 BC bore the head of Jupiter on the obverse and a Victory

crowning a trophy on the reverse. The images stamped on a cast bronze bar (*aes signatum*)—an elephant facing right on the obverse and a sow facing left on the reverse—seem to relate to Pyrrhus' Italian wars against the Romans, to the episode in which his great elephants were put to flight by a herd of menacing pigs.

From the end of the second century BC an increasingly common feature of coins was depictions of influential ancestors of the magistrate who issued the coin, or the exploits of this ancestor. These magistrates, the *triumviri monetales*, thus used the opportunity to record the glories of their own family history. The allusions in these tiny images are sometimes of great complexity, as for example on the obverse of the *denarius* minted in 91 BC by Decimus Junius Silanus. A small plow surmounted by a head of Silenus is depicted, within a

Rome, Republic. Silver *denarius* with the head of Jupiter on the obverse and a depiction of Victory placing a wreath on a trophy on the reverse. End of the third to beginning of the second century BC.

wreath (*torquis*). While the inclusion of Silenus is an obvious reference to Silanus' *cognomen*, the significance of the *torquis* and the plow would have been understood only by those with a detailed knowledge of the history of this branch of the family: it was descended from a certain Manlius Torquatus who, having been adopted by the powerful Iunii family, had held the post of praetor in 141 BC—hence the presence of the *torquis*. The family was also closely related to the Iunii Bubulci. *Bubulcus* means plowman, which probably explains the appearance of the plow, symbolizing the surname.

In other cases the family's mythical ancestor appears, as on the *denarius* issued by Lucius Marcius Censorinus in about 85 BC. This shows the statue of the Silenus Marsyas which Gaius Marcius Censorinus had consecrated in the Forum

Rome, Republic. Obverse of a gold *sestertius* from the end of the third century BC featuring the head of the god Mars.

in 294 BC. Another coin, minted in 82 BC by Gaius Manilius Limetanus, depicts Ulysses—a supposed ancestor.

The images on the coins of this period began to include buildings erected by the minter's ancestors. These buildings—as the etymology of the Latin word *monumentum* suggests (from *monere*, to remind)—were to be enduring reminders of the family's glorious history. Thus in 62 BC Lucius Scribonius Libo reproduced on a coin a well (*puteal*) decorated with lyres and garlands. The inscription identifies it as the *puteal Scribonianum*, built in the Forum by the ancestor who was tribune of the plebs in 149 BC, who had also borne the name Scribonius.

A large building occupies the whole of one side of the *denarius* minted in 61 BC by Marcus Emilius Lepidus, who became one of the triumvirate in 43 BC. Lepidus

Rome, Republic. *Denarius* of L. Marcius Censorinus from 85 BC depicting Silenus Marsyas on the reverse.

Rome, Republic. *Denarius* of C. Manilius Limetanus minted in 82 BC and showing Odysseus after his return home on the reverse.

was the younger son of the consul in 78 BC, a member of a family of ancient lineage that had invented a legend about its origins that was closely interwoven with the history of Rome itself. The myth claimed Trojan descent via a daughter of Aeneas and Lavinia, as well as a Sabine line of descent via a son of Numa Pompilius.

The building represented on the coin had two floors with porticos, separated by a high balustrade bearing large round shields aligned with the columns of the porticos. The inscription tells us that this is the Basilica Aemilia as it appeared after its restoration by the consul in 78 BC. At this time the consul was at the peak of his political and military career, which had culminated in 82 BC with the conquest of Norba, the last stronghold of Marius in Latium.

The first portrait that the Senate allowed to be struck on a coin was that of Julius Caesar. Henceforth self-celebratory images were to be increasingly explicit. Even Caesar's assassins had no hesitation in reproducing the head of Brutus on the obverse of a silver *denarius* (with a naval and terrestrial trophy on the reverse). However, it was with the empire that coins

Rome, Republic.
Denarius of L. Scribonius Libo (62 BC) depicting the *puteal Scribonianum* on the reverse.

Rome, Republic. *Aureus* of M. Junius Brutus from 43 BC with his portrait on the obverse and a triumphal monument made of weapons and parts of ships on the reverse. Milan, Civiche Raccolte Numismatiche del Castello Sforzesco.

Rome, Empire.
Aureus minted in Spain between 18 and 17 BC under Augustus. The reverse shows the Parthian Arch on the Forum Romanum erected by the emperor. Naples, Museo Archeologico Nazionale.

became a real propaganda tool to celebrate the emperor's deeds and official acts.

Here, as in other fields of craftsmanship, it was Augustus who blazed the trail, followed by all his successors until late antiquity. The eagle of Jupiter bearing in its claws the *corona civica* (civic garland) of oak leaves depicted on an *aureus* of 27 BC recalls the honor bestowed on Augustus that year by the Senate, an event referred to in Augustus' official record of his reign, the *Res Gestae*. The *clipeus virtutis* awarded to Augustus as restorer of the state also appears on an *aureus* together with another symbol of his glory, the military standards captured from the armies of Crassus and Mark Antony, returned by the Parthians in 20 BC.

Detailed representations of buildings erected or restored by Augustus appear on other coins: an *aureus* minted in 18 or 17 BC shows a three-vaulted arch with a *quadriga* (chariot) on top, a representation of the great Arch of Augustus erected in the Forum alongside the Temple of Divus (Divine) Julius. Another *aureus* commemorates the restoration of a road (possibly the Via Flaminia), with a viaduct on arches, and a triumphal arch decorated with rostra and a triumphal *quadriga*.

Together with acts of imperial generosity, military exploits are the most frequent images on coins minted during the empire. A coin issued by Claudius, perhaps from the period of his campaign in Britain, shows a military camp with the *sacrarium* of the military standards visible in the center, as well as a statue of Claudius. A scene depicting a speech delivered to soldiers—which seems to foreshadow the *adlocutiones* on Trajan's Column—can be found on a *sestertius* issued by Galba dating from AD 69.

The military repertory appears repeatedly, but without many new features, on late antique coins—the period of greatest crisis for the empire during which professional soldiers frequently became emperor. With the transformation of the empire into a theocracy, the images on coins were expanded to include striking allegorical references to the power of the sovereign, a trend influenced by the figurative language established in the eastern empire. A coin

Rome, Empire. *Sestertius* of the emperor Galba (AD 69) depicting an *adlocutio*, an address to the troops, on the reverse.

issued by Constans I (323–50) is a good illustration of this. The emperor, in full armor, carrying a spear and crowned with a Winged Victory, drags a prisoner by the hair. At his feet a kneeling woman begs in a gesture of submission. The scene is more reminiscent of the devastating fury of the ancient Pharaohs as depicted on Egyptian reliefs than of the calm lord of the world portrayed on a coin issued by Antoninus Pius, in which the emperor, dressed in a toga, holds a terrestrial globe in his right hand.

Fabrizio Pesando

(Unless otherwise indicated, all the coins pictured above are held in Rome, Museo Nazionale Romano in the Palazzo Massimo alle Terme, Medallion Collection, Collection of F. Gnecchi.)

Art, Power, and Consensus: From Trajan to Constantine

Domitian and Nerva

The sudden and bloody termination of a political regime makes it difficult to distinguish between elements of social transformation and those which perpetuate the old orders of power. This problem exists mainly because of the rapid adaptation to the new that is generally exhibited by the dominant classes.

This ambiguity was not avoided in the moment of passage between the last Flavian emperor, Domitian, murdered in a palace conspiracy in AD 96, and his successor, the elderly Nerva (AD 96–98). As dramatic tremors in imperial political institutions had demonstrated a century earlier, one of the problems of the grandiose Roman state remained the need to balance the autocratic impersonal tendencies of the emperor and the space for action claimed by the senatorial class. This class was given to oscillate, depending on circumstances, between astute adulation of, and conscious opposition toward, the emperor.

The brief reign of Nerva signaled dominance of the senators over the excessive orientalism that had characterized the rule of not only Domitian, but others too, particularly Caligula and Nero. Opposition to the absolutist desires of the emperor, an opposition found expressed in the history writing of the senatorial class (which, at least in the case of Tacitus, was far from friendly), found a way to be appeased, thanks to two important decisions taken by Nerva. The first was the emperor's solemn promise not to prosecute the senators. The second was his designation of a successor, Trajan, from outside his own blood family, beginning a practice that would secure the empire for almost a century.

But however incisive—and, in their way, revolutionary—transformations such as these may have been, they did not substantially alter the structure in which the governing head consisted of a tiny elite. This structure would remain the distinctive characteristic of the Roman state for a long time.

The rule of Nerva offers clues about continuity and discontinuity compared with the preceding period in the field of what we would today call the ideology of images, where the propagandistic function of images served also to enhance the political consensus (an ancient phenomenon).

The Bronze Equestrian Statue

Our analysis will begin with an artistic product that did not belong to a specific area of the city of Rome, though it deals with a work inspired by the very center of imperial power. A fortunate archaeological discovery made about thirty years ago at Misenum, the celebrated port on the bay of Naples where the Roman military fleet was based, was of a bronze equestrian statue, part of the Sacellum of the Augustales, an edifice reserved for the imperial cult typical

Detail from a bronze equestrian statue of the emperor Domitian, which was raised from the sea floor near Miseno. After the emperor's violent death and the subsequent declaration of a *damnatio memoriae*—the abolition of his memory—the head of this statue was reworked into a portrait of his successor, Nerva. Naples, Museo Archeologico Nazionale.

of every more or less important place within the Roman state. One of the most interesting aspects of this bronze is the reworking of the portrait head. It was originally conceived as an image of Domitian, in a pose that clearly denoted a typological parallel with equestrian statues of Alexander the Great—a guide for every absolutist political design. Following the bloody exit from the scene in which Domitian had styled himself "lord and god" (*dominus et deus*), and the subsequent senatorial *damnatio memoriae* (a decision by the Senate that the memory of a condemned man must not be perpetuated and that his name must be erased from inscriptions), the face of the figure was recut to assume the wrinkled features of Nerva.

There is no doubt that for this portrait, as for others depicting rulers, immediate physiognomic realism had a dual significance. It signaled simultaneously the detachment from a Hellenistic tradition of idealization, which had inspired the portaits of Domitian, and the need for a pro-Senate emperor like Nerva to reconnect himself with the typology of the late republican veristic portrait, dear to the ideology of recapturing power that was held by the senatorial class.

It is indisputable, therefore, that the change of style observable in this case between Domitian and Nerva was not implemented in order to rub out signs—in a sense contradictory—of continuity between the two regimes. In the imperial cult at Misenum, the "new" equestrian statue—however different the face of the emperor appeared—continued to portray for Nerva (in ways completely other than superficial) a heroization that was still modeled on the example of Alexander. What is remarkable is that the bronze cult statue was not destroyed in order to forge an effigy suitable to the new situation. This confirms the theory of the German scholar Tonio Hölscher, who emphasizes the importance of artistic and ideological continuity over a long period, even in a schema that seems to recognize the existence of "period" styles.

Trajan

Remaining in the field of public buildings, we continue our analysis with examples of the art of Trajan's reign (AD 98–117). The careful scrutiny of works executed for the public realm remains crucial on account of the frequent possibility of dating them with precision, as well as because of the objective importance of their context, theoretically the unlimited contemporary public—and perhaps not only contemporary—that the imperial court intended to reach.

The Forum of Trajan

Trajan, of Iberian origin, whose army career helped propel him to the helm of the state, was committed to a great project of urban transformation in the center of Rome. The Forum of Trajan, the last and most extensive of the imperial forums, was unfortunately excavated in the 1930s in such a way as to prevent the modern observer from seeing its totality. The construction of the Forum was undertaken at the conclusion of the victorious war against the Dacians (in modern Romania), with two prolonged campaigns in AD 101–2 and AD 105–6.

The spoils of war, the Dacian gold which was one of the principal motivations for the conquest of these faraway Danubian territories, permitted the realization of a complex of squares and buildings unprecedented in the history of the city. To have an idea of the grandeur and scale of the Forum of Trajan, we must consider that in order to obtain the open space for the complex it was necessary first to cut away the saddle that connected the slopes of the Quirinal and the Capitoline Hills. The best-preserved monument in the Forum, the celebrated Trajan's Column, had among its functions precisely that of indicating through its own height (one hundred Roman feet, equivalent to slightly less than ninety-eight feet) the height of the hill formerly there. This is documented by the inscription on the base of the column.

The intrinsic monumentality of the Forum and its adherence to an urban tradition initiated more than a century and a half earlier by Julius Caesar and followed by the Flavian emperors is integral

Axonometric view of a reconstruction of the Forum of Trajan and the adjacent Markets of Trajan. Designed by Trajan's architect, Apollodorus of Damascus, the scale of this complex overshadowed the fora built by both Caesar and Augustus, and formed the single largest complex in the heart of ancient Rome.

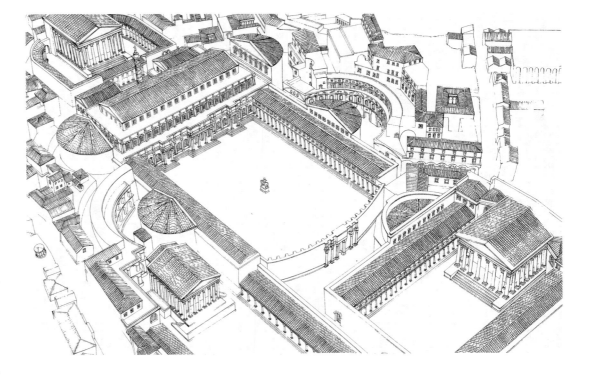

OPPOSITE:
Trajan's Column has survived almost completely intact, and is one of the finest monuments of imperial Rome. Only the column shafts from the former Basilica Ulpia have survived and are seen here in the foreground. The church of Santa Maria di Loreto, to the left in the background, was designed by Antonio di Sangallo the Younger.

In antiquity the pedestal of Trajan's Column, with its superb reliefs showing captured Dacian weapons, housed an urn containing the emperor's ashes. Trajan was the first emperor to be buried within the sacred precincts of the city. The legal basis for this act was provided by an old custom which held that only those who had celebrated a triumph might be buried in the city.

to the ideology of power pursued by Trajan and his collaborators through the urban model. In this the great architect Apollodorus of Damascus, recorded in the sources, played a key role. Although he was tied to imperial propagandistic notions, it is likely that he agreed with them.

As the German archaeologist Paul Zanker emphasized a generation ago, the disposition of buildings and spaces unearthed in the Forum of Trajan would have obeyed a guiding idea that was probably close to the ideological intentions of Trajan himself. The architectural sequences of the complex appear to be modeled on military encampments, with an explicit emphasis on the part of Trajan—demonstrated by the intention of reproducing military forts in the very heart of the empire—on the decisive importance that the army had for the state (already demonstrated by the very means through which Trajan had come to power).

The main square of the Forum, corresponding to the central square in a military camp (the *praetorium*), had a curved entrance side. It was pierced by a monumental colonnaded arch, the appearance of which can be reconstructed from images of it on coins. On it towered a bronze quadriga with an effigy of the emperor. In imitation of the adjacent Forum of Augustus, the main courtyard had porticod colonnades with two large facing lateral exedras. A paved street, still visible, separated the northeast exedra from the adjacent Markets of Trajan, located on the slopes of the Quirinal Hill.

A monumental bronze equestrian statue of Trajan (now lost), the focus of the entire square, was sited on the principal visual and geometric axes of the precinct. The *praetorium* of the military camps was replaced by the *principia* (headquarters building), the area where soldiers were addressed and justice was meted out. The far end of the Forum was closed by the flank of an enormous basilica, called the Basilica Ulpia in honor of Trajan's *gens* (clan). Of gigantic proportions, it was sumptuously decorated and articulated in a vast central space entirely surrounded by a double colonnade, which on its short sides opened on to two large exedras. In the older imperial forums the preference had been to close off the far end with a temple, not a basilica. This difference reinforces Zanker's hypothesis of a strong link between military camps and the Forum of Trajan. Further evidence for such a link is found in the structure of the Forum.

From the Basilica Ulpia one entered a small courtyard, dominated at the center by Trajan's Column and flanked by two libraries located symmetrically to the column. Here too, we see a reflection of army camps, in the way that the complex of libraries and columns echoes the function and placement of an analogous ensemble formed by the legion's archives and the sanctuary of the legion's insignia (the *vexilla*).

Behind the smaller courtyard with the column, the Forum continued further in an uncovered space, conceived by Trajan and completed by his successor Hadrian. This porticod courtyard, unusual in plan (the rear side was strongly curved), contained the Temple of the Deified Trajan, the building reserved for the cult of the emperor (and his wife Plotina, likewise deified) who had allegedly ascended to heaven after death, through apotheosis, a characteristic Roman ritual modeled on Hellenistic and oriental customs.

Trajan's Column

The centrality of the theme of overcoming death through superhuman and supertemporal glorification of the emperor, results evidently from one circumstance. In the vault of the column, in a small room, Trajan had the space for his own tomb excavated. This prepared the way for a series of ideological cross-references between the emperor's positive military-political action, exemplified by the column and its friezes, and his deification, sanctified by the temple that closed off the Forum.

In a recent analysis of the column, which is both profound and timely, Salvatore Settis has noted that the column embodies an elaborate eulogistic plan that rested on a double platform. There was the affirmation of the cult of the *optimus princeps* (highest ruler), formally recognized by the Senate and probably achieved by

Depiction of Victory listing on a shield all the conquests made under Trajan's leadership. She is standing in front of a tropaion, a victory monument constructed from captured enemy weapons. Within the frieze she performs a connecting function, linking the depictions of both expeditions against the Dacians into a continuous narrative.

the other, in an uninterrupted spatial continuum. The two military campaigns are separated by an allegorical representation in which Victory, enclosed in a large trophy of arms, writes the successes of Trajan on a shield.

Notable is the scrupulously chronicled documentary of the narrative through extraordinary images. The sculptors dwell on a group of episodes that give full information about the Roman war machine. Battle scenes alternate with, among others, moments that are specifically logistical and organizational (such as the construction of encampments and roads), or political and ritual (such as the emperor's speeches to the troops or the purificatory and propitiatory sacrifices), as well as events that are strictly military. In addition to battles, there are also scenes of siege, surrender, the taking of prisoners, and so on.

A not unimportant space is reserved for the Dacian enemy, whose famous leader Decebalus appears many times until his dramatic suicide to avoid capture by the Romans, given the inevitability of defeat. As is obvious, in a great number of the episodes—around seventy—Trajan is depicted in the various managing duties connected to his rank. The frequency of the emperor's image can be considered a confirmation of that subtle mixture of calculated propaganda and more or less accurate reconstruction of the events of war, which distinguishes the conception of the entire column.

It has been noted many times, with respect to the way Trajan is depicted, that from a stylistic and ideological point of view he is portrayed as a rational and moderate *princeps* (leader). This is undoubtedly true if one puts the accent on the lack of emphasis given to the figure of Trajan in individual episodes. Most famous in this sense are the scenes in which Trajan is portrayed together with his staff, without either symbolic or dimensional distortions compared to his underlings.

This idea of balanced wisdom—commonplace in modern historiography—becomes less convincing when we consider the general conception of the frieze and its context. As we have indicated, it always occurs in the presence of a monumental urban apparatus conceived in order to broadcast the absolute power of the emperor.

In connection with this last point, it is interesting to examine aspects of the critical discussion of Trajan's Column by one of the greatest historians of ancient art, Ranuccio Bianchi Bandinelli, who dedicated many intense and noteworthy pages to the column. Without taking away anything from the intellectual tension present in his interpretation, some of his avenues of research concerning Trajanic art do not stand up to analysis.

Trajan by virtue of his shrewd administration of power. There was also the more subtle conviction that such ideological apparatus guaranteed the cohesion of the state through devotion, oscillating between superstitious adherence to, and ancestral need for, potent symbols.

The masterpiece in this eulogy is the spiral frieze throughout the entire height of the column. It imitates a bolt of material or, more likely, papyrus—its curving form, perhaps not by chance, resembles the typical structure of a rolled-up scroll (*volumen*). The column was once surmounted by a bronze statue of Trajan (likewise full of meaning). The statue, destroyed in the Middle Ages, was eventually replaced by Sixtus V with a statue of St. Peter.

The subject of the frieze is the two Dacian campaigns, illustrated in 155 scenes, one after

This is especially the case with the artistic autonomy of the individual whom Bianchi Bandinelli called the "Master of the Deeds of Trajan." Bianchi Bandinelli succumbed to the strong temptation to identify him as Apollodorus of Damascus—who, as has already been seen, the literary sources record as designer and architect—making Apollodorus coordinator of the workshop of sculptors who executed the great frieze. Leaving aside the question— probably unanswerable—of the identity of the director of works (who must have existed, at the least as a guide for the overall stylistic unity of the decoration), it is important to pay particular attention to the following argument of Bianchi Bandinelli. Departing from the difficulty of a continuous reading of the frieze, he held that the sculptor was permitted a great deal of creative freedom by his imperial client in the execution of the work.

In support of this thesis, he cited the celebrated scene of the suicide of Decebalus. The stirring participation and fundamental respect for the sad fate of the vanquished, and the heroic dignity of his suicide, would have found fertile ground in the substantive ideological and emotional sharing of a similar destiny on the part of an eastern Greek, such as Apollodorus of Damascus, who was born of a land that had long been subject to the Roman yoke. Like every true great artist, continued Bianchi Bandinelli, Apollodorus' fundamental creation would have been in the name of his own aesthetic and intellectual needs, in a climate of illuminated tolerance that culminated in casting a further light of balance and wisdom on his patron Trajan, thus continuing to feed the myth of the *optimus princeps.*

In evaluating this undoubtedly fascinating theory, even if we do not perhaps totally share it, it is necessary to consider that Bianchi Bandinelli described the so-called Master of the Deeds of Trajan as a luminous exception in the panorama of Roman art. A fundamental assumption of this profound conviction was the idea that the sculptor of the column had been gradually giving voice to his own originality thanks to the characteristics of the monument, that these had allowed him to carve out for himself a concrete freedom of action. Having recognized the high level of sculptural quality of the frieze, Bianchi Bandinelli then found it natural to imbue the master with traits that made him more similar to an artist modeled on examples of formal autonomy in the Renaissance, or in the nineteenth-century avant-garde, rather than with characteristics that might match the excellent craftsmanship typical of ancient culture.

Even if in this critical reading important suggestions abound, it is still necessary to

recognize that the essential pillars of Bianchi Bandinelli's theory today appear somewhat fragile. As for his discussion of the vanquished enemy, Hölscher has demonstrated the different nature of such a characteristic, which fits into a figurative stylistic tradition that goes back—as recognized by Bianchi Bandinelli himself—at least to the Hellenistic period. We are reminded of the celebrated Pergamum statues of the *Dying Gaul* and the *Gaul Killing Himself and His Wife.* An increased emphasis in the portrayal of the valor—even the moral stature—of the defeated makes the deeds of the victors seem even more glorious because of the difficulties they have had to overcome. In other words, the pause in the narrative at the suicide of Decebalus is not—or is at least not only—a generous act of sympathy for the Dacian chief, but

One of the most famous episodes in the frieze is the depiction of the suicide of the Dacian prince, Decebalus. An atmosphere of the greatest tension is produced by combining, in the narrowest possible space, the desperate but proud self-destruction of the Dacian leader with the charging Roman cavalry.

The images on Trajan's Column are not only notable for their bold artistry, but also constitute an important historical record. This section of the frieze vividly illustrates the painstaking accuracy of the depictions. The lower register shows the crossing of the Danube by a pontoon bridge. Above this and to the left is an *adlocutio*, a depiction of the emperor addressing his troops, followed by a scene showing the construction of a military encampment.

rather a propaganda emphasis on the power of the Roman emperor. It is this very emphasis that is to play an essential role.

The problem of the impossibility of a continuous integrated reading of the frieze has recently been restated by Settis, in very different terms. The modalities of reading the meaning of the scenes by the beholder could have rested—notwithstanding the undoubted novelty of the typology of the column—either on visible pre-existing models (for example, triumphal pictures paraded on banners in the republican era) or on the fame of the political and military events represented on the frieze.

In the ambience of such perceptual adaptability, a place of first rank is occupied by the vertical axis as a clue to understanding the frieze. The scene of the suicide of Decebalus high up is one of the last episodes of the second Dacian campaign. The scene is vertically aligned, both with the allegorical Victory, which separates (and unites) the two Dacian campaigns, and with an enigmatic scene from the second band, which has been convincingly interpreted as representing Trajan in the presence of a favorable omen. This vertical axis is positioned significantly on the side of the column facing the Temple of the Deified Trajan. All the episodes on this axis would have constituted a coherent sequence centered on the fortunate outcome of the Dacian wars and on imperial glory. The sequence would have been appropriately conceived, as in other cases, with a preferred direction for reading that converged—like the plan of the entire Forum—on a propagandistic celebration of the *princeps*.

What has been said up till now does not in itself exclude a complementary possibility. Among the strategies of communication through elaborate images of the column, consideration of its general symbolic value must also have played a significant role. This means, in other words, that to the already described criteria for precise reading of the frieze (vertical, oblique, casual, and so on) was to be added—placing it thereby in real life—the global perception of the column as a self-referential *signum* (sign) of the glorious Dacian campaigns, without a need to focus on specific events. Anyone wanting a detailed record of the Dacian wars could have consulted Trajan's account in his *Dacica*, unfortunately lost, in the adjacent libraries.

It is clear that whatever was the modality of reading selected by the beholder—analytic observation of episodes or groups of episodes, however bound by the characteristics of the monument (that is, the symbolic and synthetic perception of the message contained in the frieze)—the semantic system of the column

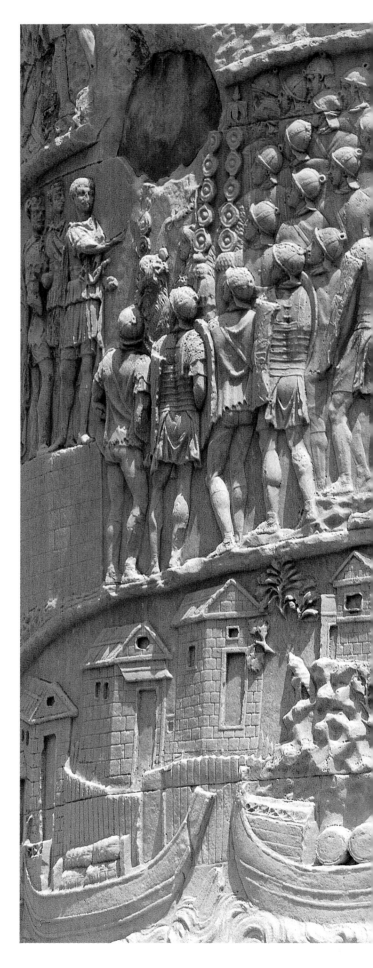

Illustration of a *suovetaurilia*, a ritual sacrifice made before the start of a military offensive. At the bottom, a pig and a sheep are being led to the sacrificial altar. The ox which was also destined for sacrifice cannot be seen in this view. The emperor is shown with a veiled head in front of the altar carrying out a libation, a drink-offering to the gods.

OPPOSITE:
Although the spiral arrangement of the frieze on Trajan's Column did not favor a detailed reading of the work, the wealth of its materials and decoration had an imposing effect on the contemporary viewer, and therefore served to glorify the emperor.

rested in the end on the glorification of Trajan, with little margin for independent work reserved for the sculptor.

It is important to clarify that recognition in the work of an unknown artisan of precise functional mechanisms designed for the political needs of the imperial court does not diminish the artistic value of the frieze. It is precisely the exceptional compositional proportions and the calibrated attention to strategies of communication through images which constitute the mark of a coherent *Kunstwollen* (intention of the work of art), to use the famous keyword of Alois Riegl—an artistic intention born from the regime's propagandistic aims, but also, as we have observed, the direct expression of an intimate ideological fusion between Trajan and the talented sculptor of the column, who must

have shared the principles that inspired the imperial project.

The Forum of Trajan was thus an impressive figurative apparatus that as an emblem of power stood in a position to restrain the Roman people, who recognized it as such, with its propaganda trappings of power, because there were no practical alternatives.

This evaluation appears to be confirmed by a formal and stylistic examination of the column reliefs. Although the author largely shares the affirmation—repeated many times—that the spiral frieze contains the happy coincidence of a naturalistic Graeco–Hellenistic conception and the needs of a programmatic narrative clarity typical of the Roman mind, he believes further investigation is warranted. It is important to recognize that the reliefs are part of a technical and aesthetic conception, blending characteristics that are properly sculptural with those that are properly pictorial. The sculptural effects, obtained in the presence of a notably reduced depth of relief, coexist with the dominant tendency to introduce spatial and dimensional registers one above the other. With this last expedient—clearly pictorial in origin—the sculptor avoided making each band correspond to a single unified space. Only in rare cases does the height of the band equal that of the human figures. In the meantime, the sculptor overcame the convention typical of archaic and classical Greek relief which rendered the arrangement of every single episode against a neutral background.

It is not certain that Trajan's Column put into place—for the first time in the ancient world—such a marked pictorialism in the art of relief. One of the earliest examples of this kind of pictorial language is the small frieze depicting the myth of Telephus on the Altar of Pergamon, dated to the mid-Hellenistic period (second century BC).

A comparison between the unfortunately fragmentary Telephus frieze and the column reliefs demonstrates, apart from the undeniable affinities, significant differences. In the Pergamon frieze, the disposition of the scene across several panels never sacrifices the essential adherence to the principle of spatial–temporal unity. An example is the famous episode of the boat of Auge, in which the heroine Auge, Telephus' mother, observes from above (on an upper register) the materials for constructing the boat. In contrast, on Trajan's Column episodes occurring at different times or in different places are often placed within a single panel. The principle of compositional unity does not apply.

One of the best examples of this is the solemn sacrifice (scene CIII) celebrated by Trajan in a military encampment. It deals with a ceremony of *suovetaurilia*, during which a pig, a sheep, and a bull are sacrificed on a pyre after they have been ritually paraded for purification. The scene is constructed on a division in terms of both perspective and space as well as narrative. Trajan is represented from a bird's-eye view, together with other individuals, on the inside of the *castrum*, while he engages, head covered (as in other representations of Roman ritual), in pouring a libation on the altar. Outside the wall of the encampment—no longer seen from above but frontally—the procession with the animals destined for sacrifice proceeds around the fortified circuit.

In the same panel, therefore, are not only two different representations of space side by side, but also—in all probability—two moments that are temporally distinct. It seems reasonable to suppose that the libation operations would have started at the moment when the procession and animals for sacrifice would have entered the *castrum*, having completed the tour of the perimeter. The most convincing explanation of this narrative and compositional detail is, undoubtedly, in a search for pregnant, symbolic meaning that might specify, without the possibility of misunderstanding, that it deals precisely with that particular sacrifice with its more substantial and significant religious and ritual prerogatives. Such a language is already manifest in well-known examples of Roman republican art, such as the so-called altar of Domitius Ahenobarbus (late second century BC).

In the case of the *suovetaurilia* on Trajan's Column, it seems evident that even if the sculptor, in the execution of numerous scenes, was close to a formal sensibility oriented toward Hellenistic naturalism, he was disposed to relinquish it in favor of the need for easy decipherability of content by the public for whom the monument was destined.

If this is the case, we will have isolated a nodal point in not only the stylistic conception of the frieze but also in the basic mechanisms of Roman art itself. In it appears a dominant need to communicate the message clearly and independently of stylistic unity. Naturally this does not mean to deny that from time to time the Romans carefully considered that style (or a mixture of styles) could be used for specific ends in communicating through images. From this perspective, Roman eclecticism, far from being an arbitrary oscillation in taste, assumes a valuable and meaningful significance.

If hoping to find a unified aesthetic principle in the execution of the reliefs on Trajan's Column, it would be a mistake to seek the prevalence of formal reasons for effective and pragmatic transmission of the message. The anonymous sculptor had at his disposition for the conception and

LIBERATORIVRBIS

The so-called Great Trajanic frieze, which was reused for the Arch of Constantine at the beginning of the fourth century, shows Trajan's victories over the Dacians. The sheer might of the attack shown in this scene seems to be patterned on depictions of Alexander the Great's military achievements.

execution of the frieze a baggage of earlier formal models extending back more than half a millennium. As has been seen, the column contains naturalistic as well as synthetic–symbolic approaches. Both are deducible from a long iconographic tradition employable without the preoccupation of rendering the monument stylistically unified, in ways that are revealed as incredibly distant from the purist, literary precepts of every epoch.

If unity exists, it resides in the continuous force of clarity in the narrative, a veritable constant present for centuries in Roman art, and certainly more important than a superficial phenomenon like the oscillation of stylistic characteristics examined period by period. It goes without saying that for modern scholars of Roman art the individualization of styles typical for each period is a precious instrument, needed essentially to create a basic chronological grid for the great number of products of Roman artistic culture, which are often lacking in context. However, what is more interesting is the effort to collect, where possible, the coordinates of a long period of a system little accustomed, on account of its socio-political structure, to traumatic events that could subvert its longstanding equilibrium.

The Great Trajanic Frieze

Stylistic heterogeneity, determined by precise needs, seems therefore to be the dominant *Kunstwollen* of Roman art. This is demonstrated by another official frieze from the Trajanic period. The original purpose and location of this sculpted decoration are unfortunately unknown (perhaps the Forum of Trajan). The frieze was reused successively in the attic and on the inside of the principal vault of the Arch of Constantine. In this other example of historical relief, conventionally called the Great Trajanic Frieze on account of its size—about ten feet high by a (surviving) length of more than fifty-eight feet, though it was originally longer—the subject is likewise the celebration of Trajan's victorious Dacian campaigns.

What survives is a narrative of three thematic nuclei: the bloody conquest of a Dacian village by the Roman army, with decapitated villagers; a cavalry charge personally commanded by Trajan with a strong following of standard-bearers, trumpeters, and horsemen, with the necessary complement of dead or dying enemies represented dramatically on the ground; and Trajan's triumphal entry into Rome, emphasized by a winged Victory,

Detail of the famous Alexander mosaic from the House of the Faun at Pompeii. This section shows the great Macedonian king on his favorite horse, Bucephalus. The number of depictions of his heroic deeds in a range of different genres demonstrates Alexander's function as a model for the antique world. Naples, Museo Archeologico Nazionale.

who crowns him, and by a Virtue dressed as an Amazon, allegory of the imperial city.

Even more interesting than the repetition of the figure of Trajan within a single space of the figured narrative, is the ideological and iconographic model on which the depiction of the emperor in the episode of the cavalry charge is based. There is no doubt that this recalls the sweeping and victorious driving force of the battles of Alexander the Great, of which there was a long tradition of representation, known to us especially through the famous mosaic discovered in the nineteenth century in the House of the Faun, in Pompeii.

If on Trajan's Column the image of the emperor conforms to iconographic traits that are more calm without obviously negating the affirmation of his power (compare the way in which Trajan conducts a battle in scene XCVII), the effects of the Great Trajanic Frieze are different. Here a rhetorical emphasis flung at full speed dominates, with an intense dynamism not too far in its formal style from the so-called Pergamon Hellenistic baroque. It would almost seem that the destination of this monumental frieze must have required (or suggested) the explicit recalling of Alexander the Great, with the automatic superimposition of Alexander and

Trajan, an affirmation of the imperial aspiration toward absolute dominion.

Trajan's Column and the Great Trajanic Frieze, therefore, appear to represent two stylistic positions, different but complementary, finalized—even if by different means—with the same objective of glorifying the emperor. Such an element alone already demonstrated that in the same epoch, and in the same orbit of patronage, heterogeneous languages could coexist, manipulated with shrewdness according to the type of message to be delivered.

Even more indicative in this regard is that both cycles seem to come from the same workshop, given the close correspondence in execution of detail. This reinforces how much until now has been sustained on the predominance of the needs of pragmatic content—ideological clarity compared to the reasons for an abstract stylistic unity. The same workshop could use different formal languages—Hellenistic pathos, composed classicism, or a synthetic–symbolic tone. These variations obviously derived from patronage strategies, where those responsible for the execution of the frieze would not be required to fit them neatly into stylistically coherent forms. This had been characteristic of some of the Greek tradition and what it would come to represent, but a very different consciousness and potency began to achieve visible results, especially in contemporary art.

Trajan's Markets

Here, the scrutiny of works of art executed in Rome during Trajan's rule is completed with Trajan's Markets, a complement, on the ideological and the functional plane, of the Forum of Trajan. Though the brickstamps establish that the erection of the Markets preceded that of the Forum's main square, the unity of the two projects seems certain. Such a circumstance is assured by the fact that Trajan's Markets, an inventive and utilitarian complex designed by Apollodorus of Damascus, are arranged organically on many levels on the slopes of the Quirinal Hill. Further confirmation is the presence, at the closest point between the Forum of Trajan and the Markets, and together with the structures, of the same compositional module, founded on a large semicircular exedra.

In the brick hemicycle of Trajan's Markets, closed on the sides by two semicircular rooms, ten shops (*tabernae*) are arranged. Their doors were made of travertine and the roof was vaulted. Above this a series of elegant, arched windows gave light to a covered corridor onto which another group of shops faced. At a still higher level—the buildings were connected by stairways and ramps—is an ancient street, winding and sloping, lined by more *tabernae*. These last—or at least some of them—may have been reserved for the sale of beverages, as indicated by the medieval name of the street on to which they faced, Via Biberatica.

From this street a steep ramp led to a large room, covered by six notable and daring cross-vaults on travertine corbels. Onto this luminous space—perhaps the ancient entrance to the Markets—open two more levels of *tabernae*. Towards the south is another series of rooms, also on two floors, probably the management area for the whole complex.

The whole structure of Trajan's Markets, intended for commerce, wholesale (with a predominantly state administration), or retail, has numerous points of interest. An adaptable design contrived by Apollodorus of Damascus could pass from the rigidly axial and frontal arrangement of the Forum, to an architectural ensemble animated by lively but arbitrary asymmetries and perfectly inserted into the slope of the hill. This was made possible by engineering—the use of the arch, the vault, and concrete.

The increasingly noticeable urbanistic tendency removed even more definitively from the original Forum its economic and commercial functions. The process had already begun in the late republican era. Confirmation of Trajan's ability to administer public affairs was made visible in the gigantic building operation, which, together with the Forum bearing his name, in one extraordinary move multiplied approval. The Markets of Trajan provided a solution to a problem for the city, marrying the easiest distribution of provisions, especially food, to a massive employment of labor—a symbiosis between good government and demagogic astuteness that characterizes Trajan's political action, not just his shrewd use of art and architecture.

Hadrian

After Trajan's nearly twenty-year-rule the reign of Hadrian (AD 117–38) followed. Hadrian, a cousin of Trajan, was, like him, born in Italica, near modern Seville. A complex figure, Hadrian's name is associated with his declared admiration for Hellenistic culture, which suggested to him the guidelines for his stewardship of the empire.

One of the principal merits of this cultivated and refined emperor, who had aspirations as poet and architect, is apparent in the political and ideological astuteness with which he successfully administered the empire. Despite his interest in the culture of the Hellenistic eastern Mediterranean, Hadrian never took up the models of autocratic rule which so often prevailed there. This is apparent in the cult of Hadrian in Athens, preferred also in Rome (not without opposition from the more traditional and partisan senatorial circles). During a stay there, Hadrian took up the post of the ancient and prestigious office of archon, a magistracy that had had its chief moment of glory during the period of the city state before the fall of Athens into Macedonian domination.

Hadrian's choices are not to be considered superficially as the fruit of a simple aestheticizing orientation, a fortunate result of a cultural program dear to a man who had the good fortune of having been chosen to guide the empire. If there was a strong philosophical–literary component—perhaps exaggerated in Marguerite Yourcenar's fascinating historical evocation of Hadrian's mental world—Hadrian's behavior also sprang from the need to co-opt to the administration of power the influential and rich eastern elites. One of Hadrian's primary objectives was the cohesion of the empire. This was pursued through careful measures of a pro-Hellenistic policy capable of acquiring approval in the eastern Mediterranean, and a moderate ideology—in a way even anti-tyrannical—in the choice of reference models, which succeeded in being substantially acceptable in the rest of the empire and, especially, in Rome.

A glance at Hadrian's principal accomplishments in architecture in Rome is sufficient to understand how much was due to the need to offer a solid image of power. To maintain—as has recently been proposed by Giorgio Gullini—that Hadrian's architectural activity is configured as antithetical to Trajan's misses the point. Especially in public buildings, the symbolic–ideological mechanisms were fundamentally unchanged.

The Pantheon

The Pantheon is among the most representative edifices of Hadrian's rule. The often lamented stylistic incoherence of the construction—caused by the mixture of a Greek-style colonnaded facade and Roman-style internal space, with its strong monumental impact—should be modified since the present view of the building does not coincide with how it was intended to look. The current simultaneous perception of the pronaos and the ensemble, formed by drum and dome was avoided in antiquity because the two lateral porticod colonnades enclosing the space in front of the building hid the great construction behind. The space in front was also much larger than the present piazza, with more harmonious proportional relationships.

On the other hand however, still recognizable in Hadrian's building is a certain stylistic ambivalence, perhaps to be understood as the significant combination of substantially evocative philhellenism with a grandiose political-propagandistic apparatus that hinges on the huge rotunda. Here were the most profound ideological messages. The interior of the Pantheon, with its imposing hemispherical dome with a diameter equal to the height of the entire structure, was conceived to suggest unmovable geometric perfection. The ensemble of relationships between the architectural components, the synthetic rhythms centered on regularity and symmetry, achieve with extraordinary effectiveness a spatial effect of complex immobility. The architecture translates perfectly the protections and expectations of permanence of the imperial Roman court into a symbolic message—at once tangible and ideal—of the eternal empire (*aeternitas imperii*), laden with unequivocal political and ideological meaning.

The universalism sought by the Pantheon finds its most obvious demonstration in the relationship between the great dome and the celestial vault, as was noted by Dio Cassius in a well-known passage (LIII, 27). Such correspondence was facilitated and suggested by the oculus, the large circular opening (about twenty-six feet across), at the top of the dome.

Among the elements that made the Pantheon a building of exceptional importance is the engineering skill expressed in it. This was the result of an architectural tradition that in the Roman world had been seen previously in works such as the circular baths in Rome and in Baia.

One of the most important devices was the scrupulous attention paid to calculating the solids and voids, which allows the drum to support the weight of the gigantic dome. The vault of the dome has a thickness that diminishes progressively from the base to the top. Its structural logic is such that in the Renaissance it was studied by Filippo Brunelleschi, who in the *modo di murare* (manner of building) of this—as in other ancient Roman buildings—found more than one creative starting point.

Also of great interest is the sumptuous decorative scheme, in large part preserved, distinguished in the pavement as well as in the walls by a pleasing chromatic play obtained by the use of colored marble.

The Mausoleum of Hadrian

Substantially analogous language is also visible in another key monument of Hadrian's rule, the mausoleum on the flat area between the Vatican Hill and the Tiber river, close to the riverbank. Transformed in late antiquity into a fortress, the building retained this function under the papacy and became, as Castel Sant'Angelo, the key point of the defense of the papal palace.

The original Mausoleum of Hadrian, which held the ashes of the emperors up to Caracalla, can be considered in its main lines a copy of the Mausoleum of Augustus, which inspired its structure and form. A large square precinct in brickwork, formerly covered by a marble decorative revetment, functioned as the base for the imposing circular drum of the sepulcher, built from blocks of peperino, tufa, and travertine, and originally adorned with fluted marble decoration. Above the drum was an earthen tumulus, planted with trees and surrounded by marble statues. These were surmounted by a central-plan structure with a smaller diameter, intended to carry a bronze quadriga with a statue of Hadrian.

The interior of the mausoleum had its center in the large square burial room where the imperial ashes were collected in niches, preserved together with portrait statues of the emperors. Heads of Hadrian and his successor, Antoninus Pius, survive.

Hadrian's enthusiasm for Greek sculpture is demonstrated by this portrait modeled on a cult image by the sculptor Alkamenes from the Temple of Ares in Athens from around 420 BC; here, the emperor's head replaces that of the god. Rome, Capitoline Museums.

From the point of view of urban renewal, there is no doubt that the Mausoleum of Hadrian—whose outline even today symbolizes Rome—signaled effectively to the inhabitants of the imperial capital, in a way even more direct and immediate than the Pantheon, the stability of state institutions. This was made manifest especially in the fact that Hadrian was able, with his mausoleum (completed only in AD 139, a year after his death), to set himself in a continuous line with Augustus, within a historical–political direction that truly, at the base of this ascendency, declared itself as unshakable.

The Mausoleum of Hadrian, so similar to the Mausoleum of Augustus, must not be seen in contrast to it but rather as its twin in meaning, function, and typology. The legitimization of absolute power and its aspiration to perpetuate the system had to pass through this dense scheme of refined, but also extremely comprehensible, historical–symbolic references.

Alongside such explicit links to the imperial autocratic tradition, it is possible to read in Hadrian's urban model signs specifically centered on his person. This is particularly so in the case of the Mausoleum of Hadrian, an important part of the urban project centered on the Aelian Bridge, named in honor of Hadrian's clan (*gens*), the Aelius. The bridge, which is still well-preserved, was originally constructed to connect the Mausoleum of Hadrian across the river to the Campus Martius.

The present short road from the mausoleum originally led across the bridge to the area in which, as Eugenio La Rocca has demonstrated, stood the memorial of Agrippa, the same eminent supporter of Augustus whose dedicatory inscription on the Pantheon was preserved by Hadrian. Thus the ideological–urban relationship stabilized between the funerary apparatus intended for Hadrian and Agrippa's monument further confirms how Hadrian's dynastic program, directed toward immortalizing his own memory, was simultaneously intended to emphasize a precise connection with earlier emperors, and in particular with Augustus. An important link, therefore, existed between continuity with the past and affirmation of Hadrian's personal glory, one of the clearest indications we have to evaluate Hadrian's shrewd political–ideological equilibrium.

The Temple of Venus and Roma

If this hypothesis is true, we must consider in more or less analogous terms another important building erected under Hadrian, the huge Temple of Venus and Roma. It is possible to reconstruct its original appearance, notwithstanding the major

Nineteenth-century drawing showing a view of the long side of the Pantheon. Built by Hadrian, the Pantheon replaced a previous structure from 27 BC by Agrippa, friend and later son-in-law of Augustus. Originally a temple dedicated to the twelve gods of heaven and focused on the cult of Augustus, the new Hadrianic building retained this religious dedication in spite of being thoroughly reconfigured. Paris, École Nationale Supérieure des Beaux Arts.

The construction of the Pantheon under Hadrian was made easier by the destruction of its Augustinian predecessor in a fire. Hadrian skillfully used this opportunity to establish a sense of continuity with the founder of the principate: this can be seen in the respectful treatment of Agrippa's dedicatory inscription. Hadrian's building consisted of a columned porch on the site of the former temple, an intermediate area of brick, and the majestic rotunda.

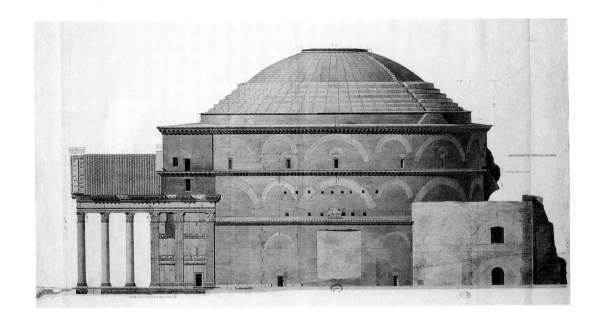

The striking silhouette of the Mausoleum of Hadrian is one of Rome's most dominant features. Since late antiquity the monumental structure has repeatedly been used as a defensive fortification. The name it is commonly known by today, Castel Sant'Angelo, is based on the legendary appearance of the Archangel Michael during a plague epidemic at the time of the pontificate of Gregory the Great.

modifications carried out under Maxentius and the crumbling and demolitions of the medieval and early modern eras. The design is attributed to Hadrian himself, who in order to create space for the building had an enormous rectangular platform–podium constructed, which ended up destroying what remained of the monumental atrium of Nero's Golden House. Hadrian, like the Flavian emperors and Trajan, pursued an obvious program of further canceling the building accomplishments—and memory itself—of Nero.

In the Temple of Venus and Roma the long sides of the platform held a double portico, opening at the center of each side through a propylaeum with gray granite columns. In this manner the two facades of the temple were fully visible, on axis with the short sides of the podium. The cult building, at the center of the platform on a low socle (a Hellenic trait), had ten Corinthian columns. It had two cellas oriented in opposite directions, with their back walls adjacent. The cella toward the Forum was

Nineteenth-century reconstruction of the long side of Hadrian's Temple of Venus and Roma on the Forum Romanum. This perspective allows the viewer to gain an impression of the former magnificence of the structure. The design for the temple, which lies between the Basilica Maxentius and the Colosseum, was drawn up by Hadrian himself. Apollodorus of Damascus, Trajan's architect, objected violently to this and as a consequence paid with his life. Paris, École Nationale Supérieure des Beaux Arts.

Using at least two dozen elephants for transport, Hadrian saw to it that Nero's colossal bronze statue was moved close to the Colosseum, thus originating the name "Colosseum." Nero had conceived the statue, which stood at the center of the entrance to his palace, in order to favor his identification with the sun-god Helios, though it was naturally considered only an image of that deity. With a symbolism of clear universalist mold, Hadrian would have wanted to place as a symmetrical pendant to the colossal statue of the Sun an analogous effigy of Luna, the Moon, but that project never came to fruition.

reserved for the cult of the goddess Roma. The other, which faced the Colosseum, was dedicated to Venus.

Before considering the ideological and cult aspects of such an arrangement, the probable reasons for this unusual ground plan should be emphasized. The Temple of Venus and Roma constituted a link between the eastern part of the Forum and the Colosseum area. The back-to-back orientation of the two cellas facilitated the perception of the role of urban axis played by the huge temple. In that central area of the city, toward which the beginning of the access road to the imperial palace on the Palatine also gravitated, the Temple of Venus and Roma constituted a nerve center out of which roads ran in every direction, all equally important and meaningful.

Not being able or willing to proceed with the creation of a new forum square, like some of his predecessors (Trajan for example), Hadrian assigned to the Temple of Venus and Roma the role of representing the basic values that inspired his principate. The weighty ideological message to the Roman people lay in the cult

(LXIX, 4) of Hadrian's condemnation to death of Apollodorus of Damascus for criticizing his choices in the Temple of Venus and Roma as too Hellenic. It appears likely that the great architect paid with his life for his courage and his intellectual independence, not so much for his past as main architect of Trajan's court. Thus, it is possible to affirm that in the panorama of Roman art, Apollodorus represented one of those rare exceptions of aesthetic self-consciousness, achieved probably through his

characteristics of the Temple more than in its style: to unite in religious devotion (*pietas*) the goddess Venus, who in myth had given birth to the ancestors of the first emperor, Augustus, with the goddess Roma, who embodied the divine destiny of the city. This was to demonstrate how much Hadrian considered himself the heir of a precise historical–political tradition that belonged in every way also to his direct predecessor, Trajan. This sort of ideal appears much more meaningful than the formal difference that characterized the Hadrianic style compared to the past.

Nor in this formulation can one invoke the celebrated episode related by Dio Cassius

unique architectural skill, a practice that was far more prestigious than the other arts.

However, as should have been demonstrated, that does not mean—acknowledging that Apollodorus may have undertaken the execution of Trajan's Column—that he would have been permitted to take an independent stylistic or ideological direction away from imperial directives.

One of the eight so-called Hadrianic Roundels, depicting a wild boar hunt. The roundels, which originally decorated an official monument, were reused in the construction of the Arch of Constantine.

Roundel depicting a sacrifice to Apollo. The scene vividly illustrates the use of classical elements common to many art works of the period.

The Hadrianic Roundels

The sculpture of this period offers interesting confirmation of the plurality of stylistic directions. This is demonstrated by a group of reliefs dating from Hadrian's reign, some of which are executed in a classicizing mode in the narrow sense while others are closer to Hellenistic art. Not infrequently both these sources of formal inspiration coexist.

An example is the so-called Hadrianic Roundels. Part of an official Roman monument that does not survive, these were reused under Constantine on the famous Arch of Constantine near the Colosseum. Of the eight marble circular reliefs, four represent hunting scenes and four sacrificial scenes in woods. Their substantial classicism in the execution of drapery and bodies, as well as in the composition, lives without distasteful clashes alongside landscape passages of clear Hellenistic derivation.

In other cases, for example in the two reliefs of the so-called Arco di Portogallo now in the Capitoline Museums, which focus on the deification of Sabina (Hadrian's wife, who died in AD 137, a year before her husband), the form presents a classicizing tone, in itself somewhat scholastic and measured, partially enlivened by insertions of painterly taste. If we turn to the reception of the figural messages by the public, it seems likely that such stylistic differences were hardly perceptible, and that the symbolic–narrative and political–ideological content were definite presences in these types of images.

Antoninus Pius: Differences and Continuities

Hadrian's successor Antoninus Pius (AD 138–61) is one of the most famous archetypes of the figure of the good monarch, careful in his conduct of state affairs to preserve a balance between the classes and capable of reviving a broad consensus thanks to few autocratic excesses. This means, of course, that the measured character and slight grayness of the most long-lived Antonine emperor did not prevent a return to the apparatus and ideological–symbolic rituals designed to emphasize the absolute centrality of the emperor.

The Column of Antoninus Pius

One of the strongest pieces of evidence for this is the monument that, in line with the deep-seated political–religious usage of the Roman world, sealed the apotheosis of Antoninus Pius immediately after his death. Not far from the funeral pyre (*ustrinum*) was erected, in the Campus Martius, a column dedicated to the deified emperor. Unlike Trajan's Column, this column was made of a monolithic block of red granite without any reliefs. Figured panels were instead present on three of the four sides of the column base (the fourth side held the dedicatory inscription). This plinth, large and decorated with reliefs, has come down to us in good condition and is today in the Vatican Museums.

The subjects of the decoration were the apotheosis of Antoninus Pius and his wife Faustina (who died twenty years before him), and a ritual cavalry parade of horsemen and praetorians, the so-called *decursio*, represented twice with minimal differences on the other two panels of the base.

The reliefs on the Column of Antoninus Pius are further confirmation of the stylistic adaptability of Roman art, explicable once again by the predominant necessity of didactic clarity in the narrative content. The imperial apotheosis fits perfectly into the Roman tradition of historical reliefs, closer to a "scholastic" type of classicism in its spatial and plastic renderings, but substantially without soul in its inspiration. From this last impression one must subtract, at least in part, the two eagles symbolizing the ascent of the deified imperial couple toward the gods, due to the liveliness with which they are depicted.

The eagles and the busts of Antoninus Pius and Faustina are gathered together under the broad wings of an imposing allegorical figure, a personification of Aion (eternal and absolute time), a clear allusion to the overcoming of every contingency of immortality culminating in apotheosis. From the compositional point of view, the winged genius is the pivot around which the entire composition is arranged.

In the lower portion of the panel are two more allegories, the goddess Roma dressed as an Amazon and, on the left, the Campus Martius (site of the ceremony), with the significant attribute of the obelisk from the Augustan sundial, a subtle but explicit sign of continuity with the first emperor. The choice of a classicizing language is not simply linked to a generic aesthetic but is probably derived from the value placed on the communicative efficacy of this formal structure. For a subject such as apotheosis, intimately imbued with immortalizing worth, recalling a stylistic model of enduring prestige constituted in a way a further allusion to the most profound meanings connected to this particular iconography.

The panels with the *decursio* manifest a completely different foundation in the stylistic

One of four reliefs from a monument erected by the emperor Commodus for his father Marcus Aurelius and reused to decorate the attic area of the Arch of Constantine. It shows an *adlocutio* scene in which Marcus Aurelius addresses his troops.

Antonine relief depicting the *suovetaurilia*, the ritual sacrifice of a pig, a sheep and an ox before a military expedition, and reused in the Arch of Constantine. The style of this depiction is marked by a combination of sculptural values in the foreground with painterly effects in the more flatly worked background.

Relief from the base of the Column of Antoninus Pius. Only the marble pedestal has remained of this monument erected in honor of the emperor and his wife Faustina, who had died twenty years earlier. The illustration shows an allegorical depiction of the apotheosis of the royal couple. Both figures are shown as busts being borne up by Aion, the symbol of eternity. The allegorical figures of the goddess Roma on her throne and the Campus Martius with the obelisk from the Augustan sundial mark the place where the event took place. Rome, Vatican Museums.

Depiction on the base of the Column of Antoninus Pius of a *decursio*, a military review carried out as part of the funeral exercises for the royal couple. This relief clearly contrasts with the style of the apotheosis scene and was probably made by a different artist. Rome, Vatican Museums.

realm, but have the same preoccupation of making unambiguously explicit the sense and content of the figural message. The *decursio* was a ritual in which a company of horsemen and the praetorian guard circled three times around the pyre during the funeral ceremony, as a sign of deference and homage toward the imperial couple just deified.

To maximize comprehension of the aspects deemed fundamental in this particular scene, the anonymous sculptor did not hesitate to renounce fully the classicizing principle of temporal and compositional unity. The two armed companies appear on the same panel, the infantrymen on the inside of the circle delineated by the cavalry—although in reality the two groups would have followed each other. There is no doubt that, whatever was lost in the objective configuration of events was recovered, so to speak, in effective narrative. Anyone looking at the monument would have had to consider whether someone had actually participated in the *decursio* (cavalry and praetorian guard) or whether such a ceremony consisted fundamentally in a parade around a focal center. The apparent margins for ambivalence in this representation—in point of fact, how much one saw in the relief would have made one think of a group of horsemen (*equites*) surrounding a squad of infantrymen—were naturally overcome on account of the fame of the ritual and the modalities of the *decursio* for the Roman people, the principal target of the images.

It is also important to note the technical and stylistic choice of high relief, with frequent recourse to effects of sculpted forms fully in the round, to produce an animated and pictorial play of light and dark. Thus, here too, is the simultaneous presence of two artistic languages, one close to classical conventions, the other almost totally antithetical to them.

Marcus Aurelius

Successor to Antoninus Pius, Marcus Aurelius (AD 161–80) was a follower of Stoicism and an intellectual with a strong and independent personality, as is clear from his *Meditations*, a fascinating book of philosophical reflection. At first in power together with his adoptive brother Lucius Verus, a fragile man with a superficial moral temperament, Marcus Aurelius found himself reigning alone in AD 169 following Lucius' death. With a decision that almost broke the long tradition of the adoptive succession, Marcus Aurelius—the first emperor since the time of Nerva to have a natural descendant—in AD 176–77 associated his young son Commodus with the rulership of the state. In the wake of Marcus Aurelius' death in

AD 180, Commodus revealed himself as an autocrat with limited intellectual abilities.

Unlike his son, Marcus Aurelius brought noteworthy capacities in government to the fore. Despite this, his rule was tormented by dangerous skirmishes, crises, quarrels (for instance, the persecution of Christians in Lyons in AD 177) and, especially, by almost constant border instability. The main border problems—as yet always resolved victoriously by the Roman army—were in the Danube area on account of pressure from the Germanic peoples.

The Column of Marcus Aurelius and Faustina

One of the most typical monuments of Marcus Aurelius' rule deals with imperial glorification through the celebration of wars conducted successfully by the emperor against the barbarians. The Column of Marcus Aurelius and Faustina was erected in the Campus Martius immediately after Marcus Aurelius' death. It was a worthy reminder—in addition to the war activities—of the same ceremony of deification that had occurred nearby. It seems probable that the work on the column lasted well into the reign of Commodus.

It is possible that the column—which today towers in isolation in the piazza that shares its name—formed part of a more articulated urban complex, including at the very least a temple, built under Commodus and, perhaps (though this is not demonstrable) an arch. The marble reliefs that were later reused on the Arch of Constantine would have belonged to this arch.

In many studies there is particular insistence on the stylistic novelties of the column compared to the immediately preceding periods, and an identification of a definite point of change and radical formal transformation in the art of Marcus Aurelius. Behind this critical proposition is the need to distinguish the anticipation, or even the first significant manifestations, of the late antique style—believed to be a language that must be almost completely distinct from the preceding naturalistic tradition of classical and Hellenistic origins.

The historical–stylistic question depends essentially on comparison between the Column of Marcus Aurelius and its model, Trajan's Column. The two have significant differences but it is certain that, especially for the ancient public for whom they were designed, there was a stylistic affinity.

The sculptures of the base of the Column of Marcus Aurelius have unfortunately been lost, on account of the ill-advised work by

Constructed between AD 180 and 196 on the northern part of the Campus Martius, the Column of Marcus Aurelius was clearly modeled on Trajan's Column. Like that of its famous predecessor, the base of the Column of Marcus Aurelius was decorated with reliefs. Its depictions of barbarians submitting to the emperor were destroyed at the end of the sixteenth century.

Domenico Fontana at the end of the sixteenth century. The column, made entirely from Carrara marble, is articulated by a long spiral narrative the entire height of the shaft. A primary difference from the Trajanic model is the height of the frieze, an element that affords a smaller number of bands and a shorter length, inclusive of the narration.

The narrative subject, divided into two segments by a Victory writing on a shield—like the similar figure on Trajan's Column—is the war against the Germans and the Marcomanni (AD 171–73), and against the Quadi and the Sarmatians (AD 174–75). Following Trajan's Column, the account of the wars is structured in episodes directly known from events of war—combat, sieges, capture of prisoners, surrenders—and in scenes that might be called infrastructural, such as marches, sacrifices, and construction of encampments.

details, both columns are effective propaganda tools for imperial deification, functioning in an analogous manner.

Should one wish to find a substantial difference between the two monuments, it would be best to stay with the subject matter and examine the content of a number of scenes on the Column of Marcus Aurelius. The most famous example is the scene—known also from a literary source—of the so-called miracle of the rain, in one of the lower registers. It represents Roman victory in battle, dominated by an immense winged and bearded *genius* who evokes a providential downpour, pictured as a supernatural intervention that permitted the favorable outcome of the battle. It is significant that in this difficult situation the achievement of victory was attributed more to the benevolence of divine forces than to the prowess of the Roman army. In this scene, one observes an irrational change unknown in Trajanic mentality, an index of the psychological unrest that was to make its effects felt in the years to come.

An echo of this state of mind, uncertain and insecure about the complex value of human existence, is evident in some of the reflections of Marcus Aurelius, as for example in his celebrated aphorism (*Meditations*, VI, 29): "It is a terrible thing that the soul becomes weary of life before the body is even tired."

Mystical and irrational components are also evident in another characteristic of the frieze. In the many portraits of Marcus Aurelius, who is often depicted as commander of the council of war, most common is a completely frontal representation. The emperor's figure and face appear in a dimension almost entirely free of contact with his deputy lieutenants, in a sort of divine aura. Comparison with Trajan's Column shows a difference: Trajan, in council with his generals, appears intent on realistic discussion. However, such difference must not be overvalued. It is not sufficient in itself to indicate a break in continuity between two epochs, between rational equilibrium and mystical–symbolism.

The insistence in the Column of Marcus Aurelius on almost supernatural frontality in the depiction of the emperor is probably connected to an absolutist idea of majesty (*maiestas*), united with the ancient theocratic rituals of eastern origin, remote from the Roman Empire. The frontal nature of the reliefs must be equivalent to appearances of the mighty ruler, immobile and imposing, in perfect axiality with respect to the seats where his subjects remain. But even admitting that this could have been the model, the imperial iconography of the Column of Marcus Aurelius would not be other than one of the many stages in which Roman power had no

Reliefs from the Column of Marcus Aurelius showing the miracle of rain, one of the most astonishing scenes on this monument. The bearded personification of rain which appears to the rear of the relief, Jupiter Pluvius, brings a long period of drought to an end and destroys the enemies of the Romans with floods. The Roman soldiers themselves appear to regard this divine miracle with a mixture of astonishment and relief.

One might agree with whoever recognized in the column less care in narrative development. There are repetitions, sometimes disconnected, of scenes that are frankly propagandistic, for example the many scenes that show the surrender and submission of the barbarian tribes. It should be noted, however, that this does not mean that in Trajan's Column less importance was given to the ideological–persuasive function of the images only because in it, there is greater attention to the coherence of the chronological plan of the campaigns. Even if their narrative structures differ in important

impediment to presenting itself with its most absolutist face.

It is probable that the reliefs derived from the conception of a dynasty superior to anything else, belonging to Commodus, during whose rule the execution of the column was carried out. In the charged glorification of the supernatural *maiestas* of his father, Commodus would have followed indirect but highly-effective propaganda, which in reality focused on his

Depiction of Marcus Aurelius with his imperial advisers in a fortified complex. This view shows the emperor from the front, an unusual perspective for the official Roman art of the day, but one which was later to become much more widespread.

own person. Insofar as this may correspond to the truth, the difference between the modes of representing Trajan and Marcus Aurelius on the two columns would not be the result of a formal evolution concluded in favor of the more recent style, that is, frontality.

The history of the Roman politics of images reveals a prolonged oscillation between forms of autocratic representation, that might be called moderate, and more unbridled exhibitions of power. Both these forms corresponded to observed stylistic choices, characterized by a full knowledge of the effects each could achieve.

Immobile and absolute frontality, although destined to become—especially in late antiquity—an element almost not relinquishable in imperial self-representation, remained for a long while after Commodus as a possibility, though not without linguistic–stylistic alternatives. It would be equally imprecise to think

that from the Column of Marcus Aurelius onwards, official Roman art avoided recourse to a naturalistic plan, especially if it is true that the column constitutes an initial moment of such important anti-classical tendencies.

One final specifically iconographic element merits analysis before proceeding to a formal examination of the Column of Marcus Aurelius: the representation of the defeated barbarians. The evaluation of this element is often attended by a sort of critical squinting, deriving in the final analysis from the necessity of demonstrating at any cost the spiritual and aesthetic difference, even ahead of a stylistic difference, between the Column of Marcus Aurelius and Trajan's Column. As already seen with respect to Trajan's Column, it seems opportune to abandon the commonplace according to which a fundamental respect for the tragic destiny of the enemy found a place on the monument. The indulgence of the frieze on a pivotal scene, such as the suicide of Decebalus, reveals the nearly opposite intention—it makes the glory and military ability of the Roman army shine more than ever. On the Column of Marcus Aurelius, on the other hand, a felicitous tradition of scholarship has restored to prominence the excessive dramatic sentimentality that the anonymous Roman sculptors would have reserved for the representation of the defeated barbarians. Notable are the faces, with often spirited and intense eyes and mouths expressively closed in suffering grimaces. But even these sinuous and vaguely disjointed poses reveal a fundamental disdain toward the enemy.

Apart from the fact that in Trajan's Column there are approved and effective scenes of pathos and the dramatic overcoming of the classical balance of the composition, an ideological difference between the two columns remains to be demonstrated. Rather than compare the sentiment toward the defeated, it appears more constructive to infer from both friezes the presence of the same unlimited affirmation of the military and political right of the strongest. Most probably this was the essential message conveyed to the populace, who would have seen it operating in a substantially analogous way on both Trajan's Column and the Column of Marcus Aurelius. Such a message was decipherable precisely because there was full symbolic and semantic affinity between the two columns, decisive for that type of public monument.

It is not unhelpful to demonstrate such an assumption through a deliberate paradox. Among the scenes on the Column of Marcus Aurelius, barbarian women are pictured with their young children. In scene XX, for example, a young mother, with a gesture of desperate resistance, tries with her child to escape capture by a Roman soldier who grasps her by the hair.

If limiting oneself to a superficial analysis, it would be possible to push forward and sustain the idea that in the desperation of the woman, depicted with profound emotion, the sculptor has manifested a feeling of pity toward someone who, along with her defenseless child, is about to lose her freedom. But such a conclusion is as misleading as would be the interpretation of the scene of the suicide of Decebalus on Trajan's Column as a generous and equal recognition of the dignity of the enemy. Equally far from an interpretive reading in pity is the scene on the Column of Marcus Aurelius we have taken as an example.

It is essential to remember that the ancient conception of freedom was very different from that prevailing in Western culture since the Enlightenment. For the moderns—or at least for whoever of the moderns is linked to an elaborate ethic, as in the eighteenth century—freedom consists essentially in the reciprocity of duties and limits imposed on the autonomy of the individual out of respect for the rights of other individuals. For the ancients, in contrast (leaving aside minority philosophical positions) freedom was manifested in its fullness only in action and, in a particular way, in either the subjection or enslavement of others. In the light of this consideration, it seems more convincing to believe that the way the barbarians are portrayed on the columns should be connected to the ideological–propagandistic need of emphasizing Roman superiority toward all enemies.

It is misleading to distinguish between the style of the two columns, as many scholars have done. What would be much closer to historical truth arises from the inextricable mixture between newness and continuity pointed out earlier. It is convenient to start from a characteristic that at first would incline toward the thesis of substantial change between the reliefs on Trajan's Column and those on the Column of Marcus Aurelius. In the scenes on the Column of Marcus Aurelius, the figures are made by deep undercutting obtained using a technical instrument, the so-called running drill, the use of which spread among stonemasons precisely during the rule of Marcus Aurelius. Made of iron, it had a spiral cutting edge that was set into action by two ends of rope, and was capable of incising deep into the surface of the marble. On account of this, many figures in the reliefs undergo a sort of dissolution from sculptural solidity, with powerful chiaroscuro effects of pictorial ascendency that appear to annul the naturalistic consistency of the form.

This stylistic characteristic—which indicates a formal construction different from that of

Roman troops ravaging a barbarian settlement. The futile attempt of the barbarian woman in the foreground to save herself and her child from her attackers intensifies the drama of this scene from the Column of Marcus Aurelius.

Trajan's Column—must, however, be valued within the context of the general objectives of the sculptors of the Column of Marcus Aurelius. A fundamental choice is recognizable in the tendency toward high relief, with the various elements of the story (people, animals, objects, landscapes) strongly detached from the background plane, and achieving noteworthy, sculptural three-dimensional results compared to the earlier frieze on Trajan's Column. Such expressive orientation must be connected to the need to facilitate the reading of the frieze as much as possible, with scenes and figures that, precisely because of their accentuated volume, produce effects of great didactic clarity. In light of this, it appears possible to argue that the deep undercutting produced in each figure by the action of the running drill converged with the play of violent chiaroscuro to promote a "naturalistic" readability of the whole, more than to encourage the anti-naturalistic dissolution of the form.

In this regard, we must also remember the need to remove the perceptual problem that would have occurred on account of the distance separating those who were looking at the figured frieze, a condition resulting from the structure and general characteristics of the column. High relief, and plays of light and shadow certainly aided the beholder, perhaps in ways that were even more effective than on Trajan's Column, to decode the salient elements of this complex pictorial narrative.

This stylistic discussion of the Column of Marcus Aurelius is not intended to negate the fact that the column has important formal differences from Trajan's Column. The lesson of this comparison is the fundamental need to analyze in Roman art the crucial role played by elements of sign-expressive continuities, recognizable even from a distance of centuries. Such intimately conservative modes were intended to imprint themselves with great force on the minds of the public, beyond differences between individual monuments. Such differences include the narrative simplification found in the Column of Marcus Aurelius, where for example soldiers on the march are depicted in monotonous sequence, with none of the spatial sense found on Trajan's Column.

If we wanted, however, to extend to the entire Column of Marcus Aurelius the characteristic of major narrative simplification, regarding it as absolute proof of a definitive change in artistic language compared to that of the classical–Hellenistic tradition to which Trajan's Column still belongs, there would still be some risk of misunderstanding.

An example is an element such as the union of different spatial arrangements, as in scenes CI and CII of the Column of Marcus Aurelius. In

the first, a council of war (*consilium princeps*) appears in a view from above, while in the adjacent panel the representation of the episode is presented—as often occurs on the Column of Marcus Aurelius—in full frontality. But similar indifference to the classicizing conventions of unity and spatial representation is not a new stylistic prerogative among the sculptors of the Marcus Aurelius frieze. It is already perfectly observable, as noted earlier in the scene with the *suovetaurilia*, on Trajan's Column.

The true unifying factor of the two friezes, especially in their diversity and the major formal simplification presented in the Column of Marcus Aurelius, is the stylistic–expressive adaptability—a direct function, as has been pointed out, of the higher needs of didactic narrative clarity.

The Marcus Aurelius Reliefs

The recurring theme of formal adaptability is confirmed by another famous ensemble of marble panels, the eight large reliefs of Marcus Aurelius reused in the Arch of Constantine. To these must be added another three panels of the same dimension but of different style in the Capitoline Museums.

For a long time scholars debated whether these two sets of reliefs (to this last group might perhaps be added a small fragment of a fourth panel with a portrait of Marcus Aurelius, now in the Ny Carlsburg Glyptothek, Copenhagen) might have been part of a single monument. Mario Torelli recently argued for this, hypothesizing that the panels belonged to an arch of Marcus Aurelius. That arch, still visible in the late Middle Ages, when it was called *arcus panis aurei* or *arcus argentariorum*, was on the Capitoline Hill in the area of the church of Santi Luca e Martina.

The two sets of panels, both illustrating official acts of the emperor in specific relation to his anti-barbarian military activity, must have been divided by a slight chronological difference, distinguishable on the basis of the subjects and of the identification of several individuals. The eight reliefs reused by Constantine, which have no triumph scenes, must date from AD 173, Marcus Aurelius' return to Rome from war. The other three (or four), in contrast, would have been executed for the imperial triumph of AD 176.

Even allowing (which does not seem necessary) that the two groups of panels must have belonged to two distinct monuments, their historical–aesthetic evaluation remains analogous in terms of the adaptability of Roman art. As has been noted, it is a question of two series of

Aurelian relief showing a *deditio*. The defeated barbarians kneel before the emperor Marcus Aurelius and beg for mercy. Rome, Capitoline Museums.

reliefs that, despite their almost coincidental chronological horizon and dependence on the same patron (the imperial court), result from different formal canons, even if they share some stylistic traits.

To conclude: a comparison between two panels, one from each series, to form a clear idea of their formal characteristics. In the scene of the *deditio*—the surrender (in the group in the Capitoline Museums)—Marcus Aurelius is shown on horseback engaged in an act of clemency toward barbarians, who entreat him on bended knee. One should note the still relevant importance of a solid amount of mass, generically defined as classicizing. Pictorial effects, however, are not lacking. For instance, the presence in the background in low relief of several figures effectively expands the spatial rendering into many planes of depth. The trees, and especially the standards play an important role in completing the background space. In particular, the depiction of an oblique and undulating standard above left adds, beyond the general spaciousness in which the scene is set, a level of atmospheric dynamism that is translated into the lively mobility of the whole group of figures, even if each is portrayed in the graphic stability of its own gesture.

In examining the relief with *liberalitas* (the ceremony in which the emperor distributed gifts), which belongs to the series later reused on the Arch of Constantine, one notes a wide use of the running drill. The use of this tool has an important consequence, on a par with what would occur several years later on the Column of Marcus Aurelius: the appearance of deep chiaroscuro cleavages in drapery, beards, and hair, with a more visible pictorialism compared to the panels in the Capitoline Museums. This does not, however, deny the persistence of a taste still linked to three-dimensional plasticity.

Without any doubt, the two groups of reliefs reveal more stylistic differences than similarities. But their substantial contemporaneousness and shared patronage, as well as the possibility that they came from the same building, are further proof of how little modern criteria of aesthetic and formal criticism apply to the study of Roman art. Stylistic variants and delays, generally ignored since the artistic theories of the Renaissance (for example Vasari) must have had an unbiased appearance in the eyes of the public of the imperial period, guided in their judgment by an obviously different approach.

A possible indication of this lies in the entire literary work of Lucian of Samosata, a Greek intellectual of Syriac origin, who lived in the reigns of Antoninus Pius and Marcus Aurelius and wrote passionately about art. In a celebrated passage (*Imagines*, 6), Lucian argued that, in order to be able to model the form of a beautiful woman, the maker must know how to take from the great Greek artists of the past—who belonged to a temporal arc that stretched back from the Severan era to early Hellenism—those individual parts in which they had achieved excellence.

An eclectic taste, therefore, that was already alive in late Hellenism, reverberates not only in the polymorphous character of official imperial art but also in an imposing artistic and cultural phenomenon of the second century after Christ—the copying and reworking of great masterpieces. These sculptures were often the result of love for the deliberate contaminations between classical and Hellenistic elements, between details inspired by the technical traditions of the marble worker and those derived from those of the bronzeworker.

Commodus

To conclude, mention must be made of a celebrated imperial portrait, the marble bust of Commodus, perhaps originally from the Esquiline Hill and now in the Capitoline Museums. If this bust appears new, whether in the mind of the patron or in the eyes of his subjects, it was less because of the vague pictorial treatment of the hairstyle and the beard-traits already present in the famous portraits of Commodus' father Marcus Aurelius as, for example, the bronze equestrian

statue on the Capitoline Hill, than because of the surprising and daring iconography.

Commodus, an autocrat without any sense of restraint, had himself portrayed like a new Hercules, the deified hero beloved by the urban masses with whom he preferred to identify himself. With his head framed by a lionskin (the remains of the Nemean lion), his right hand holding the club, and his left the apples of the Hesperides, the portrait was imbued with an absolutist exhibitionism. Not long after, this must have provoked the bloody palace conspiracy, which, on the last day of AD 192, brought the era of the Antonines to an end.

The Art of the Severans

The dramatic end of Commodus' reign left the door open for a political battle that created even more upheaval than in the past. In AD 193 Septimius Severus, from the African city of Leptis Magna, became emperor with the support of the army garrisoned in Pannonia, the province of which he was governor.

But the difficult and hard-fought series of events that took Commodus to power illustrate the profound changes taking place within the Roman empire. At one time the agreement of the Senate and the praetorian guard was decisive, more than enough to guarantee that the imperial court remained in power. This was now swept aside by the increasing importance of elements whose influence was a determining factor despite their distance from Rome—the provinces and, above all, the military units garrisoned along the far from secure confines of the empire.

Leaving this new state of affairs to one side, two further factors contributed to the pervasive climate of unrest and instability characteristic of the Severan era that persisted, despite repeated attempts to bolster the foundations of the state. These destabilizing elements were, first, the chronic problem of imperial succession. The Severan emperors once again adopted the criteria of dynastic succession. This produced dramatic results, such as the murder of Septimius Severus' son Geta by his brother Caracalla in AD 212, or the accession of adolescent emperors such as Elagabalus (AD 218–22) and Alexander Severus (AD 222–35), puppets in the hands of female family members and unable to govern with the necessary authority.

Secondly, the spiritual climate was ever more inclined to devalue worldly experience in favor of the irrational spread of the hope of salvation in another realm, as prophesied by countless mystical doctrines from the east. These were especially popular among the troops. Out of

The megalomania of the emperor Commodus is illustrated by the affected artistry of this marble bust portraying him as Hercules. Rome, Museo dei Conservatori.

Aurelian relief later reused in the attic area of the Arch of Constantine. It shows a *liberalitas* ceremony in which Marcus Aurelius is dispensing gifts to the waiting figures below at the end of a triumphal procession.

Bust of the North African Septimius Severus, the founder of the Severan dynasty which determined Rome's fate for more than forty years. Rome, Capitoline Museums.

Severan relief from the Palazzo Sacchetti in Rome. This fine work depicts a ceremony which probably took place in the year AD 205 when Geta and Caracalla were made consuls.

these, Christianity finally emerged, but not without deep divisions and violent persecutions.

There is no doubt that such an unusual situation must have influenced art in the Severan era. Changes did occur in a number of areas relating to style and form compared to the past. Despite this, however, it is true that in the wide-ranging artistic output produced between the reign of Septimius Severus and Alexander Severus it is possible to identify the far from minor role of longstanding ways of working. There is evidence that these link back to earlier Roman traditions of figurative culture. Three sculptural monuments, all completed in the first decade of the third century, in the reign of the dynasty's founder, Septimius Severus, are typical.

The Palazzo Sacchetti Relief

The first is a relief, today in Palazzo Sacchetti, whose original position is unknown. It depicts a public ceremony, which has recently been identified as the nomination of Septimius Severus' sons Geta and Caracalla as consuls in AD 205. Although the composition shows a single scene, the figures are clearly divided into two separate groups. Both groups are set against an architectural background of the imperial Palatine palace and, on the far left, the Arch of Titus. On the right of the relief, set on a low podium, are the members of the imperial family and court. Among them we should notice in particular the seated figure of Septimius Severus (whose head is unfortunately

lost), who appears to be giving an official speech (*adulocutio*). In the center and on the left, a dozen senators in togas listen to the oration.

The stylistic and compositional elements are interesting. First of all, the portrait of the emperor is not a frontal view, which would isolate him in an unattainable, symbolic hierarchy. Instead he is positioned at a slight, three-quarters angle. This gives naturalism to his speech-making, even though his rank is clearly defined by the podium and the curule chair on which he is seated. This means that the relief would appear to confirm in full everything said earlier about the way in which the ideologically more moderate naturalistic tradition of portraying the still-living emperor was used.

As far as the composition itself is concerned, it should be noted that the sculptor sought to place the two groups of characters within a curved and embracing space. There is no doubt that this was a deliberate attempt to link into the naturalistic style found in the earlier tradition of historical reliefs (for instance the panels on the Arch of Titus). Here, however, it was only partially successful, since the sculptor resorted to simplification, above all in the somewhat mechanical way in which he arranged the figures.

The Arch of Septimius Severus

The usual difficulty in outlining a convincing synthesis covering the stylistic features of each era in Roman art recurs in comparing the Palazzo Sacchetti relief and other remains from the same time, such as the Arch of Septimius Severus and the Arch of the Argentarii (money-changers). The Arch of Septimius Severus, commissioned by the Senate, was constructed in AD 202–3 in a striking setting at the northeast end of the Forum, at the foot of the Capitoline Hill. It celebrated the emperor's victory, secured in two long and difficult campaigns, over the Romans' most dangerous and stubborn opponent on their eastern frontier, the Parthians.

The monument, with three arches, is of considerable architectural interest, since it introduced architectural and structural innovations that modified the older type of triumphal and honorary arches. The most prominent modification was the use of free-standing columns on high plinths, with full use of chiaroscuro effects, instead of the traditional half-columns. A further novelty was the insertion of large figurative panels, each telling multi-layered stories instead of the usual single-subject panels.

However, there is no doubt that the main interest of the arch is the carved decoration. The first significant feature is the simultaneous presence of no fewer than three distinct stylistic trends, each of which involves a specific set of figurative decoration. These sets correspond to the symbolic –allegorical reliefs on the plinths, and on the spaces immediately surrounding each of the three arches—the four large panels relating military events above the arched side openings and the small frieze showing the triumphal procession immediately below them. The symbolic–allegorical stories are also told in a section dedicated to underlining the universality of Septimius Severus' military campaigns and political role. A particularly important role is played by four Victories on either side of the arch, above the central arch, made to stand out still further by four youthful figures symbolizing the seasons of the year.

This type of framework, emphasizing the eternal, makes use of what is essentially a classical style adapted to the needs of the moment. It is, therefore, heir to an ancient tradition, which on its own is thus able to allude to meanings beyond time.

A different stylistic trend, though not entirely opposite, can be recognized in the main section of decoration on the Arch, the panels depicting the Parthian campaigns. An invaluable note by the historian Herodian (*History*, III 9,12) tells how, while at the front, Septimius Severus sent back to Rome a number of paintings about the progress of the war. It seems a reasonable assumption that these were used as source material for the reliefs on the arch. This could well account for the overwhelmingly pictorial taste of the panels, with a strong use of chiaroscuro, far more than in the symbolic–allegorical panels.

As well as the triumphal paintings, another important factor must be considered. This is the close connection—which does not exclude specific differences in form—with the style and narrative of the columns of Trajan and Marcus Aurelius. In the genre of historical relief the columns were famous, and relatively recent, precursors of the Arch of Septimius Severus. They used the device of multi-layered scenes, where the timeline makes sense on both the arch and the columns, reading the pictures, as the beholder was expected to, from bottom to top. This narrative device places the Arch of Septimius Severus firmly in line as a successor to the monument–symbols of the two great second-century emperors.

It is not inconceivable that by making this obvious allusion to the recent tradition of historical reliefs, Septimius Severus—founder of the Severan dynasty, whose rise to power was not straightforward—was seeking to affirm his political legitimacy as well as the prestige derived from the victory over the Parthians.

A number of stylistic elements are specific to Severan artistic language. To a far greater degree

The immense and richly decorated triumphal Arch of Septimius Severus dominates the Forum Romanum below the Capitol. The reliefs on this structure, which was built in AD 203, depict the military successes of the emperor against the Parthians, one of imperial Rome's most feared enemies.

Detail of the so-called Arch of the *Argentarii* and its extraordinarily ornate sculpture which has been integrated into the church of San Giorgio in Velabro. This monument was dedicated to the emperor Septimius Severus and his wife, Julia Domna, by the *argentarii* (money lenders) and the livestock traders who had their businesses in this area.

The portraits of Septimius Severus stand out for the symbolic steadfastness of his figure, which is an accurate physical portrait. These characteristics come to the fore in the scenes where he addresses the troops. Conversely, the soldiers stand out only because they are all portrayed in substantially the same manner, turning them into an amorphous mass (partly a result of the chaotic narrative style).

As already touched on, the Arch of Septimius Severus contains a third figurative element, which stands out for yet another stylistic feature. This is the small frieze that shows the triumphal procession. It is made up of small figures carved in high relief, though on the face of it this does not convey the fact that the sculptors chose an organic and naturalistic vocabulary in which to interpret the event. The opposite is true. Men, animals, and chariots are portrayed in a mechanically coordinated manner, which displays a disregard for anatomical and proportional accuracy, not to mention harmony of movement.

The most plausible explanation for this peculiarity is that this specific type of subject matter, which encompasses processional and triumphal rituals, is of Etruscan–Italic origins. It had been present in Roman artistic culture for a long time, as can repeatedly be seen in official art, for example the Ara Pacis. This dated from the time of Augustus, and is proof, if it were needed, of the persistence of certain stylistic models in connection to specific subjects that could, therefore, be readily identified precisely thanks to the repeated use of the same forms. Thus the decoration on the Arch of Septimius Severus exemplifies the coexistence of different stylistic models.

The Arch of the *Argentarii*

A further key element, however, can be found on the Arch of the Argentarii. This is in fact an architraved gateway decorated with reliefs in the Velabrum area, at the entrance to the Cattle Market (Forum Boarium), where bankers and merchants plied their trade. It was they who erected the monument in honor of the imperial family. The arch has since been partly absorbed into the side of the medieval church of San Giorgio in Velabro.

Among a number of interesting things about this small "arch", two features in particular should be mentioned. First, its ornament is particularly exuberant, full of foliage and decorated cornices, which give a strong chiaroscuro effect, though it must be said that this effect is present throughout all the sculpted surfaces. The ornamentation is almost as extensive as the figurative scenes.

than those on the Column of Marcus Aurelius, the panels on the Arch of Septimius Severus show a definite—if not total—departure from the stylistic-compositional unity originally from Graeco-Hellenistic art. The somewhat chaotic jumble of scenes and convulsed groups of figures reinforce this assessment on several levels. Naturally this in no way dispensed with the didactic requirement typically found in all Roman art, since the loss of the unity is counterbalanced by an increase in the use of symbolic–expressive devices.

This can be illustrated by a close investigation of details. In order to underline the power of the Roman war machine, a primary role is given to depictions of weapons such as battering rams, often shown on their own or in sharp visual prominence in scenes showing besieged Parthian towns (Edessa, Seleucia, Ctesiphon). The capture of these towns, especially Seleucia (lower part of the northwest panel) is highlighted by a clever and balanced use of the dominant lines. The walled city, in the center of the panel, is seen in bird's-eye perspective. The city is under attack by the Roman troops armed with battering rams, who are shown in frontal view (bottom right). Meanwhile in the three remaining sectors (top left, bottom left, and top right) the Parthians, also depicted frontally, run away on foot or on horseback as fast as they can. The whole scene is depicted with a strong narrative flair.

Second, the peculiar stylistic and iconographic characteristics of the arch lie in the way in which the members of the imperial family are portrayed, in particular Septimius Severus' wife, the highly influential Julia Domna. She is depicted alongside her husband in one of the sacrificial scenes of the main panel to the right of the supporting arch. (Originally Geta also appeared in this scene but Caracalla had him chiseled off after murdering him.) Here we see a very clear hierarchy. The members of the group are fully frontal—unlike Septimius, who is turned slightly around in a three-quarter view. Their gazes are solemn, staring out in front. The empress also stands out for an unmissable lack of plasticity in the way the lower part of her body is carved. This underlines once again the profoundly symbolic nature of the image, almost totally lacking in naturalism.

However important this aspect may be, in these reliefs the way the imperial family is depicted incorporates other fundamental symbolic and stylistic components. To start with, the panels with scenes of the imperial family differ from those next to them (which show allegories and sacrifices, and the officiating priests) in that the figures they show are far bigger in scale to those depicted in the others. This makes the Arch of the Argentarii one of the first places with the explicit use of a stylistic device that was to enjoy widespread favor, not only in late antiquity, but throughout medieval art. Hierarchical proportion, that is, giving larger dimensions to figures according to their political or social rank (or, later, their religious status), deliberately sets aside the unitary coherence imposed by naturalism. The accentuated symbolism of this monument, therefore, represents a new, and significant, departure in sculptural art in the first decade of the third century.

The Baths of Caracalla

The most remarkable Severan architectural construction is undoubtedly the imposing Baths of Caracalla, among the most monumental and imposing archaeological complexes of the entire imperial epoch. The baths are situated a short distance away from the Circus Maximus, just along the built-up section at the start of the Appian Way. They were built by Caracalla (AD 211–17) between AD 212 and AD 216 for overtly demagogical motives, entirely in keeping with his political ideology.

The Baths, which continued in use until the end of the sixth century, took their main reference point from Trajan's Baths on the Oppian Hill. Caracalla's Baths use essentially the same

Portrait of the emperor Septimius Severus (AD 146–211), the first of the so-called soldier emperors. Hailing from North Africa, Septimius Severus attempted to avert the impending imperial crisis by strengthening the power of the emperor.

Portrait of Julia Domna, wife of Septimius Severus. Born in Edessa in Syria and descended from a priestly caste who worshipped the sun-god, Julia encouraged the influence of Eastern culture at the Roman court. This process reached its peak during the short reign of her nephew Elagabalus (AD 218–22).

ground plan and alignment as the earlier ones, taking full advantage of the heat of the sun. A major innovation, however, was the separation of the baths themselves from ancillary services, such as the libraries and walkways.

The Baths of Caracalla were built entirely in brick over a huge artificial terrain. The complex was contained within an enormous wall, almost square in layout, which contained shops at the rear and two enormous exedras at each end of the side elevations. A covered walkway ran around the inside of the wall. Half of the courtyard closest to the entrance was taken up by the buildings containing the baths themselves. The remaining sector was given over to spacious gardens, terminating at the back in tiered seating forming half a stadium, used for spectators watching sporting contests. On either side were two large chambers of symmetrical layout, probably libraries. The stadium steps hid the huge water cisterns, which had a capacity of nearly three thousand cubic feet. These were fed from specially constructed extensions running from the ancient Acqua Marcia. Each of the two exedras contained three spacious halls, of which particular mention should go to an octagonal chamber whose roof was a dome supported by pendentives.

The thermal complex, on the other hand, was divided into two symmetrical areas, separated by a central axis containing large halls and the swimming pool, which together provided baths at various temperatures. Each area was reached either through a vestibule alongside the swimming pool or through a room from which the visitor walked straight out into an open courtyard, with colonnades around three sides with the far end forming a huge semi-circle. This courtyard was undoubtedly used as the exercise court (*palaestra*) for gymnastic and sporting exercise. Between the courtyard and the vestibule was a changing area divided into five rooms. Beyond the *palaestra* the visitor went

into another series of rooms, including a hall for steam baths (*laconicum*), laid out along interesting curved lines. The steam room had small access doors so as not to lower the temperature. At this point, the order of the two symmetrical areas unifies, feeding back into the central axis.

Along the central axis we find the obligatory succession of facilities. These were the *caldarium* (a huge circular chamber for hot baths, enclosed by a dome and lit by bold windows aligned to get as much light and heat as possible), the *tepidarium* (a smaller chamber for washing in warm water), the *frigidarium* (an enormous hall containing four cold pools and two fountains, roofed with three cross vaults supported by eight pillars, a design that was to inspire the builders of the Basilica of Maxentius among others), and the *natatio* (a large openair swimming pool adorned around the edge with statues in niches). The cold baths and the swimming pool had direct access to the vestibules and the changing rooms, where you

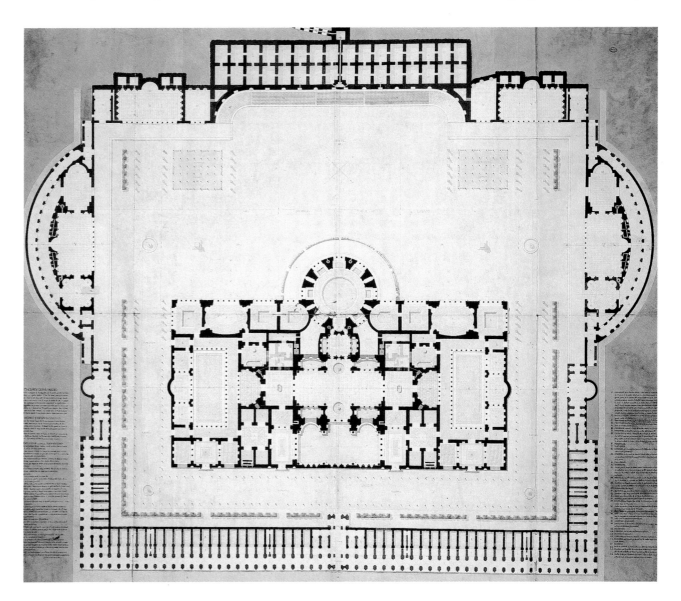

Planimetric reconstruction from the nineteenth century of the Baths of Caracalla. This imposing complex, begun under Septimius Severus, was one of Rome's favorite recreation spots. Paris, École Nationale Supérieure des Beaux Arts.

142

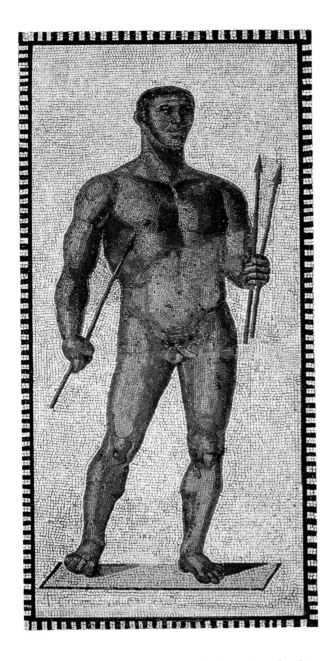 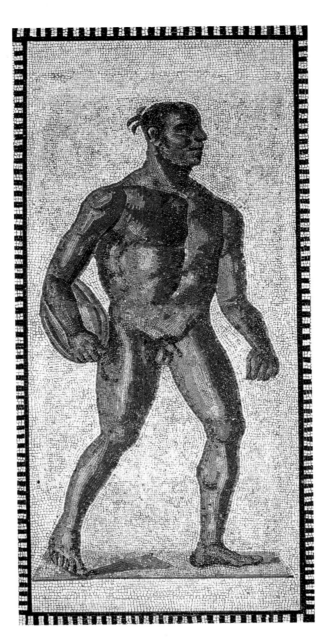

Depiction of two athletes from the famed polychromic floor mosaic of the side exedra in the Baths of Caracalla. The choice of this type of illustration for the baths can only be understood in the context of the enormous popularity of athletic contests at the time. The baths were also the traditional training ground for gymnastics. Rome, Vatican Museums.

ended up after the extended and refreshing bathing routine.

The Baths of Caracalla were public and, in general, access was free of charge. A fundamental feature of the baths was the luxurious decoration, which included mosaic flooring and rich marbles, as well as precious statues. Together they gave a feeling of Baroque wealth and abundance.

From the engineering viewpoint, the ability of the architects deserves mention. They came up with complicated plans in which static and dynamic elements are counterbalanced, and found workable solutions to the problems of vaulted and domed ceilings when dealing with huge internal spaces.

The floor mosaics in one of the two large side exedras, now in the Vatican Museums, deserve special mention. They are made up of a series of pictures divided by a braided decorative motif. Against a white background, the pictures show competition judges and the figures (or busts) of athletes. The nakedness of the athletes distinguishes them from the judges. The equipment the athletes carry reveals what competition they have entered or what prize they have won. Occasionally their names are shown. They are depicted in such a way that the viewer cannot fail to notice their muscular strength and intense athletic energy; the athletes are not without a degree of puffed-up force.

Stylistically speaking the depictions are naturalistic, but they are charged with violent color contrast and contain deliberate highlights in a symbolic and expressive manner. An example is the large but rather dulled eyes of the athletes. The aim of the entire mosaic is, in fact, totally directed toward a specific end, namely to create particularly striking images of these figures, who were doubtless popular with the public who came to the baths.

The immense underground chambers below the Baths of Caracalla housed among other things one of the many mithraea, or shrines of Mithras, in Rome. There is one famous for its frescos in the church of Santa Prisca on the Aventine Hill. The shrines were used for the cult of Mithras, one of the most widespread divinities concerned with human salvation to come out of the east. The religion was one of the most revealing among the phenomena pointing toward the substantial spiritual unease that is a hallmark of the period.

The Third Century

It is arguable that the fifty years between the death of Severus Alexander (AD 235) and the accession of Diocletian to the imperial throne (AD 284) are the most uncertain and tormented period in the entire history of Rome. Deep-seated problems had been allowed to continue without any convincing or definitive solutions being found for them. On several occasions the delicate socio-political workings of such a vast and composite state structure as the empire fell apart.

The main destabilizing factors, masked in a complex mass of elements, are briefly outlined below. There was the ever more determining role that the army played in the political arena. This in turn derived from the essential part that the army had in containing the increasing barbarian pressure. As a consequence of the

army's role, the military made pronouncements with alarming frequency, often dramatically clashing with each other, supporting emperors who were in reality hostage to the changing will of the troops. Apart from a few rare cases where there existed unity of purpose with the remnants of authority left to the Senate, emperors reigned for too short a time to be able to set in motion any kind of truly incisive political action.

At the same time, Christianity was spreading further and further. It had permeated the highest social classes and was by now able to trigger a deep crisis in the ideological basis of the empire, such as the cult of the emperor. Christianity affected the already unstable power of the emperors. Consequently, in some cases this encouraged them to unleash harsh anti-Christian repression.

Portrait Heads

The most impressive artistic testimony of this highly precarious and agitated phase of Roman history can be found in official portraits of the emperors. The faces are of autocrats, almost totally bereft of any values of rational balance that come from the Greek type of intellectual training, as had been the case with Marcus Aurelius. They remained so for almost fifty years. The portraits almost always reveal the likeness of a political and military leader who has an intrinsic and expressive hardness in his features, allowed to show through without any attempt to idealize or conceal it.

Among the more revealing examples of portraits of this type are the marble likenesses of emperors such as Maximinus (AD 235–38), Philip "the Arabian" (AD 244–49), Trajan Decius (AD 249–51), Trebonianus Gallus (AD 251–53), and Probus (AD 276–82). Their physiognomic depiction combines with a clear attempt at precise portraiture to give a strong image of some of their specifically barbarian and military origins. The images convey energetic and lively authoritarianism, which—with unintentional irony—appears is in sharp contrast to their weakness in the actual exercise of power. Nonetheless the portraits, especially the portrait of Decius now in the Capitoline Museums, betray clear expressive signs of unease and melancholy. Although these signs coexist with unmistakable affirmations of power, the portraits convey perhaps the deepest sense of the psychological character of this whole period of military anarchy.

A partial exception to the stylistic and ideological model of imperial portraiture in this phase can be found in the famous marble image of Gallienus (AD 253–68) in the Museo Nazionale Romano. Gallienus ruled for a comparatively long period of time, including the initial seven years alongside his father Valerian, one of the rare phases of this tormented epoch in which institutional and military reform could be attempted. The effort to rationalize the state encountered serious obstacles. These came within an overall framework that continued to be plagued by countless factors leading to internal imbalance and by constant pressure across a number of fronts from armies on the borders of the empire.

Gallienus himself was a cultured man, deeply tied to the Hellenistic tradition. His court was home to the celebrated Neoplatonist philosopher Plotinus. Gallienus' personal inclinations are revealed in the conception and style of his portraits, especially those done in later life, such as the Museo Nazionale Romano likeness. Here, there is no trace of expressionistic accents so often found, as has been seen, in the imperial portraiture of most emperors at this time. Gallienus' portrait, on the contrary, returns to a high degree of sculptural unity, underlined by the softness of the chiaroscuro transitions. It is also present in the far more naturalistic manner in which both hair and beard are treated, compared to the simplification found in so many other third-century, official portraits.

More important than any of this is the fact that Gallienus clearly took his ideological inspiration from Alexander the Great. Like statues of Alexander made centuries earlier, Gallienus' portrait stands out for the slight, but clearly visible, twist of the head. The large

Marble bust of the emperor Philip "the Arabian" (AD 244–49), an oriental member of the empire, who gained the throne with the help of troops rebelling against the emperor Gordianus. Compared with earlier imperial portraits, the strongly expressive features of this work were intended to indicate vitality, and are characteristic of the era of soldier emperors. Rome, Vatican Museums.

intense eyes look upwards, underlining the constant contact with the heavens and the Olympian deities.

Neither should we overlook another class of monument: the famous carved sarcophagi. These include extraordinary works, such as the Ludovisi sarcophagus in the Museo Nazionale Romano. With a heterogeneous stylistic trend, they illustrate the often dramatic climate of this troubled phase.

The Aurelian Walls

However, the most striking record of the difficult political and military situation in the third century is undoubtedly found in the walls that Aurelian (AD 270–75) built around Rome. In order to understand the profound historical change represented by these imposing walls—the largest surviving Roman construction—we must take into account the fact that, during the centuries of large-scale territorial conquest the idea that Rome might be attacked was inconceivable, so much so that over the years the far older Servian Wall had even been dismantled in places. The appearance of the first Germanic barbarian hordes in Italy changed this. Aurelian, who was engaged in the revolt of Palmyra in the east, felt that action could no longer be delayed and started the gigantic building project.

The walls followed the contours of the hills surrounding the city, enclosing it within a twelve-mile circle. An indicator of the haste with which work was undertaken was the inclusion in the walls of a number of already existing large buildings such as Castra Praetoria, Porta

Maggiore, and the pyramid of Cestius, taking advantage of their position. Access was provided by numerous gates, the more important of which had twin arches defended by two semi-circular towers. Square towers were positioned every hundred feet or so, containing rooms equipped to use ballistas (large mounted crossbows).

The walls were completed under Probus (AD 276–82) but Maxentius had to reinforce them as early as AD 310, as can be seen from the layered restoration work (horizontal courses of tufa alternating with brick). In AD 401–2 the threat from the Goths obliged Honorius to take radical action, doubling the height of the walls, incorporating the Mausoleum of Hadrian into the walls by turning it into a bastion, and re-inforcing the gates, which now looked like highly equipped fortresses. Much of what we see today dates from Honorius' time.

One of the most spectacular and best pre-served stretches of wall runs from Porta San Sebastiano (the Via Appia) to Porta San Paolo. The walls continued to be used in the defense of Rome, with varying degrees of success, until recent times, with the defense of the papal state in 1870 or the events of 1943. Their imposing monumental quality not only captures the grandeur of an entire civilization, but also fore-shadows the historic decline, which just a few decades later was to remove Rome from the cen-ter of the world stage.

From Diocletian to Constantine

Diocletian's rise to power in AD 284 coincided with the start of an attempt to bring stability through the reorganization of the institutions of the empire. Despite the fact that, in historical terms, this was essentially a failure, it marks the birth of a new era.

Diocletian, who was of Illyrian origin, had managed to reunite various branches of the army under his command. His name is con-nected to a constitutional arrangement, the Tetrarchy (rule of four), which diverged totally from anything tried before. Its intention was to resolve the recurring problems of the imperial succession. In the Tetrarchy the empire was divided into four interdependent districts, bound to uphold the unitary cohesion of its wideranging territory. The state was run on a

The changed military and political situation at the end of the imperial era forced the emperor Aurelius (AD 270–75) to throw up a great chain of fortifications around the capital. The so-called Aurelian Walls, which still determine the shape of the city, integrated a series of structures into the defensive ring, such as the Pyramid of Cestius, a tomb from the Augustinian era.

joint basis, with two emperors (*Augusti*) as leaders, assisted by two junior emperors (*Caesars*). After twenty years the Augusti were to abdicate and hand power over to the Caesars, who would in turn nominate new deputies. There would thus be a chain of succession destined to go on forever in a mechanical fashion.

The intention of its creator was that—despite its unwieldiness—this system would guarantee political and military continuity within the empire. But, as we shall see, the Tetrarchy was unable to withstand the impact of violent conflict between the holders of power, which was triggered by the inevitable desire to establish a dynasty that followed the first, and only, abdication of the Augusti—Diocletian and Maximian—in AD 305.

Among other basic elements in Diocletian's policy was the clearly authoritarian way in which he restated the prerogatives that came with the position of emperor. One example of this was the name of Jovius (Jupiter) that Diocletian took, while Maximian was given the name Herculius. This was a way of recalling the divine origin of the autocratic *maiestas*, which translated into iron-clad rituals of power centered around emphasis on the imperial cult. This was the main reason for the bloody persecution—the last—that the Roman state was to unleash against the ever-increasing followers of Christianity.

The Temple of Minerva Medica

Apart from the vast Baths of Diocletian, architecture of the Tetrarchy is represented in Rome by the so-called Temple of Minerva Medica, which is one of the best-preserved buildings from late antique Rome. It stands close to the railroad terminus in what was once the gardens (*horti*) of the Licinii, which belonged to the emperor himself.

The temple is a large brick building built on a complex, ten-sided ground plan and roofed with a semi-circular dome. The building present today is not as it originally was at the beginning of the fourth century, since a twin-apsed atrium and two semi-circular side chambers have been added. The main chamber has ten sides, nine of which open on to apsed exedras (the side facing the entrance has two columns). Four of the exedras were originally open and decorated with columns, but were later walled up following the construction of the two semi-circular chambers mentioned above. The huge space was lit by ten majestic windows.

The interest of the building—not a temple but an official meeting hall—lies in two things: the bold building techniques, using a concrete dome supported by an ingenious system of brick ribs, and the complexity of the plan itself, rich with curvatures. Such curved lines had existed in the tradition of imperial building for two centuries, as in constructions from the time of Nero and Hadrian. Here, however, they also point forward to early Christian and Byzantine religious buildings with a central layout.

The Decennalia Base

Widespread evidence of the trends in sculpture that prevailed during the Tetrarchy survive. First is the Decennalia Base, a four-sided column pedestal sculpted on all sides, not far from the Arch of Septimius Severus in the Forum. It is the only remaining base from five that supported five honorary columns erected during the Tetrarchy. The front of the base has an inscription inside a shield borne by winged Victories above crouching barbarians. It celebrates the tenth anniversary of the two Caesars (Costantius Chlorus and Galerius) of the first Tetrarchy, celebrated in AD 303, the year Diocletian visited Rome. The five honorary columns were

Porphyry sculpture of the four emperors of the Tetrarchy. It shows the four rulers in a cordial embrace intended as an expression of *concordia*, or agreement. Originally located in Constantinople, the sculpture was plundered during the Crusade of 1204, taken back to Venice and incorporated into the facade of San Marco.

originally erected on the Rostra, as revealed in one of the reliefs on the Arch of Constantine. This depicts each one supporting a statue of one of the four Tetrarchs and, in the center, the god Jupiter, of overwhelming political and ideological importance.

The right and left sides show the ritual sacrifice of a pig, sheep, and bull (*suovetaurilia*), and Senate procession. On the face opposite the inscription Costantius Chlorus, crowned by a Victory, in the act of making a sacrifice on a portable altar. He performs the ritual in the presence of the seated goddess Roma, above whom the radiant head of the Sun divinity appears. Also in the scene are the tutelary genius of the Senate (to the right of Costantius Chlorus), two young servants, a priest of the cult of Mars wearing the typical pointed headgear, Mars himself—to whom the sacrifice was clearly dedicated—and a man in a toga identified as Maximian, the emperor to whom Costantius Chlorus was junior.

In this period, the style of the reliefs clearly shows a desire for heterogeneity. Two almost totally antithetic concepts can be found side by side on the Decennalia Base. The image shows the strong but primitive use of plastic elements and carving, seen also in the famous porphyry group of the four Tetrarchs in Venice. This vision tends to give geometric form to the solidity of the available volume. On the other hand, the other two scenes show a marked predilection for pictorial techniques in order to achieve

a three-dimensional effect. Extensive use is made of drilling and grooving, a perfect example of late antique classicism in which organic unity and plastic dissolution exist side by side.

Maxentius

The abdication of Diocletian and Maximian was followed by a long period of internecine fighting for power, complicated by factors such as the unexpected death of Costantius Chlorus in AD 306 and by the structural weaknesses in the tetrarchic system of succession, which failed to eliminate the ambitions of those wishing to push claims based on dynastic reasons. This turbulent phase produced Constantine as the almost absolute victor. Son of Costantius Chlorus, Constantine came to power after defeating Maxentius, the son of Maximian, in the famous battle at the Milvian Bridge in AD 312.

Maxentius himself is a significant figure. He was elected in Rome due to the support of the praetorian guard and the plebs, or people, of Rome. During his brief reign (AD 306–12), political expediency pushed him into an enormous program of public donations and monumental works, which still today shape the face of the city. The famous Villa of Maxentius, whose evocative remains lie between the Appian Way and the Via Appia Pignatelli, was constructed at this time.

The Basilica Nova

However, perhaps the most famous monument to come out of this propaganda-driven building frenzy was the Basilica Nova. Even today this imposing brick construction remains in reasonable condition. During the Renaissance, it exerted enormous fascination over artistic culture. This fascination can be seen in the wonderful architectural background reminiscent of Bramante's work that Raphael painted for *School of Athens* in the Stanze in the Vatican Palace in about 1510.

The basilica stands between the Via Sacra and the small Velia Hill, into the side of which it is partly built. Maxentius conceived of the basilica as an imperial reception hall. It had three aisles, accessed originally through a narrow doorway on the east side. This also had a large semi-circular apse which terminated the center nave. It was here that fragments of a colossal statue of Constantine were found, now in the Capitoline Museums.

Under Constantine the basilica was radically realigned. The new entrance, highlighted by the addition of a propylaeum, was at the center of

Depiction of the *suovetaurilia* on the base of the Decennalia. This plinth belongs to a five-columned memorial erected near the Arch of Septimius Severus on the Forum Romanum. The columns of this ensemble were originally crowned by the statues of the four Tetrarchs, who in turn were arranged around a standing figure of Jupiter. The monument was erected to commemorate the twentieth anniversary of the rule of the *Augusti* (Diocletian and Maximian) and the tenth anniversary of that of their younger colleagues, the *Cesares* (Constantius Chlorus and Galerius).

the side facing the Via Sacra. This created a new main axis, emphasized by a new apse complete with niches and lacunars. The apse was not built symmetrically to the new entrance but was positioned halfway along the west side. The side aisles, divided into three communicating spans, had beautiful coffered barrel vault ceilings (surviving only on the north) perpendicular to the axis of the central nave but taller than it (114 feet). The nave itself was roofed with bold cross vaults supported by eight marble columns. The basilica was lit by wide arched windows let into the side naves. The internal decoration was likewise stunning, though little remains today—a few facings in plaster and precious marble, all multi-colored.

For the prototype of the Basilica Nova we must look to the huge halls in the baths, which had already so brilliantly resolved the problems inherent in roofing huge internal spaces by articulating them into vaults. Here this technique achieves wonderful effects of balance and compactness. The structural plan of the basilica should also be emphasized (as it was in Maxentius' time). The apse placed in emphatic relation to the porticod entrance became the preferred model for early Christian buildings, such as the original Vatican basilica of St. Peter's.

The Arch of Constantine

The reign of Maxentius' victorious rival, Constantine, was without question of critical importance to the history of imperial Rome. To drastically generalize history, it can be said that the energetic Constantine took two significant decisions with long-reaching consequences: allowing freedom of worship to Christians in the Edict of Milan in AD 313 and ending Rome's historic role as capital of the empire (already thrown into crisis by the creation of the tetrarchy). In AD 330 Constantine transferred his court to the city he founded at Constantinople, with a building and town planning program on a scale never before seen.

All the same, as a memory of Constantine's era Rome preserves one of the most extraordinary monuments ever produced by Roman art. The triumphal Arch of Constantine was erected next to the Colosseum in AD 315 to commemorate Constantine's victory over Maxentius three years earlier. Though bigger, the marble monument essentially copies the structure and features of the Arch of Septimius Severus in the Forum. Three supporting arches are framed by pillars broken by free-standing Corinthian columns mounted on tall plinths. Recently, archaeological investigation has indicated that the foundation of the arch may date from a much earlier period, possibly even from the rule of Antoninus Pius.

The Basilica Nova on the Forum Romanum is one of the most impressive buildings from late antiquity. It was begun under Maxentius, the rival of Constantine. The gigantic structure was designed as an imperial reception area and completed after Maxentius crushing defeat by Constantine at the battle of the Milvian Bridge in AD 312.

Even supposing that this is true—and it has not been proven—what is definitely datable to Constantine's age is one of the most interesting and significant features of the monument. This is the fact that the carved decoration invented a composite pastiche in which a few, albeit extremely important, reliefs produced in Constantine's reign were placed alongside figurative panels from earlier periods. What this means is that when the arch was decorated, friezes on other public monuments were simply dismantled. All of them can be dated to various periods in the second century after Christ. Their selection does not appear to have been random. The Arch is, therefore, a valuable anthology of official imperial sculpture, including reliefs from the reigns of Trajan, Hadrian, and Marcus Aurelius.

The coffered ceiling of the Basilica Nova was an important source of inspiration for a number of influential Renaissance architects.

Various explanations have been proposed for this unique phenomenon, each probably containing part of the truth. Thus a crisis in sculptors' workshops in the fourth century is proposed, with sculptors unable to cope with decorating such a huge surface as the monumental triumphal arch erected for Constantine. Alternatively there is the suggestion that in terms of ideology the regime looked back to periods of past greatness, as nostalgia for times gone by grew stronger with the beginning of Rome's

decline. There was also another ideological reason. For obvious political reasons Constantine wanted to base his own autocratic legitimacy—which in fact had derived from a disastrous civil war that brutally swept away constitutional order—on a semblance of continuity with the greatest and most revered emperors of the past.

For whatever reason Constantine's court decided to adopt the composite solution. The result was an arch that is perhaps the most definitive and convincing demonstration of the stylistic moment sought here to define. Among the characteristics of Roman art, a special place is held by the substantial indifference toward abstract principles of formal unity. So true is this, that the second-century styles—already varied between themselves, though bound together by their overall naturalistic line—were readily slotted in alongside the language of the age of Constantine, where the narrative is mainly symbolic. Even the decoration on the arch produced in Constantine's reign is anything but unified in style, since it still contains a residual but important echo of classical traditions of form.

It is interesting to note that one of the first people to recognize the composite character of the Arch of Constantine was Flaminio Vacca, an obscure sculptor who worked in Rome during the late Mannerist period. In his *Memorie di varia antichità* (Notes on antiquities), written in 1594 but published only in 1704, Vacca describes: "prisoners similar to those that are on the Arch said to be of Constantine that are in the same manner. I inspected it carefully and am certain that they are by the same hand, and by the same master who fashioned the column [Trajan's Column]. It is certain that they were transported to the Arch of Constantine because on the base I saw clumsy carving done in Constantine's day, when the art of sculpture had been lost."

What is extraordinary about this passage is above all the sharp distinction Vacca makes between the sculpture dating from Trajan's day (the prisoners which, with a stroke of genius, Vacca connects to the manner of a sculptor to whose hand he attributes the reliefs on Trajan's Column) and the friezes of Constantine's era. He wrote them off as clumsy, due to his own prejudice for the classical, something which no longer prevails.

To attempt a summary description, it should be remembered that the eight statues of Dacian prisoners referred to by Vacca on top of the columns, date from Trajan's rule, as does the Great Trajan Frieze (and indeed the other second-century decorations reused on the arch). The frieze was dismembered in four sections and reinstalled inside the main supporting arch and along the short sides of the attic. From Hadrian's rule, on the other hand, date eight truly elegant roundels installed over the secondary supporting arches. From the era of Marcus Aurelius date eight large panels installed on the long sides of the attic alongside the two dedicatory inscriptions, which have identical texts.

As further proof of Constantine's ideological acuity, it is worth mentioning that in all of these reused friezes the portraits of the emperors' heads were reworked to make them look like either Constantine himself or his colleague Licinius, who held power beside him until AD 324.

The remaining decoration on the arch all dates from Constantine's day. This includes plinths with Victories, barbarian trophies, deities on the keystones of the arches, personi-fications of rivers in the archivolts of the lateral supporting arches, and Victories and the seasons in the central supporting arch and two roundels (complementing those from Hadrian's reign) showing the Sun and the Moon, on the short sides of the arch.

Above all, however, there is a fascinating historical frieze in six scenes that runs around the minor supporting arches and, at the same height, across the short sides of the monument. This relief, about three feet high, tells the story of the bloody struggle between Constantine and Maxentius. The narrative starts on the short west side, with the departure of Constantine from Milan. On the south face, the two sections of frieze show military events: the siege of Verona and the battle of the Milvian Bridge, recognizable from the bridge and the figure of

Rome's arches of triumph and honor are among the best known structures of antiquity. Dedicated to members of the imperial household or famous personalities, they performed an important propaganda function in public life, especially in communicating military victories. Only a handful of the 50 arches known from official sources have survived the centuries. The Arch of Constantine, with its decorative program constituted from spolia, represents a special case.

Allegorical depiction of the Sun with a *quadriga* from the Arch of Constantine. The *tondo* is one of the few examples of sculpture from the Constantine era to be combined with the mainly second-century spolia. This phenomenon is less a symptom of cultural decline than the expression of the new aesthetic concept of *varietas*.

the river Tiber on the far left. On the short east side we see Constantine entering Rome after his victory over Maxentius. On the north face are two scenes of peace, one showing Constantine making a speech in the Forum, the other showing him giving largesse to the people, an event that occurred in the Forum of Caesar in AD 313.

There is no doubt that in this historical relief we can see the expression of a formal vocabulary that makes use of stylistic expedients now far removed from classical tradition, but which were foreshadowed by a number of important earlier works, whose roots went right back to their Etruscan and Italic origins. The effect is to enhance their power of visual communication, due to the efficacy and immediacy of a narrative symbolism, redolent with meaning. One aspect of this is the hierarchic proportions of the figures according to their status on the social scale. In the final relief no fewer than five proportional models are used for human figures.

Equally significant for the departure from the naturalistic style is the way in which scenes are reversed. In the fifth relief, the crowd listening to the emperor's speech is depicted standing at the sides of the tribune, whereas in reality it stood in front of it. Another important feature is the insistence on showing the emperor in

frontal view, a tradition which goes back to Commodus (compare the Column of Marcus Aurelius), alluding to the divine and intangible dimension of imperial majesty. The Constantinian frieze on the arch also makes widespread use of drilling. This leads to a substantial reduction in the carved concreteness of the figures, which are used for clear decorative purposes. It is almost superfluous to mention that all the aspects listed were to play a primary role in shaping early medieval art, which had its beginnings around this time.

A totally different stylistic trend, though not immune to the tendency just described, can be found in the symbolic and allegorical subject matter on the arch. Victories, rivers, seasons, and barbarians are all clearly derived from a repertory or from a tradition that was far fuller with classicism, the same phenomenon we discussed earlier in connection with the Arch of Septimius Severus. In this case too, it proves that in Roman art, given the same point in time and within the framework of the same monument, two completely separate stylistic expressions could coexist.

Moreover, the allegories on the Arch of Constantine permit us to clarify an essential point concerning the emperor's ideology, even the political choices he made about Christians. The inclusion of figurative roundels that pay explicit homage to divinities such as the Sun and the Moon—quite clearly universalist in meaning—proves beyond any doubt that Constantine, at least this early in his reign, thought of himself as an autocrat who essentially derived his power from the values of the pagan tradition.

Pointing in exactly the same direction is the way in which Constantine's own political role is highlighted, emphasized by portraits in an absolutist vein both on the arch and in the famous colossal statue, fragments of which are now in the Capitoline Museums. This means that the Edict of Milan, by which Constantine gave Christians freedom of worship—which is naturally read as a religious choice on his part—was in fact an act of political astuteness. It was inspired by the fact that Christianity had become ever more widespread among holders of key positions in the social and institutional structures of the empire.

Constantine's conversion to Christianity came long after the battle of the Milvian Bridge, the source of the well-known legend about Christ's cross protecting Constantine's army. During a reign which lasted roughly a quarter of a century, Constantine sought to strike a workable and intelligent balance between the increasing strength of Christianity and the pagan aristocracy, which was still thriving albeit in retreat, and little inclined to see itself sidelined in matters of state.

It can be said, therefore, that Constantine managed to be an absolute monarch in the mold of imperial tradition. It is no accident that Constantine's triumphal arch, right next to the Colosseum—an affirmation of such a specific and recurrent political practice should have been included by the great German scholar Aby Warburg in his project for an atlas of images which have molded the European world-picture, entitled *Mnemosyne*, the Greek goddess of memory. The Arch of Constantine is depicted in the Gemma Augustea in Vienna, the apotheosis of the Sabines taken from the so-called Arco di Portogallo, and the similar scene depicted at the base of the Column of Antoninus Pius, showing the posthumous deification of Antoninus Pius and Faustina.

Emidio De Albentiis

Roundel on the western side of the Arch of Constantine depicting the Moon on a two-horse chariot. The pendant depictions of the Sun and the Moon set the cosmic framework for the sculptural program of the arch, which features the heroic deeds of the emperor Constantine.

The City of the First Christians

When Christian Rome was officially born with Constantine's Edict of Milan in AD 313 in favor of the Christians, Christianity was already amply represented at all levels of society. The numerous followers of Christianity had gradually become organized and were dealing with increasingly complex needs, needs that had been evident since the first century and the first preaching of the apostles in Rome.

most part the funerary repertory of painting and sculpture in the catacombs and cemeteries. Of these, well-known and important examples in painting are the fresco of the Virgin and the prophet, perhaps the decoration of the so-called Greek Chapel in the catacombs of Priscilla, the "gallery of the sacraments" in the catacombs of St. Callistus, and the Christ depicted as Helios, the sun-god, in the necropolis under St. Peter's.

Mid-third-century chest sarcophagus from Santa Maria Antiqua. The relief at the front shows a combination of Christian and pagan motifs. These are, from left to right: the *ketos* (whale) from the story of Jonah; Jonah in the shade of the gourd; a woman praying; a philosopher; the Good Shepherd; and the baptism of Christ. Rome, Santa Maria Antiqua.

The endurance and resistance Christians had demonstrated in the frequent persecutions of the first centuries of the empire until the last terrible edicts of the early fourth century were certainly not the only qualities that turned public attention towards Christianity. The new creed's ability to attract all levels of society was also crucial and was the main reason why Christianity was victorious even over religions like Mithraism, which had many followers and centers of worship, particularly in Rome.

Christian Iconography

Christian art did not emerge in the fourth century but gradually became discernible at least from the second half of the second century, part of a cultural climate which would still be predominantly pagan for a long time. The only expressions that have come down to us from the earliest period are iconographic, for the

In sculpture, just as important—even if still showing strong ties with the classical tradition—is the much debated Via Salaria sarcophagus, while those of Santa Maria Antiqua and the Via della Lungara are equally important.

Out of such examples a Christian repertory of highly symbolic content developed during the third century, chiefly concerning the Resurrection and Christ as redeemer. Over time this grew more distinct, becoming the substrate of Christian art of the early Christian period, even when the reasons for its formulation had changed and the abundance of new themes deriving from an almost exclusively religious content or from political inspiration, had relegated it to the background.

From the fourth century onwards, the need was felt to evoke the glorious story of the Christian faith in detail, through the stages indicated in the Old and New Testaments. For this, an iconographic language of a predominantly narrative character would develop. From the end of the fourth century and throughout the Middle Ages, the stories of the saints were also recounted, almost in the manner of fantastical fiction. These stories made use of the rich literary tradition of saints' lives which, especially between the fifth and seventh centuries, fed and conditioned the iconography of the martyrs.

In contrast, there are no characteristic or even discernible examples of Christian architecture in this period, since Christianity could not be expressed in official buildings. Instead, existing buildings were adapted. Given the difficult situation of the Christians and the frequent persecution, this was also a way to live discreetly as a Christian.

Architecture

For these reasons, while in the fourth century the pictorial repertory had already evolved, both in terms of complex symbolic and narrative representation and also in the choice of purely decorative ornament, architectural forms had to be invented. Above all, they had to be inserted into the dense pre-existing urban network which expressed the implementation of the complex construction plans of Rome. The first thing this required was new planning, which would literally overturn the previous

The catacombs of Sts. Peter and Marcellinus on the Via Labicana. Detail of a ceiling fresco from the reign of Constantine, with a central depiction of the Good Shepherd and scenes from the life of Jonah in the axes of the cross. The areas in between are decorated with images of men and women at prayer.

The so-called Claudianus sarcophagus. The front of the work depicts, from left to right: St. Peter bringing forth water from the prison wall; the arrest of St. Peter; the miracle at Cana; a woman at prayer; the Miracle of the Feeding of the Five Thousand; St. Peter's denial of Christ; the Resurrection of Lazarus. The relief on the lid shows the birth of Christ, the healing of the woman with hemorrhage; and the sacrifice of Isaac. Rome, Museo Nazionale Romano in the Palazzo Massimo alle Terme.

155

organization, but which needed to be carried out in order to define the new Christian Rome, despite opposition from some of the most important class of Romans, the Senate.

Furthermore, it must not be forgotten that together with the needs of the bishopric of Rome and the local community with respect to the construction of buildings of worship inside the city walls, provision had to be made immediately for the presentation of the "city of martyrs." Christian martyrs lay buried in various locations in the outskirts of Rome, a city that was to call back to it all the peoples of the Christian world. This area had to be envisaged as a satellite area which would extend directly beyond the walls, like a monumental ring, and absorb the heterogeneous influx of all the peoples of the Christian world. With such a project, the management of the area beyond the walls became one with that of the city. For much of the fourth century at least, the question of this building outside the walls was of concern to popes and emperors.

Rome Beyond the City Walls

The most characteristic Christian buildings in Rome, apart from the urban episcopal complex, were erected in the area outside the Aurelian walls. Within the walls of the city, once the fervor centering on the construction of the episcopal center of St. John Lateran had subsided, there was a slowing down in the construction of large cultural complexes. Instead a series of *tituli* (meeting places) could be found, similar to modern parishes, to which were entrusted the leadership and development of the local community.

The new religion, as mentioned, had numerous powerful opponents, while Constantine himself, after the unsuccessful celebrations of the twentieth anniversary of his proclamation as emperor in AD 326, left Rome for good. For these reasons too, there was greater potential outside the walls for constructing numerous large basilicas. The importance of such an operation outside the walls—a way of attacking the city from the outside—of surrounding it with a number of poles of attraction comprising great martyrial complexes whose importance could not be ignored, had perhaps already been intuited by the emperor Maxentius. It is not by chance that it was on Maxentius' estates on the Via Appia, in front of the great circus and mausoleum that Maxentius had had built, that a great complex was raised. Later dedicated to St. Sebastian, it was related to the veneration of Sts. Peter and Paul, whose remains were probably transferred here for a period.

The Mausoleum of St. Helena. This rotunda was designed as the tomb of Constantine's mother; because of its status it was built in a privileged position close to the ambulatory of Santi Pietro e Marcellino. This structure from the first half of the fourth century is a monumental record of the practice of *ad sanctos* burial - that is, of burial close to the graves of venerated martyrs.

Constantine

When he became emperor, Constantine continued along the same lines as his rival Maxentius. Because of his intervention, the church of Santi Pietro e Paolo (Sts. Peter and Paul), the mausoleum of St. Helen, and the church of Santi Pietro e Marcellino, and possibly, though not definitely, the Prenestina basilica were built, as well as the basilica commemorating St. Lawrence on the Via Tiburtina (San Lorenzo fuori le Mura). In the first half of the fourth century, grandiose complexes were being erected, similar to those already mentioned. Among these was probably the great basilica recently discovered between Via Appia and the Via Ardeatina, which may date from the time of Constantine and may have been founded by Pope Mark (AD 336). The church of Sant'Agnese was also built on the Via Nomentana.

All these were significant complexes of separate buildings with distinct functions. All of them, with the exception of Santi Pietro e Paolo, but including that attributed to Maxentius, had a characteristic structure known as a circular or ambulatory basilica, because its plan resembles that of a circus. It is now generally agreed that these buildings are essentially large covered cemeteries rather than churches, in which liturgical services could also take place. Arising from the search for ways of organizing large areas near the tombs of the martyrs and the process of turning them into monuments, they are the most grandiose and imposing expressions of Christian complexes in the area outside the walls. These complexes were supplied with a number of rooms and services for their maintenance and for receiving the faithful. They were an irreplaceable source of experience for analogous building solutions, both at the time and later, and would be among the examples that would become the standard for universal imitation.

At the same time as Constantine and his descendants were establishing imperial foundations, the popes were also doing their best to set up buildings in the area outside the walls. The work continued with alacrity in the second half of the fourth century. The outcome of this activity is not always recognizable today and often nothing of the buildings has been found, even though there is precise information concerning them. Thus the identification of the church which contained the tomb of Pope Silvester (AD 314–35) above the catacombs of Priscilla on the Via Salaria remains in doubt.

Early Martyrs' Churches

The same is true of the three foundations of Julius I (AD 337–52). The first, set up in honor of St. Callistus, above the catacombs of Calepodius on the Via Aurelia, has not been identified. The second was on the Via Portuense, in the name of the martyr, Felix; no traces of it have been found. The third, on the Via Flaminia, honored St. Valentine. Despite efforts to create a planimetric reconstruction on the basis of some possibly fourth-century wall

structures there is no agreement among scholars in this respect.

In the second half of the fourth century, Damasus I (AD 366–84), who commemorated his veneration for the tombs of the martyrs in poetic compositions, built a church on the Via Ardeatina, where he buried his mother and sister and where he himself wished to be interred. No information about the identity of the pope who promoted the building of other fourth-century complexes, such as the catacombs of Domitilla (Santi Nereo e Achille) is available.

Other cultural complexes, often no longer in existence, which are referred to for the first time in early medieval sources, may date from this period. This is the case with the complex dedicated to St. Saturninus on the Via Salaria Nuova, restored in the fourth century by Felix IV (AD 526–30).

The chamber of the millers in the catacombs of Domitilla on the Via Ardeatina, with a mural from the late fourth century. The apse is decorated with an image of the Good Shepherd surrounded by depictions of the seasons. The inscription above the pedestal contains information on the activities of the millers, as well as those of the surveyors.

At this time not all churches were completely above ground level in the countryside. A church might be partly built as a hypogeum (underground), since it was intended to be in close contact with the tombs of the martyrs in the catacombs, or even be completely underground. Thus we have the semi-hypogeum basilica of the martyr Ermete on the Via Salaria Antica, while on the Via Salaria Nuova, beside the church with the tomb of Pope Silvester near the catacombs of Priscilla, the church of San Saturnino and that of Santi Crisanto and Daria may also date from the fourth century. On the Via Tiburtina were two churches, of which one is a hypogeum and can be visited. The other, which has disappeared, was in honor of the martyr Hippolytus. In the same area, a basilica in honor of the martyr Genesius must also have been built. Numerous hypogeum churches are to be found near San Lorenzo.

The catacombs of Domitilla on the Via Ardeatina. View of the apse of the Santi Nereo e Achilleo basilica. The remains of the fourth-century basilica, excavated in 1874, have been restored.

Along the Via Tiburtina, beyond the above-mentioned circular basilica of the first half of the fourth century today almost completely lost, is the *martyrium* (burial place of a martyr) of Sts. Processus and Martinianus on the Via Aurelia, attested from the time of the usurping emperor Flavius Eugenius (AD 392–94), but also lost, together with the catacombs below. To date at least, despite some interesting hypotheses, these catacombs have not been identified with any certainty.

San Paolo fuori le Mura

The most important site associated with the early Christian martyrs of the last decade of the fourth century is the rebuilding of the Constantinian basilica of San Paolo fuori le Mura on the Via Ostiense. The desire to create a lavish complex was expressed in AD 386 in an

imperial edict, in which the western and eastern emperors, Valentinian II and Theodosius I, and Theodosius' son, Arcadius, ordered the prefect of Rome, Sallustius, to organize the project and adapt the surrounding territory to the magnificence of the new building. It was eventually completed by Emperor Honorius (AD 393–423) in the early fifth century.

It is likely that Constantine's basilica of St. Paul was not as imposing as this new one, though it cannot have been as absurdly small (the size of an oratory) as it was until recently reputed to be. The new church, with its five aisles and great transept, must be considered the last grandiose imperial intervention in the outskirts of Rome, not only in the fourth century, but at any time.

Expansion of the City

These vast complexes outside the city walls must however always be considered in close relationship with the life of the city of Rome. The great ring of sites outside the walls did not isolate the city within the walls, but contributed to extending it, favoring the creation of numerous residential nuclei. These too have to be considered as one of the causes of the process connected to a new way of living in Rome, anticipating the gradual phenomenon of the abandonment of the area inside the walls of the city in favor of extending substantial settlements outside. This flight from, and thinning out of, the crowded city was not, strictly speaking, a phenomenon unique to Rome, even if Rome was a special case because of its history and the characteristics of its territory.

Part of this enlargement of the urban area was the creation of imposing porticos which

View of the facade of Santa Maria in Trastevere. The building seen today was constructed in the twelfth century on top of an early Christian structure from the time of Pope Julius I (AD 337–52).

connected the city to three of its most important sanctuaries: St. Peter's, San Paolo fuori le Mura, and San Lorenzo. In time these were connected to a series of buildings, with San Mena outside Porta San Paolo and San Gennaro outside Porta Tiburtina. In this way, the outer sections of Via Cornelia, Via Ostiense, and Via Tiburtina along the tract that connects the walls to these centers of worship were monumentalized. Later, in the early Middle Ages, these centers became fortified citadels.

Aristocratic Rome

On the other hand, as the historian Olympiodorus recorded in the fifth century, vast residences belonging to patricians of the late empire existed in Rome, so well protected as to appear to be citadels. Rutilius Namatianus (*De reditu*, I, 110–11) alludes to others surrounded by woods, which had probably already existed for some time. The importance of these estates is that they were located not in the center of the city, but on the periphery. A splendid and vast residence of the Anicii family, with a private basilica, rose near the walls. This may have been connected to the large residence which must have occupied part of the Esquiline Hill and probably extended beyond the walls. There were also numerous important patrician residences in the Esquiline and Quirinal areas, far from the heart of the city, centers of attraction for the life of its affluent urban residents.

St. John Lateran

In the same period and in an urban context, nothing could equal the completion of the episcopal complex of St. John Lateran. Constantine wanted to take the credit for construction himself, depriving for the purpose the area of the encampment of the mounted bodyguard of the emperor (*equites singulares imperatoris*), who had been faithful to his rival Maxentius. The outer area of the Caelian Hill, where the new foundation arose, was almost on top of the Aurelian walls and thus in a markedly decentralized position. But this was not a sign of lesser importance, since this part of the city had substantial imperial residences, those of the emperor's family and of his intimates who had resided here since at least the first half of the second century. Part of the garden estate (*horti*) of Domitia Lucilla, mother of Marcus Aurelius, where it is known that Marcus Aurelius spent his childhood, has been identified near the hospital of San Giovanni, perhaps near the house of Constantine's paternal grandfather, Annius

Verus, although the precise location is not certain. In the vicinity of the Lateran complex must have been the *domus* of Titus Sextus Lateranus, who had received the land from his friend, the emperor Septimius Severus.

The relatives of Constantine similarly had their residences in this area. In particular, it is believed that the residence of Fausta, Constantine's wife, was here, though there is disagreement over its precise location. The palace of Fausta was also known as the seat of the episcopal tribunal against the Donatists that Pope Militades convened in AD 313. The land was probably given to the pope in whole or in part on that occasion. This original building has been identified in the imposing ruins discovered during construction of the new INPS (National Institute for Social Security) building on Via dei Laterani. Whatever they are, these ruins are certainly the remains of an important residence.

Helena, mother of Constantine, had chosen to make her home not far from St. John Lateran, in the property of Sessorius. The surviving part of this elaborate complex near the Aurelian walls around the basilica of Santa Croce in Gerusalemme, built out of a hall of the imperial palace itself, can be visited today. The complex was set up in the third century and extended beyond the walls until it included the *possessio ad duas lauros* (at the two laurels) complex on the Via Labicana, the great cemetery area dedicated to the martyrs Sts. Peter and Marcellinus. Helena's presence in the *domus sessoriana* enlivened a huge area terminating in a martyr's church. This was given an imposing building complex by Constantine himself in honor of Sts. Peter and Marcellinus, including a mausoleum for Helena, which Constantine had originally intended for himself.

The site of the residence of the bishop of Rome was thus chosen to be in close contact with the most important imperial environment. It was less exposed than a papal residence in the area of the Palatine would have been. Even the Palatine had not always been the preferred location for imperial residences. As early as the third century, Emperor Gallienus (AD 253–67) had transferred his residence and the entire imperial administration to the Esquiline Hill. Diocletian and the emperors of the Tetrarchy deserted the Palatine, and Constantine lived there only occasionally. After brief periods when emperors stayed there and its restoration by Theodoric (AD 493-526)—who never lived there—the Palatine was to become the headquarters of the functionaries of the Byzantine empire. Many, however, such as Belisarius, preferred a residence away from the center, such as the *palatium in Pincis* (palace on the Pincio Hill) recorded by Cassiodorus (*Variae*, III, 10).

With this type of preference, therefore, residences were often located on the outskirts of the city or outside it altogether. This was in harmony with the trend of enlarging the urbanized area, as shown by the martyrs' churches. Given this context, the location chosen for the residence of the bishop of Rome should not be surprizing.

The Lateran complex was certainly grandiose. The many services incorporated into it called for numerous spaces for their efficient rendering, as well as many rooms for clergy and staff. Unfortunately the reconstruction of much of it is uncertain. Constantine's basilica probably had five aisles, even if today only three of them are certain and can be reconstructed on the basis of what remains of the building. These three are the only proof of its existence, except for a few doubtful fragments of walls, which seem to be from the outermost aisles.

The difficulty of reconstructing the original building is due to its history, one in which collapse, fires, and disasters of various kinds must have further radically altered its appearance. This was further confused by Borromini's restoration and by the nineteenth-century enlargement of the apse. According to recent interpretation, besides the nave and double aisles, there was also a transept, a prototype of the series of such cross naves between the apse and the longitudinal body of the basilica. It is likely that the church had a portico, since the restoration of the atria, which the *Liber pontificalis* mentions under the life of Hadrian I (AD 772–95), could well refer to those designed at the time of Constantine.

Thus even the first official papal residence has to be considered as part of the Constantinian structure. This residence would constitute the first nucleus of the complex of the bishop of Rome and may perhaps be identified with the *domus* of Fausta.

It is impossible that the great basilica would not have been furnished with a baptismal structure, as was proposed some time ago. The Easter baptismal ceremonies were among the most important of the functions of the bishop of Rome for the community, since they marked its growth. For most of the fourth century at least, the pope had to carry them out personally. This solemn ceremony called for a special space, certainly the great round baptistery, the remains of which can be seen under the floor of the present octagonal baptistery which dates, in all probability, from the papacy of Sixtus III (AD 432–40).

The *Tituli*

As mentioned, in the fourth century, the city of Rome did not experience within its walls the multiplication and impressiveness of the complex cultural centers that studded the area outside the walls. All the same, it must be pointed out that in this period a considerable number of religious buildings were constructed, forming solid foundations for the gradual Christian transformation of the city.

The most important of these constructions, around which the new settlements gravitated, were those set up to promote the growth of the Christian community in the city and to direct its life. The process by which they were planned was slow, marking the growth and organization of the new Christian community. In this respect, the third century was an important period. These new settlements were distinguished with the name of *tituli*, but only in the fourth century did they correspond almost fully to modern parishes. They had the task of caring for the souls and, when necessary, the material well-being of the followers, who were assigned to them according to where they lived. This task of seeing to the material well-being of its members was always at the center of the Church's concern. For this purpose its organization was extended, at the time of Gregory the Great (AD 590–604) if not earlier, in particular when state food provision ceased to exist.

The process of spiritual education or preparation for the Christian life, as well as its organization, was managed by the *tituli*. These tasks would later be more clearly specified and increased with the addition of baptisteries, from at least the fifth century, and with their being entrusted with the care of the cemeteries. The relationship between these basic institutions of ecclesiastical management and the episcopal see was mediated by the regional deacons who supervised the districts into which the city had been divided for the purpose of Church management. In these districts, the centers of Christian life were the *tituli*.

Earlier, at the time of Constantine, Pope Silvester founded two *tituli*. It could be said that these, overlooking the *Clivus* (street) *Suburanus*, "grabbed" one of the more lively and populated areas of Rome. One of the two had the name of Silvester himself, the other that of his presbyter, Equitius. Unfortunately, the present situation concerning the location of monuments is not very clear in this regard and it is possible to indicate their position only approximately, in the vicinity of the early medieval church of San Martino ai Monti.

The *titulus* of Pope Mark (AD 336), Silvester's successor, has recently been recognized according to its original plan. Though it was not based on a great church but was a single hall with no aisles, it had a strategic position in the center of Rome, at the foot of the Capitoline Hill. Julius I also wanted to set up a *titulus* in the densely

FOLLOWING PAGES:
The pictorial motif of the Lamb of God, popular in the founding years of Christianity, was also widespread in the following centuries, as can be seen in this mosaic from the apse of Santi Cosma e Damiano from the first half of the sixth century.

IOR D

VS MEDICIS PO

SACRO

Depiction of the Good Shepherd (second half of the third to first half of the fourth century). The mode of representation of the figures is strongly reminiscent of antique statues of the gods. Rome, Museo Pio Cristiano in Vaticano.

populated area of Trastevere. This, the church of Santa Maria in Trastevere, like earlier churches, was given the name of its founder while also commemorating Julius' great predecessor Callistus. After a recent preliminary excavation, systematic excavations are now expected to find the remains of an early Christian construction of primary importance.

Damasus built his *titulus* in his name and on his property in honor of St. Lawrence (San Lorenzo in Damaso), next to the Theater of Pompey, in an area involved in the animated environment of the factions tied to the horse-races. Recently the remains of this *titulus* were found under the Palazzo della Cancelleria.

In Damasus' time other areas of the city were already marked by titular structures. Thus the *titulus* of Anastasia was established at the foot of the Palatine Hill, an area of great importance, connected to the imperial residences and, later, to the Greek population of Rome. This church of Sant'Anastasia, in all probability already fully functioning in the first half of the fourth century, was the object of an intervention by Damasus in the second half of the century. Not far from the Appia Gate, in the section of the Via Appia inside the walls, was the *titulus Fasciolae*, now Santi Nereo e Achilleo, while the *titulus* of Pudentiana on the Viminal Hill is now the church of Santa Pudenziana. Santa Pudenziana retraces an important artery of the crowded Subura district. The church would later be renovated by Siricius (AD 384–99) and Innocent I (AD 401–17). Finally, by the year AD 399, Anastasius I (AD 399–401) had instituted the *titulus* of Crescenziana, the location of which is uncertain.

The numerous papal *tituli*, covering more than half of the fourth century, are indicative of the aims of the particular attention of the popes with regard to these institutions, almost as if to keep them mainly linked to their conduct, and, perhaps, also in order to guarantee a more protected existence in a Rome where the echoes of paganism still affected many of the aristocracy. Besides those mentioned above, other titular buildings may have been instituted in the fourth century, though they cannot be dated accurately. Among these may be San Clemente and San Marcello, known from AD 418.

Certainly not all known *tituli* have their origins in the fourth, or even the third century, and were preceded by a *domus ecclesia*, a house or building made available to the community by its owners in the early period of the Church. These foundations were established where it was necessary to set up and maintain a connection with the faithful, and they retained their position above all in relation to the influx of these faithful. There is no certainty that, once the need for them no longer existed and they were closed, they were replaced, perhaps with another name. Thus institutions such as the *tituli* of Tigride, Romanus, Nicodemus, and Matthew disappeared. Their origins and, in the case of the first three, their location, are unknown. Other foundations that did not already have the function of *titulus* acquired it or were created on purpose, independently of the suppression of *tituli*.

Other Buildings

Other important religious buildings also brought life to the city of Rome in the fourth century, even though it has not always been possible to determine their precise function. Some scholars have presumed they were titular, others considered them devotional buildings or even alternatives to the patriarchal buildings. This is the case with the lost church of Monte di Giustizia (dated to the fifth century), numbered among the Christian buildings in Rome of the followers of Arianism, the basilica of Julius I near Trajan's Forum, the basilica of Liberius, near the slaughterhouse on the Esquiline Hill, and others known in the first half of the fifth century, which probably dated back to the fourth century at least.

In the same period, a series of places must have come to be considered centers of worship, because tradition associated them with martyrs. Indeed, without this previous work and preparation, the choice of location for a large number of buildings of worship connected closely to the memory of martyrs would be inexplicable. Among these are those dedicated to Callistus and, possibly, Marcellus (although the legend in this case was not old). Others were dedicated to Sts. Cecilia, Lawrence, John, and Paul.

Monastic Foundations

Another phenomenon, monasticism, also has its roots in the fourth century. This phenomenon is not akin to that of the monastic hermit life of Upper Egypt or to oriental Christianity in general. On the other hand, the monastic foundations that began to be founded in Rome from at least the first half of the fifth century cannot be explained without a preparatory process of gaining awareness. Already under the pontificate of Julius I, Athanasius of Alexandria had amply illustrated the Egyptian monastic experience and its importance in the Church during his long stay in Rome, which stimulated the interest of the Christians there. Certainly the forms of individual monasticism which arose in response to such suggestions, favored in the second half of the fourth century by strong

characters such as St. Jerome, did not result in a full manifestation of the phenomenon. All the same, they contributed to the creation of a store of experience that, by the beginning of the fifth century with the great monk Cassian, had become consolidated and oriented more to cenobitic formulations.

part of the original decoration of the nave, but it is more likely that these iconographic ensembles, like those of St. Peter's and San Paolo fuori le Mura, ought to be considered a fifth-century intervention inspired by Leo I.

Of the entire iconographic production pertinent to the Roman churches of the fourth century (if a fifth-century dating is not accepted), only the theme represented in the apse of the so-called oratory, now destroyed, of the Monte di Giustizia is known. This was described as having a scene with "the Apostles seated around the master, at whose feet is a casket. On the wall below were fishing scenes with genies guiding the boats." This theme, formulated in this way reminiscent of scenes of Nile riverscapes, again brings to mind fourth-century iconography.

There is no doubt that the Roman churches were decorated at this time. Sant'Anastasia, for example, was decorated by Damasus and it can be assumed that this was not an isolated case. Our ignorance of such interventions limits our understanding of the premises of the Christian inconographic repertory which is amply represented in the churches of the fifth century. This repertory, a broad one, can be deduced partly from the sources, partly from important surviving examples.

St. John Lateran. Detail of the apse mosaic with a half-portrait of Christ. This copy from the nineteenth century is the only surviving trace of the original decoration for the apse from the fourth and fifth centuries.

Catacomb Painting

The painting of the catacombs and cemetery decoration, along with funerary sculpture, partially solves this question, at least from the thematic point of view. In this context it is possible to follow the development of more than one iconographical theme in most cases. The above-mentioned scene of Christ among the Apostles provides an example. It is known that it was also used in the important context of the Mausoleum of Constantia attached to the *martyrium* of Sant'Agnese on the Via Nomentana even before it was used in the little Monte di Giustizia oratory in the fourth century. We also know that the scene recurred in the apses of religious buildings, the focus of their decorative scheme. But the subject was older. It is found frequently in catacombs from the third century onwards, where we can also follow the shift from scenes of Christ as a teacher preaching to his disciples to Christ represented as king among the Apostles. Variations on this scene can also be recognized on fourth-century sarcophaguses.

In general, knowledge of fourth-century figurative themes comes from work found in the cemeteries, of which a large amount survives. In contrast to the third century, in this period an enrichment of the repertory

Mosaic and Frescos

Virtually no trace of fourth-century figurative art in Roman churches survives. It is known that the original decoration of the apse of St. John Lateran had provided solely (if lavishly) for the application of gold leaf (as with mosaic), preferring a non-figurative decoration for the apse. Only later, in the fifth century, did this decoration receive a figurative component, known today only from the splendid image of the head of Christ of which a copy has survived, placed in the context of the medieval mosaic which was reproduced in the nineteenth-century apse of the present basilica. It is not known if the parallel Old and New Testament scenes were

167

developed earlier, related to a theme of Christ as redeemer, can be seen.

A narrative intention was also connected to the Old and New Testament themes. The contribution of New Testament themes offered the greatest novelty, which would be highly successful and would characterize a number of iconographic cycles, such as the one expressed in the so-called Passion sarcophaguses, depicting scenes from the Passion of Christ. The formulation, fundamental to the economy of ecclesiastical policy, of the important scenes of the *traditio legis* (the handing over of the law) and the *traditio clavium* (handing over the keys to St. Peter) is also new. These scenes found meaningful, if particular, expression in the mosaics of the two semi-circular niches of the Mausoleum of Constantia in the Sant'Agnese complex on the Via Nomentana. The earliest scenes of the deaths of the martyrs, beginning with Sts. Peter and Paul, were also new.

But apart from the expressions of official art, often repetitious and even banal, there is also evidence of private cemetery art which has revealed, through its choice of unusual themes, the depth and breadth of the knowledge of the more educated members of the Christian community in the fourth century, and their capacity to develop its content, probably using the codification of early writing connected to the production of decorated manuscripts.

The Via Dino Compagni Hypogeum

In this respect, the most important example is the Via Dino Compagni catacomb on Via Latina. The decorative context of the hypogeum not only demonstrates the choice of new themes, but was also the result of the work of highly skilled craftsmen not usually engaged in repeating the stereotypical formulas of the repertory of the community cemeteries, which by that time were already classical. This implies that when they tackled the usual themes—not to mention the new scenes—they did so without relying on standard formulas, and with excellent results. Furthermore, the decorative themes chosen in this cemetery provide a window on the life of the Romans in the fourth century, still deeply affected by pagan culture, here significantly documented together with Christian culture without any noticeable stylistic differences, in a symbiosis that seems unaffected by contrasting elements. The Via Dino Compagni catacomb is certainly not an isolated case, even if it can be considered the most complex and most important private hypogeum of the fourth century.

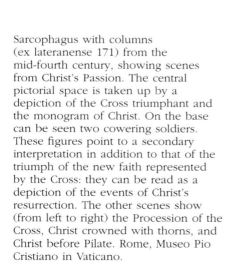

Sarcophagus with columns (ex lateranense 171) from the mid-fourth century, showing scenes from Christ's Passion. The central pictorial space is taken up by a depiction of the Cross triumphant and the monogram of Christ. On the base can be seen two cowering soldiers. These figures point to a secondary interpretation in addition to that of the triumph of the new faith represented by the Cross: they can be read as a depiction of the events of Christ's resurrection. The other scenes show (from left to right) the Procession of the Cross, Christ crowned with thorns, and Christ before Pilate. Rome, Museo Pio Cristiano in Vaticano.

Minor Arts

Abundant evidence of the multiplicity of iconographic themes of the period can be found in the so-called minor arts, which include luxurious textiles as well as crafts for everyday use, such as lamps, the decoration of which for this very reason should be considered the most genuine expression of the themes most familiar to the Christian community. Those characteristics of syncretism that typify an aristocratic clientele were not dissimilar to those mentioned in connection with the decoration of the Via Dino Compagni catacombs.

In this context, the Proiecta Casket, a silver wedding casket, should be noted. Part of the Esquiline treasure, it is covered entirely in decoration, representing a series of subjects from the pagan repertory. It refers to the married couple, Secundus and Proiecta, with the wish that they live *in Christo* (in Christ), and is signed with the Christ monogram, alpha and omega.

However, in many precious objects the ornamental context is totally Christian, such as the little ivory casket discovered outside Pula, which has caused much discussion about its decoration, which possibly refers to the basilica of St. Peter's, and the Berlin ciborium. The so-called gilded cemetery windows in which, apart from the images of Sts. Peter and Paul, those of other martyrs such as Sixtus II, Lawrence, Hippolytus, and Cyprian make an early appearance, belong to a class of their own.

The importance connected to the organization of the life of the Christian community of the fourth century emerges from all this. It is part of a climate that saw the beginning of a different conception of the city, one less urban and with a changed attitude to the conservation of the distinctive values of Rome. These too turned out to have changed, and they came to include certain characteristics of the territory. Churches inside the walls and cemetery complexes revitalized this new Rome, soon to be one of the most important destinations of pilgrimage in the Christian world, if not the most important. At the same time, artistic expression acquired maturity and breadth of content as well as a style of its own. All the achievements of this period mentioned above obtained mainly because the strong sense of Romanness was still so deeply rooted as to constitute the stimulus for these renovations, despite the fact that the power of imperial Rome was already in decline.

Art and Architecture in the Fifth Century

By the beginning of the fifth century, much had been achieved, and all the premises for the establishment of the new Christian Rome had been established. Without the groundwork of the previous century, certain important objectives achieved in this period of time, a continuation along pathways already begun, would not be comprehensible.

The fifth century was a period of crisis. Early on, Rome was devastated by the invasion of Alaric and the Goths. The danger of the invasion of the Goths, even if this is not commonly remembered, had the effect of keeping Innocent I (AD 401–17) far away from Rome for a long time. It was a period of exile from Rome which the pope, then on mission to the imperial court at Ravenna, had to tolerate.

Innocent I

However, a strong character such as Innocent could draw on such an experience to create useful ideas for carrying out his mandate more fully and with greater awareness. Innocent participated personally in the climate that had become established in northern Italy, where the effects of the imperial power in Milan, as well as Ambrose's period as bishop there, were recent. In Ravenna, Innocent became involved

Anonymous catacomb on the Via Latina (Via Dino Compagni). Detail with the bust of the Samaritan woman from the scene of her encounter with Christ at the well. Fourth-century mural from the chamber of Samson.

Via Salaria. Hypogeum on the Via Livenza with a fourth-century depiction of Diana, the goddess of hunting.

170

in the pastoral administration of Illyricum (the southeast Balkans), a strategic territory for contacts with the east, summoning Rufus, bishop of Thessalonica, to work with him.

When he returned to Rome, Innocent was the first pope to introduce the veneration of non-Roman martyrs, which, apart from some illustrious exceptions included in the calendar of the Roman church in the first half of the fourth century, was finally expressed in an organized way. Using the legacy and the earnings of an illustrious woman, Vestina, Innocent had the titular churches of Santi Gervasio e Protasio and, later, San Vitale built. This choice of dedication, clear evidence of Innocent's experience, revealed too the adoption of typically eastern building features. San Vitale is the first Roman church which can be dated with certainty in which a dosseret can be found.

Innocent was also responsible for introducing the veneration of St. Crisogonus, the famous martyr of the Aquileia area. Recent excavations have made it possible to attribute with probability the building of the titular church of San Crisogono in Trastevere to the first half of the fifth century.

Invasion and Crisis

All the same, it is not possible to minimize the importance of a calamity as disastrous as the sack of Rome by Alaric. Innocent's absence from Rome must likewise be considered in negative terms, even if, after his return, he lost no time and was untiring in his efforts to rebuild Rome's image. Moreover, the event that ravaged Rome in the papacy of Innocent was not an isolated case during the fifth century. The second half of the century saw the new and no less tragic invasion of the Vandal Gaiseric, the fall of the Western Roman Empire, and the conquest of Italy by Theodoric's Ostrogoths.

Indirect, if no less serious, damage also struck the Church's patrimony. Of the great land donations of the emperors and landowners, and of the estates that the Church had come to own in Africa, Gaul, and Spain, all was lost in the invasions of the Vandals, Burgundians, Franks, and Visigoths. Only the territories in central and southern Italy and the Italian islands remained.

Fifth-Century Popes

In the meantime, the election of the pope in Rome took place amid much dissent, something that was certainly not new and had already produced serious disputes, especially in the second half of the fourth century. Boniface I (AD 418–22) had to endure the opposition of the anti-pope Eulalius (AD 418–19), forcing him to live outside the city,

TOP:
Silver wedding casket belonging to a woman called Proiecta, from the Esquiline treasure. Despite the obviously Christian inscription referring to the young couple ("Secunde et Proiecta vivatis in Christo"), the depictions on this box show scenes of pagan origin. London, British Museum.

ABOVE:
Fifth- or sixth-century cylindrical container with lid (pyxis) from the church of Santi Quattro Coronati. This superb piece of silver work was probably originally used as a cult vessel to celebrate the Eucharist, and later still to store the head of St. Sebastian. Rome, Museo Sacro Vaticano.

near the cemetery of Sts. Maximus and Felicity near the Nomentana Gate, and to carry out the Easter baptismal functions near the catacombs of St. Agnes. The episode shows once more that the area outside the walls was well-equipped even for such an occurrence. In a very similar situation in the fourth century, anti-popes such as Felix II (AD 355–65) and popes such as Liberius (AD 352–66) had also found refuge there.

The election of Sixtus III in AD 432 was also challenged. He was humiliated by a trial for rape which embittered the beginning of his pastoral mandate. At the close of the century, the election of Symmachus (AD 498–514) was blocked by the power of the anti-pope Lawrence (AD 498–99, AD 501–6) and his supporters. To settle the question, the presence of the Gothic king Theodoric was invoked.

Rome was also the scene of the Pelagian schism, when the monk Pelagius and, even more, his disciple Celestius, attracted a large number of patricians, resulting in a serious blow to the Christian community. In this climate, the Nestorian heresy was debated, which, like the Arian heresy of the previous century, compromised relations with the eastern empire. The councils of Ephesus in AD 431 and Chalcedon in AD 451 were important stages in the victory of orthodoxy, for which the contribution of the Church of Rome was of fundamental importance, especially with popes Celestine I (AD 422–32), Sixtus III (AD 432–40), and Leo the Great (AD 440–61). The specter of heresy, always a threat in Rome, recurred with the arrival of the Arian Goths of Theodoric. At the end of the century, apart from the pope, even the bishop of the Goths had his residence in Rome.

In this climate, once again the city owed its conquests and its progress to the values, doctrine, and capacity to govern of its popes. Besides those mentioned, individuals such as Siricius, Simplicius (AD 468–83), and Gelasius I (AD 492–6) cannot be forgotten. However, all the fifth-century popes, despite the ordeals and difficulties they had to face, contributed to the growth of Christian Rome and to the development of the guidelines that had already been clearly indicated in the previous period.

A fifth-century revival has been mentioned, especially in architecture. Perhaps this is not an appropriate definition, even if it is certain that construction in this period implied a growth and consolidation of past experience and that this substantial enrichment made it possible to strengthen the image of Christian Rome. As far as the area outside the city walls is concerned, however, probably nothing built in this century could have the importance and exceptional characteristics of St. Peter's or San Paolo fuori le Mura, built by three emperors and exalted in verse by Prudentius.

It is also certain that, in the sanctuaries of the martyrs, work was undertaken to improve the functioning of the complexes, which in many cases was able to guarantee their autonomous management. Thus, for example—as has already been mentioned—Boniface I had taken care of the memorial to St. Felicity on the Via Salaria Nuova, with the building of a basilica in her honor (possibly two, one a hypogeum, the other above ground). The establishment of a residence nearby, for the period in which Boniface was forced to live outside Rome due to conflict with the anti-pope Eulalius, is also attributed to him.

The first of the monastic structures of Rome was established outside the walls by Sixtus III, next to the center of the Sts. Peter and Paul complex on the Via Appia. Also on the Via Appia, but near the catacombs of Callistus, Leo the Great built a church in the name of his celebrated predecessor Cornelius (AD 251–53). Leo was also the founder of the most important of the five monasteries that made up the basilica of St. Peter at the Vatican, dedicated to Sts. John and Paul. St. Peter's, perhaps in the fifth century or the beginning of the sixth, had a female monastic institution, that of Santo Stefano Maggiore, in which, as reported by Gregory the Great, the aristocrat Galla retired to pass the rest of her life in sanctity.

Santo Stefano Rotondo

Leo also gave his assent and encouragement for the foundation of the church of Santo Stefano Rotondo on the third mile of the Via Latina, promoted by the patrician Demetriade, of the Anicii family. The complex is important because it includes a baptistery. It inaugurated the cult of St. Stephen, archdeacon of the eastern church, instituted in the context of the *martyria* foundations beyond the walls of Rome. Some decades earlier, the relics of St. Stephen had been found. Demetriade put them in the memorial set up in the apse of the church. This foundation was important not only for its memorial value but, above all, for the attraction of the baptistery for the inhabitants of the surrounding area, who could consider themselves the beneficiaries of a cultural structure that was not the object of pilgrims' visits, but had been set up for the local community. Unfortunately, the poor condition of the archaeological area of Santo Stefano and the poorly documented excavations do not permit the study it merits. It may be possible to identify the existence of an early monastic structure associated with the church in significant remains in front of the facade.

Mosaic from the right wall of the nave of Santa Maria Maggiore, showing scenes from the life of Joshua.
ABOVE: The Ark of the Covenant crosses the Jordan.
BELOW: Joshua's spies are sent out to Jericho.

Symmachus

The *martyrium* of St. Lawrence on the Via Tiburtina was the site of important works. A male monastery, perhaps with a nunnery in the fifth century (attested in the early eighth century), and baths, libraries, and an aristocratic residence were built. At the end of the fifth and the beginning of the sixth century, Symmachus concerned himself with the Via Aurelia, building a basilica with a *balneum* attached in the name of the martyr Pancras (San Pancrazio). The construction of a church with a baptistery in honor of St. Agatha is also due to Symmachus. It might be defined as a foundation for the use of the inhabitants of the Roman outlying areas, like Santo Stefano Rotondo on Via Latina. It was almost certainly in the area of the cemetery of Sts. Processus and Martinianus, on the Via Aurelia Nuova.

The original nucleus of the Vatican palace may also be attributed to Symmachus. His sensitivity to the poor encouraged him to set up hostels for the poor, the *habitacula*, near the great sanctuaries of St. Peter's, San Paolo, and San Lorenzo. With this operation, Symmachus ingeniously achieved his goal of bringing to general awareness an aspect of Church activity inherent in the problem of charity and assistance, putting it into the context of the work involved in running the more important *martyria*. This stimulated not only the offerings of the local community but pilgrims' charity.

In the fifth century, building outside the walls of Rome and its goals were therefore important. The popes took steps to improve what had been created in the fourth century and make it more functional, contributing to enlarging the structures outside the walls and refining their features. However, no great complex could equal those of the previous layout.

Building inside the city walls is treated separately here only for convenience; it should be considered together with the area outside the walls, as will be clear from the observations that have been made about this area. The situation within the walls has important peculiarities. It can be said that it was precisely the operations that were brought to a conclusion here that brought to mind a revival of early Christian architecture.

Sixtus III

If these interventions are taken into consideration, among those that can be attributed to this period is a series of constructions built either completely or almost completely anew, without noticeable reuse of previous buildings, as can frequently be observed in early Christian churches. Moreover, it can be pointed out in any case that the most important period for Christian building in the fifth century is the period up to the papacy of Sixtus III. With Sixtus, echoes of the victory of the council of Ephesus could still be heard and the distance between the consequences of the sack of Rome by Alaric and the events of the later devastation by Gaiseric is the same. This was a propitious period for refining and enriching the layout of Christian buildings in Rome, bringing to completion a series of buildings that seem to have been part of a common project.

Rather than a revival, the papacy of Sixtus III was a period when building activity was brought to a grandiose conclusion. This activity, despite the sack of the city by the Goths, did not seem to suffer from problems of continuity. As in the first decades of the century, Innocent I, who had completed Santa Pudenziana, also built San Vitale, as well, perhaps, as San Crisogono in Trastevere. In any case San Crisogono was built not long after his papacy, soon after (if such an early dating is accepted) San Clemente. Sixtus III also finished Santa Sabina on the Aventine Hill, begun by his predecessor Celestine I.

Santa Maria Maggiore

The peak of Sixtus's activity as a builder of churches is Santa Maria Maggiore, with which he wanted to celebrate the victory at the council of Ephesus (though recently an opinion to the contrary has been expressed). Placed on the Cispian summit of the Esquiline hill, it was the first church with a baptistery, apart from the recent discoveries in the area of the Sessorian basilica of Santa Croce in Gerusalemme, the dating of which will depend mainly on new excavations. In any case it must be considered a highly unusual *martyrium* within the walls. Santa Maria Maggiore immediately became one of the most important churches in Rome. The quality of its role also emerged, for example, in the context of the great procession ceremonies between the basilicas.

Fortunately, the building survives. Its impressiveness can be evaluated almost completely and even its substructure examined. It is not only a great basilica with three aisles but also a daring construction. It cannot have been easy to set it on the top of the Cispian summit, at a great height over the surrounding area. The fourth-century basilica of St. John Lateran was also at a certain height, but it is not possible to compare it with the other churches of the period except for Sant'Anastasia.

Nevertheless, this became a characteristic of fifth-century churches, a way of displaying eminence in relation to the surrounding context of buildings. In the same way, the churches of San Clemente, Santi Giovanni e Paolo, Santa Pudenziana, Santa Sabina, San Lorenzo in Lucina, and the oratory of Monte di Giustizia are also built at a higher level.

Santa Sabina is part of the above-mentioned group of buildings by Sixtus III, who completed the construction that his predecessor Celestine I had left unfinished. Sixtus was also responsible for the rebuilding of San Pietro in Vincoli, the origin of which may well go back to the fourth century, as well as the rebuilding of the Lateran baptistery (though this is sometimes contested). It is likely that San Lorenzo in Lucina and San Sisto Vecchio were also part of Sixtus' work.

Indeed, as if numerous and authoritative opinions were not sufficient in this regard, attentive examination of the masonry of all these buildings, whose elevations were entirely built in precise stonework, has confirmed the affinity of many features of the masonry. The masonry has identical-sized modules. Equal care is also shown in the choice and laying of the materials, to the extent that the group of churches of Sixtus III can be considered the work of a single group of craftsmen.

The Later Fifth Century

Little indeed of the construction of Roman cultural buildings within the walls changes after the enormous contribution of this period. Hilarius (AD 461–68) annexed three beautiful oratories (four, if Santo Stefano is included) to the Lateran baptistery. Of these, two (one decorated with mosaic) remain. They are dedicated to St. John the Baptist and St. John the Evangelist. That of Santa Croce was destroyed in the Renaissance.

A church like Santo Stefano Rotondo, unique in Rome for its round plan, and for the grandeur and peculiarities of its construction, almost certainly cannot be considered part of the building picture of the second half of the fifth century. Recent studies have dated its construction to the emperor Valentinian III (AD 423–55), so that it would fall within the papacy of Sixtus III, above all because of the characteristics of the facings.

Except for Santo Stefano, the churches built by Simplicius are much less important. It was to Simplicius that the cultural complex had previously been attributed, but today it is considered

Mosaic from the right wall of the nave of Santa Maria Maggiore, showing scenes from the life of Joshua.
ABOVE: The angel appears to Joshua.
BELOW: Rahab helps the spies to descend from the walls of Jericho; the spies report what they have seen to Joshua.

that he was only the person who dedicated it. These churches are Santa Bibiana and Sant'Andrea, both on the Esquiline Hill, the only Roman churches that can be attributed with certainty to the troubled period of the second half of the fifth century. Of the two buildings, the first was actually built, while the second was only laid out in a splendid private basilica of the fourth century which had been part of the property of the aristocratic Bassi family. The area of the basilica of Santa Maria Maggiore was probably also included in this property.

Doubts exist, finally, as to the third Roman church attributed to the papacy of Simplicius. This is the enigmatic church in the Subura dedicated to St. Agatha, Sant'Agata dei Goti. This church is still substantially complete despite the later interior rearrangement and the effect of careless restoration, which has made it impossible to read the rare and important late antique masonry. It is striking for a period in which it was certainly connected to the Arian heresy. This peculiarity was pointed out by Gregory the Great, who described his inauguration of the church, numbering it definitively among those of the Catholic rite, with the name of Sant'Agata. It must, however, be pointed out that the complex of the cult changed its chronological determina-tion at the time of Simplicius, essentially from its relationship with the memorial of the barbarian noble Ricimer, to whom many radical changes of the imperial situation in the second half of the fifth century are due. The inscription that could be read on the base of the bowl-shaped vault of the apse seemed to refer to Ricimer. It is possible that this inscription refers to another Ricimer, a consul of the second half of the fourth century, with the same name, position, and aristocratic status. Ricimer may only have decorated the basilica, as the inscription says: *pro voto suo adornavit* (he decorated it to fulfil his vow).

Members of the imperial family and Christian aristocrats in general received excellent publicity from this kind of operation, which certainly cost less than raising an entire building. Nothing was a more effective form of advertising than the use of their name in memory of the decoration of all or part of a basilica. There are many examples, beginning with the second half of the fourth century: Anastasius, with the martyr Martinianus, Longinianus, who contributed to the baptistery of St. Peter's and that of Sant'Anastasia, Felix and Padusia, who had the apse of St. John Lateran decorated (AD 428–30), and Valentinian II, Theodosius, Arcadius, and Galla Placidia, who

Aerial view of the church of Santo Stefano Rotondo on the Celian Hill. This centralized structure was founded by an imperial patron, possibly Valentinian III, and built in the fifth century on the site of a former barracks. The remains of the *castra peregrina*, including an important mithraeum below the church, provide an impressive picture of the dimensions of this military complex.

covered the apse of San Paolo fuori le Mura with mosaic, and Placidia and Honoria, who decorated the so-called chapel of St. Helena in Santa Croce in Gerusalemme.

What has been discovered more recently, and is a characteristic of the fifth century, are the installations of baptismal structures attached to the *tituli*. In reality, their dating is in many cases uncertain and it cannot be hypothesized that these annexes date from earlier than the second half of the fourth century. It is certain, however, that precisely in this period, with the increased requirements of a large community, the need was felt to distribute the baptismal ceremony over many points of the city instead of its previous concentration in St. John Lateran. With their parish-like functions, the *tituli* seemed to be best suited to this task.

This changed situation finds important confirmation not only in the sources, which often allude to the liturgical baptismal furnishings of the *tituli*, but also in the ever more numerous archaeological findings which attest to them. The baptistery of San Marcello on the Corso was already known, but recently those of Santa Cecilia (in Trastevere), San Marco (in Piazza Venezia), San Lorenzo in Lucina, and San Clemente have also been discovered. The number of fourth-century baptismal structures is proof of the strengthening of the urban cultural centers in parallel with similar operations outside the walls including, between the fourth and fifth century, many baptisteries.

The fifth century can seem much richer than the previous century, at least as far as Rome inside the walls is concerned, in part because numerous buildings have come down to us, which are rich in original evidence, providing large sections of the decoration that adorned them. While the fourth century has bequeathed mainly evidence of hypogeum painting outside the walls, the following period begins with the imposing mosaic of Santa Pudenziana of Innocent I.

From the period of Sixtus III the stories of the Old Testament and the childhood of Christ have survived in Santa Maria Maggiore, splendid examples of the work of Roman mosaicists. Similarly the mosaics of the inner wall of the facade of Santa Sabina and the atrium of the Lateran baptistery have survived. In San Paolo fuori le Mura, even if it has been much restored, the mosaic of the triumphal arch of Leo I has come down to us, with the acclamation of the twenty-four elders of the Apocalypse, a theme of Leo's own theological speculations. There remains the mosaic of the vault of the chapel of St. John the Evangelist in the Lateran Baptistery, built by Hilarus (AD 461–68).

Missorium depicting the hunt of Meleager, evidence of the liturgical use of profane objects in late antiquity (end of the fifth to beginning of the sixth century). Rome, Museo Pio Cristiano in Vaticano.

Church Furnishings

Much ancient and Renaissance evidence helps to reconstruct the lost decoration of other churches, enhancing our understanding of those that have survived. The archaeological finds of luxurious liturgical furnishings provide a more detailed picture of the religious buildings of the period. An example of this is a document of AD 471 concerning the foundation of a church in the countryside near Via Tiburtina by a Catholic Goth called Valila. This lists church furnishings: a rich series of precious silks and linens woven with gold and embroidered, as well as precious vessels and an abundance of lamps. If a country church was so well endowed, what must the churches in Rome have been like?

Examples of such precious archaeological finds can still be found: secular objects such as the dish of Flavius Ardabur Aspar, consul in AD 434, in the archaeological museum in Florence, or that of the hunt of Meleager in the Vatican Museums, which were used for the offertory, and thus for liturgical use, without being excessively subtle about it.

Moreover, even if all this monumental and written documentation is available, it should not be forgotten that, despite the excellence of certain results, the second half of the fifth century marks a different historical climate. All the above-mentioned construction in Christian Rome did no more than confirm the results that had already been amply achieved in the fourth century, in accordance with a line of continuity that showed signs of decline only in the second half of the following century.

Margherita Cecchelli

Art in the Paleochristian Period

An Absence of Images

It is generally accepted that Christian art did not emerge or spread in Rome or elsewhere in the ancient world at the same time as Christianity did. For almost two hundred years there was an artistic vacuum, just at the time when the new religion was with difficulty taking root in the sophisticated polytheistic culture that developed in Rome and the empire in the first two centuries after Christ.

This absence—a total silence—can be accounted for in a number of ways. The veto on representational images in the Ten Commandments is usually referred to: "You shall not make a carved image for yourself... You shall not bow down to them or worship them" (Exodus, 20, 4–5). The veto, which had had tremendous influence on Jewish culture—already unfavorable to representational art—influenced the outlook of the early Christians.

The authoritative Fathers of the Church of the first centuries constantly returned to the subject, stressing the attention that Christians needed to pay to representations of the sacred. In practice, images of God the Father were forbidden, given the fear that reverence for images might turn into idolatry. Christian writers of the first centuries, from Clement of Alexandria and Origen in the east to Tertullian and Minucius Felix in the west, wrestled with the problem of the dividing-line between reverence for images and idolatry. The debate continued for centuries, even after Constantine's conversion to Christianity. Epiphanius and Eusebius were highly critical of any who dared to represent the sacred.

The debate reached Rome, as is attested by a passage in Minucius Felix's *Octavius* in the second century. In a discussion of the pagan custom of making images of gods, Minucius expounded the Christian view: "Why should I carve an image of God when, if you think about it, man himself is the image of God?" (*Octavius*, 32).

In the first and second centuries after Christ, Christianity was becoming widespread in Rome, as is attested by St. Paul's letter to the church there, written between AD 57 and AD 58 (Romans, 1, 8). The Christian community in Rome was evidently by this time well known throughout the ancient world. Later, notably in AD 64, during Nero's persecution, Rome saw

mass executions of Christians, including the martyrdom of Sts. Peter and Paul; the persecution is referred to by Tacitus (*Annals*, 15, 44) and Clement of Rome (*To the Corinthians*, 5–6).

Over time Christianity spread to the highest social classes, even to members of the Senate. Under Domitian severe measures were taken against relatives of the emperor himself, as is recorded by Dio Cassius in his *Roman History* (47, 14) and Suetonius in his *Lives of the Emperors* (*Domitian*, 15, 1).

Though, with the institution of the priesthood, diaconate, and episcopate, the Christian community of Rome was becoming organized into a hierarchical structure. Separate and distinct places of worship and burial did not yet exist. The liturgy still took place in private homes, the so-called *domus ecclesiae* (house churches), as mentioned by St. Paul (Romans, 16, 5).

Christians were buried in pagan necropolises, as with the tombs of St. Peter, on the Vatican hill, and St. Paul, on the Via Ostiense. Despite the general tendency in second-century art and architecture to size and grandeur, Sts. Peter and Paul were not buried in large elaborate tombs but in a smallish *tropaion*, according to Gaius the priest, as recorded by Eusebius in his *Ecclesiastical History* (2, 25, 6–7).

Despite these burials, and despite the early establishment and organization of the Christian church in Rome, nothing whatsoever survives from the first two centuries after Christ to suggest any artistic or building activity. Nor do any historical sources suggest such activity. It would be a long time before Christian artistic and architectural commissions emerged; they had been deterred by persecution and by political, religious, and social obstacles. Romans had always been cautious about new religions from the East, especially when they were monotheistic. For all these reasons, as well as the traditional Jewish ban on images, the first Christian artistic manifestations in Rome are both cautious and neutral, and reveal a distinct use of symbolism.

The Earliest Christian Art

Scholars used to assume that this use of symbolism was a useful expedient to allow Christians to live undetected within Roman society and to avoid recurring accusations that Christians were to be found not only among pagans but also, and above all, among Jews. It was believed that Christians therefore invented a symbolic language that only they could decode. A short passage in Minucius Felix's *Octavius* was interpreted in this way: listing the accusations of unspeakable behavior that were leveled against Christians, Minucius records that they both communicated with, and recognized each other by means of signs (*Octavius*, 9, 2). However, the passage can in fact be interpreted in a number of ways, in effect it merely describes mysterious, incomprehensible behavior.

All the same, over and beyond these signs of a secret Christian language, such symbols should be recognized as the first, primitive, artistic expression of the Roman Christians. It was in the second half of the second century, almost contemporaneously with Minucius Felix's *Octavius*, that the first terse Christian artistic manifestations appear, as a rule in a funerary context.

Inscriptions and Signs

The earliest known example is a group of inscriptions on the closure of burial niches in the *piazzuola* of the catacombs of St. Sebastian.

View into a hypogeum, a subterranean burial chamber, from the complex of St. Sebastian on the Via Appia.

Epitaph of Atimetus from the catacombs of St Sebastian on the Via Appia. The style of the inscription is virtually the same as those of contemporary pagan inscriptions. Only the two flanking symbols of the anchor and the fish indicate that the deceased was a member of a Christian congregation.

Second-century wall paintings from a house below the church of San Sebastiano on the Via Appia. The formal principles of this type of domestic decoration were taken up in the murals of underground burial sites in the third century.

The language of these early Christian inscriptions is exactly that of contemporary pagan epitaphs, but in addition there are seemingly neutral symbols, such as anchors and fish, which have a clear Christian significance. Thus the burial niche of Atimetus, who died at the age of eight, was decorated with an anchor and a fish, as was the niche of Ancotia Auxeis, dedicated by his parents.

Even more significant in this sense is the tombstone of Licinia Amias, discovered on the hillside behind St. Peter's, where the standard phrase D[iis] M[anibus] is followed by a formula in Greek meaning "fish of the living" and an anchor with a fish each side. The tombstone, which appears to be probably early third-century, is a striking blend of pagan and Christian elements, such as the Greek acrostic ("Jesus Christ, son of God the Savior"), recalling a well-known passage in Tertullian's *Baptism*: "But we are born like little fish in water following our Lord Jesus Christ, and only by water can we be saved" ("Sed nos pisciculi secundum nostrum Iesum Christum in aqua nascimur necaliterquam in aqua permanendo salvi sumus," *Baptism*, 1, 3).

Christian Symbols

The fish is thus one of the neutral symbols used by the early Christians to accompany epitaphs. The fish, however, compared to the anchor and other early symbols, had a wealth of meanings, ranging from the esoteric to meanings derived from the New Testament—echoes of the miracle of the loaves and fishes, and eucharistic implications. Through these entwined meanings, the Christian baptismal significance already referred to is dominant.

The symbolic language of these early images seems to be supported by a well-known passage in Clement of Alexandria's *Tutor* (3, 11, 59–60) where anchors, fish, doves, and ships are recommended for use for seals on rings belonging to Christians. The images on the earliest Christian inscriptions seem to reflect this passage: that of Faustinianus, with a sheep, a dove on a branch, and an anchor; that of Urbica, on which the inscription, inside a round mirror, is flanked by a fish and a dove; and that of Valeria in the catacombs of Priscilla, where anchors and palms are added to the inscription, and painted in red on the bricks closing the burial niche.

In Rome, artistic expressions of Christianity suffered from this drastic limitation, which recalls the use among the Jews of symbolism in places of burial or worship as well as in objects for private use. However, pictorial expressions of Christianity were beginning to appear. Deriving from contemporary artistic models, these began to give expression to the new messages and the new religious ideas emerging with the growth of Christianity.

Catacomb Decoration

The years around AD 200 saw a distinct development in domestic wall fresco decoration. Inspired by the Pompeian style of decoration, which emulated architectural forms, and the "Fourth Style" of painting, a sophisticated geometrical art emerged. Thin lines, usually red or green, would be drawn on perfectly white walls to form frames in which scenes with figures would be placed. This pattern of continuous or broken lines is also found on catacomb walls as well as on the vaults in many *cubicula* (small rooms used as family vaults). Below, on the bases, was *opus sectile* (mosaic of colored marble cut in geometrical shapes) or frescos of palisades and charming flower gardens. Space was still conceived of as in Hellenistic domestic decoration, with three horizontal registers: base, figurative frieze, and vault.

In the *cubicula* of the catacombs, this subdivision was maintained as if creating the idea of an eternal home (*domus aeterna*). There are many points of contact between the late antique Roman house (*domus*), as excavated in Rome and Ostia, the mausoleums of pagan necropolises, and the *cubicula*. All-private houses, public buildings, Christian basilicas, pagan hypogea, and *cubicula* shared a common form of decoration, which might vary according to the form of the building and the particular wishes of the patron.

In the years around AD 200, a number of frescoed interiors allow us to understand the sensitive moment of transition between a pictorial language which was still infused with mythological, pastoral, sacred, and Dionysian elements, and a new language which, while continuing to employ imagery from astrology and the four seasons, was already introducing biblical scenes. These buildings are on the cusp between these two very different pictorial worlds, reflecting both the traditional syncretic, or neutral, pictorial language and the new ideas.

The Aurelii Hypogeum

Examples of such buildings are the so-called "small villa" in the complex of St. Sebastian and the buildings discovered under the basilica of St. John Lateran. The best record of this transitional period is the Aurelii family hypogeum, discovered at the beginning of the twentieth

The Aurelii Hypogeum in Viale Manzoni. Detail of a fresco from the first half of the third century, with a depiction of a shepherd shown as a scholar.

century in Viale Manzoni. The burial place, probably dating from the first half of the third century, comprises an area bounded by an enclosure, a semi-hypogeum *cubiculum*, and two underground rooms.

The three rooms are entirely decorated with fresco. The upper niche has images of philosophers with a background of townscapes, along with striking groups of figures which appear to depict the creation of Adam and the expulsion from the Garden of Eden. The two underground rooms are completely taken up by panelled walls with red and green lines. The iconography is in part still informed by Dionysian–cosmic topics, but is in part already sensitive to Christian themes. The floor of one of the rooms has a mosaic funerary inscription, recording three deceased persons and a dedication, all from the aristocratic Aurelii family. The only other marble inscription in the complex, discovered re-used in the floor, refers to another member of the Aurelii family.

The figures in the fresco frieze halfway up the wall seem to be the three members of the Aurelii family mentioned in the mosaic dedication. They comprise a striking "shepherd-scholar" tending his flock of sheep, a horseman making a triumphant entry to a city and giving a speech in the forum, and a woman at a banquet. The three also appear to be represented in the central scene of the vault of the other room.

These and other figurative scenes in the hypogeum have been interpreted variously—a heretical patron or agnostic sect—but the interpretation now gaining favor is that of a complex private religious syncretism, a mix of many of the religious and mystic strands then current. Among the most frequent images in the hypogeum are philosophers and shepherds, two images which were spreading through the Mediterranean world at just this time, reaching Rome in the years around AD 200.

The Aurelii Hypogeum in Viale Manzoni. Detail of the ceiling paintings in one of the rooms. The central clipeus shows three standing figures who are identified by the inscriptions as the three Aurelii who commissioned the structure.

Late third-century sarcophagus with scenes from the life of Jonah. On the bottom frieze the prophet is cast into the waters and swallowed by the *ketos*, the great whale. The next scenes show the monster vomiting Jonah up onto dry land, and the prophet resting in the shade of the giant gourd. They are separated by a miniature portrayal of Noah in the ark. In addition to the episodes of Jonah, the resurrection of Lazarus and St. Peter's miracle of the spring are shown in the upper register. Rome, Museo Pio Cristiano in Vaticano.

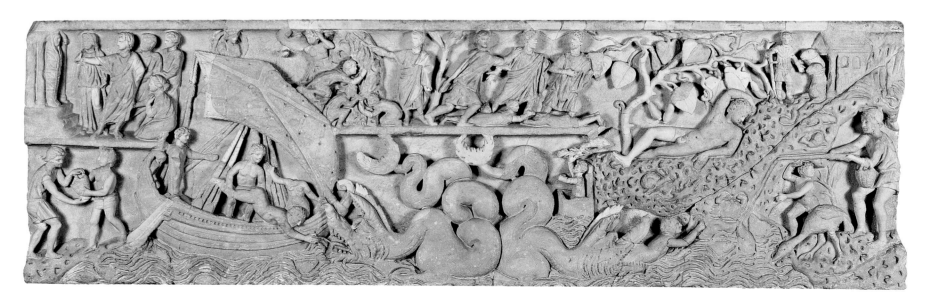

The Good Shepherd and the Philosopher

Philosophers and shepherds are also depicted, together with praying figures and fishermen, on a group of marble sarcophagi, probably of Roman manufacture, which have always been regarded as the precursors of Christian funerary sculpture. The earliest and most complete examples are considered to be those in La Gayolle and Basle. These include all four images and are suggestive of the air of symbolism typically found in this type of material. Though in the past the figures were identified as the deceased, it is now believed that they allude to moral virtues and to intense spiritual states. In the La Gayolle and Basle sarcophagi, it is easy to understand the significance of the different figures and the reasons why they are placed in pairs: the shepherd and the fisherman represent tranquillity and security in a distant place where earth and sea meet in absolute peace; the praying figure and the philosopher evoke wisdom and the transmission of knowledge.

Of the four figures, the praying figure and the Good Shepherd were the most popular. They embody the traditional ideas of piety (*pietas*) and good works but also had new significance, representing respectively the deceased reunited with God and the shepherd with the lost sheep, in other words, Christ the Savior. This shift, already evident in the sarcophagi of Via Salaria and Via della Lungara, finds its fullest expression in the Santa Maria Antiqua sarcophagus. The triad of praying figure, shepherd, and philosopher form the center of a frieze that by now includes biblical scenes, with a terse baptism of Christ and the story of Jonah resting under the pergola.

The Story of Jonah

The story of Jonah, the Hebrew prophet who was thrown overboard the ship in which he was fleeing from god, swallowed by a whale and then spat out onto dry land after three days, was popular in early Christianity because of the parallel with the resurrection of Christ. The figure of Jonah came to replace the symbolic figure of the fisherman since he prefigured Christ and his resurrection. The story, often depicted in the ancient Christian world, was divided into three or four scenes: Jonah cast into the sea, Jonah swallowed then regurgitated by the whale, and Jonah resting under the arbor and the withered gourd.

The story of Jonah reached Rome early and appeared simultaneously both in sculpture and painting. As far as sculpture is concerned, the so-called late third-century Sarcophagus of Jonah in the Vatican Museums is significant. The story of Jonah occupies the entire lower register and part of the upper, where it is accompanied by scenes of the raising of Lazarus and St. Peter's imprisonment in Rome.

The Catacombs of St. Callistus

Scenes from the story of Jonah soon appeared in funerary art, starting with the "gallery of the sacraments" in the catacombs of St. Callistus on Via Appia Antica. This part of the catacombs was the heart of the great complex of St. Callistus, the official burial place of the bishops of Rome, organized by Pope Zephyrinus (AD 199–217) and entrusted to the supervision of Callistus when he was still a deacon. This part consisted of an almost rectangular area of land within which were excavated two parallel staircases serving two galleries. Over time a number of passages branched off, creating a grid pattern. The catacombs were deepened several times, and in the first half of the third century a number of *cubicula* were dug, including the "crypt of the popes," where many

Rear wall of the sacramental chamber in the catacombs of St. Callistus. The third-century murals show a supper scene framed by two praying figures.

third-century popes were buried, and the "gallery of the sacraments."

These *cubicula*, with flat ceilings and large burial niches in the walls, were frescoed with the usual red and green lines against a white background. Small scenes with figures were set in the resulting frames. The abbreviated scenes, which have only a few figures and are difficult to interpret, are halfway up the wall, as if suspended in the frames reserved for them, creating an illusionistic effect and underlining their symbolic purpose.

images that hover between realism and allegory. These are the banquet scenes and the images of the grave-diggers who constructed the catacombs, responsible for excavating the galleries. The images of the grave-diggers have several levels of meaning. As well as simple representation, suggesting a group which was rising fast both economically and in the Christian community, there is a complex and symbolic transposition of the ancient idea of the *genius loci* (guardians): the grave-diggers, rep-

Detail of the "crypt of Lucina" in the catacombs of St. Callistus, with the eucharistic symbols of fish and bread.

Between about AD 320 and 350, the whole range of biblical scenes can be found in these *cubicula*, beginning, as has been said, with the popular Jonah story and continuing with the equally popular figure of the Good Shepherd (in the center of the ceiling) and the philosopher, praying figure, and—now rare—fisherman. The fisherman was to disappear altogether a few years later, his place being taken by Jonah. The "gallery of the sacraments" is decorated with scenes from the Old and the New Testaments: the sacrifice of Isaac, Moses striking water from the rock, the baptism of Christ, the Samaritan woman at the well, the raising of Lazarus, and the healing of the paralyzed man.

These elaborate and eclectic decorative programs included the ancient Dionysian and seasonal artistic subject-matter, but also original

resented on the entrance walls of the *cubicula*, take on the role of *vigilantes*, guardians of the burial place.

The banquet scenes consist of small groups of companions arranged around a C-shaped table laden with baskets of bread. Before them are three-legged tables with plates of fish. The scenes have two layers of meaning. On the one hand, they recall *refrigeria*, the funeral feasts organized on the anniversary of a person's death (the *dies natalis*). On the other, they allude to the heavenly banquet and thus to a blessed state of paradise.

As well as these fundamental and significant readings, there can be a eucharistic implication, as in the "crypts of Lucina" from the early third century, where two large fish support two baskets of bread and two beakers of red wine. The "crypts of Lucina" are another important element in the catacombs of St. Callistus. Here too, with great illusionistic effect, is the red-green painted framework. Here too, biblical episodes are associated with the standard images of the Good Shepherd and the praying figure, as well as with Hellenistic elements: the ubiquitous story of Jonah, Daniel in the lions' den, and a lively and original baptism of Christ, where Christ is helped by St. John the Baptist to step out of the waters of the Jordan as the dove of the Holy Spirit hovers above his head.

The Catacombs of Praetextatus

Scenes from the life of Christ were also the inspiration for the decoration of the *cubiculum* of the "coronation" in the aristocratic catacombs of Praetextatus on Via Appia Pignatelli, in the heart of *Triopion*, the estate brought as a dowry to Herodes Atticus by his wife, Annia Regilla, and after her death absorbed into imperial property. The catacombs of Praetextatus, precisely because of their pagan antecedents as an aristocratic burial ground, including the tomb of the emperor Balbinus (AD 238), continued to fulfil a prestigious role among the Via Appia catacombs. The *cubicula* opened on to the *spelunca magna* (great cave), a majestic gallery carved out of a disused cistern. Here were the burial places of the martyr saints Janvier, Felicissimus, and Agapitus, whose tombs were inscribed with epigrams in honor of them by Pope Damasus (AD 366–84).

The *cubiculum* of the "coronation" is linked to the more important of the two staircases leading down from the large cemetery above ground. Its subject-matter and decoration is typical of the first half of the third century, with the customary red-green frames. Themes of the seasons and earth and sky are kept for the background, while scenes from the New Testament have pride of place. Only a few New Testament images survive intact, but it is possible to recognize the raising of Lazarus, the healing of the woman with an issue of blood, the meeting with the Samaritan woman at the well, and Christ with the crown of thorns.

This last image is most unusual. Christian art had systematically avoided violent and negative images and had given pride of place to those of redemption. The scene of the crowning with thorns should perhaps be regarded as an exception, perhaps made on the insistence of a demanding client, diverging from church guidelines.

The Catacombs of Priscilla

Also unusual is a fresco from the years AD 320 or 330, in the central *arenario* (probably originally a disused quarry) of the catacombs of

Mural from the first half of the third century in the so-called burial chamber of the "coronation"—the crowning with thorns—in the catacombs of Praetextatus. Detail with the scene of the Samaritan woman at the well.

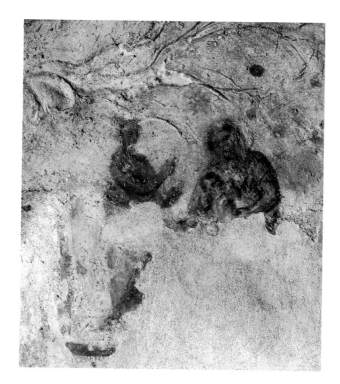

Fresco from the catacombs of Priscilla depicting the Virgin in dialogue with a prophet.

Catacombs of Priscilla. Central picture of the ceiling painting from the chamber of the Annunciation, with a scene of the biblical event reduced to a minimum of narrative elements.

Priscilla on the Via Salaria. On an irregular wall, a burial niche was first decorated with two shepherds in stucco, then with an unusual image in fresco, the earliest representation of the Virgin and Child. The Virgin stands in front of a prophet, perhaps Balaam or Isaiah, who points to a star to signify the messianic prophecy.

This charming fresco, executed in a careful impressionistic technique—only the soft light of the oil lamps could reveal its full quality—is effectively a political and religious declaration of Christian orthodoxy in the face of heretical and schismatic movements which questioned the divine nature of Christ and the teaching of the Bible. The simple scene shows how it was possible to express even complex theological ideas in simple language, with just three figures.

A few decades later, and with the same intention, the scene of the Annunciation was depicted at the catacombs of Priscilla in a *cubiculum*, along with scenes of the raising of Lazarus and Jonah, against a cheerful background of flowers. A complex theological issue is now conveyed with just two figures: the Annunciation succeeds in alluding to the mystery of the Incarnation. The Virgin, seated on a throne, directly faces the angel Gabriel who, with his right hand raised, makes his grave announcement.

Still in the catacombs of Priscilla, images from the second half of the third century include the *cubiculum* of the "veiling," on the edge of the *arenario*, dating from AD 260–70. The decoration again draws on Old Testament stories, with Jonah, Abraham, and the three Jews in the fiery furnace in Babylon, all standard examples of salvation which were held to prefigure the salvation of the faithful at the end of time. On the vault a particularly harmonious image of the Good Shepherd stands at the center of a symbolic cosmos, with peacocks (signifying the sky) and quails (signifying earth).

The lunette contains one of the most striking representations of the Christian earthly and spiritual journey. The woman buried in the *cubiculum* of the "veiling" is represented in three separate scenes: in marriage, standing with her husband before the elderly priest administering the sacrament; holding her baby; and received into paradise, where she makes a significant sweeping gesture with her raised arms, either to express a song of praise to the Lord or to indicate her blessed state.

These images are noteworthy, since they are a depiction of everyday life, seldom found in the catacombs. Catacomb art concerned itself with the redemptive themes of resurrection, baptism, and, more rarely, the eucharist. Significant events in a woman's earthly life alternate with her after-life, giving rise to that hazy

View of the rear wall of the chamber of the "veiling" in the catacombs of Priscilla. The fresco, from around AD 260–70, shows episodes from the life of a woman. The wedding scene on the left is balanced by motherhood on the right. The scene in the middle shows a large-scale figure of the woman praying.

Mural from the burial chamber of the coopers in the catacombs of Priscilla. The depiction on the rear wall shows a scene connected with this trade.

boundary between real and symbolic which we have already seen in the images of grave-diggers and banquets.

A further intriguing aspect is the intense expression of the deceased woman. Her gaze is suspended, inspired, almost hypnotic. This is in accordance with the contemporary conventions of late antique portraiture, more concerned with psychological tension than with verisimilitude. It is telling to see how early Christian visual and spiritual language was influenced by the secular pictorial and stylistic tradition.

This trend is also apparent in the late fourth century in the so-called *cubiculum* of the coopers, also in the catacombs of Priscilla, and in the so-called *cubiculum* of the bakers in the catacombs of Domitilla (also known as the catacombs of Sts. Nereus and Achilleus), as well as in tombstones carved with images of blacksmiths, fishmongers, and horse drovers.

The Greek Chapel

The cemetery of Priscilla also contains the best example of third-century art, the Greek Chapel. Recent restoration has revealed its complexity, from both a technical and a stylistic point of view. The area, re-using a nymphaeum, is a double *cubiculum*.

The inner room has a triple apse with a long bench, used perhaps for funeral feasts, around the walls. The decoration has a base frescoed to resemble marble and stucco. Superbly executed stucco acanthus scroll decoration is repeated in the underside of the vaults. The first room has a light background with an extensive biblical cycle, including the story of Susanna and the Elders, in which Susanna was falsely accused by two elders of the community but finally, with the help of Daniel, was exonerated. On the

View into the Greek Chapel in the catacombs of Priscilla. This chamber was named after the Greek inscriptions found here and is decorated with frescos, imitation marble incrustations and plaster profiles. The scene painted on the arch dividing the room shows the Adoration of the Magi; their Phrygian caps mark them out as coming from the Orient.

entrance wall are the three Jews in the fiery furnace in Babylon, on the arch dividing the room the Adoration of the Magi. A phoenix surrounded by flames is prominent on the right-hand wall. The phoenix, a pagan image which was used by Christians to signify the resurrection of the body (as the phoenix was reborn from the flames), recurs on the vault, where there is also a bust representing summer, which is part of the cycle of the four seasons that, suggesting rebirth and renewal, alludes to the Resurrection.

In the inner room, against a background of Pompeian red, are scenes of Abraham, Noah, Daniel, and Lazarus. The most significant and effective scene, and that with the greatest emotional impact, is a banquet in the center of the front arch. An evocative scene, strongly suggestive of symbolism, it suggests a heavenly, perhaps even eucharistic, context rather than a funeral feast.

The artistic techniques used suggest the involvement of skilled craftsmen, expert fresco painters, who had evolved a specialized technique for hypogea where the high humidity made it impossible to carry out conventional fresco, but instead suggested the use of *fresco secco*, that is, fresco which is executed on dry plaster. Stylistically, compact solid volumes alternate with the more familiar "twilight painting," in a balance between impressionism and expressionism.

The Museo Nazionale Romano Panels

From the same time is an important work, the polychrome marble panels in the Museo Nazionale Romano. Decorated in low relief, with traces of gold, yellow, green, and brown color, these must have belonged to the cover of a tomb rather than a sarcophagus. The style and subject-matter, with an expressionist disharmony and an anatomical disjunction, suggest a date about AD 300.

The decoration is in two registers, with New Testament scenes which take their inspiration from the central scene of the Sermon on the Mount, in which Christ, dressed as a Cynical philosopher, raises his right hand in a rhetorical gesture. The scene is flanked by scenes of miracles: the blind man, the paralyzed man, the woman with a flux of blood, the miracle of the loaves and fishes, and the raising of the son of the widow of Nain. The choice of scenes is revealing: all reflect the miraculous healing power of Christ. For this reason, Christ is given the hieratic face of Jupiter-Aesculapius. The

sequence of scenes is not haphazard, as had previously been the norm.

The Catacombs of Sts. Peter and Marcellinus

Such a preoccupation finds its fullest and most mature manifestation in the art of the age of Constantine, particularly catacomb painting, and above all in the catacombs of Sts. Peter and Marcellinus which saw new impetus in the creation of burial areas with the construction above the cemetery of the great circular mausoleum by the family of Constantine.

The *cubiculum* of the "two banquets," so-called because of the images in the two *arcosolia* (niches topped with an arch), is typical. While the walls have geometrical and plant decoration as well as full-length portraits of a deceased man and woman, the vault has a complex cycle of New and Old Testament scenes around the ubiquitous Good Shepherd, placed in a careful order. They include baptism, Job, Moses striking water from the rock, the raising of Lazarus, Daniel in the lions' den, the healing

The catacombs of Sts. Peter and Marcellinus. Ceiling painting from the burial chamber of the "two banquets". A series of both Old and New Testament scenes is arranged around the clipeus in the centre which depicts the Good Shepherd.

of the paralyzed man, Noah and the Ark, and the miracle of the loaves and fishes.

Sarcophagi

Such a biblical sequence, with key scenes suggesting salvation in order to evoke salvation for the deceased, who is usually represented at the center of the scenes, recurs in the many sarcophagi with a continuous frieze produced under Constantine, such as the Sabine sarcophagus in the Vatican Museums. Around the figure of the deceased, who is represented as praying and must therefore already be in paradise, are scenes from the Bible: the miracle of the spring produced by St. Peter on his arrest, the marriage at Cana, the healing of the blind man, the miracle of the loaves and fishes, and the raising of Lazarus, scenes which recall the simple prayers of the time when the salvation of the individual believer was compared to—and almost identified with—the miracles recounted in the Bible. This convergence of pictorial, patristic, and liturgical elements reveals how for early Christians the Bible was at the center of religion and spirituality.

In the mid-fourth century, the production of sarcophagi saw its artistic peak, with the number of scenes increasing. There was still a continuous frieze, but it was now organized in two registers, as in the sarcophagus of the "two brothers." In the center are portraits of two men of very similar appearance, perhaps brothers. On the two registers, in high, almost detached relief, is a harmonious sequence of biblical scenes: the raising of Lazarus, the denial of Peter, Moses and the Ten Commandments, the sacrifice of Abraham, Pontius Pilate washing his hands, St. Peter with the miracle of the spring and his arrest, Daniel in the lions' den, the denial of St. Peter, the miracle of the blind man, and the miracle of the loaves and fishes.

The frequency with which St. Peter appears is explained by the popularity of his cult in Rome, marked by the construction of the great basilica of St. Peter's on the Vatican hill, as well as the basilica dedicated at this time to the "memory of the Apostles" (*memoria apostolorum*), later dedicated to St. Sebastian, at the third milestone of the Via Appia at the catacombs of St. Sebastian.

Three scenes from St. Peter's life—his denial of Christ, his arrest, and the miracle of the spring—decorate the lower register of the so-called "dogmatic" sarcophagus in the Vatican Museums, along with the Adoration of the Magi, the healing of the blind man, and Daniel in the lions' den. On the upper register are the raising of Lazarus, the miracle of the loaves and fishes, and the marriage at Cana, as well as the

The sarcophagus of the "two brothers" from the middle of the fourth century. The casket gets its name from the portrait busts of two very similar figures depicted in a conch between two registers with scenes from the Old and New Testaments. The style of this sarcophagus is very close to work of the same era from Constantinople. Rome, Museo Pio Cristiano in Vaticano.

FOLLOWING PAGES:
The sarcophagus of Junius Bassus. This monumental work, made for the Municipal Prefect of Rome, who died in 359, was found in the sixteenth century beneath old St. Peter's near the Apostle's grave. The upper register shows, from left to right: Abraham's sacrifice, the arrest of St. Peter, Christ enthroned over Caelus (the personification of Heaven) between Sts. Peter and Paul, and Christ before Pilate. The bottom register shows, from left to right: Job covered in boils, the Fall, Christ's procession into Jerusalem, Daniel in the lions' den, and the martyrdom of the Apostle Paul. Rome, Museo del Tesoro di San Pietro.

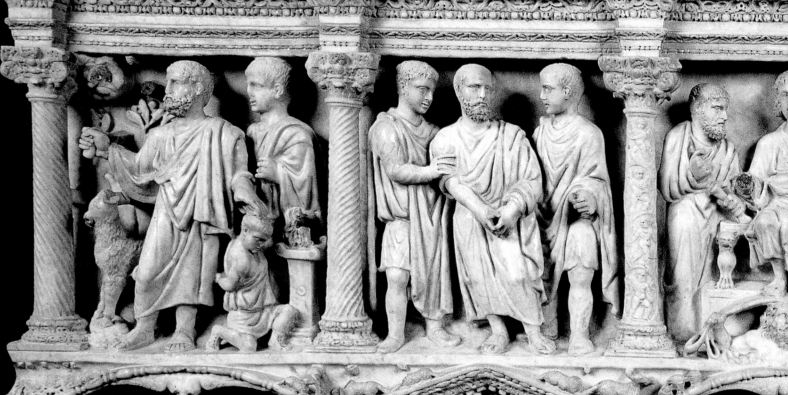

IVNBASSVSVCQVIVIXITANNISXLIIMEN·II·INIPSAPRAEFECTVRAVRBINEOFI·

well-known scene of Creation with the three figures of the Trinity who have identical faces, thus stressing the doctrine of the Trinity, then the subject of fierce theological controversy.

However, the best-known sarcophagus, which can be dated with certainty to AD 359, is that of the prefect Junius Bassus, found near the Vatican and now in the treasury of St. Peter's. The splendid front, with two horizontal rows of columns, as if imitating the women's galleries in basilicas, is in high relief. It is smooth and treated in the classical manner, in a style that demonstrates all the signs of an astonishing artistic renaissance.

Narrative scenes are framed between the regularly spaced columns. In the center are a solemn and ceremonial Christ in majesty (*maies-*

tas Domini) and Christ's triumphal entry into Jerusalem. Elsewhere are the sacrifice of Isaac, the arrest of Christ, the arrest of Peter, Pilate washing his hands, Job, Adam and Eve, Daniel in the lions' den, and the beheading of St. Paul.

Three scenes—the Christ in majesty, Christ enthroned handing over the law (*traditio legis*), and Christ giving the keys to St. Peter (*traditio clavium*)—of great symbolic and Christ-centered significance, were usually reserved for the decoration of churches. It is clear that these scenes were first used on sarcophagi before being used for the most prestigious parts of basilicas. The emergence of the scenes reflects the politico–religious upheavals of the first half of the fourth century or even before. With the adoption of Christianity by Constantine, the Christian community had achieved a degree of tranquillity and security within the Roman state, but it began to suffer internal problems and to be undermined by theological controversies, especially about the nature of Christ, with the spread of Arianism.

Christ and the Apostles

This is the background to the emergence of the image of the apostolic college, the twelve Apostles seated around Christ, which translated into pictorial form represents the strength and unity of the church of Rome, faced with attempts to destabilize it. From the time of Constantine the image is found in all artistic forms—from painting to funerary sculpture, from *objets d'art* to mosaic. It expresses a second, political, fundamental tension. After Constantine's adoption of Christianity as an official religion of the empire, there was conflict over the responsibilities of pope and emperor. It is significant that at the first council of the Church, in Arles in AD 314, it was Constantine who presided, not Pope Silvester, who made his protest felt by not attending.

The continuing and unresolved conflict between state and Church, which was to erupt in the Middle Ages, encouraged the development of the image of Christ with the Apostles. It expressed a constant anti-imperial stance, particularly as the iconography was drawn from official images of the emperor surrounded by his dignitaries. A comparison of the images of Christ with the Apostles from the age of Constantine and the reliefs on the Arch of Constantine, where the emperor appears with his retinue, is revealing. In a play of reflections, the apostolic college is a celestial image of earthly authority and unity. Representations of Christ with the Apostles in apses of churches—and thus in line with the *subsellia* (episcopal

Detail of the mosaic from the left apse of Santa Costanza, the former mausoleum of Constantia, the daughter of the emperor Constantine. This work from the middle of the fourth century is the earliest surviving monumental example of the tradition of depicting the *traditio legis*, the transmission of divine law from Christ to St. Peter. This motif was prominent in Roman apse ornamentation up to the ninth century.

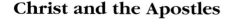

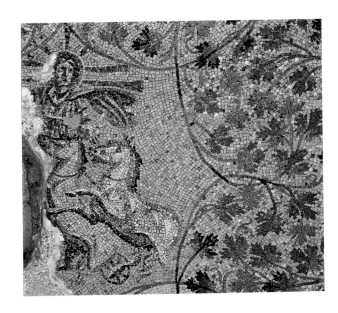

Detail of the mid-third-century ceiling mosaic of the mausoleum of the Julii, with Christ as the sun-god, Helios. The appropriation of the pagan motif of the chariot-driving god, which was also used to portray the apotheosis of kings, was intended to symbolize the triumph of the resurrected Savior over death. Rome, Vatican Necropolis.

seat) reserved for the bishop surrounded by priests and deacons—created a further reflection, suggesting parallels between earthly and heavenly hierarchies.

Sometimes only Christ and Sts. Peter and Paul, the most important Apostles, were represented, rather than all twelve. Between these three figures, a highly hierarchical relationship was established, influenced by the ceremony of the imperial court. They include the stately gesture of the *traditio legis*, whereby Christ as *imperator* (emperor) sits in splendor on a throne or stands majestically on the mount of paradise and entrusts the law, in the form of a scroll, to St. Peter in the presence of a reverent and attentive St. Paul.

The image was intended to express symbolically the continuity of the Church and the authority of the bishop of Rome, assuring the primacy of the Roman Church which, just as it was becoming established, was being challenged. The solemn ceremonial scene of the *traditio legis* appears to have been thought suitable for the most important funerary monuments, such as the sarcophagus with columns from St. Sebastian, dating from the first half of the fourth century, and the carved slab from a cemetery on Via Salaria, now in Anagni.

Detail of the mosaic from the right apse of Santa Costanza. The *traditio clavium*—Christ handing over the keys of heaven to St. Peter—was conceived as the counterpart to the *traditio legis*, the transmission of divine law. St. Peter is shown receiving the key from Christ enthroned with covered hands, a sign of his reverence.

OPPOSITE:
View of the apse of the chamber of the
millers in the catacombs of Domitilla.
As well as scenes illustrating the
activities of the deceased, the most
prominent position in the apse was
taken up by individual depictions with
theological themes.

The Mausoleum of Constantia

However, the finest example of the scene is in
one of the two semi-circular side niches of the
Mausoleum of Constantia, part of the Sant'Agnese
complex on the Via Nomentana. The mausoleum is closely linked to the basilica built by
Constantia, Constantine's daughter, while she
was living in Rome between AD 338 and 350.
The basilica, which has a large atrium and
aisles, is about 325 feet long and 132 feet wide.
It was linked to the mausoleum by an apsidal
porch. The mausoleum, built by Constantia for
herself and for her sister Helena around AD 350,
has extensive mosaic decoration, both on the
barrel vaulting and in the semi-circular niches
each side.

Mosaic had always been popular in Greek
and Roman art and was even more widely used
in late antiquity, especially for Christian buildings, perhaps because of the implication of the
"eternal light" (*lux aeterna*) of the hereafter and
the illumination acquired through baptism.
Mosaic is occasionally found in the catacombs,
while the celebrated mausoleum of the Giuli
family from the Vatican necropolis, one of the
earliest Christian burials there, is almost entirely covered with mosaic made of glass tesserae.
The most striking part of the mausoleum is the
splendid image of Christ–Helios on the ceiling,
represented as the "unconquerable sun" (*sol
invictus*) on an astonishing chariot of light. A

mid-third century date is likely from the themes
on the walls, which include the traditional
Good Shepherd, fisherman, and Jonah.

In contrast, at the Mausoleum of Constantia
the polychrome mosaic has been partly lost,
especially in the dome. To judge by sixteenth-
and seventeenth-century drawings, the scenes
were popular biblical stories. In the vaulting, in
contrast, large sections of mosaic survive, with
geometric designs, vines, still-lifes, imitations of
unswept floors, and agitated Dionysian scenes,
with *erotes* (Venus' baby companions) picking
and treading grapes. These motifs are also to be
found, with a symbolic intent, on the porphyry
sarcophagus from inside the mausoleum, now
in the Museo Pio-Clementino in the Vatican
Museums.

The two semi-circular side niches also have
mosaic decoration, now however damaged
from past restorations. In the small niche on the
right is the *traditio legis*, with Christ giving St.
Peter a scroll on which can be read *Dominus
pacem dat* ("The Lord gives us peace"), a
variant on the usual phrase, *Dominus legem
dat* ("The Lord gives us the law"). The image,
with a rejoicing St. Paul at the side, has a
background of paradise, with palm trees and
buildings which stand for the Churches of the
Gentiles and of the Jews. Sheep (representing
the Apostles) walk away from the buildings.
While Christ descends a staircase of clouds
from the mystical mountain out of which
flow the four rivers of paradise, the other
niche has Christ handing the keys to St. Peter.
Christ is seated in state on the earthly globe,
again in a paradisical setting of clouds and
palm trees.

These scenes, which have no biblical source,
suggest the influence of imperial ceremony.
This appears also to have been the case with
the decoration of the apses in the principal
basilicas, starting with St. Peter's. Although the
decoration of the apse of St. Peter's has not survived, if the argument that the cover of the
ivory reliquary casket of Samagher reproduces
its iconography is accepted, it must have
included the scene of the *traditio legis*. The
apparently late fifth-century casket of Samagher,
discovered outside Pula and now in the
archaeological museum in Venice, appears to
have depictions of faithful reconstructions of
the most important early Christian sites of Rome
and Jerusalem. On the cover is a harmonious
scene of the *traditio* which may have been
inspired by the decoration on the apse at
St. Peter's.

Mural from the hypogeum of Trebius
Justus depicting the construction of his
country villa. The entire decorative
program of this tomb seems to have
been created solely for Trebius Justus,
an entrepreneur of the fourth century.

Emergence and diversification

The Hypogeum of Trebius Justus and the *Cubiculum* of the Millers

In the second half of the fourth century, Christian iconography diversified, with the emergence of new narrative, cyclical, and Christocentric forms. The trend was reinforced by the diffusion of illustrated manuscripts of the Bible. This new taste for cycles is apparent in funerary art, as is shown by some private hypogea, starting with the hypogeum of Trebius Justus on Via Latina, from the time of Constantine. The large burial chamber, within a Christian catacomb, as indicated by inscriptions and drawings in the galleries, is entirely decorated with frescos which recall with a wealth of detail the twenty-year-old Trebius Justus, nicknamed *Asellus*.

Trebius was a *parvenu* of the new fourth-century Roman bourgeoisie. His qualities are praised in the images on the walls: supervising building a country villa and working on his family's agrarian property. On the end wall are a scene of Trebius' parents showing him the family treasures, arranged carefully on a table-cloth, and a portrait of the young man with writing instruments and scrolls, as if to emphasise a level of education higher than in reality. The decoration has no Christian content and is imbued with representations of real objects, but the vault has a generic spiritual air: a

View of part of the anonymous catacomb on the Via Latina (Via Dino Compagni). The rich decorative and architectural furnishings of this complex indicate patrons with considerable financial influence. Both Christian and pagan themes are represented in the decorative program, but all the representations are of an extremely high artistic standard.

central roundel contains a Good Shepherd surrounded by flowers and birds, an allusion to a blessed afterlife.

Another cycle representing everyday life can be found in the large *cubiculum* of the "millers" in the catacombs of Domitilla, again dating from the latter part of Constantine's rule. Here the decoration is much more complex. Alongside representations of the various stages of milling— buying grain, milling, and selling flour—are traditional Christian images such as the scenes of Jonah in the four lunettes of the *arcosolia*. Other scenes are inspired by the new Christocentric ideas: the two large semi-circular niches contain the Apostles, with Sts. Peter and Paul seated in the foreground each side of Christ, and a symbolic scene of the Good Shepherd and personifications of the four seasons.

The Via Dino Compagni Hypogeum

Moving from public catacombs to private hypogea, and in particular to the small Via Dino Compagni hypogeum discovered in 1955 near the second milestone of Via Latina, the iconography becomes more complex, with subtle expressions of the religious beliefs of the deceased. Disentangling these is difficult. The Via Dino Compagni hypogeum has particularly daring "negative architecture": *cubicula* with columns carved out of tufa. Corbels and stucco enrich the structures and makes them heavier, while fresco covers all the available space. This suggests the patronage of a wealthy and aristocratic family, perhaps from senatorial circles, some time between the middle and end of the fourth century.

The family responsible seems to have had in mind a set of scenes so eclectic in its inspiration and so complex in its iconography as to suggest a freedom of thought within a particular cultural milieu. The iconography is rich and varied, but has a common thread of Hellenistic themes, with animal and plant life with vaguely cosmic, seasonal, or Dionysian overtones. The bases emulate marble or garden scenes with fountains, palms, and trellises—idyllic pastoral images. Within this unusual context are scenes with figures, comprising about a hundred different subjects. The subjects come variously from different religious, mystic, or simply allegorical sources.

The biblical scenes, with many from the Old Testament, include a number which are rare or unknown elsewhere in Christian funerary art, such as the story of Finees killing Zamri and Cozbi, Samson turning jackals into the fields of

the Philistines and killing the Philistines with the jawbone of an ass, Balaam and the angel, the drunkenness of Noah, the supper of Isaac, the blessing of Ephraim and Manasse, Absalom hanging by his hair, Job and his wife, the Flood, the ascension of Elijah, Tobias and the fish, Lot fleeing from Sodom, and the sacrifice of Isaac. There are even short cycles, again from the Old Testament, of Moses for example (rescued as an infant from the Nile, passing through the Red Sea, and striking water from the rock), Joseph (meeting his brothers, dreaming, and Jacob's arrival in Egypt with his sons), the vision of Mambre, the vision of Bethel, the expulsion from the Garden of Eden, the sacrifice of Cain and Abel, Jonah, the three men in the fiery furnace in Babylon, Susanna and the Elders, Daniel in the lions' den, and the prophet pointing to the star.

Scenes from the New Testament are rarer. The raising of Lazarus from the dead appears in two virtually identical images. There is also Christ and the Samaritan woman at the well, the miracle of the loaves and fishes, and the Roman soldiers gambling over Christ's clothes.

Of particular interest is the cycle of the Virgin, which extends over the vault of the *cubiculum* at the entrance to the hypogeum. Recent restoration has revealed that the three surviving images on the vault represent the Adoration of the Magi, the Annunciation, and the bitter waters (derived from the apocrypha, in particular, the gospel of Pseudo-James).

In the same *cubiculum* on the large arch at the end is a majestic group of the twelve Apostles, following the format used in the second half of the fourth century for apses and for sarcophagus fronts. The iconography, as has been pointed out, is derived from images of the emperor and served to underline the majesty of Christ, represented as teacher, emperor, and judge. These meanings are also clear in two more images of Christ. In one he is an isolated figure seated on a throne, between chests (*cistae*) of scrolls, in an eloquent attitude of philosophical teaching. In the other, a dignified bearded Christ, seated between Sts. Peter and Paul in a pose suggestive of hierarchical *maiestas*, makes a sweeping rhetorical gesture with his arms. This latter scene is in a hexagonal space with a theme of philosophy: on the walls are full-length figures of philosophers, and on the vault dignified busts alternate with chests (*cistae*) and books (*volumina*).

The high point of the program is the pendant of this *maiestas Domini* in the niche opposite, the large mysterious scene traditionally known as the lesson of medicine, surgery, or anatomy. At the center of the scene is the severe figure of a philosopher, dressed as a Cynic, with his pallium thrown over his bare back. On each side of him sit other philosophers clad in tunic and pallium, one of whom points with a rod to a naked young man who seems to have a hole in his belly.

When the hypogeum was discovered, this scene was interpreted as a scene of medicine, but it must rather be associated with the general philosophical theme and should accordingly be interpreted as a philosophy lesson in which the protagonist has the features and physiognomy of Aristotle or Socrates discussing man and his soul. The positioning of the philosophy lesson and the Christ in majesty opposite each other suggests a deliberate parallel, in which the philosophy of the past is presented as an alternative—or precursor—of the true philosophy of Christ, the teacher, between Sts. Peter and Paul. The context is the politico–religious world of the late fourth century, when the pagan revival under Julian the Apostate (AD 361–63) seemed to express the mentality of the Senate, which did not surrender before Christianity but saw itself as an important and popular alternative.

Another *cubiculum* with a neutral, not fully Christian, theme is that which its finder called the "hypogeum of Cleopatra." The most important scene is that on the lunette of the *arcosolium* at the end: a half-clad woman lies leaning against a basket of fruit in a cornfield, with a snake in front of her. The woman has a halo and the background is a cave. The subject would seem to be Cleopatra killing herself but on closer examination, it is clearly a personification of earth (*Tellus*). On the walls and vault are conventional themes of earth and the heavens, including animals and birds and personifications of air, fire, winds, and the breeze, around a head of Medusa in the center. Medusa offers the beholder the snake ends of her hair, as if to soften the evil force of the figure.

As well as these neutral themes, another *cubiculum* has unequivocally pagan or, rather, mythological cycles of the Labors of Hercules and the myth of Admetus and Alcestis. These themes, of clear funerary significance and suggestive of sympathy with Orphic and mystery cults, strongly evoke the deep-seated pagan reaction in senatorial circles of the late fourth century.

The Proiecta Casket

The same spirit seems to inspire the decoration of objects of daily or ritual use from this period, ranging from the *lanx* (dish) of Parabiago to the silver amphora from Porto Baratti. The best example of this spirit is an example with Christian content and among the most significant late antique silverware, the Proiecta Casket. The

Detail from the wooden doors of the church of Santa Sabina on the Aventine. The crucifixion scene dates from the fifth century and is considered the earliest surviving example of this critical event in Christ's Passion.

casket, decorated in light relief with traces of gilding, was part of a valuable find of objects discovered on the Esquiline Hill and is now in the British Museum. Its subject-matter is entirely secular, with the portrait of a young female aristocrat, who is praised in an epigram by Pope Damasus, together with her husband. The inscription reads "Secundus and Proiecta, may you live in Christ" ("Secunde et Proiecta vivatis in Christe"). On the four sides of the lid are Venus in a seashell surrounded by sea creatures, a Nereid on a seahorse, and a procession approaching thermal baths. On the sides of the casket, servants bring objects to Proiecta for her bath.

"Passion" Sarcophagi

During this urgent revival of paganism in the late fourth century, Christian artistic language was shifting midway through the century. A new element in western culture was an interest in the next world. The resulting iconography is especially apparent in funerary sculpture, in particular in the so-called "passion" sarcophagi, with scenes inspired by the final events in the lives of Christ and Sts. Peter and Paul, arrest and judgment. The meaning of these scenes is suggested by what is effectively an emblem in the center of the front, a cross with a crown with the name of Christ on it and at its foot the two sleeping soldiers. The symbolic allusion to the Resurrection is clear, as is the triumphal significance that pervades the decoration.

The best example of an artistic expression of this new mentality is the columned sarcophagus in the Museo Pio-Clementino in the Vatican Museums, with the symbol of the Resurrection at its center, and on the sides, the arrest of Christ, Christ's crowning with thorns, the judgment of Pilate, and Simon the Cyrenean carrying the cross. The Museo Pio-Clementino has more examples of this type, such as the splendid sarcophagus *ad alberi*, with scenes of the arrest of

Sts. Peter and Paul, Job and his wife, and the sacrifice of Cain and Abel, as well as the "stars and crowns" sarcophagus, with a procession of saints, perhaps the Apostles, converging on the symbol of the Resurrection, under a star-studded sky.

Images of Martyrdom

Though suffering and triumph co-existed in this late fourth-century art, until now Christian art in Rome had never included violent scenes, even martyrdoms or Christ's passion. The first surviving image of the Crucifixion is the fifth-century wooden panel on the doors of the church of Santa Sabina.

However, there are rare and moving scenes of martyrdom. The earliest is the fourth-century carving on the column of a small tabernacle in the underground basilica of Santi Nereo e Achilleo in the catacombs of Domitilla. The martyrdom of Achilleus is represented, led to death by a Roman soldier, his hands bound behind his back.

Other scenes of arrest and martyrdom can be recognized in the small cycle in the *confessio* (crypt under the high altar) under the basilica of Santi Giovanni e Paolo on the Caelian Hill, dating from the early fifth century. The scenes, which are difficult to interpret, appear to allude

One of the earliest known martyrdom scenes depicted on a shaft of the former ciborium of the church of Santi Nereo e Achilleo. The fourth-century depiction shows St. Achilleus being led by a henchman towards his place of execution.

to the legends of the martyrdom of Sts. Crispin, Crispianus, and Benedicta, celebrated martyrs buried here.

Guardian Saints

More common are scenes in which martyrs enjoy the peace of paradise and intercede for Christians who have died, as in the well-known fresco in the *arcosolium* of Veneranda in the catacombs of Domitilla, where the dead woman is accompanied affectionately by St. Petronilla to paradise. The fresco, from the second half of the fourth century, is evidence of the intimate relationship which came to exist between the protectors and the protected. This had obvious implications for funerary sculpture, as Christians now wished to be buried near the sepulchres of the martyrs, creating thus a heavy concentration of tombs, conventionally called *retrosanctos* (behind the saints).

Representations of guardian saints began in Rome in the late fourth century, first in the minor arts, in particular in gilded glass, with Sts. Agnes, Laurence, Hippolytus, Peter, and Paul, and in the frescos in the catacombs. They increased in the early Middle Ages, when pilgrims from all over Europe began to visit the Roman catacombs.

A fresco in the catacombs of Sts. Peter and Marcellinus on Via Casilina is valuable evidence of this trend. The great panel decorating the ceiling of one of the *cubicula*, thought to date from the early fifth century, has a complex iconographical program which seems to revive the apsidal decoration of early Christian basilicas. The panel, with two horizontal registers, is dominated by a powerful bearded Christ seated on a throne, clad in a sumptuous purple tunic and with a halo, with the apocalyptic letters alpha and omega. To each side Sts. Peter and Paul acclaim Christ. On the lower register is a lively procession of saints who were venerated in this complex *ad duas lauros* (at the two laurels), including Sts. Peter, Marcellinus, Tiburtius, and Gorgonius. The saints, identified by captions in red, acclaim Christ and Sts. Peter and Paul in the upper register, but seem to be proceeding towards the focal point, a lamb on the mount of paradise from which four rivers flow. The whole scene is set in a delightful paradisical garden, suggested by festoons and garlands. Christ's pose also suggests the day of judgment: Christ appears as a severe judge surrounded by his intimates, by the celestial court of Sts. Peter and Paul and the martyr saints.

Arcosolium tomb of Veneranda in the catacombs of Domitilla. The fresco decoration of the grave from the second half of the fourth century shows the entry of the deceased into paradise accompanied by the martyr Petronilla; this scene shows the expectations bound up with an *ad sanctos* burial— that is, a burial close to the grave of a venerated martyr.

204

OPPOSITE:
Ceiling fresco from the catacombs of Sts. Peter and Marcellinus. The depiction from the early fifth century shows Christ enthroned between Sts. Peter and Paul who acclaim him. In the lower register the saints venerated in this catacomb are seen praising Christ. Between the saints can be seen the Lamb of God on the summit of paradise. The depiction shows clear analogies in its composition to officially produced art works.

Detail of the early fifth-century apse mosaic from Santa Pudenziana. This section shows the central figure, Christ seated on a gem-encrusted throne. The text of the open book indicates that Christ is the protector of the church.

205

Santa Pudenziana

This same mood can be found in the apse mosaic in the church of Santa Pudenziana, in the valley between the Esquiline and Viminale Hills. The church, built at the end of the fourth century on an old thermal hall, appears to be near the ancient *titulus* (meeting house) of Pudenziana, but it retains little of its early Christian form apart from the apse decoration,

sign of acclamation, are Sts. Peter and Paul. Gold crowns are being placed on their heads by two women, personifications of the Church of the Gentiles (*ecclesia ex gentibus*) and the Church of the Jews (*ecclesia ex circumcisione*).

As a background to this complex of figures, deriving from the conventional iconography of triumph and apotheosis, with its symbolic head in the figure of the Christ as king and teacher, is a portico in a semi-ellipsis. Behind it is the ideal city, the celestial Jerusalem, in which buildings

View of the entire mosaic of Santa Pudenziana, which was reduced from its original size by changes made at the end of the sixteenth century. Christ is shown in the centre of a college of Apostles with two allegorical female figures at either side. This monumental composition combines the familar theme of Christ teaching with elements of imperial art.

which has suffered damage and restoration which here drastically reduced its extent and subject-matter.

All the same, the basic scheme is still apparent. The focal point is a regal Christ, bearded and wearing a gold tunic and pallium, seated on a glittering throne studded with gems and draped with purple and blue. He has a large gold halo and raises his right hand in the solemn gesture of *adlocutio* (addressing listeners). In his left hand he holds an open book on which can be read "Lord God, protector of the church of Pudenziana" (*Dominus conservator ecclesiae Pudentianae*), stressing the antiquity and prestige of Santa Pudenziana compared to other churches in this part of Rome. A second inscription, now lost, recorded the names of the patrons, Ilicius, Maximus, and Leopardus, who lived during the papacy of Innocent I (AD 401–17).

Around Christ stand the twelve Apostles in a semi-circle, at a slightly lower level. Their animated mood is very different from the inert, fixed stance of early Apostle groups. Prominent each side of Christ, raising their right hands in a

from the Holy Land have been identified. The portico itself may allude to the Resurrection, while the buildings in the distance may refer to buildings on Golgotha and the Mount of Olives, and the church of the Nativity in Bethlehem.

In the middle of this partly realistic, partly idealized townscape, a hill rises on which stands a majestic gold cross, studded with gems. Around it, in a sky with purple clouds, are the symbols of the Evangelists (man, lion, ox, and eagle). Corresponding to the cross and Christ on the throne, before the disastrous restorations of the past, stood the mystic lamb on the mountain with, according to drawings, the dove of the Holy Spirit above.

From a solely iconographic point of view, the Santa Pudenziana mosaic reveals audacious and revolutionary artistic ideas, with a wealth of new or revived iconography. Above all, it represents the Revelation of St. John, translated and commented on by Ticonius for the Latin west between AD 380 and 400 and beginning to be accepted as part of official scripture. Like the Apocrypha, it had hovered for centuries on the

Mosaic inscription from the entry wall of the church of Santa Sabina, the only section of the original mosaic which still survives. The text, framed by two female figures, tells of the construction of the church from a donation by Peter the Illyrian during the pontificate of Celestine I (422–32).

edge of orthodoxy. Despite this novel iconography, from the stylistic and formal point of view, the Santa Pudenziana mosaic adheres to Roman tradition and shows no sign of the new manneristic and illusionistic tendencies which from the time of the eastern emperor Theodosius (AD 379–95) were becoming widespread in Rome and the west.

This adhesion to Roman classical artistic canons is especially clear in the figures, with their stereometric rendering of volume, particularly the solid figure of Christ and the dignified images of Sts. Peter and Paul, but also the solemn figures of the two female figures who symbolize the Churches of the Gentiles and of the Jews.

Equally, in the way space is organized and in the depiction of the celestial city and the original creation of a sky stormy with the apparition of Christ, there is no indulgence in illusionism, excessive symbolism, or airy or weak metaphor. Everything is solid, massive, consistent, and in proportion. Every single element and figure is essential to a composition which does not use perspective, but orders the size of figures in accordance with their importance and the relationship between them.

A move to the ethereal

Santa Sabina

A few years later, this balance between realism and symbolism seemed to collapse, to be replaced by a more metaphorical, ethereal language. The decoration of the church of Santa Sabina on the Aventine Hill reflects this trend. Santa Sabina was begun by Peter of Illyria, a priest from Dalmatia, during the papacy of Celestine I (AD 422–32) and was completed under Sixtus III (AD 432–40). The shift in figurative style entailed the abandonment of traditional classical forms used until now in senatorial circles, which made a strenuous effort to retain the stately language of the Roman aristocracy. The mosaics of the triumphal arch and the apse are largely lost, though as far as the apse is concerned, in the sixteenth century Taddeo Zuccari

preserved the original design in his fresco, which seems to record the most important elements of the early Christian mosaic. There was presumably an abbreviated Apostle group of only six figures in the conventional semi-circle around Christ, as if depicting the key moment of Christ giving authority to the Apostles.

The decoration of the triumphal arch also has to be reconstructed through drawings. The drawings, however, record not only the early Christian image but also the changes which were made in the early Middle Ages: in the early ninth century, work was carried out which may have affected the triumphal arch mosaic. However, in all probability the original design survives. The drawings suggest that under the triumphal arch was a series of busts (more than twelve and therefore not Apostles) around a bust of Christ. The busts were perhaps of saints and martyrs or, more likely, prophets and other biblical figures. The small procession of doves at the top of the arch must refer to the Apostles. Contemporary, or slightly later, parallels for the doves/Apostles can be found in western early Christian art, including the lost apse at Cimitile, described by Paulinus of Nola, and the mosaic in the baptistery in Albenga in Liguria.

If these images suggest artistic experiments carried out in a deeply Roman cultural milieu, the decoration of the inside of the entrance wall of Santa Sabina is in a more original language, one which was sensitive to new ideas from the East. The focus of the carefully executed mosaic is a long dedicatory inscription:

"When Celestine had reached the highest level of apostolic dignity, and was shining brightly throughout the world as the first among bishops, this splendid monument was created by Peter, a priest from Illyria in Rome, a man who was worthy of bearing this name since he grew up following Christ's teaching—rich for the poor but poor for himself. Fleeing the comforts of earthly life, he now merits those of the life hereafter."

On each side of the inscription are personifications of the Church of the Gentiles and the Church of the Jews in the form of two women, alluding to the Jewish and Gentile origins of

Detail of the inscription in Santa Sabina depicting the *ecclesia ex circumcisione*, the Jewish church. The allegorical female figure is identifiable through the subtitle and the codex, the Old Testament.

View of the mosaic on the triumphal arch in Santa Maria Maggiore, with episodes from Christ's youth. The pictorial narrative accords the Virgin Mary an important role, as befits the dedication of the church, and is arranged in several horizontal registers. In addition to being of a high artistic standard, the mosaic in this church is the best preserved late antique ensemble of pictorial narratives.

the Church. On the left is a synagogue with the scroll of the Old Testament, on the right a church with the New Testament. Originally, emphasizing the double nature of the church, there were also Sts. Peter and Paul, with Evangelist symbols.

The decoration and structure of Santa Sabina is homogenous, dating from the mid-fifth century. Thus in the nave a sumptuous *opus sectile* frieze survives over the imposing colonnade. The motif is taken from the classic model of a wall topped by a band of geometric elements. Parallel with the single columns is a banner, perhaps alluding to Christ's triumph.

The splendid cedarwood door, still in one of the main entrances, dates from the same time. It has a decorative cycle on each side, with geometric and plant motifs on the inside and biblical scenes on the outside. Four rows of oblong and square panels alternately show scenes from the Old and New Testament, probably inspired by decorated scrolls and manuscripts of the Bible. They concentrate on the stories of Moses, Elijah, and Christ.

The climax of the narrative is, as has been said, the Crucifixion. Christ is in the center between the two thieves, larger than them and in an unusual dramatic posture, with his hands held out (*expansis manibus*). Along with the purely narrative scenes are less familiar episodes from the book of Exodus, such as the fall of manna from heaven and the capture of quails,

as well as traditional New Testament scenes, such as scenes of healing, the miracle of the loaves and fishes, and the marriage at Cana. There is a sense of experimentation with entirely new and original designs, which suggests eastern influence. This is especially true of the celebrated Christocentric panel which has on the same axis Christ in Judgment, between the symbols of the Evangelists, and a female figure, possibly the Virgin, but most probably a personification of the Church, between Sts. Peter and Paul, who hold up a symbol of triumphant martyrdom.

Santa Maria Maggiore

A convergence of old and new images pervades almost all fifth-century art and architecture. It achieves its fullest expression in the complex decorative program of the basilica of Santa Maria Maggiore on the Esquiline Hill, as conceived by Sixtus III, who probably commissioned the church.

Despite repeated alterations and restorations between the Middle Ages and Ferdinando Fuga's alterations in the mid-eighteenth century, Santa Maria Maggiore has maintained its early Christian plan, with three aisles defined by two rows of twenty columns. The columns, bases of varying heights and Ionic capitals, are linked by a marble architrave. Above is a long cycle of mosaic panels, the length of the church, mostly in two rows, with scenes from the Old Testament. On the left-hand wall are stories from Genesis, on the right, stories from Exodus, Numbers, and Joshua. The scenes have a wealth of detail which reveals an affinity with the cyclical tendency which in these years was inspiring the decoration not only of major decorated manuscripts but also of complex cycles—in mosaic or fresco—in early Christian basilicas. The classic example, unfortunately lost, was the procession of Pope Leo the Great at San Paolo fuori le Mura.

We know little of the original decorative program of the apse in Santa Maria Maggiore, though the Virgin as Queen of Heaven was in all probability its theme, following the doctrine sanctioned by the Council of Ephesus in AD 431. However, the majestic triumphal arch mosaic does survive, strongly influenced by the cult of the Queen of Heaven. Here everything moves from the zenith, with a symbolic clipeus accommodating the empty throne. Below is an inscription recording Sixtus' dedication, "Bishop Sixtus made this for God's people," towards which Sts. Peter and Paul raise their arms in acclamation.

Themes from the apocryphal gospels, in particular the gospels of Pseudo-James and Matthew, are represented here in three registers, closed off below by representations of the cities of Jerusalem and Bethlehem. Even scenes which by now had a fixed iconography are marked by the influence of these new sources. Thus the classic scene of the Annunciation is embellished by the legend that at the moment of the Annunciation the Virgin was spinning purple cloth for the Temple, while in the Adoration of the Magi the infant Christ is sumptuously dressed and placed on a rich bench.

In substance, all the themes in the registers of the arch—the Presentation in the Temple, the Flight to Egypt, the dramatic slaughter of the innocents, and the apocryphal welcoming of the Holy Family by Afrodisius at Sotinen in Egypt—while emphasizing the redeeming role of the Virgin, suggested in the scenes in the nave, never lose from sight the central focus on Christ.

From the purely formal point of view, the stylistic language of the mosaic artists in Sistus' workyard at Santa Maria Maggiore is eclectic, composed of a notoriously composite figurative language. Though the lively small scenes of the nave, full of color and shadow, pools of light, and superimposed levels, are influenced by the impressionistic tradition found in catacombs from the mid-third century as well as in domestic decoration in Rome or Ostia, where neutral white backgrounds contained agitated small figures in an atmosphere that was pure illusion, the

Detail of the mosaic in the left spandrel of the triumphal arch in Santa Maria Maggiore. In the upper register, the Adoration of the Magi is shown. Individual pictorial elements such as the Christ child seated on the throne, as well as the ranks of angels arranged behind, are evidence of appropriations from imperial ceremonies. The register below shows the Massacre of the Innocents. The very bottom register depicts the town of Bethlehem.

images of the triumphal arch are of quite different registers, setting, allusions, and color range.

Everything is horizontal, as if to retrieve the rhythm of the spiral column. Everything is projected into the foreground, to such an extent that the background disappears, apart from a few buildings crucial to the understanding of the story. The figures dominate. Occupying all the vertical space, they invade much of the register with the volume of their bodies, appearing as powerful statues, with serious and controlled gestures. In short, the decoration of the triumphal arch seems to have much in common with sculptural relief.

Apse Mosaics

A mosaic survives of the head of St. Peter, now in the Vatican Grottos but recognized as coming from the decoration of the triumphal arch of San Paolo, as restored by Leo I. The imposing decoration, with large evenly arranged figures, seems to have influenced apse decoration in two lost fifth-century churches.

In the dome of the church of Sant'Agata dei Goti, decorated between AD 462 and 470 on a commission from the Gothic military leader Ricimer, Christ was seated solemnly on a globe. In his left hand he held a book and with his right made a sweeping rhetorical gesture (*adlocutio*). On each side, Sts. Peter and Paul headed the Apostles, silhouetted against a golden heaven.

The decoration, also lost, of the apse of San Andrea in Catabarbara dated from the papacy of Simplicius (AD 468–83). To judge by drawings, it again represented the Apostles, in an abbreviated form, with six Apostles beside Christ on the mystical mountain and the four rivers of paradise. Christ held a scroll in his left hand and raised his right arm in a rhetorical gesture.

Santi Cosma e Damiano

All these images are precursors of a mosaic which is the climax of early Christian art but also the starting-point of Byzantine art, the apse of the church of Santi Cosma e Damiano, commissioned by Felix IV (AD 526–30). The decoration is still sensitive to Roman tradition, even if pictures and objects appear to be in a suspended atmosphere, almost in a dream. An imposing figure of Christ, clad in a golden tunic and pallium, holds a scroll in his left hand and makes a rhetorical gesture with his right. He appears to hover on blue and pink clouds. Wearing a crown and raising his hand, he surveys the scene of paradise, as indicated by the two palm trees that close off the scene at the sides, and the river Jordan below.

On each side, Sts. Cosmas and Damian, with crowns of martyrdom in their veiled hands, are presented to Christ by Sts. Peter and Paul. The procession ends with Felix IV, who holds a model of the basilica, and St. Theodore. Below is a procession of twelve lambs, representing the Apostles, leaving the cities of Jerusalem and Bethlehem and proceeding towards the mystic lamb, which stands on the mountain of paradise.

In this clear expression of Christ in majesty, with its origins in traditional religious and secular high ritual and ceremony, can be seen the new stress on judgment and the next world. Images of the imperial *adventus* (formal arrival) were adopted for images of Christ, creating a new language. Roman artistic canons survive in the figures, their interrelationship, and their gestures, but the first signs of a new rhythm can be seen, with more chilly representations, less coherent in the figurative interrelations and closer to the Byzantine artistic forms which had already reached Rome and would influence pictorial language for centuries.

Fabrizio Bisconti

Mosaic in the apse of Santi Cosma e Damiano. Rooted in local Roman tradition, this monumental depiction represents an expansion on the popular scene of the *traditio legis* by adding the image of Sts. Peter and Paul presenting the patron saints of the church to Christ.

Medieval Architecture

The Sixth Century

The great building campaigns begun by Constantine and continued by the bishops of Rome in the fourth and fifth centuries continued in the following centuries, though not without interruptions. By now the city of Rome had a strongly Christian appearance, not only in the outer districts—given importance by the great basilicas of St. Peter's at the Vatican and San Paolo fuori le Mura on the Via Ostiense, but also within the city walls. A lavish building program had been carried out by Sixtus III (432–40). Sixtus had created one of the most significant Christian centers of the city, the magnificent basilica of Santa Maria Maggiore on the Esquiline Hill.

The sixth century was marked by tragic events and barbarian invasions. Belisarius, Justinian's general, conquered Rome in 536, annexing it to the eastern Roman empire. After a lengthy siege by the Ostrogoths led by Vitigis in 537, Rome was reconquered by Narses in 552. In 560 the Lombards invaded Italy. Nevertheless, the city preserved its antique appearance at the same time as undergoing a Christian transformation, by now in full swing.

While many classical buildings remained intact, Christian buildings were becoming more evident. Regarded as the best way of carrying out the task of evangelization, as early as the beginning of the sixth century there were already no fewer than twenty-five churches. Pope Symmachus (498–514), forced by his rivals to abandon the Lateran Palace to take refuge in the Vatican, initiated a long building program. He transformed the older of the two rotundas remaining near St. Peter's into an oratory dedicated to St. Andrew, placing a baldacchino of pure silver in it. Around the baptismal font, dating from the time of Damasus (366–84), he consecrated three oratories bearing the same dedications as those that Hilarus (461–68) had built near the baptistery of the Lateran—the Cross, St. John the Evangelist, and St. John the Baptist. Symmachus embellished St. Peter's with marble and decorated both the

Detail from a mosaic in the apse of Santi Cosma e Damiano depicting Felix IV (526–30) presenting a model of the church to Christ. Despite several sections having been altered in the seventeenth century, this work remains the oldest known example of a mosaic depiction of a donor pope.

fountain (*cantharus*) and the quadriporticus with marble and mosaic. He also improved the steps leading up to the basilica and those below the *platea*, or *campus*. To the right and left of these lower steps, perhaps at the top, he had two *episcopia* built, reception buildings for the use of bishops visiting St. Peter's.

Within the walls, on the Oppian Hill, Symmachus initiated the construction of a basilica dedicated to St. Martin of Tours, next to the church of San Silvestro, originally the *titulus*, or meeting house, of a Christian called Equitius—or possibly in place of it, since a number of medieval texts refer to the new church as *ecclesia Sancti Silvestri et Martini* (the church of Sts. Silvester and Martin).

With the advent of Felix IV (526–30), the Christianization of the city began to extend as far as the Imperial Fora with the conversion on the Via Sacra near the round temple "of Romulus" of an *aula* (hall), or part of an *aula*, originally used as a census and land registry archive. There is a reference to the transformation of this secular *aula* into an *aula Dei* (hall of God) in the mosaic in the apse of the church of Santi Cosma e Damiano, the first representation of a donor pope, holding a model of the basilica. Unfortunately the decoration is not easily seen today on account of the raising of the church floor in the seventeenth century under Urban VIII.

A few decades later another Roman building, nearby at the foot of the Palatine, was converted into a church dedicated to the Virgin. The site was of particular importance as it included the so-called Temple of Divus Augustus and the temples of Castor, Minerva, and Vesta. The church, Santa Maria Antiqua, stands on what was probably the site of the monumental vestibule near the imperial palace, used to house the guards on duty in the palace. A coin from the time of Justin III (565–78) discovered under a column in the nave provides a possible date for construction.

The church consists of two main elements, the atrium and the church proper. In front is a courtyard with a portico. Off this on the left is a rectangular hall, converted into the oratory of the Forty Martyrs of Sebastea.

The atrium, originally covered by a masonry vault, has walls with alternating semi-circular and rectangular niches. The church is subdivided into two clearly defined areas, the nave and the sanctuary. The aisles seem to originate from a columned quadriporticus, with passages on all four sides, so that the side corresponding to the entrance takes on the appearance and function of a narthex while the side opposite in front of the presbytery forms the crossing. There is archaeological evidence that brick piers once

St. Cosma being presented to Christ by St. Peter. Part of the decoration of the apse of Santi Cosma e Damiano illustrating the impressive figurative style of the sixth century.

occupied the positions of the columns. The central nave once had a schola cantorum parallel with the colonnades, of which masonry traces survive. The presbytery, rectangular in shape with an enclosed semi-circular apse, is flanked by two chapels. The models for the building as a whole are found above all in the east, between Greece and Syria.

When responsibility for the care of the poor and sick passed from the civil authorities to the church, Santa Maria Antiqua quickly became a diaconate. As such, it benefited from attention from the popes, evidence of which can be found in the wealth of painted decoration that from the end of the sixth century to the ninth century covered its walls, the layers often superimposed one on another, making the church an archive of early medieval painting in Rome. Frequent donations to Santa Maria Antiqua are recorded in the *Liber Pontificalis*.

During the iconoclastic period, the church became identified with the cult of a number of eastern saints, encouraged perhaps by the several popes of Greek origin in this period. Monks fleeing from Constantinople sought refuge in Rome, with the result that Santa Maria Antiqua became from the devotional, artistic, and cultural point of view a significant meeting point between east and west, a miniature Byzantium in the heart of Rome.

Not far from the Capitoline Hill, possibly on the site of an earlier fourth-century church, Pelagius I (556–61) embarked on the construction of the basilica of Santi Apostoli, dedicated to Sts. Philip and James. It was completed and consecrated by Pelagius' successor, John III (561–74). A verse inscription on the lintel of the main door (removed at the end of the fifteenth century) records the work of the two popes. The original construction, in which Narses played a part, must have been influenced by Byzantine architecture such as that in a slightly earlier building, the first church dedicated to Santi Quirico e Giulitta near the Forum of Nerva, built between 537 and 545. Here we see a triconch presbytery and polygonal apse,

Interior of the Pantheon, a temple built at the time of Hadrian and converted to a church dedicated to the Virgin and all the martyrs at the instigation of Boniface IV (608–15). In spite of various changes made over the centuries, this view conveys an impression of the effect of space in the great buildings of ancient Rome. In addition to its function as a Christian church, the Pantheon was also used as a tomb. As well as the grave of Raphael, the building contains the final resting places of the first two Italian kings and the first Italian queen.

following a model from Constantinople which was widespread in the eastern empire, found also in the three-sided apse of the basilica of San Giovanni a Porta Latina, dating from the same period or a few decades earlier.

Thus the official face of Rome was taking on an ever more Christian appearance. The building of the churches of Santi Cosma e Damiano and Santa Maria Antiqua was the signal for significant change in the appearance of public buildings. An important stimulus to this process was the establishment of the diaconates as centers for charitable assistance for the poor. The Roman market inspector's office

(*Statio Annonae*) became the church of Santa Maria in Cosmedin, the grain warehouse (*Horrea Agrippiana*) San Teodoro, the *Portica Minucii* San Giorgio in Velabro, the Curia Sant'Adriano, the *Secretarium Senatus* Santa Martina, the *Saepta Julia* Santa Maria in Via Lata, and so on.

Perhaps the most noteworthy event, an event which was to put the final seal on the christianization of Rome, was the conversion of the Pantheon into a church dedicated to the Virgin and all the martyrs by Boniface IV (608–15). The temple, which became known as Santa Maria Rotonda, retained its original splendor, with bronze doors, an imposing colonnade in the vestibule, wooden roof beams that were covered with gilded bronze, and the original marble decoration.

Equally significant was the new dedication to the Archangel Michael of the Castel Sant'Angelo by Boniface, after he had built a chapel there commemorating the appearance of the archangel on the top of the mausoleum during the papacy of his predecessor, Gregory the Great (590–604).

Gregory the Great to Leo II

The period of Gregory the Great, which coincided with the conversion to Christianity of the Lombards, especially Queen Theodolinda, was a period of splendor and great prestige for the papacy. The people of Rome became accustomed to the idea that the pope was their ruler, though they continued officially to be subjects of the eastern Roman empire.

Architecturally this was a period of transition. With the exception of the commissioning of a monastery on the Caelian Hill by Gregory the Great, where rooms and chapels were constructed out of the classical remains, the majority of building projects in the sixth and seventh centuries seem to have involved the outlying burial areas near the Vatican and on the Via Tiburtina and Via Nomentana.

It was thanks to Gregory the Great that the basilica of St. Peter's received the attention it deserved. A new arrangement of the apse was created, involving the raising of the floor by five feet above the Constantinian floor level. This meant that only a third of the height of the marble shrine containing the tomb of St. Peter, parallelepiped in form, rose above the new floor level. This upper part was used as an altar for the celebration of mass. Beneath the raised presbytery, around the curved apse, a crypt was created, with a straight central passage that led directly to the back of St. Peter's tomb. A *fenestrella* was placed in the front part of the raised area, while the spiral columns of the original baldacchino were aligned in front of the confessio to create a kind of iconostasis.

This was copied in the basilica of San Pancrazio in about 630, then in the alterations made to San Crisogono by Gregory III (731–41). By the ninth century this typology was widespread not only in other Roman churches but in numerous other churches in Italy and north of the Alps.

On the site of the tomb of the martyr saint Lawrence, Pelagius II (579–90) built one of the most beautiful basilicas of the period, San Lorenzo fuori le Mura. The presbytery of the original building still survives. The influence of the Byzantine occupation of Rome is apparent in the restrained style of the basilica, arranged on two levels, with a narthex and matroneum (women's gallery), where fine classical materials (columns, capitals, and architraves) have been reused. Of exquisite workmanship, the Corinthian capitals were in some cases adapted for their new function by adding carved crosses. The capitals of the matroneum are surmounted by cushion-shaped impost blocks supporting the arcades. The apse had a small central window and two broad windows on each side that lit the area behind (*retro sanctos*), described by archaeologists as the "subterranean area," access to which was gained from the end of both side aisles.

Here a rectangular chapel was created in which wall paintings from different periods have been discovered, perhaps dating from the period between John VII (705–7) and Gregory III. Later the easternmost part of the subterranean area was given a particularly solid apse, used as a crypt or choir, reached directly from the original church apse, first by steps built into the apse itself and later through a passageway cut through it.

Today the original basilica commissioned by Pelagius forms the presbytery of the existing thirteenth-century church. The floor level is considerably higher than that of the original church and the orientation has been inverted. Although the old apse does not survive, the mosaic of the vault above it does. On what is now the chancel arch, it includes Pelagius as donor, holding a model of the church and presented to Christ by St. Lawrence.

Pelagius' church seems to have been the model for the church of Sant'Agnese on Via Nomentana, built over the tomb of St. Agnes by Honorius I (625–28) a few decades later, on the site of a burial chapel. Besides a narthex and galleries that face the three sides of the central nave, there are other Byzantine architectural elements such as impost blocks above the capitals of the lower colonnade, and a matroneum. The mosaic with St. Agnes dressed

View of the interior of San Lorenzo fuori le Mura, built during the reign of Honorius III (1217–24). Parts of a previous building by Pelagius II (579–90), erected close to the grave of the martyred St. Lawrence, were integrated into the church, including the presbytery pictured here. St. Lawrence was the subject of special veneration, and this basilica numbered among the *Sette Chiese* (Seven Churches), the most important of Rome's sacred Christian sites.

Sixth-century mosaic from the triumphal arch of San Lorenzo fuori le Mura, depicting Christ enthroned on a sphere between the Apostles Peter and Paul. The central group is approached from the right by Sts. Stephen and Hippolytus and from the left by St. Lawrence and the patron, Pelagius.

as an empress, Honorius holding a model of the church, and a second pope (possibly Symmachus) also reveals Byzantine elements, not only in the stylized and frontal depiction of the figures, with their clearly marked linear outlines, but also in the plain gold background.

Apart from these two Byzantine-influenced martyr churches, the following period produced no particularly notable buildings. John IV (640–42) constructed the chapel of San Veneziano off the Lateran baptistery, making use of an existing building. Theodore I (642–49) had the relics of Sts. Primus and Felician moved from the cemetery on Via Nomentana to the church of Santo Stefano Rotondo on the Caelian Hill, where a chapel was built to house them. The mosaic in the apse shows the two saints in military dress standing on each side of a large cross in the center of the composition.

Leo II (682–83), a highly cultivated man, was fully occupied in the struggle to defend Roman orthodoxy. Among the few artistic projects with which he was involved was the construction of the church of San Giorgio in Velabro, though the building seen today dates from the ninth century.

The Early Carolingian Renaissance

The end of the seventh century and the first half of the eighth were characterized not so much by the appearance of new buildings as by the

Antique Corinthian capital, re-used in the nave of Sant'Agnese fuori le Mura.

restoration of ancient ones, both within and outside the city walls. From 726, the papacy was to pass through a difficult period on account of the continuing disagreements with the eastern church over the cult of images. Politically there was also reason for alarm, especially after the Lombard advance into the Roman countryside by the troops of Gisulph.

The building programs undertaken were modest in scale, an example being the enlargement and ornamentation of the Lateran, where Zacharias (741–52) erected an entrance tower and portico with columns in front of the papal residence. At St. Peter's, Zacharias' successor, Stephen II (752–57), erected a bell tower, probably of wood, which was covered with gold and silver, the first recorded campanile in Rome. Stephen also oversaw the transformation of Honorius' mausoleum next to St. Peter's into the chapel of St. Petronilla. In this same period, perhaps in 755, the church of Sant'Angelo in Pescheria was built.

In the last thirty years of the eighth century, with the papacy of Hadrian I (772–95) and the changing political climate, new building began. The alliance of the papacy with the Franks encouraged a renaissance of the Roman empire based on the supremacy of the pope as the heir to St. Peter and on the protection of Charlemagne, seen as the heir of Constantine. Never had there been such a frenzy of building. This was made possibly by Hadrian's recruitment of a large workforce drawn not only from the city but also from distant parts of the Campagna. As far as the restoration of the great basilicas went, the supply of materials necessary for repairs to the roofs was guaranteed by Charlemagne himself.

With the aim of restoring the physical aspect of the city, Hadrian made it his concern to repair the Aurelian walls and towers as well as the aqueducts that supplied the city and mills with water. Hadrian built embankments on the Tiber near the Vatican to protect the many pilgrims who came to worship at the tomb of St. Peter against flooding.

During Hadrian's papacy, major work was carried out on the diaconal church of Santa Maria in Cosmedin, enlarging and improving it with the addition of three apses and a sham matroneum, suggested by the existing galleries. A crypt with an oratory was excavated below the presbytery, with a nave divided by columns supporting architraves, a unique arrangement. The relics of martyrs were brought to the crypt from the catacombs and placed in wall niches resembling ancient *colombaria*.

Hadrian took a particular interest in the diaconiates, the number of which was increased to meet the needs of the poor of the city. It was

View of the nave of Santa Maria in Cosmedin, with its well-preserved and unique liturgical ensemble, consisting of the *schola cantorum* (twelfth century) and, behind it, the altar ciborium with its Gothic canopy from the thirteenth century.

The church of Santa Prassede, remodelled during the time of Paschal I (817–24). Its opulent inlay work is an outstanding example of papal patronage in the Carolingian era.

decreed that every day a hundred or more poor people should be given food, distributed beneath the portico of the Lateran. Food supplies were to be guaranteed by produce from church farms (*domus cultae*) in the countryside outside Rome, which were being expanded at this time.

The Later Carolingian Renaissance

The popes in the first half of the ninth century pursued a similar political and religious policy, continuing to stress the importance of renewing the physical fabric of the city, restoring its places of worship to their former glory, and reviving the cult of its martyrs within the city walls.

Leo III (795–816), who officiated at Charlemagne's coronation, was keen to improve the papal residence at the Lateran, erecting two triclinia, or ceremonial rooms, decorated with painting and mosaic, the first with three apses and the second with eleven, in imitation of similar eastern buildings. The intention was clearly to emulate the magnificence of the palace of the Byzantine emperors in Constantinople. Access to the second triclinium, later known as the *aula concilii*, was either directly from the neighboring Constantinian basilica by a staircase, or from the main entrance to the palace, along a long connecting corridor (*macrona*) with an open gallery (*solarium*) that led to the second floor of the palace.

In 1589 this palace complex was almost completely demolished on the orders of Sixtus V to make space for the present palazzo designed by Domenico Fontana. Only a few sections of the original construction remain, including the main apse of the first triclinium with its mosaic. The mosaic was restored in the eighteenth century, however, and can be seen today, detached from its original context, in a niche behind the Scala Santa.

As well as the work carried out at the Lateran, Leo III rebuilt the church of Sant'Anastasia on the slopes of the Palatine and made changes to the church of Santi Nereo ed Achilleo, possibly giving it two towers flanking the apse, following a design of Syrian–Palestinian origin not found elsewhere in Rome. He also embellished Santi Nereo ed Achilleo with mosaic, of which those in the apsidal arch remain, showing the Transfiguration. Leo paid attention to the papal residence at the Vatican, where he built a triconch triclinium similar to that at the Lateran, as well as encouraging the development of the Borgo district there in general.

Not content merely to restore and decorate churches in the city, Leo also sought to embellish them with precious gifts—gold and silver liturgical vessels, vestments and hangings, silver lamps, and other liturgical furnishings. The long list of gifts made in 807 is an invaluable historical record.

Rome's revival in the Carolingian period finds its most mature expression in the patronage of Paschal I (817–24). Paschal's name is connected above all with the reconstruction and mosaic embellishment of Santa Prassede, Santa Maria in Domnica, and Santa Cecilia in Trastevere.

Founded on the Esquiline near Via Merulana towards the end of the fifth century, Santa Prassede (the *titulus Praxedis*) was in a sorry condition despite restoration by Hadrian a few years earlier. Paschal decided to rebuild it entirely nearby, in order to deposit there the remains of a large number of martyrs from the now ruined catacombs. The martyrs' names are recorded on a long list in Santa Prassede. Still well preserved, the church is a small-scale copy of the Constantinian basilica of St. Peter's, with which it has many similarities. The differences seem less significant if viewed in the light of the contemporary approach to construction, which, in the reproduction of models, placed greater emphasis on the search for the ideal element or the general idea than on the formal aspect. The quadriporticus at the entrance, the annular crypt, and the trabeated colonnades that extend at right angles to separate the aisles from the transepts are all direct borrowings from St. Peter's.

Opening off the right-hand aisle of the church is the chapel of St. Zeno, where the pope's mother, Theodora, was to have been buried. Square in plan, with a groin vault on corner columns, the oratory reproduces the typology of the late antique mausoleums outside the city walls. It is clad in rich mosaic decoration shimmering with light and color.

As at Santa Prassede, so too in the other churches restored by Paschal we see a trend towards a shortening of the overall length, while the nave becomes wider. There is less light since the windows are concentrated in the upper walls of the nave.

Santa Maria in Domnica (also known as Santa Maria alla Navicella) is near Santo Stefano Rotondo. Despite later restorations, particularly in the sixteenth century, the nucleus of the church is still well preserved—the three apses of the facade, the aisle walls, and those of the central nave, supported by eighteen reused classical granite columns with beautiful Corinthian capitals, each different in form and similarly, for the most part, of antique origin. The semi-circular apse is marked at the corners by two porphyry columns that give the appearance of supporting the apsidal arch.

Santa Cecilia in Trastevere was built on the same site as an earlier basilica, first a house

Mosaic clipeus of Christ supported by four caryatid angels in the vault of the chapel of St. Zeno in Santa Prassede. Paschal had originally intended the chapel to be a tomb for his mother.

church (*domus ecclesia*) then a *titulus*. It housed the relics of St. Cecilia, brought here from her tomb in the catacombs of Praetextatus. A striking characteristic of this basilica, besides the architectural structure and mosaic, was its precious marble furnishings, including plutei, screens, candelabras, and ambos. According to the *Liber Pontificalis*, the area around the choir was particularly magnificent, with its cladding of precious marble, ciborium of black and white columns—incorporated by Arnolfo di Cambio in the present baldacchino—supporting semi-circular arcades covered with sheets of silver, and iconostasis surmounted with silver statues.

Santa Cecilia today, with its nave and aisles, and one particularly wide nave, differs from its original appearance, because the colonnades have been concealed within massive square piers. The annular crypt—more of a *martyrium*, on account of the presence of a large number of saints' bodies in six precious marble sarcophagi—contains a silver statue of St. Cecilia weighing nearly seventy pounds placed there by Paschal I.

Paschal also built a monastery near the church (as at Santa Prassede), a community of monks being the only way to provide the

Santa Cecilia in Trastevere is a church complex which was remodeled by Paschal at the beginning of the ninth century; the campanile and the right wing, with its convent and cloister, were added in the twelfth and thirteenth centuries.

Tower above the entrance to the cloister and church of Santi Quattro Coronati, erected at the end of the ninth century using building materials taken from antique sites. This complex, dedicated to the martyrdom of four Roman soldiers, was built on an ancient connecting road between the Colosseum and the Lateran.

day-to-day services required for a reliquary church. The portico, the campanile, and part of the monastery are additions from the time of Paschal II (1099–1118).

Similarly from the first half of the ninth century is the building work carried out by Gregory IV (827–44) at San Marco near modern Piazza Venezia, rebuilt from the foundations up with an inversion of the orientation of the original church, and at the diaconate church of San Giorgio in Velabro, where the apse and spacious hall were completely reconstructed. The somewhat irregular plan of San Giorgio, with its converging colonnades, was determined by the existing church. The portico (recently damaged but subsequently rebuilt) was added at the early thirteenth century along with the campanile.

By the middle of the ninth century, the favorable political situation which had emerged from a balance of power between the pope and the emperor had begun to deteriorate. If it was the intention of Charlemagne's heirs to extend their influence over church affairs and over the city of Rome, papal policy was increasingly to pursue its own path. In this climate of tension and political uncertainty, which in 846 saw the destruction of the basilicas of San Paolo fuori le Mura and St. Peter's, and in 887 was to lead to the collapse of the Carolingian empire itself, the last substantial building project took place during the papacy of Leo IV (847–55). This was the church of San Martino ai Monti, originally known as *Equizio* after Equitius, a Roman

Christian who had set up an oratory in a *titulus* on this site.

The church, which has changed little over the course of time, is one of the best examples of the later Carolingian Renaissance. The use of trabeated colonnades and the probable existence of an annular crypt, as well perhaps of an atrium, recall the alterations made by Leo to the Quattro Coronati, where a massive tower opening over the atrium strategically dominates the road leading from the Colosseum to the Lateran (the Via Maior). One of the two chapels that were added to either side, of a type structurally similar to the chapel of St. Zeno at Santa Prassede, survives in a remarkably good state of preservation, with the beautifully carved corbels of the vault, of reused Roman materials, still *in situ*.

Nearly contemporary are Santo Stefano Maggiore (now Santo Stefano degli Abissini) near St. Peter's, also with trabeated colonnades and an annular crypt, and Santa Maria Nova (now Santa Francesca Romana), built not far from the Basilica of Maxentius or Constantine, on the high ground to the east of the Forum, in the place of Santa Maria Antiqua, abandoned after the earthquake of 847.

The *Civitas Leonina*

Leo IV's major building project is generally considered to be the fortification of the Vatican area. After the devastation wrought by the Saracens in St. Peter's, profoundly shocking to the Christian world, it was decided to fortify the area around St. Peter's tomb. Leo III had already made this decision, but little had been done because of the theft of the materials set aside for the job. Leo IV, who had already undertaken the repair of the Aurelian walls, gates, and towers, organized the work in such a way that within four years he saw it complete. On June 27, 852 the ceremony of consecration of the walls was performed, in the presence of the pope and clergy, who, barefoot and with heads smeared with ashes, processed round the entire circuit of the fortifications, sprinkling them with holy water and at every gate calling on divine protection against the enemy that threatened the inhabitants.

The enclosed area was to take on the status of a city in its own right, which was both separate and distinct from the *Urbe* of Rome, despite its proximity to it. The new *civitas*, dubbed *leonina* after the pope, came to be seen as an exceptional event, so much so that it can be considered the most significant urban event of the early Middle Ages.

The walls, surviving only in places, followed a largely horseshoe shape. It may have been the allocation of the work or, more likely, the use of the foundations begun by Leo III that determined the sinuous profile of the north side, not otherwise explicable in terms of the topography. Starting from the Castel Sant'Angelo, the wall ran along the section known as the Passetto di Borgo, extending westwards to embrace St. Peter's, then possibly climbing to the top of the hill and joining the Tiber on the south, passing eastwards across the present Porta Cavalleggieri and Santo Spirito (now separate).

Interrupted only at the four points of access into the *civitas*, the walls had forty-six fortified towers (*turres castellatae*), standing out on both sides of the wall and surmounted with embrasures in the place of the usual castellations with passageways, as had been used in the Aurelian walls. The sections of internal wall were marked by arcades that gave it an appearance more reminiscent of an aqueduct rather than a fortification.

Despite the work carried out at later dates, the Carolingian parts of the walls are visible in the north section, near the Vatican gardens, and along the section that joins the papal palaces with Castel Sant'Angelo. Technically they consist of undulating courses of reused red brick held together by thick mortar with irregular fragments of marble.

Well-preserved portion of the wall erected at the initiative of Leo IV (847–55) to protect the Vatican from Saracen attack. The fortifications on the city side are organised into a series of arcades, like an aqueduct.

The defensive character of Leo's walls underlines the importance of the Vatican area from not only the religious but also the political point of view. The *palatium Caroli* (palace of Charlemagne), intended for the emperor, formerly stood in the immediate vicinity of St. Peter's. Built by Charlemagne himself behind the diaconate of Santi Sergio e Bacco as a two-story structure not unlike the Lombard *laubiae* (buildings with a portico at ground level and arcades above), the building served to symbolize the control exercised over Rome by the imperial power, despite the animosity and opposition of the Roman aristocracy.

The Vatican area was beginning to be seen as a papal residence, if not yet a permanent one. Many masonry buildings had already been constructed for this purpose: Symmachus' two *episcopia*, an attractive *domus* by Hadrian I, a triclinium by Leo III. Gregory IV added reception rooms to this last building and it was here that the emperor Lothair was received in the time of Leo IV. Within the *civitas*, along with similar residential buildings of a hall type, lesser buildings in a diversified style developed, characterized by a spontaneous and heterogeneous approach. They were built of less permanent materials and followed uses and customs imported by those who were beginning to take up residence around St. Peter's.

The increase in population took place in conditions of extreme physical discomfort, while the number of poor people and pilgrims who streamed into the area every day was causing disquiet. It was with these people in mind that the secular and ecclesiastical authorities set up a number of centers that offered assistance. To these were attached hospitals, hostels for pilgrims, and small churches. Between the eighth and the ninth centuries, there were five diaconiates, similar to those found elsewhere in Rome, concerned chiefly with the poor, and four *scholae*, reception centers for foreign pilgrims.

Despite defeat in 849 and 916 in the coastal cites of Naples, Gaeta, and Amalfi, the Saracens continued to lay waste to the countryside and sack the outskirts of Rome, causing the already precarious living conditions of the urban population to deteriorate still further. In face of this continuing external threat, not only was the Vatican area fortified, but the churches of San Sebastiano on the Appian Way, Sant'Agnese on Via Nomentana, and San Lorenzo on Via Tiburtina were strengthened. In addition, a new district, along the lines of the *civitas leonina*, was created around St. Paolo fuori le Mura, given the name of Giovannipoli after the pope, John VIII (872–82), who took over construction in 880.

From Otto I to Gregory VII

The climate of uncertainty became constant towards the end of the ninth century and throughout the tenth century. The internal situation was complicated by the struggle between the papacy and the old and new aristocracies. Driven by ambition to take over control of Rome, these families often ended up in head-on confrontation.

The architectural and pictorial works produced in Rome at this time are few, but they include the conversion of the Temple of Fortuna Virilis (Temple of Portunus) into Santa Maria *ad gradellis* (subsequently called Santa Maria Egiziaca) by John VIII, who had it adorned with wall paintings, as well as the construction of a number of small churches such as Santa Barbara dei Librai, constructed after 900 within the remains of the Theater of Pompey, or Santa Maria in Pallara (now San Sebastiano al Palatino), built between 970 and 999 and also decorated with frescos.

A scheme that seems to have been more demanding was the restoration carried out as a result of the energetic and enthusiastic Sergius III (904–11) at the Lateran after the devastating earthquake of 896 that brought down the church "from the altar to the doors," as described in the *Liber Pontificalis*. The basilica was closed for at least seven years, during which time mass was not said. According to the *Liber Pontificalis*, the basilica was rebuilt *a solo* (literally, from the ground), that is, almost completely. It is not possible however to reconstruct precisely what was done.

Despite the uncertain political situation, the papacy and the Ottonian imperial ruling dynasty both wished for a *renovatio imperii Romanorum* (renewal of the empire of the Romans) that would restore Rome to the glory it had known at the time of Charlemagne. The coronation of Otto I in St. Peter's in 962 led to the creation of the Holy Roman Empire.

Emperor Otto III (995–1002), advised by one of the greatest minds of his day, Gerbert d'Aurillac (later Silvester II (999–1003), seemed the embodiment of the ideals of his time. His premature death saw the end of dreams of restoration and marked the end of an era. The period had produced little important architecture, with the exception of San Bartolomeo on the Tiber Island, built in 977 by Otto II in honour of St. Adalbert on the site of a temple to Aesculapius, god of medicine and of healing, to whom the island was dedicated. The relics of St. Bartholomew were brought from Benevento, giving the new church its dedication. Later, perhaps as early as 1113 with Paschal II, then between 1130 and 1180, the church was completely restored. From this period it is still possible to see the arcaded colonnade, in the place of a trabeated colonnade, and, below the raised transept, the remains of a crypt with a vault supported on columns.

In the first half of the eleventh century little changed. On the one hand the papacy became increasingly secular, expanding into areas outside its spiritual domain. On the other, the empire was increasing its interference in ecclesiastical matters, taking upon itself the right to appoint the so-called prince bishops. Meanwhile the great Roman families, who regarded themselves as the only true descendants and keepers of the destiny of the city, attempted to built a third, alternative, power base between the papacy and the empire.

Under the patronage of the Pierleoni family, who had increased their power to include the Tiber Island and Trastevere, the church of San Cosimato was rebuilt in 1066, though today little can be seen of this earlier restoration. The diaconate of San Nicola in Carcere was restored or reconstructed, without any features of particular note, on the site of earlier Roman buildings, still partly visible (the Temple of Peace and what is thought to be a prison), in the former Forum Holitorium (vegetable market). In the right wall, reconsecrated in 1128, is a stone dating from 1088 which mentions donations to the diaconate from one of its rectors at the time of Urban II (1088–99).

More modest in scale was the work carried out at Sant'Urbano alla Caffarella (created in 1011 out of a magnificent brick Roman building), at Santa Maria in Via Lata, first recorded in 1042, when it must have been a small chapel, later replaced by the present sixteenth-century church), at San Lorenzo in Damaso (rebuilt in a reduced form in the first half of the eleventh century after a fire had destroyed an earlier church, as recently discovered by archaeologists, in the area of the Palazzo della Cancelleria alongside the present Renaissance church the present Renaissance church), at San Giorgio Nazianzeno, in the Campus Martius (rebuilt between 1061 and 1071), and at Santa Pudenziana (endowed with an oratory to the Virgin behind the apse about 1080).

After 1050, the desire to restore a lost past was expressed by a number of popes, such as Alexander II (1061–73) and Gregory VII (1073–85). This essentially religious desire also took the form, under the influence of the Cluniac monasteries, of a reform movement based on the return of the Church to the purity of early Christianity. To Gregory we owe the *Dictatus papae*, one of the most important documents exalting the mystique of the papacy, written in 1075, the catalyst that led to the famous episode

when Emperor Henry IV sought penitence at Canossa in 1077. The seemingly intractable conflict over investitures, the right to appoint bishops, which ensued between papacy and empire, was concluded only in 1122 with the concordat signed at Worms between Lothair and Callistus II (1119–24).

A firm upholder of papal authority, Callistus wanted to commemorate the event with a fresco in his apartment at the Lateran Palace. He also had a chapel dedicated to St. Nicholas erected nearby, the decoration of which, according to later descriptions, represented Callistus' apotheosis, victorious over the schisms that had emerged during this period of disputes with the emperor.

In 1084 the Normans arrived in Rome, to support Gregory VII who was threatened by Henry IV. The event was to be disastrous for the city, which was damaged by a huge fire between the Colosseum and the Lateran.

The Twelfth-Century Renaissance

From the early twelfth century economic improvement and the strengthening of papal power led to a flowering of the arts, the second great Roman renaissance, after that of the Carolingian era. It took the form of a revival of early Christian style in both architecture and decoration. This rebirth was probably stimulated by the reconstruction at the abbey of Monte Cassino, begun in 1066–71 by the abbot, Desiderius, who, as a disciple of Hildebrand (later Gregory VII), had sought to express the ideas of a reforming papacy through the formal revival of models from the past, one such being the early Christian basilica of San Paolo fuori le Mura. It was not coincidental that San Paolo was also the most important Benedictine abbey in Rome.

On the basis of the surviving evidence, it would appear that the typological characteristics of Desiderius' vanished abbey at Monte Cassino were widely copied in the Romanesque buildings of the period. From it for example, were copied individual elements such as the raised crossing, higher than the nave, the triumphal arch resting on columns, a cloister in the neighboring monastery buildings, and the addition of a campanile and a portico to the facade. These elements were to become common in religious buildings in the twelfth and thirteenth centuries.

The influence of Monte Cassino, which was widely admired by contemporaries, appears also to have been important from the point of view of decoration. It encouraged the revival of wall painting and, particularly, mosaic, neglected

FOLLOWING PAGES:
Detail of an Easter candlestick from San Lorenzo fuori le Mura. This sculpted piece is a fine example of elaborate liturgical furnishings.

Detail from the paving of San Clemente, executed in *opus sectile*, an inlay technique using brightly colored pieces of marble. This floor ornamentation is an early example of a type which was later widely used, especially by the Cosmati and Vassalletto families of *marmorari* (marbleworkers).

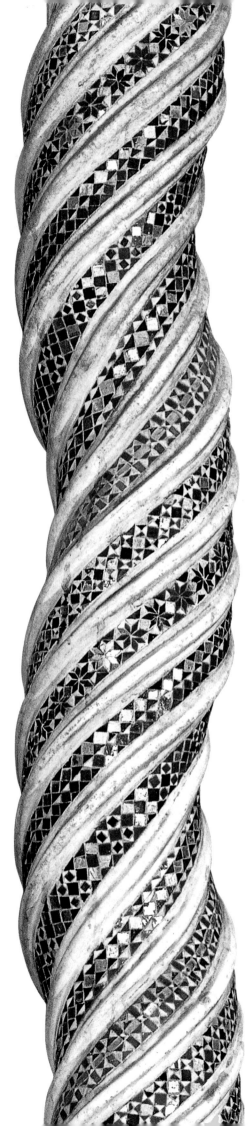

for more than two centuries, and stimulated—following a fashion brought from Byzantium and the Muslim world—the production of liturgical furnishings such as ciboria, ambos, Easter candlesticks, and cathedrae, as well as pavements with geometric inlaid patterns of colored marble (*opus sectile*).

Such work became associated with two Roman families of marbleworkers (*marmorari*), the Cosmati and the Vassalletto, who operated on a vast scale at this period. All these elements, together with local tradition, such as the widespread use of available classical carvings, and the use of lintels instead of arcades to link the columns each side of the nave, together with a wider ornamental repertory derived directly from early Christian buildings in Rome, can be found in the three churches that sum up the new Roman renaissance: San Clemente, Quattro Coronati, and Santa Maria in Trastevere.

Although attempts were made to continue to use the church of San Clemente, the damage inflicted by the Normans meant that demolition was necessary, though the walls were only partly removed. Anastasius, titular cardinal at the time of Paschal II (1099–1118), decided to reconstruct the church, but on a higher level, since the ground level had risen because of the ruins and burials. The new church, built over the previous one, was completed by a certain Pietro, perhaps Pietro Pisano, the author of the papal biographies from Leo IX to Paschal II found in the *Liber Pontificalis*.

The entrance to the upper basilica, to the east of the quadriporticus, has a gabled porch. Built in brick, it has the appearance of a baldacchino supported by two Ionic columns and marble brackets. It appears to be contemporary with the quadriporticus, the supports of which seem partly to stand on the atrium of the lower church. Similar porches appear in this period in San Cosimato, Santa Prassede, Santa Saba, Santa Maria in Cosmedin, and Old St. Peter's. As it appears today, the narthex contrasts with the sides, with sloping roofs on architraved lintels supported by columns whose Ionic capitals are either reused antique ones or medieval imitations.

The basilica has three aisles, the central nave ending in a particularly broad apse. The internal arrangement is marked by the two rows of eight columns interrupted in the middle by rectangular piers, topped with capitals similar to those of the quadriporticus. Today there are three large windows in the walls on either side of the nave. Bricked-up traces of the original windows (ten each side) can be seen from the exterior. The coffered ceiling dates from the eighteenth century, but the roof may originally have had exposed wooden beams, as in a drawing by Ciampini of about 1690.

Although it has been restored several times, the *opus sectile* pavement is one of the most beautiful of its type, with inlaid colored marble arranged in geometric patterns within a marble border made up of slabs of white marble taken from cemeteries outside the city. The presbytery is preceded by a schola cantorum, both with marble enclosures from the old church dating from the time of John II (533–35; his monogram can be seen on some of the slabs), made in Constantinople. The colored insertions are additions by twelfth-century marbleworkers. Dating from this period too are the ambos, the twisted Paschal candlestick, the baldacchino, and the papal cathedra with its raised circular back with an inscription recording the work of Cardinal Anastasius.

San Clemente's structure was copied in the renovations and decoration commissioned in 1123 by the papal *camerlengo* Alfano in Santa Maria in Cosmedin, where the central piers recur, interrupting the rhythm of the columns, as well as the style of the pavement and the furnishings with a schola cantorum, ambos, candlestick, bishop's throne, and ciborium, though that seen today is a thirteenth-century replacement. Probably dating from the same period is the work at Santa Prassede, where piers supporting transverse arcades interrupt the rhythm of the Carolingian colonnades.

Fires started by the Normans between the Lateran and the Colosseum also caused damage to the church of the Quattro Coronati. Previously restored by Leo IV, it was now repaired by Paschal II, who had important changes made. Two walls were built to divide the side aisles from the central nave, which was shortened in length. The present internal subdivision of the nave was affected by the addition of two rows of eight columns, with a matroneum over the newly created side aisles. Two atria remained in front of the new church, the earlier being that next to the massive entrance tower, now partly altered, while the second relates to that part of the Carolingian church still visible in the columns buried in the side walls. Reused fragments of marble were employed in the reconstruction—these are still visible in the parapets of the matronea—in the Cosmatesque pavement, and around the high altar.

To the left of the church a vast monastery was built, possibly replacing an older one. The cloister—perhaps the first built in Rome—dating from 1116 or shortly afterwards, has piers alternating with closely placed arcades, arranged in groups of eight on the longer sides and six on the shorter. In the twelfth century Benedictine monks took over the basilica, building the famous chapel of St. Silvester, consecrated in 1246.

The return to early Christian forms is particularly apparent in Santa Maria in Trastevere, whose reconstruction from the ground up was begun around 1120 by the antipope Anacletus II, a member of the Pierleoni family, titular cardinal of the church. The work was almost complete by 1143, under Innocent II (1130–43), who came from Trastevere and belonged to the Papareschi family. The church had monumental proportions, both in the transepts and in the impressively spacious nave and aisles, where the colonnades are architraved, following the example of Santa Maria Maggiore. The imposing granite columns are surmounted with vigorous Ionic capitals, some reused classical, some medieval.

Outside, to the right of the portico, originally trabeated, is the campanile. The exterior of the apse, with its arrangement of spaces divided up by flat pilaster strips connected by arcading, has echoes of the Lombard Romanesque style. This can also be seen in the apse of Santi Giovanni e Paolo, where a pseudo-loggia has been added—the only example of its kind in Rome.

Roughly contemporary with the initial rebuilding of Santa Maria in Trastevere is the reconstruction of the nearby church of San

View into the cloister flanking the church of Santi Quattro Coronati. Built shortly after 1116, the complex is one of the earliest examples of this type of structure in Rome.

OPPOSITE:
View of the nave of San Clemente, with the *schola cantorum* and an ornate mosaic in the foreground. This work is an excellent example of the deliberate return to the forms of early Christian art in Rome that was characteristic of the twelfth century.

Interior of Santi Quattro Coronati, whose appearance today is largely the result of renovations carried out in the twelfth century.

Crisogono (1123–29). Despite the seventeenth-century restoration, the three-aisle arrangement can still be seen, divided by granite columns supporting architraves, and a triumphal arch supported by two gigantic porphyry columns.

In the course of the twelfth century, therefore, Rome was enriched by a number of great churches, monumental in conception and with rich decoration and furnishings. In other churches of more modest dimensions, the number of columns dividing the aisles might go from four to seven, as in Santo Stefano del Cacco, near Piazza del Collegio Romano, or in San Salvatore in Onda, near Ponte Sisto, though these were rebuilt in the seventeenth and nineteenth centuries respectively. The most important example is the rebuilding of the church of San Giovanni a Porta Latina, consecrated in 1191, incorporating the sixth-century apse and two side rooms, where the aisles were separated by two rows of only five columns.

The Abbey of Tre Fontane

Standing out from the relatively homogeneous artistic panorama of twelfth-century Rome is the abbey of Santi Vincenzo e Anastasio alle Tre Fontane. Its construction presents characteristics totally different from the architectural context described so far.

Founded in 1140 by monks from Clairvaux on the spot where according to tradition St. Paul was beheaded, Tre Fontane is one of the first and most typical examples in Europe of early Cistercian architecture, following the strict dictates of the founder of the Cistercian order, St. Bernard of Clairvaux (1091–1153). The work was carried out by a well-organized teaching workshop, as can be discerned from the ground plan, based on square modular units, which governs the whole of the interior of the church and the monastic buildings.

The church, with walls of reused brick, has a nave and aisles divided by massive rectangular piles of similar material, with transepts and the typical Cistercian flat east end with a choir and square side chapels. The roofing saw the introduction of groin vaults over the aisles and choir, with barrel vaults over the transepts and chapels, where the vault rises immediately out of the curving walls without a stringcourse. A barrel vault was begun over the nave, but was quickly replaced—for reasons that are unclear—by a wooden beamed roof.

The essentially architectural aspect of the building is emphasized by the total absence of decoration, in conformity with St. Bernard's strict principles. His austere rule recommended the abolition of all superfluous decoration,

which he considered was pointless and dangerous in buildings intended to be strictly functional, the main aim of a church being prayer and contemplation.

The originality of the design of Santi Vincenzo e Anastasio, associated with the presence of Burgundian monks and fidelity to the precise architectural plan laid down by St. Bernard for every abbey of the new order, remains an isolated case in the context of Romanesque twelfth-century architecture in Rome, characterized, as has been seen, by a virtually exclusive use of forms derived from the city's own late antique and early Christian models.

Although unique, Santi Vincenzo ed Anastasio still nods in the direction of Roman tradition in the addition to the facade of a portico. This structure, dated to the time of the consecration of the church by Honorius III (1216–27) in about 1221, has Ionic capitals on reused columns supporting a marble architrave with a dignified Latin inscription, surrounded with a delicate cornice with multiple projections.

Porticos, Campaniles, Cloisters, and Towers

It was not only at Tre Fontane that a portico with trabeated columns appeared. The feature had become widespread in plans for the modernization of early Christian or early medieval buildings. Porticos were added—in place of, or as a less costly version of, the old quadriporticus—to a number of churches during the papacies of Innocent III (1198–1216) and Honorius III (1217–24), becoming a typical feature of Roman architecture by the end of the twelfth century and the first three decades of the thirteenth.

A good example of such a portico can be found at San Lorenzo in Lucina (1130). A portico existed at Santa Maria Maggiore (1145) until Fuga's alterations, while the seventeenth-century portico of San Crisogono reused granite columns from the earlier medieval portico of 1129. Santa Maria in Trastevere has one (1141), altered by Carlo Fontana in 1702, and there is one at San Giorgio in Velabro, commissioned by the prior, Stefano di Stella, named in the inscription that runs along the architrave. The destroyed diaconate church of Santi Sergio e Bacco by the Forum, reconstructed by Innocent III before he became pope, had a portico added some time after 1198 to the facade, which was open at the side as at San Giorgio in Velabro. A succession of additions of a similar type followed at Santa Cecilia in Trastevere, St. John Lateran, and San Lorenzo fuori le Mura, where the carving and mosaic decoration are Cosmati and Vassalletti work.

In the entrance portico of Santa Cecilia in Trastevere, supported by four antique Ionic columns and two piers with Corinthian capitals, the mosaic inlay of the architrave is set in medallions representing those saints whose relics had been placed in the confessio by Paschal I. At St. John Lateran the new portico on the facade was executed in part between 1159 and 1181 by the *marmorario* Nicola d'Angelo, in the same style as the portico of San Lorenzo fuori le Mura, though it was not completed for many years.

Removed in 1732 when the new facade by Alessandro Galilei was built, the portico consisted of six columns beneath a continuous lintel decorated with a small mosaic frieze, with animal heads, and a two-line inscription continuing to the right on to the masonry. The portico, originally intended to extend right along the front of the basilica, corresponded only to the width of the nave and the two northern aisles. The remaining space was taken up with the chapel of St. Thomas, built at the time of John XII (956–64) as a *secretarium*, the place where the pope put on his sacred vestments before mass.

The transformation of Pelagius' church of San Lorenzo fuori le Mura was begun by Cardinal Cencio Savelli before his election as Honorius III. The church had its apse removed and, with the orientation reversed, was used as a presbytery for the new church added on the western side. This consisted of three aisles divided by powerful Ionic colonnades with architraves. A portico was added to the facade, though it was rebuilt, together with part of the church, as a result of bomb damage in the Second World War. The work of Vassalletto, the portico has as well as a decorated lintel fine capitals, stylistically similar to those in the nave, indicating a continuity of workshop style between the two building campaigns. Notable too in the local Verano masonry was the introduction of the use of small blocks of tufa (*opus saracinescum*) as cladding for the outer walls of Honorius' church, while inside the use of brick continued (*opus testaceum*).

Another group of churches with the same type of portico with architrave has, in addition, an upper story or gallery. This is the case with Santa Croce in Gerusalemme, dated to the

Facade of the church of San Giorgio in Velabro, with an entry portico and a Roman campanile to the side. Adjoining the church at the left and integrated into the building is the so-called Arch of the *Argentarii*. This area was severely damaged by a car bomb in 1993, but extensive repair work has restored it to its original state.

Cloister and exterior of San Paolo fuori le Mura. The cloister is one of the few areas of the complex which escaped damage in a fire which broke out on the night of 15 to 16 July, 1823.

papacy of Lucius II (1144–45) but known today only through eighteenth-century drawings. A clearer example is that of Santi Giovanni e Paolo on the Caelian Hill, originally commissioned by the titular cardinal Giovanni da Sutri in 1154. Later work initiated in 1216 by Cardinal Cencio Savelli seems to have been confined to the heightening of the portico with a gallery in reused brick, characterized by alternating rectangular single and twin openings.

On similar lines is the church of Santa Saba, whose facade has a trabeated portico with a gallery above, where originally single and twin openings alternated. Here the Cosmatesque entrance portico, dated 1205, provides a useful reference point for dating.

From what we have seen so far, the cultural climate appears to have remained somewhat inward-looking, with a passive repetition, or simplification, of earlier buildings, in particular, early Christian models. As has been said, the portico placed against the facade can be regarded as a simpler version of the earlier quadriporticus. Thus there appear to have been no aspirations towards innovation and therefore no stimulus to develop new typologies or styles. This conservatism persisted throughout the entire Romanesque period, failing to find a justification for change in the desire to express the fervor of religious reform and instead repeating the forms sanctioned by the earliest years of Christianity.

Yet this apparent fidelity to tradition and the lack—albeit deliberate and convenient—of an innovative impulse is astonishing when one remembers that in the 1220s, when work on San Lorenzo fuori le Mura was coming to its conclusion, the cathedral of Chartres in France had just been completed and the Gothic style had dominated for a hundred years. The new style introduced by the Cistercian monks active at Tre Fontane did not catch on. Not even Lombard culture, rapidly assimilated elsewhere in Italy, seemed capable of penetrating Rome's cultural isolation.

The single modest contribution to the architectural landscape—apart from the isolated examples already referred to, the apses of Santi Giovanni e Paolo and of Santa Maria in Trastevere—was one imported from the Po valley. Like those in Lombardy, the campaniles built in Rome in the twelfth century and later are all brick, square in plan, and of several stories. Yet they are distinguished by characteristics of their own—the slightly lighter construction, the emphasis on openings (two- or three-light) on each level, the use of colored brick enlivened here and there with pottery, gleaming paterae, crosses of serpentine or porphyry, mosaics depicting little niches containing sacred images, and ornate stringcourses with marble corbels marking the division between each story.

Among the oldest of such campaniles are the modestly proportioned examples of Santa Maria in Cappella and San Benedetto in Piscinula, dating from the end of the eleventh century and the first half of the twelfth respectively. At San Giorgio in Velabro, the campanile, which is from a slightly later period than the nearby portico, reveals a similarity with that of Santa Pudenziana, erected at the time of the rebuilding there under Cardinal Pietro Sassone (1210). Another early campanile is that of San Sisto Vecchio, which can be dated with certainty to 1215–22. Other campaniles built in conjunction with a portico or at the time of more general building programs are Santa Croce in Gerusalemme, San Lorenzo fuori le Mura, San Crisogono, Santa Maria in Trastevere, Santa Maria in Cosmedin, San Silvestro in Capite, Santa Maria Nuova, and Sant'Alessio, as well as the slender towers of Santi Giovanni e Paolo and Santa Maria in Cosmedin.

Possibly influenced by the cloister at Montecassino, cloisters began to appear in Rome alongside religious buildings. Among the first examples are those of the Quattro Coronati, already mentioned, and of San Lorenzo fuori le Mura (1187–91), the second rather austere and lacking mosaic decoration. Much more richly decorated from this point of view are the cloisters of San Paolo fuori le Mura and St. John Lateran. The colonnettes are twisted and encrusted with mosaic, cornices sculpted with luxuriant foliage, masks, lions' heads, and palmettes, and friezes decorated with geometric marble inlay.

The cloister at San Paolo fuori le Mura, though conceived as a single work, reveals two building phases. The original nucleus, commissioned by Cardinal Pietro Capuano of Amalfi between 1208 and 1214, developed along the east, south, and west sides. The north, completed some fifteen years later, between 1230 and 1235, is certainly the work of the Vassalletto workshop which had just completed the Lateran cloister. When work recommenced, the style of the cloister continued as before, covered with a wooden roof and arranged into five groups of arcades divided by rectangular piles.

The same scheme of a modular treatment of the surfaces is found in the Lateran cloister, where responsibility for the entire work can be attributed to the Vassalletto workshop, in particular to the father and son who are mentioned in an inscription on one of the piers of the south side: "Vassalletto, skilled in this art, began this noble task with his father and completed it himself" (*Nobiliter doctus hoc Vassalectus in arte cum patre cepit opus quod perficit ipse*).

View of a part of the Cosmati-like cloister of St. John Lateran, built by the Vassalletto workshop between 1216 and 1230.

Coat-of-arms of the Savelli family, from the church of Santa Maria in Aracoeli. The bands in the lower part of the emblem are probably a reference to the holding of an office in the ecclesiastical courts.

The Torre delle Milizie, one of the most imposing remnants of civil architecture from the Roman Middle Ages. A landmark of the city, this dominating structure was built adjoining the Markets of Trajan in the thirteenth century.

They were working there between 1216 and 1230. Here the workers acted as skilled architects as well, constructing a roof for the walks with a series of groin vaults supported by corbels on columns attached to piers, and corbels on pilasters along the wall running round the cloister.

Less certain in date, but less elaborate in terms of formal solutions compared with the cloisters of San Paolo fuori le Mura and at the Lateran, are those with simple leaf capitals at Santa Cecilia, San Cosimato, and San Sisto Vecchio (on the two-light chapter house opening), as well as at Santa Sabina, where there is an alternation of twin and single colonnettes.

The thirteenth century saw the development of a phenomenon which was to condition the political and artistic life of the city. Acting as a counterweight to the universality and centrality of papal power was the local bias of the great

Roman families. Documents from as early as the twelfth century record the custom of these families of fortifying their residences, mainly to be found on the sites of the ruins of ancient buildings between the Imperial Fora and the Mausoleum of Augustus. Numerous tower-houses appeared, generally rectangular in ground plan, a type of construction seen as a sign of importance, as it confirmed the nobility of a family that could boast of the rights that accompanied their status. Within the tower, a family could entrench itself against its neighbor—who for the same reasons and with the same aims built and fortified his own tower. Only nobles were allowed to erect towers to defend and ornament their houses and defend their power.

The typology of such houses—closely linked with the tower, as can be seen in the surviving house of the Pierleoni family opposite San Nicola in Carcere, or in that of the Anguillara family, at the beginning of Viale Trastevere just after the river—was to become the basis of the Roman house style in the fourteenth century. The Frangipani family, which along with the Pierleoni was the most powerful around 1100, boasted fortified houses in several parts of the city—in the Forum, on the Palatine, and in the Colosseum. The Savelli built their residence on the Theater of Marcellus then near the church of Santa Sabina on the Aventine. The Colonna were on the Capitoline Hill, the Orsini at Monte Giordano, the Crescenzi near Santa Maria in Cosmedin, the Pierleoni family on the Tiber Island, the Anguillara in Trastevere, and so on.

Notable among these fortified constructions are the towers of the Conti and Milizie families (Torre de' Conti and Torre delle Milizie). The massive Torre de' Conti was erected behind the Forum of Nerva for Riccardo Conti, brother of Innocent III. It was reinforced around the base with a sloping wall of flint and limestone in alternating bands, typical of a building style also found close by in a stretch of wall next to the convent of San Francesco di Paola near San Pietro in Vincoli.

The Torre delle Milizie, still today two-thirds of its height, was probably in existence towards the end of the twelfth century. It reused part of an old garrison, possibly Byzantine. From its elevated site near the Markets of Trajan, the impressive construction still dominates the whole city. The fresco depicting the city of Rome painted by Cimabue in San Francesco in Assis, in the vault of the Evangelists, next to the figure of St. Mark, shows its original appearance. Its construction, reminiscent of a telescope, is formed of three superimposed parallelepipeds, each smaller than the one below. The tower, once part of a genuine fortress, passed from the Frangipane family to the Annibaldi, then in 1301 to Pietro Caetani, nephew of Boniface VIII.

The rest of the buildings of this period can only be reconstructed hypothetically, given the small number of surviving medieval houses, and given the alterations to their original appearance. The most important survival is the so-called Casa dei Crescenzi, a few yards from the Temple of Fortuna Virilis, built around 1200 by Niccolò Crescenzi, a member of this powerful family. The building has brick cladding decorated with reused antique fragments. Long inscriptions on marble were inserted into the facade, in which Niccolò proclaims his intention of restoring Rome to its former glory.

The Mendicant Orders

The early thirteenth century saw the birth of the mendicant orders. In December 1219 the early Christian church of San Sisto Vecchio, together with its associated buildings, was entrusted to the Dominicans. Work was started on the monastic buildings, while Innocent III had the church converted into a single hall through the demolition of the two aisles. The Dominican residence at San Sisto was only brief, however, for in 1221 they found a permanent home in

View of external sections of the Casa dei Crescenzi, which was built at the beginning of the thirteenth century making heavy use of antique building materials. The emblematic use of these materials and their inscriptions illustrates the efforts made at the time to restore the glories of ancient Rome.

Santa Sabina on the Aventine, within the Savelli fortress, where they began work on monastic buildings, starting with a cloister.

Tradition has it that in 1219 the Franciscans established themselves in Trastevere, thanks to a noblewoman, Jacopa dei Settesoli, near the Benedictine hospice of San Biagio, obtaining possession of San Biagio in 1229 through a papal bull of Gregory IX. Within a few years, the church and monastery of San Francesco a Ripa was completed on this site. The thirteenth-century church, today concealed behind Peruzzi's late seventeenth-century building, contained a cycle of frescos commissioned by Pandolfo II d'Anguillara around 1285, generally attributed to Cavallini, depicting the many miracles of St. Francis.

It was to the Franciscans again that Gregory IX gave a small church in the northern part of the city, near Porta San Valentino. This they reconstructed, dedicating it to the Virgin. Shortly afterwards, at the same time as the Franciscans moved to the Benedictine monastery of Santa Maria *de Capitolio* or in Aracoeli and the beginning of work on the nearby town hall, the Palazzo dei Conservatori,

the church and its attached monastery passed to the Augustinians. Now known as Santa Maria del Popolo, the church acquired its present Renaissance appearance from the Augustinians.

Alterations to Santa Maria in Aracoeli began in the mid-thirteenth century. Built of brick, the church stands on the foundations of an earlier Benedictine church that may have stood at right angles to the present building. Imposing transepts were added, marked on the exterior by corbels with female heads supporting the arms of the Savelli family in mosaic. The financial contribution of the Savelli earned its members the right to be buried in the south transept. The tombs of the senator Luca Savelli (d. 1266) and his wife Vanna Savelli are portrayed in a style reminiscent of van Eyck's famous Arnolfini portrait, with a recumbent effigy of their son, Honorius IV (d. 1287).

In the reconstruction of Santa Maria in Aracoeli, extending from the apse to the main body of the three-aisled church and the facade with cavetto moldings, we can see possible involvement of the architect and sculptor Arnolfo di Cambio. His influence can be seen in some of the Gothic detail, particularly the

The Franciscan church of Santa Maria in Aracoeli on the Capitoline Hill. While sparingly decorated on the outside, the interior of the church contains a number of extraordinary works of art from various eras, including the San Bambino, a famous and much revered image of the Christ child.

insertion in the end walls of the transepts of an imposing three-light window surmounted by a rose window, flanked by a series of smaller two-light windows, as can be seen in a number of sixteenth-century drawings showing the church from the Palazzo Senatorio side. Unfortunately later restoration removed these windows, though fragments of an original two-light window seem to have links with the drilling technique used by Arnolfo di Cambio on his ciboria in San Paolo fuori le Mura and Santa Cecilia in Trastevere.

Access to the church was by a little street by the church of San Biagio *de mercato* lower down, and through a side entrance on Piazza del Campidoglio. The monumental flight of steps that now leads up to the main entrance was built in 1348.

Nicholas III

To understand the complex picture of the artistic flowering in Rome in the latter part of the thirteenth century, it is necessary to examine the role of the Roman pope, Nicholas III (1277–80). A member of the Orsini family, he made a significant contribution to his native city through large donations. During his brief but active papacy, Nicholas paid particular attention to architectural matters. He was concerned to see the buildings and institutions that fell within the care of the papal Curia (monasteries, hospitals, churches, and chapels) prosper, and to ensure that the general decay of the city should be remedied.

The poor state of the city's buildings had come about in part because of those popes who between 1261 and 1272 had chosen to live permanently far away from the historic seat of the papacy, in Viterbo, Perugia, Orvieto, Rieti, and other smaller centers within the papal states. Nicholas III took up residence in Rome, where he decided to build a "new palace" (*nova palatia*) and gardens in the area around St. Peter's. His project was able to advance relatively rapidly thanks to the radical reconstruction work that almost entirely changed the topography of the Borgo area. The original roads were closed off, creating axes in new directions, and many private houses of the *civitas leonina* were demolished. Houses had been so crammed that, despite the interdicts of the chapter of St. Peter's and the intervention of the city magistrates responsible for building and the roads (*magistri aedificiorum* and *magistri viarum*), they even intruded on to the steps leading up to the front of the basilica.

Eugenius III (1145–53) and Innocent III had begun to erect a series of buildings in the area

Detail of a mosaic decoration showing Christ Pantocrator in the Sancta Sanctorum in the Lateran. The chapel is one of the few areas of the former Lateran palace not affected by renovations carried out by Sixtus V (1585–90).

NON·EST·IN·TOTO·SANCTIOR·ORBE·LOCVS

around St. Peter's, intended for the most part for administration and defense, or simply as annexes to the Lateran. The palace planned by Nicholas III, by contrast, was clearly intended as a residence, as an alternative to the Lateran palace. The core of the building was around the Pappagallo, Borgia, and San Damaso courtyards of the present Vatican Palace, incorporating the so-called tower of Innocent III, dating in fact from the time of Innocent IV (1243–54). Part of the palace was reserved as accommodation for the *penitenzieri* of St. Peter's, priests who saw to the needs of visitors, particularly of pilgrims. The entire structure was protected by a wall, thus taking on the appearance of a magnificent and secure residence, with spacious gardens planted with a wealth of different species.

By order of the pope, the Vatican palace was connected with Castel Sant'Angelo by a corridor (later known as the Passetto di Borgo), which was cut through a stretch of the Leonine walls. Now belonging to the Orsini family, Castel Sant'Angelo, created out of the Mausoleum of Hadrian, was able to guarantee even greater security for the new papal residence.

In religious architecture, a number of restorations were carried out that are worthy of mention. The Franciscan church of Santa Maria in Aracoeli enjoyed a prosperous period, particularly as a result of the adoption of the larger chapels by the Roman aristocracy (the Orsini, Savelli, Colonna, and Capocci). The basilicas of St. Peter's, San Paolo fuori le Mura, and St. John Lateran were similarly embellished. At St. Peter's, where a new papal altar was consecrated on June 11, 1279, Nicholas III chose a burial place in a chapel that he dedicated to St. Nicholas at the end of the right aisle, near the crossing.

Perhaps the most significant moment of all of Nicholas's building campaign was the construction of the palatine chapel of the Sancta Sanctorum at the Lateran, the only well-preserved example of late thirteenth-century religious architecture. In 1227, immediately after the death of Honorius III, a violent earthquake struck Rome, damaging, among other buildings, the original chapel, dedicated since its construction to St. Lawrence. In the second half of the thirteenth century, Fra' Tolomeo da Lucca, a Dominican who became bishop of Torcello near Venice, wrote in his *Ecclesiastical History* that the palace chapel was in a ruinous state and Nicholas III had had it rebuilt from the foundations up and ornamented with splendid marble, mosaic, and paintings.

A fresco displayed on the inner walls immortalizes the pope who, accompanied by Sts. Peter and Paul, presents a model of the new building to an enthroned Christ surrounded by angels. The chapel has a more or less square ground plan. Small in size but richly elegant, it expresses a striking fusion of tradition and innovation, showing an attachment to traditional styles while standing as a manifesto of a controlled reception of the new mature Gothic becoming widespread outside Rome. Inside there are important similarities with the transepts of the upper church of San Francesco at Assisi and with examples in France, including the Sainte-Chapelle in Paris (1248).

On the other hand, the treatment of the exterior, the spaciousness of the interior, the cladding of the internal walls in large sheets of

marble, and the fresco and mosaic decoration, as well as the Cosmatesque pavement, are indicative of a mature blend, in other words, of a successful revival of schemes and solutions already present in Roman medieval architecture. An unidentified *magister Cosmatus* has proudly set his name to this work in a slab set in the small passageway at the entrance, ensuring his primacy over any other craftsman involved in the project.

The same compositional elements, despite their projection upwards, retain the old peaceful and harmonious proportions, with solid walls and small windows at the Sancta Sanctorum. The Gothic elements of the interior are canceled out by the antique marble revetment, the mosaic, and the wall painting in a happy synthesis that makes the building as a

Detail from a mosaic in the Sancta Sanctorum, with a depiction of an episode from the life of St. Nicholas.

whole a unique expression of the eclectic tastes of Rome in a period which was poised between innovation and tradition.

Last in chronological order of Nicholas III's recorded commissions is the church of Santa Maria sopra Minerva. Nicholas' protection of the mendicant orders saw concrete expression in the confirmation of the Franciscan rule. He also showed his esteem for the Dominicans by often allowing himself to be represented by Cardinal Aldobrandino Cavalcanti and Latino Malabranca Orsini, Dominicans and important figures in the affairs of the Florentine Dominican church of Santa Maria Novella, as well as those of Santa Maria sopra Minerva in Rome. The similarities between these two churches are so striking that it is likely that the architects of Santa Maria sopra Minerva (not identified) were inspired by the Florentine church designed by Fra' Sisto and Ristoro da Campi.

Particularly reminiscent of Santa Maria Novella are the pointed arches, and the slim columns on bare walls. The aisles, originally covered with a beam roof, were not vaulted until the fourteenth century over the side aisles, while the central nave was vaulted in 1453. Unfortunately nineteenth-century restoration has partly altered the general proportions of the building.

St. John Lateran and Santa Maria Maggiore

Towards the end of the thirteenth century, there were no important initiatives in architecture, apart from the Sancta Sanctorum and Santa Maria sopra Minerva. North of the Alps, as mentioned, Gothic had been dominant for more than a century. Nevertheless, it is fair to say that in these years the spirit of innovation, stimulated by the Franciscans and Dominicans, influenced St. John Lateran and Santa Maria Maggiore, which both saw building work in the apse and the facade. The inspiration behind these changes was Nicholas IV (1228–92), the first Franciscan pope.

At St. John Lateran, where Nicholas initiated radical restoration, work must have begun, if not at the same time as, then shortly before work on Santa Maria Maggiore, to judge from the decoration. Together with two mosaic inscriptions in the apse at St. John Lateran, another inscription, the so-called Tabula Magna, now next to the sacristy, commemorates the restoration and alludes to the dream in which, according to the description by St. Bonaventura, Innocent III had a vision of St. Francis supporting a collapsing St. John Lateran. Innocent

interpreted the dream as a warning of the need for physical restoration of the church that must have had real problems of instability. As can be learnt from the same inscription, the work undertaken by Nicholas concentrated on the rear of the basilica, particularly on the western side, on the apse and the ambulatory running round the outside of it, which had been added at the time of Leo the Great (440–461) known as the Portico Leoniano, demolished and rebuilt using the old foundations. The ambulatory, divided internally into two aisles by five columns, was given a vault. Via a door with a few steps, it communicated with the area and buildings behind. At this time too, the transepts were built, though it is possible that they were built on the site of existing transepts in 1130–40.

At St. John Lateran the transepts were almost as wide as the aisles, while at Santa Maria Maggiore the hilltop site made it necessary to make then narrower. Nicholas IV also commissioned the mosaic decoration of the apse, replacing the fifth-century mosaic but without entirely changing the original subject matter and retaining the bust of the Savior, believed to have appeared miraculously at the time of the basilica's consecration. The task was given to Jacopo Torriti, who left the Lateran workshop around 1291 to assist the work at Santa Maria Maggiore. Unfortunately Torriti's Lateran mosaic was redone in the nineteenth century when restoration enlarged the presbytery and moved the apse forward.

The basilica of Santa Maria Maggiore, the restoration of which was planned by Nicholas IV immediately after his election as pope, had its early Christian tribune removed and acquired greater spaciousness through the creation of transepts of the same height as the nave. The apse was given a pentagonal profile similar to that of Santa Maria sopra Minerva. The additional structures were richly decorated: the apse with Torriti's wonderful mosaic (completed around 1296), the transepts with frescos by different painters, the exterior of the apse with a cycle of mosaics of the Virgin, destroyed in the seventeenth century.

The work in the time of Nicholas IV probably also involved the rebuilding of the chapel of the Holy Crib, executed by Arnolfo di Cambio, and the restoration of the facade in the part decorated with mosaics by Filippo Rusuti.

Arnolfo da Cambio and His School

The mixture of tradition and innovation reached its highest point in the work of the Tuscan Arnolfo di Cambio during the period he spent in Rome. Architecture, sculpture, and mosaic Cosmatesque decoration came together to form an organic whole, as in the ciboria at San Paolo fuori le Mura (1285) and Santa Cecilia in Trastevere (1293)—possibly inspired by the slightly earlier double ciborium in the Sainte-Chapelle—or in the tomb of the papal notary Annibaldi, who died in 1289, in St. John Lateran and the tomb of Boniface VIII, from some time before 1296, in St. Peter's. The San

The mosaic from the apse of Santa Maria Maggiore by Jacopo Torriti, completed in 1296 and featuring a monumental image of the crowning of Mary by Christ.

Paolo ciborium was executed in collaboration with a certain Pietro who may perhaps be identified with the still somewhat mysterious figure of Pietro di Oderisio, who made the tomb of Clement IV in the church of San Francesco in Viterbo.

Equally problematic is the work that Arnolfo carried out at Santa Maria in Aracoeli and in the chapel of the Holy Crib in Santa Maria Maggiore. Arnolfo created this latter chapel on the site of a much older place of worship containing the relics of the Nativity in 1291, probably at the same time as the work commissioned by Nicholas IV. For the burial place of Boniface VIII, Arnolfo collaborated with Jacopo Torriti, who executed the dedicatory mosaic panel. Crowning the tomb was a little cupola, later destroyed, masked by an open gallery with pinnacles in the Rayonnant style, of the type characterizing the two ciboria.

Arnolfo da Cambio's work, architectural and sculptural, gave rise to a school in Rome, where a number of marbleworkers, rather than develop Arnolfo's ingenious solutions, limited themselves to reproducing similar objects, ciboria and tombs. Deodato has left his name on the ciborium at Santa Maria in Cosmedin and the dismantled one in the cloister of St. John Lateran, which must originally have stood above the altar of

St. Mary Magdalene, consecrated in 1297 by Cardinal Gerardo Bianchi.

Deodato's brother, Giovanni di Cosma, was responsible for the tomb of Cardinal Stefano Surdi (d. 1295), now removed from its original position to Santa Balbina, the monument to Cardinal Guglielmo Durando (d. 1296) in Santa Maria sopra Minerva, and the monument to Consalvo Garcia Gudiel (d. 1299) in Santa Maria Maggiore.

Palazzo Senatorio

In the fourteenth century the Capitoline Hill once again became a focus, with its traditional role in Roman history of providing a mediating point between the Vatican and the Lateran. The new communal palace, which was built in the mid-thirteenth century, was on top of the walls of the late first century BC Tabularium. A short stretch of its original structure can still be seen at the sides of the present Palazzo Senatorio. In 1299 a loggia was added, which survives in the present Sala del Consiglio Comunale, with arcading on antique columns with medieval Ionic capitals. This was followed by the construction of a number of reinforcing towers which gave the palace the appearance of a castle.

Cosmati altar from the Cappella del Presepe, the chapel for the relics of Christ's manger in Santa Maria Maggiore.

Frontal view of the Stefaneschi Triptych in the Pinacoteca Vaticana, made by Giotto and members of his workshop. The double-sided painting of this retable from 1300 is an early example of an altar conceived of as visible from all sides.

The third-floor hall had extensive decoration, partly surviving, together with a series of Orsini arms, alternating with those of the Senate. The building was depicted by Cimabue in San Francesco in Assisi, in the vault of the Evangelists mentioned above, with the presence on the exterior of two Orsini coats of arms and four shields with the letters SPQR. A tower was added in 1300 by Boniface VIII. The palace was further reinforced with an eye to defense in 1344 by Cola di Rienzo. The addition by Boniface IX in 1389 and 1404 of further towers made it even more fortress-like.

The Fourteenth Century

The works completed by Nicholas IV at the Lateran found completion in the construction of the benediction loggia by Boniface VIII in the complex, behind the facade of the *aula concilii*, demolished in 1586 under Sixtus V. This was a complex structure, generally associated with the jubilee of 1300 on account of the surviving fresco from the pictorial decoration of the loggia itself, now attached to the third pier of St. John Lateran, sometimes attributed to Giotto.

In reality the fresco, rather than depicting the proclamation of the first jublilee—or, according to another interpretation, the takeover of the Lateran by Boniface VIII in 1297—shows Boniface, accompanied by a cardinal (perhaps Matteo Rosso Orsini) and a deacon, performing some kind of solemn ceremony such as the proclamation of a bull, as seems to be confirmed by the *Incipit* that can still be read on the scroll held by the deacon. The loggia, arranged on three levels, had at the middle level a balcony supported by a number of columns rising from the lower level. It was framed by three arcades, the central one of which was trefoil, similarly supported by columns. On the third level a triangular front flanked by small gables included two statues and a coat of arms. Overall the original structure was an excellent example of the formal style of fourteenth-century Roman Gothic, owing more than a little to Arnolfo di Cambio. The small church of San Nicola dates from the

death of Boniface VIII. It is a single aisled building with transverse arches clearly punctuated by buttresses with oblique terminals.

The elements of the rich culture that in the last years of the thirteenth century had contributed to the revival of the city and produced a profound change in the general culture, traditionally inclined to evolve slowly, and only on the basis of its own inheritance. In this period Rome took on the appearance both of a well-organized capital from the political and spiritual point of view, as well as a cultural and artistic center able to compete with other cities—Siena, Florence and Venice—that were beginning to emerge as important centers. Rome was praised in the *Marvels* (*Mirabilia*) guidebook intended for use by pilgrims, exalted in Master Gregory's *Narrative*, celebrated in the poem by Ildeberto of Lavardin, and depicted in many painted townscapes, from Cimabue's in Assisi to the Golden Bull of Louis of Bavaria, where pagan Rome was depicted as incorporated into the Christian city.

Political events eventually put an end to this remarkable flowering of medieval Rome. With the exile of the papacy to Avignon between 1304 and 1376, the city found itself in a state of anarchy, impoverishment, and decadence. Constant quarreling and violence broke out between the rival families who supported the Orsini or the Colonna and were split between the Guelph and the Ghibelline factions. From the artistic point of view, apart from the patronage of Cardinal Jacopo Stefaneschi, responsible for Giotto's work in St. Peter's, little of importance was produced. Even the most important masters preferred to move elsewhere.

With the popes absent, building came to a halt, while the ancient buildings, Christian basilicas, and aqueducts fell into disrepair. In 1349 an earthquake affected whole districts, damaging numerous monuments. The Lateran Palace fell into disuse and St. John Lateran, harmed not only by neglect but also by fire in 1308 and 1361, was reduced to such a state that Petrarch felt impelled to appeal to Urban V (1362–70) to intervene to save the ancient basilica.

In the second half of the thirteenth century, after the devastation of the Black Death of 1348 that spread throughout Italy and Europe but spared Rome, signs of revival began to be felt. The steps leading up to Santa Maria in Aracoeli were built in 1348 by Lorenzo di Simone Andreozio as an *ex voto* (thanks offering) for the freedom of Rome from plague. The traditional visual axis that favored the Forum over the new directional axis represented by St. Peter's on the Vatican was reasserted. San Paolo fuori le Mura saw restoration in 1349, as well as the campanile, now replaced by the new bell tower by Poletti next to the apse.

The jubilee of 1350 saw an influx of pilgrims greater that could have been imagined. Between 1367 and 1370 Urban V (1362–70) took up residence in Rome. In 1368, after a number of restorations, St. John Lateran was given a new ciborium—still on the high altar today—by a Sienese sculptor, suggesting that there were at that time no sculptors in Rome. In Santa Maria Maggiore, between 1370 and 1378, the present campanile was rebuilt in place of the earlier Romanesque one, the highest and most elegant of Roman campaniles, with a slim pyramid-shape. On the Capitoline Hill, Palazzo Senatorio, as we have seen, was the object of further work.

In 1376 Gregory XI (1370–80) re-established the papacy in Rome, bringing an end to the Avignon exile. Yet the crisis was far from resolved. Scarcely a year after Gregory's return, Christendom was divided by the profound internal dispute known as the Great Schism, which saw popes in Rome opposing popes in Avignon. It was concluded only in 1417, with the election of Martin V (1417–31) and the

View into the loggia of the facade of Santa Maria Maggiore, which was built from a design by Ferdinando Fuga between 1743 and 1750. At the left of the picture the mosaic decoration of the previous facade is visible; it was completed by Filippo Rusuti at the end of the thirteenth century.

resignation of the rival popes. Only then was Rome able to emerge from the crisis and return to a stable role.

Martin's building work aimed for the most part to improve the fabric of the city. He was concerned less with the construction of new buildings than with the rescue of existing ones. The basilica of Santi Apostoli was restored, together with the nearby house of the Colonna family (to which Martin belonged). In 1425 a new floor was laid, with marble reused from St. John Lateran. Shortly afterwards Palazzo Senatorio on the Capitoline Hill was fortified with a tower, still visible on the left of the facade.

In this period, several major artists appeared in Rome, including Masolino and Masaccio, both perhaps involved in the decoration of the chapel of St. Catherine in San Clemente. All in all, even the later schemes of Eugenius IV (1431–47), including the palazzo attached to Santa Maria in Cosmedin and Palazzo Capranica—still without any clearly defined stylistic character of their own—can be said to be, on the one hand, the final examples of a long period of transition that brought the Middle Ages in Rome to a close, or, on the other, the first hints of a change that was to lay the foundations of a new Renaissance.

Mario D'Onofrio

The campanile of Santa Maria Maggiore, built at the end of the fourteenth century, dominates the roofscape of the Esquiline through its brooding mass and its height (75 m).

Medieval Sculpture

As in architecture and painting, though with specific characteristics of its own, the evolution of the sculptural arts in the course of the Middle Ages in Rome seems to have been marked by an intimate dialectical relationship with the antique. This, with the maturing of historico-ideological knowledge and motivation, was expressed, often synchronously, in the reuse of *spolia* (fragments of Roman sculpture or architecture) in a more or less conscious anti-classical experimenting, with deliberately significant quotations and autonomous revisions.

With the decline of imperial patronage, as early as the fourth century after Christ a decline in the figurative sculpture intended to celebrate the ideology of secular power on a monumental scale can be seen. In parallel with this, a new functional and symbolic specificity was being developed for sculpture in Christian buildings. Initially this transition took place through the adaptation and reuse of elements of architectural and decorative sculpture such as architraves, columns, bases, and capitals which, due to the neutral or generic character of their iconography, better lent themselves to a new context.

In this process Rome was favored by the ample availability of antique marble, which afforded notable practical advantages both at the economic level and in the time it took to carry out the work. At the same time it made up for the lack of skilled master stonecutters. As evidenced by the earliest Christian basilicas, materials were selected with a great deal of care and placed in accordance with exact criteria of homogeneity, among which were then distributed the necessary variations to highlight focal points at a structural, liturgical, as well as symbolic level.

The progressive despoliation of classical buildings—the removal of materials and their reuse in new works—must have been organized early on by workshops of marblecutters. Pieces not otherwise reusable were turned into lime for building in the limekilns, whose presence is amply documented in the proximity of, or inside, the largest and most materials-rich buildings.

This phenomenon of reusing the antique period, therefore, immediately demonstrates its extremely practical and functional nature. But at the same time it is charged with symbolic values that are considerably deeper: an awareness of the high artistic level of Graeco-Roman culture, a profound admiration for the numerous vestiges of the past which were scattered throughout the city, and the will to express the pride provided by an awareness of being the legitimate heirs of Rome.

The development of a line of continuity with this high artistic tradition, which from the first centuries of Christianity had been achieved in architecture and painting through a process of recovery and reworking of formal models—though cleansed of their original contents—does not find an immediate parallel in sculpture. In this sector of the figurative arts, the late Roman spirit left behind the most intense and suggestive witnesses of its own mimetic and expressive ability. It was perhaps just this evocative charge of ancient statuary and portraiture that made manifest the memory of pagan idolatry in the most evident way, even when this no longer constituted a threat for Christianity. It is probable that the Roman

Fifteenth-century tomb of Cardinal Venier in the church of San Clemente, which reused some of the original liturgical fittings from the lower church. These sixth-century pieces attest to the artistic influence that Constantinople wielded at the time: they have characteristically slim, elegant columns, with botanical motifs and basket capitals. Rome, San Clemente.

Church's prejudice against "false idols" played an influential part from the outset in interrupting the continuity of the tradition of ancient sculpture, intended as an expressive form with its autonomous spatial placing in the full round and with the specific characteristics of the expectant naturalism of materials.

In this process of abandoning the ancient *mimesis*, several other equally determining factors also played their part. This concerned, above all, the birth of a new, typically medieval, two-dimensional, abstract language which was based on the fundamental expressive value of the line of symbolic or, more simply, evocative values. However, there has also been discussion of a progressive and concrete loss of operating capacity, due to the general economic crisis and to the emergence—as often occurs in such cases—of popular art forms, in contact with the ornamental tendencies in use by the various populations of barbarian Europe.

It may be said therefore that in Rome in the course of the early medieval centuries, stone sculpture, together with and beyond the different ways of its reuse, was expressed almost exclusively in anti-iconic formulae, with motifs of prevalently phytomorphic, zoomorphic, and geometric character. These decorations were normally carried out on ancient marble, which had been recovered through the use of rather poor instruments, mainly points and flat or toothed scalpels, on the part of individual stonecutters. An embryonic organization of workshops occurs only from the ninth century onwards. Surviving reliefs are, in general, flat and of simplified execution, with schemes that are more or less symmetrically ordered, in distinct subordination to the space allocated to them on elements of liturgical and architectural furnishings, for example altars, tabernacles, chancel enclosures, and *scholae cantorum*

The *schola cantorum* in the upper church of San Clemente. This ornate liturgical ensemble was created in the twelfth century by Roman sculptors, who used a large number of stone blocks from the walls of the original sixth-century enclosure.

(enclosures for choristers in the nave), *pergulae*, and iconostases (screens), as well as windows and portals. The reconstruction of the original typology is often arduous because of the lack of context and the fragmentary state in which the majority of the nevertheless numerous, surviving testimonies have come down to posterity—arch slabs, plutei, transepts, newel posts, capitals, dosserets, architraves, jambs, cornices, and shelves—walled or reused in subsequent centuries in Roman churches, or now in museums.

Byzantine Culture

If remains of the local production in stone intended for early Christian buildings between the fourth and the fifth centuries are rare, in general limited to a few fragments of slabs with late Roman motifs on gates, pierced for daylight or reduced to bas-relief in the sixth century as a result of the dominating Byzantine class in Rome and the oriental monastic element, significant phenomena of more or less direct importation are not lacking.

Clear evidence of this is provided by works obviously influenced by Constantinople, such as the notable remains of furnishings made by Byzantine artists for the early Christian church of San Clemente, commissioned by the priest Mercurius during the years of the papacy of St. Hormisdas (514–23) and when Mercurius himself became Pope John II (533–35). Of these, above all, two capitals remain of clear Justinian stamp, arranged on small columns fully covered in shoots and leaves. Perhaps originally intended for a tabernacle or an iconostasis, they were subsequently reused in the fifteenth-century tomb of Cardinal Venier. Apart from these, parts

of the sixth-century sanctuary have survived, reused in the twelfth-century sanctuary, and made up of a series of marble newel posts and plutei with sharp squares with the monogram of John II in the middle, between crowns of leaves and lateral crosses.

These are evidence of the Byzantine taste in the era of Justinian for clear geometrical spacing, carved with elegance and without filling decoration, and found in other contemporary panels, such as those in Santa Maria in Cosmedin, with their assumption of a decorative theme of lozenges and geometric figures inscribed and intersected in various ways, rare in Rome but frequent in Constantinople, and well known in the Byzantine world from Asia Minor to the Adriatic.

The Carolingian Age

As attested to by the greater amount of surviving evidence from the end of the eighth to halfway through the ninth century, the development of architectural sculpture of local production is related, above all, to the economic and political recovery of the papacy and the flowering of patronage on a large scale which was characteristic of the Carolingian Renaissance.

Among the first examples to come down to us of the new language that was already partly in evidence, is a fragmentary slab in Santa Maria in Cosmedin, reformulated and reused in the sanctuary but considered as having originally been part of an altar dating from the pontificate of Hadrian I (772–95). In the arms of the central cross this shows the symmetrical repetition—though not rigidly preordained—of two motifs composed with the tendency to occupy all the available space, in accordance with the distinctly anti-classical taste of the *horror vacui* (literally, a horror of emptiness, a reluctance to leave any space undecorated), widespread in the barbarian medieval west. In the upper part, two peacocks, symbols of immortality, face each other in the act of drinking, and thus take up the theme of early Christian origin of the "refreshment" which would be applied widely, with a clear eschatological reference, on panels that not by chance are related above all to altars and tabernacles.

This is demonstrated not only in the contemporary pluteus now in the portico of Santa Maria in Trastevere, which reveals a similar graphic and superficial working of the relief in minimum projection, but also in various pieces of evidence of tabernacle arch slabs which arrange the motif in two lateral triangles placed between the upper cornice and the crowning

Stone slab from the twelfth-century presbytery of San Clemente, with the framed double cross monogram of John II (532–35).

251

of the arch. Among these, two in particular are of note, now in the wall of the church of Sant'Alessandro on the Via Nomentana and which are considered among the most notable realizations of the early Middle Ages due to the singular variety of their animal repertory (sheep, peacocks, griffins, lions, crocodiles) and their references to motifs in work from the upper Adriatic area.

Other elements present in the lower part of the slab in Santa Maria in Cosmedin form part of a diffuse repertory in addition to this: tufts of vegetation, clipeated rosettes with petals, and, above all, wicker strips, a typical motif of barbarian entwining sculpture, found here for the first time in Rome on the inside of the cross. These and other decorative themes appear successively on stone slabs from the ninth century, relating to

eastern influence in general—like those found in the common decorative milieu which developed in the west in the barbarian period—found their diverse development.

An example of such characteristics can be seen in one of the various slabs remade in the reconstruction of the *schola cantorum* in Santa Sabina, dating from the pontificate of Eugenius II (824–27). On the right of the enclosure, heavily restored, it has a complex composition of motifs (butterfly palmettes, heart-shaped leaves, lilies, and birds), arranged in a rigid geometric scheme formed by two large circles of double-grooved wicker bands next to each other and knotted, in which lozenges of ribbon are crossed diagonally by four wicker braids. Here, with the addition of the braided ornament and the various filling motifs, the geometrical theme

Tombstone from the eighth century used as part of the choir screen in the church of Santa Maria in Cosmedin. Its decoration is evidence of the emergence of a new ornamental vocabulary in the early Middle Ages, whose characteristics were a tendency to cover entire surfaces and a use of strongly stylised forms.

furnishings in the numerous ecclesiastical establishments, which in this first Roman artistic renaissance were entirely rebuilt and redesigned at the structural and decorative level or, more simply, were reworked, restored, and enriched with precious donations.

While it is difficult to define a clear stylistic evolution among products that were often qualitatively diverse, historians have nevertheless found in the reliefs of the Carolingian age, in particular those from the papacy of Paschal I (817–24), a sharper and more rigorous organization of the compositional schemes in clear and balanced formulae, in which various motifs of late antique, early Christian, Byzantine, and

is again developed, which derived from the examples already mentioned of the Justinian age. These had already been used in a group of elegant panels from the papacy of Paschal I in Santa Prassede and Santa Cecilia, similar airy compositions of circles, squares, lozenges, and rectangles, inscribed and intersected between each other in various ways, and revealing technical characteristics shared to such an extent with the Santa Sabina slab that they have been referred to a single workshop, which perhaps had the benefit of drawings for the reproduction of models.

This exceptional renaissance of the arts in Rome in the Carolingian age thus found a

parallel also in the more elegant and spacious stylization of sculptural decoration. At the same time, at the first signs of a conscious recovery in a political and ideological style of early Christian architectural and figurative models, it found a new relationship with antique sculptural elements, which were now no longer simply reused with slight changes, but were completed or remade on the basis of antique models so as to supply the missing parts or pieces.

Significant evidence of this is found in the decoration of the little chapel of St. Zeno in Santa Prassede. At the entrance, the ninth-century stonecutter made the two capitals *ex novo,* providing a free interpretation in the Ionic style, no longer in use in Rome since the fifth century. He also "completed" summarily on the sawn sides the motifs of the splendid reused architrave. Inside he roughly reproduced on three of the pedestals of the four corner columns the tendrils present on the despoiled fourth, dating back to the fifth century.

The Origins of Cosmatesque Work

A large part of the subsequent development of sculptural production refers, between the twelfth and thirteenth centuries, to the activity of the families of marbleworkers traditionally known as *Cosmati* but subsequently renamed by art historians as *magistri doctissimi romani* (expert Roman masters), in accordance with the definition they themselves used on inscriptions. They seem to be already contained in this emblematic, dialectical relationship with the ancient world. These elements can be summarized in the prevailing subordination of the sculptural element to architectural support and the consequent tendency to decorate the relief in limited projection, the rooted diffidence and preclusion towards human figures, the decided lack of interest in story-telling, and the taste for antique commemoration in reference to iconographic and formal models of specifically Roman–classical, late antique, and early Christian tradition.

This was in perfect harmony with the ideology of the papacy, in its tendency towards a conservation of the decorative types and formulae already reworked and consolidated, and in its attachment to the familiar craft tradition from which no artistic personalities seemed to emerge that are harmoniously distinct, in the judgment of the critics, for their original stylistic creativity.

The "classicism" of Paschal I in the reuses of the little chapel of St. Zeno constitutes therefore a significant conjecture, but one not sufficient to justify the origins and the continuity of an antique-type sculptural tradition, whose traces up to the second half of the twelfth century seem lost. The question of the most immediate precedents of Cosmatesque production remains open. In particular, what is still the object of study is the problem of the paucity and stylistic and qualitative heterogeneity of its sculptural testimonies, dating, among the various hypotheses, not only from the period of general crisis of the papacy, between the end of the ninth century and the mid-eleventh century, but above all between the last quarter of the eleventh century and the end of the next, when the first Cosmatesque works appeared. The gap is more evident if it is linked to the significant architectural and pictorial works created in Rome in just this period, around 1100, in order to represent symbolically and ideologically the political and religious fervor connected to the reform of the Church and the investiture contest (the struggle for power between the papacy and the Holy Roman Empire).

Based on these considerations, the traditional thesis recognizes the impulse deriving from the reconstruction of the abbey of Monte Cassino by Desiderio, which is clearly identifiable in Rome in the rebirth of architecture and mosaic, as the origin of the antique taste of Cosmatesque production—particularly the obvious classical-type accents in the iconography and the compositional balance of the decoration of the three facade portals, rebuilt on the basis of surviving fragments and reproductions. Between the two despoiled cornices of the lateral portals, the central one shows up as created for the occasion, returning to and reworking originally the Roman motif of lacunars in the elegant succession of molded lozenges with sculptured flowers in the center, against a mosaic background.

According to recent studies, however, on its own Monte Cassino does not fully use up the definition of the presuppositions of subsequent developments in Roman sculpture. Above all it does not justify the figurative aspects which, even if limited, are nevertheless well-represented, as shall be seen, in Cosmatesque work, starting with the paschal candlestick of San Paolo fuori le Mura from the end of the twelfth century. In order to define the framework of the evidence of the eleventh and twelfth centuries, it is necessary therefore to consider—albeit briefly, and without going into complex reconstruction and chronological problems—that group of works which has been re-evaluated by recent criticism and recognized as works preceding, or contemporary with, the artistic climate of the age of Pope Gregory.

A first appearance of figured motifs is evident in works such as the tenth-century wellhead of the church of San Bartolomeo on the Tiber Island, unique in Rome for the return to Carolingian models in the elegant and complex bas-reliefs which represent, between rich shrines, Christ, St. Paolinus of Nola, St. Bartholomew, and Otto III, or the altar-reliquary of Santa Maria del Priorato, which has on one side the symbols of the Evangelists on the four corners of the cross, and on the front the early Christian motifs of the Lamb of God (*Agnus Dei*) and the door, framed by vinescrolls.

A first significant Roman revision of the early Christian theme of the inhabited vinescroll, in line with the ideological and cultural program of the reforming papacy, is encountered, however, on the surviving group of fragmentary, newly handled, and decontextualized cornices relating to the portals of the churches of San Giorgio al Velabro, Santa Maria in Cosmedin, Santa Maria in Trastevere, Santo Stefano degli Abissini, Santa Pudenziana, and Sant'Apollinare. Apart from the obvious heterogeneity of the delivery and the various hypotheses regarding dating, the cornices have in common the decoration of spirals of vinescroll, often interrupted by animal motifs, simple figured representations of clipeated pictures.

Among the others, because of the elegant naturalistic sensitivity of the reliefs of late antique influence and their classic compositional balance, the fragmentary cornices of Santa Pudenziana and Sant'Apollinare stand out, among the prototypes of the Romanesque portal with vegetable spirals. On the basis of reconstructions, these present a similar composition of vinescrolls interrupted by clipeated busts representing, in the first case, the Lamb of God and Sts. Pudenziana, Prassede, Pastore, and Pudente and, in the second, Christ and Sts. Peter and Apollinaris. The fragments of the cornice of Santa Pudenziana can today be seen as the architrave of the portal of the church, while the seven fragments of the cornice of Sant'Apollinare, recently attributed to an entrance on the right of St. Peter's leading to an oratory of the same name, can now be seen in room seven in the Vatican Grottos.

Both works, linked by iconographic and stylistic affinities, have thus been dated to the end of the eleventh century and placed, along with the frescos in San Clemente, as a direct reflection of the Gregorian culture of reform. They help make the artistic manifestations of the period clearer and more faceted, and therefore, in their shared ideological reference to early Christian models, they are inserted as an alternative testimony into the Cosmatesque milieu, which would come to maturity in the coming decades because of two factors: the recovery of their own early medieval traditions and, above all, more or less direct contact with the most up-to-date Byzantine craftsmen who were working at Monte Cassino.

From these in particular, in parallel with the discovery of mosaic, the recovery of the antique *opus sectile* (mosaic or paving of thin pieces of colored marble cut in geometrical shapes) in numerous floor decorations of the first half of the twelfth century is derived, directly connected to the origins of the taste for polychrome ornamentation and marble inlay or mosaic insertions, which became almost synonymous with it, characterizing all Cosmatesque production. In reality, the activity of the *magistri doctissimi romani*—of whom the Cosmati were just one of five or six families in a total of about sixty craftsmen working between the twelfth and thirteenth centuries—was not limited to this certainly typical decoration but comprised an intense architectural production, distinguished by the modernization of structural typologies, both installations, such as cloisters, porticos, and belltowers, and liturgical furnishings, such as tabernacles, bishops' thrones, candelabra, and tombs.

Furthermore, their traditional role as stonecutters did not end in the inheritance of the organized workshops, which monopolized the despoiling and reuse of antique marble, even if the symbolic value of the materials used fulfilled an important role in that recovery of a sense of Romanness, of which they, with pride, considered themselves the creators and interpreters. A result of this mature awareness is the new interest of the marbleworkers in antique models, which were not only reused but closely studied and imitated (as is demonstrated by the Ionic capitals in San Lorenzo fuori le Mura) or reworked to create a "medieval antique," as attested by the mosaic insertions in the two panels of John II on the frontal of the San Clemente *schola cantorum.*

Is it possible to speak of sculptors, or were they just competent artisan decorators who restricted themselves to applying some sculptural relief to architectural structures, showing little interest in the sculptural development of the forms or in human representations and narrative scenes? This is the question that has been asked by some historians on the basis of a comparison with contemporary Romanesque production in other areas of Italy and areas north of the Alps.

The negative judgment of reduced and late development deriving from this can be overcome in part only by considering the general closed nature of Roman circles to external cultural imports and its conservative ideological language, which for the whole course of the Middle Ages, and in the different arts, was renewed only through successive and modernized recoveries to its own antique and early Christian tradition. In the expectation of broader comparisons, which will also include those with contemporary realizations in other materials such as wood or plaster, most studies complete the picture of possible justifications by calling upon the above-mentioned theory of "false idols," according to which since its earliest days the Roman Church, for fear of idolatrous interpretations, had forbidden all images which could not be distinguished unequivo-cally for their apotropaic value—precisely those lions, sphinxes, masks, and corbel heads that appear in Cosmatesque work. It is not by chance that it was just to these images, which stand out for their sculptural and formal autonomy and their exceptional expressive vigor, that the artistic restoration of the Roman marble-workers was entrusted, in a position to express themselves also as sculptors on those rare occasions, and in the specific ways, in which this was permitted to them.

The *Magistri Doctissimi Romani*

In order not to enter into diverse and complex problems of attribution and dating, only some of the more typical works of the vast and diver-sified artistic Cosmatesque production will be examined here. For convenience and clarity of exposition, they will be presented in accordance with a typological evolutionary criterion, without necessarily respecting their chronological order or location.

After the liturgical reform of 1095, in which Urban II introduced obligatory choral singing for all clergy, the building of *scholae cantorum* was encouraged and, with them, the complete renewal of church furnishings. To the central enclosure, candelabra for the paschal (Easter) candle, and two ambos (pulpits) were connected. The ambo where the Epistle was read was simpler; that where the Gospel was read was more complex, with a double ramp and projecting lectern. This pattern was immediately adopted, as is clear from the twelfth-century examples in Santa Maria in Cosmedin and San Clemente. The same type of furnishing with enclosure panels, ambos, and candelabra, to which in the presbytery were linked the altar, the tabernacle, and the bishop's chair, remained practically unchanged in the work of the Roman marble-workers for more than a century and a half.

A later, more monumental version is found in the divided remains of the original arrangement of San Lorenzo fuori le Mura, referring to two successive work campaigns. The first, linked to

One of the two ambos of San Lorenzo fuori le Mura, part of the liturgical ensemble in this famous place of pilgrimage. The basilica was renovated under Innocent IV (1243–54); the two ambos, the bishop's throne and an Easter candlestick were executed in Cosmati work.

Honorius III (1216–27) and the marbleworkers of the Vassalletto family, includes, apart from the portico and the capitals of the nave, the rich plutei visible at the sides of the bishop's chair and the two lions' heads at the edges of the chancel benches.

The second, associated with Innocent IV (1243–54), refers to the bishop's chair and the two ambos. The ambos, like the enclosure panels of San Lorenzo, bear witness to the evolution in a monumental sense of the typology and the development of a more complex, regular ordering of decoration, composed of geometrical shapes in porphyry and serpentine between alternating marble and mosaic frames and cornices, enriched with elegant sculptured ornamental motifs. The plutei are crowned by an architrave supported by newel posts and small spiral columns, in accordance with a pattern which found reflection in the similar panels presently in the wall in the right aisle of Santa Saba, which belonged to the enclosure of the iconostasis and was also carried out by the Vassalletto workshop in the second quarter of the thirteenth century.

However, linked to the families of the first generation of marbleworkers—and fundamental for their precocity and quality of their work—are two examples of works, for the development of their relative typologies: the San Lorenzo tabernacle and the San Paolo fuori le Mura candelabra.

The first, signed by Paolo's sons—Giovanni, Pietro, Angelo, and Sasso—and dated to 1148, is one of the rare surviving original testimonies of the structural evolution immediately preceding the innovations of Arnolfo di Cambio. The tabernacle, placed on four columns, has two galleries of small superimposed columns with an architrave and is crowned by a truncated pyramid-shaped cover on an octagonal base, with an upper lantern pierced in turn by columns and a pyramidal termination.

The spread in Rome and the surrounding region of this new typology, deriving from the early twelfth-century simplified model of San Clemente and based on the recovery of the architraved structure and cage cover probably of early Christian origin, is due to the ancient and well-known family of the Cosmati. It is difficult to reconstruct precisely possible prototypes and early medieval developments of the tabernacle, both because the sources—while attesting to its ample diffusion in Rome from the fourth century and the richness of the materials used—do not provide precise structural indications, as well as because, as has been seen, the testimonies of slabs from the eighth and ninth centuries are fragmentary and out of context.

FOLLOWING PAGES:
The richly decorated balustrade on either side of the bishop's throne, or cathedra, in San Lorenzo was made by the Vassalletto family of marbleworkers under Honorius III (1216–27).

Aspects of the color and form of the bishop's throne in San Lorenzo—such as the use of mosaic discs and canopy—attest to the maturity of thirteenth-century sculpture in Rome.

257

OPPOSITE:
The complex iconographic program of
the Easter candlestick of San Paolo is
situated 5.6m above the ground, and
combines depictions of plants and
animals with more complicated
figurative scenes illustrating the Passion
and Resurrection of Christ.

BELOW:
The Easter candlestick in San Paolo
fuori le Mura, signed by Niccoló
d'Angelo and Pietro Vassalletto, with its
richly decorated shaft, is a rare example
of this kind of liturgical object from the
end of the twelfth to the beginning of
the thirteenth century.

It is, however, to the classic models of pagan
candelabra that the structure of the San Paolo
paschal candlestick refers, although this was not
at the origin of the new typology expressed in
the numerous subsequent examples of more
simple spiral columns, decorated with mosaic
insertions and at times accompanied on the
base with sphinxes or lions. It is an extraordinary and unique testimony of its type in
Rome, above all for the early dating, between
the end of the twelfth and the beginning of the
thirteenth century, and for the exceptional
sculptural decoration. This is arranged between
eight superimposed registers in which the high
(seventeen-foot) shaft is subdivided in accordance with a complex iconographical program,
which marries the themes of monastic patronage
with the specific symbolism of furnishing created
for the liturgy of Holy Saturday, alluding to the
cathartic progression from obscurity of demoniac
figures and pagan presences from the base to
the light of the resurrection on Easter Day, in an
intertwined complex of elaborate references
precisely from the world of the Benedictine
monastery of Monte Cassino.

On the wide base are four richly attired
women, alternating with sphinxes, rams, and
lions, interpreted in symbolic and ideological
style, projecting from the background. Four registers of similar dimensions follow. The first has
intertwined plants and animal insertions while
the other three develop in sculptural relief
scenes of Christ's Passion and Resurrection. A
wide fascia, divided into two sectors by a central enlargement and decorated with picturesque vinescrolls, precedes the last level with
eight monstrous sculpted animals which support the cup of the candle holder.

The authorship of the work, like its date,
is linked to an inscription beneath the Christ
cycle with the names of the sculptors: Niccolò
d'Angelo, who was the son of one of the
above-mentioned sculptors of the San Lorenzo
tabernacle, and Pietro Vassalletto, recognized as
active in the cloister of St. John Lateran and
perhaps also in the cloister of San Paolo fuori le
Mura. The concept of the work is unanimously
attributed to Pietro Vassalletto, while the
attribution of the different parts remains
controversial since other works definitely by
Niccolò d'Angelo with which it would be
possible to make comparisons are not known.

What is certain, however, is the direct reference to classical and early Christian models in
the compositional organization of the scenes,
the sculptural rendering of the reliefs which
betrays the use of the drill, and the consistent
stylistic seeking after pictorial effects and movement, as in the frequent citations of typological
and iconographic character. The work is to be

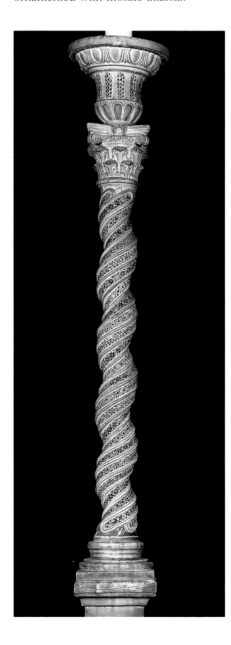

placed, therefore, at a formal level among the most complete testimonies of the sculptural, figurative, and narrative capabilities of Roman marbleworkers. Equally, it is charged with liturgical, symbolical, and ideological value in relation to the specific nature of the commission, linked to the first manifestations at Monte Cassino of the demands of the reforming papacy.

The type of furnishing in which these demands found most obvious expression is, however, the bishop's chair. In Rome this assumed the specific prerogative of the symbolic incarnation of papal authority, founded on *sanctitas* (sanctity) and the *imperium* (temporal authority) on the basis of the affirmation of the dual spiritual and temporal inheritance of the papacy, consciously elaborated in the Donation of Constantine and developed further in the dictates of the *dictatus papae* (papal claims; 1075) of Gregory VII.

From the earliest examples, in San Clemente and Santa Maria in Cosmedin, bishops' chairs were meaningful references both to the early Christian age-evoking memories of martyrs, saints, and reminding the beholder of the direct descendence of the first popes from Peter—and also to the symbolism of the secular power, present in the attributes of the imperial emblems, such as the lions or the sphinxes used in Roman imperial decoration.

The most complete iconographic elaborations can be seen in the examples at Santa Saba (1205) and Santa Maria in Trastevere (1215), attributed in different ways to Jacopo di Lorenzo, founder of an active workshop operating in the first three decades of the thirteenth century, at the same time as the Vassalletto workshop mentioned earlier.

In Santa Saba, evidence can be seen crowning the dossal, of a marble disk decorated in mosaic with a central palmate cross, an explicit reference to the cruciform halo of Christ and thus to the divine origins of papal power. In Santa Maria in Trastevere the development of the iconography of the armrests is associated to the simpler reintroduction of the plain unadorned disk. This iconography substitutes for the usual lions two elegant full figures of winged and horned lions, alluding to flight and thus to the glorification of the ruler, according with Hellenic models which are returned to here in testimony of the specific supernatural dimension of the authority of the pope as vicar of Christ.

In subsequent examples from the mid-thirteenth century in Santa Balbina and San Lorenzo, the symbolic evidence faded, favoring the development of polychrome decoration, which retained, however, the halo-disk in the central position, adding a trilobed crowning to

give the idea of a baldacchino, again a reference to the attributes of rule.

A precise antiquarian symbolism is assumed also by the two different types of burial monument which were introduced and developed from the eleventh century onwards, that is, reused antique sarcophaguses and wall tombs, excluding the earth graves predominating in the preceding centuries, even for popes. The reuse of classical marble sarcophaguses is clearly linked to the ideology of *spolia*, which was probably extended to burials since they were included in those imperial insignia due to the pontiff in accordance with the *dictatus papae*. This practice is attested to from the mid-eleventh century, with the tomb of Leo IX (1054). In the twelfth century it was made even more explicit with the reuse of porphyry examples taken from imperial burial places, as in the striking case of the sarcophagus of Hadrian, removed from Castel Sant'Angelo for the tomb of Innocent II (1143), once in St. John Lateran but now lost. Also based on the fusion of elements of antique origin was the new structure of wall tombs which, from the first developments of the beginning of the twelfth century leading from the tomb of Cardinal Alfano (1123) in the portico of Santa Maria in Cosmedin developed a tripartite structure. On to the base sarcophagus was superimposed a figured lunette, deriving from the catacomb model of *arcosolium* tombs

Decorated spandrel of the cloister of San Paolo fuori le Mura, depicting a "wolf at school". The wolf, disguised as a monk, is attempting to learn the alphabet. The moral of this scene was intended as a warning to the monks not to allow themselves to be distracted by worldly thoughts while praying.

(niches topped with an arch) and thus a gabled cover on small columns, deriving from the classical shrine.

This essential pattern would survive until the later thirteenth-century, pre-Gothic examples, among which is the tomb of Cardinal Fieschi (1256) in San Lorenzo fuori le Mura, which reunites and combines the two models developed earlier, composing them to form the basic structure in which successive revolutionizing contributions would intervene. Here the motif of the classical nuptial sarcophagus, symbolically reused, is inserted in the inside of the wall type, formed by frescos (lost), showing the presentation of the deceased man to Christ, and by the triangular gable cover, enriched by the architraved baldacchino motif with a gallery of small columns inspired by the structure of contemporary tabernacles, like that described above inside the same church.

The successive evolution of funerary typology in works by Arnolfo di Cambio, with the introduction of the recumbent figure on the sarcophagus and the Gothic development of the architectural complex, would be mediated by the contribution of French models in the tomb of Clement IV (about 1270) in San Francesco in Viterbo. These were ascribed to Pietro d'Oderisio, who was a Roman sculptor, probably with a wide range of production, but as yet not well defined by historians.

The list of examples of the different typologies of furnishing renewed in the structure and decoration of the work of Roman marbleworkers is concluded here with an examination of the cloisters of St. John Lateran and San Paolo fuori le Mura, constructions of more specifically architectural nature but characterized by the introduction of numerous sculptural reliefs—or more correctly, sculptured relief—together with rich polychrome ornamentation of the common Cosmatesque repertory.

The decorative program of the cloister of St. John Lateran, carried out together with the structural program between 1215 and 1232, included, apart from the pedestals, small columns, and mainly composite-type capitals, various figured examples. The upper pendentives contain a rich series of bas-reliefs with plant and animal motifs and numerous figures, of which only one depicts a biblical subject (that of Original Sin), while all the others derive from classical mythology, alluding generally to the contrast between good and evil. Three fascias decorated with mosaic and marble follow, the first two superimposed, and the third preceded and supported by a thick line of small corbels with leaves. Crowning the whole is an exuberance of sculptural plant braids from which, at regular intervals, emerge the heads of lions and grotesque human heads, almost fully in the round. The picture is completed by sculptured pairs of lions and sphinxes which flank the three openings of the podium towards the central garden.

An inscription on one of the pillars of the south side attributes the work to two members of the Vassalletto family, father and son, without stating their exact identity. In the first some critics have recognized the Pietro Vassalletto of the San Paolo fuori le Mura candlestick, subsequently active in the narthex of San Lorenzo fuori le Mura, dated to the papacy of Honorius III (1216–27).

Beyond the specific attributive hypotheses, however, the stylistic and formal characteristics, evident above all in the sculptural decoration of the cloister, confirm the presence of two distinct personalities. The "father" would have carried out the whole of the podium, including the lions and the sphinxes, as well as the north and east sides. The other two sides would have been brought to completion by Vassalletto, "the son." The reliefs of the first sculptor are distinguished by a greater creative variety of iconographic motifs in heavily populated and exuberant decoration, by their more marked expressive characterization of the heads on the cornices, and by the more meticulous care for detail in the relief carried out with soft and vigorous carving. The second style, while in the simplification of the ornamental repertory, develops instead greater formal elegance of classical taste in the essential but effective delivery of the relief in clear projection from the background, and in the more sober and airy compositions.

Historians have recognized the work of this same Vassalletto "son" inside the cloister of San Paolo fuori le Mura, in particular in the execution of the north side, finally realized between 1230 and 1235 and clearly distinct in its characteristic decoration from the other three sides, which pertain to a first period of work dating from around 1210. The general concept of the structural complex and its ornament is similar to that of the Lateran cloister, but despite the notable evolutionary divergence of the different phases, more declaredly classical taste is encountered there.

This is already visible in the first timid appearance of grooves on the newel posts and marbled panels in the under-arches of the most archaic sides (east, south, west), features of the general simplification of the polychrome ornament and relief, limited to the monotonous succession of lions' heads on the cornice and the almost graphic formal rendering of the capitals.

A clearer and more coherent antiquarian accent, however, informs the whole decoration

Another moral lesson on the dangers of secular life can be seen in a different spandrel of the same cloister. It shows the chimaera, a mythological beast composed of a lion, a goat, and a snake.

265

The ciborium over the altar of San Paolo fuori le Mura dates from 1285 and is the earliest piece that can be attributed with any certainty to Arnolfo di Cambio's Roman period. It combines architectural, sculptural and painted elements from a variety of sources to create a highly innovative work of the Gothic type. The corner figure visible here is the Apostle Paul, the patron saint of the basilica.

FOLLOWING PAGES:
LEFT:
In his work on the ciborium in San Paolo, Arnolfo di Cambio was assisted by a number of colleagues. Foremost among them was the "socio Petro" ("colleague Peter") mentioned in the inscription on the ciborium, who is thought to have created the elegant figurative capital below the depiction of St. Timothy.

RIGHT:
The statue of St. Benedict from the ciborium in San Paolo.

of the most recent north side and the spans adjacent to it. These are decorations that are taken up again and develop the iconographic motifs and formal solutions of the Lateran cloister—the figured capitals, the sculptural ornament of the pendentives with subjects of decorative character or allusions to moralizing themes, the spreading of soft vinescroll on the top with, at regular intervals, the clear emergence of the animal heads or the three naturalistic human heads. Innovative solutions are numerous, such as the grooves on the half-pilasters and the classic caisson motif with central rosettes in the under-arches, the placing of the bas-reliefs also on the pendentives turning towards the inside of the ambulatory, the insertion of small sculpted animals among the bases, the introduction of subjects such as the chimera or the wolf scene, where were unknown in Rome, but widespread in the repertory of medieval sculpture.

In the absence of precise documentary sources, the determining of the possible sculptors of the two subsequent interventions in the cloister is based mainly on technical and stylistic analysis, and has thus been found to be more complex and controversial for the more archaic, the less characterized, parts of the east, south, and west sides. Recent hypotheses propose Niccolò d'Angelo and Pietro Vassalletto, already active in the workshop in San Paolo on the paschal candlestick.

Very differently outlined and harmonious, however, is the attribution of the north side to Vassalletto, the son of Pietro, whose work can already be recognized in the decoration of the south and west sides of the cloister of St. John Lateran. To the stringent affinities with the formal characteristics shown in this is added a more finished evolutionary synthesis that binds together the antiquarian traditionalism of the quotations and a mature recovery of classical naturalism to the conciseness of the clear and decisive inlay and the essentiality of a typically medieval sculptural rendering.

These works of the 1230s mark a point of arrival in the formal research on the Roman marbleworkers, who reached the highest point of their originality in the creation of what has been defined "medieval antique," in direct relation with the strong ideological thrust which gave life to the theocratic affirmation of the papacies of Innocent III and Honorius III.

In the subsequent realizations leading up to the advent of Arnolfo di Cambio, like the untidily recomposed furnishings in San Cesareo, at the same time as the decrease in political tension, occurred a corresponding reduction in the expression of images in a phenomenon of self-quotation and a repetition of by now codified typologies, in which the only evidence

CVMSVOSO
O PETRO

267

of development is seen in the increased richness of the materials and the chromatic and decorative effects.

The final Cosmatesque work, which will be dealt with later, took place in the last two decades of the thirteenth century, before the papacy's move to Avignon in 1309. It is represented mainly by some exponents of the Mellini family who knew how to express the taste and more limited requirements of their patrons in a moderate updating of traditional typologies.

Arnolfo di Cambio

At the beginning of the thirteenth century, Roman artistic culture opened up to profound and radical renewal. While reaffirming the ideological constants that had characterized its evolution in the course of the Middle Ages, it was now ready for fertile contact with the most modern and revolutionary lines of development in Italian and European art. The indisputable protagonist of this renewal was Arnolfo di Cambio, sculptor, architect, and perhaps painter. Arnolfo was born in Colle Val d'Elsa in Tuscany between 1240 and 1245. His training was complex and was strengthened by contact with the most modern workshops—the Cistercian craftsmen active on Siena Cathedral— and thus, indirectly, with the classicism of the artistic culture of Frederick II, with the *Rayonnant* Gothic style that developed in the cathedrals of the Ile de France around the years 1270 and 1280, and, above all, with the original synthesis of these same factors worked on by the sculpture of Nicola Pisano and his followers, among whom Arnolfo himself is documented between 1265 and 1268.

The first knowledge of Arnolfo's presence in Rome is linked to the figure of Charles of Anjou. Arnolfo may have been in Rome as early as 1270, since in 1277 a formal request was made for him to go to work on a fountain for the government of Perugia, of which the surviving sculpture is now in the National Gallery of Umbria in Perugia. However, all the indisputable testimonies to Arnolfo's activity in Rome are placed after the execution in 1282 of the tomb of Cardinal de Braye in San Domenico in Orvieto, in the last two decades of the century, when the sculptor reached his stylistic maturity and had obtained patronage of the greatest prestige.

Rome must have exercised a strong cultural stimulus on Arnolfo, bringing him into contact with the numerous vestiges of antique sculpture, early Christian sculpture, the original permeation of architectural, sculptural, and coloristic values in the works of the marbleworkers, and, not least, with the direct influence of French Gothic architecture recognized in the workyard of Santa Maria in Aracoeli and leading to the presence of the Angevin court and the succession of popes from beyond the Alps in the third quarter of the century.

The San Paolo fuori le Mura Tabernacle

The quotation and development of these different contributions is clear in the tabernacle of San Paolo fuori le Mura, the first documented work of Arnolfo in Rome, attested to by three inscriptions on the main elevation towards the entrance. The central inscription is dated 1285 and identifies the patron as the Abbot Bartolomeo, who between 1282 and 1297 ruled the Benedictine monastery next to the basilica. The two lateral panels reveal the paternity of the work: *Hoc opus fecit Arnolfus cum suo socio Petro* (Arnolfo and his partner Pietro sculpted this work).

The concept of the tabernacle and the execution of various parts of the unmistakable stylistic stamp have therefore been attributed to Arnolfo. The definition of the workshop interventions has remained problematic, above all in relation to the uncertainty of the identity of the "partner Pietro" and his role in the realization of the whole. Critics, in the absence of definitive historical documentary proof, waver between the traditional identification with Pietro Cavallini, who in those same years had worked on San Paolo, and Pietro d'Oderisio, mentioned above, sculptor of the tomb of Clement IV at Viterbo.

The tabernacle, above the main altar with the relics of St. Paul, appears profoundly innovative compared with the previously developed typology, due to the original and harmonious composition of architectural, sculptural, and pictorial elements, and also because of its adoption of the elements and stylistic features peculiar to Gothic *Rayonnant* taste.

The work, on a square plan, appears to be crowned by a rich endowment of spires, pinnacles, and gables, culminating in the base of the dome which concludes all the linear tension and the upward slope of the single structural and decorative elements. The sides are marked by four gables decorated with Gothic leaves, pierced by the same number of small rose windows supported by pairs of angels in flight against a background of mosaic and polychrome marble.

Beneath are four acute trefoil arches, at the sides of which, in the pendentives issuing from

The recumbent figure of the notary
Annibaldi, removed from its original
context. Rome, St. John Lateran.

the mosaic background, are arranged figures in relief: Abbot Bartolomeo, who offers a model of the tabernacle to St. Paul, Adam and Eve, the prophets David and Solomon unwinding scrolls, and Cain and Abel sacrificing. At the corners, almost in the round, rise the majestic figures of Sts. Peter, Paul, Timothy, and Benedict. They are counterbalanced on the inside of the structure on the same level, by four angels, two of which are in flight from above with censers and two are standing holding candelabra. Apart from the angels, the internal decoration has at the top of the ribbed cross an ostentatious keystone formed by a plant roundel surrounded by the busts of four angels with open wings. The walls are enriched by mosaic decoration with figures of animals inside clipei. The four base capitals complete the structure. One, figured, is attributed, together with the keystone, to "the partner Pietro," as well as the columns which were substituted for the porphyry originals during the restoration that took place after the fire of 1823, which destroyed the basilica.

At that time, the tabernacle, which fortunately suffered minimal damage concentrated in particular on the supports and the crowning, was dismantled and reconstructed. Observation of the back of the panels revealed an ample reuse of antique marble that had been reworked on the rough side. This detail, even if it fits into the common Roman practice of reuse, reflects the complex framework of cultural quotations and ideological cross-references present in Arnolfo's work. Among these, the reference to the antique is apparent, for example in the direct recovery of the classical winged victory motif in the angels holding the clipeus, and in the choice of triangular gable, in addition to, stylistically, the formal balance of the four corner saints, certainly the work of Arnolfo.

The use of polychrome figured mosaic rich with early Christian motifs, was widespread in the Romanesque tradition in central and southern Italy, just as the placing of mosaic next to sculptural relief was developed by Roman marbleworkers and thus added to their value. Arnolfo, a Tuscan, thus showed that he knew about abstract graphic and geometrical intellectualism and the dematerializing and vertical tension of French Gothic, but he translated this into a more solid and calm whole, in which the straight line prevailed over the arch and the capable integration of the structural, sculptural, and decorative elements combined to create a new typology of tabernacle that was no longer a simple liturgical furnishing but possessed a well-defined individuality of its own and an architectural autonomy in space.

The Tomb of Riccardo Annibaldi

Chronologically, the next stage in Arnolfo's artistic journey is the tomb of the notary Riccardo Annibaldi, executed in St. John Lateran after Annibaldi's death in 1289, according to information recently acquired. The work has been passed down as fragmentary and decontextualized, and has been the object of long and complex study directed towards the plausible reconstruction of the original and a dating consistent with the evolution of Arnolfo's style and the recognition of the identity of the deceased.

The question is introduced here of the difficulty of reconstruction of Arnolfo's oeuvre, owing to the fragmentary state in which numerous works have reached us, a situation even more deplorable, as it concerns a sculptor who expressed a substantial part of his own personality in the creation of complex spatial links between sculpture, architectural structures, and the scenographic and optical perspective of which these were part.

Of the Annibaldi tomb remain the recumbent figure and a frieze, divided into two panels of mosaic background on which, one after the other, rhythmically spaced, are six clerics and a bishop celebrating a liturgical service, a mass for the deceased, according to what has been

hypothesized on the basis of the request in a funerary inscription relating to the notary Annibaldi, visible in the cloister of St. John Lateran and connected with the tomb.

A plausible reconstruction of the whole has been arrived at through a comparison of the surviving elements with the funerary typologies widespread in those years, and, above all, through the observation of the formal characteristics of execution of the relief. In this, as in all other works that are definitely by Arnolfo on which it is possible to carry out close analysis, an attentive optical study on the part of Arnolfo has been noted, which is proceeded by carefully refining only the parts directly visible to the spectator, leaving the others roughly drafted. All this took place in accordance with an operating procedure which was both rigorous and systematic. It has been called a "criterion of visibility" and has been ascribed to the characteristic style of Arnolfo.

Study of the unworked parts of the Annibaldi relief has thus made it possible to establish that it was a tomb with walls. The figure of the deceased was framed by two raised curtains and sloped steeply towards the spectator. In an upper position, and in consistent relation with the optical axes of the recumbent figure, there must have been the two panels of the frieze, which were arranged at right angles to form

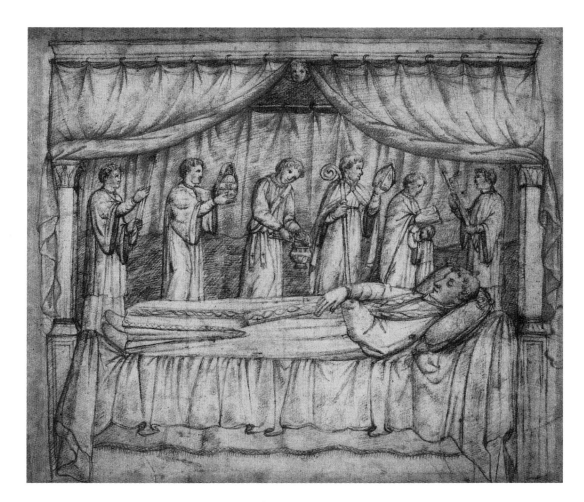

Another of Arnolfo di Cambio's works is known only from fragments—the Nativity scene in Santa Maria Maggiore, which dates from 1291. The two standing figures of the Magi have been attributed to di Cambio's colleagues, as they differ in style from the figures of Joseph and the kneeling king.

between them a sort of caisson with the cleric candelabra-holder of the minor panel on the short side. The low unfinished parts of the frieze, and the consequent disproportion and greater projection of the heads of the persons, are thus attributable to the high position and the visibility of the "caisson" from below, apart from the presence of the small columns in the ample spaces between the figures, forming an inhabited gallery in accordance with models once again derived from the court style of French Gothic.

Various components of Arnolfo's artistic language recur therefore in the Annibaldi tomb. It is especially from sculpture progressing at the same time in workyards beyond the Alps that the sensitive attention to realistic information that Arnolfo absorbed and then reworked in his very personal style—of which there is particular evidence in this work—took its inspiration.

What strikes the observer is the spontaneity of the movements, poses, and attitudes of the figures in the funeral ceremony. The liveliness of the gestures and the clearly intended portraiture, recognizable above all in the faces of both the bishop celebrating mass and the deceased, marry together perfectly and indeed increase the credibility and solemnity of the rite, so that, as in Gothic naturalism, it is fused and substantiated by Arnolfo with the classic composure and monumentality of the volume, the balance and rhythm of the movement and composition, as well as the organized synthesis of line in the treatment of the drapery and the hair.

Finally, the structural and compositional variants that Arnolfo introduced into the development of tomb typology seem significant, in the same way as it was being revised previously, in relation to his first interpretation in the de Braye tomb in Orvieto. Where the recumbent figure tended to be placed low down and the theophanic representation in a higher position, in the Annibaldi tomb—going by the reconstructions—this latter was lacking altogether and was substituted at the top of the composition by a liturgical ceremony made real by the naturalistic rendering of the personalities. As has been underlined in recent studies, the representation of death is humanized and the daily joining together in commemorative celebration is substituted for the intercession of the saints, involving, with the immediate expressiveness of the images, real space and the compassionate participation of the observer.

The Santa Maria Maggiore Chapel of the Relics

The evolution of the stylistic characteristics until now evidenced in the field of a more ample autonomy of volumetric and spatial relationships is joined in the surviving figures of the nativity scene in the Chapel of the Relics in Santa Maria Maggiore in 1291. The date, which comes to us from sources on the basis of a lost inscription, places the intervention of Arnolfo in the works commissioned in the basilica by Nicholas IV (1288–92). As the first Franciscan pope, Nicholas must have had at heart the reuse of a small ancient chapel, annexed to the right aisle already towards the mid-seventh century to safeguard relics of the Nativity.

The exact reconstruction of Arnolfo's work presents difficulties in this case, too, because of the decontextualized and fragmentary nature of the surviving pieces. During the papacy of Sixtus V (1585–90) the chapel, together with its precious relics, was transferred and adapted for the new Chapel of the Holy Sacrament, built by Domenico Fontana in the right aisle.

Of the sculpted decoration of the original there remains an arcade decorated with two prophets on the mosaic pendentive and arranged to frame the real crypt. Above all— apart from a sixteenth-century Virgin and

The figure of the kneeling king from the Nativity scene in Santa Maria Maggiore is a striking illustration of the expressive values which characterize Arnolfo di Cambio's personal style.

OPPOSITE PAGE:
In his altar ciborium for Santa Cecilia in Trastevere of 1293, Arnolfo di Cambio once again adopted the design he had developed for San Paolo fuori le Mura. Compared with its predecessor, however, the Gothic elements of his work in Santa Cecilia are more restrained.

The figures of the ciborium of Santa Cecilia are allowed a greater degree of independence from their architectural frame, as can be seen here in the mounted figure of St. Tiburtius.

Child—there are figures of St. Joseph, the Magi, and the ox and the ass in a niche at the end of the ambulatory. Of the rich Cosmatesque decoration, testified to by sources and probably predating the work of Arnolfo, an altar frontal and a porphyry roundel on the floor are still conserved.

The attribution of this work to Arnolfo dates from Vasari and is still now accepted by critics insofar as the general concept of the project is concerned. This, in consistent evolution with Arnolfo's stereometric and spatial interests, had by now freed sculpture almost completely from architectural support, and arranged it freely within a consciously calculated setting which related elements to each other and to the beholder. Not by chance, just as the two standing Magi have been attributed to a different member of the workshop, so the St. Joseph and, especially, the kneeling king, because of their unmistakable stylistic characteristics, have been attributed to Arnolfo himself. They present that typical use of the "criterion of visibility" which plays such a large part in the hypothetical reconstruction of the original ensemble.

According to the most recent studies, the characters of the scene were arranged by Arnolfo in a dialectic relationship with the background niche on the altar of the ancient chapel. The Virgin and Child would have thus occupied the center of the scene, represented, in accordance with the usual iconography of the period of Syrian–Byzantine origin, in a semi-recumbent position on a couch, with the ox and the little donkey on the left in a small cavity. Turned towards the Virgin, on the right of the niche, would have been the kneeling king. St. Joseph and the two standing Magi would have framed the scene on the outside walls, positioned on the left and right respectively. The whole would have then been framed by a baldacchino crowned at the top by a low arcade with the prophets (which may also have been outside the chapel towards the nave).

The Santa Cecilia Tabernacle

The tabernacle on the altar of Santa Cecilia in Trastevere seems to be complete in its state of conservation. According to a recently discovered inscription, it was made by Arnolfo in 1293. It forms part of the final moment of an ample and consistent effort at restoration of the entire decorative system of the church of Santa Cecilia, which included the well-known Cavallini frescos, the liturgical furnishings, and sculptural ornament.

The obvious Gothic *Rayonnant* character of this revision has recently been attributed to the

patronage of a French cardinal, while the direction of the whole project has been attributed to Arnolfo, who, working in the last decades of the thirteenth century in the service of the major families, the new preaching orders, and the popes, without a shadow of doubt dominated the panorama of the most innovative Roman trends in the artistic field.

The tabernacle repeats the structural complex and decorative scheme of the San Paolo fuori le Mura tabernacle but simplifies and strengthens the Gothic forms, creating a new proportional balance between the parts and reworking the concept of the whole in the light of a more mature assimilation of the classical references. With respect to his first interpretation in *Rayonnant* taste, here Arnolfo reduced and redirected the ascending elements of the base of the cupola and the pendentives of the crown, and in addition attenuated the vertical soaring of the four gables and the trefoil arcades of the baldacchino, but created a notable development in the height of the supporting columns, to which he also added the original solution of cube-shaped dosserets, decorated with Cosmatesque mosaic.

Detail of the Santa Cecilia ciborium, showing the particularly innovative use of the base. Arnolfo di Cambio transformed this traditional element into a fragile cube whose outer surfaces are decorated with mosaic circles.

What is unfamiliar is the three-dimensional measurement which can be identified in the relationship between the upper, obliquely cut corners of the baldacchino and the sculpture placed nearby, which acquires—thanks to this new perspective arrangement, greater size, and reduced background of the cover niches—a positioning in space which is still more mature in autonomy and monumentality compared to the corresponding figures of the St. Paolo tabernacle. It is, in particular, the four small statues representing the legend of St. Cecilia—Sts. Cecilia, Valerian, Tiburtius, and Urban—emerging as fulcra of the greater structural, sculptural, and symbolic emphasis of the whole, that underline the general equilibrium of the proportions and, with this, the high quality of sculpted work which is indisputably by Arnolfo.

It is to these that is entrusted the role of documenting the maturing development of Arnolfo's sculpture which, revising its own cultural references in a new synthesis, now freed the volume of architectonic support almost completely, or otherwise framed it in a bold perspective view, as is shown by the celebrated St. Tiburtius on horseback that emerges forcefully in lively projection from the square panel behind it. The equestrian statue of Marcus Aurelius has often been quoted as emblematic testimony of the classical nature of the work, visible in numerous iconographical details as well as in the above-mentioned general balance of the proportions and the sculptural–architectural decoration.

The personal Gothic interpretation of Arnolfo remains significant, however, based on the synthesis of the forms in clear relief and, at the same time, on the tension of the linear outline of the drapery, the profiles, and movements, thanks to which the volumetric, perspective, and dynamic indications of the figures are defined. The remaining sculptural decoration is applied to the mosaic background of the resulting spaces of the complex and includes motifs similar to the San Paolo tabernacle—the angels holding up the rose-windows and the prophets unrolling scrolls—while the figures of the Evangelists and the Wise Virgins of the pendentives stand in contrast, just as the Annunciation and the angel at the base of the newel posts are new.

Here too there is much discussion over the distinction between the signed parts and the interventions by Arnolfo's workshop, whose members must certainly have participated in the execution of the reliefs, as is demonstrated by the more rigid and awkward rendering of the angels holding the rose-window, and the Virgins. To Arnolfo are attributed, apart from the four corner statues that have already been referred to, the reliefs of the four Evangelists and of the two prophets with scrolls in the pendentives. If the first are distinguished for the dynamic freedom of the arrangement of the bodies in space, the second, in the soft pictorial relaxation of the model and the rhythmic sinuosity of the lines, enables us to appreciate the evolution in Arnolfo's style, compared with Nicola Pisano and the similar figures already encountered in the San Paolo tabernacle and the arcade of the Chapel of the Relics in Santa Maria Maggiore.

The Tomb of Boniface VIII

Particularly significant on the plane of historical documentation, let alone typology and style—but bristling with problems because of the reconstruction of a whole that has reached us only fragmentarily and out of context—is the tomb of Boniface VIII, executed by Arnolfo in St. Peter's between 1294 and 1296. The principal remains, at present in the Vatican Grottos, include two angels holding back curtains and the recumbent figure in pontifical robes on the sarcophagus, which is covered with rich draped fabrics and embroidered with the arms of the Caetani family, repeated below in the mosaic of the plinth. Further, a series of architectural and sculptural fragments with Cosmatesque decoration of uncertain provenance survives,

Preserved sections from the funerary chapel of Boniface VIII. The chapel was built under the supervision of Arnolfo di Cambio between 1294 and 1296, and originally formed part of the interior facade of Old St. Peter's. In addition to the recumbent figure of the deceased, there are two angels who originally pulled back a curtain framing the tomb, thus making a uniquely dramatic contribution to the spectacle of the pope's grave. Rome, Vatican Grottos.

The realistic portrayal of Boniface VIII's slackened features is evidence for the rebirth of the genre of portraiture based on living models at the end of the thirteenth century. Rome, Vatican Grottos.

with further complicated attempts at reconstruction of the whole, destroyed in 1605 together with Old St. Peter's, but fortunately documented by a series of different sources, both graphic and documentary.

Based on these, it has been possible to determine the original structure of the tomb. It took the form of a small chapel, placed behind the counter-facade of the early Christian basilica, bounded by an iron enclosure containing at its center an altar dedicated to Pope Boniface IV (608–15). The ceiling of the chapel, consistent with Arnolfo's designs for the dome of the Duomo in Florence, and in evolutionary line with the preceding interpretations in *Rayonnant* Gothic in the San Paolo and Santa Cecilia tabernacles, presented an extrados cupola decorated at the base with a rich gallery of gables and standing on four architraved columns. Inside, on the back wall, opposite the altar and under a mosaic panel, the recumbent figure was placed on the sarcophagus between a niche framed with drapery and flanked by two curtain-holding angels.

The authorship is based on epigraphical sources, referring the mosaic to Jacopo Torriti *pictor* (painter) and the definition of the structural project to Arnolfo *architectus* (architect). Recognition of Arnolfo's hand in the realization of the surviving sculpted parts remains dependent on stylistic and formal analyses. The main difficulties are establishing the effective pertinence to the tomb of the two curtain-holding angels which figure typologically in the iconography of the work as it has come down to us from the graphic sources, but which in the past were referred to the tomb of Nicolas V. Furthermore, they present obvious incongruences and gaps in their formal execution, since once liberated from subsequent additions and mishandling, they both appeared to have an arm missing as well as an edge of a robe and a part of the leg.

That they belong to the chapel of Boniface VIII and are to be attributed to the workshop of Arnolfo has been demonstrated by a close comparison between the three surviving pieces and an analysis of their relationships in general composition and the criteria of the visibility of the work. It was noted that the missing legs of the angels were in exact correspondence and had been planned deliberately to allow the recumbent figure below to be lodged in them. In the same way, the two arms that would have been covered by the curtains were not actually made. The use of these characteristic deformations seems quite obvious, and was carried to the extreme in the recumbent figure, in which every detail seems to have been meticulously studied and realized more or less accurately in function of a highly calculated study of visual perspective.

The consistent concept of the architectural and sculptural work in function of the direct involvement of the beholder in a spatial perspective of scenic and symbolic nature had already been experimented with by Arnolfo, respectively in the Chapel of the Relics in Santa Maria Maggiore and the liturgical ceremony of the Annibaldi tomb. The implicit theatricality in these works was further developed in the tomb, which presupposes the actual celebration of the funeral mass, with the priest before the altar, turning towards the niche with the recumbent figure. Furthermore, what is significant in its ideological function is the introduction of the variant of the angels in the place of the usual curtain-holding deacons—in other words, a supernatural element next to the image of the mortal remains of the pope, made even more realistic by the mimetic features of the face made while Boniface was still alive.

Historically, this is an image of great importance which testifies, after centuries of neglect, to the rebirth of the portrait taken from life. Its coinciding with the figure of Boniface VIII loads it with both political and ideological value in relation to the ultimate affirmation of the theocratic power of the medieval papacy. In this context, the positioning of the angels near a figure so realistically expressed in its individuality appears to be significant; eliminating the margin generally present in tombs between the volume of the earthly remains and the pictorial transfiguration of the otherworldly space signifies a clear affirmation of the sanctity of the pope on earth.

Boniface VIII was not new to this type of representation from real life. Indeed, he had various self-glorifying portraits made as political manifestos of immediate visual impact, which were also the cause of accusations of idolatry on the part of the French court. One of these is the fragmentary half-bust in the Vatican Museums, attributed by the sources to the decoration of the same chapel, though its position is not certain, perhaps inside a cornice with an overhanging gable, as if the pope was looking out of a window.

Dated to 1300, the occasion of the jubilee, it has been attributed to Arnolfo because of the absolute prestige of the commission and, above all, the stylistic quality, even more obvious when the additions of restoration were eliminated. As in most of Arnolfo's work, here too the relief does not reach the full round but is placed on a reused slab, reworked and decorated, probably in mosaic. The pope is represented in a solemn frontal position, with his right hand blessing and the symbolic attributes

of personal power in clear evidence. In his left hand are the keys and on his head the papal tiara, the triple crown which had been introduced by Boniface VIII himself.

The most innovative element in the iconography is, however, the rendering of the pope's face, a portrait from real life and as if he were alive, just like the self-glorifying images of his temporal power but now placed inside a church. With the lesson of the classicizing pseudo-portrait of the age of Frederick II already assimilated, perhaps through Nicola Pisano or at the Angevin court, Arnolfo, with the figure of Cardinal de Braye, had revived the mimetic effect of the old face, experimenting with the use of a cast taken directly from the deceased. In Boniface's tomb, this realistic representation was taken from a person who was still alive and was intended to allude symbolically to the theocratic synthesis of the pope's dual power: immortal sanctity embodied in the reality of the image of earthly remains, as well as temporal power, figuring in the portrait bust placed by Boniface VIII right in the heart of Christendom, a consistent ideological progression from the earlier distribution of other self-celebrating statues in places of symbolic and visual importance, distributed strategically in the main centers of the papal states.

The bust of Boniface thus constitutes one of the earliest examples of the rebirth of the post-classical portrait and the height of the evolution of pre-humanistic impulses evident in the attention to real facts, and in the original reworking of antique references in Arnolfo's work can thus be seen.

The Bronze *San Pietro*

Further and significant testimony to these antiquarian experiments is a work that for centuries has been the object of critical discussion centered on the dating and authorship problem. Only recently has it been confirmed that it should be attributed to Arnolfo. The work in question is the statue of San Pietro, one of the few medieval bronze works to survive, from 1605 placed in front of the first column on the right of the dome in St. Peter's, but made for the apse of the oratory of San Martino situated externally, near the right side of the apse of Constantine.

The majestic figure looks grave and solemn, with dense curls in the hair and beard, and is dressed, antique style, with tunic, heavy mantle (*cinctus gabinus*), and sandals, while holding the symbolic keys of St. Peter in his left hand and giving a blessing with his right.

Between the two main hypotheses of date, the one that refers the *San Pietro* to the late classical period (dominant until 1863 but returned to also after 1943) is based mainly on these iconographic details, apart from the general stylistic characteristics and documentary references, subsequently revealed as not crucial, since they were not necessarily pertinent to this particular image among the many of St. Peter in the basilica of St. Peter's since classical times.

The second hypothesis arose in the mid-nineteenth century and is based essentially on stylistic analysis, sustaining a dating of the second half of the thirteenth century. It is accepted by the majority of historians and proposes an attribution to Arnolfo, with which many agree. The evident and marked influence of iconographic and formal late classical models has been referred on the one hand to the specific needs of historical, political, and ideological order, which, as seen a number of times, gave substance to the symbolism of the images of the medieval Church. On the other hand, it was placed in the thirteenth-century classicism of sculpture, more especially in the framework of the cultural tendencies combining in the formation of Arnolfo, from his first experiences in the milieu of Frederick II to the school of Nicola Pisano and, at the same time, at the Angevin court, where the results of mature French Gothic were reflected.

A recent review of the whole problem of the San Pietro, conducted at historico-documentary, stylistic, and iconographic levels, combined with technical investigations on the material data of execution and thermo-luminescence measurement, has proved a late thirteenth-century dating of the work, placing it more precisely in the years around 1300. At the same time, the attribution to Arnolfo has been evaluated on the basis of precise comparisons of iconographic, stylistic, and formal character with works definitely by Arnolfo. The execution of the hair and beard recurs, for example, in the figure of the paralytic man for the Perugia fountain of Perugia and in the St. John in the Berlin *Death of the Virgin*, and is just as precise in the superimposing of the gesture of blessing and the symbolism of the keys with the bust of Boniface VIII.

At a stylistic level, as already revealed several times, the use of classical models does not yet reach the full and mature three-dimensionality of the full round, both because it remains linked to an element of support—the original chair, however, must have been without arms—and also, and above all, because the sculptural rendering of volume is explicated in the typical linear and abstract profiling of the two-dimensional planes, as is shown clearly by the complex and tense geometry of the drapery. To this general concept of the work some significant

stylistic peculiarities of Arnolfo are highlighted, for example, the style of the ears and eyes.

Finally, at a formal level, also in *St. Peter* is found the typical working to a "criterion of visibility" which calculates accurately—and thus neglects—the parts not directly perceptible from the viewing points from which the work should be enjoyed, which in this case made it possible to hypothesize about its original context.

The absence of superficial vibration effects, so typical of Arnolfo in rendering the modeling, has finally been led back by the most recent studies to the technique of smelting bronze together with the fourteenth-century scraping to eliminate the color which, as has been proved by analysis, covered the statue in accordance with the widespread taste in medieval sculpture, a system not unknown to Arnolfo himself who applied it in the de Braye tomb. In this case, however, the coloring of the bronze was exceptional, as at the time it was a rare metal of complex working and thus intrinsically precious. This testifies again to the original deep penetration of the trends of diverse tastes in the art of Arnolfo.

The Circle of Arnolfo: Doubtful Works

Apart from the masterpieces analyzed, a series of works grouped generally in the last quarter of the thirteenth century and of uncertain attribution exists in Roman sculpture. Distinguished by their stylistic quality, these have been attributed by some studies to Arnolfo himself, by others to his workshop—in any case, to persons not more easily identified who moved in the same artistic and cultural circle, characterized by the influence of French Gothic and the classicizing circle of Frederick II.

The existence of a workshop of collaborators of greater or lesser ability has been proved by the disparities in the making, evidenced in the works signed by Arnolfo and by the entity of some commissions assigned to Arnolfo in precisely the years in which he is documented to have been in Rome or Florence. It is probable that, especially in the last period, Arnolfo concentrated on the planning of calculated architectural and decorative projects and on the accurate drawing of models which he then left to be carved by his assistants, limiting his own intervention to the most important parts and the most prestigious commissions. Of the ample production of Arnolfo's circle and the complex attributive problems that have developed around this, the most representative works will now be discussed.

The Portrait of Charles of Anjou

The portrait of Charles of Anjou in the Capitoline Museum is distinguished for its exceptional historical–documentary value and for the complexity of its political and ideological meaning. Linked recently to Charles' third term as senator in Rome (1281–84), but perhaps of earlier date, the sculpture fulfills an important role of geographical and temporal link between the different artistic and cultural contributions brought together in the process of rebirth of late classical portraiture, culminating in Arnolfo's realistic representation of Boniface VIII and the classic setting of the *St. Peter*.

In the evolution of the secular portrait, given the specificity of the commission, the *Charles of Anjou* reflects, on the one hand, the experience of the French Gothic images of the king represented on a throne of the twelfth and thirteenth centuries as a patron of important ecclesiastical foundations. On the other, it reconnects with classical models by means of the classic-style experimentation of statuary in the style of Frederick II, of Italian and southern European circles. The figure clearly shows evidence, therefore, through its whole iconographic and formal concept, of the different matrixes of power met together in the person of the Angevin king.

The stylistic characteristics of the Gothic style from north of the Alps, the majesty of the image, and its attributes of regality—the gem-studded crown, the scepter in the right hand, and the lost globe, which must have been in the open-curving left hand—all allude explicitly to Charles' direct blood link with the French crown and to the political significance inherent in the acquisition of the Swabian kingdom in southern Italy. Frederick II's inheritance seems, however, to be symbolized by references to the visible classical art, apart from details such as the arrangement of the draped mantle over the shoulder and the statu lion heads, reminders of the heraldic leonine heads each side of the Roman official *sella curulis*. At the same time the lions are a direct reference to the senatorial dignity conferred on Charles by the city of Rome, while, with their attitude of opposition, they allude to the diverse faces of justice consistent with the resonances of the image of the judge, and the place it was intended for.

On the basis of reconstruction, this was originally between a baldacchino structure crowned by a trefoil arcade, on which were placed two symmetrical high-relief figures of trumpeters or heralds. The whole representation would then have been situated at the entrance or the inside of the so-called capitoline *tribunal*, a complex intended for the administration of justice which Charles had erected, but whose exact position has remained controversial since the traditional identification with the three thirteenth-century chapels that were added on the right-hand side of Santa Maria in Aracoeli has recently been placed in doubt.

If the stylistic and formal characteristics are considered, the monumental concept of the work and its political and symbolic value in relation to the historical stature of the patron do not find a qualitative response in the execution of the work such that it can be sure of a certain attribution to Arnolfo, as shown by the rigid geometrical cut of the head, the static frontality of the corporal mass, the hard sculptural rendering of the face, and the sharp cut of the drapery folds. No determining element for attributive purposes has emerged from the recent restoration which—apart from the heavy successive mishandling—has revealed the presence of pigments that provide evidence of an original lively coloring. Restoration has also underlined the summary working of the parts behind, in confirmation of the frontal setting of the image.

The Franciscan Workshop at Santa Maria in Aracoeli

In parallel with the supposed attribution of the statue of Charles of Anjou, numerous Arnolfo references and echoes have been recognized in the new architectural and decorative programs for the Capitoline Hill in the second half of the thirteenth century. Not by chance, since these are due precisely to the direct impulse of two commissions outside Roman circles—the Franciscans and the Angevin court—to which Arnolfo was linked in various ways, to express their innovative requirements. Already the object of political and ideological advances with the construction of the Palazzo Senatorio and the arrangement of the symbols of Romanness, the Capitoline Hill was involved in the complex reconstruction of the ancient Benedictine church of Santa Maria in Aracoeli after its assignment to the Franciscans by Innocent IV in 1249.

The intervention of Arnolfo in the workshop at the church and his role as designer and director of works has been recognized in the transept architecture and decoration, financed in the 1280s and 1290s by the Savelli family, who had their family chapel and arms inserted there, applied on the outside head. As has been seen, Arnolfo had already directed a similar large-scale intervention at Santa Cecilia, but leaving aside the complex question of the architecture and decoration of the transept of Santa Maria in Aracoeli and its more or less direct attribution to Arnolfo, it is necessary to proceed to the analysis of what remains of the sculpture, traceable in the inside and outside of the right wing of the building.

Under the cornice of the buttresses limiting the head of the transept, two arms of the Savelli family in mosaic are still visible, supported at the base by two marble shelves with female faces, which, because of the softness of the modeling and the quality of execution, have been attributed to a sculptor in Arnolfo's circle. The absence of direct typological and stylistic parallels in Rome at this time has led historians to recognize in these one of the rare reflections of the production of the circle present in the city, using the style of Frederick II. The only possible parallels have been identified not so much in the heads in the St. John Lateran and San Paolo cloisters, of a considerably more rigid and contracted concept, but in the classical faces decorating the remains of the basin and lid of a marble fountain in the cloister at St. John Lateran.

The chapel built in the right wing of the transept by Pandolfo Savelli, who was a senator in Rome and brother of Giacomo Savelli, who became pope as Honorius IV (1285-87), contains the two facing tombs of their parents: that of the senator Luca Savelli the Elder seen on the left and his wife, Vanna Aldobrandeschi, positioned on the right. The present appearance of the chapel is the result of a succession of interventions and interpolations that have changed the original arrangement. In particular, according to the oldest drawings, both tombs were framed by Gothic baldacchinos with trefoil arcades, while on Luca Savelli's tomb was a panel depicting him with his wife.

The tomb of Luca Savelli is now composed of a classical sarcophagus with garlands, surmounted by a fascia with inscriptions and a rich Gothic crowning. The decoration is mosaic, comprising in the lower part three family arms framed with pinnacles and Gothic leaf decoration. In the middle of the gable in a small niche is a Virgin and Child, which often attributed to Arnolfo himself.

The tomb of Vanna Aldobrandeschi is also composed of a mosaic sarcophagus with family arms, two Savelli and one Aldobrandeschi in the middle, and a high plinth, formed in this case by three superimposed elements, the upper two of which have Cosmatesque decoration.

The recumbent figure of Honorius IV presently on the sarcophagus does not belong to the

FOLLOWING PAGES:
LEFT:
Among the finest works produced by the group around Arnolfo di Cambio are the tombs in the Chapel of the Savelli in the church of Santa Maria in Aracoeli. The antique and garlanded sarcophagus of Luca Savelli's tomb was crowned by an ornate Gothic superstructure.

RIGHT:
The tomb of Vanna Aldobrandeschi, the wife of Luca Savelli, consists of a sarcophagus with a coat-of-arms in Cosmati work, and was positioned on an elevated pedestal. The recumbent figure of Honorius IV, the son of the deceased, was transferred to the family chapel together with his remains in the sixteenth century.

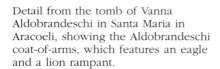

Detail from the tomb of Vanna Aldobrandeschi in Santa Maria in Aracoeli, showing the Aldobrandeschi coat-of-arms, which features an eagle and a lion rampant.

Now in the Museo del Palazzo di Venezia, but discovered in 1887 at St. John Lateran, the image is the subject of critical debate regarding its original architectural destination (two-light mullioned window, cloister, portico, loggia) and provenance, as well as the identification of the pope, its date, and attribution. Without going into the problems which, in the absence of certain archival data and with the stylistic evidence compromised by the poor state of conservation remain difficult to solve, it is nevertheless important to place into evidence the attribution of the work to a sculptor who, even if he cannot be identified as Arnolfo as some would propose, certainly was in the circle of Arnolfo's collaborators, and reveals so precise a Gothic inflection that recent scholars have suggested that it was directly imported by the Angevin court, but thoroughly modernized in line with the major Roman works of the period.

Last Cosmatesque Work

Placed next to the production, between the end of the thirteenth century and the papacy's move to Avignon in 1309, of the most direct Arnolfo influence, and therefore the cause of wavering in critical judgment between direct attributions to Arnolfo and general referrals to Arnolfo's workshop, a series of works was produced that was stylistically further away from these and thus more clearly identifiable as the products of different personalities, even in the various modes and measures that could be considered to be in the orbit—or in the trail—of the language of Arnolfo.

This concerns, in particular, the activity carried out by the last descendents of the Roman families of marbleworkers, who concentrated on attempting to reconcile the traditionalism of their patrons with the simplified and popular development of single innovative elements introduced by Arnolfo.

Among these, clear signed testimonies have been left by Deodato and Giovanni, the sons of Pietro Mellini, who distinguished themselves in the modernizing of the architectural and decorative typologies of tabernacles and tombs, starting from the work by Arnolfo, but deriving from these only the most obvious structural characteristics and some Gothic elements. However, besides the works of these two most defined personalities, at least some of the varied and more or less fragmentary surviving works of uncertain authorship, generally attributed to the circles of the last production of the Roman marbleworkers, should be noted. These, despite their mediocre level, seem grouped by an appreciable attempt at modernization in the Cosmatesque decorative tradition inspired by

tomb, even though it constitutes what is left of Honorius' tomb, originally in St. Peter's and transferred here, together with the pope's remains, in the sixteenth century. The image slopes towards the outside, with the head raised high on two pillows. The execution is characterized by the soft rendering of the modeling in the draperies and, above all, in the face, and by meticulous attention to the decoration of the pontifical vestments, the tiara, as well as the pillows themselves.

The presence of remains of the curtains at the end of the figure, which recall the sepulchral typology Arnolfo introduced into the de Braye tomb combined with the quality of sculptural execution, brings the image of Honorius into a proximity of similarity with Arnolfo's other recumbent figures, even if recent studies suggest that it is not by Arnolfo himself but is, instead, by the sculptor of the standing Magi in the Chapel of the Relics in Santa Maria Maggiore.

The Pope on the Faldstool

Significant testimony of the influence of the Gothic style from beyond the Alps, introduced into Rome by the Angevin court, is the pope seated on the faldstool, and applied frontally on the fragment of impost of two arches, on the back of which can be seen an angel with its wings spread wide.

Arnolfo, in particular with the insertion of more evident sculptural elements, and with their attention turned to human representation.

In the Cappella del Crocifisso in St. John Lateran is a figure in clear relief with the rigid and marked features of a pope kneeling in prayer. Its original context is unknown. Some archival clues, and above all the similarities discovered in recent studies to the Vatican statues of Boniface VIII, both in distinctive iconographical characteristics such as the papal tiara as well as the Arnolfo-inspired stylistic rendering, have led to the identification of the image of the pope and the hypothesis of its placing in the area of the benediction loggia which Boniface had built next to the Lateran palace.

Included in the decorative program of this loggia were perhaps also the statues of Sts. Peter and Paul in the Lateran Museum, distinguished by their monumentality and the careful development of the classical modules of the iconography of early Christian origin. They reveal the modest artistic personality of the sculptor in their rather awkward and rigid rendering, and inert and blocked expressive ability.

A particular evolution of the typology of the eucharistic tabernacle—of which numerous testimonies survive in Roman churches—is shown by the late thirteenth-century San Clemente, also indirectly linked to the patronage of Boniface VIII. According to some, it should be placed in the context of the cult of the Eucharist resulting from the miracle at Bolsena in 1263. The novelties of this late Cosmatesque work are the Gothic modernization of the structure and the insertion on the internal lunette of a sculptured relief of the Virgin and Child flanked by St. Clement and Boniface VIII, in the act of presenting his nephew Giacomo Caetani, who commissioned the work in 1299 when he was the titular cardinal of the church, as attested by the mosaic inscription.

It is interesting that in the iconography of the pope has been recognized the first known example of a portrait which identifies the depicted person with a saint; the halo behind the pope's head identifies him with a saint, perhaps St. James, though the figure has the unequivocal face of Boniface VIII.

At the stylistic level, despite a certain relaxation in the spatial composition and in the treatment of the drapery, the treatment of the faces brings this work too into the modest panorama of derivative production of these anonymous Roman marbleworkers of the end of the thirteenth century.

Giovanni di Cosma

More original and definable for its expressive quality is the work of renewal and diffusion of the tomb typology testified to in Rome by the three signed works of Giovanni di Cosma, all executed when he was at the peak of his artistic maturity, as is proved by the style and the high status of the patron.

The first was executed around 1295 for the papal chaplain Stefano Surdi, nephew of Cardinal Riccardo Annibaldi. Now in Santa Balbina, on the right wall of the counter-facade, it shows the recumbent figure above a sarcophagus covered by a draped curtain, all placed on a high podium formed by a caisson with mosaic and family arms.

The position of the recumbent figure, with head inclined towards the beholder and arms crossed, is inspired by the similar position on the

Tomb of Cardinal Garcia Gudiel in Santa Maria Maggiore. Produced between 1299 and 1303, this work marks the highpoint of Giovanni di Cosma's artistic career. The status of the deceased is elevated still further by the tabernacle architecture on the rear wall with its mosaic of the Virgin enthroned.

Annibaldi tomb and reflects equally the flat and synthetic rendering of the modeling. However, already in this first work Giovanni differentiates himself not only from Arnolfo but also from the Arnolfo milieu through an original style that succeeds in marrying a taste for volumetric rendering with the sharp linear tension of the carving.

Dated around 1300 is the tomb executed by Giovanni for Cardinal Guglielmo Durando, bishop of Mende (1296), in Santa Maria sopra Minerva, where it is now embedded in a niche in the back wall of the right transept framed by a trefoil arcade decorated with Gothic leaves, on small newel posts. It is composed of a sarcophagus with drapery and family arms against a mosaic background, with the recumbent figure above flanked by two angels holding back the curtain. The mosaic under the arcade, of uncertain attribution because of frequent restoration, represents, flanking the Virgin enthroned with the Child, St. Dominic on the right and on the left St. Privato, second bishop of Mende, in the act of presenting the deceased, who kneels.

As far as the execution is concerned, even in this case the decorative ability and idiosyncratic, rather hard and tense rendering of the nevertheless robust volume, come next to obvious references to Arnolfo's work, in particular, the tomb of Boniface VIII, from which details have been drawn, such as the draping of the funeral cloth, the family arms, the angels holding the curtains, the mosaic, and, in the reclining figure, the treatment of volume and drapery, and the motif of the head turning upwards.

Giovanni's mature artistic language is apparent in the tomb of Cardinal Consalvo Garcia

FOLLOWING PAGES:
The mosaic above the recumbent figure on the tomb of Cardinal Garcia Gudiel. The kneeling Cardinal is presented to the Virgin by the interceding saints.

Detail of the recumbent figure of Cardinal Garcia Gudiel. The deceased is flanked by angels who raise a curtain. The composition is similar to Arnolfo di Cambio's tomb for Boniface VIII.

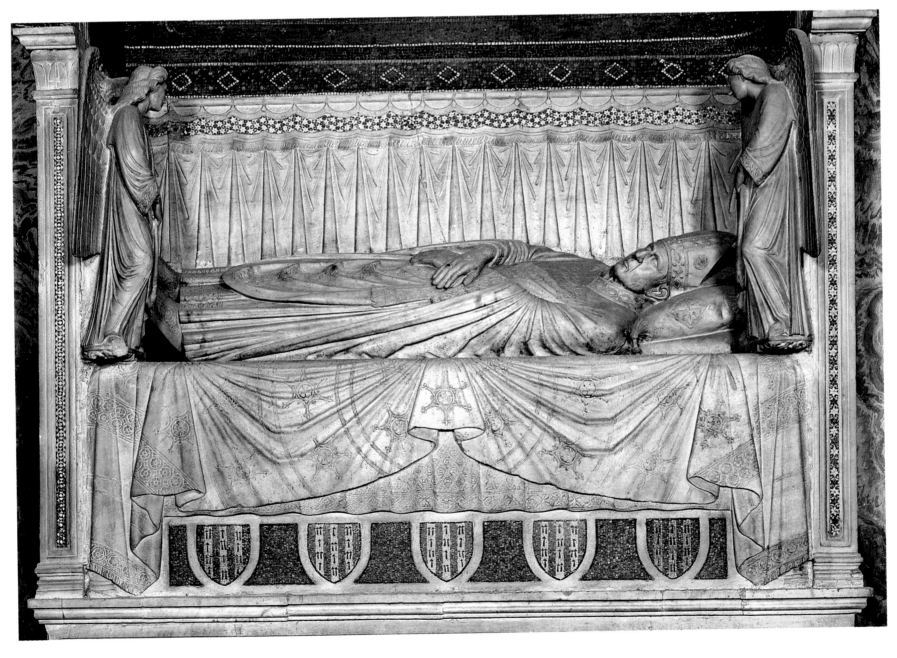

Gudiel, dated between 1299 and 1303, in the right aisle of Santa Maria Maggiore. At the structural and architectural level, the tomb is similar to that of Guglielmo Durando, but it differs from it above all in its greater consistency and compositional integrity, and in the stylistic rendering, which is developed in the richer and softer modeling of the drapery, the more relaxed and elegant forms of the angels, and the intensity of the representation of the face of the recumbent figure. The mosaic has a similar pattern with the Virgin enthroned and the deceased kneeling at her feet, but the interceding saints are in this case Sts. Matthew and Jerome.

With this work Giovanni di Cosma reached his stylistic and expressive peak, and at the same time represented and consolidated in the taste of the period that skillful deep penetration of architectural, sculptural, and color elements which, as in his other works, Arnolfo had applied also to the tomb, renewing its typology with the introduction of the figure of the deceased, already developed from French models by Pietro d'Oderisio in the tomb of Clement IV at Viterbo. In this way the sculptor marked the hierarchical and symbolic subdivision between the sculptural evidence of the recumbent figure, the mediation of the angels who close the curtains of his mortal parenthesis, and the ethereal, pictorial evocation of the next world, in which the kneeling deceased is presented to Christ by interceding saints.

The compositional scheme was widely used even if, with respect to Arnolfo's prototypes, a progressive loss of sculptural and structural energy was apparent in the complex, which would tend to assume a sloping typology, set in a higher position and always at the end of the wall, as can be seen in several fourteenth-century examples.

Apart from the diffusion of wall tombs—first backed then increasingly enclosed and raised from the floor—some examples of different traditions remain. Among these in particular is the tomb now in the Cappella del Crocifisso in Santa Prassede on the wall opposite the altar, but probably originally detached from the wall and standing independently, in accordance with French typology. This contains the remains of Cardinal Pantaleon of Troyes, titular cardinal of Santa Prassede, where he was killed in 1286 during a riot. It shows the recumbent figure resting on a mosaic sarcophagus, with small columns at intervals, and covered by ample drapes. The quality of the execution, apart from obvious Cosmatesque and Arnolfo allusions, confirms in the elegant linear rendering of the drapery an inspiration that is more or less directly taken from French models.

Deodato di Cosma

Active in the years around 1300, Deodato, like his brother Giovanni, must have enjoyed considerable fame in the conservative circles of the Rome of this period, as is shown by the prestigious patrons of his few surviving works and the moderately innovative character of his artistic language. The novelty of Deodato's style lies in his attempt to modernize the rooted classical taste of family tradition in line with the Gothic novelties introduced into Rome at the end of the thirteenth century by Arnolfo and his collaborators and followers.

Basing himself on works by Arnolfo in San Paolo and Santa Cecilia, Deodato developed his own version of the tabernacle, in which, eliminating the traditional formulae of the enclosure and the confessional, developed the architecture of the baldacchino in a Gothic sense. This is the characteristic that groups the three works attributed to him. One has survived whole, the second is fragmentary, and the third is documented only from sources.

The first is the tabernacle of Santa Maria in Cosmedin executed for Francesco Caetani, nephew of Boniface VIII, as is attested to by the arms visible on the gables. The dating of the work has been established as 1295, the year in which Caetani was ordained cardinal deacon of Santa Maria in Cosmedin.

The structure has four pointed trilobed arches on columns, bounded at the corners by high newel posts and surmounted by gables decorated with Gothic leaves and a fretwork of rosettes. A small cupola base crowns it all, corresponding to the crossing of the roof pitches and the internal groined cross. The general scheme and some typically Gothic motifs, such as the small newel posts and the pointed trilobed arches decorated with Gothic leaves, seem to be clearly derived from the San Paolo example, but are accompanied by an extreme simplification of style and structure. The sculptural decoration is substituted by mosaic, of which some fragments remain. But in the thin two-dimensional drawing of the forms, the robust structural energy of Arnolfo's tabernacles is missing. Arnolfo had understood how to distinguish the bearing elements from the decorative, in a powerful three-dimensional architectural complex.

The second tabernacle signed by Deodato can now be seen in the cloister of St. John Lateran. It has been reduced into single fragments, some reassembled in an incongruous fashion. The whole comprised various elements, all with more or less diffuse traces of mosaic decoration: three pinnacles and three newel posts, two groups of three spiral columns, a marble base, a spire culminating in a sphere, and, above all, three gables with Gothic leaf decoration and central rosettes that were surmounted by family arms.

The object of successive removals, and demolished during Innocent X's (1644–55) rebuilding of St. John Lateran, the tabernacle must originally have been inside the church, on the altar of St. Mary Magdalene, which was consecrated in 1297 by Cardinal Gerardo Bianchi on Boniface VIII's instructions. The hypothetical reconstructions, which were based on archival sources and analyses of the surviving fragments, placed the work inside the layout of the tabernacle-reliquary, a new typology of French origin, widely used in Rome around 1300. This was composed of two superimposed levels, since it was intended to keep the relics in a higher and safer position, sometimes made conspicuous by a grille.

Belonging to this type, according to the reconstructions, was a series of lost examples among which was the third work signed by Deodato, carried out around 1290 for a chapel in Santa Maria in Campitelli.

The topmost section of the monumental ciborium in St. John Lateran shows the influence of the French Gothic in its strong vertical lines.

The St. John Lateran Tabernacle-Reliquary

The best-known example of the evolution of this type of tabernacle at two levels is dated now as late fourteenth-century. It reveals considerable development in the vertical sense of the structural complex for the insertion of the cage-reliquary between the columns of the base and the covering system. This is found on the main altar of St. John Lateran, commissioned by Urban V (1362–70) during rebuilding following a fire in 1360.

The execution of the work, which was financed by Emperor Charles IV and was associated with the intended re-establishment in Rome of the papacy after its absence in Avignon, was laden with intense symbolic significance with regard to the dual political and religious stress on the value of continuity with the early Christian tradition, which the place itself provided explicitly, with the memory of the previous fourth-century tabernacle. Charles wanted to allude to his own close relationship with the papacy by recalling the similar donation of the original tabernacle by Constantine, while the Church wished to reaffirm the continuity and centrality of papal power by means of that complex strategy of the image that had developed in ever more explicit political functions throughout the Middle Ages.

OPPOSITE:
View of the ciborium in Santa Maria in Cosmedin made by Deodato di Cosma, the brother of Giovanni. This piece is a restrained example of the artistic design developed by Arnolfo di Cambio for this type of liturgical piece.

Detail of the ciborium in St. John Lateran. This hybrid form of ciborium and reliquary, with its strong verticals, has clearly been influenced by French sources. The area for storing and displaying relics from the skulls of St. Peter and St. Paul was designed to be isolated behind a grill, and yet visible from the outside.

Apart from the specific value of its placement at the heart of one of the first Christian foundations, the tabernacle of Urban V proclaimed his connection with the age of Constantine and the continuity between Old and New Testaments through the presence of the venerated texts of Sts. Peter and Paul, in relation to the relics of the original tabernacle, and also to the iconographic allusions of the sculptural decoration.

The architectural structure of the whole, attributed to the Sienese artist Giovanni di Stefano and his workshop, consists of four base columns linked by three rounded arcades divided inside by two pointed coupled and pierced arches. On these is a cross vault on which is placed a cubic box, decorated on all four sides with twelve frescoed panels, perhaps originally by Barna da Siena (1367–68) but redone in the following century, and refined on the corners by four pairs of fourteenth-century statuettes with saints and personifications of virtues inside

gables. On the box stands a vault-covered loggia enclosed by railings, inside which are the relics. Finally, the whole is crowned by a spire and four gables, flanked by high pinnacles.

The structure of the work, while obviously influenced by Arnolfo's work, diverges from these, on the one hand, for the more marked influence of French Gothic (explicable by its patronage) visible in the Gothic verticalism and the decorative exuberance of almost Flamboyant character, and on the other, for its direct reference to the stylistic archaism of Deodato, in particular in the St. Mary Magdalene tabernacle, found by critics in the massive rigidity and frontality in both the complex and in the added sculpture.

Apart from the St. John Lateran tabernacle, few works were completed in Rome during the fourteenth century, when the transfer of the papacy and the papal court to Avignon provoked a collapse of patronage and of the

economy of the city, with a consequent dispersion of artists. The rare works which exist were associated with a modest production of tombs for individual important personages, often from the great Roman families. A slight recovery occurred in the last twenty years of the century with the return of the papal court, even if by now—as is shown by the summary execution of the nevertheless monumental statue of Boniface IX (1389–1404) now in the cloister of San Paolo fuori le Mura—for new testimonies of Roman sculpture it was necessary to wait for the end of the Great Schism (1417), the subsequent restoration of the economic and material prosperity of the city, and the new thrust provided by the activities of Tuscan sculptors such as Donatello and Filarete in the 1430s.

Virginia Leonardis

Medieval Metalwork

Numerous intriguing passages in the *Liber Pontificalis* reveal how, from the time of Constantine onwards, the churches of Rome owned numerous precious images in metal and enamel. It is not known whether these objects were imported from the east or made in local workshops.

Only a fraction of the treasures described survive. The reasons for their destruction can be found in the events that overtook the city—the barbarian invasions and the raids of the Saracens (846) and the Normans (1084), the Sack of Rome in 1527, the requisitions ordered by Pius VI in 1797 to satisfy the conditions imposed by Napoleon in the Treaty of Tolentino, and, finally, the plundering of churches during the Roman Republic (1798–99).

To have an idea of the richness of church ornaments, it need only be noted that the font in the Lateran baptistery was decorated with gold statues and that on its tabernacles were silver arches. The great doors of St. Peter's were made of silver with reliefs of the Apostles, as Honorius I wished. Such a demand encouraged Roman workshops. Demand for goldwork also came from as far away as the east and the north.

Among the earliest works completed in Rome, from the mid-fourth century, is a gilded silver casket discovered in the neighborhood of the church of San Martino ai Monti and now in the British Museum. It formed part of the wedding gifts of a Christian noblewoman, Proiecta, the wife of Secundus, as the acclamatory inscription relates. This was perhaps the woman for whom Damasus (366–84) wrote a solemn epitaph in the church of San Martino. The scenes portrayed on the casket have a narrative character and mix pagan images with Christian symbols: the maiden taken to her new home, guests bringing gifts, the bride beautifying herself.

A few isolated examples of fretwork survive. The earliest is a silver votive lamp—a rare example of a liturgical lamp—also from San Martino ai Monti. It was considered to be either a crown or tiara of Pope Silvester (314–35) when it was found in 1632. Its discovery was described as follows: "Father Maestro Medici began an excavation in our little garden next to the garden of San Silvestro. Among other antiquities he found a silver crown five inches tall, as broad as a man's head. The crown was given to the most excellent Barberini and was kept among his most outstanding antiquities." The lamp was handed back by Cardinal Barberini in 1641 and authenticated as a relic.

Precious gifts might come from the Byzantine court, presented to bishops or churches. Justinian I gave Hormisdas (514–23) gold and silver vases, evangelistaries with golden jeweled clasps, a gold paten with oriental hyacinths, and another two in silver. Among other objects, two which came to Rome are now in the Vatican Museums. One is an oval casket embossed with silver with a jeweled cross on the lid and busts of saints between clypei. Formerly kept in a tabernacle, it may date from the early sixth century. The other is the great reliquary of the true cross, in gilded silver leaf, which was given by Justinian II (565–78) and his consort Sophia.

In the eighth and ninth centuries Byzantine forms dominated Roman goldwork. As a result of opposition to iconoclasm, the goldsmith's art acquired the character of monumental sculpture realised in precious metal. Thus Santa Maria Maggiore possessed a gold statue depicting the Virgin and child dating from the time of Stephen II (752). San Paolo fuori le Mura had a silver Christ with angels, St. Peter's an iconostasis decorated with silver images of Christ and the Apostles, and the Virgin among the ten virgins, both of which can be dated to the pontificate of Gregory III (731–41). St. Peter's also had an image of St. Andrew in gold and precious stones. The silver statues of the Savior and of Sts. Processus and Martinian, in the chapel dedicated to them, were commissioned by Paschal I (817–24).

Roman churches, such as Santa Prassede, San Giorgio al Velabro, and Santa Maria in Trastevere, had altars covered in silver plate and often gilded. The silver of the tabernacle of Sant'Agata dei Goti weighed 720 pounds, while the gold on the reliquary in St. Peter's ordered by Leo II (795–816) weighed 453 pounds.

A magnificent cruciform candelabra that could hold 1,465 candles is of Roman workmanship, commissioned by Hadrian I (771–95) for St. Peter's. There are only two silver casket reliquaries. One of these, commissioned by Paschal I, is cruciform and embossed with images from the

Cruciform reliquary case in embossed gilded silver showing scenes from the gospels, commissioned by Paschal I. Rome, Vatican Museums.

Vatican cross given by
Justinian II (565–78), with Latin
inscription and figures of the
emperor and empress praying.
Rome, Treasury of St. Peter's.

Reliquary case in embossed silver depicting Christ between Sts. Peter and Paul, the work of a Roman artist from the time of Paschal I (817–24). Rome, Vatican Museums.

gospels, in low relief and lightly gilded (Vatican Museums). The other casket, in embossed silver, depicts Christ between Sts. Peter and Paul (Vatican Museums).

Still in the sphere of goldwork, enamel from Limoges reached Italy. One precious image, in typical Limoges style but perhaps Roman, may date from the tenth or eleventh century—the Virgin in Santa Maria in Campitelli. The Virgin is depicted against a blue background. Her head is veiled and she holds the infant Jesus in her arms. At the sides are oak and olive branches (perhaps an allusion to the tree of the knowledge of good and evil) under an arch supported by two columns with Ionic capitals. In the corners above are the haloed heads of Sts. Peter and Paul.

The Virgin of Santa Maria in Portico, now in the treasury of the church of Santa Maria in Campitelli.

During the eleventh and twelfth centuries, lay craftsmen became increasingly important. They are often identifiable from inscriptions on the gold objects they produced. This is the case with a partly gilded silver reliquary of the cross in Santa Maria in Campitelli. Engraved and embossed, it dates from the twelfth century. On the longer arm is the inscription "G G AURI FE SERBUS DE SERBUS DEI." The inscription continues on the back: "G AUR CU BENEDICTA CONIUGE MEA." Its maker must therefore have been a goldsmith named Gregorio, who gave a votive reliquary together with his wife Benedetta.

Reverse of the twelfth-century pseudo-altar of San Gregorio Nazianzeno by Gregorius Aurifex, now in the treasury of the church of Santa Maria in Campitelli.

The mark of Rome is only found on a tiny number of objects. Thus the embossed silver arm reliquary in Santa Maria in Campitelli, dated to the beginning of the thirteenth century, with one of the first examples of such marks, is of enormous historical and artistic importance. On a base of carved gilded wood, it contains a relic of St. Marcellinus.

At the beginning of the thirteenth century, the enamel art of Limoges found an enthusiast in Innocent III, whose support encouraged the spread of objects from Limoges. An interesting example is the reliquary casket in gilded, enameled bronze in Santa Maria in Via Lata.

Outside Rome two forces are apparent during the Middle Ages. One is that of Siena, which dominated the nearby region of Viterbo. The other is that of the Abruzzi, to the east. Trends that began in the Abruzzi were apparent in the Frosinone area, particularly in the treasuries of the cathedrals of Veroli and Anagni. Viterbo and the surrounding area were enriched by Sienese artists and master craftsmen. In 1352, for example, Vannuccio di Viva da Siena made a splendid processional cross formerly in the cathedral but now in the diocesan museum in Orte, the most important example of Sienese influence. Vannuccio was the son of Viva di Lando, who together with

Silver reliquary of the cross by Gregorius Aurifex in the treasury of the church of Santa Maria in Campitelli.

Arm reliquary of St. Marcellinus in the treasury of the church of Santa Maria in Campitelli.

Ugolino di Vieri made the reliquary of the holy corporal and the reliquary of St. Savino in Orvieto Cathedral. Vannuccio interpreted Sienese goldwork in the light of Florentine influence, especially for the decorative elements. Giacomo di Guerrino, a contemporary Sienese artist, signed only one known work, the reliquary bust of St. Felicity, in the cathedral of Montefiascone.

Fourteenth-century Rieti, meanwhile, reflected the influence of the Abruzzi.

Thirteenth-century evangeliary cover in gilded bronze, enamel, and semiprecious stone, originally held in the collegiate church of Santa Maria di Amaseno. Rome, Museo Nazionale di Palazzo Venezia.

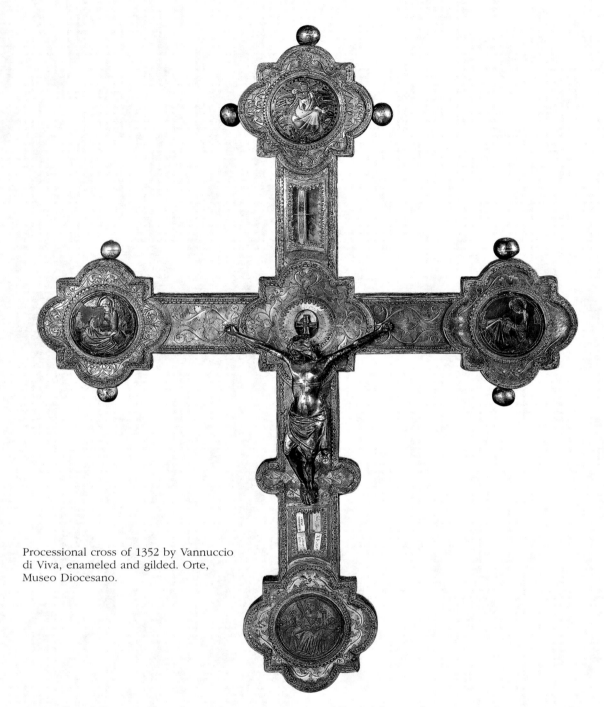

Processional cross of 1352 by Vannuccio di Viva, enameled and gilded. Orte, Museo Diocesano.

Eleventh-century cross in the treasury of the cathedral of Veroli.

Apart from the small embossed crosses in gilded copper laminate and the embossed silver cross from the church of San Venanzio in Mercetelli, all of which come from Sulmona workshops, of note is the cross from the church of Santa Croce in Borbona, which has similar features both to the famous Orsini cross (1344) from Rosciolo (which could be seen until recently in the Museo del Palazzo di Venezia in Rome) and to the cross of the parish of Forcella, in the Abruzzi.

Veroli, near Frosinone, has precious goldwork that reflects varied influences from Benedictine (compare the cross in the cathedral, dating from the eleventh century, formerly in the Benedictine monastery of Sant'Erasmo) to that of Sulmona.

The abbey of Montecassino is another important treasury, together with the lost monastery of Santa Maria in Flumine in Ceccano and the abbeys of Casamuri and Trivulsi. The area around Latina, open to influence from Naples, reveals significant Byzantine influence, for example in two crosses from Gaeta Cathedral, an enameled cross with half-figures and a Greek inscription from the eleventh century, and a Pantocrator in gold and enamel, from the same period.

The Rome–Lazio area has many objects from more distant origins. To cite just one example, there is the group of objects conserved in part in the sanctuary of Santa Maria in Vulturella near Palestrina. Among them is a gilded metal lunette, from the twelfth or thirteenth century, decorated with figures in relief on one side and engraved on the other, and two candelabra from the school of Mosul. In bronze with inlaid silver and jeweled decoration, they are decorated with figures between medallions, inscriptions, and geometric designs.

Maria Giulia Barberini

Pictorial Art from the Fifth to the Fourteenth Century

Late Antique and Early Medieval Mosaic

There is almost no surviving trace of works of monumental pictorial art executed in Rome in the first half of the fourth century, following the establishment of Christianity as the official religion of the Roman empire. This dearth makes it virtually impossible to recreate the cultural developments from which the stylistic and iconographic principles of early Christian art emerged.

Mausoleum of Constantia, Santa Pudenziana, St. Peter's, and St. Paolo

The few examples of the art of this period that do survive fill only a small part of the gap in our knowledge. One of these is the mosaic decoration of the Mausoleum of Constantia, a building with a centralized ground plan originally erected as the tomb of Constantine's daughter, and therefore a very private kind of monument. The ceiling of the gallery running around the circumference of the building is covered in superb mosaic, executed in about 360, with scenes of grape-harvesting and leafy tendrils with figures and realistically portrayed birds, a somewhat vague allegory of salvation. A much more explicit evocation of the Christian message is to be found in the mosaic decoration of the semi-circular niches in the mausoleum, where the *traditio clavium* (the handing over of the keys) and the *traditio legis* (the handing over of the Ten Commandments) symbolize the direct derivation from Christ of the Church's authority.

The apse mosaic in the church of Santa Pudenziana, probably dating from the time of Innocent I (402–17), is the earliest example of its kind to have come down to us. Christ is shown between the Apostles and two allegorical

Mid-fourth-century mosaics from a barrel-vaulted walkway in the former Mausoleum of Constantia, today the church of Santa Costanza. The profusion of scenes depicting country life can be seen as expressing joy as well as the hope for a peaceful afterlife.

Detail from a mosaic in the ambulatory of the former Mausoleum of Constantia, which illustrates the "microstructure" of the vine pattern; it is composed of animals and various other objects.

figures representing the converted Jews and the converted Gentiles, the roots from which the new Christian community had sprung. The scene is represented against a background of architecture which is proudly classical in style. On top of a hill in the center stands a triumphant jeweled cross, silhouetted against a sky which is heavy with clouds but at the same time splashed with bright patches of light and color. In this sky the four symbols of the Evangelists appear: an eagle standing for John, an ox for Luke, a lion for Mark, and a man for Matthew. The quality of the Santa Pudenziana mosaic and its lofty and monumental style suggest that, right from the beginning of official Christian art, this must have been the preferred technique for decorating new sacred buildings.

However, frescos also soon began to assume an important role. Leo the Great (440–61) had two cycles of biblical scenes executed, one in the original basilica of St. Peter's, the other in San Paolo fuori le Mura, the ancient basilica founded by Constantine. Unfortunately all these frescos are lost. Those in St. Peter's were destroyed during reconstruction in the sixteenth and seventeenth centuries, those of San Paolo in the fire which devastated the basilica in 1823. Watercolor copies made in the sixteenth and seventeenth centuries give a fairly accurate idea of the subject matter of these lost frescos, but cannot compensate for the impossibility of evaluating and interpreting their stylistic features, which are lost forever.

Santa Maria Maggiore

What has come down to us almost intact is the mosaic decoration in the basilica of Santa Maria Maggiore. Twenty-seven panels along the walls of the nave depict Old Testament scenes, narrating the stories of Abraham, Isaac, Jacob, Moses, and Joshua. On the triumphal arch are scenes from the childhood of Christ, most of them taken from the apocryphal gospels.

Santa Maria Maggiore has a special role in the history of early Christian art. It was the first basilica directly commissioned by the papacy, which took over what had previously been the imperial authority to build and decorate places of worship for the now triumphant Christian religion. Begun around 429, the basilica was completed and decorated during the papacy of Sixtus III (431–40). Sixtus had his name included in the mosaic at the top of the triumphal arch facing the nave, dedicating the work to the community of the faithful: "XYSTUS EPISCOPUS PLEBI DEI" (Bishop Sixtus to the people of God).

The Santa Maria Maggiore mosaics represent the peak of pictorial art in Rome in the first half of the fifth century. In the nave panels, the composition is rhythmically balanced and free-flowing. The landscape setting of the various scenes is carefully represented, the figures are solidly naturalistic, and color is skillfully used. These mosaics clearly observe the stylistic and compositional principles typical of late antique classical art, here applied to the new Christian iconography.

The cycle on the triumphal arch, with stories from the childhood of Christ, displays a number of differences in style and technique when compared with the nave panels. This mosaic must have been done by different artists, trained in another manner and of course using different models. However, it was not—as was once surmised—a separate project. The mosaic decoration in Santa Maria Maggiore, in both style and

Mosaic depicting the apparition of three angels to Abraham, and Abraham's hospitality towards them, from the north wall of the nave in the basilica of Santa Maria Maggiore. Abraham, as the chief protagonist in these two episodes, is portrayed three times in order to generate a sense of narrative continuity.

content, was definitely the product of a single, unified plan.

The nave panels, particularly the story of Moses, have close stylistic parallels in the Vatican Virgil, the masterpiece of early fifth-century book illustration. This manuscript, containing the works of the poet who symbolizes classical Roman culture (Vatican Library, Ms. Vat. lat. 3225), was decorated just a few years before Santa Maria Maggiore was embellished with Sixtus' mosaics. In it examples of compositional layout that resemble those of the Santa Maria Maggiore mosaics can be found, as well as a very similar representation of the human figure, with the concept of volume clearly indicated despite certain distortions.

It is of considerable significance that there should be such similarities between a mosaic directly commissioned by the papacy and a highly sophisticated manuscript belonging to pagan culture, probably made for a member of one of Rome's leading families. It suggests that the language of painting of late antiquity must have become an integral part of the figurative style of early Christian art, and that the people for whom both works of art were intended could be regarded as belonging to the same social group.

Santi Cosma e Damiano

One of the most important early medieval examples of mosaic apse decoration in Rome is that of Santi Cosma e Damiano in the Forum, dating from the second quarter of the sixth century. It was commissioned by Felix IV (526–30), who is portrayed in the mosaic holding a model of the church. In the center of the composition is a bearded Christ, against the background of an extraordinarily lumininous dark-blue sky, streaked with bright red clouds. The huge full-length figure of Christ, enveloped in a resplendent golden robe, dominates the scene below, where Sts. Peter and Paul present the two dedicatees of the church, Sts. Cosmas and Damian, holding crowns of martyrdom. Sts. Peter and Paul are depicted as painted statues; the sense of monumental volume and form links them directly to late antique sculpture.

On either side of the apse are portrayed, on the left, Felix IV (drastically restored in the seventeenth century) and, on the right, St. Theodore. On the dome of the apse a procession of angels symbolizes the apostles. On the apse arch there is traditional apocalyptic iconography: the twenty-four Elders of the Apocalypse (almost entirely obliterated by seventeenth-century restoration), the seven candlesticks, the seven angels, and the Mystic Lamb.

The arch mosaic has notable differences of style and technique compared with that in the

apse itself. These differences are not the result of the decoration having been carried out in stages or of a delay in execution, rather they reveal how in this crucial moment of transition between antiquity and the Middle Ages several figurative trends coexisted, without wholly coinciding.

The mosaic reveals a strikingly monumental concept of the human figure, a characteristic inherited from the pictorial language of late antiquity. The powerful modeling of the figures gives them a clearly plastic quality, although it seems that the skill in the use of chiaroscuro and the subtle blending of colors, which is so evident in the Santa Maria Maggiore mosaics, was by now disappearing. The figures of Sts. Cosmas and Damian are splashed with marked color contrasts, sometimes by sharp clashing of one color against another, though always to

TOP:
The shepherdess Rachel returning from the fields to report the arrival of Abraham to her father Laban. North wall of the nave, basilica of Santa Maria Maggiore.

ABOVE:
The Ark of the Covenant being carried across the Jordan, from the life of the Old Testament hero, Joshua. South wall of the nave, basilica of Santa Maria Maggiore.

The juxtaposition of these two images, separated by the nave, serves to illustrate the similarities in their composition. A pronounced feature of the Old Testament scenes is the narrow gold strip which acts as a connecting element between the figurative scenes in the foreground and the landscape of the background.

Mid-fifth-century mosaic panel from the south wall of the nave in Santa Maria Maggiore. Moses is shown as an infant being taken into the court of the Pharaoh in the upper part of the picture, while in the lower part Moses is seen debating with scholars.

OPPOSITE:
Detail of the mosaic in the apse of Santi Cosma e Damiano, commissioned by Felix IV (526–30). The depiction of Christ descending on a carpet of clouds is impressive in its monumentality and marks the highpoint of late antique mosaics in Rome.

great effect, powerfully evocative of the great event that is taking place—Christ's appearance.

The representation of this scene is all the more significant in that the church of Santi Cosma e Damiano was the first to be erected within the monumental center of pagan Rome, an area regarded in the preceding centuries as full of negative associations—even, in popular belief, as inhabited by evil spirits.

San Teodoro and San Lorenzo fuori le Mura

Two mosaics executed in the second half of the sixth century demonstrate an intermingling of two pictorial styles, Roman and Byzantine. They are the decoration in San Teodoro, on the slopes of the Palatine Hill, and that on the triumphal arch of San Lorenzo fuori le Mura. In the apse of San Teodoro, the figure of Christ standing on the globe is shown with Sts. Peter, Paul, and Theodore, to whom the church is dedicated. The background of uniform gold tesserae has the effect of dematerializing the figures, eliminating any impression of depth or sense of place or landscape, even though the figures seem to be based on those in Santi Cosma e Damiano.

The mosaic on the triumphal arch at San Lorenzo fuori le Mura, executed under Pelagius II (579–60), has the subject matter normal for apse decoration: Christ standing on the globe with the traditional figures of Sts. Peter and Paul, accompanied by Sts. Lawrence, Stephen, and Hippolitus, and by Pelagius himself. This mosaic was no longer visible from the original nave after the early thirteenth century, when Honorius III (1216–27) extended the basilica and reversed the orientation of the church.

The Capital of Medieval Christendom

The turn of the century was dominated by the figure of Gregory the Great (590–604), who provided the decisive momentum that transformed Rome into the capital of medieval Christendom. Gregory, of aristocratic descent, a member of the powerful Anicii family whose origins were steeped in classical culture, devoted himself to reorganizing the religious and civic life of Rome, undertaking major public works. Gradually the Church took over political and administrative control of the city, replacing the Byzantine rulers, who in any case regarded Rome as no more than a provincial city of little importance, entrusting its rule to governors.

It was under Gregory that the definitive Christianization of pagan Rome got underway. The most obvious manifestation of this process was the dedication of the Pantheon—the temple that was the symbol of paganism—to the Virgin of the Martyrs (Santa Maria ad Martyres). Its consecration in 609, a project of Boniface IV (698–15), had to be authorized by the Byzantine Emperor, Phocas. It was perhaps for the consecration that the icon of the Virgin and Child was painted, a work that has stylistic similarities with the Santi Cosma e Damiano mosaic. Other icons were probably produced between the sixth and seventh centuries in the Rome area, such as the Virgin and Child in Santa Francesca Romana (formerly Santa Maria Nova) and the Virgin in Santa Maria in Trastevere (though this is believed by some to date from the time of John VII, 705–7).

Santa Maria Antiqua

The best example of early medieval painting is the frescos originally in Santa Maria Antiqua, a place of worship created in the second half of the sixth century out of buildings on the northwest side of the Palatine Hill, which had formed a kind of monumental prelude to the imperial palace. The church underwent various decoration projects up to the year 847, when a landslip and the consequent collapse of some of the buildings that stood above it caused it to virtually disappear. Lying under a huge mass of rubble, it was abandoned. Its possessions, including the greatly venerated icon of the Virgin, were transferred to the nearby church of Santa Maria Nova.

Partially rediscovered in 1702, Santa Maria Antiqua was fully brought back to light in the early years of the twentieth century. Excavations revealed a formidable pictorial anthology of over three centuries of painting. The complex history of this long period of artistic production is exemplified in the so-called palimpsest wall to the right of the apse arch, with no fewer than four superimposed layers of fresco, painted between the second quarter of the sixth century and the time of John VII. The earliest fresco depicts the Virgin as Queen of Heaven enthroned between angels. Its frontal image with its air of imperial solemnity places it between 536 and mid-century.

On the second layer are fragments of a splendid Annunciation, probably from the early seventh century. The face of the Archangel Gabriel is rendered with areas of chiaroscuro and subtle use of color in a manner reminiscent of the most refined Hellenistic painting, a tradition that influenced painting in the Byzantine Empire over a long period.

The third layer dates from around the mid-seventh century, probably from the time of Martin I (649–54). It shows Sts. Basil and John Chrysostom, linked to the images of the Fathers of the Eastern Church on the left wall of the apse arch, holding scrolls bearing text from the Lateran Council of 649. Finally, the fourth layer, from the time of John VII, depicting St. Gregory of Nazianzus, was executed as part of a much larger redecoration project for the presbytery.

There are also some large fragments of surviving wall painting in the nave which record other phases in the development of painting in the seventh century. In particular, there is a group of frescos dating from the first decades of the century, showing scenes of Solomon and the Maccabean martyrs and an Annunciation on a pilaster in the nave. These are strongly evocative of Hellenistic painting. In their use of powerful modeling and their elegant free-flowing lines, they show affinity with the Annunciation on the palimpsest wall.

Mosaics and Icons

The most important seventh-century mosaic is in the apse at Sant'Agnese fuori le Mura on Via Nomentana. The work marks the resumption of commissioning by the papacy: it was executed on the orders of Honorius I (625–38), who had the apse seen today constructed near the tomb of the martyr saint, Agnes. The mosaic shows St. Agnes with the kneeling pope, who presents a model of the church, and another figure, identifiable as Pope Symmachus (498–514). The figures, completely frontal in presentation, are depicted against a background of gold tesserae, which helps to give the image a sense of insubstantiality and transcendence in accordance with the stylistic trend of contemporary Byzantine painting.

John IV (640–42) founded near the Lateran Baptistery an oratory dedicated to St. Venantius to house the relics of martyrs from Dalmatia and Istria. The oratory was decorated with mosaic that must have been executed later at the time of John IV's successor, Theodore I (642–49), since both popes are portrayed on the lower half of the apse, together with Sts. Peter, Paul, John the Baptist, John the Evangelist, and Venantius. These saints, four on each side, flank a praying Virgin. In the center of the apse is a bust of Christ with archangels on each side, while on the arch are the symbols of the Evangelists and representations of the cities of Jerusalem and Bethlehem above four figures of Dalmatian saints.

Two interesting icons that are probably seventh-century survive, although it is impossible to date them precisely. One is the so-called Virgin *salus populi Romani* (salvation of the Roman people) in the Cappella Paolina in Santa Maria Maggiore, whose original appearance has been greatly altered by successive repainting. The other is the Santa Maria *de Tempulo* icon, now kept in the Oratory of the Rosario, clearly of Byzantine provenance.

Painting

These and other works bear witness to the profound influence that the figurative tradition of the eastern Empire had on the Roman artistic world. This influence came partly through the growing volume of precious objects such as ivories, textiles, and jewelry, important vehicles for the transfer of stylistic and iconographic features. Another factor was the number of Greeks who occupied the papal throne in the seventh century and who commissioned major works of figurative art. Many monastic communities from the east also chose to make Rome their base. It was in these circumstances that the Byzantine painting style made steady progress, leaving its mark on traditional Roman pictorial language, for which works such as the mosaics of Santa Maria Maggiore and those of Santi Cosma e Damiano represented authoritative models, providing both artistic and technical inspiration.

In the same context is a group of paintings of great interest, though it is difficult to analyse their stylistic features and equally difficult to pin down their chronology, partly because of their poor state of conservation. These are the paintings in the church of Santa Maria in Via Lata, which was founded in the years around 500 and appears in records from the end of the eighth century onwards. A fresco representing the Seven Sleepers of Ephesus has been discovered in the underground space below the building, with stylistic features that are clearly Byzantine. It dates from somewhere between the end of the sixth century to the second half of the seventh. What is certain is that its origin is eastern, from the point of view of both style and iconography (it has Greek inscriptions). Another scene, the judgment of Solomon, was painted in the same period, while a brief cycle of stories from the life of St. Erasmus was probably painted in the eighth century.

However, it was John VII (705–7), responsible in his brief time as pope for commissioning a large number of works, who left an indelible—and perhaps the most significant—mark on eighth-century painting. Greek by origin, John was the son of the official responsible for the maintenance of the imperial palaces and a man of great learning ("natione Graecus... vir eruditissimus"), according to the *Liber pontificalis*.

The Oratory of the Virgin

John is linked with two important pictorial works, a mosaic and a fresco. The first relates to the famous oratory dedicated to the Virgin, consecrated on March 21, 706 by John himself, who was described in an inscription as *servus Sanctae Mariae* (servant of the Virgin). Situated against the inner facade of St. Peter's, it was demolished when the basilica was rebuilt in the first decade of the seventeenth century. Something is known of its general appearance, however, from drawings in Giacomo Grimaldi's *Instrumenta autentica* (Vatican Library, Ms. Barb. Lat. 2733), and from other illustrated and descriptive sources.

The interior of the oratory was completely covered with mosaic depicting a cycle of scenes from the childhood of Christ and his Passion. Only fragments, and those not in good condition, have come down to us: the Adoration of the Magi (now in Santa Maria in Cosmedin), the bathing of the infant Jesus, the portrait of John VII with the square halo used for a person still living, the Entry into Jerusalem in the Lambertini deposit in St. Peter's, a praying Virgin in the Ricci Chapel in San Marco in Florence, the Virgin of the Nativity in the Museo Diocesano in Orte, St. Joseph of the Nativity in the Pushkin Museum in Moscow, and part of a Crucifixion, almost totally reworked, in the Studio del Mosaico in the Vatican.

The exceptional quality of these mosaics is unparalleled in Roman artistic output at this time. Nor do any works outside the city come anywhere near them in quality. Greek culture—or rather, that of Constantinople—which had been an integral part of John's education, is apparent as an ineradicable background, not only for the stylistic features so strongly impregnated with Hellenism, but also for a number of details regarding the technical execution, such as the use of marble tesserae to represent the flesh of the faces portrayed.

Painting in the Eighth Century

The second great group of pictorial works for which John VII was responsible is the series of wall paintings in Santa Maria Antiqua, already mentioned. Here John had the decoration of the *schola cantorum* and the presbytery refurbished, with the addition of biblical scenes. These too reveal the influence, albeit to a different degree, of Hellenistic molding and chiaroscuro that had characterized the Annunciation painted about a century earlier, and which had given the palimpsest wall an air of antiquity even then.

The pictorial output of the first decades of the eighth century is almost totally lost. All that remains, as a faint testimony of that output, are a few wall paintings in the nave of the lower church of San Crisogono in Trastevere, fragments of a Christ cycle, and a number of figures of saints. It can be dated to the time of Gregory III (731–41) and seems to contain echoes, in the use of chiaroscuro, of the paintings commissioned by John VII.

Still in the church of Santa Maria Antiqua, at the time of Zacharias I (741–52), a small chapel dedicated to Sts. Cyriacus and Julitta was decorated with fresco, commissioned by the dean (*primicerius*) Theodotus. On the rear wall was an enthroned Virgin with Sts. Peter and Paul, together with Zacharias and the donor. The donor also appears in two other decorations in

FOLLOWING PAGES:
Detail of a mosaic from the triumphal arch of Santi Cosma e Damiano. The work has survived only in fragments; this view shows the Lamb of God in front of a cross lying on a throne encrusted with gems.

Crucifixion scene from the chapel of Sts. Cyriacus and Julitta in Santa Maria Antiqua. This fresco forms the centerpiece of a large private endowment made by the dean of the church, Theodotus, between 741 and 752. The art historical value of the scene lies in its combination of eastern pictorial elements, such as the *colobium* worn by Christ—an item otherwise known only from Syrian manuscripts—and the Latin characters which identify the Savior.

the chapel, in one accompanied by members of his family. The portraits are executed with great care and with obvious attention to accuracy. The rest of the frescos show various images of saints, the scene of the martyrdom of Cyriacus and Julitta—noteworthy for its unusually powerful sense of narrative—and a Crucifixion scene of remarkably complex iconography on the wall above the altar, in which Christ wears a *colobium*, a long tunic. This, together with other stylistic features, testifies to the influence which Palestinian painting, in particular the painting linked with a number of icons in the monastery of St. Catherine in Sinai, had on Roman figurative style in the eighth century.

This influence is also discernible in the frescos that represent stories of Christ and in

medallions with busts of saints in Santa Saba on the Little Aventine, the most important religious community of eastern monks in Rome. It can also be seen in the stories from the life of St. Erasmus in one of the underground bays of the *diaconia* (early Christian welfare center) of Santa Maria in Via Lata, although these have inscriptions in Latin.

The High Middle Ages

The crucial transition between the eighth and the ninth century was symbolically marked by the coronation of Charlemagne by Leo III (795–816) in St. Peter's on Christmas Day of the year 800. It was also marked by a decisive change of direction in figurative painting towards western models, and the consequent progressive abandonment of subject matter and stylistic formulae of eastern derivation. Roman pictorial art of these decades looks to its own early Christian origins or, at most, to the late imperial age, and rediscovers in large-scale mosaic decorations its own expressive medium *par excellence*.

Leo III was responsible for important projects of this kind, starting with the Triclinium in the Lateran Palace, where the apse mosaic depicted Christ on the Celestial Mountain, flanked by Sts. Peter and Paul, to represent the *Missio apostolorum* (Christ sending forth the Apostles to preach the Gospel). On the pendentives of the arch, on the left Christ was shown entrusting the keys to Peter (the figure is perhaps also identifiable as St. Sylvester) and the imperial standard to Constantine, while on the right hand side St. Peter passed the papal pallium or stole to Leo III and the imperial standard to Charlemagne. The mosaic was badly damaged and entirely remade around 1600. Finally, in about 1730, the Triclinium was dismantled and reconstructed on the Piazza di San Giovanni in Laterano, where it can still be seen. The new mosaic was made by the painter Pier Leone Ghezzi, using old records as a guide. Only a fragment of the medieval work survives: the face of an apostle is preserved in the Museo Sacro in the Vatican Museums. The choice of iconography was clearly determined by a desire to reaffirm the supremacy of theocratic power and the derivation from this power of all earthly authority, including that of the emperor.

Other important mosaics were carried out under Leo III. They include the decoration of the so-called *Aula Concilii*, also in the Lateran Palace, and that in the apse of Santa Susanna. Both are now lost but have been recorded in illustrated and literary sources. Another is the decoration in Santi Nereo e Achilleo, which has

been partially preserved, at least on the apse arch, where the Transfiguration of Christ, the Annunciation, and a Virgin appear.

The Mosaics of Paschal I

A work commissioned by Paschal I (817–24) marked the start of another significant phase in mosaic decoration. His principal undertakings were in the churches of Santa Maria in Domnica, Santa Prassede, and Santa Cecilia in Trastevere, where the apses are decorated with the most finely executed mosaic. Paschal appears in them all, with the square halo indicating a living person.

At Santa Maria in Domnica the pope kneels at the feet of a monumental image of the Virgin and Child, while in the others he is shown standing, at the far left of the apse, at the end of a row of saints ranged on either side of the Christ in Majesty flanked by Sts. Peter and Paul, a composition based on the apse of Santi Cosma e Damiano.

The triumphal arch at Santa Prassede has an unusual representation of the Celestial (New) Jerusalem. The richly jeweled walls enclose Christ among angels, with the Apostles in two rows on either side, the Virgin, St. John the Baptist, the prophets Moses and Elijah, and clear allusions to the Apocalypse (Revelation of St. John). The interior of the small chapel of

St. Zeno, which opens off the south aisle, is entirely covered with mosaic in glowing colors, which extends to the front of the entrance, where a large lunette contains a double circle of busts of saints. Inside, on the ceiling, there is an *imago clipeata* (image within a medallion, or circular frame) of Christ, supported by four full-length angels that occupy the space of the pendentives of the arch. In the lunettes on the walls are representations of the Transfiguration and Resurrection, busts of saints, and a portrait of the pope's mother, Theodora, for whom the chapel was built as a mausoleum.

The style of these mosaics is based firmly on the desire to communicate the essential message of the images. This is achieved through giving the surfaces a flat appearance and using extremely clear outlines. In addition, the intensity of color is quite new and in some ways unusual, with patches of color placed side by side and an abundant use of orange and red highlights, which, especially in the representation of flesh, produce wonderfully realistic but subtle effects.

Decline

Up until the time of Paschal I it is not too difficult to trace—with the help in some cases of written sources giving information about lost works—a continuous line in terms of style and

Depiction of the Celestial Jerusalem on the triumphal arch of Santa Prassede. The city of the Elect is shown as a town whose walls are encrusted with precious stones and guarded by angels. The college of the Apostles appears in two groups, which approach Christ standing in the center. The group on the right is led by the Virgin and St. John the Baptist, and that on the left by the eponymous saint, Praxedes.

the commissioning of works of art, running right through the early Middle Ages. However, the second half of the ninth century and the tenth century was a period in which such large-scale works became steadily more rare. There are nevertheless one or two interesting works from this time, such as the apse mosaic in San Marco, which depicts the pope who commissioned it, Gregory IV (827–44), the last example—and certainly a less accomplished one—of the style of the mosaics commissioned by Paschal I.

A devastating raid on the city by the Saracens in 846 and an earthquake in 847 exacerbated the economic problems that were already affecting the papacy and led to a further reduc-

Mosaic above the entrance to the chapel of St. Zeno in Santa Prassede, an endowment by Paschal I (817–24). The window over the entrance is framed by two rows of busts of saints. The inner row shows the Virgin and Christ child in the middle along with two male and eight female saints, while in the outer row half portraits of the twelve apostles are grouped around a portrait of Christ.

tion in the number of new works of art commissioned. The decoration of San Martino ai Monti, now lost, was executed in the time of Leo IV (847–55), as was probably a mosaic depicting St. Peter, in St. Peter's basilica. There are also a number of frescos painted in the second half of the ninth century, such as the cycle of the life of Christ in the lower church of San Clemente and the frescos in the chapel of St. Barbara in Santi Quattro Coronati.

Through almost the whole tenth century the difficult political and economic conditions Rome was suffering led to a drastic reduction in the number of major commissions. Moreover, the paucity of surviving evidence, both figurative and written, means it is not possible to

reconstruct the artistic culture of the time other than in the most fragmentary fashion. Among the most interesting artistic works were the frescos of Santa Maria in Pallara (now San Sebastiano al Palatino), which narrated the stories of Christ and the saints. These frescos have disappeared and are known to us only through the usual seventeenth-century copies, but in the apse there is still a figure of Christ between saints and, below, a praying Virgin between archangels and female saints. The frescos were commissioned between 973 and 999 by a physician named Pietro and his wife Joanna, who had themselves portrayed in the apsidal arch together with the Elders of the Apocalypse and figures of prophets carrying the Apostles on their shoulders.

The Eleventh Century: Rome and Monte Cassino

The eleventh century saw a number of important events concerning pictorial art in Rome, which foreshadowed the trend towards a revival of the antique style, a trend that was to develop more fully in the next century. In this context, it is still open to debate whether there existed from the middle of the century a network of relations between Rome and the abbey of Monte Cassino, which under the rule of the abbot Desiderio occupied a privileged position in relation to Rome, not only in religious matters. Unfortunately the fragmentary surviving figurative art of this period makes it impossible to work out exactly what these relations were. It is not known whether the return to subject matter and stylistic themes from late antiquity and early Christianity in Rome was a reflection of works executed at Monte Cassino for Desiderio, who had mosaic artists brought from Constantinople, or whether, on the contrary, it was the works commissioned by the popes in Rome that in some way were responsible for the classicism that characterized pictorial art at Monte Cassino. What is certain is that a deep interest in antiquity was not a new phenomenon. As has been seen, it had been a fundamental component of art in Rome from the earliest Middle Ages.

On the other hand, if Desiderio was obliged to make use of artists from Constantinople to execute the mosaic decoration of the new abbey church at Monte Cassino, it is probable that in Rome there was a lack of skilled craftsmen able to plan and carry out a decoration that would adhere to early Christian models, in the spirit of the archaism that was beginning to take hold and which soon, from mid-century onwards, would become firmly established.

Frescos

In this context, some of the most interesting of frescos from the early eleventh century are those in Sant'Urbano alla Caffarella near the Via Appia, a church created through the conversion of a second-century Roman building. The decoration comprises a Christ cycle and a series of scenes relating to Sts. Urban, Cecilia, Lawrence, and other martyrs. It can be dated to 1011, due to an inscription below the Crucifixion—at the foot of which there appears a lay donor—which states "BONIZZO FRI A.XPI MXI" (in the year 1011).

The choice of scenes and their arrangement—in two bands, framed within false marble columns that emphasize the architectural structure of the whole composition—recall wall paintings with scenes from the Old and New Testaments in St. Peter's. The style, although difficult to make out because the decoration has undergone extensive reworking, shows clear signs in the iconography and elsewhere of the growing trend of archaism that was soon to become dominant in Rome.

The frescos in the south aisle of the lower church of San Crisogono in Trastevere, with scenes from the life of St. Benedict, probably belong to the years immediately after the middle of the century, though they were formerly ascribed to the tenth century. They have been correctly identified as connected with the pictorial art of Monte Cassino. The important linking figure is Abbot Federico of Monte Cassino (1057–58), who was also cardinal archpriest of San Crisogono. A clear relationship has been identified between these frescos and the iconography in some of the miniatures in the famous lectionary of Abbot Desiderio (Vatican Library, Ms. Vat. lat. 1202), executed shortly after 1071, the year in which the new abbey church of Monte Cassino was consecrated.

The last quarter of the century is marked by the pontificate of Gregory VII (1073–85). Gregory was responsible for a program of religious reform whose influence on the output of figurative art has been studied in depth. It is clear that there was a conscious desire to achieve an archaic tone in works of art, as well as a return to early Christian iconographic themes. An interesting example of this trend is provided by the frescos in the Oratorium Marianum in Santa Pudenziana, showing stories from the life of Sts. Pudentiana and Praxedes, and an enthroned Virgin and Child flanked by these two saints, datable to 1080.

The San Clemente School

However, the work offering the most extensive evidence of the richness and originality of the pictorial art of those years is without doubt the frescos in the lower church of San Clemente, with stories from the lives of Sts. Clement and Alexis, datable to the last two decades of the century. They were commissioned by two members of the lay community, Beno di Rapiza and Maria Macellaria, who are identified by an inscription and are portrayed in the lower part of the scene with the miracle of the child found alive in a church at the bottom of the sea, close to St. Clement, and together with their children Clemente and Altilia. This is particularly interesting, showing as it does subjects from everyday life for the first time in commissioned works of art.

The other scenes in this cycle, between the narthex and the nave, depict the translation of

Fresco from around 1080 from the Oratorium Marianum in Santa Pudenziana, showing the sisters Pudentiana and Praxedes presenting the crowns of their martyrdom to the Virgin and Christ child.

history of Roman painting, particularly from the manner in which the compositional and structural elements were utilized within the painted area, such as the *vela*, the architectural framing of the scenes, or the buildings themselves that are depicted. A new direction is also evident here and there in touches of naturalism, as for example in the surprising variety of fish present in the miracle of the church at the bottom of the sea, or in the lifelike representation of the villains in the miracle of the column. In the last scene is also one of the earliest examples of written Italian.

Another group of frescos displaying the decorative repertory of late antiquity and early Christianity is those in the nave of Santa Maria in Cosmedin. These frescos, in very poor condition, are dated 1123. Originally they may have depicted scenes from the Old and New Testaments. A series of decorative elements including foliage, dancing putti, medallions containing masks, candelabra, and cornucopias is evidence that Roman artists at this time were making a careful study of classical models.

There are also decorative elements based on models from antiquity in the meager remains of frescos in the church of Santi Quattro Coronati, visible between the apse and the roof. These were painted by two painters called Gregorio and Petrolino between 1111 and 1116, as part of the reconstruction work at the church undertaken by Paschal II (1099–1118).

The fullest expression of this revival of the ancient style is to be found in the apse mosaics in the upper church of San Clemente, which probably date from the 1120s. Here the choice of mosaic as the artistic medium is a clear demonstration of a deliberate turning back to the tradition of late antiquity: mosaics had not been made in Rome on this scale for centuries and production of the materials used in this technique must have, therefore, largely died out. Considering the quality of the work, it is hard to know where the craftsmen can have come from, although it is possible that they came from Campania in the 1130s, bringing with them knowledge of the latest Byzantine stylistic features, similar to those displayed in the illuminated manuscripts produced by the scriptorum of the abbey of Monte Cassino in the years around 1100.

Above all, though, it is the subject matter of the San Clemente mosaic that demonstrates links with early Christian figurative art. A cross with the dead Christ, flanked by the Virgin and St. John the Evangelist, is surrounded by thick whorls of acanthus populated by a multitude of figures, Christian and secular, putti, shepherds, all kinds of animals, and genre scenes. All these can be traced back to models in early Christian

TOP:
Fresco from the lower church of San Clemente, showing the miracle of St. Clement's grave. The miraculous event occurs under water, and is given a lively rendering in the detailed depiction of various types of fish.

ABOVE:
Fresco depicting the life of St. Alexis from the lower church of San Clemente. It shows a narrative intensity, as well as a number of compositional and naturalistic elements new to eleventh-century painting.

the relics of St. Clement, the Mass of St. Clement, the miracle of the column (when heathens ordered to seize the pope were struck blind and carried off a column instead), Christ enthroned between the archangels Gabriel and Michael and Sts. Clement and Nicholas, and St. Clement enthroned. There are also two episodes from the life of St. Alexis and figures of saints and prophets.

The stories of Sts. Clement and Alexis display a liveliness and narrative immediacy which delineates a turning-point in this phase of the

catacomb painting and also to monumental painting from the fourth and fifth centuries.

The sparse but important remains of the frescos formerly in the crypt of San Nicola in Carcere belong to both the same period and the same figurative milieu. What is left comprises medallions with prophets, the baptism of Christ, and fragments of decorative elements, with animals among foliage motifs, all clearly showing an early Christian derivation.

The path of the artists working at San Clemente is continued in the mosaic of the apse at Santa Maria in Trastevere, a work dating from the papacy of Innocent II (1130–43). Here, in the center of the apse, Christ and the Virgin, as Queen of Heaven and bride of Christ (*Sponsa Christi*), are depicted seated on a single jeweled throne. The throne, an innovation for a subject depicted in an apse of a Roman church, relates to a passage from the Song of Songs. Two stylistic trends can be discerned: one, apparent on the apse arch, is closer to the stylistically archaic model at San Clemente while the other, a more rigid and strongly linear style, is visible in the decoration of the apse, particularly in the figures of saints flanking Christ and the Virgin. It is worth noting that the faces of the divine personages in this composition are thought by some to be an almost direct copy, stylistically as well as in the features portrayed, of the two most venerated Roman icons, the Savior in the *Sancta Sanctorum* (the private chapel of the Pope in the Lateran Palace) and the Virgin in Santa Maria Nova (now Santa Francesca Romana).

In the apse of Santa Francesca Romana is a mosaic showing an enthroned Virgin and Child within an archway in classical style, flanked by four saints. The date of this work must coincide with the consecration of the church, 1161. It fits into the trend that began with the San Clemente mosaic and continued with Santa Maria in Trastevere—which it most closely resembles—a trend that was marked by an archaic feel, and an emphasis on strong outlines and a simplified representation of figures.

The three mosaics—San Clemente, Santa Maria in Trastevere, and Santa Francesca Romana—are linked not only in terms of stylistic features but also by the effects of political and religious events in Rome between 1130 and 1161. It is indeed reasonable to surmise that a single workshop was involved in producing these three mosaics, with craftsmen from Campania, which over the years was responsible for creating an entire figurative lexicon based on early Christian Roman art, giving rise to the revival of an archaic culture. This trend was to enter a new phase in the next century, when it would be more profoundly and systematically developed.

Detail of a mosaic in the apse of the upper church of San Clemente. The center of the composition is occupied by a crucifix flanked by the Virgin and St. John the Baptist. The lower end of the cross is in the shape of an acanthus whose vines spread out across the entire surface of the conch, symbolizing *Ecclesia* (the Church), whose root is the Cross, or Tree of Life.

Santa Croce in Gerusalemme

A mural painting, which is decidedly distant stylistically from the works discussed so far, is that in the basilica of Santa Croce in Gerusalemme, which can be dated to the 1120s or 1130s. It was commissioned by Lucius II (1144–45), who had been titular cardinal of the basilica since 1125, making it likely that he had commissioned work in the building even before he became pope. The fresco cycle, which survives only in fragments mostly detached from

FOLLOWING PAGES:
Lower section of an early twelfth-century mosaic from the apse of the upper church of San Clemente. The four rivers of Paradise are shown on the central axis of the composition, the presence of various animals on the banks of these rivers lending the scene an idyllic quality.

...VCIS IACOBI DENS IGNATII Q...

...ISVPRA SCRIPTI · REQVIE SCVN...

San Paolo fuori le Mura. Detail of the mosaic in the apse with a figure of Christ enthroned, flanked by the Apostles Peter and Paul. The version seen today is a nineteenth-century replica of a thirteenth-century original which was destroyed by fire in 1823.

Head of the Apostle Peter. One of the few remaining sections of the original apse mosaic from the thirteenth century. Sacristy of San Paolo fuori le Mura.

FOLLOWING PAGES:
Fresco in the oratory of St. Sylvester in the church of Santi Quattro Coronati, showing the emperor Constantine giving the tiara to Pope Sylvester.

the wall and preserved in the church, included in the nave a series of tondi with figures of patriarchs and an elaborate decorative frieze. There is no way of knowing whether the iconographic program also included stories from the Old and New Testaments. Other frescos on the triumphal arch, now almost completely indecipherable, show a Last Judgment scene, with an *imago clipeata* that must have contained a bust of Christ or the Lamb of God, between the symbols of the Evangelists and the seven candlesticks. The Santa Croce frescos, the work of at least three different painters, testify to the extent to which Rome had been penetrated by Byzantine stylistic features that were clearly of Venetian derivation.

As far as painting on wood is concerned, the icons in Sant'Angelo in Pescheria (signed by Pietro di Belizo and Belluomo), now in the Santissimo Nome di Maria church and the Magnani collection in Reggio Emilia, all seem to belong to the same stylistic milieu and may even be from the same workshop. They display convincing stylistic similarities to the San Nicola in Carcere fresos and it is possible therefore for them to be assigned a significant chronological marker, at around the end of the 1120s.

San Giovanni a Porta Latina

One of the most important groups of pictorial works—and one of the most difficult to assess—dates from the last decade of the twelfth century. This is the cycle of stories from the Old and New Testaments in the basilica of San Giovanni a Porta Latina on the walls of the nave. In addition there is a Last Judgment on the apse arch, with angels presenting the Bible, flanked by the symbols of the Evangelists. Other frescos at the end of the right aisle have been identified as scenes from the life of St. Elizabeth. On the inner facade are stories from the lives of Sts. Anne and Joachim, and on the walls of the choir are the twenty-four Elders of the Apocalypse and the four Evangelists.

Traditionally these frescos have been dated to 1190, the year in which the church was dedicated, as recorded in an inscription that was formerly on the interior facade but is now clumsily inserted in a modern lectern. The cycle is the sole example in Rome to have come down to us relatively entire, more in terms of its composition than for its style, given that the finishing layers of color have been almost completely lost. It reveals the same reversion to early Christian features that marks most of the pictorial work of the twelfth century, though in other ways it is unusual. It is difficult to identify the model for the cycle or the origins of the craftsmen who painted it. Comparisons, not altogether satisfactory, have been made with other frescos and, especially with regard to iconography, with the Umbro–Roman Atlantic Bibles. Certainly the San Giovanni a Porta Latina frescos draw in equal measure from local and, more generally, central Italian Byzantine tradition and from the innovative trends demonstrated by Roman artists in this century.

The Later Middle Ages

The election in 1198 of Cardinal Lotario of the family of the counts of Segni as Innocent III (d. 1216) marked the start of a new phase of development in monumental art whose focal points are to be found in St. Peter's and in San Paolo fuori le Mura.

St. Peter's

As part of a large-scale program of works in Constantine's ancient basilica of St. Peter's, Innocent III had the early Christian mosaic in the apse redone. The new mosaic could be seen until 1592, when it was destroyed during

OPPOSITE:
Mid-twelfth-century depiction, in tempera on wood, of the Last Judgment. The artists, Nicola and Giovanni, structured the narrative in five horizontal registers, one on top of the other. In the bottom register can be seen the two patrons of the work, Costanza and Benedetta; these two Benedictines are shown kneeling before the Virgin who is seated on a throne. Rome, Vatican Picture Gallery.

Detail of an early thirteenth-century fresco cycle in the oratory of St. Sylvester in Santi Quattro Coronati, showing the three messengers sent from Constantine to Pope Sylvester. The work is an outstanding example of medieval Roman art: it relates the legend of the Pope miraculously curing Emperor Constantine by baptizing him—an event which led to the establishment of papal sovereignty.

the rebuilding of St. Peter's. However, it was carefully copied in Giacomo Grimaldi's *Instrumenta autentica.*

The new mosaic, which was probably completed in about 1209–12, showed Christ enthroned in the center flanked by the standing figures of Sts. Peter and Paul, against a background of a classical river landscape with the mountain of Paradise, with the four rivers of Paradise and stags representing the faithful. In the middle of the wide band below was the throne and the Lamb of God, flanked by twelve angels approaching from the cities of Jerusalem and Bethlehem. On either side of the throne were images of the Church of Rome (*Ecclesia Romana*), holding a standard, and Innocent III, commissioner of the mosaic. These last two images are the only surviving parts of the work, together with a medallion containing a phoenix (now in the Museo di Roma). From an iconographic viewpoint, the St. Peter's apse mosaic was an explicit reaffirmation of both the authority of the pope, directly derived from God, and the importance of the basilica of St. Peter's over St. John Lateran; for centuries they had vied for the position of the most important church in western Christianity.

From a stylistic viewpoint, the fragments that survive seem to show the influence of Sicilian mosaics. This had spread through central Italy thanks to the itinerant artistic workshops, such as that which produced the mosaic in the abbey of Grottaferrata depicting the descent of the Holy Ghost.

San Paolo fuori le Mura

The other large-scale work that Innocent III must have planned as part of his program of artistic commissions was the redecoration of the apse of San Paolo fuori le Mura. This project was in fact undertaken by Honorius III (1216–27), who brought in mosaic craftsmen from Venice, having requested them from the doge, Pietro Ziani. The mosaic was seriously damaged in the disastrous fire of 1823. In 1836 work began on replacing the mosaic almost in its entirety with a replica which faithfully reproduced the original iconography and incorporated the parts of the old mosaic that had been saved from the fire.

In the center of the apse is Christ enthroned, flanked on the right by Sts. Peter and Andrew and on the left by Sts. Paul and Luke, standing on a strip of flowery meadow with numerous animals. In the lower part of the mosaic the other Apostles are portrayed, together with the Evangelists and St. Barnabas. Below the throne are five Holy Innocents, whose relics were preserved in the basilica. Another three figures, identified by inscriptions, complete the composition: Honorius III, prostrate before the right foot of Christ, the sacristan Adinolfo, and the abbot Giovanni Caetani.

According to the dedicatory inscription, which was transcribed before 1823, Giovanni Caetani was responsible for the completion of the mosaic. This part of the mosaic appears to have been carried out slightly later than the upper part and by a different artist, who perhaps had already worked on Innocent III's commission at St. Peter's. Other fragments of mosaic have been detached and are now kept in the sacristy. They show the heads of St. Peter and two other Apostles and four birds, originally from the strip of ground at the lower edge of the semi-dome of the apse.

The San Paolo fuori le Mura mosaic had a determining influence on the course of Roman figurative language in the early thirteenth century. In the decades that followed this new trend was evident in ambitious works such as the frescos in the chapel of St. Sylvester in Santi Quattro Coronati and also those by the artist

ICCE...

+ REGNVM·PERCIPITE·BENEDICTI·QVIQ·VENITE· VOBIS·PARATVM·PER·SECLA·CVNCTA·DONATVM·

VENI
TE·BE
NEDIC
TI·PA
TRIS·
MEIS·
PER
CIPI
TE·RE
GNVM

DISCE
DITE·
QANE·MALE
DICTI
INIG
NE·QV
MIE·E
VIB

+ OFFERET·VT·PAVLVS·FVERIT·QDOVISQ·LVCRATVS·QD·MARTYR·STEPHANVS·CLAMAT·GREX·ISTE·PVSILL·MEQ·APA·ISTI·POT·P·SEPE·DEDISTI·VEL·SI·MVL·IN·DVTO·REPARASTI·CORPORE·NV·
VDICAT·ORBE·ADVEN·ET·BLANDVS·IVST·FR·VG·REMD·IVST·PVTENISV·MANINERE·RGNIDI·RISOVOQ·TARTRE·INIVSTOS·INIGNE·MI·CLI·PVI

C·ME·GENVS·VOLVCRV·VEL·REPTILIS·ATQ·FERARV·REDDVNT·HVMANA·PISCES·QVOQ·MENBRA·VORATA·
CLANGORE·TVBAE·SVRGVNT·DE·PVLVRE·TERRAE·NIQ·QVE·IOHS·PI·

...TIS·EST...·TES·PARADISI·...DES·HOS·RT·......·AB·ELIS·IRA·

DA·BENEDIC·ANCILLAE·DI·CONSTANTIA·ABBATISSA·

known as the Maestro Ornatista in the crypt of Anagni Cathedral.

The Chapel of St. Sylvester and the Tre Fontane

Other works from this period are smaller in scale but nevertheless of considerable interest. One that is unfortunately lost, although its overall composition is known to us through seventeenth-century copies, is the series of frescos in the chapel of St. Sylvester in the convent of San Martino ai Monti, painted between 1219 and 1227. The only cycle of wall paintings from these years that can be dated precisely, it was probably commissioned by Cardinal Guala Bicchieri, who became titular cardinal of San Martino in 1211. Also worth noting are a mosaic icon depicting the Virgin and Child in the chapel of the Sacrament in San Paolo fuori le Mura, whose style only vaguely resembles that of the apse mosaics, the apse frescos in San Bartolomeo all'Isola, those in the oratory of San Sebastiano fuori le Mura, and those on the arch of Charlemagne in the Cistercian Abbazia delle Tre Fontane on Via Laurentina.

The Tre Fontane cycle is particularly interesting because of its historical theme, unique in thirteenth-century Roman pictorial art. The work consists of two large lunettes on which a series of narrative scenes are painted in a fresh and lively style. These relate the events surrounding Charlemagne's capture of Ansedonia, a victory achieved thanks to the intervention of the miraculous relic of the Tre Fontane—the head of St. Anastasius—and the subsequent donation of the conquered towns to the Cistercian community. The cycle was probably painted during the first two decades of the thirteenth century.

St. Peter's

Another important mosaic, dating from the time of Gregory IX (1227–41), is that on the facade of St. Peter's, which replaced the earlier mid-fifth-century decoration. This was executed by local craftsmen, probably influenced by Venetian masters working at San Paolo fuori le Mura. Little is known about its stylistic features from the surviving fragments and thanks to the usual seventeenth-century copies we know its iconography. The mosaic had an apocalyptic theme—traditional in the interior of religious buildings—with an image of Christ enthroned, flanked by the Virgin and St. Peter and the symbols of the Evangelists. Beneath these was the kneeling figure of Gregory. In the lower part of the mosaic were the Evangelists and beneath them the twenty-four Elders of the Apocalypse and the lambs emerging from the walls of Jerusalem and Bethlehem.

For years there was only one known surviving fragment of this work, depicting the face of Gregory IX. This fragment, preserved in the Museo di Roma, was in poor condition, with large patches of wall fabric showing. In recent times, however, two new fragments of the work have been identified: the faces of St. Luke (Vatican Picture Gallery) and of the Virgin (Pushkin Museum, Moscow). Finely executed, they seem to derive stylistic features from the apse of San Paolo fuori le Mura.

Frescos

The 1240s were dominated by the struggle between pope and emperor. Innocent IV (1243–54) and Frederick II (1194–1250) confronted each other not only in the political and religious arena but also on the battlefield. Rome was threatened by imperial troops. In 1244 Innocent fled to Lyons and the protection of the king of France. The following year he promulgated a papal bull from Lyons excommunicating Frederick. In Rome, Stefano Conti, in charge of the city (*vicarius Urbis*) and titular cardinal of Santa Maria in Trastevere, had the monastery of the Santi Quattro Coronati on the Caelian Hill fortified as a place of refuge in case of attack by Frederick's troops. A marble inscription on the south wall records that on the Friday before Palm Sunday 1246 a chapel dedicated to St. Sylvester was consecrated by Rinaldo, bishop of Ostia.

The chapel is decorated with a frescoed cycle narrating stories from the lives of St. Sylvester and Constantine. Everything in the frescos emphasizes the subordination of imperial power to divine power—and therefore to the authority of the pope, God's representative on earth. The cycle closes with scenes from the life of St. Sylvester and a Last Judgment above the entrance. From a stylistic point of view, the frescos derive details of their style and composition from the mosaics in the cathedral of Monreale in Sicily. However, it is also possible to detect signs of a new influence, that of the Venetian mosaic craftsmen working at San Paolo fuori le Mura twenty years earlier, particularly in the treatment of drapery.

The frescos in the left aisle of the basilica of Santi Giovanni e Paolo also belong to this milieu. Executed about a decade later than those in the chapel of St. Sylvester, they are less original and lifelike, with rather dull figures of saints placed in the spaces of a simple arcade.

An icon of the Virgin suckling the Infant Christ, the so-called *Virgin of the Chain* (Madonna della Catena) in San Silvestro al Quirinale, displays stylistic points of contact with the St. Sylvester frescos. Two other paintings on panel, which in the seventeenth century were referred to as being in the oratory of San Gregorio Nazianzeno, seem to have been influenced by Byzantine painting from the late Comnenus era. These are the Virgin in the Galleria Nazionale d'Arte Antica in Palazzo Barberini and the panel depicting the Last Judgment in the Vatican Picture Gallery, signed by painters named Nicola and Giovanni.

After the St. Sylvester cycle, however, for about a quarter of a century there seems to have been no painting on so large a scale. There is evidence nevertheless that figurative traditions persisted and that a considerable amount of commissioning of works of art was still going on. An example is a mosaic panel from a tabernacle commissioned in 1256 by Giovanni Giacomo Capocci and his wife Vinia. The panel, formerly in Santa Maria Maggiore and now in the parish church of Vico near Frosinone, shows an enthroned Virgin and Child in the center, with donors presenting a model of the tabernacle. The panel almost certainly came out of one of the Cosmati marble workshops, whose craftsmen were accustomed to producing mosaics and were consequently skilled in the relevant artistic and production techniques. The use of color and the way in which the tesserae are laid down seem to echo motifs in the mosaic icon depicting the Virgin and Child in the chapel of the Sacrament in San Paolo fuori le Mura.

The Sancta Sanctorum

In 1277 Giovanni Gaetano Orsini ascended the papal throne, taking the name Nicholas III (1277–80). The new pope commissioned one of the most important complexes of pictorial works that was to be undertaken in the thirteenth century, the frescos and mosaic of the Sancta Sanctorum, the pope's private chapel in the Lateran Palace. Nicholas ordered the complete rebuilding and redecoration of the old chapel, dedicated to St. Lawrence and in existence since at least the eighth century. For centuries the most precious relics of Christianity had been preserved and venerated here, together with an ancient and miraculous image of the Savior, known as the Acheiropoeton (meaning that it was believed not to have been made by human hand).

The decoration was in both mosaic and fresco. The mosaic decorating the vault above the altar must have been of considerable significance for subsequent developments in this technique that had not been used for any large-scale works in Rome for several decades, not since the apse decoration of St. Peter's and San Paolo fuori le Mura. This return to the use of mosaic, essentially Roman, was decidedly archaistic in stylistic terms.

In the middle of the presbytery vault, on a gold background, is a bust of the Savior within a multicolored medallion supported by four full-length angels. The mosaic in the lunettes has busts of saints. The *imago clipeata* of Christ is striking because of the archaic style of the features of this hollow-cheeked solemn face, staring fixedly and, because of the frontality of the figure, which was almost certainly inspired by the Acheiropoeton icon below. The mosaic reveals a number of interesting technical and stylistic details. One of the most unusual formal characteristics is the use of rows of orange and red tesserae, with tonal gradations, not only as outlines for faces, hands, arms, and ears, but also as scattered highlights, creating a kind of relief and intended perhaps to enhance the luminosity of the composition, which was in a dark position.

The decoration of the chapel has frequently been linked, directly or indirectly, with the stay in Rome of the Florentine artist Cimabue. Evidence of Cimabue's presence in Rome is contained in a notary deed dated 1272, preserved in the archive of Santa Maria Maggiore. However, no work survives that has any connection with this visit, and the artists carrying out the mosaics and frescos in the Sancta Sanctorum do not seem to have been influenced by Cimabue.

The scenes painted on the walls above the gallery depict Nicholas III between Sts. Peter and Paul, presenting the model of the Sancta Sanctorum to Christ enthroned, the crucifixion of St. Peter, the beheading of St. Paul, the stoning of St. Stephen, the martyrdom of Sts. Lawrence and Agnes, and the miracle of St. Nicholas. Above, in the semilunettes, are two figures of angels on each wall, arranged symmetrically on either side of the windows. On the cross-vaulted ceiling over the main body of the chapel are the symbols of the four Evangelists, against a star-studded sky.

The choice of subjects, with scenes of martyrdom of saints, clearly shows the wish of the pope to reaffirm the importance of the apostolic tradition as the indisputable basis of papal authority. As for the stylistic features displayed, these were to become a rich source for exponents of the classical revival. It is important to stress the significance of this project in this regard: it was responsible for the development

of iconographic as well as stylistic themes that would subsequently dominate figurative art during the last quarter of the century. Its influence would extend to the work carried out in the upper church of San Francesco in Assisi.

Thanks to the recent restoration of the frescos, which removed some heavy repainting done in the late sixteenth century, new and important information about this remarkable complex has emerged. First, it has revealed the frescos' extraordinarily brilliant, shining colors, which are in almost perfect condition, having been protected for four centuries by the layer of paint that covered them. There are Pompeian reds, intense yellows and blues, and areas of chiaroscuro, none of which could have been guessed at. Altogether there is an entire repertory of artistic elements representing an archaic revival that left its mark on subsequent painting during the last quarter of the thirteenth century to a degree that cannot be overestimated.

St. Peter's and San Paolo fuori le Mura

Another work apparently from the same milieu survives in just two fragments, of outstanding figurative quality. These fragments were part of a cycle showing stories from the lives of Sts. Peter and Paul which decorated the front of the portico of St. Peter's. The cycle was destroyed in 1606 during the building of the new facade. The fragments, preserved today in St. Peter's, were part of a scene depicting the apparition of Christ in a dream to Constantine, with the heads of Sts. Peter and Paul. The cycle, which is mentioned by Vasari as the work of Margaritone d'Arezzo, was painted during the papacy of Urban IV (1261–64). It comprised at least sixteen scenes, reproduced in the *Album* of Domenico Tasselli da Lugo (Vatican Library, Archivio San Pietro, A 64 ter).

The two fragments, which at one time were identified as probably belonging to the circle of

Jacopo Torriti, should in fact be associated with the frescos of the Sancta Sanctorum and are datable to about the end of the 1280s. This connection is discernible in their solemn, monumental, and consciously archaic air and in the general layout of the composition, in accordance with the guidelines established in the work commissioned by Nicholas III.

Other important pictorial works are connected with Nicholas, including the series of portraits of popes within medallions in St. Peter's, St. John Lateran, and San Paolo fuori le Mura. In San Paolo's, Nicholas must have commissioned a thorough restoration of at least part of the frescos in the nave and put the abbot Giovanni (1278–79) in charge of the work. Unfortunately the 1823 fire resulted in the almost total loss of these works. Copies survive, but although they give a faithful reproduction of the subject matter, they do not reproduce the style.

According to Ghiberti, Pietro Cavallini was responsible for the painting, but it is difficult to assess this attribution with any certainty given the almost complete disappearance of the work itself. Only four portraits of popes escaped the fire. One of these, recently restored, turns out to be a work of high quality. It exemplifies a trend in Roman painting that combined a Byzantine stylistic intonation with a western pictorial language—the latter permeated by classical references but already showing a certain Gothic influence in the use of line, although in no way similar to Cavallini's style.

After the death of Nicholas III, other prominent personages left their mark on the figurative art of Rome, which became a crossroads of artists and ideas. The results of this intense activity spread to the rest of Italy and Europe.

Jacopo Torriti

The election as pope of Fra Girolamo Masci from Lisciano (near Ascoli Piceno) as Nicholas IV (1288–92) was a significant event in the history of the medieval papacy. Nicholas was from the Franciscan order, the first Franciscan to ascend the throne of St. Peter. His election was important from an historical viewpoint, because the choice of the conclave of cardinals fell not on a member of one of the great Roman families but on a representative of the religious order, which in those years, embodied the demand for spiritual renewal in the Church. It was also important for the history of art. During the four years of Nicholas' papacy some of the most important artistic projects not only in Rome, but anywhere, were planned and executed, most of them directly promoted by Nicholas himself and supported by the cardinals.

Nicholas IV was not new to undertakings of this kind. Between 1274 and 1279 he had been head of the Franciscan order. He was then elevated to the rank of cardinal by Nicholas III. It was as representative of the Pope that Fra Girolamo must have taken a close interest in the frescos being painted in the transept of the upper church of San Francesco in Assisi, a project promoted by the future pope and carried out by Cimabue and his workshop. Immediately after his election, Nicholas gave new impetus to the work in San Francesco, taking charge of the decoration of the nave, which depicted scenes from the Old and New Testaments. The painter chosen by the pope to carry out this work was Jacopo Torriti. In the years immediately following this commission, Nicholas entrusted Torriti with the decoration of the rebuilt apses of St. John Lateran and Santa Maria Maggiore.

The former facade of Santa Maria Maggiore, whose mosaics were completed by Filippo Rusuti around 1290. The upper section shows Christ enthroned in an aureole of glory supported by angels, towards which a procession of saints is moving. The lower section shows the legendary founding of the basilica by Pope Liberius.

Detail of the Last Judgment fresco in Santa Cecilia in Trastevere, showing Christ enthroned among angels. This important work of Roman painting from the end of the thirteenth century is by Pietro Cavallini. It remained hidden until the beginning of this century, when it was revealed by the removal of a layer of paint.

At St. John Lateran, the walls of the apse and its ambulatory, the so-called Leonine Portico, were restored. The huge mosaic decoration of the apse was completed in 1291 and was signed by Torriti as well as by Fra Jacopo da Camerino *socius magistri operis* (associate of the master in the work). A mosaic depicting a half-figure of Christ, probably fifth-century, preserved from the original decoration, was inserted in the new composition. Tradition held that this image had appeared miraculously in the basilica. It was placed above a large jeweled cross, with the Virgin and St. John the Baptist on one side and Sts. Peter, Paul, John the Evangelist, and Andrew on the other. In addition there are smaller figures of Sts. Francis and Antony of Padua. Unfortunately, today there is only a late nineteenth-century replica of Torriti's mosaic in

the apse, the original having fallen victim to heavy-handed restoration.

Santa Maria Maggiore

At Santa Maria Maggiore Nicholas IV commissioned the construction of a transept at the end of the nave of the old basilica of Sixtus III (432–40). The former apsidal arch now became the triumphal arch of the new presbytery area. Nicholas also had a new apse built. This was decorated with a mosaic completed in 1296, after his death, with the support of Cardinal Jacopo Colonna, archpriest of the church.

The new apse was embellished with an iconographic scheme which glorified the Virgin. In the center of the composition, within a

medallion and against the background of a starry sky, was the Coronation of the Virgin, and the nine angelic choirs. At the sides are Sts. Peter, Paul, Francis, John the Baptist, John the Evangelist, and Antony of Padua. As in St. John Lateran, a kneeling Nicholas IV is portrayed. On the opposite side is the figure of Cardinal Colonna, in recognition of his part in the completion of the decoration. In the semi-dome of the apse, between the windows, are five scenes from the life of the Virgin. The series is completed with an Apocalyptic vision with the twenty-four Elders and two panels representing St. Matthias' sermon to the Jews and St. Jerome with Paula and Eustachium.

The use of a theme from the repertory of monumental sculpture of the Gothic cathedral—the Coronation of the Virgin had been a widely-used theme since the end of the twelfth century—in the apse of a fifth-century church, was an innovation. Alongside this iconography, which is distinctly northern in character, the decorative element of coils of foliage displays a conscious and sophisticated revival of classical and early Christian stylistic features.

In these years Santa Maria Maggiore became a workshop in which some of the most important artists of the day were employed. In about 1290 Arnolfo di Cambio, commissioned by the Pope, produced the Chapel of the Relics. Perhaps a little later, Filippo Rusuti started work on the mosaic decoration of the facade. In the center of this mosaic, within a medallion with figures of angels, Christ enthroned is flanked by the Virgin and by Sts. Paul, James, Jerome, and John the Baptist on the left and Sts. Peter, Andrew, and

Matthias on the right. At the top were the symbols of the four Evangelists. On the bottom edge of the medallion the artist placed his signature.

In the left transept an unknown but skilled artist painted frescos of high quality. It is difficult to give this work an attribution. It was a project planned but never completed. As far as can be seen, it was to have consisted of an Old Testament cycle in the left transept with corresponding stories from the New Testament in the right transept. Above is a decorative band with large medallions enclosing figures of prophets alternating with whorls of foliage and framed by painted architectural motifs, with small coffered arches resting on corbels.

The frescoed scenes, partially carried out in the left transept, were probably never even started in the right transept, since no trace of paint has been found there. Of the scenes planned for the left transept, only the figure of God in the first scene of the Creation remains, but the decorative band showing the prophets was painted in its entirety.

The reason for the work being halted was almost certainly connected with the historical events concerning the Colonna family, who were traditionally linked to the patronage of the basilica, and Boniface VIII, their implacable enemy. After the death of Nicholas IV (April 4, 1292) and the election and abdication of Celestine V (July 5–December 13, 1294), Benedetto Caetani was elected pope on December 24, 1294 in Naples. On January 23 the following year he was consecrated in Rome, with the name Boniface VIII (d. 1303). Soon quarrels broke out between the Caetani and Colonna families, culminating in the excommunication of the Colonna in 1297. The family were outlawed, their titles and property confiscated, and military action was launched against their castles.

It is therefore not surprising that the painting of the frescos in the transept of Santa Maria Maggiore, probably begun when the mosaic decoration of the apse was almost complete, in about 1296, stopped when the Colonna family fell into disgrace. The part completed, however, reveals the skills of a great painter. Attempts at identifying this artist have produced a varied list of names—Gaddi, Giotto, Cavallini, Rusuti—but none of these suggestions seems supported by convincing evidence.

On the other hand, it seems reasonable to compare the frescos stylistically, even if only at a superficial level, with the celebrated stories from the life of Isaac in the Upper Church of San Francesco in Assisi. The most notable feature of the frescos in the transept of Santa Maria Maggiore is their sense of volume, which makes the figures stand out sharply from the background and gives them a sense of existing in real space. The treatment of the background is done in wide sweeps of color with soft chiaroscuro, crossed by vivid highlights. The prophets are strongly individualized in their expressions and facial features, drawn with dark clear-cut lines, particularly noticeable in the furrows on the forehead and around the eyes.

The mosaic showing the story of the foundation of the basilica in the lower part of the facade probably dates from around 1310. The top part of the mosaic was made and signed by Filippo Rusuti, probably not later than 1297, the year in which the basilica's patrons, the Colonna family, were deprived of the post of cardinal and exiled. The figures of Cardinal Giacomo and, perhaps, Cardinal Pietro, were portrayed kneeling, together with the Colonna arms, at the bottom of the medallion depicting Christ blessing.

It is unlikely that the work continued after that date, given that the family who commissioned it were no longer in Rome. More probably, work was resumed after 1306, the year in which Clement V (1378–94), who was in Avignon, readmitted the Colonna as patrons of the basilica. Gregory XI had already authorized their political and ecclesiastical rehabilitation on September 23, 1303.

The striking feature of the scenes of the foundation of the basilica in the lower zone of the mosaic is the complex way in which architectural space is structured. The buildings forming the background to the scenes are arranged in three-dimensional schemes quite unknown in Roman late thirteenth-century painting. They must have been influenced by Giotto's work in Assisi and Padua. In general they show distinct Gothic features far removed from the classical architecture painted by Torriti and Cavallini towards the close of the thirteenth century. For example, the interior in which are portrayed the kneeling figures of the patrician Giovanni and his entourage in front of Pope Liberius is covered with a series of rib-vaulted ceilings seen in perspective. This detail alone is an indication of how much this work owed to knowledge—perhaps direct knowledge—of Giotto's ideas on the representation of space.

Pietro Cavallini

Between the end of the thirteenth century and the beginning of the fourteenth, Pietro Cavallini, without a doubt the most important Roman painter of the day, was active on other major projects in Rome. The discovery by Hermanin in 1905 of frescos on the inner facade of Santa Cecilia in Trastevere marked a turning-point in the interpretation of the pictorial art of the late thirteenth century. The extraordinary quality of

these paintings, their mature sense of molding, the skillful and measured use of chiaroscuro, and the naturalness of the faces, challenged the traditional view of Roman pictorial art as trapped in a worn-out Byzantine tradition. The discovery had the same effect on the equally deep-rooted view that Cavallini was a pupil of Giotto, a theory inherited from Vasari, who was anxious to place the Renaissance of Florentine painting above that of Rome.

The large composition depicting the Last Judgment includes a number of iconographic elements from the Byzantine tradition, but in stylistic terms it represents a revolution in the way in which it portrays the human figure. The bodies of the figures are constructed with a clear sense of plasticity that was entirely new at that time. The sense of their physical presence is achieved by means of a masterly use of chiaroscuro based on subtle tonal variations, which interact with the luminous highlights that are spread across wide areas of painted background.

These frescos on the inner facade are not the only remains of the decoration of Santa Cecilia. In addition to the architectural motifs already mentioned, on the right wall of the church there are fragments of three scenes of Isaac and Jacob while on the left wall there is part of an Annunciation and a large figure of the Archangel Michael. It is immediately obvious that these are the work of more than one artist. Moreover, the lower part of the Last Judgment displays clear differences in style and technique from those of the upper part. While the Annunciation appears to have been done by a more maladroit painter who worked rather roughly, the artist responsible for the stories of Isaac and Jacob displays a sureness and originality of structure and line which place him on a level of true excellence. Like Cavallini, he constructs his figures by means of broad sweeps of color. However, on this he lays bright incisive flashes of light and he draws the figures with quick nervous strokes, which distance him from the classical and calm monumentality of the artist of the Last Judgment.

The dating of the cycle must be close to that of the ciborium (tabernacle) executed there by Arnolfo di Cambio. This, dated 1293, must have represented the conclusion of an extensive project for redecorating the building.

Cavallini's other major work in Rome is the cycle of the life of the Virgin in the apse of Santa Maria in Trastevere, across the bowl of the apse below the already mentioned mosaic commissioned by Innocent II. Cavallini's mosaics comprise a problematic counterpart to Torriti's similar cycle at Santa Maria Maggiore. It is not easy to say which came first; they must have been executed within a very short time of each other.

Another work that must have been the product of Cavallini's workshop is the fresco in the apse of the church of San Giorgio in Velabro, of about 1296. This painting, though in a very poor state, bears a close resemblance to both the Santa Cecilia frescos and the mosaics in Santa Maria in Trastevere. However, it is not altogether easy to recognize in it the hand of Cavallini himself.

In another important Roman church, Santa Maria in Aracoeli on the Capitoline Hill, the first Franciscan establishment in Rome, Cavallini carried out various works, possibly over a period of several years. His work here must have come to an end at the same time as the painting of the fresco on the tomb of Cardinal Matteo d'Acquasparta, who died in 1302; the fresco depicts the Virgin and Child between Sts. Peter and Francis, who present the deceased prelate.

In the same church are fragments of fresco in the ceiling of the Savelli Chapel, with an enthroned Lamb of God, a haloed figure, and fragments of architectural framework with foreshortened corbels. These fragments are part of what must have been the redecoration carried out at the same time—and in a similar stylistic manner—as the remodeling of the church in Gothic style, a project directed by Arnolfo di Cambio from the early 1290s.

Little remains of what might be called the connective tissue of pictorial art from the last two decades of the thirteenth century, and which alone could provide a deep understanding of the network of influences and similarities making up such a complex figurative culture. However, it is still possible to recognize from the works that do survive how rich this artistic output is in cultural elements gleaned from a variety of sources—though this is too often overlooked or misunderstood. Evidence of this richness is to be found, for example, in the frescos in the Abbazia delle Tre Fontane, those in the so-called fourth aisle of Santa Saba, the painted cross for Santa Maria in Aracoeli (which are now in the Museo del Palazzo di Venezia), and the frescoed cycles in Sant'Agnese fuori le Mura (now in the Vatican Picture Gallery), and the cycle on the portico of San Lorenzo fuori le Mura, to cite just a few of the most interesting examples.

In the ancient sacristy of the Cistercian abbey church of Tre Fontane, a painter who was strongly influenced by Torriti's apse mosaic in Santa Maria Maggiore frescoed in two lunettes a Coronation of the Virgin and a Nativity scene, which clearly derived their typology and compositional cadences from Torriti. However, the artist did not intend—or did not know how—to interpret Torriti's all-embracing classicism and grandiose layout schemes. His style in fact was completely unlike Torriti's sweeping, but carefully modulated lines. Another group of frescos in Tre Fontane, with allegorical scenes of human life, has some intriguing motifs that reveal on the one hand that the work has undeniable points of contact with some of the most significant Roman works of art of the 1290s, but on the other, signs of European—particularly Franco-English—figurative influences, as well as broader ones.

Giotto

The painted cross in the little church of San Tommaso de' Cenci, transferred from Santa Maria in Aracoeli in the mid-fifteenth century, is one of the few surviving examples of this particular kind of figurative typology. Among others is the much more ancient crucifix in the convent of Sant'Alberto. Given its high quality and the originality of its style, which is still discernible despite the loss of a substantial part of the painted surface, the cross also provides an important means of reconstructing the fabric of figurative art in the late thirteenth century. When first studied by art historians, it was thought to have been by an artist from Assisi. Later it was linked to Giotto or his circle, although still with much uncertainty. However, given that the work shows discernible Roman influence, with the image of the Savior for example—a typology deriving from the Acheiropoeton in the Sancta Sanctorum—and also given the facial features of the crucified Christ, the Aracoeli cross must surely be seen in the context of the frescos of Old and New Testament scenes in the upper church of San Francesco in Assisi.

Works of this kind must have contributed in more than a marginal way to Giotto's artistic development. The young Florentine painter would have been able to see them in their full splendor during his numerous visits to Rome. Roman pictorial art was in a phase of great vitality just as Assisi was experiencing its most significant artistic period. Thanks to Arnolfo di Cambio, it had assimilated and reworked the most recent trends in figurative art, always against its own enduring classical background.

Within the cultural framework outlined so far, the election of Boniface VIII (1294–1303), the links between current figurative art and the papal court, and the jubilee of 1300 all combined together to produce a period of great progress in artistic life, an artistic life that during these years, as has been seen, was mutually influenced by the art of Giotto. The great excitement that permeated Rome at that time could not have failed to attract Giotto, who

had completed work on the cycle of St. Francis in the upper church of San Francesco in Assisi.

It is difficult to work out the pattern of commissioning by Boniface VIII—who perhaps had been responsible for Giotto's first visit to Rome—given the apparent lack of any systematic planning behind the projects he promoted. One of the first works known to have been commissioned by Boniface VIII was his own tomb. The planning and execution of this monument was entrusted to Arnolfo di Cambio in 1296. Jacopo Torriti was called to produce a mosaic panel for the base, now lost apart from two fragments, one in the Pushkin Museum in Moscow and the other in the Brooklyn Museum of Art in New York. The panel represented the Virgin holding the Child within a medallion. On one side was St. Paul, on the other St. Peter presenting a kneeling Boniface.

The Jubilee Fresco

The first work Giotto is traditionally believed to have done in Rome is the so-called Jubilee fresco, of which only a fragment remains, attached to the third pilaster in the right aisle of St. John Lateran. It came from the Benediction Loggia which Boniface VIII had had constructed on the north side of the *Aula Concilii* of the Lateran Palace. In its present state the fragment shows Boniface proclaiming the jubilee of 1300, flanked by two ecclesiastics within a loggia. The cleric on the left is unrolling a scroll which, when the abbreviations are interpreted, reads: "Bishop Boniface, the servant of the servants of God, in everlasting memory" (Bonifacius episcopus servus servorum Dei ad perpetuam rei memoriam). On the far right of the scene, between two columns, is a bearded figure in profile, dressed in a brownish-grey tunic.

Thanks to a watercolor drawing from the end of the sixteenth century preserved in the Biblioteca Ambrosiana in Milan, the scene can be completed. In the lower half, of which the original is lost, a group of the faithful acclaiming the pope was represented. On either side of the loggia were ecclesiastics and dignitaries of the papal court. The Caetani family arms alternate with the insignia with the *umbraculum*, an imperial emblem, along the parapet of the architectural structure.

The *Navicella*

The other Roman work that sources attributed to Giotto is the mosaic of the Navicella, now almost totally lost, in the atrium of Old St. Peter's. It was commissioned by Cardinal

Jacopo Stefaneschi, without a doubt the leading artistic patron in the papal court of the first half of the fourteenth century. Originally in Rome under Boniface VIII, then in Avignon after the move there of the papacy, he was responsible for some of the most important artistic undertakings of the day.

The Navicella, for which Stefaneschi composed a verse caption, must have aroused enormous fascination among contemporaries immediately after it was completed as several replicas are known, starting with a fresco in the Jung Sankt Peterkirche in Strasbourg, datable to the 1320s. Numerous other copies followed, including a drawing attributed to Parri Spinelli (Hewitt Fund, Metropolitan Museum of Art, New York) and a series of sixteenth- and seventeenth-century engravings.

All that remains of the original are two medallions enclosing busts of angels (Vatican Grottos, St. Peter's; San Pietro Ispano, Boville Ernica). The technical details of their execution display the involvement of a mosaic artist to whom Giotto must have entrusted the execution of the work, having put together the general lines of the composition and, probably, having made a cartoon or preparatory drawing. From this point of view, what is striking is how similar—almost identical—the technique used for the Navicella and Cavallini's mosaic in Santa Maria in Trastevere is, even if the actual stylistic results are different.

Giotto was subsequently commissioned by Cardinal Stefaneschi for the great triptych for St. Peter's, large parts of which were the work of artists from his workshop. In this same period, also as a commission from Stefaneschi, Giotto was busy painting frescos in the apse of St. Peter's. These are unfortunately all lost, but it is known they represented five stories from the life of Christ.

The Navicella, rich in symbolism and executed with great technical expertise, must have revitalized the tradition of mosaic workshops in Rome, even if for only a few years. About ten years later, Cavallini—if Ghiberti's testimony is to be trusted—was engaged in what can be regarded as the last great mosaic work of medieval Rome, the facade of San Paolo fuori le Mura. In this case the commission came directly from the papal court at Avignon, albeit at the request of the abbot of St. Paul's. In a letter dated January 31, 1325, John XXII (1316–34) ordered that the income from the high altar of San Paolo's be spent for a period of five years on the mosaic. Two years before this, in 1323, the pope had displayed interest in this church, having allocated 1,000 florins for restoration there. Again in 1326 he renewed the five-year concession and donated a further 1,000 florins for the work.

Reverse of the Stefaneschi Triptych, a work commissioned by Cardinal Jacopo Stefaneschi from Giotto and his workshop around 1310 for the basilica of St. Peter's. This is one of the few remaining works made by the Florentine artist during his time in Rome. The central panel shows Christ seated on a throne bestowing his blessing, while the side panels depict the martyrdoms of Sts. Peter and Paul, the two Apostles of greatest importance to Rome. The predella shows the Virgin on a throne, holding the Christ child and flanked by the Apostles. Rome, Vatican Picture Gallery.

Fresco showing a scene from the life of St. Benedict; part of a fresco cycle originally in the church of Sant'Agnese fuori le Mura attributed to Lello da Orvieto. Rome, Vatican Picture Gallery.

The original appearance of the mosaic is known through a number of drawings. On the top was a medallion depicting Christ the Redeemer, supported by angels and flanked by the symbols of the Evangelists. Below, between the windows, were from the left St. Paul, the Virgin and Child enthroned, St. John the Baptist presenting a kneeling donor to the Virgin, and St. Peter.

The Avignon Papacy

The transfer of the papal court to Avignon was formalized in 1309 by Clement V (1305–14), formerly bishop of Bordeaux, who had continued to live in France even after he had been elected as pope. It was a traumatic event for Rome and its cultural life, the consequences of which was a drastic fall in the number of artistic commissions, until then virtually the monopoly of the cardinals and high prelates of the Curia. However, not all figurative art came to a halt. The presence of a patron such as Stefaneschi, the production of works like those by Giotto's followers, the completion of the Santa Maria Maggiore mosaic, and Cavallini's work at San Paolo fuori le Mura in 1325, all testify to the fact that commissions went ahead, in some cases on a monumental scale.

Between around 1310 and 1340 a number of interesting artistic projects were undertaken.

They include the cycle of stories from the lives of Christ and the Virgin in San Sisto Vecchio, showing the direct influence of Cavallini, and the works recently attributed to the painter Lello da Orvieto—formerly active at the court of Naples—such as the detached frescos depicting stories from the life of St. Benedict originally in Sant'Agnese fuori le Mura and now in the Vatican Picture Gallery, and the panels with Sts. Louis of Toulouse and Antony Abbot, which are markedly Angevin in style (convent of San Francesco a Ripa).

Cola di Rienzo and Painting

Paintings, now lost, were associated with Cola di Rienzo. Commissioned by him for the Capitoline Hill and the facade of the church of Sant'Angelo in Pescheria, they were allegorical representations of political themes relating to the disastrous situation of Rome without a pope. The extraordinary story of Cola di Rienzo, the leading political figure in Rome from 1343 to 1354, had no lasting effect in the sphere of artistic production, but it coincided with a significant moment in the history of figurative art. The famous anonymous *Cronica* provides a detailed description of the images used in the paintings commissioned by Cola di Rienzo. In narrating the events surrounding the figure of Cola, the author describes the paintings in question, probably executed during the period of Cola's senatorship, between 1343 and 1347.

The works on the Capitoline Hill showed a ship in a stormy sea on the point of sinking. On board there was a woman dressed in black, which an inscription identified as representing Rome. The cities of Troy, Babylon, Jerusalem, and Carthage were also symbolically represented on half-sinking ships. In addition there were three islands. On one was another woman, personifying Italy, on the second an image of the Church, on the last, the cardinal virtues. The complex allegory included animals (wolves, bears, goats, hares), which symbolized elements harmful to the life of the city of Rome, such as fraudulent councillors, the oppressed populace, and corrupt judges. They blew into horns, from which sprang the storm agitating the sea. Divine justice was represented by God with a sword issuing from his mouth, in the manner of archaic apocalyptic iconography, flanked by Sts. Peter and Paul.

In a painting in Sant'Angelo in Pescheria, however, Rome was seen as an old woman who was surrounded by flames and supported by an angel, together with Sts. Peter and Paul. A painting on another church, Santa Maria Maddalena, showed an angel holding a sword

in the act of trampling a lion, a dragon, a basilisk, and a serpent. There were also other so-called defamatory paintings (*pittura infamante*) on political themes and a coat of arms, on the Capitoline Hill.

These images, symbolically echoing the events that the city of Rome was living through, were intended to appeal to the people of Rome and urge them to re-establish civic harmony. They were of an entirely civic and political nature, which sharply separated them from the

Roman iconographical tradition—even though they adopted some of its most important images. The new manner perhaps constituted an attempt to take Rome closer to what was going on in other Italian cities, including the choice of subjects depicted in paintings.

The death on October 8, 1354 of Cola di Rienzo, at the hands of the very citizens who had once enthusiastically supported him, ended this attempt to revive figurative art in the city. As Dupré-Theseider puts it, the city "seems to settle down into a rhythmn without history for about twenty years." This period without history also related to the figurative arts. Only a few examples, though some were quite important, stand out during this period of stagnation.

Fresco showing St. Catherine disputing with the philosophers before the emperor, painted for the church of Sant'Agnese fuori le Mura between the late twelfth and early fourteenth century. Rome, Vatican Picture Gallery.

PIVS·IX·PONT·MAX

One of the four bands of frescos that decorate the monumental ciborium reliquary above the high altar of St. John Lateran.

Return and Renewal

In 1367, for example, Urban V (1362–70) took the unexpected decision to return the papacy to Rome, even if only for three years (he returned to Avignon a few months before his death). On visiting St. John Lateran on March 1, 1368, he ordered the opening of the altar in the Sancta Sanctorum, the pope's private chapel. The most precious relics, the heads of Sts. Peter and Paul, were "rediscovered." This rediscovery was judged an event of the greatest importance, not just for the city of Rome. Urban decided that the relics required a more prestigious housing, in a new ciborium above the high altar of the basilica. New reliquaries were made, with enamel decorations representing stories from the lives of the Apostles. The king of France, Charles V, sent two golden lilies for the reliquaries and the queen of Naples, Joanna, also sent precious objects, as did the queen of Navarre. The Sienese goldsmith Giovanni di Bartolo, assisted by Giovanni di Marco, was commissioned to make the reliquaries.

The Sienese architect Giovanni di Stefano, with several collaborators, was entrusted with producing the ciborium, which was markedly Gothic in its structure but in its decoration used the typology of late thirteenth-century Roman tradition. The arms of Urban V and of Cardinal Albornoz figured prominently. The decoration of the ciborium was completed with a short cycle of frescos depicting the Annunciation, the coronation of the Virgin, the Good Shepherd, Christ's Passion, images of saints whose relics were preserved in the basilica, and a kneeling cardinal, possibly Albornoz.

It is difficult to assess these paintings because of the successive repainting that they have undergone over the years, but they have been linked to the work mentioned in the *Libro di Antonio Billi*, carried out by Giottino at St. John Lateran in 1369.

Urban V's expressed desire to re-establish Rome as the papal seat, and his involvement in restoring the city's great basilicas, aroused excitement in the city, as was demonstrated by

ANNO · D · MDCCCLI

various images made of him, the originals of which are now lost but recorded in seventeenth-century copies. One of the interesting portrayals shows Urban holding a model of the ciborium—a traditional gesture that is associated with patrons. Another shows an icon with Sts. Peter and Paul, an obvious allusion to the rediscovery of the relics of their heads. These images, which in their original forms were probably frescos, have also been linked to the activity of Giottino in Rome, although this is no more than conjecture.

Urban V was not able to accomplish the papacy's definitive return to Rome. This fell to his successor, Gregory XI (1370–78) who, despite the fact that many cities of central Italy led by Florence, were in revolt against the papacy, chose to return to Rome, convinced that only by this gesture could the prestige and authority of the papacy be re-established. After considerable hesitation due to the complicated political and military situation in Italy, but due partly to the impassioned pleas of St. Catherine

of Siena, he at last entered Rome on January 17, 1377, accompanied by a splendid procession.

Thus ended one of the most difficult periods in the history of Rome. The death of Gregory XI on March 27, 1378 signaled a new phase of great uncertainty for the papacy, with the election in Rome of a new pope, Urban VI (1378–89), opposed in France by the antipope Clemente VII (1378–94), elected by the French clergy. The Great Schism which thus opened was not healed until 1417 and the election of Martin V.

Alessandro Tomei

The Fifteenth Century: the Early Renaissance

Architecture

"She seemed to us old and sad in her manner. I could see that her dress was torn and dishevelled" and that her face "was wet with tears."
This was how the personification of the city of Rome appeared to Fazio degli Uberti and the philosopher Solinus in the mid-fourteenth-century *Dittamondo*. Dressed in widow's weeds, the woman tells the travelers of the sad state of the buildings of ancient Rome, inside city walls far too large for the shrinking urban population.

By the beginning of the fifteenth century the neglected state of the city's ancient monuments had worsened still further. The two jubilees under Pope Boniface IX (1389–1404) in 1390 and 1400 did not revive the city, and the pontificate of Boniface's successor, Innocent VII (1404–6), was disrupted by continual attacks by Ladislas Durazzo, king of Naples. Furthermore, the Great Schism, with rival popes in Rome and Avignon from 1378 to 1417, and struggles between the great Roman families—the Colonna, Orsini, Savelli, and Caetani—meant that the popes in Rome in the years around 1400 were more concerned with military affairs than with artistic patronage.

Coat of arms of Pope Martin V, from the tower built during his pontificate beside Palazzo Senatorio on the Capitoline Hill. The quartering features the column emblem of the Colonna (column) family.

The Revival of Classicism

When Pope Martin V (1417–31), elected in 1417 at the Council of Constance which ended the Schism, entered Rome in 1420, he found it, according to the later description by Platina in his *Lives of the Popes*, "so broken and ruined that it did not resemble Rome in the least. Houses stood ruined, temples were collapsing, the countryside was abandoned, and the city full of mud. There was dearth and poverty everywhere."

The decline in population, to some 17,000, had led to the decay of whole areas. The basilica of San Paolo fuori le Mura was now used to house cattle. The Forum and the Capitoline Hill had acquired the revealing names of Campo Vaccino (Field of the Cows) and Monte Caprino (Goat Hill), since they were used for grazing. In their descriptions of, and guides to, ancient Rome, scholars lamented the city's lost greatness and nostalgically recalled her past glory, as, for example, in the *Antiquities and Sites of Rome* (*Tractatus de rebus antiquis et situ urbis Romae*) of about 1411, Niccolò Signorili's *Description of the City of Rome* (*Descriptio urbis Romae*) of the late 1430s, and Poggio Bracciolini's *The Vicissitudes of Fortune* (*De varietate fortunae*), which was completed in 1448.

Martin V made the reconstruction of the city a central preoccupation of his papacy. Some decades after his death in 1431, his work as bringer of peace and restorer of the city was remembered in Platina's words of praise (1474). For Martin, collecting ancient sculpture and inscriptions reflecting Rome's magnificence, Christian and pagan alike, and the recovery of her immense antiquarian and classical heritage was the first step toward a cultural and political revival. A number of initiatives were associated with this program, including the task, assigned to Niccolò Signorili, of cataloguing the monu-

One of three towers from the corner bastions of Castel Sant'Angelo built under Nicholas V in the mid-fifteenth century. On the right can be seen the beginning of the fortified corridor built under Nicholas III.

Drawing attributed to Filippino Lippi depicting Castel Sant'Angelo and Ponte Sant'Angelo, leading to it.

ments of the city. From this was born the *Laws and Glories of the City of Rome* (*De iuris et excellentiis urbis Romae)*, a catalog of streets, bridges, gates, basilicas, churches, and inscriptions.

In 1420 Martin allocated the first sums of money for the repair of the chapel of St. Nicholas in St. Peter's, the Passaggio delle Benedizioni, and the Vatican Palace. In 1423 instructions were issued for the restoration of the basilica of San Paolo fuori le Mura. The four-arch portico of St. Peter's was consolidated, as were the churches of the Santi Quattro Coronati and San Lorenzo in Lucina. Martin also had the pavement of the basilica of San Giovani in Laterano remade with marble from ruined churches.

Prominent among his projects was the restoration of Palazzo Senatorio on the Capitoline Hill, begun in 1427. It was probably at this date that the so-called Tower of Martin V was built, on which the pope's arms can still be seen. Martin also had part of the dome of the Pantheon covered with sheet bronze tiles, repaired the Ponte

Castel Sant'Angelo and Ponte
Sant'Angelo altered by Bernini in the
sixteenth century. In the background is
the great dome of St. Peter's.

Senatorio and the Milvian Bridge, and restored stretches of the city walls. In 1425 he revived the institution of the "magistrates of the streets" (*magistri viarum*), who were given the responsibility of preventing the theft of stone and sculpture from the surviving ancient buildings and controlling the dealing in excavated antiquities and the occupation of buildings such as the Teatro Marcello by artisans and traders.

The pontificate of Eugenius IV, the Venetian Gabriele Condulmer, who was elected on March 3, 1431, was of lesser significance, as Eugenius spent only a short time in Rome, fleeing to Florence on July 4, 1434 in the face of a popular insurrection and returning only in September 1443. Meanwhile the council of the Church which was to bring about union between the eastern and the Roman churches (1437–39) had sat, first in Ferrara and then in Florence, solemnized by the presence of the Byzantine emperor, John VIII Palaeologus, who was accompanied by a large entourage of ecclesiastics and theologians including Cardinal Bessarion and Gemistus Pletho. These last two remained in Italy, where they were to make an important contribution to the spread of Greek and classical learning.

Among those clerics at the council was Leon Battista Alberti, who had moved to Rome in 1432, where he was appointed papal secretary in the Curia, the papal civil service. He was also appointed prior of Gangalandi. From this time Alberti worked in the Curia for Eugenius IV, closely involved in the events that led up to the union of the Roman and eastern churches. His intellectual and personal development took place within the climate of the rediscovery of classical culture and renewed interest in antiquarian studies. In all, Alberti was to spend almost forty years of his life in Rome.

Alberti's scientific and artistic knowledge, and his studies of architecture and topography, were to find application under Pope Nicholas V (1447–55), when he wrote his *Description of the City of Rome* (*Descriptio urbis Romae*) and *On Architecture* (*De re aedificatoria*), a treatise inspired by the Roman author Vitruvius' *On Architecture*. Alberti followed Vitruvius' arrangement of the treatise into ten sections, the last reflecting Nicholas' plans for the city.

The encounter between the great humanist and the cultivated pope was a significant meeting of minds. However, Alberti was also critical of Nicholas's utopian dreams. Although Nicholas had a great love of ancient texts and regard for the splendors of ancient Rome, he had less respect for antique statues and marble, using them to produce lime for mortar for his new buildings, obsessed as he was with the idea of competing with the greatness of the past. His projects fall into two periods: 1450, the

year of the jubilee, and 1452, when he began a number of town-planning projects.

The third point of Nicholas' program provided for extensive work in the Borgo area, between the Vatican Palace and the river. In addition, the plans provided for a large piazza in front of the basilica of St. Peter's and extensive work both around Castel Sant'Angelo and on Castel Sant'Angelo itself, with the addition of round bastions on the four corners of the ancient square foundations. In 1452–53 Nicholas had the statue of the Archangel Michael made for it, recalling the legend of an angel's appearance to Pope Gregory the Great in 590 to mark the end of the plague. This statue can be seen as early as 1459 in a miniature in Niccolò Polani's manuscript of Augustine's *City of God*. Nicholas also

created three major roads linking Castel Sant'Angelo on the river with the rest of the city—the Via Peregrinorum, the Via Papalis, and the Via Recta—following Alberti's insistence on the need for "straight and wide [main roads] which give the city greatness and majesty."

The fourth point of the program was the rebuilding of the papal palace at the Vatican. This was assigned to a certain Antonio di Francesco from Florence, of whom only his name is known. The palace was turned into a seemingly impregnable fortress bristling with towers, "accessible only to the birds of the air," as Manetti put it. Another important feature of Nicholas' plans were the Vatican gardens, an early reflection of the ideal of the heavenly city, defined by Manetti as "a beautiful place of

Coat of arms of Paul II (from the Venetian Barbo family) featuring a lion rampant. The carving is from a richly decorated marble doorframe in Palazzo San Marco (now di Venezia).

Palazzo San Marco (now di Venezia), the earliest example of a Renaissance city residence in Rome. Dominant features such as the corner tower and crenellated gallery are evidence of the persistence of architectural elements from medieval fortified palaces.

paradise," rich with every kind of plant and adorned with a central fountain.

A drawing attributed to Federico Zuccari records an important feature of Nicholas' building, a cross-form window, where the transom and mullion form a cross. The idea came from a fourth-century relief of Peter's denial of Christ after the Crucifixion in the ex-Lateran collection in the Vatican Museums. The earliest example in Rome seems to be in the *diaconia* (Christian welfare center) of Santa Maria in Cosmedin.

Nicholas also used this architectural detail of the cross-form window on the facade of Palazzo Senatorio on the Capitoline Hill in his rebuilding between 1450 and 1453. The appearance of Palazzo Senatorio after Nicholas' restoration is recorded in an engraving by Hieronimus Cook made before Michelangelo's work on New St. Peter's in the mid-sixteenth century.

The most important element of Nicholas' plans was that which Manetti saved for the end of his account: the restoration of the basilica of St. Peter's. This, according to Vasari, was carried out by Bernardo Rossellino, who planned to provide a new setting for the high altar, with a splendid tribune and a broad transept. In his treatise, Alberti expressed himself cautiously where this project was concerned, expressing doubts about the weakness of the buildings and praising the nearby late-antique rotondas which too ambitious a project would condemn to destruction (as was to happen in the sixteenth century). It is impossible to know how much influence so authoritative an opinion had, but rebuilding did come to a halt after barely a year.

It seems likely that Alberti was involved in the repairs to the aqueduct of the Acqua Vergine in order to feed an early version of the Trevi Fountain. This, a pet project of the pope, fitted in with Alberti's stress in his writings on the need to restore the ancient aqueducts.

The latter part of Nicholas' pontificate was marked by a number of difficulties. The fall of Constantinople—the ancient capital of the eastern Roman empire—to the Ottoman Turks in 1453 led to accusations that the pope had squandered a fortune in building and book collecting not helping to defend Constantinople. That same year Stefano Porcari's republican conspiracy against the pope marked the beginning of a conflict between clerics and humanists which was to harden with the alleged "humanist conspiracy" of 1468, led by Pomponio Leto, when there was tension even between Alberti and the pope and Curia. By the time of his death in 1472, Alberti was an isolated figure, seeing only the scholars and artists who visited his house in the Banchi quarter, where Florentines resident in Rome congregated.

The executor of Alberti's will was Mattia Palmieri from Pisa, a translator of Greek and secretary until 1463 to Cardinal Prospero Colonna. In 1447 Colonna had given Alberti the task of locating the Roman ships that had been sunk in Lake Nemi, in the Alban Hills south of Rome. This project formed the basis of Alberti's lost treatise *The Ship* (*Navis*).

A portrait survives from this last tragic period of Alberti's life. An anonymous drawing in a manuscript of Alberti's dialogue *Profugiorum ab aerumna*, otherwise known as *On Peace of Mind*, which Alberti had written in happier times, around 1441–42, represents him as a cleric with a book in his hand.

The papacy of Paul II (Pietro Barbo, 1464–71) was marked by a major building project, begun when Paul was still a cardinal, the construction of

The vertical arrangement of the classical orders of architecture in the arcades of the courtyard of Palazzo San Marco is a clear sign of a return to classical models. This stacked pattern, known as a tabularium motif, appears in a number of important buildings from the end of the Roman republic such as the Colosseum.

the palazzo now known as Palazzo di Venezia, then called Palazzo San Marco, after the neighboring church of San Marco. It seems to have been inspired by the Albertian concept of architecture as having a moral function. Thus the cardinal's palace was to be "a place worthy of worthy actions by worthy people." The notion of the moral function of a dwelling was later elaborated by Paolo Cortesi in 1510 in *The Cardinalate* (*De cardinalatu*), which starts out from the Albertian scheme and must have had this palace in mind.

A contemporary source describes Paul II as having "a fine majesty of figure, commensurate with the dignity of his position. His height is also in proportion to the dignity of his status: in public he is always taller than those around him. He has a cheerful, pleasant, and kind face." Of noble Venetian family, Paul was arrogant and ambitious for ecclesiastical advancement, but also open-minded and genuinely religious. Although surrounded by the greatest humanists of the day (George of Trebizond, Leonardo Dati, and Francesco Barbaro), Paul was also rigorously orthodox, to the point of waging war on the Roman academy of Pomponio Leto and on the public teaching of the classics. Aware of the importance of both winning over and impressing the populace, Paul gave great prominence to spectacular events, ceremonies, and festivals, especially those of a popular kind. He revived the Carnival celebrations which recalled the *Saturnalia* of ancient times.

The facade of the church of San Marco was built under Paul II and integrated into Palazzo San Marco. The facade is modeled on the benediction loggia of Old St. Peter's, built under Pius II, the predecessor of Paul II.

Paul II's collection of works of art was celebrated. It included both modern and antique sculpture, much of which was subsequently sold to the Medici of Florence by Pope Sixtus IV in an attempt to ingratiate himself with them. The most important part of the collection consisted of coins, bronzes, gems, icons, textiles, glass, and silverware. Around the middle of the century the pope was buying almost anything that appeared on the market—particularly objects from the East—through his emissaries, one of whom was the traveler Ciriaco d'Ancona.

A telling letter of November 1466 from Antonio de' Rossi, papal ambassador to the duke of Milan, was to the duke's secretary, Cicco Simonetta, and described "the customs and intolerable display of the entire court, above all the pope, who passes the entire day counting and sorting coins and handling pearls rather than the rosary."

Paul's passion seems to have had a number of motives. One, the desire to appear rich and powerful, led him to turn his public appearances into sumptuous events in which the display of pomp and jewels played a dramatic role. Paul enhanced the magnificence of his court with the exaggerated ritual of the eastern church, which had long fascinated the western imagination and had been lost with the fall of Constantinople.

In 1451 the future Paul II was made cardinal-deacon of the church of San Marco. The church, a modest and relatively small structure built on the remains of a Roman building, stood in an area of intense commercial activity. Construction of Palazzo San Marco began in 1455. The appearance of the palazzo now is not the original one, as it was altered in the early twentieth century during work on the Victor Emmanuel II Monument. The choice of site was significant, both symbolically and from the point of view of town-planning. It stood at the end of the Corso, the last stretch of the Via Flaminia, the principal road leading to Rome from the north; it thus marked a break between modern Rome and the ancient city, represented by the Capitoline Hill. From the exterior, the fabric appeared strong and of moderate height, with brick cladding and cross-form windows, completed with a panoramic tower.

The model for Palazzo San Marco seems to have been the palazzo which had been completed by Cardinal Domenico Capranica in 1451 (Palazzo Capranica). The architecture of Capranica's palace is transitional, retaining Gothic elements while revealing the influence of the new ideas from Florence. Particularly significant is a classicizing portal with a tympanum supported by brackets, previously used only in ecclesiastical architecture. The barrel vault with square coffering in the atrium, based on the Pantheon, and the loggia in the inner courtyard,

imitating the orders used on the exterior of the Colosseum, were carried out by Alberti, whose relations with Paul II were to become stormy. The courtyard represents a new element, which was to be a distinctive feature of the Roman Renaissance palazzo. Another innovation was the garden—completely altered in 1911 during work to create the present Piazza Venezia—which had a precedent in the garden planned by Nicholas V at the Vatican Palace.

The internal arrangement of Palazzo San Marco revealed a clear division between the public and private rooms. In the private quarters, the pope's bedroom opened onto the Sala del Pappagallo (Hall of the Parrot) and the Sala dei Paramenti (Hall of Tapestries). Three public rooms—the Sala del Mappamondo (Hall of the Map), the Sala del Concistoro (Hall of the Consistory), and the Sala Regia (Royal Hall)—made up a plush suite of rooms which the pope would pass through on his way to audiences.

The construction of Palazzo San Marco resulted in major changes in the surrounding area, with the acquisition of houses and gardens, and their demolition. In 1468 the enormous enterprise caused the duke of Milan's ambassador to write of "the ruins alongside the palazzo of the houses which have been demolished in order to enlarge the palazzo and make it more splendid. It covers a vast area, and could accommodate not just many men, but a whole army."

The main victims of Paul's building scheme were the ancient monuments that for years were to provide the primary building materials, according to rumor "an infinity of travertine blocks which were dug up from gardens near the Arch of Constantine, together with stone and fragments from the Colosseum, Castel Sant'Angelo, and a temple on the Capitoline Hill."

After the conspiracy of Pomponio Leto, Paul took to living much more in the Vatican Palace and recommenced the restoration of St. Peter's, begun under Nicholas V. As a result, he delegated responsibility for work on Palazzo San Marco to his nephew, Marco Barbo. Among the parts of the palazzo completed under Barbo's direction, of particular note are the north entrance portal and the double order loggia of the great internal courtyard.

Dated to around 1470, this loggia represents the most obvious contribution of Florentine architecture in the palazzo. It has been described as effectively "a huge Florentine tabernacle," with columns replacing the pilaster strips and high plinths which take their inspiration from the arches of Septimius Severus and Constantine. The loggia in the courtyard—something entirely new for Rome—was later taken up by Antonio da Sangallo the Younger in Palazzo Farnese. It was inspired by ancient

Roman models: the Tabularium (Archive) on the Capitoline Hill, the Theater of Marcellus, and, above all, the Colosseum.

There is a close stylistic relationship between the portico and the first order of the loggia of the church of San Marco, which from the very beginning of his pontificate, Paul II had intended to turn into the chapel of his palace. Pope Gregory IV (827–44) had originally restored the church, which had a nave and aisles, a raised sanctuary, and a porticoed facade. The interior was altered by Barbo. The roof was covered with gilded lead tiles and the coffered ceiling, with Paul's arms in the center, was painted and gilded. Marble two-light windows replaced the medieval brick, colored glass was brought from Murano, and a porphyry altar, brought by Paul in 1467 from the Mausoleum of Constantia, was placed in the sanctuary.

The reconstruction of the portico, begun in 1467, was of great importance for Paul. New additions were the central door, with a frame with swags, and a marble and travertine loggia, unfinished in 1470, which has recently been attributed to Giovannino de' Dolci. This had a sole precedent, the *Benedizione* in St. Peter's, commissioned by Pius II, which had replaced the wooden pulpit used until Pius' death.

The new pulpit had columns of granite and cipollino marble taken from the Portico of Octavia, as well as "nine small columns" from San Giovanni in Laterano. Begun in 1460, work on the pulpit continued under Paul II and was completed under Alexander VI. The pulpit was destroyed by Paul V between 1610 and 1616. Numerous drawings survive, however, including one by Maarten van Heemskerck, which show how it too was inspired by the orders on the outside of the Colosseum.

It is not clear who was the architect at Palazzo San Marco. Given the scale of the project and the long period over which construction continued, it seems unlikely that there was a single plan. Funds for the work on the palazzo were cut off in the autumn of 1471, shortly after the death of Paul II. In the last accounts the names of a number of craftsmen can be found, including the stonecarvers Meo del Caprino and Giovannino de' Dolci, the latter of whom in the second half of 1471 is named as the master of works.

Recent attention has focussed on Francesco di Benedetto Cereo from Borgo Sansepolcro, who first appears in Rome during the pontificate of Nicholas V. Cereo was a papal secretary under Calixtus III and prefect under Pius II and Paul II. He was thus responsible for all organizational, administrative, and financial matters concerning papal building works. Described as "architect" in two lives of Paul II—Gaspare da Verona's *The Accomplishments of Paul II* (*De gestis Pauli Secundi*) and Michele Canense's *The Life and Papacy of Paul II* (*De vita et pontificatu Pauli Secundi*)—Cereo's interest in humanism and learning is clear from his writings now in the Vatican Library, Latin translations of Euclid, Archimedes, and Ptolomy, with geometrical and perspectival illustrations possibly by Cereo himself. He probably had links with Alberti, who may have recommended him to Pius II to oversee building work at the Vatican.

Paul II died on July 26, 1471 in his beloved garden at San Marco, after dining (and perhaps, according to Platina's account, eating too many melons, of which he was particularly fond). Some people alleged magical practices, claiming that "he was strangled by certain devils he kept shut up." This echoed the opinion of the populace, who had always regarded Paul's collection of jewels and gemstones with suspicion, attributing magical healing powers to them.

Paul left a splendid palazzo and church that were to have great influence on Roman architecture in the last quarter of the fifteenth century. The loggia of the internal courtyard would be a model for the facade of the church of the Santi Apostoli and the portico of San Pietro in Vincoli, while the loggia of the church of San Marco was to inspire the Palazzina Riario in Palazzo Colonna and the Chiostro dei Genovesi. The facade of Palazzo San Marco would be repeated in the palazzo of Cardinal Domenico della Rovere (now the Palazzo dei Penitenzieri), with different proportions and scale.

Sixtus IV, Restorer of Rome

Pope Sixtus IV (1471–84), who came from Liguria, was elected pope on August 9, 1471. He was a man of great humanist learning, as was recorded by Bessarion. A learned theologian, he was the author of an important treatise, *The Blood of Christ* (*De sanguine Christi*, 1471), and of a work that defended the doctrine of the Immaculate Conception.

Sixtus' papacy was marked by violent political events, including the Pazzi conspiracy against the Medici family in Florence in 1478, when Sixtus sided with the faction hostile to the Medici, headed by his nephew Girolamo Riario and the Pazzi family. Though Giuliano de' Medici, Lorenzo's brother, was killed, the plot failed. Lorenzo escaped, and in the aftermath of the conspiracy had a number of ecclesiastics close to Sixtus IV executed, for which Sixtus excommunicated him. Only then did Lorenzo free Girolamo Riario, but he threatened to call a council of the Church. These events were the background for a war in which Sixtus, allied with Siena and Naples, clashed with Florence, allied in turn with Milan, Venice, and the king of France. Peace was made in 1480.

In addition, the Ottoman Turkish threat was drawing ever closer. In 1477, under Sultan Mehmed II, they had penetrated Venetian territory as far as the Isonzo and Tagliamento rivers and in 1480 the town of Otranto in the heel of Italy was captured; it was liberated the following year. Girolamo Riario continued to pursue his expansionist goals, turning now towards Ferrara, where he tried to oust Ercole I d'Este. The war sparked off by this action ended in 1484, the year of Sixtus' death, with the Peace of Bagnolo.

A few months after being elected, Sixtus made the first step in his plans for Rome. It was of symbolic significance: the establishment of the Capitoline Museum, with the gift of six bronze sculptures from the papal collection at the Lateran Palace—the *She-Wolf*, the *Spinario* (boy removing a thorn from his foot), the colossal head of Constantius II, the hand of a colossal statue, the *Palla Sansonis*, and the *Camillus*—sculptures that for the Romans represented the memory of their great past. The gift was indicative of Sixtus' plans for the city. He was to be more concerned with restoration and re-evaluation than with emulating ancient Rome—which

had obsessed Nicholas V. Sixtus' austere outlook, his background in the Franciscan order, and the political difficulties of the time ruled out the kind of lavish display sought by his predecessor. This is how the title *Urbis Restaurator* (Restorer of Rome) over the door to the left of the Palazzo Senatorio should be understood, and the approving words of the Englishman Robert Fleming in 1477, which emphasize that Sixtus had not filled the city with sumptuous buildings, but had concentrated on churches and sober buildings.

Even the work carried out for the jubilee of 1475 was characterized by utilitarian needs rather than outward appearance. Sigismondo de' Conti, an early sixteenth-century diarist, recorded that there was no chapel that the pope did not have restored for the jubilee. Sixtus also had the main street of the city repaved, the hospital of Santo Spirito improved, and the remains of an old Roman bridge rebuilt as the Ponte Sisto.

As Sixtus wished, the church of Santa Maria del Popolo was rebuilt between 1472 and 1477 as the burial place of those linked to him by bonds of family or politics. The church had been given to an Augustinian congregation from Lombardy in 1472 and the rebuilding was in Lombard style, with three aisles, pentagonal chapels, a crossing

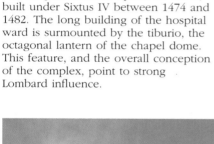

The hospital of Santo Spirito in Sassia, built under Sixtus IV between 1474 and 1482. The long building of the hospital ward is surmounted by the tiburio, the octagonal lantern of the chapel dome. This feature, and the overall conception of the complex, point to strong Lombard influence.

with a dome on an octagonal support, transepts with apses, a large main chapel behind the altar, with two chapels on either side, and groin vaults in the central and side aisles. If the plan shows considerable similarities with San Pietro in Gessate in Milan, designed by Guiniforte Solari, the building technique is distinctly Roman, deriving from the works at Palazzo Venezia. The facade is attributed to Baccio Pontelli, who was responsible for various architectural works of the Sistine period, from Santa Maria della Pace to San Pietro in Montorio, and the cathedral of Sant'Aura in Ostia Antica to the campanile of Santo Spirito in Sassia.

Sixtus' most important project, one with a clearly symbolic and celebratory intent, was the Sistine Chapel in the Vatican Palace, whose external fortress-like medieval appearance was fitting for the warlike times. Construction began on the site of a thirteenth-century palace chapel in 1473. A poem of 1478 describes how Sixtus has built a chapel that is "beautiful and outstanding" (*pulchrum et praestans*).

As far as the architect of this work is concerned, Vasari claimed that the chapel was built according to a design by Baccio Pontelli. However, it is known that Pontelli was occupied between 1471 and 1479 on the intarsia work in Pisa cathedral. From a document of October 1481 it appears that the superintendent of works at the Vatican Palace was Giovannino de' Dolci.

The architectural structure of the Sistine Chapel appears to allude to the biblical Temple of Solomon, a reference apt for Sixtus IV, who was referred to as the heir of Solomon in 1513 by his nephew Pope Julius II in a papal bull. There are parallels between the Temple of Solomon and the Sistine Chapel: the description of the Temple in the Old Testament (Kings, 1) states that it was sixty cubits long, twenty cubits wide, and thirty cubits high, with either two halls or a two-part hall preceded by a portico. The Sistine Chapel is divided into two parts by a screen, and its measurements coincide almost perfectly with those of the Temple, if the biblical measurements are calculated using the Palestinian cubit.

Moreover, Perugino's fresco *Christ Giving the Keys to St. Peter* in the chapel refers directly to Solomon. In the background two triumphal arches reminiscent of the Arch of Constantine flank the central building. On each, above the central arch, is an inscription. These explicitly compare Sixtus and Constantine but place Sixtus above Constantine, declaring that Sixtus is "lesser in wealth but greater in religion." The implication is that the avoidance of luxurious display indicates the choice of austerity made by the Christian faith and the superiority of a choice: the pope is superior to Solomon, Christ to Moses, and the New Testament to the Old.

The name of Baccio Pontelli recurs in one of the earliest examples of a cardinal's palace, the palazzo built by Domenico della Rovere, now Palazzo dei Penitenzieri. Born around 1440 in Piedmont and related to Sixtus IV, Domenico della Rovere was a generous patron of ecclesiastical buildings, particularly in connection with the church of Santa Maria del Popolo, where he was buried with solemn rites in 1501, the funeral

The travertine facade of the church of Santa Maria del Popolo by Andrea Bregno, perhaps the earliest Renaissance church facade in Rome. Several details were altered by Bernini in the seventeenth century.

Palazzo dei Penitenzieri in the Borgo, commissioned by Cardinal Domenico della Rovere and built by Baccio Pontelli.

oration being given by the humanist Raffaele Brandolini, who praised his activities as an architectural sponsor. Patron of the re-established Roman academy of Pomponio Leto from 1478, Della Rovere was one of the principal promoters of the interest in antiquarian decoration, which was to find such a magnificent interpreter in Pinturicchio, whom he called in to decorate some of the rooms of his palazzo.

Built over a number of phases, the palazzo reveals similarities with Pietro Barbo's Palazzo San Marco (now Palazzo Venezia), particularly in the cross-form windows and corner tower. Recently, because of these echoes of Palazzo San Marco, the design for the building has been attributed to Meo del Caprino, who had worked at Palazzo San Marco and who left Rome for Turin in 1491, where he was employed in the construction of the cathedral there, commissioned by Domenico della Rovere himself, who had been appointed archbishop of Turin in 1483.

The other great palazzo built for a cardinal in this period is the Palazzo della Cancelleria, commissioned by Raffaele Sansoni Riario. A noted figure in the world of Roman humanism, and friend of Ermolao Barbaro, Riario commissioned manuscripts of Cicero's works from the illuminators Bartolomeo Sanvito and Lauro Padovano. He also financed the first printed edition of Vitruvius' *On Architecture* in 1486.

It is not known precisely when work started on Riario's palazzo, but the diarist Stefano

Detail of the Palazzo della Cancelleria, showing its facade curving outwards towards the Campo de' Fiori. At the corner can be seen the coat of arms of the Riario family. The richly sculptured balcony has been attributed to Andrea Bregno.

Work on the Palazzo della Cancelleria began in 1489 on commission from Cardinal Raffaele Riario, but it did not become the seat of the papal chancery until later.
Although its design was clearly influenced by Palazzo San Marco, the building is a landmark in Renaissance palace architecture and a source of inspiration for Renaissance buildings.

Infessura recorded in 1489 that a palazzo with a corner tower was being built. It is known that Riario took up residence there in 1496, when the building was still unfinished. Vasari suggests that Bramante was involved in the design of the palazzo, but this seems doubtful, as Bramante arrived in Rome only in 1499, the year of the rift between Riario and Pope Alexander VI, which led to Riario's departure from Rome. Riario did not return until 1503 for the conclave to elect Alexander's successor. It is more likely that the visit to Rome by Bramante which Vasari refers to was in order to consult Riario on work still outstanding during Riario's absence in Rome.

The palazzo, stylistically mixed, seems to be the result of a joint effort. Construction was slow, continuing almost until Riario's fall from favor. In 1516 Riario was to be accused of plotting against Pope Leo X, and died in the palazzo where now he was a mere guest—Leo had confiscated it and given it to his nephew, Cardinal Giulio de' Medici.

Alexander VI: the Jubilee of 1500

Before their quarrel in 1499, Riario had had much influence over Pope Alexander VI (1492–1503), who entrusted him with the project for Via Alessandrina (the grandest of his pontificate), the fortification of Castel Sant'Angelo, and the rebuilding of the Borgo. Originally built as the mausoleum of the Emperor Hadrian, under Alexander, it became a crucial node between the two parts of the city on each side of the river. A moat was created around it, with a fortified bridge with a tower. It was part of the scheme for rebuilding that included the bridge and area on the other side of the Tiber, with the fortification of the Tor di Nona.

The creation of the Via Alessandrina, begun in 1499 with the jubilee of 1500 in mind, and prompted by the need for easier access, required the demolition of part of the medieval Borgo district. On the side of this road was a pyramidal funerary monument, the *Meta Romuli* (Pyramid of Romulus), of similar dimensions to the surviving Pyramid of Cestius at Porta San Paolo. In the past its stone cladding had been used to pave the portico and build the steps leading up to St. Peter's. It is not clear if Alexander completely demolished the *Meta Romuli*. Some historians have suggested that it was made a focal point of the scheme. This would have had great symbolic value for Alexander, as the pyramid evoked the Egyptian Osiris and the heraldic bull Apis (the Borgia emblem was a bull).

Over the next two decades, with the construction of palazzi directly inspired by antique buildings, the Via Alessandrina became a showpiece,

complete with all the elements (castle, palazzo, temple, mausoleum, gate) of the tragic stageset described in Vitruvius' *On Architecture*. A note by Sebastiano Serlio on Vitruvius' recommendations and a drawing by Battista da Sangallo in the margin of a copy of Vitruvius show a street with aristocratic and ecclesiastical buildings, and a triumphal arch or gate through which can be glimpsed a pyramid that appears in the street in precisely the position of the *Meta Romuli*.

Historians have suggested that Bramante, who probably arrived in Rome in the summer of 1499, may have been instrumental in saving the *Meta Romuli*. He was immediately drawn into work for the jubilee of 1500. Vasari described his role as "under-architect," supervising the restoration of the fountain of Santa Maria in Trastevere under Cardinal Juan Lopez from Valencia, who died in 1501. Vasari also claims that Bramante restored the fountain in the square in front of St. Peter's, though this is uncertain. This fountain, consisting of two basins on a pedestal, had been built during the pontificate of Innocent VIII and was only decorated and enlarged under Alexander VI. It marked the end of the Via Alessandrina.

Gioia Mori

The courtyard of Palazzo della Cancelleria is dominated by the arcades on two floors. Baccio Pontelli, Cardinal Riario's architect, borrowed this motif from the Palazzo Ducale in Urbino but elevated it to a new level of monumentality.

Sculpture

FOLLOWING PAGE:
Carved stone slab from the tomb of Giovanni Crivelli in the church of Santa Maria in Aracoeli. This relief, made between 1432 and 1433, is the only signed example of Donatello's work from his Roman period.

This marble ciborium by Donatello, today in the Treasury of the Sagrestia dei Benificiati in St. Peter's, dates from the same time as the Crivelli tomb. The upper relief shows the deposition of Christ. The image in it of the Virgin, the Madonna della Febbre, is attributed to Lippo Memmi.

Tomb of Cardinal Philippe d'Alençon (d. 1397) by Giovanni d'Ambrogio in Santa Maria in Trastevere. The relief below the gisant figure of the Cardinal depicts the death of the Virgin. The two sections of the tomb are connected by architectural elements from antique models.

At the beginning of the fifteenth century, sculpture in Rome is represented by a number of tombs by Florentine and Umbrian sculptors. Attributed to the Florentine Giovanni d'Ambrogio is the monument to Cardinal Philippe d'Alençon in the church of Santa Maria in Trastevere, dating from after 1397, the year of the cardinal's death, and the monument of Cardinal Adam Easton in Santa Cecilia in Trastevere. The d'Alençon monument was later dismantled, and its original appearance as a ciborium with altar was lost when it was converted into a wall monument. Surviving from the original elaborate tomb are the recumbent figure representing d'Alençon, the reliefs of the Dormition and Assumption of the Virgin, and a series of small statues, some of which are now in the portico.

The only sculptor whose activities and name are documented in this period is a certain "Magister Paulus" (Master Paul), whose signature appears on the tombs of Bartolomeo Carafa (died 1405) in Santa Maria del Priorato and Cardinal Pietro Stefaneschi (died 1417) in Santa Maria in Trastevere. Both tombs were subsequently dismantled and rearranged.

The signature of "Magister Paulus" has led to disagreement over attribution, as there were two sculptors of this name active at the time, the Umbrian Paolo da Gualdo Cattaneo—responsible for a number of stylistically mixed works outside Rome in which Late Gothic elements appear alongside designs with an often rather archaic sense of volume—and a certain Paulus Salvati, or Salvatelli, who may have been responsible for the statue of Pope Boniface IX now in the cloisters of San Paolo fuori le Mura, which is also ascribed to Cattaneo. Grimaldi's opinion of 1620 that the statue had formed part of Boniface's tomb is now rejected and the statue is believed to have been a tribute to Boniface's memory, perhaps on the occasion of the jubilee of 1400.

Donatello and Filarete

It was during the pontificate of Eugenius IV that Donatello made one of his visits to Rome. There was a revival of the tradition of major commissions, which were now entrusted to Donatello or to Filarete. As a result, a new artistic language, inspired by the most modern humanist ideas, emerged in Rome. According to Vasari, Donatello had already been in Rome in his youth with Brunelleschi, when both men had been so busy with the excavation of antiquities that they were known as "the treasure-hunters." Donatello must have been in Rome in 1430, since a letter dated September 1430 from Poggio Bracciolini to Niccolò Niccoli in Florence records that "Donatello saw [it] and praised it greatly" ("Donatellus vidit, et summe laudavit").

Donatello's ciborium in St. Peter's (now in the Treasury of the Cappella della Sagrestia dei Beneficiati), a frame for the painting of the Madonna della Febbre, can be dated to this stay. On the ciborium, designed as an architectural facade, the upper relief with the Deposition of Christ is believed to be by Donatello himself, inserted into a structure which is probably by his workshop. The relief is horizontal, framed by curtains drawn back by two putti to reveal Christ. There are references to antique sculpture, from the scenes of mourning over the dead Meleager to representations of maenads with raised arms. The position of the relief on the attic of the ciborium recalls Roman triumphal archs.

There is controversy over the involvement of Michelozzo, who collaborated with Donatello for

many years. According to Vasari, "[Michelozzo] was skilled in working in marble and in matters concerning bronze-casting." It is known from a document of April 1, 1433 that Pagno di Lapo had to go to Rome to collect "Donatello and his *compagno* [partner]" so that they could finish the pulpit for Prato Cathedral. The "compagno" would appear to have been Michelozzo.

However, John Pope-Hennessy suggested that it was unlikely that the two men could have opened a workshop in Rome in the short time that they spent there. He also rejected the dating of the ciborium as 1432–33. Since the ciborium is composed of different elements which could be easily transported and assembled, he suggested that the various pieces were made in Florence in the late 1430s and that the ciborium was commissioned by Eugenius IV, following the advice of Alberti, who spent much time in Florence between 1434 and 1443.

The only signed work by Donatello which was definitely made in Rome is the marble tomb slab in the church of Santa Maria in Aracoeli of Giovanni Crivelli, archdeacon of Aquileia. On the slab, which originally lay on the ground, the body of the dead man is represented within a niche with a shell vault. Crivelli died on July 29, 1432, and the slab is traditionally dated between then and the spring of the following year, when Donatello returned to Florence. It seems more likely that the work was commissioned and executed before Crivelli's death. Crivelli may even have been involved in the choice of image, which is markedly traditional in style.

The other probable work by Donatello in Rome is the tomb slab for Pope Martin V, originally placed, following the pope's wish, before the high altar of San Giovanni in Laterano. It is known that the tomb arrived by sea: two customs declarations of April 1445 mention the tomb slab being landed in Rome from a papal galley commanded by a Florentine. The attribution to Donatello is not certain. Other art historians have suggested that the tomb was executed in a workshop following designs by Donatello after he moved to Padua in 1443, or was by Simone Ghini, after a design by Donatello. It is possible that Donatello carved only the face. Pope-Hennessy attributed the entire work to Michelozzo, Donatello's "compagno."

In the same year, 1445, the other significant piece of work to be carried out under Eugenius IV was completed. This was the bronze doors made by the Florentine Filarete (Antonio Averlino), which Filarete referred to with pride in the dedication of his *Treatise on Architecture* (*Trattato d'architettura*) to the duke of Milan, Francesco Sforza, and Piero de' Medici. Vasari was more critical: "If Pope Eugenius IV, when he decided to have the doors of St. Peter's in Rome made of bronze, had tried harder to find excellent men for the task, it would not have been done in as disgraceful a manner as can be see today." According to Vasari, "they labored twelve years to finish it." It appears that the execution of the doors can be dated from between 1433, the year Filarete arrived in Rome and was present at the coronation of Sigismund as Holy

Roman Emperor, and 1445, as can be seen from the inscription on the back of the door, which includes a representation of Filarete and his assistants. Filarete's doors are mentioned by Flavio Biondo in his *Rome Restored* (*Roma instaurata*) of about 1446 as the most successful artistic enterprise of Eugenius' papacy. Biondo considered Filarete's doors superior to the silver doors executed under Pope Leo IV.

With its "disgraceful" manner and eclectic iconography, the doors are a crucial record of the contemporary passion for antiquarian study. They have a pleasing sense of narrative, confidently handled in those places where contemporary events and episodes from mythology and Roman history are depicted.

The scenes on the door include Christ the Pantocrator, the Annunciation, St. Paul, and St. Peter with Eugenius IV. At the bottom are two scenes of martyrdom, the beheading of St. Paul (apparently based on the general layout of the same scene in Giotto's Stefaneschi Triptych,

which then stood on the high altar in St. Peter's) and the crucifixion of St. Peter, where the townscape in the background is based on the descriptions in the medieval guide to Rome, the *Marvels of Rome* (*Mirabiliaurbis*), with depictions of actual buildings such as Castel Sant'Angelo and imaginary reconstructions of vanished buildings. Between the larger reliefs are four smaller reliefs intended to glorify Eugenius IV: the Emperor John VIII Palaeologus on the sea-voyage to Italy and his reception by Eugenius; a session of the Council of Ferrara/ Florence and the departure of the Greeks from Venice; the coronation of Sigismund and his procession with the pope through Rome; Abbot Andrew of the monastery of St. Anthony in Egypt receiving in Florence the papal bull on the union of the two churches; and the arrival of Abbot Andrew in Rome to worship at the tombs of the Apostles, the latest event depicted, having taken place in 1441.

Filarete's archeological and antiquarian interests and his figurative skills are demonstrated in

the framework of the panels. Subjects from myths in Ovid, Livy's Roman history, and Virgil's *Eclogues* emerge out of entwining acanthus. There are also medallions with profiles of Roman emperors, adopted from Roman coins or manuscripts such as Giovanni de Matociis' *History of the Emperors* (*Historia imperialis*), decorated around 1320. In other words, the bronze border is treated like the decorated margin of a manuscript. Rome and the Church, the papacy and its martyrs, are glorified in a timeless *continuum*, from myth and ancient history to the present.

Donatello influenced to some extent Isaia da Pisa, son of the sculptor Pippo di Gante da Pisa. Isaia knew Donatello and as a result of a number of important commissions had links with the family of Eugenius IV. Isaia is thought to have come to Rome as early as the 1430s. There are also later references to him there between 1447 and 1464. In 1448 he took on an important commission, the tomb of Cardinal Antonio de Chiaves (died 1447) in San Giovanni in Laterano. The commission had originally been given to Filarete, who probably left the tomb at the design stage when he was forced to flee Rome in 1448, wrongly accused of the theft of reliquaries. The tomb, which was dismantled and reassembled in the course of work for the jubilee of 1650 during the papacy of Innocent X, has echoes of Donatello and antique art and is executed with great delicacy.

Paolo Romano

The obsession with building that tormented Nicholas V during his life was to pursue him even after his death. It was as a result of works being carried out at St. Peter's that his body found no permanent resting place. Nicholas was buried in St. Peter's. According to Canon Tiberio Alfarani da Gerace, who published a precise plan of St. Peter's in 1571, Nicholas' tomb was moved for the first time between 1506 and 1513, during the papacy of Julius II. It was moved again in 1576, when part of Old St. Peter's was demolished, while the meticulous description of St. Peter's by the notary Giacomo Grimani published in 1619 also relates that on September 11, 1606 the body of the pope was exhumed.

Some fragments of this wall tomb, originally more than nineteen feet high, are now in the Vatican Grottos. They include part of the original pediment with two flying angels, the side pilasters with niches with rounded shell vaults containing Apostles, the recumbent figure of the pope, and a verse inscription composed by Aeneas Silvius Piccolomini on a tablet supported by two cherubs.

The name of the sculptor is unknown but the most plausible theory identifies the tomb as an early work by Paolo Romano (Paolo Taccone) because of the influence of antique sculpture

Relief from the tomb of Pius II in Sant'Andrea della Valle, depicting the presentation of the head of St. Andrew, one of the central events during the pontificate of Pius.
The execution of the relief is attributed to the so-called Master of Pius II, one of the artists active in the group around Paolo Romano.

Another of Isaia's works, carried out between 1447 and 1453, is the tomb of Eugenius IV, originally in St. Peter's and now in the convent of San Giorgio in Alga, adjoining San Salvatore in Lauro. The work regarded as Isaia's most successful is that made in the early 1450s, the *Virgin Enthroned with Sts. Peter and Paul and Donors*. The donors have recently been identified as Eugenius IV as well as Cardinal Pietro Barbo, his nephew.

and because of similarities to another work that can be attributed to him with certainty, the tomb of Pope Pius II. Paolo Romano, son of a certain Mariano di Tuccio Taccone da Sezze mentioned by Filarete as a sculptor and goldsmith, was already active in 1451 on the Palazzo dei Conservatori on the Capitoline Hill. In 1542 he was working on the chapels which had been commissioned by Nicholas V for each end of Ponte Sant'Angelo.

Tomb of Pius II, made under the artistic direction of Paolo Romano. In 1614 it was transferred from St. Peter's to the church of Sant'Andrea della Valle. The relief depicting the presentation of St. Andrew's relics was placed over the epitaph at the bottom. Above the central gisant figure of the pope is a relief showing Sts. Peter and Paul presenting the pope and Cardinal Piccolomini to the Virgin. The figures in the side niches portray the virtues of the deceased.

Most of Paolo Romano's work dates from the pontificates of Pius II and Paul II. Between 1461 and 1462 he made the statues of Sts. Peter and Paul, now in the Vatican Library, which originally stood on the steps leading up to St. Peter's. After 1461 they were replaced by two statues of St. Andrew which celebrated the arrival in Rome of the relic of St. Andrew's head, a gift from Thomas Palaeologus, who had brought the head from Patras and presented it to the pope near the Milvian Bridge, just north of the city.

The presentation of the relic of St. Andrew's head was a particularly solemn ceremony. It was recorded in Pius II's *Commentaries* (*Commentarii*) and celebrated in the relief that decorates Pius' tomb, the last work executed by Paolo Romano, who is believed to have died in 1473. The tomb, which was eventually moved from St. Peter's and reassembled in Sant'Andrea della Valle, was commissioned by Cardinal Francesco Todeschini and executed by several sculptors, one of whom can be identified as the "Maestro di Pio II" (Master of Pius II).

The design of the tomb, a wall monument with three orders with architraves and three niches with shell vaults on each side, is attributed to Paolo Romano, who executed for it an unfinished recumbent figure of the pope, as well, perhaps, as the upper relief with Sts. Peter and Paul, who are shown presenting the donors, Pius II and Cardinal Francesco Todeschini, to the Virgin. The central relief, on the other hand, depicting the presentation of the relic of St. Andrew's head, and the virtues standing in the flanking niches, is attributed to the Master of Pius II, whose style shows the influence of Paolo Romano and Mino da Fiesole, the Florentine sculptor who had been a pupil of the Rossellino brothers.

Mino da Fiesole had already been in Rome between 1453 and 1455, during the papacy of Nicholas V, a stay documented by a signed and dated 1454 bust of Niccolò Strozzi now in Berlin. Mino's longest stay in Rome can be placed some time before 1461, the date of the ciborium of Santa Maria Maggiore, now dismantled, which was commissioned by Cardinal Guglielmo d'Estouteville. Mino also made an altar dedicated to St. Jerome for the cardinal; four reliefs from it survive in the Museo del Palazzo Venezia.

Tuscan and Lombard Workshops

It may have been on the occasion of the jubilee of 1475 that Sixtus IV initiated restoration work on the ciborium in St. Peter's. Now dismantled, it had stood on the *confessio* in front of the high altar from at least the time of Pope Callixtus II (1119–24) and had been restored by Pius II. Sixtus IV had reliefs added, that depicted the crucifixion of St. Peter, the beheading of St. Paul, Christ giving the keys to St. Peter, the healing of the paralytic man, and the fall of Simon Magus, all apparently gilded.

The reliefs are dated to between 1471, the year of Sixtus' election, and 1478, the year of the death of Cardinal Giovanni Battista Mellini, who was in charge of the work. Two names have been

suggested for the sculptor: a Florentine master close to Antonio Rossellino, who may have been responsible for the general decorative scheme and could have executed some of it, and a Roman master close to Mino da Fiesole and Paolo Romano. There is no doubt that the ciborium is iconographically related to the old stories of the Apostles as they appear in St. Peter's: the thirteenth-century frescos in the portico and the martyrdoms of Sts. Peter and Paul depicted on Filarete's doors. The reliefs reveal close study of the antique, not only in the narrative style but also in the technique of drilling used to represent hair and the careful attention to details of clothing, the principal source for which seems to be the reliefs on Trajan's Column.

Relief showing the crucifixion of St. Peter. This work belongs to Antonio Rossellini's decorative program for the ciborium over the high altar of Old St. Peter's, which was redesigned from a commission by Sixtus IV. St. Peter's, Vatican Grottos.

Part of the relief from the ciborium of Sixtus IV showing a group of Roman soldiers. The archaeologically precise rendering of the armor reveals a close study of antique Roman monuments, particularly the reliefs on Trajan's Column. St. Peter's, Vatican Grottos.

In contrast with this, which has been described as "an extraordinary hotchpotch of antique formulae," in the 1470s a number of beautifully executed sculptures were produced in Rome, mainly the work of Lombard and Venetian sculptors. The most famous of the Lombards was Andrea Bregno, one of a family of sculptors from Como, who arrived in Rome in the mid-1460s. A friend of Jacopo Ripanda and Platina, Bregno was to be one of those recommended to Lorenzo de' Medici as "a celebrated

sculptor and close to me" (*sculptor egregius et vicinus meus*). Andrea da Montecavallo (as Bregno was known from the part of Rome he lived in, Montecavallo) had a wide knowledge of antiquarian matters and owned an important collection of antique sculpture including the Sarcophagus of Adonis and the Belvedere Torso.

Bregno's most impressive work is the high altar in Santa Maria del Popolo, a large architectural structure in the form of a triumphal arch. He signed and dated the altar in memory of a

Detail from the ciborium of Sixtus IV showing the beheading of St. Paul. Antonio Rossellini endowed the scene with a particularly intense quality by creating different levels within the relief.

FOLLOWING PAGE:
Marble ciborium for the main altar of Santa Maria del Popolo. Commissioned by Rodrigo Borgia (later Alexander VI), it was made by Andrea Bregno in 1474. The architecture of the work shows a clear return to the forms of ancient triumphal arches. In the course of Bernini's redesign of the altar, Bregno's work was re-erected in the sacristy.

tragedy that occurred in 1473 while he was working on it—the death of his son, Marcantonio, at the age of seven. The size of the altar (it was to reach a height of almost fifteen feet and a width of about nine) and its typology were unusual for the time, although Bregno had completed a work in 1469 that anticipated it, a ciborium to contain the communion bread and wine for San Gregorio al Celio, commissioned by the abbot of the monastery, Gregorio Amatisco. This was in the form of a triumphal arch, based on the Arch of Constantine. A carefully designed perspectival scene decorating the top section of this ciborium shows the penitential procession of Pope Gregory the Great, when an angel appeared on the Castel Sant'Angelo to signal an end to the plague. In this miniature depiction of the Castel Sant'Angelo, perfect in its rendering of perspective, Bregno's knowledge of the most advanced theories of architecture appears clearly.

The triumphal arch of the altar of Santa Maria del Popolo was conceived by Bregno almost as an iconostasis. Among its numerous innovations, the use of shell motifs alternately pointing up and down is especially striking. The shell design is repeated, on a bigger scale, in the apse of the church. Here it has been attributed to Bramante, but because this motif is typical of Bregno, it has also been seen as forming part of the original plan, modernized by Bramante.

It was not only in his work in Santa Maria del Popolo that Bregno was responsible for important innovations in figurative art in Rome. The quiet assurance of his sculpture and the balance of the architectural whole of his work for the tomb of the Cardinal d'Albret in Santa Maria in Aracoeli, dated 1465 in an inscription, and the tomb of Cardinal Alain Coëtivy in Santa Prassede, of later date and only recently attributed to Bregno, reached new heights of novel, classical harmony.

The structure of the Albret tomb was to be repeated in the tombs of two cardinals, Domenico Capranica (about 1470) and Giovanni de Coca (about 1477) in Santa Maria sopra Minerva, with the architrave supported by double pilasters and surmounted by a shell pediment. This typically Lombard solution is further embellished in the tomb of Cardinal Pietro Riario (about 1477) in Santi Apostoli, with niches in the pilasters and a mixtilinear tympanum.

A more classical version, with an arch with a lunette, is found on the tomb of Cristoforo della Rovere in Santa Maria del Popolo of about 1478, commissioned by Cristoforo's brother, Domenico della Rovere. As it is known that Mino da Fiesole was present in the Santa Maria del Popolo workshop at this time, it has been suggested that he executed the Della Rovere tomb and that Bregno's role was that of designer, concerned

The tomb of Cardinal d'Albret from 1465 in the church of Santa Maria in Aracoeli, Andrea Bregno's earliest Roman work. It consists of a lower zone for the epitaph, the deceased's statue in the center, and fenestrated architecture with busts of the Apostles, representing the secular world, the tomb, and the realm of the divine.

SEDENTE · PAVLO · II ·

LVDOVICVS · DE · LEBRETTO · REGIVS · SANGVIS ·
SANCTORVM · PETRI · ET · MARCELLINI · PRESBYTER ·
CARDINALIS · NOBILITATE · ANIMI · INNOCENTIA ·
ET · FIDE · PRAECLARVS · SACRI · APOSTOLICI · SENATVS ·
AMOR · ET · DELITIAE · HOC · MONIMENTO · CONDITVS · EST ·
M · CCCC · LXV · DIE · IIII · SEPTEMBRIS ~

with planning the chapel as a whole, as for the nearby Cibo, Basso della Rovere, and Costa chapels. Common to these chapels is the concept of a space designed according to the principle of *canditus ornatus*, architectural clarity and balance, and the importance given to sculptural decoration designed to provide a framework for the frescos.

Andrea Bregno's style can be contrasted with the work in the same period of Giovanni Dalmata (also known as Giovanni da Traù), a sensitive and educated sculptor who arrived in Rome in the late 1460s. Though Giovanni had worked on his own outside Rome, in Rome he worked in collaboration with Bregno and, in the 1470s, with Mino da Fiesole.

The tabernacle in San Marco of about 1476 is the work of the two sculptors Giovanni Dalmata and Mino da Fiesole, as was the tomb of Pope Paul II, which was, according to Vasari, "held at that time to be the richest tomb for ornamentation and figures ever made for a pope." The tomb was commissioned by Cardinal Marco Barbo, perhaps before his journey to Hungary as papal legate between 1472 and 1474. An inscription on it records that it was completed in 1477. During the rebuilding of St. Peter's under Bramante, the tomb was dismantled. It was re-erected in 1574 but was dismantled again after 1607, part remaining in St. Peter's and part going to the Vatican Grottos. Two fragments of sculpture from the base of the tomb were used in 1616 to decorate the Casino of Villa Borghese. They were acquired on behalf of Napoleon, brother-in-law of Camillo Borghese in 1808, and ended up in the Louvre, where they can still be found.

The original appearance of the tomb (over thirty-two feet high and sixteen feet wide), is known from a number of contemporary drawings, including a detailed sketch by Giovanni Antonio Dosio. The two sculptors signed their names on two of the figures of the virtues: Mino da Fiesole on that of Charity, Giovanni Dalmata on Hope. The overall plan had been entrusted to Giovanni Dalmata, who had originally turned to Barbo, a fellow Venetian, for assistance. Mino da Fiesole's contribution seems to date from 1474, perhaps a result of the urgency of completing so ambitious a work in a short time. He was assigned the figures of Faith and Charity, a scene from the Fall of Man (now lacking the figures of Adam and Eve), Sts. John and Luke, the angels of the upper arch, and the seraphim on the lintel. In turn, Giovanni Dalmata was responsible for Hope, the recumbent figure of Paul II, the creation of Eve, the Resurrection, Christ blessing, two angels bearing the monogram of Christ on the ceiling of the cella, Sts. Mark and Matthew, and the four angels to the right of the arch.

At the beginning of the 1480s, these two north Italian sculptors, who over the previous decade had left their mark on Roman sculpture, now moved on. Andrea Bregno, invited by Cardinal Francesco Piccolomini, who was the nephew of Pius II, to work on the Piccolomini altar in Siena Cathedral, was to be away from Rome from 1481 to 1485. Giovanni Dalmata, already summoned to Hungary in 1481, possibly through the recommendation of Cardinal Marco Barbo, was to return there around 1485 to the court of King Matthias Corvinus, where he was appointed court sculptor. He was not to return to Italy until the early sixteenth century, when he worked in Venice and the Marches, in 1509 signing the tomb of Girolamo Giannelli in Ancona Cathedral, his last known work.

Bregno reappeared in Rome in 1485, where he was active in the workshop of Santa Maria del Popolo, still an important center of artistic production. In Siena he had collaborated with the Milanese sculptor Luigi di Giovanpietro Capponi. Capponi is recorded in Rome from 1485, where he was active for about ten years. His style, showing the influence of the Padua school, is marked by a taste for descriptive detail and a pleasing expressiveness. In 1485 he was given the commission for the tomb of Archbishop Giovanni Francesco Brusati in San Clemente, and the following year the commission for the altar with a crucified Christ between the Virgin and St. John, today in the sacristy of Santa Maria della Consolazione. Another important work by Capponi is the altarpiece with scenes from the life of St. Gregory the Great in San Gregorio al Celio, dating from about 1490.

Though he was the preferred sculptor of the Della Rovere family, Bregno was not responsible for the tomb of Sixtus IV (died 1484) since he was busy in Siena at that time. Instead the Pollaiuolo brothers, Antonio and Piero, were called to Rome that year to take on the work. They were eventually to execute two papal tombs in Rome.

The first tomb was that of Sixtus IV, commissioned from Antonio Pollaiuolo by Sixtus' nephew, Cardinal Giuliano della Rovere (later Pope Julius II). It was completed in 1493, as can be seen from the inscription, which also praises the sculptor: "*FLORENTINI ARG. AVR. / PICT. AERE CLARI*" (illustrious for his work in silver, gold, and painting).

The second was that of Innocent VIII, who died on July 25, 1492. It was commissioned by Innocent's nephew Cardinal Lorenzo Cibo and

Marble altar in the sacristy of San Marco, made by Mino da Fiesole and Giovanni Dalmata in 1474. The figures of the angels and the relief depicting Melchizedec with Abraham, as well as the deception of Jacob, are attributed to Andrea Dalmata.

Tomb of Cardinals Cristoforo and Domenico della Rovere in Santa Maria del Popolo, by Andrea Bregno and Mino da Fiesole, who is thought to have created the relief depicting the Virgin.

Bronze tomb of Sixtus IV, made by Antonio and Piero Pollaiuolo between 1484 and 1493, one of the great sculptural achievements of the fifteenth century. Surrounding the recumbent figure of the Pope, and set on a slightly lower level, are depictions of the seven virtues. The concave base of the tomb is decorated with ten reliefs depicting allegories of the liberal arts. St. Peter's, Vatican Grottos.

completed by January 30, 1498, when the pope's remains were placed in the new tomb. A few days later, on February 4, Antonio Pollaiuolo died, his brother having died in 1496. The two brothers were buried in San Pietro in Vincoli, Giuliano della Rovere's titular church.

Vasari described Sixtus IV's tomb as "completed at great expense." The bronze tomb, on a raised platform, looks like the scaled-up product of a goldsmith's workshop, of chased metalwork and bronze tracery. It alone would be enough to justify the words of praise for Pollaiuolo in the goldsmith Benvenuto Cellini's *Treatise on Goldsmithing* (*Trattato di Oreficeria*) of 1568. The figure of the recumbent pope is surrounded by figures of the theological and cardinal virtues in rectangular compartments while the liberal arts are depicted around the base.

Michelangelo

It was Cardinal Riario who arranged for the young Michelangelo to come to Rome in June 1496. The underlying reason for the invitation was Riario's passion for antique sculpture; his collection, displayed in the courtyard of his palazzo, with capitals, lintels, and columns, was one of the most prestigious in Rome, conforming with Vitruvius' writings. It included larger sculptures such as the Muses recorded in the *Antiquarian Prospects* (*Antiquarie Prospettiche*) compiled at the end of the century.

Inside the palazzo were smaller statues. For a time these included a *Sleeping Cupid,* made by Michelangelo in 1496. Michelangelo had given it an "antique" patina selling it to Riario for a high price as a genuine Roman piece. The sale gained Michelangelo access to the powerful Roman cardinal, who gave him hospitality for almost a year. When Riario realized that the *Cupid* was a fake, it passed to Isabella d'Este, in 1502.

Michelangelo's *Bacchus*, (now in the Bargello Museum Florence), was also commissioned by Riario. The sculpture was ready in July 1497, but soon passed from his antiquities' collection to the banker Jacopo Galli, and placed in the garden of his house near San Lorenzo in Damaso. The free-standing statue of the drunken young god is life-size. He balances precariously on an irregular plinth, in a serpentine pose, accompanied by a satyr. The sculpture does not conform to the canons of the classical models admired by Riario, showing instead Michelangelo's personal interpretation of the antique pervaded with sensuality.

Michelangelo's *Pietà*, commissioned by Cardinal Jean Bilhères de Langraulas, abbot of St. Denis and ambassador of Charles VIII, king of France, to Pope Alexander VI, was finished in 1499. It was originally placed in the chapel of Santa Petronilla in St. Peter's, from where it was moved around 1517, reaching its present home in the first chapel on the right in 1749. In this intense sculpture, Michelangelo brought to bear all the values of balance and harmony typical of Florentine art, expressed in a refined and smooth sculptural technique. The carefully composed and modeled figures are exquisitely finished. Iconographically related to northern European sculpture and the school of Ferrara, the theme of the Virgin with the dead Christ on her lap had been treated by Perugino in 1495, and twice by Botticelli, again at the end of the century. Botticelli's paintings are of a more intense pathos. Michelangelo's decision to show the Virgin as a young woman may have been inspired by St. Bernard's prayer in Dante's *Divine Comedy* (*Paradise*, XXXIII, l. 1), where she is called "daughter of your son" (*figlia del tuo figlio*).

Gioia Mori

Painting

In the early years of the fifteenth century painting in Rome, culturally and economically impoverished by the lack of major commissions, was little affected by the great innovations which elsewhere led to the emergence of important schools of painting.

Among the fragmentary pieces of evidence from the first two decades of the fifteenth century—a few devotional paintings, tired imitations of Umbrian, Tuscan, or southern Italian schools—the Brancacci tabernacle in Santa Maria in Trastevere stands out. This was commissioned by Cardinal Rainaldo Brancacci, who had received Santa Maria in Trastevere *in commenda* from Pope Innocent VII (1404–6), an occasion celebrated in this work, which is perhaps by a Florentine painter.

Another notable artistic work from this period is the series of frescos in the church of San Sisto Vecchio, which includes portraits of a number of Dominican saints and a large scene in which various events from the life of St. Catherine of Siena are depicted within a single frame. The coat of arms painted on it has been identified as that of the Sant'Eustachio family, which had close links with the convent of San Sisto, where female members of the family destined to be nuns went. The choice of scenes from the life of St. Catherine of Siena relates to the process of her canonization, which reached a crucial

Detail of the Masolino fresco above the entrance to the Barda Castiglioni Chapel in San Clemente. This section shows the Virgin of the Annunciation.

Fresco by Masolino in San Clemente depicting the disputation between St. Catherine of Alexandria and pagan philosophers before the Emperor. San Clemente, Barda Castiglioni Chapel.

stage in 1411. This would place the frescos in the second decade of the fifteenth century. Once again, the commission did not go to a local artist, but to a painter of Sienese training, who also reveals Neapolitan influence.

Harder to date is a fragment of elaborate decoration on the tympanum over the apsidal arch of San Clemente, with two groups of angels with peacock feather wings, crowned with flowers. It seems likely that this was executed at a time when San Clemente was experiencing a period of renewal. In poor condition at the end of the fourteenth century, the monastery had passed to the Ambrosian order in 1403–04. In 1419 Pope Martin V suppressed the collegiate church and assigned the prebends to the Ambrosians, who then took over the restoration. The decoration may, therefore, date from the 1420s. It was entrusted to an Abruzzi workshop and shows remarkable similarities to the Late Gothic school of the town of Loreto Aprutino.

Gentile da Fabriano, Pisanello, Masaccio, and Masolino

In 1423 Martin V decreed a jubilee for 1425, intended to reinforce the role of Rome as the center of Christendom. The artistic commissions on this occasion had specific aims and programs. Since lack of commissions meant that artists' workshops had barely existed in Rome over the years the papacy was based in Avignon, it was necessary to summon painters such as Gentile da Fabriano and Arcangelo di Cola da Camerino from Florence and the Marches.

Martin gave his most important commission for painting in San Giovanni in Laterano to Gentile da Fabriano. He had met Gentile in Brescia in 1418 when Gentile was working on the decoration of the Broletto (town hall) there. Martin had also received as a gift from Malatesta an altarpiece by Gentile, which is now lost. Martin took particular care over the restoration of San Giovanni in Laterano, where he had once been archpriest and where he had elected to be buried. He was assisted during his pontificate by his nephew, Prospero di Marcantonio Colonna.

The first thing Martin did was to restore the king-post, probably in 1425, the eleventh centenary of the foundation of the church by Constantine. In July that year the floor of the nave was repaired using precious marble from antique ruins, and including the Colonna arms in the decoration. The canons' choir in the center of the nave was removed and the space subsequently used for Martin's tomb.

Discussions began on the painting of the frescos in September 1426.

Gentile da Fabriano's fresco cycle, destroyed when San Giovanni in Laterano was altered by Borromini for the jubilee of 1650, was impressive. According to calculations, there were sixteen sections, each some twelve feet wide. Of this extensive decoration there survives only a fragment and some drawings, including one by Borromini showing the complicated structure: scenes from the life of St. John the Baptist are surmounted by a frieze in which painted curtains alternate with Gothic tabernacles containing half-bust figures with scrolls. Between the eight windows the surface was painted to look like richly decorated and pierced stonework, with painted niches containing the colossal figures of prophets painted to look like marble, a technique much used in Flemish painting.

Two ink and silver-point drawings of scenes from the life of St. John the Baptist attributed to Pisanello probably reproduce two more of Gentile's frescos, the baptism of Christ and St. John the Baptist in prison. A detached fresco in the Vatican Library with a fragment of decoration and perhaps a bust of King David probably came from the area above the scenes.

Much use was made of lapis lazuli, with apparently no regard for cost. Visitors to Rome frequently referred to this in amazement, as did Vasari, who speaks of the use made by Gentile of "a kind of ultramarine blue given to him by the pope, so beautiful and of so glowing a color that it still has no rival."

Gentile died between August and October 14, 1428, leaving the cycle unfinished. Pisanello, whose presence in Rome is documented between April 1431 and March 1432, was summoned by Eugenius IV to complete it. Eugenius, a Venetian, must have been aware of Pisanello's painting, since Pisanello had painted an episode from the war between the emperor Frederick Barbarossa and Pope Alexander III in the Sala del Maggior Consiglio in the ducal palace in Venice, also to complete a cycle begun by Gentile da Fabriano.

Of Pisanello's work in San Giovanni in Laterano equally little remains, merely a few drawings of scenes from the life of St. John the Evangelist. This bears out the description by Paolo Giovio, according to which each side of the nave was painted, one side with the life of St. John the Baptist, and the other with the life of St. John the Evangelist, the latter executed by Pisanello and his workshop.

During his stay in Rome, Gentile was overwhelmed with commissions. To the decoration of San Giovanni in Laterano can be added a number of other works. One was a panel, now lost, representing Martin V with ten cardinals.

Possibly commissioned to mark the election of new cardinals on May 24, 1426, this introduced to Rome the genre of the official portrait. Gentile was also commissioned to paint a Virgin and Child tempera panel for the church of Santi Cosma e Damiano on the occasion of the celebrations for the ninth centenary of the foundation of the church (under Felix IV, 526–30). The commission may have come from Arcidino della Porta, bishop of Novara and one of the cardinals elected in May 1426, who was associated with Santi Cosma e Damiano. The painting was taken to the town of Velletri near Rome in 1633.

In the church of Santa Maria Nova (now Santa Francesca Romana), where Gentile had stayed in the monastery and where he was eventually buried, a *Virgin and Child with Sts. Benedict and Joseph* (now lost) was painted in the lunette over the tomb of Cardinal Alemanno Adimari. According to Vasari, it was "held in esteem by the divine Michelangelo."

Martyrdom of St. Catherine of Alexandria. The wheel on which Catherine was to have been broken was destroyed by divine intervention, and the saint was eventually beheaded. Scene from the lives of the saints cycle in the Barda Castiglioni Chapel in San Clemente by Masolino, c. 1428.

The first work to be commissioned by Martin V was from a Florentine artist. While in Florence in 1419, Martin asked Lorenzo Ghiberti to provide him with a golden miter with eight figures of angels and a cope button in embossed gold; they are described by Ghiberti in his *Commentaries* (*Commentarii*).

The exquisite button embossed with various figures, including Christ as the man of sorrows, seems to be echoed in the cope button of St. Martin of Tours, who is depicted with the features of Martin V, in the so-called *Snow Triptych* by Masolino and Masaccio, a work probably planned in 1423 with reference to the coming jubilee and originally intended for Santa Maria Maggiore. It was later divided into six panels, now dispersed in various galleries and collections. The triptych can be read as a powerful celebration of Martin V and the renewal of the papacy after the Council of Constance (1414–18), which had challenged the pope's authority. It is probably no accident that the pope entrusted this message to a work for Santa Maria Maggiore, because the connection between the Colonna family and Santa Maria Maggiore is documented from the thirteenth century, when Cardinals Pietro and Giacomo Colonna had commissioned the external mosaic of the old portal.

The theme of the *Snow Triptych* is the refoundation of Santa Maria Maggiore by Martin V, a political and cultural program which is equated with the ancient foundation of the basilica. This is the message conveyed by the scene of the *Miracle of the Snow*, which relates the foundation of Santa Maria Maggiore by Pope Liberius on the spot where snow fell in August 352. Similarly celebrated is the Holy Roman Emperor Sigismund, who had played an important role in the organization of the Council of Constance. He is portrayed next to Martin in the guise of St. John the Evangelist. The idea of rebirth is also conveyed by the figure of St. Jerome, who holds up his Vulgate translation of the Bible, open at the first page of Genesis, and displays a model of the church. Dominating the triptych are the arms of Martin V, while the pope's emblem, the column that echoes the name of the Colonna (column) family, is grasped by St. John the Baptist and decorates the cope worn by St. Martin of Tours.

Masolino and Masaccio were also responsible for the decoration of the chapel of St. Catherine in San Clemente for Branda Castiglioni. The chapel was probably begun around 1425, when Castiglioni returned to Rome, where he stayed until 1431. The decoration was probably carried out between 1428 and 1430.

Cardinal Branda Castiglioni was one of the most influential figures in the Curia. An astute diplomat, he was born in Castiglione Olona near Como and began his diplomatic career in 1401 with a mission to Cologne to Sigismund. He remained with the emperor for several years, mostly in Hungary. He was created bishop of Piacenza in 1404 and cardinal in 1411. In 1417 he was one of the cardinals who elected Pope Martin V, who showed his gratitude by entrusting Castiglioni with important responsibilities. Between 1421 and 1425 Castiglioni traveled in central Europe in order to mobilize powers against the Hussite heresy in Bohemia. After Martin V's death in 1431, he supported the election of Eugenius IV and was present at the coronation of Sigismund in Rome. He is documented as being with Eugenius in exile in Florence in 1435. He died in 1443, not long after the completion of a cycle of frescos by Masolino in the baptistery at Castiglione Olona.

The chapel of St. Catherine in San Clemente has an Annunciation on the exterior and above, in the center, Castiglioni's arms. The inner side is decorated with figures of the twelve Apostles. Inside, on the groin vault are depicted the four Evangelists and the Fathers of the Church. On the left wall are scenes from the life of St. Catherine of Alexandria, and on the right scenes from the life of St. Ambrose. The rear wall has a Crucifixion.

The choice of scenes from the lives of these two saints is related to Cardinal Branda Castiglioni's own life: St. Ambrose, bishop of Milan and a doctor of the church, had spent the greater part of his life in the fight against the Arian heresy, while St. Catherine, famous for her learning and the patron saint of education, was particularly important to Castiglioni, who founded schools in Rome and Pavia. Furthermore, Catherine's fight against heresy and her mission as ambassador of the faith recall Castiglioni's campaign against the Hussite heretics and his diplomatic career.

Between 1430 and 1432 Masolino painted a cycle, which is now lost. Contemporaries, however, considered it to be one of the most important and extensive secular cycles. This was the cycle of frescos decorating the so-called Sala Theatri in Cardinal Giordano Orsini's palazzo at Montegiordano, which was destroyed as early as 1485 in a fire started by supporters of the rival Colonna family.

The tradition of celebrating ancient heroes, using their example to incite the beholder to virtue, had its origins in the courts of the fourteenth century, inspired by Provençal literature. From the time of Giotto, who had painted a cycle for Robert of Anjou at Castelnuovo in Naples in 1330, there were many elaborations of this theme in Italy. Examples include the Sala Virorum del Livianum in Padua, with ancient

Paintings in the Chapel of Nicholas V in the Vatican, executed by Fra Angelico and others, including Benozzo Gozzoli, between 1454 and 1455, feature episodes from the lives of Sts. Lawrence and Stephen. On the left, Lawrence is consecrated as deacon, while in the upper register on the opposite wall St. Stephen is depicted preaching to the people and the scholars. Below this, Lawrence is shown receiving the church's treasury and distributing it to the poor.

FOLLOWING PAGES:
Detail from Fra Angelico's decorative program in the Chapel of Nicholas V showing St. Lawrence receiving the wealth of the church and distributing it to the poor. One of his predecessors, Sixtus II (257–258), had charged archdeacon Lawrence with dispersing the church's wealth to the needy. This deed aroused the ire of Emperor Valerian who had claimed the treasure for himself, and formed the basis for the charges brought against Lawrence and his eventual execution.

Roman heroes, the Sala Imperatorum in Palazzo Trinci in Foligno, with emperors, the Villa della Legnaia near Florence, with illustrious men and women by Andrea del Castagno (about 1450), and the Sala dei Gigli in the Palazzo della Signoria (town hall) in Florence (now Palazzo Vecchio), with Roman heroes by Ghirlandaio.

Masolino's cycle at Montegiordano was planned with great erudition, following a program perhaps designed by Cardinal Orsini himself, a cultivated man who collected ancient texts. An idea of the scale of the cycle and of the famous men depicted can be gained from contemporary descriptions. The overall plan was that of a "universal chronicle," a history of humanity through its most celebrated characters, following a division of history into six ages, as elaborated in the medieval treatises of Eusebius and Isidore of Seville, with additions from Vincent of Beauvais' encyclopedia.

At Montegiordano, the literary tradition was expanded with additions reflecting the political and cultural ideas of the patron, Cardinal Orsini. As a Guelph (supporter of the papacy against the Holy Roman Emperor's claim to sovereignty in Italy), Orsini was a fervent upholder of the supremacy of the Church. He had portraits of his ancestor, Pope Nicholas III and Boniface VIII added to the other figures. Some 300 life-size figures adorned the walls of the hall, while on the vault were a salamander, chameleon, anchovy, and mole, representing the four elements of fire, air, water, and earth.

The extensive and well-planned cycle immediately became the model for others. Filarete mentions it in 1464, in the context of a scheme of decoration to be carried out in his imaginary city of Sforzinda. It was not long before drawings of the Montegiordano cycle began to circulate, though only a few remain today. There are five series of copies, some taken from the original. Of these five, only one is complete, that of the Lombard Leonardo da Besozzo. Dated to around 1436–42, it consists of sheets painted in tempera on both sides, divided horizontally into three bands, which may reproduce the arrangement of the walls of the great hall.

Fra Angelico and Benozzo Gozzoli

It is still not known exactly when Fra Angelico arrived in Rome. Some historians assert that he was summoned by Eugenius IV for the decoration of "the chapel of the basilica of St. Peter's" ("majori cappella ecclesiae Sancti Petri"). According to Vasari he was summoned by Nicholas V to decorate the chapel of the Sacrament in the Vatican Palace (destroyed in the sixteenth century) with "scenes from the life

of Christ" and a cycle of famous men, including, as Pietro Aretino recalled, a portrait of "the emperor Frederick [III], who came to Italy at that time, Fra Antonino, later archbishop of Florence [St. Antonino]," and Flavio Biondo, who had been papal secretary under Eugenius IV.

pursued by Nicholas V of a link between Christian and classical culture. Fra Angelico's figures have a "Roman" appearance: they stand solemn and serious, like heroes from antiquity, against a background of theatrical architecture, reminding the beholder of the buildings of

Part of the fresco in the Chapel of Nicholas V depicting the arrest and stoning of St. Stephen. Stephen had been blessed by the Apostles and was the first to be ordained a deacon. Accused of blasphemy, he was stoned to death in Jerusalem. According to legend his remains were taken to Rome in the fifth century and buried beside those of St. Lawrence.

Fra Angelico was entrusted with a number of commissions for the Vatican Palace. The one that involved the most work was the decoration of the small room in the ancient tower of Pope Innocent III that Nicholas V had turned into his private chapel, a rectangular space with a groin vault. The floor installed at this time survives. It displays the emblem of Nicholas V, a radiant sun. The frescos show scenes from the lives of Sts. Stephen and Laurence, in two horizontal bands. On the rear wall was a *Deposition*, also by Fra Angelico and mentioned by Vasari, but now lost. On the arches are the eight Doctors of the Church in Gothic aedicules. The Evangelists are on the vault, while on the window jambs rosettes with the head of Christ alternate with heads of patriarchs and prophets.

The cycle, probably painted between 1448 and 1449, is generally attributed to Fra Angelico and his workshop. The hand of Benozzo Gozzoli has been identified in some of the scenes from the life of St. Stephen. Painted for the jubilee of 1450, the cycle clearly reveals the program

ancient Rome. The intention was to underline the continuity between imperial and Christian Rome which the pope wished to assert.

The work undertaken by Nicholas V in the Vatican Palace was considerable, but for the most part only a few fragments of dubious attribution and date survive. One of the pope's projects was the Greek Library (Biblioteca Graeca), constructed, according to recent research, on the ground floor of the Vatican Palace around 1450 to house the manuscripts of the pope's library. In addition to building, Nicholas V had another expensive passion—Latin and Greek manuscripts. The Florentine bookseller Vespasiano da Bisticci described how in the jubilee year "a huge sum of money came into the apostolic see. For this reason [Nicholas] began to build in many places and to send for Greek and Latin books everywhere he could find them, with no thought for price."

Of the decoration in the library dating from Nicholas' time there remains a *trompe-l'œil* painting of a Roman colonnade, through which landscapes can be glimpsed, and the arms of Nicholas V on the bosses of the vault. This has recently been attributed to Andrea del Castagno, who is identified with a certain "Andrea from Florence, painter" ("Andreino da Firenze pittore") named in a payment of 1454.

Fragments of fifteenth-century decoration can also be found in some of the rooms on the first and second floors of the Vatican Palace, in the so-called Cubicolo of Nicholas V, the Sala del Concistoro (Hall of the Consistory), the Sala del Pappagallo (Hall of the Parrot), and the Sala Vecchia degli Svizzeri (Old Swiss Guards' Hall). In this last room—originally a robing room, where the cardinals put on their liturgical vestments before going into the pope's presence to accompany him during ceremonies and religious rituals—fragments of fifteenth-century painting survive, with playful putti chasing butterflies, riding storks, practising archery, or playing the bagpipes. The representations of the cardinal virtues, here symbolizing good government and provided with inscriptions in Gothic letters listing their attributes, taken from the classical sources of Macrobius and Cicero, probably date from this period.

The intense artistic activity of Nicholas V's papacy was also determined by the 1450 jubilee. Although most of the works are lost, the archival records survive, providing evidence of the revival of activity in the workshops of Roman artists. The account books record "palace painters," who provided displays for ceremonies, and "painters of the holy face," who specialized in the reproduction of the venerated reliquary of St. Peter's, a highly lucrative industry aimed at pilgrims.

In addition, artists from Umbria and northern Lazio came to Rome, including Benedetto Buonfigli, Simone da Viterbo, Antonio da Orte, and Bartolomeo di Tommaso, who was summoned by the Roman senate to work on the Capitoline Hill. The arrival in Rome of artists from Umbria and the Marches led to the diffusion of a style that, compared with that of Florence, was still archaic and Late Gothic. An example is the triptych commissioned by the Catellini family, the *Virgin and Child with Sts. John the Baptist and Michael*, today in San Carlo ai Catinari, but intended originally for Santa Barbara dei Librai. It is signed in an inscription by Leonardo da Roma and dated 1453.

Among the painters who introduced the more modern Florentine style to Rome, Benozzo Gozzoli became particularly celebrated. He returned to Rome in 1453, where he remained, despite visits to central Italy, until 1458–59, when he went to Florence to paint the chapel of the Medici palace. During this long stay in Rome, he painted the fresco of *St. Antony of*

Padua with Two Donors in the Albertoni Chapel in Santa Maria in Aracoeli, a severe heraldic work, reminiscent of the figures painted by Fra Angelico in the chapel of St. Nicholas in the Vatican Palace. It is framed by two angels and has the two donors below.

Datable to the same period is a banner with a Virgin and Child, recently attributed to Gozzoli and now kept in the chapel where Fra Angelico lies buried in Santa Maria sopra Minerva. Formerly attributed to Gozzoli is the fresco of the *Virgin and Child with Angels*, originally in a tabernacle on the outer wall of the parish house adjoining the church of Sant'Angelo in Pescheria. It is now generally thought to be by a painter from Gozzoli's school. This school emerged at this time in Rome and its style was to last a long time.

Superimposed onto Gozzoli's style was an assimilation of Piero della Francesca's lucid synthesis of form and color. The only surviving record of Piero's presence in Rome is a payment during the pontificate of Pius II, by the Vatican in

Triptych with the Virgin between St. John the Baptist and the Archangel Michael. Painted by Leonardo da Roma in 1453, this work is evidence of the persistence of a late Gothic formal language in Roman art of the mid-fifteenth century. San Carlo ai Catinari.

April 1459, of 150 florins "for part of [Piero's] work on a number of paintings which he is executing in the pope's apartments [in the Vatican Palace]." These paintings were destroyed when Raphael started work on the Stanza d'Eliodoro.

The one surviving work which may be by Piero della Francesca is a fragment of a fresco depicting St. Luke in the chapel of St. Michael in Santa Maria Maggiore. Attributed to Gozzoli by Vasari, it has also been ascribed to Lorenzo da Viterbo, the painter who best combined Gozzoli's figurative and narrative ability with the austere spatial sense of Piero della Francesca.

Antoniazzo Romano and Melozzo da Forlì

The public rooms in Palazzo San Marco (now Palazzo di Venezia), where Pope Paul II lived as a cardinal, were decorated throughout, even if

Fresco by Melozzo da Forlì showing the appointment of the humanist Bartolomeo Sacchi, known as Platina, as head of the Vatican Library by Sixtus IV. Between Sixtus and the kneeling Platina stands the pope's nephew who, as Julius II, would later rule the papal State himself. Vatican Museums, Pinacoteca.

the quality of the painting was somewhat mediocre. The most impressive decorative scheme was that of the Sala del Mappamondo (Hall of the Map). The first reference to the great map of the world that gave the room its name is a 1495 diary entry of Alexander VI's master of ceremonies, Jacob Burchard. It appears that the map was not painted directly onto the wall but was on paper or vellum. It was completed some time between 1464 and 1469 by the Venetian Gerolamo Bellavista, described as the pope's "geographical advisor," and was inspired by the maps made by the Venetian geographers Antonio de' Leonardi and Fra Mauro.

The building accounts for Palazzo San Marco include a payment in 1466 to one "master Antonio di Benedetto, painter from Rome" ("magister Antonio Benedicti pictori de Urbe") for the decoration of a room. This was Antoniazzo Romano, a painter from the Colonna *rione* (quarter) of Rome, who worked in the city for more than forty years and whose figurative style was enriched over the years by Umbrian and Florentine influences. Antoniazzo's importance as an entrepreneur was evidently considerable: he made it his business to associate with painters not yet well-known in Rome, guaranteeing them major commissions, which he was able to obtain thanks to his contacts with patrons. This position was confirmed when in 1478 he became the head of the guild of painters and illuminators of Rome. It was Antoniazzo who revised the guild's statutes, together with the painter Cola Saccoccia and the illuminator Jacopo Rivaldi.

The task entrusted to Antoniazzo by Pope Paul II in 1466 was not his first papal commission. In 1464 he had been asked to provide the decorations for the pope's coronation, succeeding Pietro di Giovenale as official painter after Pietro's death. Pietro di Giovenale, from the Sant'Eustachio *rione*, had dominated the Roman artistic scene during the pontificate of Pius II. Among many other things, he had been responsible for the papal arms on the vault of the tower of Pius II in the Vatican Palace in 1463, and for two chapels in St. Peter's, the chapel of Santa Petronilla (1463) and the vault of the chapel of St. Andrew (1464).

The first mention of a work by Antoniazzo is in 1464, the year he was commissioned to decorate the funerary chapel of Cardinal Bessarion in the church of the Santi Apostoli, completed in 1467. Along with Pius II, Bessarion, a Greek, had had an important role in the diffusion of Greek learning in Rome, where he founded an informal academy of Greek theologians and Italian humanists, including Cardinal Francesco della Rovere, the future Sixtus IV. The principal activity of the academy was the collection of Greek texts that had escaped the Ottoman conquest or had been preserved in the Greek monasteries of southern Italy. Bessarion bequeathed the collection, the most important in western Europe, to Venice, where it formed the nucleus of the Marciana Library.

For his chapel in Santi Apostoli—of which a few fragments remain—Bessarion chose the Byzantine theme of the Archangel Michael. In the center was a icon of the Virgin, now in the chapel of St. Anthony, which can be dated to between 1467 and 1472, the year of Bessarion's death. This was a copy of the *Teotokos Virgin* in Santa Maria in Cosmedin, which from the seventh century had been the church of the Greeks in Rome.

The icon of the Virgin in Santi Apostoli is one of the most remarkable examples of Antoniazzo Romano's considerable production of Virgins, generally taken from Byzantine models. Antoniazzo was a much sought-after copier of icons. His access to such works was facilitated by his post as *camerlengo* (treasurer) of the confraternity of the Raccomandati from 1470, the year he painted the Virgin for the church of Santa Maria della Consolazione.

In the years between 1475 and 1480 Antoniazzo's production of altarpieces and panels with images of the Virgin increased as a result of the encouragement of the cult of the Virgin by Sixtus IV. One such painting is the *Virgin and Child with Donor* now in Houston, framed within an aedicola, with a donor wearing the velvet cloak of a person of importance.

In the oratory in the *casa santa* (holy house) of the monastery of Tor de' Specchi, near the Theater of Marcellus, is a fresco cycle dating from the late 1460s, showing the influence of Antoniazzo, with scenes from the life of St. Francesca Romana. St. Francesca Romana (Francesca Bussi Ponziani) died in 1440 and was canonized in 1460. The frescos are dated 1468. The twenty-six scenes, illustrating the saint's miracles, her visions, the foundation of the order of Oblates, her death, and her ascent into Heaven, represent an important stage in fifteenth-century Roman art, pervaded as they are with a figurative style which blends the influences of both Piero della Francesca and Benozzo Gozzoli.

Another cycle of frescos of the Roman school is that painted between 1476 and 1480 in the hospital of Santo Spirito, showing the life of Sixtus IV. Depicting his parents' dream in which Sts. Anthony and Francis announce their son's future membership of the Franciscan order, the miraculous events of Sixtus' youth, his ecclesiastical career, and the events of his papacy, the frescos are a hymn of praise to Sixtus' deeds

and abilities. Completed while the pope was still alive, the cycle includes events that were intended to occur after his death: the presentation of his works—architectural models representing the churches of Santa Maria del Popolo and Santa Maria della Pace, the Ponte Sisto, and the hospital of Santo Spirito—carried up to heaven by angels. These, the final section of the cycle guarantees, will be sufficient to ensure Sixtus' entry into Heaven.

As the chosen artist of a commission made up of private individuals and confraternities, ecclesiastics and aristocrats from outside Rome, in the 1460s and 1470s Antoniazzo had only one rival, Melozzo da Forlì, whom Vasari described

An angel playing music. Part of the former decoration of the apse of Santi Apostoli by Melozzo da Forlì. Vatican Museums, Pinacoteca.

Baptism of Christ, a fresco by Perugino and Pinturicchio from the cycle of the life of Christ in the Sistine Chapel. Pinturicchio was probably responsible for the landscape and minor scenes. Vatican Museums, Sistine Chapel.

as "a great artist for perspective," emphasizing the painter's undisputed skill in daring foreshortening *di sotto in su* (from below looking up), a characteristic that Melozzo made his own, though it was derived from Piero della Francesca and Mantegna. In his *Verse Chronicle* (*Cronaca rimata*) of 1478, Giovanni Santi, father of Raphael, referred to him as "Melozzo, so dear to me, who has made such giant steps in perspective." Melozzo's skill in perspective was also mentioned by Luca Pacioli, in 1494, and by Sebastiano Serlio, in 1562.

Compared with the more traditional style of Antoniazzo, Melozzo's style, developed in the fertile artistic environment of Urbino, had a grandeur and modernity that Sixtus IV was quick to notice. In the 1470s, Sixtus launched one of the most important undertakings of his cultural program, refounding the Vatican Library, which was to be open to the public. The Ghirlandaio brothers were called in to decorate two of its halls in 1475. When they had finished, between 1475 and 1477, Melozzo da Forlì painted the fresco of Sixtus conferring the librarianship of the Vatican Library on Platina, a monumental scene depicting a solemn ceremony that celebrates the meeting between secular and religious culture, a reaffirmation of humanism.

Platina, a member of Pomponio Leto's Roman academy, had been imprisoned because of the alleged academy conspiracy against Paul II. Sixtus IV, described by Bessarion as the most learned person in Italy, had been in Bessarion's academy. The fresco depicts an official occasion, set in the architectural framework of an arcade, which also houses the pope, Cardinals Giuliano della Rovere and Raffaele Riario, and their nephews Giovanni della Rovere and Girolamo Riario.

Cardinal Giuliano della Rovere portrayed here, later commissioned the decoration of the apse of the Santi Apostoli, painted by Melozzo da Forlì between 1480 and 1484. Only fragments of this remain, showing the Ascension, Apostles, and music-making angels.

The Sistine Chapel

In the early 1480s painting in Rome was following two diverging lines. On the one hand there was the work of Antoniazzo Romano, which during the 1480s was particularly popular in the provinces, and on the other, the somewhat different "papal painting" that inclined towards a more modern and intellectual style. The Ghirlandaio brothers and Melozzo da Forlì were the leaders of this second style, together with the group of Umbrian and Florentine painters who were assembled by Sixtus IV for

Moses passing through the Red Sea by Cosimo Rosselli. The episodes from the life of Moses were conceived of as typological scenes prefiguring significant episodes in the life of Christ. Vatican Museums, Sistine Chapel.

the most demanding of all the schemes of his papacy, the decoration of the Sistine Chapel.

The Sistine Chapel was decorated between 1481 and 1483. A contract of October 27, 1481 records the commission agreed between Giovannino de' Dolci, master of works at the Vatican Palace, and four painters, who were listed in order of age: Cosimo Rosselli, Sandro Botticelli, Domenico Ghirlandaio, and Perugino. Contemporary sources mention the presence of other artists too. Vasari also names Luca Signorelli, Bartolomeo della Gatta, Ingegno (Andrea Aloisi), Rocco Zoppo, and Piero di Cosimo. In a manuscript of 1621, Giulio Mancini added the names of Pinturicchio and Pastura.

The barrel vault was painted at this time by Matteo d'Amelia with gold stars on a blue background. The decoration of the walls was divided into three horizontal bands. The lowest was painted with *trompe-l'œil* tapestries. The central band had frescos on all four walls showing, on the left side (facing the altar), scenes from the life of Moses and, on the right, scenes from the

life of Christ. Above this, the niches between the twenty-eight windows contain figures of the first popes.

The didactic intention of the frescos was made clear by inscriptions, or *titulae*, on each scene. These, recorded in a document of 1513 describing the conclave which chose Leo X as pope, give invaluable information about the meaning of the figures portrayed.

The paintings were to be read in pairs, one from the left and one from the right. Thus the *Baptism of Christ* faces the *Circumcision of Moses' Son* (by Perugino and Pinturicchio), the story of Moses' journey to Egypt after exile in the land of Midian, when the angel tells him to circumcise his second son. In frescos by Botticelli, the *Temptation in the Wilderness*, where Christ is tempted by the devil, is placed opposite scenes showing the trials of Moses— the killing of the Egyptian, defending the daughters of Jethro, the burning bush, and the journey to Egypt. Ghirlandaio's *Calling of Peter and Andrew* is set against the *Crossing of the Red Sea* by Cosimo Rosselli. Two frescos by

Rosselli follow, the *Sermon on the Mount* and *Moses on Mount Sinai.* Perugino's *Christ Giving the Keys to St. Peter* is opposite Botticelli's *Punishment of Korah, Dathan, and Abiram,* who rebelled against the authority of Moses and Aaron, and Cosimo Rosselli's *Last Supper* corresponds to Luca Signorelli's *Death of Moses.*

The seventh pair of frescos on the entrance wall, repainted in the sixteenth century, depicts the *Resurrection and Ascension of Christ* and *The Archangel Michael Defending the Body of Moses.* The paintings on the altar wall were destroyed to make way for Michelangelo's *Last Judgment.* According to Vasari, they were the *Nativity of Christ* and the *Finding of Moses.* In the center was an altar with a fresco of the *Assumption of the Virgin.*

As an entity, the Sistine Chapel has deep symbolic meaning both in its architectural structure and its decorative program. The program, based on parallels between the life of Moses and that of Christ, between the Old and New Testaments, develops the idea, which originated in the Middle Ages, of parallels between the

two testaments. It was also inspired by Plutarch's theory of "parallel lives." Although a pagan, Plutarch was regarded as a writer who had affinities with Christian thought, a link between the ancient and the Christian worlds. Platina, the pope's favorite humanist, was a product of the school of Vittorino da Feltre who had looked to Plutarch in his attempts to harmonize the two traditions.

It seems likely that Platina had a role in the drawing up of the program for the chapel and was responsible for the inscriptions referring to the popes on the upper band of frescos. Beginning with the period of Constantine, each pope is indicated by his name and provenance and the dates of his pontificate. The idea of the parallel between Moses and Christ is further present in the writings of Sixtus IV, which emphasize how Moses prefigured Christ. Sixtus wrote that "Moses was our Christ" (*Moises noster Christus*).

A comparison of the scenes depicted shows clearly that the principal concern was to show how the new religion of Christ was deeper

The calling of Peter and Andrew by Ghirlandaio. This scene illustrates one of the characteristics of this Florentine master—his supremely confident treatment of crowd scenes in a large composition. Vatican Museums, Sistine Chapel.

FOLLOWING PAGES:
Temptation of Christ and the healing of the leper by Botticelli, considered the most mature of the frescos Botticelli created for the lower wall of the Sistine Chapel. The large number of portrait heads is also of interest. Vatican Museums, Sistine Chapel.

Episodes from Moses' youth by Botticelli. The fresco shows Moses watering the flocks of the daughters of Jethro and driving off the shepherds; the exodus of the Jews; the burning bush; the slaying of the Egyptian; and the flight of Moses. Vatican Museums, Sistine Chapel.

The Punishment of Korah, Datan, and Arbiron by Botticelli. In this scene from the life of Moses, Botticelli placed the action in the foreground.
The rear of the picture is dominated by an archaeologically precise depiction of the Arch of Constantine. Rome, Sistine Chapel.

and more spiritual than the Jewish religion. Thus the pair of frescos showing the Baptism and the Circumcision emphasize how baptism—prefigured, according to Augustine and many of the Fathers of the Church, by circumcision—represents a "spiritual circumcision." Everything which in the Old Testament occurs through acts of violence is expressed, in the New Testament, in bloodless and symbolic ways. In the *Temptation of Christ* (where the

Temple of Solomon looks very much like the hospital of Santo Spirito that was built by Sixtus IV), the scene of sacrifice in the foreground is contrasted with the symbolic character of Christ's sacrifice perpetuated in the Eucharist. The source of this image may be the passage in Sixtus' *The Blood of Christ* (*De sanguine Christi*), which examines a passage in St. Paul's letter to the Hebrews, where the superiority of Christ's sacrifice over that of the Levites is asserted.

Equally significant is the fresco with the punishment of Korah, Dathan, and Abiram. This has been interpreted as an allusion to contemporary events and a warning to heretics. The episode alluded to may be the rebellion of Archbishop Andrea Zamometic, who in the spring of 1481 launched a violent denunciation of both the pope and the Curia, and attempted to call a council to depose Sixtus. Zamometic was imprisoned and subsequently committed suicide in Basle in November 1484. In a letter of November 1482, an apostolic referendary named Chierigati compared Zamometic to the three Old Testament rebels Kurah, Dathan, and

Abiran. However, the allusion seems rather to be to all heretics or schismatics, as well as all who rebel against papal authority, rather than to this specific incident.

In parallel with this scene of punishment, apparently holding out the promise of a reward, is *Christ Giving the Keys to St. Peter*, contrasting the supposed use of fear in Jewish law with the Christian law of love. The octagonal church in the center of the scene (reminding the beholder of the symbolic value of the number eight as an image of the resurrection) is flanked on each side by a triumphal arch similar to the Arch of Constantine, emphasizing the triumphant nature of the heavenly Church where resurrection, according to Augustine, is dual in nature, from sin to grace and from death to glory. The Arch of Constantine also symbolizes the authority and prestige of Rome. It is depicted here as surmounted with rich decorations, swags, and lozenges. In the fresco with the scene of punishment, the equivalent decoration is incomplete. In other words, the imperfection of the Old Testament is contrasted with the perfection of the New.

Christ delivering the keys to St. Peter by Perugino. This episode was of the utmost ideological importance to the papacy, and its depiction marks an artistic high point in Sixtus IV's decorative program for the Sistine Chapel. The centralized structure in the background, firmly integrated into the picture by means of perspective, is a symbolic representation of the Church which was to be built upon Peter. Vatican Museums, Sistine Chapel.

Pinturicchio

Of all the painters who worked on the Sistine Chapel, Pinturicchio was to become the most important figure on the Roman artistic scene at the end of the fifteenth century, receiving all the major private commissions as well as those of Sixtus IV's successors, Innocent VIII (1484–92) and Alexander VI (1492–1503). Pinturicchio's patrons wanted their chapels or palaces covered with the gold of his work, with its rich repertoire of antique motifs and its delightful anecdotal detail.

Around 1486 Pinturicchio carried out the decoration of the Bufalini Chapel in the church of Santa Maria in Aracoeli, with frescos showing scenes from the life of St. Bernardino of Siena. This was commissioned by the Bufalini family of Città di Castello, perhaps to celebrate the peace made between the Bufalini and Baglioni families in 1486.

The main fresco in the cycle shows the funeral of St. Bernardino, represented as taking place in a piazza in which the various miracles attributed to the saint are depicted. In the foreground stands the bier with the saint's body, surrounded by monks, friars, and members of the Bufalini family. The perspective of the scene is clearly based on Perugino's *Christ Giving the Keys to St. Peter* in the Sistine Chapel. A particularly rich image is that in a lunette, showing the investiture of St. Bernardino, where the architectural details of the building are embellished with grisaille books, weapons, helmets, masks, and musical instruments, similar to the decoration of the pilasters of the Basso della Rovere Chapel in Santa Maria del Popolo, which were painted by Pinturicchio in about 1488–90.

A particularly important commission was that of Innocent VIII for the decoration of the loggia of the Belvedere, a small palazzo built shortly before Innocent's election in August 1484. Vasari describes how Pinturicchio worked on a number of the rooms and the principal loggia, which he painted with views of Rome "in the Flemish style."

Completed probably by 1487—the date on the vault of the loggia—only fragments of the original frescos remain, but enough to show that it was another example of the *trompe-l'œil* style of decoration, with clever effects of painted stucco, grisaille animal and plant motifs, painted pilasters framing naturalistic scenes, and landscapes with figures. The literary origins of this style have been traced to Vitruvius, Alberti, and Pliny the Elder's *Natural History,* which described Roman painting of the second style, as painted by one Ludius, of whom only the name is known. The addition of the figures makes Pinturicchio's frescos a development from earlier fifteenth-century *trompe-l'œil* decorative schemes in Rome, which had solely depicted architecture and landscape. Examples are those of the House of the Knights of Rhodes (Casa dei Cavalieri di Rodi), commissioned by Cardinal Marco Barbo and completed by 1471, and those of the House of Cardinal Bessarion.

Mantegna, who arrived in Rome towards the end of 1488 and remained until he returned to Mantua at the end of 1490, was also responsible for some of the work on the Belvedere. His paintings in the chapel and in a neighboring building do not survive. According to eighteenth-century descriptions, they consisted of a

Adoration of the Christ child by Pinturicchio. This altarpiece, from around 1490, forms the center of the decorative program for the Chapel Della Rovere in Santa Maria del Popolo. Pinturicchio and Tiberio d'Assisi worked together to create the frescos in the chapel which show events in the life of St. Jerome.

DOMINICVS·RVVERE CARD·S·CLEMEN
TIS·CAPELLAM MARIAE VIRG·GENE
TRICI DEI AC DIVO HIERONIMO
DICAVIT

large number of frescoed scenes with much use of gold and blue, reported by Vasari to have been executed with great delicacy and skill.

Mantegna's stay had no lasting influence in Rome and led to the establishment of no school. The artistic world was more interested in the decorative style in the newly discovered Golden House of Nero, adopted by Pinturicchio. The only echoes of Mantegna's work which survive are in the decoration of Palazzo San Marco (now Palazzo di Venezia), from the 1490s. The main sequence of the Labors of Hercules has a northern Italian feel. The influence of Mantegna's engravings and of Venetian art is clear, as in the case of the *Hercules with the Hind*, inspired by a thirteenth-century relief on the facade of St. Mark's in Venice.

The decoration of the Sala del Mappamondo (Hall of the Map), completed in 1491 on a commission from Cardinal Lorenzo Cibo, mimics an open portico "painted architecture." It has been ascribed to a Roman workshop influenced by Mantegna. The decoration includes a wide range of antique motifs, including careful references to Roman antiquities: the winged sphinxes are derived from the lintel of the Temple of Antoninus Pius and Faustina, columns and pilasters come from the outer enclosure of the Forum of Nerva, and the bases of the columns recall those of the Arches of Septimius Severus and Constantine. The immense Sala Regia has large rectangular panels bordered by pilaster strips with candelabra, simulating marble reliefs. The frieze, with volutes, bucrania, and fauns, is interrupted at intervals by ovals containing busts of emperors. In the center of each of the three walls, Fame is represented balancing on a globe and holding a shield.

The work at Palazzo San Marco is exceptional, however. It is clear that Mantegna's style was not appreciated in Rome. In letters to his employer, Francesco Gonzaga, marquis of Mantua, Mantegna complained of the "ignorance" of the Romans, who he describes as "presumptuous and stupid."

On the other hand, perhaps Mantegna's type of painting was unsuited to Rome's cultural demands at this time. In the 1480s the study of antique topography was revived, with studies of Vitruvius being promoted by the Roman academy of Pomponio Leto under the auspices of Cardinal Raffaele Riario, culminating in the *editio princeps* of Vitruvius' *On Architecture*. This, a statement of philological methods of analysis of the antique, led to Ermolao Barbaro's manual, *Emendations of Pliny* (*Castigationes Plinianae*), published after February 1493. In this climate of erudition and philological study, Mantegna's work seemed to have been overtaken, being too

Detail from the ceiling of the Sala dei Santi in the Borgia Apartment. This section shows Pinturicchio's depiction of the story of the Apis bull. The integration of this animal, venerated in ancient Egypt, into the decorative program of Alexander VI's private apartment served as a mythical explanation for the presence of the bull in the Borgia family coat of arms.

Allegorical depiction of arithmetic, one of the liberal arts, by Pinturicchio and his assistants. The room from which this view is taken was decorated on a theme of the seven liberal arts. Borgia Apartment, Vatican Museums, Sala delle Arti Liberali.

"mystical," and perhaps not sufficiently precise compared to painters such as Pinturicchio.

Between 1488 and 1490, Pinturicchio worked in Santa Maria del Popolo on the funerary chapel of Cardinal Domenico della Rovere, a distant relative of Sixtus IV, from the Turin branch of the Della Rovere family. The chapel was dedicated to the Virgin and St. Jerome. Cardinal Domenico had commissioned Andrea Bregno to make the funerary monument in 1478. The painted decoration for this pentagonal chapel, with its details picked out in white Carrara marble, was executed by Pinturicchio in collaboration with the Bolognese artist Amico Aspertini. To the white gold of the funerary monuments and the yellow of the grotesques they added a profusion of *trompe-l'œil* architecture—grotesques, heraldic motifs, and flower and plant decoration—derived chiefly from the recently discovered painted stucco of the Golden House, here used for the first time in a sacred setting. Above the altar is Pinturicchio's *Nativity*, surrounded by a frame decorated with floral motifs and small capitals.

Towards the end of the 1480s, Cardinal Domenico della Rovere turned once again to Pinturicchio and his workshop for the decoration of his palazzo in Borgo Vecchio (the Palazzo dei Penitenzieri). The octagonally coffered ceiling of the demigods is populated with fantastic animals—sirens, sphinxes, centaurs, hybrids, and monsters—caught up in fights or embraces against a gold background painted to mimic mosaic. In both the coffered structure and the iconography, the decoration derives from the ceilings of Hadrian's Villa at Tivoli and the Golden House, as well as from antique sarcophagi. It stands alongside the medieval bestiary, with its basilisks and griffins, dragons, and allegories of an obvious Christian symbolism.

In another room of the palazzo, Pinturicchio executed a cycle of frescos divided into twelve sections, depicting the myths relating to the birth of the constellations of the zodiac, accompanied by representations of the labors of the month. Though only two sections of the cycle survive, those for June and October, they are important iconographically, since this zodiac cycle initiated an astrological typology which in the following century was to influence Giovan Maria Falconetto in the Palazzo d'Arco in Mantua and Jacopo Zucchi in his work at Palazzo Firenze in Rome.

The high point of Pinturicchio's career co-incided with the papacy of Alexander VI. Cardinal Rodrigo Borgia was elected pope in 1492 amid serious accusations of simony. Notorious for his nepotism, Borgia was a rich man who loved the most unrestrained luxury. It appears from a number of documents of 1492 that Perugino,

St. Catherine's disputation with the pagan philosophers before Emperor Maximinian by Pinturicchio and assistants, set against a classicizing backdrop. Borgia Apartment, Vatican Museums, Sala dei Santi.

along with Antoniazzo Romano and Pier Matteo d'Amelia, was involved in the preparations for his coronation, painting ephemeral decorations, including banners for the trumpeters and band of Castel Sant'Angelo.

Scarcely a year earlier, in 1491, Perugino had completed the *Torlonia Polyptych* in the chapel of the palazzo at Santi Apostoli for Cardinal

Giuliano della Rovere. This has a severe architectural structure but a more concise and less decorative narrative style than that favored by Pinturicchio, who turned away from the "gracefulness" of the Umbrian style to a style that was more archaeological and more Roman but at the same time cleverly linked to the material abundance that Alexander enjoyed.

It is no surprise then that Alexander VI entrusted the decoration of the rooms in his apartment (now known as the Borgia Rooms) to Pinturicchio. The paintings, which were executed between 1492 and 1494, drew on a complex iconographical program that used themes from medieval encyclopedias, adding an eschatological layer of meaning and cele-

among the children of the sun (his emblem). He is also celebrated in the fresco of the triumph of Venus, where the goddess's chariot is pulled not by the traditional doves but by a bull, Alexander's heraldic emblem. Among the astral decorations are twelve sibyls and prophets, exemplifying the parallel expounded here between the pagan and Christian worlds.

brating the supposedly divine origins of the Borgias.

The series begins in the Room of the Sibyls. Here trapezoidal compartments on the vault are painted with the planets and their offspring, along with the human activities associated with the different heavenly influences. Alexander chose to be depicted here with his court,

In the next room, the Room of the Creed, lunettes contain figures of the twelve Apostles each holding an inscription bearing the words of the Apostles' Creed relating to the resurrection of the body, the divinity of Christ, and life after death. Painted on the vault is the double crown of Aragon, which had been adopted by the Borgia family as its arms, surrounded by the rays of the sun, a self-glorifying reference to Alexander, who identified himself with the sun.

The Room of the Liberal Arts is particularly important for the theme of the way to salvation that inspires the program of the apartment as a whole. The presence of the personifications of the liberal arts is explained by Cassiodorus' theory that they are indispensable for a proper understanding of Scripture, allowing Christians to advance in wisdom and in theology. In accordance with the traditional iconography, Pinturicchio's figures have their closest parallel in those in the Spanish Chapel in Santa Maria Novella in Florence, and are thus more old-fashioned than the figures of the liberal arts executed at this time by Pollaiuolo for the tomb of Sixtus IV.

In the Room of the Saints, the theme is divine justice, exercised through the pope. It is in this room that Alexander's self-glorification reaches its height in the myth and triumph of the bull Apis, worshipped by the Egyptians as the living image of Osiris and conceived of as the origin of the Borgia bull.

The use of Egyptian myth is evidence of the lively interest at this period in ancient Egyptian learning, knowledge of which had been spread partly through the writings of the humanist Nanni da Viterbo, an important secretary of the Curia, who in 1498 dedicated much of his *Various Antiquities* (*Antiquitatum variarum*

volumina) to the myth of Isis and Osiris. Osiris was regarded as a model of good government, while his death at the hands of his brother Typhon (Seth) and his incarnation as the bull Apis was seen as a prefiguration of the death and resurrection of Christ.

Following this parallel, with the attributes of peace and justice, the bull is represented as an allegorical image of Alexander, as the Borgia emblem was a bull. The bull appears again in the lunette of the *Disputation between St. Catherine of Alexandria and the Emperor Maximian*, where the bull is depicted on the emperor's throne and on the triumphal arch. An inscription on the triumphal arch reads "supporter of peace" (*pacis cultoris*), referring perhaps to the fall of Granada on November 25, 1492, St. Catherine's day, and Christianity's final victory in the fight against the Moors in Spain.

The other lunettes contain depictions of other saints, chosen to represent fundamental tenets of Christianity. St. Barbara with her three-windowed tower, for example, symbolizes the Trinity; the breaking of bread of Sts. Antony and Paul refers to the Eucharist; the martyrdom of St. Sebastian refers to Christ's death; the story of Susannah and the Elders represents the persecution of the Church by the Jews and pagans; and the Visitation alludes to Alexander VI's devotion to the Virgin and the mystery of the Incarnation.

The last room is dedicated to the "mysteries of the faith," represented by seven episodes from the life of the Virgin, which refer to the Seven Joys, a devotion which emerged in the late twelfth century. The order observed by Pinturicchio follows that of a sermon by St. Vincent Ferrer. Once again this refers to the Borgia family, for St. Vincent had been active in Valencia, Alexander's birthplace. Before becoming pope, Alexander's uncle, Callixtus III, had held a synod in Valencia in 1432 in which the first of the "seven Joys of Mary" was decreed to be the Incarnation.

Vasari was critical of Pinturicchio, claiming that "in his paintings [he] would use gilded relief ornament so that they would appear more lustrous and striking in order to satisfy those who understood little of this art, which was bad taste in painting." In Alexander's largely Spanish court, whose tastes were less classical and refined, such a profusion of gilded plaster, stucco relief, gleaming gold, gilded background, and damask was highly prized.

Filippino Lippi

Shortly before the decoration of the Borgia Rooms, the Carafa Chapel in Santa Maria sopra

Altarpiece in the Carafa Chapel in Santa
Maria sopra Minerva with the
Annunciation. Filippino Lippi added the
figure of the patron of the chapel's
decoration, Cardinal Oliveiro Carafa.
Carafa is depicted being presented to
the Virgin by St. Thomas Aquinas, the
most important Dominican saint.

Minerva, dedicated to the Virgin of the
Annunciation and to St. Thomas Aquinas, was
completed. The Florentine painter Filippino
Lippi had begun work there in 1489. This was
the funerary chapel of the Neapolitan Cardinal
Oliviero Carafa, an energetic opponent of the
Ottoman Turks: in 1472 he had commanded the
papal fleet in battle against the Turks, returning
with twenty-five prisoners and twelve camels,
which were paraded in triumph through Rome.

The decoration has three main themes: Carafa
as prince of the Church, Carafa as protector of
the Dominican order (he claimed to be
descended from St. Dominic's family), and a

celebration of his qualities. On the vault are
Medici emblems and those of the Carafa, symbolizing the close relationship between the two
families. Oliviero's uncle, Diomede Carafa, had
been one of the architects of the alliance
between King Ferrante of Naples and Lorenzo
de' Medici in 1480, while Oliviero represented
Aragonese interests in Rome and hoped to
involve the pope within this alliance between
Naples and Florence.

On the right-hand wall are scenes from the
life of St. Thomas Aquinas. The central scene of
Aquinas confounding the heretics is inspired
by the fourth book of Aquinas, the *Summa
contra Gentiles*. Within an elaborate architectural stage is a central building with pilasters
ornamented with torches, that was copied from
an antique funerary monument on the Via
Ostiense. In the background are views of the
Lateran—including the equestrian statue of
Marcus Aurelius which then stood there—and
the Tiber. This may allude to Carafa's war
against the Ottoman Turks, for he had departed from the Tiber to fight the Turks and when
he returned to Rome, in January 1473, it was by
Porta San Giovanni.

In the fresco, Aquinas is surrounded by four
female figures representing Philosophy,
Astronomy, Theology, and Grammar (that is,
Latin). At the sides, in the foreground, are the
defeated heretics, among which can be identified Arius, Apollinarius, and Averroes (on the
left) and Sabellius, Euchites, and Manes (on the
right), with their books thrown down on the
ground before them. The overall architectural
structure is enlivened by elaborate grotesques
and putti bearing inscriptions, as well as by a
number of references to Carafa, such as the
prow of a Roman galley with an olive branch,
the emblem of the Carafa family, here alluding
to Carafa's naval triumph.

The altar wall has an *Assumption*, and the
central part of the wall an *Annunciation* and
Aquinas presenting Cardinal Carafa to the
Virgin. The painting appears to be on panel but
in reality is fresco, while the frame, which mimics carved wood, is of gilded stucco.

The left wall of the chapel was reworked by
Pirro Ligorio in 1559, when the monument to
Pope Paul IV, nephew of Cardinal Oliviero, was
constructed. According to Vasari, it was originally painted with a battle of virtues and vices,
or *Psychomachia*. An arched opening gave
access to the cardinal's burial place, which still
has a vault decorated with stucco and tempera
painting with ornamentation drawn from that of
the Colosseum and the Golden House.

The vault is decorated with Carafa's emblems,
scenes of sacrifice, the Roman heroine Virginia
(which was originally a pendant to a *Lucretia*),

and allegorical figures. In the center of the vault is the Carafa family crest and a pictorial image of Oliviero Carafa's name: a woman with two carafes from which emerge olive branches. On either side are scenes of sacrifice: the *libatio* (bloodless offering) and the sacrifice of a bull, both alluding to Carafa's clerical career.

The images of the Roman women Lucretia and Virginia, who for both Valerius Maximus and Petrarch were models of chastity, may allude to Carafa's well-known moral sternness: a few years later, in 1497, he was to propose a ban on allowing women into the Vatican as part of a planned reform of the Church by Alexander VI.

The allegorical paintings on the vault include many references to antique art: a naked woman on a dolphin, representing Fortune, taken from a Bacchic sarcophagus formerly in Santa Maria Maggiore and copied in numerous drawings including one attributed to the "Anonimo settentrionale" (Anonymous northerner), of 1460, and one in Amico Aspertini's *Codex Wolfegg*; the eagle with a serpent and flaming torch in its talons may come from the Trajan eagle, then in the church of the Santi Apostoli.

Thus Filippino Lippi also gave Rome a work of explicit antiquarian inspiration. The antique was now a decorative framework, bursting with objects and still-lives, the last less random than they seem, being conceived as symbols to be interpreted through analogy, following the allegorical cast of thought of the Middle Ages.

The same is true of the liturgical frieze below the Aquinas cycle, which consists of a lintel painted to look like mosaic with gold tesserae, a device Lippi was to use again in the Strozzi Chapel in Santa Maria Novella in Florence. Some ten years later Bramante also used it in his Tempietto by the church of San Pietro in Montorio. Its source is the frieze from the Temple of Vespasian, of which a number of marble fragments survived, formerly in San Lorenzo fuori le Mura and today in the Capitoline Museums. A page of the *Codex Escurialensis*, which Lippi may have seen, has drawings of fragments; they were certainly known to Carafa who in 1492 restored the ceiling of San Lorenzo fuori le Mura.

Lippi's frieze shows liturgical objects: a candlestick, a holy water sprinkler, a candle-box, papal slippers, a processional cross, a monstrance with the host, a pax with an *imago pietatis*, a miter and stole, a lamp, books, an incense-boat, and a censer. Alongside the image of Christ as the host, these are a clear reference to the Mass, in particular to the festival of Corpus Christi, when the sacrament and the pax were exhibited in a procession. The importance and position of the frieze probably refer to the feast of Corpus Christi, for which Aquinas had

composed a special office, and which had a particular significance in Carafa's life, for it was on the day of Corpus Christi in 1472 that he had departed with the papal fleet to fight the Turks.

Lippi's passion for the antique matched the ideals and studies of Cardinal Carafa, who created one of the first gardens in Rome to be ornamented with sculpture and carved stone, and in 1501 gave a home in his palazzo to the antique statue known as "Pasquino." Carafa was also the patron of the humanist and scholar Ermolao Barbaro.

missioned by the bishop of Nocera, Giovanni Cerretani of Terni, who had close links with the della Rovere family. He had been auditor of the Rota from 1448 but, because of his diplomatic work with Cardinal Giuliano della Rovere, he was not able to take up his duties until 1488–90. The panel, with its strong Peruginesque echoes, was put in place some time between 1488—the year in which Cerretani left forty ducats in his will "for the decoration" (*pro ornamento fiendo*) of the altar of the tribunal—and 1492, the year of his death.

In 1491, Antoniazzo carried out a commission for another Rota auditor, Guglielmo de Pereriis. This was a chapel dedicated to Cardinal Pietro Altissen in Santa Maria della Pace, destroyed in the seventeenth century, with a *Transfiguration of Christ with Sts. Peter, John the Evangelist, and James*. From this same period, 1490–92, is the triptych of the *Sacro Volto* (Holy Face) now in the Prado in Madrid, thought to be from the church of San Giacomo degli Spagnoli.

The frescos of the *Legend of the True Cross* were also a Spanish commission, which Antoniazzo executed with his assistants in the church of Santa Croce in Gerusalemme. The frescos were part of a much larger campaign of work in this church, involving, among others, Antoniazzo's old rival, Melozzo da Forlì, who had returned to Rome in 1489. It must have been around this date that Melozzo made the drawings for the mosaic in the vault of the chapel of St. Helena in the crypt at Santa Croce in Gerusalemme, with *Christ Borne Up by Angels and Cherubs*.

The last years of the century saw Antoniazzo particularly busy with work for the confraternity of the Annunciation, culminating in a commission for what was to be his last signed work, the *Annunciation with Cardinal Johannes de Turrecremata Presenting Three Poor Girls to the Virgin* for the chapel of the Annunciation in Santa Maria sopra Minerva. Completed in March 1500, this was intended to commemorate the founder of the confraternity, the Spaniard Cardinal Turrecremata, who had founded the confraternity to present dowries to poor girls in 1460. He died in 1468. The cardinal is shown presenting three poor girls to the Virgin, with a gesture that does not seem so distant from that depicted by Filippino Lippi in his *Annunciation* in the nearby Carafa Chapel.

Gioia Mori

Annunciation with Cardinal Juan de Torquemada presenting three girls to the Virgin, an altarpiece made by Antoniazzo Romano in 1485 for the Chapel of the Annunciation in Santa Maria sopra Minerva.

The works of Filippino Lippi, Mantegna, and Pinturicchio are the most important evidence of the passion for the antique that characterized the last decade of the fifteenth century. This is not to say that there was not some resistance to this obsession with archaeology. The most vigorous came from Antoniazzo Romano, who from the mid-1480s seems to have been influenced by his stay in Umbria, in the more restrained world of Perugino. A panel from this later phase in Antoniazzo's career is the *Virgin with Sts. Peter and Paul and the Twelve Auditors of the Rota*, originally in the auditorium of the tribunal of the Rota in the Vatican. It was com-

The Sixteenth-Century: the Golden Age

Architecture

The sixteenth century was a period of major development in Roman architecture, although it is difficult to summarise its aspects and outcomes. Though not a uniform process, it proved decisive in defining both the modern city and a European model capital destined for great things.

The century opened with an important project already under way, the Palazzo della Cancelleria, a vast building commissioned by Cardinal Raffaele Riario, which broke with the Roman fifteenth-century tradition of palaces with towers, such as Palazzo San Marco (now Palazzo di Venezia). This was ambitious architecture that introduced a demanding leap in scale, and whose challenge was quickly taken up. Its attribution is still debatable.

Bramante

According to Vasari, Bramante collaborated on the Palazzo della Cancelleria. There is no doubt

Santa Maria della Pace, the first of the buildings by Bramante in Rome. The ground floor is characterized by a rhythmic succession of arcades and pillars with pilaster facades. Above this, the first floor is surmounted by a horizontal architrave carried by a series of alternating pillars and posts.

that Bramante, arriving in Rome from Lombardy in 1499, was the most important figure at the beginning of the century. There is ample proof of his importance in the innovative cloister of Santa Maria della Pace (a church founded by Sixtus IV in 1482) which was built between 1500 and 1504 and, shortly afterward (though the exact chronology remains unclear), in the Tempietto of San Pietro in Montorio, an even more innovative work with the first centrally planned temple and the first Doric order with friezes with triglyphs since antiquity.

Town Planning under Julius II

In town planning, the opening-up of the Via Alessandrina (Borgo Nuovo) between Castel Sant'Angelo and St. Peter's for the 1500 jubilee began the series of great straight streets of early modern Rome. The moral and symbolic theme of the straight road (*via recta*) was to recur in the sixteenth-century city.

With the papacy of Julius II (1503–13), from Liguria, Bramante—who died in 1514—asserted himself as the favored interpreter of the imperial ambitions of the energetic pope. In 1504 work started on the Cortile del Belvedere in the Vatican Palace. Bramante was thus present at the change of gear which caught up all the main urban centers in an absorbing dream of material and spiritual *renovatio* (renewal), emulating the imperial Roman city but conscious of the new universal role of the Christian city, in a constantly reaffirmed classical-Christian continuity that found its architectural expression in the culture and poetics of Bramante.

The triumph of the high Renaissance characterized the first quarter of the century, with a wide range of variants and postures, work and interpretations, a unique period of grandiose visions and feverish experiments. Julius and Bramante conceived undreamed-of projects: the new St. Peter's, with its unusual mixture of practical, organizational, liturgical, symbolic, and urban problems; the reorganization of the Borgo between St. Peter's and the river, with its exemplary series of new palaces such as

Palazzo Castellesi and Palazzo Caprini; the creation of Via Giulia with the new focus of the Palazzo dei Tribunali (a colossal structure left largely incomplete); the opening-up, on the far side of the Tiber, of a new thoroughfare, Via della Lungara, to run alongside the river to the river port, Ripa (much of which never came to fruition); the planned Ponte Giulio near Santo Spirito in Sassia (of which only the fountains were built); the pleasant and well-constructed residential buildings in the Vatican Palace; and the ordering of the Canale di Ponte (Sant'Angelo) with the new church of San Celso (an innovative St. Peter's in miniature remaining incomplete, which replaced a small medieval church).

These were all projects of great significance, involving a revolutionary rethinking of urban space, which in more than one instance constrained the following generations. Bramante approached these questions with stylistic

Bramante's Tempietto in the courtyard of San Pietro in Montorio, believed to be the site of St. Peter's martyrdom. The architect clearly worked from a historical typology: individual architectural elements such as columns, entablature, and vault acknowledge a debt to classical structures. The resulting centralized building represented a new type of Christian architecture.

innovation and great technical flexibility, an unusual urban standard and extraordinary compositional control. His presence was decisive for the affirmation of the new language, but it was an open lesson, not systematic, undogmatic, and multiform and therefore not easy.

Raphael

Work continued in different directions after Bramante's death. Raphael took his place in papal projects, although he had not had architectural training. This came with the completion of the Loggia in the Vatican Palace overlooking the Cortile of San Damaso and, especially, with New St. Peter's, construction of which began in 1506 after heated debate. The rebuilding of St. Peter's was, Raphael wrote, "a great weight on my shoulders." Raphael developed Bramante's ideas in a measured, classicizing, warm pictorial language that made him the main interpreter of the High Roman Renaissance. He developed these ideas in a substantially original way; in this extraordinary period, experiences were quickly used up.

Raphael even reached the point of discarding his predecessor's plan for a centrally planned St. Peter's. This alone is enough to underline the differences between Julius's pontificate and that of Leo X (1513–21), the cultured son of Lorenzo the Magnificent who succeeded Julius. In the Chigi Chapel in Santa Maria del Popolo, Raphael created a jewel of Renaissance architecture. He also oversaw the decoration, from the mosaic to the sculpture by Lorenzetto (it was altered by Bernini in the seventeenth century.)

Antonio da Sangallo the Younger: Early Work

Raphael had an expert collaborator in St. Peter's, Antonio da Sangallo the Younger, a nephew of Giuliano da Sangallo and Antonio da Sangallo the Elder, previously an assistant to Bramante. Antonio was in the center of a solid family structure and a well-equipped workshop (which Michelangelo criticized as "the Sangallo sect"). Antonio was to dominate the scene in the 1530s and 1540s, but already in Leo's papacy he asserted himself as a first-rate architect in Palazzo Baldassini alle Coppelle and the original Palazzo Farnese (later enlarged and finished by others), in which he developed residential types that were destined to become widely used, due to their flexibility and stylistic unity: ashlared corners and portals, subtle stringcourses, and decorative brickscreens on the facade. In this field Antonio was a virtuoso without equal.

Baldassare Peruzzi and Giulio Romano

New forces of great stylistic originality came to bear on Raphael's example and the difficult problem of his legacy (in the practical sense as well, in terms of continuity of execution). Baldassare Peruzzi from Siena, and Giulio Pippi from Rome, who had both trained as painters, emerged as the most important players in this process. Peruzzi had already shown his compositional sensitivity with Agostino Chigi's Villa Farnesina, during Julius' papacy. For it he had proposed an open plan based on a C, with an airy open gallery, an innovation for Rome. Peruzzi later made a name for himself with a highly personal interpretation of Raphaelesque classicism. The finest example of this is his masterpiece, Palazzo Massimo alle

Colonne, from the porch with its binary rhythm of Doric columns and profound spaces on a convex facade embellished with an ashlarwork plaque. The result has great pictorial effect—capable of fascinating Pietro da Cortona a century later—and is a noteworthy reading of urban space (now irremediably compromised by the creation of Corso Vittorio Emmanuele in the nineteenth century). As architect of St. Peter's, after Raphael, Peruzzi took up Bramante's theme of interpenetrating accessible spaces.

Giulio Romano was also prominent through his critical, free, and highly individual interpretation of Raphael's language. He made the elements of his work contradict one another, in an investigative tension which made him an acknowledged master of Mannerism. With Palazzo Stati Maccarani he reinvented the model of a building with ashlarwork and street-level shops, following a trend begun by

OPPOSITE:
The Chigi Chapel in Santa Maria de Popolo, built between 1513 and 1515 from designs by Raphael. The dome resting on pendentives recalls Bramante's designs for St. Peter's, a structure with which Raphael was intimate as he had succeeded Bramante as chief architect of that project, the largest in Christendom.

Palazzo Massimo alle Colonne, from 1532 Baldassare Peruzzi's last project in Rome. His design marks a turning away from the facades of the Renaissance, with emphasis on harmonious design, towards an architecture which valued intellectual wit and a richness of

Villa Farnesina, built for the banker Agostino Chigi between 1510 and 1511, Baldassare Peruzzi's first Roman work and the first Renaissance villa in the city.

Bramante in Palazzo Caprini and continued by Raphael in the Palazzo of Iacopo da Brescia and Palazzo Vidoni Caffarelli. The ashlarwork, given its own vital energy, surrounds the windows of the mezzanine, compressing them against the upper trabeation, or invades the classical Raphaelesque tympanum. The facade is animated by one of Giulio Romano's highly intellectual counterpoints, in an obvious overtaking of the fragile balances of the classical ideal.

Giulio Romano also made a key contribution to the completion of Villa Madama, begun by Raphael for Cardinal Giulio de' Medici, the future Clement VII. This was a great step forward compared to Peruzzi's Villa Farnesina and a landmark (albeit of complicated gestation) in the interpretation of the villa, a typical theme of the Italian Renaissance. The more secluded Villa Turini al Gianicolo is more authentically Giulio Romano's work. The Palazzo Adimari Salviati on the Via della Lungara is another significant work, in which the established types of the villa and of the city palace were intentionally made to interact. Giulio Romano's departure for Mantua in 1524, on the eve of the Sack of Rome in 1527, deprived the city of a great craftsman. Peruzzi also left Rome, but returned in about 1532.

Coat of arms of Paul III with the fleurs-de-lis of the Farnese family, from a seventeenth-century engraving. Rome, Vatican Library.

OPPOSITE:
The surviving sections of the Villa Madama on Monte Mario represent only a fraction of the building originally planned by Raphael, together with Antonio di Sangallo the Younger and Guilio Romano, for Cardinal de Medici (later Clement VII).

Palazzo Farnese, the result of a long drawn-out design whose protagonists, Antonio di Sangallo the Younger and Michelangelo, were required to work strictly to the needs of their patron, Cardinal Alessandro Farnese (later Paul III), for a building which reflected his status.

Detail of the courtyard of Palazzo Farnese. The walls between the arcades on the ground floor are faced with Doric half columns while the Ionic order is used on the floor above.

FOLLOWING PAGES:
Model by Antonio Labacco of Antonio da Sangallo's design for St. Peter's, which required a connection between a centralized structure and the basilica. Michelangelo based his criticism of the project on this enormous and costly model. Rome, Fabbrica of St. Peter's.

Antonio da Sangallo the Younger: Later Work

After the dramatic events of 1527, Roman architecture continued its development ever more clearly dominated by Antonio da Sangallo the Younger (a member of the inner circle of Paul III, for whom he undertook the building of the Palazzo Farnese near Campo de' Fiori while Paul was still a cardinal), this was due to his tried and tested technical ability, levelheaded pragmatism, capable organization, and also a certain conformism, though he was more cultured than is generally admitted. He was in charge of important building projects such as St. Peter's (with Peruzzi 1532–36, then alone) and San Giovanni dei Fiorentini, and fortifications, with the Bastione del Sangallo, a structure built into the Aurelian walls of Rome by Porta San Sebastiano.

Antonio also undertook a vast number of projects in the region and on the Farnese estates in Lazio and Emilia. In Rome he built important thoroughfares: Via Paola, completing the "trident of bridges," and Via dei Baullari, on the axis of Palazzo Farnese. In St. Peter's he strengthened the great pillars of the dome, then concentrated his efforts on a large wooden model (carried out by Antonio Labacco), of exorbitant cost, which Michelangelo derided.

The papacy of Paul III, with its dynastic feudal grandeur and its dense implications in symbolic

The theatrical nymphaeum of Villa Giulia, designed by Bartolomeo Ammanati and built using antique spolia. The structure was organized into two levels, which were carried by herms functioning as supports. The sculptures at the sides are of the river gods Arno and Tiber.

Detail of Villa Giulia, facade by Vignola built from 1551. The presence of defensive elements, such as the rusticated triumphal arch, are explained by the location of this villa belonging to Julius III outside the city walls.

OPPOSITE:
From the beginning of the sixteenth century almost all of Rome's leading architects were involved in the planning and construction of San Giovanni dei Fiorentini, the church for the Florentine community in Rome. The end of this process was marked by the completion of the facade in 1733, from a design by Giacomo della Porta.

The dome of St. Peter's, designed by Michelangelo and based on that of Florence cathedral. The dome seen today is the result of a reworking of this design by Giacomo della Porta, not completed until 1593.

Built between 1560 and 1573, the Chapel Sforza in Santa Maria Maggiore belongs to Michelangelo's late period. Its remarkable use of space, with inward curving side walls and diagonal columns, marks this chapel out from contemporary buildings.

and religious terms, offered Europe a model of an *ancien régime* capital that was to hold sway for a long time: look only at the Palazzo Farnese and its urban layout. The papacy, albeit short, of Julius III (1550–55) offered glimpses of a new Mannerist tendency: Bartolomeo Ammannati and Giorgio Vasari worked on Julius' villa on the Via Flaminia, Villa Giulia, while Vasari and Daniele da Volterra designed chapels in San Pietro in Montorio.

Michelangelo

Antonio da Sangallo died in 1546, leaving the difficult question of who should succeed him in overseeing work on St. Peter's. Paul III answered this with a stroke of genius, giving the job to Michelangelo, who was reluctant being aware of his lack of architectural experience. However, Michelangelo took over decisively, discarding Sangallo's plans, building the tambour in the great dome, taking up the central design again, eliminating Bramante's Doric apse, and completing the wings in a unified way. Michelangelo bitterly criticized Sangallo, saying that his St. Peter's made him think of a dark alley capable of harboring all sorts of roguery, even the rape of nuns. Bramante's design, Michelangelo felt, was "pure and genuine," but he rejected it too, although he revived the central plan. In the Belvedere, Michelangelo ended up eliminating one of Bramante's most celebrated inventions, the concave–convex stair.

Though Michelangelo was an architect not through his own choice but by order of a despotic pope, he revolutionized architecture. His unique experimentation is demonstrated by other Roman initiatives, such as the celebrated Sforza Chapel in Santa Maria Maggiore and the plans for San Giovanni dei Fiorentini, where abstract centralizing geometries are shaken by energetic shivers or unexpected axial rotations.

San Giovanni dei Fiorentini, the church of the Florentine community in Rome, another complex project with a tormented history, a further St. Peter's on the other side of the Tiber—indeed, daringly laid out very close to the river—was to share the long business of construction of St. Peter's. Like St. Peter's, it was completed by Carlo Maderno. The work on the Capitoline Hill was another fundamental area of experimentation, expressed in different ways at different times, from the installation of the equestrian statue of Marcus Aurelius in 1538 to the great external staircase of Palazzo Senatorio (about 1547) and the restructuring of the Palazzo dei Conservatori, with the innovative facade on two floors solidly framed by the gigantic order, another landmark in sixteenth-century Roman architecture. Michelangelo's preeminence did not prevent significant rediscoveries

CLEMENS·XII·PONT·MAX·A·S·MDCCXXXIV·P·IV·

413

Palazzo Senatorio on the Capitoline Hill, whose appearance today is based on Giacomo della Porta and Girolamo Rainaldi's reworking of a design by Michelangelo. Only the portal of the Aula Consiliare and the double staircase at the side were retained from the original design. The porphyry and marble statue of Minerva in the center of the niche, from the first century AD, was interpreted in the Renaissance as a depiction of the goddess Roma. The flanking sculptures of the river gods of the Nile and Tiber are from the Baths of Constantine.

of Raphael's themes, like the (destroyed) Palazzo Branconio dell'Aquila in the Borgo, in the courtyard of which the young Giulio Romano collaborated, or the stucco facades by Giulio Mazzoni for Palazzo Spada Capodiferro, in mid-century.

Mid-century Rome

This rediscovery of Raphael was a tendency that the pontificate of Pius IV (1559–65) accentuated, with the mythologizing and exuberant work of Pirro Ligorio. The Casina of Pius IV in the Vatican gardens, inspired by naumachia of classical times, had rich facades with reliefs and magnificent

Seventeenth-century painting by Agostino Buonamici, known as Tassi, depicting the competion to climb the greasy pole on the Capitoline Hill. The picture records the still incomplete state of the square, lacking the counterpart to the Palazzo dei Conservatori on the left side.

decorative elements, following complex allegorical and celebratory scenes. The pontificate of Pius IV connected itself intentionally with the age of the Renaissance. The upper courtyard of Bramante's Belvedere was completed with the Nicchione, and the western wing was constructed. The idea of building Julius II's Palazzo dei Tribunali was even entertained, but this was bound to collide with the rigorism of the popes who followed, Paul IV (1555–59) and Pius V (1566–72).

Vignola (Jacopo Barozzi)

Julius III's pontificate had also witnessed the Roman debut of Vignola, with work in the villa and nearby church-mausoleum of Sant'Andrea

416

on Via Flamina, an interesting moment of friction between classicism and Mannerism. (Vignola had studied antiquity and worked with the Vitruvian academy in Rome in the early 1540s, and had spent time at Fontainebleau.) The geometric experimentation of the plan would be a constant feature of Vignola's work until the acclaimed work of Sant'Anna dei Palafrenieri in the Borgo, the first sacred building on an oval plan.

Vignola's relationship with Alessandro Farnese, the great cardinal-prince of the Catholic Reformation, opened up for him a project of central importance, that of the Gesù, the Jesuit church. He was joined for part of the work by the Jesuit architect Giovan Battista Tristano, but the building took a long time to be completed. The facade, imitated many times, is by Giacomo della Porta. Vignola was responsible for about twenty buildings in Rome. His complex internal dialectic—compare the Farnese Palace at Caprarola with the Orti Farnesiani on the Palatine—can be seen from Villa Giulia, from the middle of the century, to Sant'Anna dei Palafrenieri, an intriguing posthumous work completed by his son Giacinto (who tried unsuccessfully to put himself forward as a military architect in the courts of central Europe).

The Casino built by Pirro Ligorio as a summerhouse for Pius IV. In the facade Ligorio dispensed with traditional elements of architectural organization in favor of a classical decorative system of statues, festoons, and reliefs.

Part of the facade of Palazzo Spada on the Piazza di Capodifero. Erected after 1540 by girolamo da Carpi from a commission by Cardinal Capodifero, it was altered by Borromini after coming into the possession of Cardinal Bernadino Spada.

Courtyard of Palazzo Spada with stucco decoration by Giuliano Mazzoni showing scenes from both Greek and Roman mythology.

The small church of Sant'Andrea in Via Flaminia by Vignola, built as a memorial to the triumphal transfer to Rome of the relic of the head of St. Andrew. In architectural and historical terms, the building's combination of an ovoid dome and rectilinear floor plan is an important step in the development of this type of centralized structure.

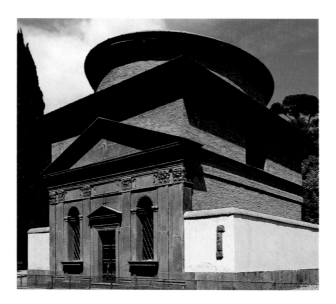

Michelangelo's Last Years

It was the aging Michelangelo who was the most innovative force, transforming part of the remains of the Baths of Diocletian into the church of Santa Maria degli Angeli and designing the striking Porta Pia, revolutionary in its language and its conception, constructed as it is with its main facade not towards the outside but towards the city. This work, which he left unfinished, was closely connected with the opening of the new axis of Via Pia. When Michelangelo died in 1564, the problem of the sculpture deriving from him found uncertain responses (for example, in Nanni di Buccio Bigio). The vexed problem of the dome of St. Peter's was entrusted to Giacomo della Porta.

The Sicilian Jacopo del Duca was the only one to confront Michelangelo's problematic path and

Construction of the church of Santa Maria di Loreto was begun around 1507 by Bramante, who was succeeded by Antonio da Sangallo the Younger. The church was completed by Jacopo del Duca in 1573 after a long delay. The strongly emphasized ribs of the dome with its round windows recall Michelangelo's design for the dome of St. Peter's.

strong creative tension, as shown in the preco-cious Savelli Chapel in San Giovanni in Laterano, openly inspired by Porta Pia. Del Duca's most important work was the completion of Santa Maria di Loreto, already begun by Sangallo, where he provided a critical interpretation of the problem of the dome with the double spherical vault, moving away from Della Porta's version in St. Peter's. The fundamental problem was that put forward by Michelangelo, whose work Del Duca brought up to date to a notable extent.

The Catholic Reformation

In 1568, amid countless difficulties and opposi-tion from powerful families who saw their interests in the area threatened, construction of the Gesù restarted. The central problem was the interpretation of how a sacred building should be after Catholic reform. The church was conse-crated in 1584, eleven years after Vignola's death. The Catholic Reformation strongly affected archi-tecture in the second half of this century. It imposed controls on the arts and demanded that architects deepen their enquiry into the essentials of architectural function. The period was marked by stylistic probity-restraint when faced by the swirling ideas of Mannerism, but also an impulse towards continual typological developments.

The years of Gregory XIII's papacy (1572–85) can be defined as the era of Della Porta, in St. Peter's, Santa Maria ai Monti (1580), and Sant'Atanasio dei Greci (1583). It is significant that Della Porta never again took up the model of the facade conceived in the Gesù. On the contrary, in San Luigi dei Francesi he developed ideas taken from Michelangelo's plans for the facade of San Lorenzo in Florence. The debate about Michelangelo was still lively. At the time of Leo X, the same projects had aroused the interest of the young Giulio Romano.

Other architects were also active. The Bolognese Ottaviano Nonni (or Ottavio Mascherino) developed Vignola's ideas in an original way in Torre dei Venti in the Vatican Palace and Palazzo del Quirinale. Martino Longhi the Elder proved himself a solid profes-sional on the model of Sangallo, constructing Palazzo Cesi in the Borgo and Palazzo Altemps.

Town Planning under Sixtus V

It is worth noting several town-planning initia-tives such as the opening of Via Gregoriana (later Merulana) and Via Ferratella. Made possi-ble by the new law regulating the expropriation passed by Gregory XIII, these show how much could happen in a short time.

Sixtus V's short pontificate (1585–90) resulted in major changes to the appearance of the city, subjected to plans aimed at the good use of the connections between the main religious sites, relaunching the hill area newly served by the Acqua Felice, establishing or enlarging centers of manufacture and commerce, and revitalising the waterflow. All this made for an undreamed-of scale, even if much of it remained on paper.

Sixtus' successor, Clement VIII (1592–1605), did not have the courage to revive the harsh policy of expropriation that Sixtus' activity demanded. In order to make wide straight roads, Sixtus remarked, you had to wring a lot of necks. But it was these same streets built by Fontana, carry-ing more carts, that were the envy of European capitals, which hastened to imitate them. The sacrifices demanded were sometimes painful, as in the case of the demolition of the ancient Septizonium, built by Septimius Severus. Even

Work on the Jesuits' church in Rome, the Gesú, was begun in 1568 from plans by Vignola, but Giacomo della Porta's design for the facade from 1571 moved in a different stylistic direction. His frontage, with its aediculas, is a classic example of the Counter-Reformation church facade, with broad nave and flanking side chapels.

419

Part of the Lateran complex remodeled by Domenico Fontana under Sixtus V with the huge benediction loggia and palace. Over the centuries it had been forced to make way for the growth of the papal residency. Fontana's new building shows the influence on his work of the palaces of Antonio da Sangallo the Younger.

Pallazzo Altemps, a result of the redesign of Palazzo Riario in the fifteenth century by Martino Longhi the Elder. Longhi's work was commissioned by the nephew of Pius V, Cardinal Marco Sittico Altemps.

the Colosseum was threatened with violent treatment, with plans to turn it into a workplace and cut it in half by a new road. Fortunately these plans were never carried out.

Domenico Fontana

Domenico Fontana was an important interpreter of this intense period. More than a great creator of new languages, he was an experienced and versatile technician. From the Ticino near Milan, he had a mentality roughly similar to Sangallo's. He had already built Villa Montalto for Sixtus V when he was still a cardinal. From the 1585 conclave emerged one of the most decisive partnerships for the history of Rome. Fontana achieved notable technical successes. His favorite project was the erection of the obelisk in the center of St. Peter's Square, earning him the title of Cavaliere della Guglia (knight of the obelisk). He also managed the difficult job of keeping to the tight schedules imposed by his energetic client, despite the size of the projects: the Lateran

Palace with the facade with benediction loggia, the Scala Santa, the Vatican Library, the Botteghe di Farfa at Termini, the Acqua Felice, the hospice in Via Giulia, the Ponte Felice in the Borghetto.

Fontana dominated the scene, and left little room for competition. Della Porta retained, in a sort of significant extraterritoriality, charge of St. Peter's, and, almost as a consequence, of San Giovanni dei Fiorentini. Martino Longhi completed the facade of San Girolamo degli Schiavoni on the Ripetta, a commission from Sixtus while he was still a cardinal, and began Santa Maria in Vallicella, the facade of which was completed in 1605 by Fausto Rughesi. Mascherino was the creator of a row of houses in Via dell'Arco di Santo Spirito, rearranged in the twentieth century, and Santa Maria in Traspontina.

The End of the Century

Fontana's monopoly ended when Sixtus died. Controversy overcame him, he moved to Naples where he became an important figure. With the new pontiff Clement VIII (1592–1603), the century closed in a fever of initiatives for the 1600 jubilee. Della Porta completed the dome of St. Peter's and worked on the transept of San Giovanni in Laterano from 1592.

New contributions were not lacking. The spatial aspect of San Giacomo in Augusta (degli Incurabili), begun in 1592, is of high quality. It was the masterpiece of Francesco Capriani from Volterra, who also began the reconstruction of San Silvestro in Capite. This monastery was the main factor in the development of the area of the Tridente of Campo Marzio, a notable aspect of the growth of the city in the sixteenth century. Capriani, who trained in Lombardy, represents a period of notable elaboration of the theme of the oval dome, whether longitudinal (San Giacomo) or transverse (San Silvestro), anticipating the shivers of Baroque spatiality.

Rome, around 1600, owed much to expert input from northern Italy. One development followed another, not just in religious architecture. In Fontana's school, Carlo Maderno is important. He worked with Domenico Fontana in Santa Susanna from the start of the work in 1593, and from 1598 was the architect of the Casa Professa of the Jesuits (begun 1599). Giovan Battista Montano planned San Giuseppe dei Falegnami from 1597. Onorio Longhi (son of Martino Longhi) worked in Santa Maria in Aracoeli and Santa Maria in Trastevere. Gaspare Guerra, Mario Arconio (linked like the Longhis with the Oratory of St. Philip Neri), Pompeo Targone, Carlo Lombardi, and Flaminio Ponzio—who arrived in 1596 and had an important role from 1605 with the new pope Paul V (1605–21)—divided the remaining

commissions between them, often linking themselves to the patronage of religious orders.

These orders were required by strict Church regulations to undertake the complex task of reevaluation—their own physical heritage, the isolation of their installations, accentuation of the decoration, and their relationship with the city. This was a dynamic situation, a huge work of transformation. There was also a proliferation of architects, itself an indication of the difference between now and Sixtus V's papacy. A whole generation of solid professionals was formed by these rich stimuli, problems, and turmoil. This was the basis of the great—and wholly Roman—era of the Baroque, which would break forth.

Stefano Borsi

Carlo Maderno's facade for the church of Santa Susanna, from 1603 already celebrated as an outstanding architectural feat at the time of its completion. By careful arranging and shaping of the individual elements of the facade, the architect succeeded in creating an effect of movement towards the center from the outside.

Sculpture

At the beginning of the century, sculpture in Rome was dominated by the rising star Michelangelo, who completed the *Pietà* in 1499, shortly after the *Bacchus* for Cardinal Raffaelle Riario. It was the eve of the jubilee of 1500, celebrated amid strong reformist expectations and clear reservations about a somewhat wordly pontificate, that of Alexander VI (1492–1503).

Sculpture at this time was in the throes of a passion for the antique, in painting expressed in the work of Pinturicchio. The city was a busy center for the trade in antiquities, fakes and restorations abounded. Not even Michelangelo was immune. His *Sleeping Cupid* was passed off as an antique and sold to Cardinal Riario. Creations in the antique style proliferated, and cardinals competed in their collections of inscriptions and sculptures. Cardinal Oliviero Carafa owned the "speaking statue" *Pasquino*, a recently discovered classical fragment, and Giuliano della Rovere exhibited the *Belvedere Apollo*.

The *Apollo Belvedere*, a Roman copy of a work by the Greek sculptor Leochares which was discovered in Italy in the fifteenth century. Part of Julius II's collection, it was displayed in the courtyard of the Belvedere. It was modified by Montesoli in 1532. In the eighteenth century Winckelmann (1717–68) made it the most admired statue of the late classical era. Vatican Museums.

The brief pontificate of Pius III (1503) made little impression on the artistic situation, though as cardinal he had been a patron both of Pinturicchio, commissioning the frescos in the Libreria Piccolomini in the Cathedral in his native Siena, and of Michelangelo, commissioning the Piccolomini Altar in the Cathedral in 1501.

The situation changed greatly with the election of the new pontiff, Julius II (1503–13). Expectations were high, particularly among artists. Rome continued to attract numerous sculptors, mainly from Lombardy and Tuscany. Among them, again, was Michelangelo, who in 1505 began the saga of the monumental tomb for Julius II—he had no hesitatation in calling this "the tragedy of the tomb," with his searching, tense, and intransigent work, the continual reductions in the scale of the tomb, oppressive conditions, and delays imposed by the patron. The saga continued after Julius' death. At least in its initial stages, it had to fit in with the not insubstantial problem of what form to give the new basilica of St. Peter's, the titanic challenge posed by Julius. The work eventually ended up in San Pietro in Vincoli.

Andrea Sansovino

The dogged Michelangelo was not the only active Roman sculptor. The young Andrea Contucci, known as Sansovino due to his birthplace (Monte

San Sovino), had already been in Rome for a year when in 1504 he executed the Manzi tomb in the Franciscan church of Santa Maria in Aracoeli. Sansovino was quickly drawn into Bramante's circle, sculpting the monumental tombs of Cardinals Ascanio Sforza and Girolamo Basso della Rovere (who died in 1505 and 1507 respectively) in Santa Maria del Popolo, remodeled by Bramante from

Sixtus IV's original church with the help of Pinturicchio. As the tombs are recorded in Francesco Albertini's *Opusculum* (1510), they must have been completed in about 1508–09.

The tombs adopt a theme of Etruscan origin, with the deceased leaning on the sarcophagus, as if on the *klīne* of the banquet in the next world. They have an insistent classicizing language, from the architectural plan to the triumphal arch with its minute decorative detail. Vasari picked out for special praise the statue of Temperance, "which for its excellence appears more antique than modern." In the atmosphere of determined classicism this was a significant judgment.

In 1512 Sansovino sculpted the *Virgin and Child with St. Anne* in Sant'Agostino, reworking an ancient model in a sacred context, confronting the language of Raphael, who painted a fresco of the prophet Isaiah on the next pillar. Sansovino's sculpture had an antique air—the face of the Virgin recalls a young Roman matron in the Flavian era—that does not, however, exclude a more austere religious inspiration. This was praised by Vasari as "the only example among modern figures that one can believe divine."

The Rediscovery of the Antique

The discovery of the *Laocoön* in 1506 and of the classical river god sculptures in the Baths of Constantine a few years later, and Bramante's reordering of the statues in the Vatican Belvedere, were important moments in this passion for the antique, relaunching the classical

Andrea Sansovino's Virgin and Child with St. Anne. Executed in 1512 for the church of Sant'Agostino, the group can be seen as an artistic response to Raphael's work in the same church.

Andrea Sansovino's tomb of Cardinal Ascanio Sforza in Santa Maria del Popolo, inspired by the tombs of Andrea Bregno.

The Laocoön, found on the Esquiline
Hill in 1506, the high point of Roman
enthusiasm for antique culture. Its
discovery deeply impressed artists
active in the city at the time, including
Raphael and Michelangelo.
Vatican Museums.

theme in sculpture. Sculpture gardens flourished, with those of Sassi, Maffei, Della Valle,
and the humanist Angelo Colocci, who placed
an Ariadne as the centerpiece of his garden.

Raphael acquired a position of absolute prestige and a complex network of collaborators. In
his circle another young Tuscan, Lorenzo di Lotti
(known as Lorenzetto) was making a name for
himself. Lorenzetto had been active in Rome for
some time, though Vasari judged his mysterious
early activity as "not meriting being remembered."

In 1519 he was given the important commission
of the statues for the funerary chapel of Agostino
Chigi in Santa Maria del Popolo. Raphael had
provided the design for the statues, but
Lorenzetto gave them a delicate, vibrant interpretation, with great skill and chiaroscuro softness.
The *Jonah* is more easily evaluated than the
Elijah, completed in 1523 with the collaboration
of Raffaelle da Montelupo. Time was short, and
the wealthy patron died in 1520, only four days
after Raphael, a key date in Italian art history.

Lorenzetto produced the *Madonna del Sasso* for Raphael's tomb in the Pantheon, again with the collaboration of Raffaelle da Montelupo. Lorenzetto lived longer than Agostino Chigi and Raphael (he was to die in 1541), but the almost simultaneous deaths of Chigi and Raphael undoubtedly heralded the decline in his fortunes. Clement VII (Giulio de' Medici) would give him an important commission, the St. Peter for Ponte Sant'Angelo and the pendant of Paolo Taccone's fifteenth-century St. Paul. The two statues seemed to have an implicit stylistic compatibility, also a subtle recognition of a certain decline. Clement was a good judge of art.

In 1524 Lorenzetto completed the tomb of Bernardino Cappella in Santo Stefano Rotondo, but in the tombs of the Medici popes in Santa Maria sopra Minerva from 1536 he contented himself with a subordinate role, with the statuary entrusted to Baccio Bandinelli. As compensation, Lorenzetto did more work (with Antonio da Sangallo the Younger) as architect-surveyor for the never-ending work on St. Peter's. This position allowed him to live in style in the house in the street Macel' de' Corvi, between the Quirinal Hill and Trajan's Column, where all the sculptors' studios were to be found, from that of Andrea Bregno to Michelangelo.

Jacopo Sansovino

A young pupil of Andrea Sansovino, Jacopo Tatti from Florence, who adopted Sansovino's name, made his debut with his collaboration on the Sforza and Della Rovere tombs in Santa Maria del Popolo, coming into contact with Perugino and Bramante's circle. Jacopo Sansovino later returned to Rome in 1518, at the height of Leo X's pontificate, and quickly established himself with important works like the *Madonna del Parto* in Sant'Agostino and the *St. James* for San Giacomo degli Spagnuoli (now the Madonna del Sacro Cuore), the Spanish national church in Piazza Navona (now in Santa Maria di Monserrato, the Catalan national church). Another important work was the monumental tomb of Cardinal Michiel in San Marcello, the church of the Servi Florentine order, for which Jacopo was also in charge of the architectural work. He overcame keen competition for this commission from Antonio da Sangallo the Younger, who got his revenge in San Giovanni dei Fiorentini, the national church of the Florentines in Rome, and was in charge of the work in San Giacomo degli Spagnoli. Jacopo, who left Rome for Venice in the fateful year of the Sack of Rome, manifested with increasing success a formal ideal that decisively broke away from the school of Michelangelo.

Jacopo Sansovino's *Madonna del Parto*, commissioned by Giovanni Francesco Martelli, made 1519–20, is one of the most venerated depictions of the Virgin in Rome. Sant'Agostino.

Double tomb of Antonio Orso and Cardinal Giovanni Michiel by Jacopo Sansovino in San Marcello al Corso.

Rome became particularly suitable territory for the development of the monumental tomb, with an accentuation of architectural impagination and expansion of its commemorative function. The architectural vocation of sixteenth-century sculpture cannot be better expressed than by this phrase from Vasari, from his life of

Baccio d'Agnolo: "Sculptors can do no less, in order to place their statues, and make ornaments on tombs and other round things." Jacopo Sansovino's solution brought up to date the type put forward by Andrea Sansovino, accentuating the role of statuary in relation to a more controlled architectural frame, which was mastered by reducing overhangs and the exuberance of decorative elements in relief. Already in about 1519–20, those expressive possibilities were apparent that made Jacopo Sansovino the great hero of Renaissance Venice, as architect, while Andrea Gritti was doge.

Julius II's death forced Michelangelo to undertake a thoroughgoing revision of his plans for Julius' tomb. It was not to be the last: the project underwent at least six reformulations before if was completed in 1542–45, by which time it was a long way from the ambitious initial plans. It was now intended for San Pietro in Vincoli, the titular church Julius had been attached to as cardinal. The *Rebellious Slave* and the *Dying Slave* in the Louvre, which date from about 1513, preceded the monumental *Moses* by two years but were rejected in the final contract of 1542, going to France in 1550. *Moses*, however, constituted a fixed point around which all successive versions rotated, becoming ever more important. In definitive arrangement it is greatly superior to the recumbent statue of Julius.

Michelangelo and Leo X

Another tale of tortuous development is that of Michelangelo's *Risen Christ* in Santa Maria sopra Minerva, inspired, significantly, by an image associated with Savonarola. Michelangelo was working on a first version around 1515, abandoned due to a fault in the marble (though this may have been a convenient excuse). A new version was hurriedly substituted in 1519–20 to fulfil the terms of the contract. Michelangelo worked on it in Florence and the final touches *in situ* were entrusted to an apprentice, Pietro Urbano, quickly replaced by Federico Frizzi after a suggestion from Sebastiano del Piombo.

Though Michelangelo lived almost as a hermit, the vigor of his work did not go unnoticed. Even the Raphaelesque Polidoro da Caravaggio did not hesitate to produce a pictorial version of the *Moses*. The classicism of the age of Leo X (1513–21) offered opportunities especially, but not exclusively, to Florentines: what they

FOLLOWING PAGES:
The original plan for Julius II's tomb included this statue of Moses, by Michelangelo between 1514 and 1516, to have been placed in the upper part of the finished structure. The figure portrays the Old Testament prophet after he has come down from Mount Sinai, when he sees the Israelites' betrayal of god. San Pietro in Vincoli.

Michelangelo's drawing for the tomb of Julius II. Never completed on the scale originally planned, it was intended to surpass every tomb from antiquity. Florence, Gabinetto dei Disegni e delle Stampe.

produced was of uneven quality. The statue of Leo X in Santa Maria in Aracoeli, sculpted in 1514 by Domenico Aimo da Varignana ten years after the Roman debut of Andrea Sansovino in the same church, is certainly not a masterpiece of the highest order, and confirms the variable quality of Roman sculpture of the High Renaissance. Varignana ended up being attracted to the circle of Raphael as architect. To him are attributed the important designs of the Mellon manuscript in the Pierpoint Morgan Library in New York, one of the most notable sketchbooks of the age.

Baldassare Peruzzi and the Tomb of Hadrian VI

The Sienese Baldassare Peruzzi also followed in Raphael's footsteps. After the notable architecture of Agostino Chigi's Villa Farnesina, he had the opportunity to seal his reputation with the theme of the monumental tomb, with that of the Netherlandish pope Hadrian VI (1522–23) in Santa Maria dell'Anima, working from 1524 to 1529. Among Peruzzi's collaborators was Niccolò Tribolo, a pupil of Jacopo Sansovino, who executed important works in Florence.

This papal tomb made way for the custom of adding reliefs with historical scenes to the architectural context, to be a feature in successive papal tombs. Peruzzi made an impression when he overcame competition from Simone Mosca and was soon attracted to Vasari's circle. He stressed the pictorialness of Sansovinian models with grand columns in polychrome marble, particularly in Lucullan black (*nero africano*), which link Hadrian's tomb with the columns Peruzzi painted in the Sala delle Prospettive in the Villa Farnesina. Peruzzi underlined the architectural installation, taking inspiration from the so-called Arco di Portogallo on the Corso (demolished in the sixteenth century), enlarging the great central arch and crowning the attic with a tympanum. Minute decoration gave way to more monumental figures and statues between orders with superimposed niches. The break with the fifteenth-century tradition of the wall architectural tomb was final.

The School of Michelangelo

The 1527 Sack of Rome resulted in a diaspora of artists. Lorenzetto, Jacopo Sansovino and his pupil Danese Cattaneo, Peruzzi, and Giovanni da Udine left the city. Even for those who were to return, Rome would never be the same, as Vasari commented in his life of Perin del Vaga.

Michelangelo's *Christ Risen*, from Santa Maria sopra Minerva. Commissioned in 1514, the piece was roughly worked between 1518 and 1521 and finally completed by Pietro Urbano in 1521 in Rome, where it had been transferred from Florence.

The papacy of the cultured Giulio de' Medici, Clement VII (1523–34), was marked in Italian politics by dramatic events and in sculpture by a preference for Michelangelo, but also by notable themes in a markedly Mannerist direction. These are exemplified by Benvenuto Cellini, based in Rome between 1519 and 1540, with spells in Florence, Venice, and France, a specialist in bronzes and bas-reliefs.

The early sculpture of Daniele da Volterra, surnamed Ricciarelli, comes under the heading of a tribute to Michelangelo. Ironically, Daniele was to conclude an honorable career as a painter, earning himself the nickname "Breeches" for the notorious operation to clothe the naked figures in Michelangelo's *Last Judgment*.

If Michelangelo was destined for Florence to work for the Medici in San Lorenzo, the school of Michelangelo dominated the Roman scene. The moment was right for Tuscan sculptors: Baccio da Montelupo, Baccio Bandinelli, Raffaele da Montelupo, Nanni di Baccio Bigio (also known as Giovanni Lippi), and Tiberio Calcagni had preferential routes and privileged opportunities, while Giovanni da Montorsoli completed the *Laocoön* in 1532, integrating the missing pieces.

As a young man Tiberio Calcagni followed in Michelangelo's footsteps. From the 1550s he took part in some of Michelangelo's important projects such as San Giovanni dei Fiorentini and the Sforza Chapel in Santa Maria Maggiore, but his age (he was born in 1532) prevented him from being counted among the heroes of Clement's pontificate.

Nanni di Baccio Bigio followed the path of grandiose monumentalism under the banner of an empty, uninspired Michelangelism, which his well-known dispute with Michelangelo could not mask. Baccio da Montelupo soon disappeared from the scene, but for some time worked under the influence of Michelangelo, who encouraged him in the first decade of the century. Michelangelo had procured Baccio the job of completing the Piccolomini Altar in Siena in his stead, as can be learnt from a letter of Ludovico Buonarroti of 1510.

Baccio Bandinelli and Guglielmo della Porta

The great official commissions for these sculptors were the tombs of the two Medici popes, Leo X and Clement VII, in Santa Maria sopra Minerva, executed under the aegis of Antonio da Sangallo the Younger. It was also their conflict, with controversial repercussions lasting for years. Baccio Bandinelli (1493–1560) took the side of Leo X and managed to rid himself of dangerous competitors such as the Ferrarese Alfonso Lombardi, who died in 1535. Lombardi, protected by Cardinal Ippolito de' Medici, moved to Bologna after his disappointment.

Baccio Bandinelli gave new dimensions to the contribution of other Tuscans. According to Vasari, Bandinelli owed his fortune to Lucrezia Salviati, the daughter of Lorenzo the Magnificent and sister of Leo X, whose influence was decisive. Bandinelli gave another version of events in his *Memoriale* (1552), allowing no room for any doubts about his superiority. The monumental complex—the contract stipulated 1536—took more than four years of work, during which the initial conditions were renegotiated. It produced a series of works now divided between galleries in Madrid, Florence, Oxford, and Vienna.

Sangallo imposed an architectural construction on the model of the triumphal arch, reducing the central supporting arch to allow the reliefs to decorate the frames in the attic, of which the crowning tympanum was interrupted by the insertion of Medici coats of arms. It displays a careful classicism, but goes beyond this as a commemorative oratory. With a marked compositional rigor and less colorism compared to Peruzzi, it is an amplification of the role of statuary, evidently thoughtful, Michelangelesque ideas. Not by chance had Michelangelo already been summoned for the task by Clement VII: he had provided designs that would inevitably be disregarded. The theme of historical and biographical reliefs was taken from the tomb of Hadrian VI, with an important scene from the life of the deceased pope. But the size accorded to these scenes in relation to the nearby reliefs on sacred themes aroused the Catholic Reformation perplexity of Vasari, who condemned the emphasis on the statue of the pope compared to those of the two saints that flanked it, even if Sangallo and Bandinelli had accented the central overhanging element to suggest an advanced perspective plane.

It was without doubt difficult to escape the influence of Michelangelo, who strongly influenced even transitory figures such as Leone Leoni, in Rome between 1538 and 1540. Leone's friendship with Michelangelo resulted in an important commission, the tomb of Giangiacomo de' Medici (brother of Pius IV), marchese di Marignano, in the Duomo in Milan (1560), an important export of the Medici-Michelangelo style outside the privileged Florence–Rome axis. In the same way, Pierino da Vinci, in Rome in 1548, was a follower of Michelangelo.

Not even Bandinelli managed to free himself completely: mentioned in Vincenzo de' Rossi's letter to Cosimo I in 1563 is the impulse that started work on the *Pietà*, the dead Christ supported by Nicodemus, in the church of the Santissima Annunziata in Florence, later entrusted to Bandinelli's son Clemente. The statue was intended for the pope's tomb: "because he had heard that in Rome Michelangelo was finishing one, he had begun a great sculpture, with five figures, for your tomb in Santa Maria Maggiore."

The inaccessible Michelangelo, ever more absorbed by architecture, found it increasingly difficult to find time for sculpture. It is not easy to discover Michelangelo's intentions, shut off as he was in virtual isolation. "Sleep is welcome to me, no longer living like a stone," "I have no friends and nor do I want any," read his sonnets and letters. Nevertheless, there was no important

Tomb of Hadrian VI (pope from 1522 to 1523) from Utrecht, the last non-Italian pope before John Paul II, in Santa Maria dell'Anima. Executed between 1524 and 1529, this work by Baldassare Peruzzi is the final expression of the medieval wall tomb in Rome.

Guglielmo della Porta's bust of Paul III. Naples, Museo Nazionale di Capodimonte.

Tomb of Paul III (1534-49) in St. Peter's. The most important work by Guglielmo della Porta, it was originally intended as a free-standing tomb. Above the allegorical figures of Justice and Wisdom is a bronze statue of the pope, depicted more as a humanist cleric and scholar than pontiff.

commission in Rome on which Michelangelo was not consulted. There was nevertheless space, in the turmoil of the mid-century, for a long wave of *bandinellism*, sculpture influenced by Bandinelli, of which the most striking example is the work of Vincenzo de' Rossi in the Cesi Chapel in Santa Maria della Pace (1560).

In the meantime the panorama of Roman sculpture in the sixteenth century was being

PAVLO·III
FARNESIO·PONT
OPT·MAX

enriched by new experiences. The monumental tomb of Clement's successor, Paul III (1534–49), was built in St. Peter's by Guglielmo della Porta. Commissioned by Cardinal Alessandro Farnese, it was supervised by Annibale Caro. The work took a long time to be completed and the tomb was inaugurated only for the jubilee of 1575, obviously in a revised version. It appears that Paul himself, aware that the end was near, had chosen an antique sarcophagus. At the end of 1552 the statue of the pope was complete, followed by the *Virtues* and the other figures. However, Della Porta himself contributed to the slowness of progress, as he was irritated by constant advice from Michelangelo and Vasari. In the end the result was modified by Bernini, who made it the pendant of the tomb of Urban VIII. Paul's gesture was inspired by the Marcus Aurelius equestrian sculpture, which Paul had had placed on the Capitoline Hill in 1538, but the Michelangelesque architectural execution in a pyramidal scheme was to be greatly weakened (recalling the fate of its predecessor, the tomb of Julius II). The full-length figures, derived from the Medici Chapel in San Lorenzo in Florence, have faces of strong archaeological connotations in conformity with Caro's aesthetic ideal.

This literary style, classicist and erudite, is noticeable even in lesser works. A good example is the sepulchral bust of the humanist Blosio Palladio (later bishop of Foligno) in Santa Maria in Aquiro, the sculptor of which is unknown.

The preferential relationship between Della Porta, the Lombard sculptor-monk, and Paul III is confirmed by the striking Capodimonte bust in two colors (white marble and Numidian yellow) of Paul, completed about 1547 in Rome. With the election of Julius III (1550–55) and the jubilee of

1550, the Florentines arrogantly took their place at the top again. The opportunity was provided by the Del Monte Chapel in San Pietro in Montorio, with the tombs of Cardinal Fabiano and Antonio del Monte, uncle and great-uncle of Julius III. Vasari was charged with the project and proposed Simone Mosca for the sculpture. Mosca had already created the reliefs in the Cesi Chapel in Santa Maria della Pace. Julius, however, submitted the designs to Michelangelo, who counseled against placing reliefs near the figures, underlining the importance of the statues. Having thus eliminated Mosca, Michelangelo placed his own conditions: not Raffaelle da Montelupo, proposed by Vasari, but a promising youth, Bartolomeo Ammannati, whose mausoleum for Marco Benavides in the church of the Eremitani in Padua (1546), in the style of Raphael and Sansovino, was his most important work to date.

It is clear that these heavy-handed interventions were not infrequent and proposed a radical reconsideration of the whole, from Vasari's architectural mould to the role of the figures and their relationship with the architecture. The strong Michelangelism of the portrait of Antonio del Monte is no surprise. Nor was the echo in the putti of the Tuscan marble balustrade of the model of these in Michelangelo's Sistine Chapel ceiling. Ammannati worked quickly, from 1550 to 1553, with the obstructive Michelangelo at his heels, while Daniele da Volterra worked on the chapel opposite. They thus ended up making a fifteenth-century church transept.

Pius IV

Michelangelo's dominance characterized artistic life during the papacy of Pius IV (1559–65). The elderly Michelangelo gave further proof of incomparable achievements, like the *Rondanini Pietà*, which remained unfinished at his death in 1564. It is no surprise that the *Treatise of Perfect Proportions* (*Trattato delle perfette proporzioni*) by Vincenzo Danti should exalt the perfection of Michelangelo as superior to all others, ancient or modern. It is, however, telling that Michelangelo's lesson was absorbed only on the level of ideal proportions of the human form. Neither the unabsorbed ethical tension nor the dramatic search for salvation were important. Catholic reform—the final session of the Council of Trent closed in 1563—affirmed the instruments of salvation entrusted to the Church, and as a result individualist positions became superfluous, if not suspect. "Neither weeping nor sculpting will make more calm/The soul turned to that Divine Love," as Michelangelo wrote in a sonnet in 1557.

There was no lack of new ideas. Roman sculpture was enriched by the Florentine Giovanni Antonio Dosio, the Neapolitan Pirro Ligorio, and the abovementioned Vincenzo Danti, from Perugia. Ligorio, the indefatigable investigator of the antique, incarnated for Paul IV's pontificate the ideal of the allegorical and secular artist, as Michelangelo was given the sacred theme. The huge distance between the two gives the measure of the variety of emphases in Roman sculpture. Pirro Ligorio, whom Guglielmo della Porta had

The Del Monte Chapel in San Pietro in Montorio, designed by Giorgio Vasari for Julius II. Vasari, author of *Lives of the Artists*, was also responsible for the altarpiece showing the conversion of St. Paul. The sculptural ornamentation in the chapel was made by Bartolomeo Ammanati from 1550 to 1553.

HELENAE SABELLAE
CONIVGI CARISSIMAE
BERNARDINVS SABELLVS

had sacked from St. Peter's in 1565, provided an unusual design for a papal tomb, with that of Paul IV (intended for St. Peter's, now in Santa Maria sopra Minerva) created in 1566–72. The whole has a clear heterodox archaeological erudition but compositional rigor, in which the Benedictine pope statue fits well. The sculptor was the relatively unknown Giacomo Cassignola.

A number of publications enriched the debate: the Giunta edition of Alberti's *On Sculpture* (*De statua*), Varchi's *Two Lessons* (*Due lezioni*), Danti's treatise, those of Benvenuto Cellini on goldwork and sculpture, published in 1568, Vasari's *Lives* (*Vite*) (1550 and 1568), and Condivi's life of Michelangelo (1553). Works sent from outside Rome also helped the process: the bronze *Rape of the Sabines* by Giambologna, an important commission now in the Capodimonte museum in Naples, reached Palazzo Farnese, while Giambologna, who worked in Florence for the grand-duke of Tuscany, was in correspondence with Ottavio Farnese in 1579.

The problem of how to follow Michelangelo dogged the work of the Sicilian Jacopo del Duca, including his architectural work. The little relief on the sepulchral tablet of Antonio Foderati in Santo Spirito in Sassia took up the theme of the *Pietà* while the completion of Porta Pia put Del Duca in the position of overseeing the conclusion of an important work by Michelangleo.

(The angels on the side of the papal arms were, however, entrusted to the most modest stone-cutter Nardo de' Rossi.) Already the tomb of Elena Savelli in San Giovanni in Laterano (1570) revealed a free analytical attitude with respect to the clear architectural model of Porta Pia. It is enriched by bronzes that follow the more distant archetype of the Sistine Chapel. The relationship with the authoritative Michelangelo appears in the little relief on the tomb of Cardinal Alessandro Savelli, *God Supporting the Dead Christ*, a free revisiting of the *Pietà*. There is a fainter echo in the group of the tympanum of the portal of Santa Maria di Loreto depicting the Virgin and Child with angels at the holy house of about 1580: not surprisingly, the attribution of this piece remains unclear.

Guglielmo della Porta was now prosperous, having obtained a dispensation allowing him to own property despite his religious vows. He had not, however, made an impression on the Roman scene for more than a decade. His last important undertaking before 1567, that of a series of altars for St. Peter's, never came to fruition and is known only from his sketch-books, now in Düsseldorf.

Della Porta's position as papal portraitist was taken by the Florentine Taddeo Landini, the sculptor of a bust of Gregory XIII now in the Staatliche Museum in Berlin and of the relief *Christ Washing the Disciples' Feet*, for the Cappella Gregoriana in St. Peter's (now in the Quirinal). Landini, who had had a typically Tuscan training took up in Rome the model of the Florentine public fountain. Baglione claimed that he provided the models for the bronze sculpture of the famous *Fontana delle Tartarughe* (*Fountain of the Turtles*) in Piazza Mattei (though the turtles were added in 1658 and the original layout is that of Giovanni Maggi in 1618).

Sixtus V

The brief but decisive papacy of the energetic Sixtus V (1585–90), crucial in creating the face of modern Rome, imparted a dynamism that affected sculpture too, even if the results were anything but uniform. Architecture was firmly in the hands of Domenico Fontana, with occasional exceptions, and painting was considered for the most part to be dominated by Giovanni Guerra and Cesare Nebbia. Sculpure, however, was more fragmented. Two Florentines, Taddeo Landini and the bronzesmith Bastiano Torrigiani (the creator of the angels that support the tabernacle of the Sistine Chapel in Santa Maria Maggiore, designed by G. Battista Ricci, from Novara) were Sixtus' portraitists. Their busts of the pope are of notable quality, with a level of

psychological penetration to be surpassed only by the Baroque. Tommaso della Porta provided the colossal bronze statues of Sts. Peter and Paul, intended to christianize the imperial columns of Trajan and Marcus Aurelius, in 1587.

It was another Lombard, Giovanni Antonio Paracca (il Valsoldo), who took the lion's share among the sculptors of the Sistine Chapel in Santa Maria Maggiore, although his previous work is not known. Vasoldo had been in Rome since his youth and, like so many others, had busied himself in the profitable business of "restoration" of ancient sculpture. Sixtus V was thinking about his tomb even before he was elected, when in 1568 he commissioned the twin tomb for Pius V (1566–72) and himself. This was begun the following year, but Sixtus did not see it completed: Valsoldo was charged with completing it by Sixtus' nephew, Cardinal Alessandro Damasceni Peretti, in 1591. In the

The unfinished *Rondanini Pietà*, which Michelangelo worked on in the last days of his life. In an expressive way it depicts the artist's own religious views, which were heavily focused on human suffering. Milan, Musei Civici del Castello Sforzesco.

Tomb of Elena Savelli by Jacopo del Duca, made from 1570, in San Giovanni in Laterano. In this work the Sicilian sculptor and architect created his own interpretation of Michelangelo's architectural motifs from the Porta Pia.

Taddeo Landini's *Fontana delle Tartarughe*, or Turtle Fountain, signaling the adoption of a type of richly decorated public fountain that was common in Florence.

435

BENEDICTVS·XIII·ORD·PRÆDIC·ALTARE·HOC·CONSECRAVIT·DIE·XXV·IVLY·MDCCXXVI·

same year Valsoldo found himself responsible for the statues of Sts. Peter and Paul for the Cesi Chapel in the Chiesa Nuova (Santa Maria in Vallicella), coming into contact with St. Philip Neri's Congregation of the Oratory.

In the Sistine Chapel Valsoldo was anything but alone. Leonardo da Sarzana was sculptor of a statue of Pius V. The historic relief underneath, showing the award of the Church's colors to Marcantonio Colonna before the battle of Lepanto, is by Egidio della Riviera, creator of other scenes from the life of Pius V, with the help of Nicolas Pippi from Arras, with whom he divided the panels. The two had displayed a certain harmony since 1575, when they worked on the tomb of Frederick of Cleves, Bavarian crown prince, in Santa Maria dell'Anima (inspired by the tomb of Hadrian VI). The statues of Dominican saints on the monument to Pius V were divided between Valsoldo (*St. Peter Martyr*) and Giacomo della Porta (*St. Dominic*). Giacomo della Porta, a Lombard maestro destined for a great career as architect for Clement VIII, was already involved in the difficult execution of the dome of St. Peter's. The statue of Sixtus V, on the tomb opposite, is by Valsoldo, while the reliefs are by Egidio della Riviera and Nicolas Pippi. The statues of the saints of the Franciscan order (to which Sixtus V belonged) are by Pier Paolo Olivieri (*St. Antony of Padua*) and Flaminio Vacca (*St. Francis*). Vacca was the author of Records of the antiquities of Rome (*Memorie delle antichità di Roma*), especially interesting for its information on excavations. An exuberant coloring characterizes these tombs, inserted into an architectural context invented by Domenico Fontana, with Prospero Bresciano in the role of iconographic deviser.

Michelangelo's influence seemed to be losing its potency, as demonstrated by the *Moses* of the Fontana dell'Acqua Felice near Santa Susanna, the work of Leonardo Sormani, assisted by Prospero Bresciano. The statue has an amplified monumentalism far removed from the ideal tension of the Michelangelesque precedent. It is conceived in terms of an expanded spatiality on an urban scale that had no precedents, in line with the scale of the great urban plans of Sixtus. The reliefs accompanying it are by Della Porta and Vacca.

The End of the Century

Sculptors were often asked to share important commissions, following a pragmatic principle that saw prompt delivery as the most important factor. So even minor projects might be executed jointly, like the angels in the corner niches of the second chapel on the right in the Gesù (about 1594), provided by the Lombards Silla Longhi and Ippolito

Buzio, and by the Romans Pier Paolo Olivieri and Flaminio Vacca. Longhi would see his reputation grow with his statues of Clement VIII and Paul V for the Borghese Chapel (Cappella Paolina) in Santa Maria Maggiore, the pendant of the Cappella Sistina. Like Vacca, Longhi was a tireless and skilful restorer of antiquity.

Bizio was a more consistent personality. In 1593, with the portrait of Alessandro Farnese he began the series of statues of important men in the Palazzo dei Conservatori, to which Bernini and Ercole de Ferrata contributed in the seventeenth century. Bizio obtained from Clement VIII (1592–1605) and Paul V (1605–21) the most important commissions, the sculpture for Clement VIII's Aldobrandini Chapel in Santa Maria sopra Minerva (with the statue of

Statue of Sixtus V by Giovanni Antonio Paracca, known as Vasoldo, in the Sistine Chapel in Santa Maria Maggiore. It shows the patron of the chapel at prayer, an act directed towards the sacramental ciborium and the reliquary. The statue was conceived as a counterpart to the tomb of Pius V, Sixtus V's predecessor.

OPPOSITE:
Bronze ciborium carried by four angels from the Sistine Chapel in Santa Maria Maggiore. Made by the bronzecaster Bartolomeo Torrigiani from a design by Giovanni Battista Ricca, this work, together with relics of Christ's manger, form a central point of reference for the decoration of the chapel.

Clement) and Della Porta's scheme for the transept of San Giovanni in Laterano (1597–1601). This was the great collective enterprise of Clement's papacy, with the angels sculpted by Bizio, Nicolas Cordier, Stefano Maderno, Camillo Mariani, Alessandro Bonvicino, and Valsoldo, the new generation under Clement, together with earlier heroes.

The undertaking was placed under the supervision of Giuseppe Cesari (the Cavalier d'Arpino) and inspired by Cardinal Cesare Baronio. Bizio would have an important role in the Borghese Chapel in Santa Maria Maggiore; he would provide the arms of Paul V supported by angels (1612) and the *St. James* for San Giacomo in Augusta (or degli Incurabili) on the Corso (about 1615).

Pier Paolo Olivieri had already had a successful career before Sixtus' pontificate, with the colossal statue of Gregory XIII in Santa Maria in Aracoeli and the monument to Gregory XI in Santa Francesca Romana (1584). He too could boast of a solid apprenticeship in the antique. At the end of the century he completed the altar of the holy sacrament in San Giovanni in Laterano, in gilded bronze. In this case the statues were divided between Silla Longhi (*Aaron*), Nicolas Pippi (*Melchizedek*), Egidio della Riviera (*Moses*), and the rising star, Camillo Mariani (*Elijah*).

The jubilee's imminence of the jubilee seemed to justify the continuation of procedures typical of Sixtus' papacy. A solid professionalism developed in the projects of the end of the century and new tendencies were not absent. The statues of prophets in the pillars of Santa Susanna by Valsoldo (*Isaiah* and *Jeremiah*) and Vacca (*Ezechiel* and *Daniel*) of 1597–99 tend to a general influence of Raphael in the decoration of the nave—the frescos by Croce were inspired by the Sala di Costantino in the Vatican Palace and the Sistine Chapel tapestries—and confirm the gradual decline in Michelangelo's influence. With his *St. Cecilia* for the church of Santa Cecilia, Stefano Maderno from Ticino, proposed an intentionally simple model of sacred art, reproducing the martyred saint in the position in which her body was found in the course of work ordered by Cardinal Sfondrati in view of the forthcoming jubilee. It was the devotional ideal, humble and recalling the early Christian Church, desired by the Catholic Reformation. Olivieri fell into line with the position of Federico Zuccari, who dominated the Roman academic world, when he produced the marble altarpiece—a typical Counter-Reformation creation—for the Caetani Chapel in Santa Pudenziana (1599).

Camillo Maiani made a much more vigorous impression. He favored coloristic taste of pure Venetian origin, borrowed from the great Alessandro Vittoria. In 1603, in the monumental

stucco decoration in San Bernardo alle Terme, he had the young Francesco Mochi at his side. Mochi was one of the great protagonists of the Baroque period. Nicolas Cordier, from Lorraine, made himself the interpreter of a refined but careful neo-Mannerism which owed much to the sophisticated lesson of Giambologna and could count on the support of Cardinal Baronio. He too would dominate the early seventeenth century in Rome, which was enriched in about 1605–06 by the arrival of Pietro Bernini. The sixteenth century closed with a great variety of accents and notable impulses. Rome was fertile territory for the great Baroque explosion of the following generation.

Stefano Borsi

Relief showing the Adoration of the Magi by Pietro Paulo Oliveiri from the Caetani Cahpel in Santa Pudenziana. This work from 1599 achieves a complex composition by combining the quality of classical material—white marble—with the ideals of a Counter-Reformation altarpiece.

OPPOSITE:
Fontana dell'Acqua Felice, made by Domenico Fontana for Sixtus V between 1585 and 1587. The dominant figure of Moses in the center, which was the work of Leonardo Sormani, takes Michelangelo's figure of the prophet as its model but elevates it still further in scale.

Painting

A penetrating gaze, absorbed in thought, a hand which grips almost violently the arm of the papal seat: thus Raphael portrayed Pope Julius II, nephew of Pope Sixtus IV, in a gesture which evoked that interior conflict between action and equilibrium, which characterised his acts. Elected in 1503, he was a combatant pope who did not shrink from putting on a warrior's garb to defend the Church's territories and to widen its bounds. The most important projects that he commissioned began in 1508. Some were entrusted to those artists with an antiquarian bent who had worked on projects for Pope

Alexander VI, such as Jacopo Ripanda from Bologna, who realized the Sala di Annibale and the Sala della Lupa in the Palazzio dei Conservatori Campidoglio (1508–13) and Pinturicchio, who painted the frescos on the vault of the choir in Santa Maria del Popolo. His study of the vaults of the Golden House is evident from his employment of geometric partition, which he modernized with illusionistic effects when he painted the background of imitation gold mosaic and inserted the imitation stucco cornices in which are gathered the *Coronation of the Virgin* in the center, four Evangelists alternating with semirecumbent Sybils at the sides between tondi, and four Doctors of the Church seated on thrones between aediculas in the pendentives.

But the most representative decorative enterprises, those which concern sites in the Vatican Palace, were entrusted to artists with a more innovative language. Michelangelo took on the task of painting the ceiling of the Sistine Chapel on May 10, 1508 and perhaps Raphael started the Stanze at the end of the same year.

Michelangelo was already committed to producing the great funerary monument which Julius had wanted to place in St. Peter's above the tomb of the apostle Peter. "He wished to finish the sepulcher. The ceiling of that chapel seemed to him a great and difficult task; considering his lack of experience in coloring, he made every effort to rid himself of this great weight on his shoulders." Thus Vasari explained the two years of anguish which intervened

Michelangelo, *ignudo*, framing scenes from Genesis in the *Separation of Light from Darkness*. Rome, Vatican Museums, Sistine Chapel.

Michelangelo, *ignudo* from the *Drunkenness of Noah*. Rome, Vatican Museums, Sistine Chapel.

Michelangelo, *ignudi* between the *Creation of Sun, Moon, and the Planets* and the *Congregation of the Waters.* The meaning of these *ignudi*, or nude figures, placed in the corners of the main pictures is still unresolved. They form a linking element between the fictive architectural framework and the Genesis scenes. Rome, Vatican Museums, Sistine Chapel.

FOLLOWING PAGES:
Michelangelo, *Creation of Adam.* The translation of this episode from the story of creation into pictorial form illustrates Michelangelo's sculptural approach. God appears as a sculptor in the process of giving life to his creation. Rome, Vatican Museums, Sistine Chapel.

Michelangelo, *Temptation and Expulsion from Paradise.* The scenes painted in February 1511 after the project had been interrupted, whose beginning is marked by the *Creation of Adam*, show a new formal and idealized conception of the human figure. Vatican Museums, Sistine Chapel.

Michelangelo, *Isaiah*. Together with the *Erythrean Sibyl*, this youthful figure flanks the *Sacrifice of Noah*. Vatican Museums, Sistine Chapel.

ESAIAS

Michelangelo, *Ezekiel*. This animated portrait of a gray-haired man in the grip of a vision is one of seven prophets. Michelangelo painted on the ceiling of the palace chapel. Together with the *Cumaean Sibyl* it frames the *Creation of Eve*. Vatican Museums, Sistine Chapel.

EZECHIEL

Michelangelo, *Delphic Sibyl*, one of five female visionaries from antiquity in the frescos of the Sistine Chapel Ceiling. Michelangelo's painting of this figure seems to have been modeled on Jacopo della Quercia's portrayal of Wisdom from the Fonte Gaia in Siena. Vatican Museums, Sistine Chapel.

Michelangelo, *Naason*. Vatican Museums, Sistine Chapel.

Michelangelo, *Aminadab*. In the Bible, Aminadab pulled the wagon carrying the Ark of the Covenant. Vatican Museums, Sistine Chapel.

449

FOLLOWING PAGE:
Detail from *Aminadab*. Vatican
Museums, Sistine Chapel.

Detail from *Naason*. Vatican Museums,
Sistine Chapel.

450

between Julius II's request for the decoration of the ceiling of the Sistine Chapel, in 1506, and the start of work. In fact, the pope had not envisaged an undertaking of such imposing proportions: the initial plan was for the twelve apostles and an architectural motif. The final result was a decoration of great formal complexity, with a clear decorated architecture and an articulated sequence of scenes taken from Genesis interspersed with figures of prophets and sibyls, nudes and sculptures in imitation marble and bronze. Perhaps the learned Egidio da Viterbo was involved in the change of plan; the textual references with which the fresco has been linked are diverse, from St. Augustine's biblical exegesis to that of St. Bonaventure's *Arbor vitae*, in turn reformulated by the theologian Marco Vigerio, who dedicated his *Decachordum Christianum* to Julius in 1507.

At the beginning several people from Ghirlandaio's studio helped with the gigantic undertaking. They were masters of the "good fresco," of smooth, enameled surfaces. Michelangelo, however, was already describing his desperate isolation in a letter of November 1509: "I am suffering from great anxiety and huge bodily fatigue; I have no friends of any sort, neither do I want any." The first half of the ceiling was unveiled for the feast of the Assumption in 1511, and on October 31, 1512 the chapel was officially opened. It revealed a harmonious system of perfect architectural scansions in a classical style, animated by imitation statues and imitation niches, of figures of powerful proportions, seated in Saturnine poses or turned in statuary torsions, clothed in changing colors or in perfect anatomies, terse, essential scenes or crowded with characters masterfully packed into tiny spaces. "Everyone is amazed," wrote Vasari, "at how he manages to depict the profundity of images, the stupendous rotundity of the contours, which have grace and lightness in themselves, turned with those beautiful proportions that can be seen in the lovely nudes." The ceiling is divided into three fascias. The first area consists in lunettes and in triangular vaulting cells in which Christ's ancestors are depicted, from Abraham to Joseph, witnesses of the human condition before its redemption: in the pendentives in the four corners some "miraculous" events tell the story of episodes of salvation of the Jewish people—Judith killing Holofernes, David conquering Goliath, the bronze serpent lifted up by divine inspiration to scatter doubts, and the punishment of Haman obtained by Esther. The second area is made up of the external fascia which contains the thrones of the seven prophets and five sibyls who predicted the coming of Christ. In the central rectangle, in spaces separated by architectural

Raphael's fresco of the prophet Isaiah on one of the piers in Sant'Agostino, painted in 1512, at the same time as Michelangelo completed the ceiling of the Sistine Chapel. Michelangelo's influence on Raphael can be clearly seen in this figure.

"Signatura Gratiae" under Paul III), probably used as the pope's private library, and decorated following a plan of neoplatonic type which was based on the relationship between Beauty, Goodness, and Truth.

The plan was developed through a tight correspondence of relationships between the figures of the ceiling, of rectangular connecting panels and walls. Thus, *Theology* (the Truth revealed) is defined in the tablet carried by a putto on "the notion of divine things" and overlooks the *Dispute about the Sacrament*, while *Philosophy* (rational Truth), which enquires into "the cognition of causes" is placed above *The School of Athens*; in correspondence with *Poetry* (Beauty), "inspired by God," is *Parnassus*, and in relation with the *Virtues* is *Justice* (Goodness), which "gives to everyone his own law." In the rectangular panels, the *Judgment of Solomon* represents a rational application of the concept of law, *Original sin* is the cause that provoked divine justice, which manifested itself in banishment from the earthly paradise, *Astronomy* refers to the harmony of the heavenly spheres, the cause of every artistic expression, and the episode of *Apollo and Marsyas* is a mythological metaphor of Christian thought

frameworks punctuated by nudes seated on plinths, nine scenes from Genesis are placed, from the *Separation of light from darkness* to *The drunkenness of Noah*. The epic account of humanity and of Christ's ancestors was one of the pictorial texts that would be a source of argument and comment for the whole century.

Michelangelo's obstinate and affected solitude, his corrosive doubts and tormented anxiety about work ("I don't have time to eat what I need," he wrote in a letter) is contrasted by the work of Raphael in the same period, in the Stanza della Segnatura. This was a work carried out "in such a delicate, sweet manner that it caused Pope Julius to reject all the work of the other maestri, ancient and modern," among whom were Lotto and Bramante. To Raphael alone fell the task of painting the pontifical apartments. Julius did not, in fact, want to live in the same rooms as Alexander VI "quem dicebat esse judaeum, et marranum et etiam circumcisum," and decided to convert the rooms on the upper floor into his own dwelling. Decoration of the apartment began with the ceiling of the Stanza della Segnatura (so called because there sat the church court of the

Detail from Raphael's *School of Athens*. Vatican Museums, Stanza della Segnatura.

which considers God as cause of all harmony. The major compositional innovations are in the frescos on the walls. The so-called *Dispute about the Sacrament* is articulated in three sections: at the top, the "cupola" of the Empyrean is brimming with light and angels which surround God; in the center is the Church triumphant, with twelve figures of saints and patriarchs arranged in a semicircle around Christ, flanked by the Virgin and John the Baptist; at the bottom is the Church militant, around the chalice, the prospective heart of the whole composition, are the saints, doctors of the church and theologians who, according to Vasari, "dispute." It is this definition of his which gives the painting its name; in reality it should be called *The Triumph of the Eucharist*, a representation of divine revelation and of the "City of God" of Augustinian memory. Between

an architecture painted with unusual solemnity is placed the *School of Athens*, where wise men of every era discuss how to reach Truth. In an ideal Temple of Knowledge, protected by tutelary gods of the arts (Apollo) and intelligence (Minerva), Aristotle and Plato indicate with a gesture (a synthesis of their own philosophical convictions) the path to take to reach Truth rationally. Plato, who has *Timeo* in his hands, raises his finger to the sky to refer to the world of ideas, while Aristotle, who holds the book of the *Ethics*, stretches his hand toward the ground to indicate that one has to enquire about the things of this world in order to know the Truth. Scientists and philosophers are grouped around them, in a suggestive scenic arrangement; many of them, as in a modern staging, are played by great contemporary characters: Plato has the face of Leonardo da Vinci, Michelangelo plays

Raphael, *School of Athens*. Painted between 1509 and 1511, the fresco shows important representatives of philosophy and the sciences in an architectural setting reminiscent of Bramante, gathered around the central figures of Aristotle and Plato. Several of the individuals bear the features of famous contemporaries of Raphael such as Michelangelo, who appears in the foreground as Heraclitus, leaning on a block of stone. Raphael himself appears together with Pietro Bembo and Sodoma at the bottom right. Vatican Museums, Stanza della Segnatura.

Raphael, *Parnassus*. The central figure of Apollo playing the violin is surrounded by the muses, as well as by a number of significant figures from Greek, Roman, and Italian literature. Dante can be seen beside the blind Homer in the upper left of the picture. Vatican Museums, Stanza della Segnatura.

Raphael, *Dispute of the Blessed Sacrament*. This depiction of the most holy sacrament forms the counterpart to the *School of Athens*. Raphael structured the composition in three semicircles arranged one on top of the other. At the bottom, grouped around the altar with its monstrance, are church teachers, popes, bishops, and monks. Above that, in the lower level of heaven, is the college of Apostles who are gathered around the central descending dove of the Holy Spirit. The topmost image shows God surrounded by angels. Vatican Museums, Stanza della Segnatura.

457

Raphael, *Galatea*. The theme is taken from Ovid's *Metamorphoses*. Raphael's pictorial rendering of the story of Galatea is evidence of his intense study of ancient culture. Villa Farnesina.

by Augustine, is on the ceiling.) There is *Fortitude* with an oak branch, Julius' heraldic sign, *Prudence* looking at itself in the mirror and *Temperance* with bridle and reins. The three theological virtues, Faith, Hope, and Charity, are represented by little putti.

While he was busy in the Vatican Palace, Raphael did not refuse commissions which often forced him to delegate large parts of his work, especially after the completion of the Stanza della Segnatura. One of his major patrons was the Sienese banker Agostino Chigi (defined by the sultan as "the great merchant of Christendom"), who involved him in the decoration of his villa outside Porta Settimana, Villa Farnesina. The scene of bizarre feasts, it was built by the Sienese architect Baldassare, who also decorated some of its rooms, including the vault of the Loggia di Galatea, with a fresco of fifteenth-century inspiration which represented the personal horoscope of the client, one of the most complex astrological images of the Renaissance (1510–11). In the same room Sebastiano del Piombo, who had been brought from Venice in 1511 by the banker himself, painted the lunettes with a series of myths connected with the element of air, of which some relate to birds, some to winds based on the *Metamorphoses* of Ovid, and a wall fresco with the figure of *Polyphemus* (of about 1512), on a monumental base, placed on a blue background. It is a work of a time of flux, which betrays the anxious meditation of the young Sebastiano on the work of Michelangelo, visible also in a painting of the same period, the *Death of Adonis*, in which the landscape of Venetian origin and tormented luminosity provides a backdrop for the sculptural figures inspired by antiquity but brought up to date in the language of Michelangelo. Next to *Polyphemus*, a giant sick with love, Raphael painted the magnificent *Galatea* who, according to the tales of Theocritus, Ovid and Politian, did not reciprocate the deformed giant's love; in fact, the marine nymph loved young Aci, who was killed by Polyphemus but transformed by Galatea into a water fountain. Raphael depicted an intense image, drenched in neoplatonic culture, a secular version of his *St. Catherine*, now in London, who looks at the Cupid holding his arrows in his hands precisely to avoid provoking passions and to encourage the exercise of virtue.

Agostino Chigi also commissioned Raphael for the plan of his funerary chapel in Santa Maria del Popolo, finished in its essential lines in 1516. Everything was designed by Raphael according to a neoplatonic plan, from the architecture to the decoration of the cupola. And between 1513 and 1514, the artist worked on the frescos of the *Sibyls* which bent over the

the part of Heraclitus in the center of the stage, Bramante gives his face to Euclid, Zoroaster has the appearance of Pietro Bembo, near which the same Raphael is to be seen, and perhaps Sodom. In the scenes of *Parnassus* and of the *Virtues*, Raphael has brilliantly resolved the spatial problem of how to arrange figures around a void. In the *Parnassus*, he places groups of classical poets on the two sides of the mountain, one sacred to the Muses and the other to Apollo. In the lunettes of the *Virtues*, he places the three cardinal virtues. (*Justice*, considered by Plato to be superior to all the other virtues, according to a concept that would be taken up

entrance arch of Chigi Chapel in Santa Maria della Pace. With this decoration he confronted compositional problems similar to those he encountered in the execution of the *Parnassus*, and the curve of the arch became the ideal slope on which to arrange the sibyls and angels

in which God enters into a direct relationship with people, and are strongly linked thematically the episodes narrated on the walls. The *Burning bush*, in which God appears to Moses in the heart of a flame, corresponds to the *Expulsion of Heliodorus*, an episode taken from

in front of an imitation cloth. The reference to Michelangelo's Sistine ceiling is clear; from it he took the twisted movement of the bodies; in the same way, the rush and torsion of the prophet *Isaiah* in Sant'Agostino recall the posture of the *Delphic sibyl*.

If the theme of the first room of Julius' apartments was of a theological and philosophical character, in the second, the Stanza di Eliodoro, the story is told of examples of God's intervention in the history of mankind, with references to contemporary events also breaking in. On the vaulting cells of the ceiling four biblical episodes are portrayed. They exemplify the way

the Book of Maccabees: the sacrilegious act of Heliodorus, a minister of King Seleucus IV of Syria, sent to Jerusalem to confiscate the treasure of the Temple for the benefit of his kingdom, was cut short by the divine intervention of a "terrible horseman" and two youths who were "extraordinary in their strength, and exquisite in their splendor." One of them, with ample clothing puffed up by the wind, is taken from a Roman sarcophagus with a Dionysian procession. The biblical tale is brought up to date by the Julius' presence: he is seated on his sedan held by dignitaries. His theatrical appearance on the theme appears is a gloss to the biblical

story, a warning which states that God is always ready to punish anyone who dares to hinder the Church's path.

The reference is to the outcome of the events of 1511 and 1512. In 1511 the papacy had lost Bologna, and had seen the recrudescence of the old Gallican doctrine which was set out again by King Louis XII of France, who had called a synod in Tours. In 1512 the French had taken Brescia and occupied the whole of Romagna: Julius II then called the Lateran Council, pushed the French out of Church territories, and, so the story goes, was acclaimed in Rome "more than Caesar or any other Roman captain." Under the *Sacrifice of Isaac* is the fresco with the *Mass of Bolsena*: if the Bible story is an example of obedience and faith, the miraculous event which happened in 1263 in Bolsena was born of doubt. The protagonist was a priest, Pietro da Praga, who harbored doubts about transubstantiation. One day, while he was saying Mass in the church of Santa Cristina, the host dripped with blood, staining his corporal. Following the miracle, Pope Urban IV announced the solemn feast of Corpus Christi on August 11, 1264. The depiction of this episode in the history of the church (on which Pope Sixtus IV had written a treatise, *De sanguine Christi*) appears in the right-hand side of the fresco, together with the pope accompanied by cardinals and canons (a group attributed to Sebastiano del Piombo) and, in the foreground, the bearers of the gestatorial chair (attributed by some to Lorenzo Lotto). Perhaps it was intended to evoke the episode of September 7, 1506, when Julius had visited the cathedral in Orvieto where the corporal with the host of Bolsena is preserved, in order to propitiate his expedition to Bologna. Otherwise, the reference is to the council of 1512. *Jacob's dream*, considered a prefiguring of the foundation of the Church, is linked with the *Liberation of St. Peter*. In this extraordinary nocturnal scene, Raphael composed an extremely effective play of light, contrasting the divine light of the angel sent to free St. Peter and guide his escape, with the artificial light of the torches and with the natural light of the moon and the imminent dawn, which illuminates the scene when the guards discover the escape. References to Julius abound in this portrayal, too: his cardinal's title had been that of San Pietro in Vincoli (St. Peter in Chains), and the chains which held St. Peter in prison in Jerusalem are preserved in that very church. Furthermore, in 1511, experts in canon law had located in the liberation of St. Peter the first source for the affirmation of the legitimacy of papal authority. And perhaps the lunettes allude to the military events of June 1512, when pontifical territories were "liberated" from French

occupation. The link between the scene show-ing Noah and *The meeting of Attila and Leo the Great* recalls that God always saves the right-eous. This happened with Noah, and again when Attila's hordes had reached Europe and were only halted when faced with the Cross of Christ. In Raphael's vision Peter and Paul repel the sovereign, who has come like a demon from the Steppes of the orient. The encounter happened in 452, but on the banks of the Mincio river, not in the area of Rome bathed in sunset while a fire blazes up at Monte Mario. The change of scene symbolized a more current

meaning: the historic event is intended to allude to the definitive retreat of French troops from pontifical territories. The fresco was certainly dreamt up by Julius, but only completed after his death, and in fact the face of the pope resembles Leo X, depicted between two cardi-nals. The expression of the group entering on horseback was probably inspired by so-called "taking of possession" by the pope, the cere-mony with which the pontifical procession went to take possession of the basilicas of the city and in particular of San Giovanni in Laterano, the seat of the bishop of Rome.

Leo X, too, demanded scenes that evoked his papacy and his name in the Stanza dell'Incendio di Borgo, in which the only fresco which can be safely attributed to Raphael is indeed the one portraying the incident which occurred in 847, when the Borgo area, in the neighborhood of St. Peter's, caught fire, endan-gering the Vatican basilica with its ancient facade decorated with mosaics. Leo IV then appeared from the benedictory loggia and the flames abated. Raphael enriched the tale with classical references, whether architectural (the colonnade on the left recalls that of the Temple of Mars the Avenger and the one on the right the Temple of Saturn) or literary (Aeneas and Anchise), and with figures in theatrical attitudes which became models for generations of artists.

Raphael's role as hidden protagonist under Julius' papacy was therefore confirmed by Giovanni de' Medici, the son of Lorenzo il Magnifico, who reached the papal seat in 1513. He was a pope of profound culture, a biblio-phile and passionate about the arts, and was painted by Raphael around 1516 seated at a table, with a finely chiseled gold and silver bell, and a magnifying glass with which he consults a precious illuminated manuscript, identified by scholars as the Hamilton Bible. During his pon-tificate, the parable of Renaissance splendor reached its apogee, and his reign coincided with the last, prolific phase of Raphael's life. To him he entrusted the direction of the works in St. Peter's, the cartoons for the tapestries that had to be placed in the Sistine, the decoration of the Logge, and the safeguarding of the antique treasures of the city. The study and presentation of antiquity was at the base of much of his work. Pietro Bembo wrote on April 3, 1516 to Cardinal Bibbiena: "Navigiero, Bazzano, Messer Baldassar Castiglione, Raphael and I shall tomorrow go to see Tivoli again [...] We shall see the old and the new and whatever is beau-tiful in that area." In that very period, Raphael himself was overseeing the construction of the apartments of Cardinal Bibbiena, on the third floor of the Vatican Palace, above the Stanze. A cultivated, refined man, Pietro Dovizi decided

to provide his new house with a *stufetta*, a place entirely decorated in the antique style with a ceiling divided geometrically which recalled the stuccoed roof of Villa Adriana, and those painted in the Golden House. The Logge are witness to the careful study of antiquity as well. Although it was the work of a team of a dozen artists, the undertaking was carried out according to Raphael's invention: according to Vasari, Raphael "made the designs of the ornaments of the stucco and the stories depicted there, and similarly of the partitions." In the loggia of the second floor, on the vaulting cells of characteristic "pavilion" style appear the fifty-two episodes of the so-called "Bible of Raphael," ideally contrasted with the severity of the Sistine, with a grotesque decoration in an abbreviated, cursive style between arboreal festoons, puttini with vegetal extremities, candelabras, and human faces with leafy beards. It was a triumph of the imagination, like that which would appear in the decorations of Villa Madama.

Only the plan is attributed to Raphael in the fresco of the fable of Eros and Psyche in the Villa Farnesina, while the two imitation tapestries with the *Council of the gods* and the *Banquet of the gods*—placed between the ribs of arboreal architecture which would be inspired by the caraccesque inventions of the gallery of Palazzo Farnese—went to Giulio Romano and Giovan Francesco Penni, as did the vaulting cells and pendentives, while the festoons of flowers and fruit were by Giovanni da Udine. The cycle must have been completed by the end of 1517, as can be seen by a letter of January 1, 1518, in which Leonardo del Sellaio announces to Michelangelo the unveiling of the vault, which he called "a disgraceful thing for a maestro." The entire complex of the Villa Farnesina must have been finished in August 1519, when the marriage of Agostino Chigi was celebrated in the Sala delle prospettive, in the presence of Pope Leo X. This room can be considered the most complete example of illusionistic painting of the period, in which the interpenetration between internal and external is achieved through an imitation open gallery with views of Rome. This was a decoration that excited great approval and which gained for Peruzzi numerous commissions for secular cycles, from Villa Stati, and Casino Mattei sul Palatino, to Palazzo Massimo alle Colonne. The particular conception of Peruzzi, a master of conceiving organic structures in which architecture and painting are in dialogue, appears also in Cappella Ponzetti in Santa Maria della Pace, commissioned by a friend of Chigi, Ferdinando Ponzetti, archdeacon of Sorrento and then cardinal. Raphael's influence is evident in the fresco of the *Madonna with child, saints, and donors*, which repeats the pyramidal scheme and

the attitude and arrangement of the figures in the *Madonna del pesce*. He looked to the *Incendio al Borgo* when he planned the *Presentation of Mary at the temple*, in the same Santa Maria della Pace, commissioned by the Sienese Filippo Sergardi, the testamentary executor of Chigi, in which the principle event is relegated to the background, immersed in a jubilation of ancient and modern architecture.

Raphael's last work was the altarpiece with the *Transfiguration*, which would be displayed together with the artist's body—he died in April 1520—in the Pantheon. Giulio de' Medici, the future Pope Clement VII, commissioned the painting: in honor of his own surname he had requested two altarpieces on the figure of Jesus as healer to take to Narbonne in France, the city of which he was bishop. He had therefore commissioned a *Transfiguration* from Sanzio and a *Resurrection of Lazarus* from Sebastiano del Piombo, who was the only artist in Rome who had understood the innovative range of Michelangelo's language, and who in the space of a few years had achieved enormously profound intellectual growth, already visible in the *Pietà* of 1515, in which nocturnal drama appears impregnated with a meditation on

Ceiling of the Loggia of Psyche in the Villa Farnesina, decorated with the *Banquet of the Gods*, attributed to Giulio Romano. The painter's portrayal of the story of Psyche is taken from the *Golden Ass* by the Roman writer Apuleius. Giulio Romano's composition, taken from a cartoon by Raphael, consciously seeks to imitate the forms and textures of a tapestry.

Michelangelo at his most tormented. The double commission of Giulio de' Medici marks the moment of direct confrontation between the two paradigms of Roman painting in the first two decades of the sixteenth century. Sebastiano del Piombo was aware of this and, in 1517, he abandoned the frescos he was working on in the Cappella Borgherini in San Pietro in Montorio, based on Michelangelesque sketches (in which he tried, in the *Flagellation*, the technique of oil on the walls). He turned instead to the *Resurrection of Lazarus*. Michelangelo sent a series of sketches from Florence, where he had returned in 1516: they were promptly utilized by his Venetian friend.

Raphael did not delegate any of the work on this altarpiece and executed the painting without involving his pupils. The *Transfiguration* may be considered the "sum" of all his previous experiences, from the play of light between the image of Christ and the clouds which recall those of the *Madonna Sistina*, to the far-off landscape which echoes that of the *Vision of Ezechiel*. The twisted, contorted figures in the lower part clearly derive, however, from the work of Michelangelo. The image refers to the words of the Gospel of Matthew, when Jesus "shone like the sun and his clothes became dazzling white," but the artist divides the panel in two, inserting beneath the Transfiguration the episode of the healing of the demoniac, which follows the moment of the glory of Christ. Both works allude to events which were afflicting the Church in that period: in 1517 Luther nailed up his ninety-five theses and in 1520 Pope Leo X pronounced his excommunication. Cardinal Giulio de' Medici was one of Luther's most staunch opponents and his convictions are finely expressed in the two paintings. In the *Transfiguration* the insertion of the healing of the demoniac is carried out by Christ, because "the disciples had not been able to heal him" because of their lack of faith, but also because, Christ adds, "this spirit is only loosed with prayer and fasting": this was almost a riposte to Luther's theories which held that faith alone was necessary for salvation. What is more, in Sebastiano del Piombo's painting, the role of Mary as mediatrix is underlined (she kneels before Christ), as is the power of God's ministers to "loose" sins (a power which Luther contested) as Christ indicates in the phrase he pronounced on this occasion: "Leave him and let him go."

The Sala di Constantino, commissioned by Leo X in 1517, was left incomplete on Raphael's death: despite Sebastiano del Piombo's requests (supported by Michelangelo), the work was entrusted, as the Venetian painter wrote regretfully, to Raphael's "apprentices"; he had left cartoons and sketches. The decoration of the room was conceived as a tapestry-work, and was coordinated by Giulio Romano, who painted the main scenes—*The Vision of the Cross*, *The Battle of Ponte Milvio*, and *The Donation of Rome*. The latter, which Clement VII had wished, was a change from the plan agreed with Leo X, and was imposed for political reasons. In fact, they wished to justify the legitimacy of the pope's temporal power which

Detail of the *Victory of Constantine at the Milvian Bridge.* Raphael's composition for this painting by Giulio Romano from 1520–24 incorporates motifs from battle scenes on Roman sarcophaghi. Vatican Museums, Sala di Constantino.

Lorenzo Valla had cast into doubt. It is in *The Battle of Ponte Milvio* that Giulio achieved his ideal of an heroic, violent Roman spirit and created with the image of the two armies which go into battle the figurative prototype for the noble Mannerism of Salviati and Vasari that followed.

Giulio Romano is without doubt the most important figure among those who were trained in Raphael's studio; he had gone into it as an apprentice at the age of ten or twelve. Until 1520 he developed in the maestro's shadow, taking his place in the execution of the least testing parts of his work. How much Giulio moved away from the maestro is already evident in the painting of the *Madonna della gatta*, completed between 1522 and 1523; the monumentalism of Raphael's invention is frayed in marginal episodes, the everyday breaks into the

sacred sphere, such as the doves inserted into the perspective that leads to San Giuseppe and the cat which peeps out, "so natural it appeared to be alive," wrote Vasari. Equally in the *Pala Fugger* in Santa Maria dell'Anima the prosaic detail of the woman feeding chicks is added to the grandiosity of the group of saints and angels that surrounds the Madonna and child, theatrically arranged in front of a drape, and the elaborate architecture of the background. When the cycle of Vatican frescos was finished, in 1524, Giulio left for Mantua, to place himself at Federico Gonzaga's service.

Perin del Vaga had left Rome in 1522 as well, having completed the Sala dei Pontefici, a commission from Leo based on an astrological plan glorifying the Medici popes. He came back to the city in 1524, perhaps accompanied by

Rosso Fiorentino, and in the autumn of the same year Parmigianino arrived. Under the reign of Clement VII, a harmony of different languages emerged which came to be called the "Clementine style," thanks to the contemporaneous presence of these three artists in the city. That figurative culture was then formed, which gave an often sophisticated formal reading of events that had only just been experienced, but which avoided deeper meditations. They preferred the theatrical set-up and the wise narrative construction in Raphael's work, and avoided the interior commitment of Michelangelo, developing instead his formal model.

Perin del Vaga presented himself as Raphael's rightful heir, as he had previously been his pupil, but his work of these years—especially in Cappella Pucci in Trinità dei Monti—depicts a crowded, often superabundant, and excessively expressive version of the marvelous, theatrical groups of figures that Raphael laid out in the Vatican frescos.

It was Parmigianino who seemed in his natural disposition to be the heir to Raphael, given that, says Vasari, it appeared that Raphael's spirit had "passed into Francesco's body, in order to see that young man in rare art and gentle, gracious manners, as Raphael had been; and, what is more, feeling how much he committed himself to imitate him in everything, but especially in painting."

Rosso Fiorentino brought his spirited manner to Rome, a certain paroxysm in lengthening figures and making them nervous, sometimes marked by an exhausted sensualism. This is evident, not in the ruined frescos of Cappella Cesi in Santa Maria della Pace (1524)—"a worse work was never painted," according to Vasari—but in the *Dead Christ supported by Angels* in Boston. Here the reading of Michelangelo's nudes finds a languid and yet innovative interpretation.

A work of greater and more profound autonomy that was produced at this time is the altarpiece by Parmigianino of the *Madonna and child, St. John the Baptist and St. Jerome*, in which the most authoritative references are harmonized in a new language, sweetened by a reading of Correggio. The group of the Madonna and child of Raphalesque origin is flanked by the vigorous Baptist, placed and contorted in the style of Michelangelo. This was the work which Parmigianino was painting on May 6, 1527 when a group of lansquenets who were sacking Rome came into his house and, Vasari tells us, "saw him working; they were so amazed by his work that, like the gentlemen they must have been, they left him alone."

Artists in that year, 1527, were forced to leave the city: Baldassare Peruzzi returned to Siena, Rosso Fiorentino who, Vasari relates, "was

imprisoned by the Germans and very badly treated" went to Sansepulcro, Polidoro da Caravaggio to Naples, followed by Giovan Francesco Penni who died the following year, Giovanni da Udine and Parmigianino to Bologna. Sebastiano del Piombo went back to Venice, Perin del Vaga left the frescos of the Cappella del Crocifisso and Cappella della Pulci incomplete after several months of siege, and went to Genoa. Pope Clement VII was present at the desecration of the city and left for Orvieto in December 1527; when he returned to Rome, in the autumn of 1528, his

attention was turned especially to Florence, which had been returned to the Medici by Carlo V.

Sebastiano del Piombo returned in 1529: his portraits as well as his sacred subjects reflect the tragedy of these events and, later, a profound spiritual crisis which calls into question his commitment to the "reformed Catholicism" of Viterbo. His point of reference was still Michelangelo, who had been consulted in 1532 for the *Birth of the Virgin* in the Cappella Chigi in Santa Maria del Popolo, already commissioned in 1526, but which was still unfinished at his death in 1547 and completed by Salviati around 1554. It is an altarpiece in which there is both technical experimentation—it is of oil on blocks of peperino—and formal research of great importance. The door in the background is the fulcrum of the composition: there the

Sebastiano del Piombo, *Birth of the Virgin*, painted on oils for the Chigi Chapel and completed by Francesco Salviati after Sebastiano del Piombo's death. Santa Maria del Popolo.

Detail of Michelangelo's *Last Judgment* in the Sistine Chapel. The scene depicted here is that of St. Bartholomew displaying, as a sign of his martyrdom, his flayed skin, which bears a self-portrait of the artist. Vatican Museums, Sistine Chapel.

OPPOSITE:
Michelangelo's monumental *Last Judgment*, painted between 1536 and 1541 on the altar wall of the Sistine Chapel. The decision to execute this theme marks the final point in a cycle of images begun almost half a century earlier with the story of the Creation. Vatican Museums, Sistine Chapel.

FOLLOWING PAGES:
Detail from Michelangelo's *Last Judgment* showing an angel blowing a trumpet and the book of judgment, as well as a damned man, an impressive illustration of Michelangelo's combination of a monumental figurative style with heightened emotion. Vatican Museums, Sistine Chapel.

light, which passes figures of sculptural solidity in the foreground in metallic incidences, is blocked. The work is the prelude to Sebastiano's later conclusions, when his paintings became of a bare rigor and a formal abstraction, which would be the model favored for painting in the years of the Council of Trent.

The Renaissances of Paul III and Julius II

With the election of Paul III in 1534 the artistic life of the city started up again. In September of that year Michelangelo returned, called back to paint the *Last Judgment* in the Sistine Chapel. Several young Tuscan artists also arrived, including Salviati and Jacopino del Conte: they had learnt from Michelangelo's art, especially in the statuary of the Medici chapel, and also from Raphael's late decorations in Rome. In 1533–34 Francesco Salviati had finished the *Annunciation* for San Francesco di Ripa, in which a quotation from Michelangelo is evident in the statuary outline and the drapery of the angel. In 1536 Jacopino del Conte began the decoration of the oratatory of San Giovanni decollato, which he would continue with the help of Salviati, in a cycle which illustrated the *Life of John the Baptist and Christ.* Jacopino's *Announcement to Zachariah* (1536) combines a reference to the last works of Raphael with an echo of one of Michelangelo's nudes, while Salviati's *Visitation* seems to reflect the influence of Perin del Vaga, from whom he derives a nervous look.

Perin del Vaga returned to Rome at the end of 1537 or the beginning of 1538, and would be the author of the general programme of *restauratio urbis*, which Paul III and the Roman nobles were pursuing, with the aim of reconstructing the artistic situation that had been destroyed by the Sack of 1527. His studio was therefore charged with the most important projects, creating decorations in which frescos and stuccos tell the stories of Roman epic poetry and tales from classical antiquity, such as the friezes in Palazzo Massimo and the Sala Regia in the Vatican Palace, begun in 1540. Perin del Vaga directed this with Antonio da Sangallo, with a decorative plan intended to reaffirm (amid reformist theses) the legitimacy of the continuity between imperial Rome and Christian Rome, the seat of the papacy. He was also responsible for the decorations in the Farnesian apartments in Castel Sant'Angelo (begun in 1543 and continued up to his death, in 1547), where he painted frescos of the *Stories of Alexander the Great and St. Paul* in the Sala Paolina, intended

to exalt the most important aspects of Paul III's pontificate, and the frieze in the Sala di Psiche, where the story is told in a gentle way, enriched with an antiquarian repertoire reminiscent of the research carried out by Polidoro da Caravaggio, visible on the facades of noble Roman houses. The presence of Pellegrino Tibaldi has been traced in the work at Castel Sant'Angelo: he was perhaps already present for the work in the Sala Regia, where a more expressive, deforming style is evident in the *Family of Darius before Alexander.* It was he, together with Jacopino del Conte, Siciolante and others who completed the Cappella di San Remigio in San Liugi dei Francesi, commissioned by Perino in March 1547.

Michelangelo's *Last Judgement* was unveiled on October 31, 1541. It is a pictorial text in which the drama of the formal solutions explains the most agonizing interior conflict of the artist between the hope of salvation and the anguish of sin, an epic of resurrection and justice in which the statuary and incomparable perfection of the sacred group—an adolescent Madonna and a Christ of Apollonian but terrible beauty—is contrasted with the faint, dreamy gestures of the elect and with the ranting rebellion of the damned. The terse luminosity of the celestial space, deprived of perspective scansion, is contrasted with the indefinite obscurity of the earth split apart by the rise of the resurrected and the fall of the damned. There is a new greatness, which was transformed by contemporaries into a repertoire of pictorial excerpts, of human figures, thus exorcising the *terribilità* of the whole. The two scenes with the *Conversion of St. Paul* and the *Crucifixion of St. Peter* in the Cappella Paolina, frescos started in 1542 and finished in 1550, were also little understood. From then on Michelangelo would paint no more, shutting himself off in an irrevocable renunciation.

While Michelangelo was working in the Cappella Paolina, Titian arrived in Rome. His was a presence that would seem not to leave a trace in figurative Roman culture. The Venetian artist saw himself taken on by Cardinal Alessandro Farnese, the nephew of Paul III, solely in the hope of gaining a canonry for his son Pomponio. In September 1544, the scholar Giovanni della Casa, apostolic nuncio in Venice, wrote to the cardinal that the artist, in order to obtain the benefice, was ready to leave and paint the whole Farnese family, "cats included." In October 1545 Titian was in the city, and was staying in the Palazzo del Belvedere. Michelangelo, accompanied by Vasari, visited him there. Vasari later reported Michelangelo's comment on the *Danae* that had been painted for Alessandro Farnese: "he more or less

praised it, saying that he greatly liked the color and style, but that it was a pity that in Venice people did not learn how to draw well from the beginning and that there were not better painters in the studio."

Despite Michelangelo's criticisms, the cardinal also commissioned a portrait of himself from Titian. The artist therefore started work on the portrait of Paul III. A masterpiece of psychological introspection, the picture illustrates the personality of the pope and the climate of intrigue in the curia. Paul avoided being depicted with his son Pier Luigi, for reasons of decency, preferring instead to surround himself with the

Francesco Salviati, *Annunciation*. In this work from 1534 the Florentine artist combined elements of Michelangelo's work with lessons he had learned from studying Raphael. San Francesco a Ripa.

less embarrassing presence of his nephews. The triple portrait, which is painted only with three colors—white, red, and black—is a manifesto of the nepotistic system and a political programme: in fact, Paul had himself represented with Ottavio, who was the heir to the duchy of Parma and Piacenza, and Alessandro, a candidate for succession to the papal seat. Ottavio, who was of a prudent temperament, which he always demonstrated with great political cunning, is portrayed in a reverential bow; Cardinal Alessandro indicates his ambition with a gesture of his hand, decisively placed on the papal seat which he would like to occupy one day; Paul is

Michelangelo's *Conversion of Saul*, painted 1542–45 representing a stylistic link to his *Last Judgment*. The drama is caused by the explosive movement radiating out from the fallen figure of Saul in the foreground, contrasted with a similar group gathered around the descending Christ. Vatican Museums, Cappella Paolina.

represented in his physical decline, bent over and gaunt, but resolutely continuing to flaunt his power and that of his family, gripping the armrest and displaying the papal ring. It is an extraordinary study of "the profit of affections" and even that unfinished right hand of the pope seems to indicate something: Titian's availability was not matched by an equal generosity on the part of the Farnese family, because, in June 1546, the painter left Rome for Venice without having first obtained the desired benefice; and it turned out that the paintings were never actually paid for.

The modestly priced work of Vasari (who was only thirty-five years old) was more attractive to the miserly Farnese family. This was in fact one of the reasons which convinced Alessandro Farnese to entrust to him the complex decoration of the Sala del cento giorni in the Cancelleria. The learned Paolo Giovo was the

intermediary: in a letter to the cardinal he described Vasari as "an energetic, expeditious, pugnacious and determined painter", that is quick and therefore cheap. Vasari had already in 1543 painted for the cardinal *The allegory of Justice* today in Capodimonte, a work full of conceits which was the prelude to the complex composition realized in only "100 days" in 1546, to the plan of Paolo Giovio in agreement with Alessandro Farnese, who had the habit of following artists' work closely. The cycle is accompanied by explanatory captions, and exalts Paul's pontificate, equating his actions with those of the ancient emperors that are represented in the busts, in a parallelism between past and present in which papal authority is underlined through a mixture of chronicle and allegory. The jumble of learned references and allegories also corresponds to an eclectic mixture of artistic suggestions: in fact, Vasari retrieved the most famous inventions of the maestri, referring to Michelangelo and the Medici tombs or to Raphael in the Stanze, in a continual play of quotations.

Daniele da Volterra came from Perin del Vaga's studio, and collaborated with him on the decorations of Palazzo Massimo with the frieze of the *Stories of Fabio Massimo*. In those years, it was only he who fully understood the problematic of Michelangelo's frescos which were a jumping-off point for strongly abstract, autonomous solutions. A new rigor, that was stripped of decorative ornaments, enlivened his compositions, in which strong luminarist scansions and divisions of light follow and define the geometric grids. He would be one of the most prolific artists of Rome in the 1540s, a period during which he worked on the frescos in the Cappella del Crocifisso in San Marcello (1540–43) which had been left unfinished by Perino; on the *Deposition* in Trinità dei Monti, originally begun in 1541, in which the magniloquence of the Mannerist decorations is confined to a few gestures of the mourners and is calmed in a rigorous compositional essentiality which can be found in frescos such as *Stories of the Virgin* in the same church (1548–55). In 1548 he was in charge of decorating a room in Palazzo Farnese in fresco and stucco, a frieze based on models from Fontainebleau, noted for incisions, and the prototype for the later decorations by Mazzoni.

The latter was considered the most authoritative of Michelangelo's followers, and it was he who in 1565 covered certain parts of the *Last Judgment* which were considered obscene and repainted the figures of St. Biagio and St. Catherine. Michelangelo himself did not live to see this vandalism: the decision to alter the *Last Judgment* was taken in January 1564 and on

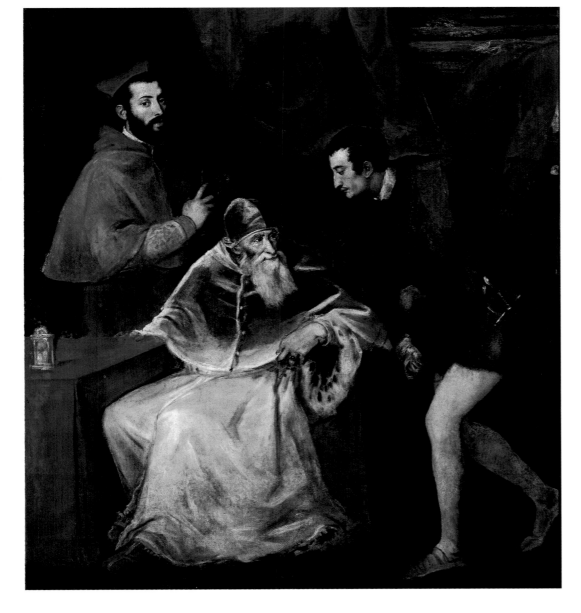

Giovanni Siciolante da Sermoneta, *Baptism of Clovis*. This fresco (1548–49) is clearly derived from the frescos by Raphael's pupils in the Sala di Costantino in the Vatican Palace. San Luigi dei Francesi.

Francesco Zuccari's *Capture of Tunis* from the Sala Regia. The dominant theme is the defense of faith by the monarchy.

Ceiling of the loggia in Villa Madama, influenced by the grotesques from the rediscovered Golden House. The figurative scenes originate from Ovid's *Metamorphoses*.

Detail from Francesco Salviati's fresco in the Salone d'Udienza or dei Mappamondi in Palazzo Ricci-Sacchetti.

February 18 of the same year the artist died in his house near the Forum of Trajan.

Paul died in 1550, without managing to inaugurate the jubilee: Pope Julius III succeeded him. In the few years of his papacy (he died in 1555) he was the protagonist of a Renaissance revival which favored the Raphaelesque style of the Logge vaticane. In 1550 he commissioned the altar piece and decoration of the Cappella Del Monte in San Pietro in Montorio, entrusted to Vasari and Ammannati. (Vasari, on the subject of his altar piece with *St. Paul blinded taken before Ananias* would say that "it did not entirely satisfy me, even if it was not unpleasing to others, and in particular to Michelangelo"). He also commissioned the construction of Villa Giulia, a project which he followed with great attention, to the point—says Vasari, who created several works for the villa—of neglecting his papal duties. He was continually taken by "new whims which had to be put underway [...] and that which he liked in the morning was worth nothing by the evening." The decoration began in 1553, under the direction of the Bolognese Prospero Fontana, who had worked with Perin del Vaga in Genoa and on the building of Castel Sant'Angelo, recalled by Malvasia for the speed which which it was completed: "It was more a work of craft than learning [...] speed was preferred to diligence, and it was so determined and hurried, that in a few days work was finished that would have taken years to complete by anyone else." Fontana organized a decorative scheme centered on allegorical images: allegories of the seasons and the liberal arts, Bacchanalia and views of the seven hills of Rome gladdened the rooms of this villa which must have competed with the the magnificence of Villa Madama. Still under his direction, decorations which were more typically commemorative of the Del Monte family were prepared between 1553 and 1555 in the first-floor loggia as well as the grand-duke's room in Palazzo Firenze, the residence of Balduino Del Monte. Here, allegorical images of myth and Roman history allude to the name of the patron and the power of his family.

A further decoration in a nostalgic, Renaissance style produced in these same years was that of the palace of Cardinal Girolamo Capodiferro, a friend of Julius, who entrusted the work to Giulio Mazzoni from Piacenza. Oil paintings on the wall, and stuccos, statues, and friezes, cycles dedicated to the elements, to the seasons, to tales from Ovid, and to Roman history, all fill the residence with lively, fantastic images, in a decorative richness that was borrowed from Fontainebleau.

Painting in the Counter-Reformation

In the middle of the century, figurative Roman language on one hand recovered its pretty story-telling tendencies of the beginning of the century, and on the other became austere when it had to communicate devotional messages. The more rigorous atmosphere is reflected in the late work of Jacopino del Conte and Salviati, who came back to Rome in 1548. In 1550, Salviati brought to a close the decoration of the cappella dei marchesi di Brandeburgo in Santa Maria dell'Anima (which had been started in about 1540) with the *Deposition*, in which Michelangelism is reduced to external constructions, monumentality, and quotations. In the same year he came back to paint in the oratory of San Giovanni decollato, realizing in 1551 *The birth of John the Baptist*, in which the figures taken from ancient reliefs have slow, restrained gestures and the chromatic range is reduced to dark tones, in a choice which takes account of the final works of Sebastiano del Piombo. In 1553–54 the frescos with *Stories of David* were completed in the saloon of Palazzo Ricci in Via Giulia (today Via Sacchetti), in which an extraordinary decorative richness is expanded through reproduced pictures, imitation tapestries and reliefs where either dreamy, faint images appear, or images in dark tones. The *Sala dei fasti farnesiani* was complex. Here the merits of the members of the Farnese family are exalted, as are Paul III's qualities as peacemaker. A few elements of the Farnese cycle are to be found in the *Stories of the Virgin* depicted in the Cappella Grifoni in San Marcello.

Marco Pino, Siciolante, and Livio Agresti also came from Peri's studios. The Sienese Marco Pino, who was brought up in Beccafiumine, had already in 1545 created the *Visitation* for Santo Spirito in Sassia. In the works that followed he would present an exasperated figuration, where Michelangelo's serpentine figure is exhausted in extended pyrimidal "enflamed" compostions, as in the *Resurrection* of the oratorio del Golfalone (1569–70) and the *Pietà* in Cappella Mattei in Santa Maria in Aracoeli.

Girolamo Siciolante da Sermoneta, who during a stay in Emilia in the 1540s had absorbed Venetian influences and the Raphaelesque lesson of *St. Cecilia* in Bologna, alternated works of marked formal preciosity (as is the case in the *Baptism of Clovis* in the Cappella Duprè in San Luigi dei Francesi) with episodes in which a strongly archeologizing tendency emerged (in the Sala Regia) or an exasperated monumentalism *Nativity of the Virgin* in the Cappella Fuggerin Santa Maria dell'Anima). His works,

which can be dated to the 1570s, demonstrate a solemn, stately composure, from the *Crucifixion* of Cappella Massimo in San Giovanni in Laterano (1573) to the *Transfiguration* of Santa Maria dell'Aracoeli (1573–5). Livio Agresti's paintings also show a recovery of the models of the early sixteenth century applied to communication of decorous devotion: in the *Pala Pellucchi* of Santa Maria della Consolazione he manages to borrow contorted anatomies from Michelangelo and models for Madonnas from Raphael.

Starting from Perin's references, Taddeo Zuccari managed to formulate a personal language. He was already present at work in Villa Giulia, where he adapted the the expressive ease of the whole decorative plan. In the cycle of the *Stories of the Passion* in Cappella Mattei

Girolamo Muziano, *Angels Appearing to Joseph*. This work illustrates the stylistic heritage of Muziano, who was from Brescia, a center of art influenced by Venice. His interpretation of the theme is an important record of the pietism which spread through Roman art from the mid-sixteenth century. Santa Caterina della Rota.

in Santa Maria della Consolazione, completed in 1556, he experimented with a language full of variables, a repertoire nevertheless up to date and thoughtful, in which several elements converge: the movement of Salviati's compositions, Michelangelism filtered through Sebastiano del Piombo and Daniele da Volterra, and a sensitivity to landscape perhaps due to Muziano's presence in Rome. The greatest stylistic unity is in the *Stories of St. Paul* in the Cappella Frangipane in San Marcello, begun in 1558–59 but never finished, where he achieved a dignified equilibrium that would become dominant and marked in the decorations of the 1560s, from the *Stories of the Virgin* in Santa Maria dell'Orto to the *Presa di Tunisi* in the Sala Regia (circa 1564) and the great decorative undertaking of Palazzo Farnese a Caprarola, where he directed the works from 1560 onwards.

In the 1560s and 1570s the devotional language of the church of the Counter-Reformation was asserted, especially in the oratories of confraternities; the last great episodes of secular decoration occurred; and the language of Flemish painting began to spread. Northern, Lombard, and Venetian influences were imported by the Brescain Girolamo Muziano (who reached Rome about 1549), who introduced Rome to an entirely northern sensitivity to landscape, making a protagonist of the landscape background in which he placed figures which reveal reflection on Michelangelo and Raphael filtered through the Venetian masters, especially Sebastiano del Piombo. (This is the case in *The apparition of the angel to Joseph* in Santa Caterina della Rota.) The influence of Taddeo Zuccari, of the clear hand, prevailed to block Venetian disintegration of color, as is clear in the *Prophets* of the Cappella Gabrielli in Santa Maria sopra Minerva, while northern elements reemerge in the *Pietà* of the Cappella Ruitz in Santa Caterina dei Funari (1562–63).

The work of Giovanni de Vecchi is visionary and mysticizing at times; after 1573 he decorated the Cappella Capranica in Santa Maria sopra Minerva with the cycle of the *Stories of St. Catherine of Siena*. The artist had reached Rome in 1558 with Santi di Tito, with whom he worked in the Belvedere vaticano on the *Stories of Nebuchadnezzar*, and in the early 1560s he was involved in the work directed by Taddeo Zuccari in Caprarola. He became autonomous and unprejudiced in *The adoration of the shepherds* in Sant'Eligio degli Orefici (circa 1575), where he does not scorn the anticlassicism of Flemish perspectives, with incongruities of dimensions. He achieved a fantastic language with the *Stories of St. Jerome* in Santa Maria all'Aracoeli: the lyrical sentiment and visionary nature of El Greco (with whom he had contact

Giovanni de Vecchi, *Adoration of the Shepherds*. The emotional values of this fresco altarpiece show the influence of the Council of Trent's rulings on the late Mannerists in Rome. Sant'Eligio degli Orefici.

Detail of the Passion cycle in the Oratorio del Gonfalone. The scene of Christ collapsing under the weight of the cross is framed by Salamonic columns which recall those in Old St. Peter's.

The frescos in the Oratorio del Gonfalone are one of the most important examples of Mannerist painting in Rome. The Passion of Christ cycle was painted between 1568 and 1575 by a group of artists that included Federico Zuccari. Raffaellino da Reggio, Cesare Nebbia, Marco Pino, and Jacopo Bertoja.

in 1570–72) make the figures both transparent and dazzling.

The decorative complex which interpreted the demands of the counter-reformation Church the most was that of the oratorio del Gonafalone, the seat of a confraternity which, as well as carrying out works of welfare, organized a famous miracle play, that of the passion, death, and resurrection of Christ, which was shown in the Colosseum. Paul banned it in 1539, because the spectators' emotional involvement was excessive, to the point that they lynched those who played Christ's executioners. The cycle was begun in early 1568 and commissioned for the jubilee in 1575. Different artists worked on it, coordinated by Jacopo Bertoja, who probably planned the whole decoration, centered on twelve scenes of the Passion of Christ framed by spiral columns and overlooked by figures of Prophets and Sibyls. Bertoja painted the scene of *The entrance of Christ into Jerusalem* in 1569 and a panel with *Prophets and Sibyls* in 1572. The only dated fresco is the notable *Flagellation* by Federico Zuccari, of 1573, judged by Baglione to be "excellently expressed." It was conceived as a scene from

theater, as if it were an episode of the miracle play organized by the confraternity.

This was an important period for grand decoration, as Giorgio Vasari returned. He was working on the chapels of the Torre Pia. Other important factors were the representations of the *Battle of Lepanto* and of the *Sacred league* in the Sala Regia: these were stories conceived with magniloquence and epic grandiosity. Vasari brought Jacopo Zucci with him; the latter went into the service of Cardinal Ferdinando de' Medici in 1572, and was entrusted with the decoration of his Roman residences. Zucchi had already, in 1575, concluded the decoration of the piano nobile of Palazzo Firenze, then a Medici property, with two rooms that saw the return of elaborate schemes based on allegory and mythology. In the Sala degli Elementi and the Sala delle Stagioni Zucchi extended a repertoire of precious images derived from learned mythological texts, polished and minutely detailed, bizarre and heaped up, but suggestive and emblematic of the influence of the Flemish Giovanni Stradano, who worked in Vasari's studio, as well as of his contacts with Spranger and Martin de Vos. This was a cultured repertoire

and a grandiose manner of conceiving the decorations which Zucchi also displayed in the "sitting room" of Villa Medici, after 1576, and then, in 1588, in the vault of Palazzo Rucellai (now Ruspoli), the climax of secular Roman decoration of the end of the century. Decorative opulence was mitigated by the demands of the destination of the works carried out about 1575 in San Silvestro al Quirinale, where Zucchi achieved a more mature control, illuminated, however, by chromatic affectation, and a range of acid colors full of metallic reflections.

In San Silvestro Zucchi found himself in contact with the other great personality of those years, Raffaellino da Reggio. Trained in Lelio Orsi's studios, Raffaellino had perhaps already come to Rome in the 1570s to work under Muziano's direction in a chapel in the palazzo di Montegiorrdano. The Cappella di San Silvestro was built in Santi Quattro Coronati in about 1570 and the election of the Bolognese Pope, Gregory XIII, in 1572 facilitated Raffaellino's entry into projects in the Vatican Palace, which were now approaching the finishing straight. He was present in the Sala Regia in 1572–73 and then in the Sala Ducale and the Gregory's *logge* (1575–77). He worked with Federico Zuccari on the frescos of the presbytery of Santa Caterina de' Funari with a fascia of putti and saints, and in 1573 he was in the Gonfalone, where he created *Christ before Caiaphas.* He was brought in to the important project perhaps by Zuccari, or by Bertoja, who had already involved him in the work at Caprarola. He did not live to finish his last work, the frescos on the ceiling and pillars of San Silvestro al Quirinale. (He died in 1578.) The altar-piece was entrusted to Venusti and the side walls to Zucchi: the result was a fragmentary decoration, but an important document which brought together in one place the most extreme and refined points of Mannerism in Rome, which by now was drawing to a close.

"To delight, to teach and to move": these were the aims of sacred painting according to Paleotti as he explained in his *Discorso intorno alle immagini sacre e profane* of 1582. These dictates were respected by painters in the 1580s, who took up an easy, cursive, involving, and communicative language already formulated in the oratorio del Crocefisso, which was placed under Alessandro Farnese's protection and painted between 1578 and 1583. The decoration was entrusted to Giovanni de Vecchi, who was given the task by Girolamo Muziano and the scholar Tommaso Cavalieri. The project consists of six scenes that are separated by plaster strips, a feature which allows a less spaced out reading compared to that of the oratorio del Gonfalone, which is easier and more continuous.

The painter dampened the visionary tone of his images, which are transparent even if shot through with burning colorism in *St. Helen commands the search for the true cross*. Already in *The finding of the cross* he reached a greater composure, which was confirmed by a fresco he painted many years later, *The stigmate of San Francesco* in San Pietro in Montorio, of about 1594. De Vecchi took his place in 1582, because he was so slow, and four other painters also got involved: Niccolò Circignani and Cesare Nebbia painted the wall frescos, Baldassare Croce and Cristoforo Roncalli those on the *contrafacciata*. Circignani already demonstrated his simple, conventional language, which was in full accord with the Church's directives in *The proof of the true cross*. In the same year, 1582, Circignani completed the *Martyrology*, thirty-two frescos in Santo Stefano Rotondo with scenes of martyrdom, following the plan created by the Jesuit Michele Laurentano. His images certainly "move" but few of them "delight", because the emphasis is on a detailed exposition of the torments suffered, with a clearness rendered even more unequivocal by the presence of explanatory captions, which are supposed to aid meditation. After these undertakings, Circagnani was to carry out many other works. He was favored by the most rigorous patrons, for whom he decorated, among other things, the Cappella della Sacra Famiglia in il Gesù (1585–87) and the *Celestial glory* in Santa Pudenzia (1587).

Cesare Nebbia, a pupil of Muziano, was responsible for the last painting in the oratorio del Crocifisso, the dignified procession of *Heraclius carrying the cross back to Jerusalem* (1584). He was to be the hero of the Sistine era, together with Giovanni Guerra from Modena. Pope Sixtus V was elected in 1585 and the five years of his pontificate were marked by a great number of commissions, aimed at extolling historic places of worship. The need to complete works quickly was satisfied by the Nebbia–Guerra team; they managed important projects in which diverse cultural components were diluted in a common idiom that was comprehensible and captivating; according to Baglioni, "Giovanni invented the subjects of the stories [...] and Cesare drew them." Of the two artists, Giovanni Guerra was the more refined, mainly in tune with the products of international Mannerism, and capable of proposing noble, complex solutions, as his frescos of 1590 in Palazzo Cenci demonstrate. In 1589 the frescos of the Scala Santa and the Sistine library were finished, and in 1593 those in the nave of Santa Maria Maggiore (which were commissioned by Cardinal Domenico Pinelli). The frescos in the Sistine library are more accurate and noble than the decorations in sacred places intended to aid public devotions. They were aimed at a cultured, restricted audience, with a cycle dedicated to the exaltation both of culture transmitted by means of the libraries of the past and of the role of the Church.

Weighty phenomena were occurring apart from Sistine projects; the panel of *The visitation* reached Rome in 1586, commissioned by Francesco Pozzomiglio in 1582 and destined for Santa Maria in Vallicella. It was a new, intense work, in which sentiments are evoked very suggestively, empathically but of a high tone: St. Philip Neri became "rapt in sweetest ecstasy" before this picture.

Federico Zuccari was not involved in Sistine projects: he was one of the most cultured artists in Rome, the user of a complex language, in which Venetian and Florentine influences are grafted onto Roman Mannerism. He was restless and intellectually curious after his stay in Florence, when he decorated the cupola of the duomo, and went to England and Spain, from where he returned in 1588. The Cappella degli Angeli in il Gesù, begun in 1594, is characterized by an elegant style, a subtle graphic line, and an archaic and cerebral compostion. The Cappella di San Giacinto in Santa Sabina, of 1600, is an interlocutory decoration, with a severe, limpid language, where quotations from fifteenth-century Florentine painting are inserted. His ideal of the intellectual artist led him to refound, in 1593, the Accademia di San Luca and to rationalize the internal processes of artistic creation in a treatise, *The idea of painters, sculptors, and architects*, published in 1607.

Scipione Pulzone's project was similar. He was only a virtuoso in portrait-painting, but achieved an absolutely individual expression in sacred painting, a "timeless" art in which diverse references are mixed with a personal tendency towards abstraction, especially after he had met Giuseppe Valeriano, the Jesuit painter. The results of this union are visible in the Cappella della Madonna in the Strada al Gesù, seven panels on the life of Mary, and in the Cappella della Passione, which followed, and which was planned by Valeriano but continued and completed after his death by Gaspare Celio, an artist of a more lyrical, visionary style. The decoration was crowned by Pulzone's *Sorrow for the dead Christ*, which has a strong emotional force. It is now in New York.

Projects of the end of the century

In the last decade of the century a general leaning towards renewal was apparent, and new needs and new projects were developing. The most clamorous novelties were put forward in the

sphere of perspective painting, in a new conception of landscape painting, a diverse orientation of great decoration, and a new enquiry into light.

Perspective painting emptied decoration of jumbles of people and objects in order to achieve a very effective rigor. Tommaso Laureti, from Palermo, had already conceived an image stripped of actions and people, inhabitated only by a fallen idol, a crucifix, and a symbolic architecture, namely the *Triumph of the Resurrection* of the ceiling of the Sala di Costantino (1586). Baldassare Croce's project was also centered on space; in the stories on the walls (1598–1600) of Santa Susanna he articulated the narration with new plays of perspective. And Giovanni and Cherubino Alberti studied new solutions to the demand for unity between architectural space and pictorial space. These were already visible of the old sacristy (1592) and the Sala Clementina (about 1600) in San Giovanni in Laterano: the ceiling divided into panels is substituted by a single vision, of great suggestiveness and involvement, which is the prelude to the amazing conclusion of the Baroque.

The wholly northern sensibility of Muziano to the landscape as protagonist of the picture was diffused at this turn of the century by Paul Brill, who had worked with Muziano on the ceiling of the Galleria delle carte geografiche. Brill achieved idyllic expressions in his decorations of the corridor of the Cappella di Santa Cecilia (1599–1600) in the church of the same name, carried out under the patronage of Cardinal Emilio Sfondrato.

Another tendency was expressed by the Cavalier d'Arpino, who would have a central role under Clement VIII's pontificate. Instead of Mannerist multiplicities he preferred the demands of symmetry and order, applied by rediscovering a reading of Raphael and returning to light, sunny painting: his influence is clear in the loggia del Pio Sodalizio dei Piceni (1594–95) which he painted under the direction of Corradine Orsini, on the theme of victorious love, and even more so in the sonorous *Ascension* of the Lateran transept (1600). This had a blinding clarity that would have a decisive influence on Guido Reni.

Researches into light are evident in the painting by Cigoli of *St. Jerome writing the Vulgate* in San Giovanni dei Fiorentini, in which the saint is absorbed in an enveloping twilight, and in the works of Cristoforo Roncalli, who would be numbered among the "friends" of Caravaggio. In Roncalli's works the contrast between the figure in the light and the background in shade is the dominating force.

The two artists who would put forward new and revolutionary ideas were already in Rome during this decade. They were Annibale Caracci

and Caravaggio. Annibale Caracci was called to Rome in 1595 by Cardinal Odoardo Farnese to decorate various spaces in Palazzo Farnese and in 1596 completed *The coronation of the Virgin* for Villa Aldobrandini, in which a Raphaelesque suggestion is still present. He painted a single-figure panel in about 1599, *St. Margaret* for Santa Caterina dei Funari. There would be a

Fresco by Giuseppe Cesari, known as Il Cavalier d'Arpino (1560–1640), depicting the battle between the Horatii and the Curatii, an event from the Roman age of kings. Palazzo dei Conservatori, Capitoline Museums.

direct comparison with Caravaggio's conclusions in 1601, in Cappella Cerasi in Santa Maria del Popolo.

Caravaggio arrived at the end of 1592, after an apprenticeship in Milan in Simone Peterzano's studio. He quickly entered the Cavalier d'Arpino's studio, where, Bellori recounts, he was "taken away from figures" and "set to paint-ing flowers and fruit," or rather that still life in the style of the Flemish masters, which was in vogue among Roman collectors. Among these was Cardinal Del Monte, who, Bellori contin-ues, "very much liked paintings and raised up Michelangelo giving him an honored place in his house with his gentlemen." Among the first works of these years are *Boy with a basket of*

Caravaggio, *The Fortune-Teller*. Painted at the beginning of Caravaggio's Roman period, this picture belongs to a group of images created for private patrons. The half-portraits generally deal with secular themes which hint at the realism of his later work. At the same time, however, these genre scenes are ambiguous, which is yet another feature of Caravaggio's work. Capitoline Museums, Pinacoteca.

fruit of the Borghese, *Bacchino malato*, and *Bacchus* in the Uffizi: they are works in which the use of a "living model" is clear. In the *Good fortune* of the Capitolina, the protagonists are expertly placed on a neutral background and play, with eloquent glances and gestures, the traditional parts of the presumptuous innocent and the cunning deceiver. Here, that study of light and color which would later characterize the Lombard painter, can already be seen. Although the palette is still light, a strip of shade stretches along the background and the masterly illumination makes the solid masses of the characters emerge very clearly. The same compositional expertise is visible in *Rest during the flight to Egypt* (1595–96), in which the most dominant feature is the mute dialogue of ges-

tures and glances between the divine musician and the very human Joseph, who holds a musical score with the transcription of a motet by the Franco-Flemish composer Noêl Balduin.

The wall oil painting of *Jove, Neptune, and Pluto* must be of after 1597. It was in the casino of Cardinal Del Monte, and in it, despite the smallness of the room, Caravaggio displays a great virtuosity in foreshortened views. Bellori tells us that the artist "felt disapproved of because of his lack of plans or perspective, so he helped himself by placing characters seen from top to bottom which he wanted to contrast with the most difficult views." The subject of the work was chosen in relation to its setting, that "little room of metals" in which numerous little bronzes were collected and which perhaps

Caravaggio, *Boy with a Basket of Fruit.* Together with depictions of fruit bowls and the *Boy Bitten by a Lizard*, this picture from 1592 belongs to a group of half-portraits of youths. These depictions of boys dressed in antique drapery secured Caravaggio the attention of Cardinal Francesco del Monte, who was to become his most important patron. Galleria Borghese.

served as a study for Cardinal Del Monte, who was passionate about alchemy and medicine. On the ceiling of this room Caravaggio therefore depicted an allegory of the passage of materials from solid to gas, symbolizing them by the divinities which preside over the earth (Pluto), the sea (Neptune), and the air (Jove). A semitransparent globe stands out in the center of the composition: it represents the universe in which the eternal process of transmutation occurs, in the same way as it was represented in treatises on alchemy.

Caravaggio's point of arrival at the end of the century was the Cappella Contarelli, acquired in 1565 by Cardinal Mathieu Cointrel, grand datary of Pope Gregory XIII. The commission for the decoration was first given to Girolamo Muziano,

but the latter had not even begun the work almost twenty years later. After Contarelli's death (in 1585) the work was entrusted to the Cavalier d'Arpino in May 1591. He only brought the ceiling fresco to completion. The testamentary executors, also pressed by the clergy of the church, passed the job to the young Merisi in July 1599, perhaps at the suggestion of Cardinal Del Monte, a prominent exponent of the pro-French faction in the curia.

The iconographic plan was fixed in 1565 by the same Contarelli: on the left of the altar the *Calling of St. Matthew* was supposed to appear, while the *Martyrdom of St. Matthew* was planned on the right. The scene of the *Calling* is set around the table of the tax-collector Levi d'Alfeo, intent on counting money—it is in this

FOLLOWING PAGES:
Details from Caravaggio's *Boy with a Basket of Fruit*, showing the realism of Caravaggio's work, executed with extraordinary technical brilliance, a skill he owed to his experience as a painter of flowers and still-lifes with Giuseppe Cesari at the very beginning of his time in Rome. Galleria Borghese.

moment that he is noted by Christ as he passes by accompanied by his disciples. Christ's entry on the scene is accompanied by a flood of light which pierces the darkness of this magisterial interior, an evident allusion to the "illumination" of the sinner touched by grace, and underlines the protagonists' gestures, caught up as they are in a mute dialogue of extraordinary expressive

Hirtacus. Everyone has been driven away from the two, a terrified altarboy flees, shouting, while the others look on surprised or contemplating the sacrifice that is about to take place in a melancholy manner, in a daring play of light which makes faces and bodies, gestures, cries, and silences stand out from the background. However, the most extraordinary invention is

Caravaggio, *Jupiter, Neptune, and Pluto,* the only work Caravaggio did in oil on plaster. The choice of subject matter for this work from 1597 came from the interest of his patron, Cardinal del Monte, in alchemy. Casino Ludovisi.

force. Matthew seems to respond to Jesus' outstretched hand, pointing to himself as if to ask for confirmation. This confirmation comes from Peter, the representative of God's will on earth, who repeats Christ's gesture. X-ray examinations have demonstrated that the figure of Peter did not appear in the first version and was added later, perhaps to underline the importance of the first pope in a period still troubled by the wars of religion.

The *Martyrdom of St. Matthew* was originally set among ancient architecture, with the weighty figure of a soldier seen from the shoulders up placed in the center of the composition, the fulcrum and hinge of the action. The artist was not satisfied with the result and completed the *Martyrdom of St. Matthew* before coming back to the scene of the martyrdom, changing it completely. The saint is portrayed in the center of the composition, at the feet of an altar, and thrown to the ground by the fury of his executioner, the soldier sent by the Ethiopian king

that rush to the bottom of the angel, hovering on the edge of a cloud, who is intent on slipping the palm of martyrdom into Matthew's hand. It is a fully "Baroque," theatrical painting, which would become very famous. In July 1600 the canvases were in place: their linguistic innovation was not immediately grasped, if what Baglione tells us is true. He records that when the principal of the Accademia di San Luca, Federico Zuccari, came to visit the church where people were flocking to see Caravaggio's work, he exclaimed maliciously: "'What is all this? And looking at it all carefully, he added, 'I don't see what all the fuss is about,' […] and grinning sarcastically, and marveling at all the noise, he turned on his heel, and went on his way."

Gioia Mori

Detail of Caravaggio, *Jupiter, Neptune, and Pluto* showing the extremely low angle from which the figures are viewed. Casino Ludovisi.

The Rome of the Saints: the Baroque

The New Architectural Face of the City

Paul V's coat of arms from a seventeenth-century engraving. Rome,

Urban VIII's coat of arms, taken from the same work. Rome, Vatican Library.

Rome and the Baroque

As with all complex phenomena, pinpointing the beginning and origins of the phenomenon known as Baroque is difficult, if not impossible. Art historians and critics have been attempting to do this since the end of the nineteenth century—Wölfflin proposed 1580—and are still trying today—Briganti proposes 1630. It goes without saying, however, that the value of such dating is relatively limited.

Harnold Hauser rightly stressed the impossibility of speaking of any kind of stylistic unity for Baroque, which was an international artistic movement. He pointed out that "the papacy had in mind a form of art that was essentially different from that found at court in Versailles. Whatever these two may have had in common would certainly not fit with the ambitions of bourgeois Calvinist Holland."

The definition itself, and the historical place of the phenomenon of Baroque, have sparked heated debate. Written off by Benedetto Croce as an expression of poor taste, Baroque had a poor reputation early on, thanks to the biting pen of Francesco Milizia, one of the foremost advocates of neoclassicism. On the other hand, Eugenio's *Del Barocco* (The Baroque), published in 1945, asserted that Baroque encapsulates the life force of that part of the human spirit which explodes into exuberant fantasy. Giulio Carlo Argan saw Baroque as the foundation of modern civilization, by which he meant the civilization of images. However, they all agree on one aspect: the central role of Rome in creating the language of Baroque. To quote Hauser again:

"By now Rome did not just play the splendid role of papal residence but was the capital of the Roman Catholic world... For the city a period was beginning in which its artistic production was to be the richest, the most luxurious, the most extravagant... The heraldic bees of the Barberini family were to be found everywhere in Baroque Rome, in the same way as the Napoleonic eagle would dominate imperial Paris. Nor were the Barberini unusual among the leading families of Rome. As well as the Barberini—and the equally celebrated Farnese and Borghese families—the Ludovisi, Pamphili, Chigi, and Rospigliosi families were all among the most active patrons of their day."

Architecture before Maderno: A Period of Transition

In the first decade of the seventeenth century, the expression of architecture and town planning in Rome was still using the language of Sixtus V. This alternated between slavishly copying Michelangelo's work (the most obvious example is the Lateran Palace by Domenico Fontana, a reworking of Palazzo Farnese) and opting for a contained vertical scansion of the facade, as in San Girolamo degli Schiavoni by Martino Longhi the Elder, close to the Tiber landing stage of Ripetta.

Giacomo della Porta was one of the dominant players in this milieu. Working with Girolamo Rainaldi (who completed the commission in 1605 after della Porta's death in 1602), della Porta changed Michelangelo's original design for the facade of Palazzo Senatorio on the Capitoline Hill and completed the project. Della Porta had earlier left his mark on Santa Maria Maggiore when he gave Flaminio Ponzio, architect of the Vatican Palace, an assignment to add a chapel on the left of the building, identical to the chapel Sixtus V had commissioned from Domenico Fontana. Ponzio subsequently changed the exterior of the right of the church, building a new sacristy on to the entrance. Work on this lasted from 1605 to 1611.

To use a modern concept, the publicity message of the city's transformation was—as Rainaldi comments—spelled out by Gunter in 1618 in his *Disegno nuovo di Roma moderna* (A New Map of Modern Rome). Though not systematic, the *disegno* explicitly compared works commissioned by Paul V (1605–28) and

494

villa, which was originally commissioned by Cardinal Scipione Caffarelli Borghese and constructed between 1613 and 1615. Its conception is still strongly influenced by the typical U-shaped Renaissance villa, the best-known example of which is the Villa Farnesina. The Casino, almost completely refurbished by Antonio Asprucci in the neoclassical period, has been restored to its original splendor.

The exterior was originally decorated with an exuberant carved motif, most of which is unfortunately lost. Devised by Giovanni Vasanzio, this was one of the innovations in seventeenth-century taste. Vasanzio (Jan van Santen), who was of Flemish origin, belonged to the same generation as Flaminio Ponzio and Carlo Maderno, and worked closely with them. All three were often employed on the same commissions, from Villa Borghese, designed by Ponzio, to the construction of Palazzo Pallavicini-Rospigliosi, commissioned by Scipione Borghese and built between 1611 and 1616. Here Vasanzio

Matthäus Gunter, A New Map of Modern Rome (Disegno nuovo di Roma moderna). This publication appeared in 1618 and served as propaganda to underpin the projects of Paul V by comparing the construction work undertaken during his pontificate with that of his predecessors.

The Acqua Paola, built for Paul V between 1610 and 1612 by Flaminio Ponzio, assisted by Giovanni Fontana. Erected on the Glanicolo, its architecture is clearly influenced by the Acqua Felice built for Sixtus V. It was modified in 1690 by Carlo Fontana for Alexander VII.

those completed under Sixtus V. Gunter framed the map with two symmetrical vertical lists of work done by the two popes. Thus the Quirinal gardens, redesigned under Paul V, are depicted opposite a view of the Vatican Belvedere on the left, to make a pair. Again, a drawing of the Fontana Paola, built between 1610 and 1612 by Ponzio with the assistance of Giovanni Fontana (and altered by Carlo Fontana in 1690), is set alongside a drawing of the Acqua Felice, its inspiration. Similarly, at the bottom of the plan, a melange of Sixtus' achievements—the plans for St. Peter's, the interior of San Giovanni in Laterano, the building housing the Scala Santa, the plan of the city itself—is offset, in a somewhat haphazard fashion, by the Palazzo Borghese (1605–13), whose distinctive harpsichord ground plan was designed by Ponzio.

The architectural parallels in Gunter's plan open with the connection between the so-called Colonna Paolina (Paul's column), the fluted cipollino column from the basilica of Constantine erected in the piazza in front of Santa Maria Maggiore, and the obelisks that Fontana erected in Rome for Sixtus V. The Colonna Paolina, erected in 1614 on a plinth celebrating the architectural prowess of Paul V, echoes the obelisk which Sixtus had placed in front of the apse of Santa Maria Maggiore. The importance Gunter's plan attaches to this amounts to a declaration of Paul V's aesthetics.

Aristocratic buildings also reveal sixteenth-century influence in their construction. An example is the Casino Rospigliosi, or garden

The Borghese Chapel (Cappella Paolina) in Santa Maria Maggiore, built from designs by Flaminio Ponzio between 1605 and 1611. It was intended as a counterpart to the Sistine Chapel on the other side of the church but was to exceed even that chapel in the sumptuousness of its materials. The decoration focuses on a venerated image of the Virgin in the center of the chapel attributed to St. Luke.

The dome of the Borghese Chapel with Cigoli's depiction of Paradise. The other frescos were painted by leading artists such as Guido Reni, Lanfranco, Giovanni Baglione, and the Cavalier d'Arpino. Their themes are the virtues of the Virgin and the worship of cult images, both central aspects of the Catholic Reformation.

worked on the nymphaeum and the garden fountains, while Maderno designed the summer villa (built by Vasanzio), also known as the Casino Aurora owing to Guido Reni's famous fresco of Aurora on the salon ceiling.

Flaminio Ponzio oversaw work commissioned by Paul V for the papal palace at the Quirinal between 1605 and 1609, when the long wing (*manica lunga*, or long arm) was added. Parallel to the wing overlooking the piazza, the new wing extended toward the garden situated on the side of the courtyard. Ponzio did little more than adapt the model, already used by Domenico Fontana, of a covered gallery topped by a series of windows, each corresponding to an arch. The differences lay firstly in the construction of an imposing four-flight staircase and landing at the south end of the gallery, and secondly in the raised central belvedere, with seven windows, which dominates the low structure of the new wing. Ponzio was not therefore proposing a new architectural vocabulary but rather was basing his work on late Mannerist ideas.

It is possible, however, to detect the beginning of a change in the Borghese Chapel (Cappella Paolina) in Santa Maria Maggiore. This is confirmed by the favorable comparison with Sixtus V's chapel (the Sistine Chapel) in the same church. The few yards dividing them takes the visitor from what is still a sixteenth-century space to one which already possesses elements of what was to become the Baroque.

Although both constructions are built on a central plan, based on almost identical Greek crosses, they reveal how the new architectural trends were about to depart from tradition. On the one hand, the elaborate canopy built in 1590 by Bartolomeo Torrigiani exalts the circularity of the interior of the Sistine Chapel by providing it with a concrete and significant center. On the other hand, the canopy installed by Ponzio emphasizes the longitudinal axis and thereby reduces the sense of centrality exclusively to the graphic elements that dominate the polished marble floor.

On the exterior, the short arm of the cruciform plan, which in Fontana's building sticks out unimaginatively at right angles, is hidden in Ponzio's scheme behind a wall, brought to life by a trapezoidal shape which joins it harmoniously to the main body of the basilica. By dividing the exterior wall finish into three broad areas, Ponzio was able to adapt the new building to fit the architectural patterns used by Michelangelo on the exterior of the apse of St. Peter's, due to a series of paired pilaster strips and niches reminiscent of Bramante.

Carlo Maderno and the Origins of Baroque

In seeking the dividing line between Mannerism and Baroque, one need look no further than the facade of Santa Susanna, designed by Carlo Maderno (1556–1629), from Lombardy. The commission came from Cardinal Rusticucci, for whom Maderno had already worked. The facade, completed in 1603, gave the architectural language of the early years of the seventeenth century a chance to catch up on the ground it had lost to painting—this was the era of Caravaggio and Annibale Carracci's majestic Galleria in Palazzo Farnese.

To understand the novelty of Maderno's first major commission—indeed his masterpiece—one need only compare Santa Susanna with the facade of Santa Maria in Vallicella, completed in 1605 by Fausto Rughesi, who was given the commission after winning a design competition. Rughesi's work is little more than a plodding imitation of Giacomo della Porta's facade for the Gesù. The only significant changes Rughesi made are the use of paired columns flanking the main entrance (instead of a series of pilaster strip-columns) and a slight extension of the volutes. Because of the way the series of pilaster strips runs, this in turn gives the corner a different appearance. The static overall impression, however, is only slightly relieved by a barely discernable chiaroscuro effect.

Maderno's work, on the other hand, is virtually sculpture. Even though his initial reference was also to della Porta, the interpretation he came up with rests on a progressive and dynamic swelling in volume as one moves toward the middle. Maderno's facade is less open than Rughesi's, though it too is divided into three by two wings and a central section, which houses the door and the balcony.

However, the Santa Susanna facade stands out for its strongly plastic quality, derived from Maderno's use of engaged columns in the lower register. These not only serve della

Porta's purpose of emphasizing the opening at the central door, but are also used to replace the pilaster strips, which are relegated to mere angular uprights. The scansion becomes tighter toward the middle. In the upper register, however, pilaster strips take center stage once more. The scansion of the surfaces remains fluid thanks to the unyielding rhythm that they impose. The final touch is a balustrade, reminiscent of Michelangelo, connecting the triangular tympanum to the heavens.

Carlo Maderno's efforts were at an end but were not in vain, since that year, 1603, he was appointed architect of St. Peter's. It was not long, however, before this honor turned sour. Maderno

Santa Maria in Vallicella (the Chiesa Nuova), built between 1594 and 1605 by Fausto Rughesi. The aedicules of the frontage are clearly derived from Giacomo della Porta's facade for the Gesù.

The Casino dell'Aurora in the Palazzo Rospigliosi, designed by Carlo Maderno, Flaminio Ponzio, and Giovanni Vasanzio, and built by Paul V for his nephew, Cardinal Scipione Borghese. The Casino takes its name from the ceiling fresco of Aurora in the hall by Guido Reni, painted in 1615.

FOLLOWING PAGES:
The monumental facade of St. Peter's was built from designs by Carlo Maderno. Of the two towers Maderno intended as a visual frame for the dome, only one was begun, on the left of the building. Engineering problems meant that this element had to be removed under the direction of Bernini. Maderno's design was altered at the start of the nineteenth century when two clock aedicules were added by Giuseppe Valadier.

497

Aerial view showing the ensemble of St. Peter's basilica and the square directly in front of it. The square for this greatest of all basilicas is framed by an imposing colonnade built for Alexander VII in 1667 from designs by Bernini. This masterpiece of Baroque theatricality was partly influenced by antique models and immortalizes the church triumphant through its opulent statuary of 140 figures of saints.

was given the task of modifying Michelangelo's design for St. Peter's. By 1595 it had become obvious that Michelangelo's design was not large enough for the services that the principal church of Christendom had to accommodate. In 1607 a competition was held which attracted numerous architects. It was won by Maderno.

Maderno's decision to alter Michelangelo's design unleashed bitter argument. His plans were opposed by Rughesi, Maggi, and even Maffeo Barberini, the future Urban VIII. The work commissioned by Paul V extended St. Peter's to a length of nearly 600 feet, enough to meet the requirements of the liturgy and to accommodate a huge number of worshippers. However, Michelangelo's architectural concept, centered on the idea of a dome dominating the entire body of the church, was completely sacrificed.

Criticism of Maderno continued for centuries. The subsequent layout of the area around St. Peter's, initially with Bernini's colonnade, and centuries later with Via della Conciliazione, all aimed at making up for his supposed mistake. In reality, however, Maderno had nothing to answer for. From the moment it became clear that the extension made it necessary to considerably lengthen the west arm of the original Greek cross, it was inevitable that the dome would lose its central role and become a mere background feature.

However, even Paul V soon realized that things were not going quite right. The facade was completed in 1612, and he immediately instructed Maderno to add a further two inter-columniations at each end to support two new towers. These were to create an optical illusion, bringing the dome forward and creating a perspective with the smaller domes of the Gregorian and Clementine Chapels. The effect Paul desired can be seen in an etching Greuter made in 1613 of Maderno's design. However, the towers were never built and even Bernini's later attempt in that direction was to come to a sorry end.

Palazzo Barberini: Bernini and Borromini's Early Work

Maderno's claim to fame rests not only on the fact that he radically altered the architectural language of the seventeenth century. In addition to this, he spotted and nurtured the two greatest talents of the age, Bernini and Borromini, who made their debut in the refurbishment of Palazzo Barberini.

Maderno was no newcomer to this type of job. He had already worked on a number of aristocratic palaces, starting with that of the Mattei di Giove family, where he had to repair and extend the original building, right through to Palazzo Borghese. In 1625 he was given the task of extending and modernizing Palazzo Sforza, recently bought by Cardinal Francesco Barberini the Elder. Little did he think this would be his last job. Due to the rate at which Rome was expanding under Sixtus' plans, the Grimani family vineyard was now right in the middle of the city's street grid, with the Via Sistina running straight through it. This meant that the site of the future Palazzo Barberini was no longer on the edge of the city but right in the heart of it. Nevertheless, the type of architecture that Maderno envisaged for the new papal family's palace was that of a rural villa, based on the typical U-layout (later it would be turned into an H-layout).

This choice was strengthened by the fact that the new Barberini palace could not run straight beside the main street laid out by Sixtus V. It was not therefore possible to design a block-shaped building along the lines of the Palazzo Farnese. It was, however, perfectly justifiable to use the space in the manner pioneered by Perruzi in the Villa Farnesina, a style which had recently been taken up again by Vasanzio in Villa Borghese.

Maderno made full use of the experience he had gained on the palazzo of Asdrubale Mattei (1598–1618), generally considered the first Baroque palazzo in Rome. Its outstanding feature was a courtyard which had no loggias around its sides. Palazzo Barberini similarly has no courtyards on its four sides (unlike Palazzo Borghese, for instance) but opens directly on to the garden by way of a three-tiered facade that features arches and windows which are reminiscent of Villa Mondragone in Frascati, designed by Martino Longhi and Vasanzio.

Maderno even made the windows of the uppermost tier, as Wittkower explained. This is proved by the fact that the windows compare favorably to the arch at the foot of the steps of Palazzo Mattei, which itself echoes the way the courtyard is connected to the atrium in Palazzo Farnese.

What is certain, however, is that not only did Bernini end up making the windows, but that they appealed enormously to the young sculptor, who later used the same design in his monument to Countess Matilda of Tuscany in St.

Stairs by Francesco Borromini for the right wing of Palazzo Barberini. Built in 1634, it is an elegant Baroque expression of a spiral staircase built on an oval groundplan, a type of structure first used by Bernini and Vignola.

Coat of arms of the Barberini on the facade of Palazzo Barberini which faces the Via delle Quattro Fontane. The palace was built from 1628 for Taddeo Barberini, nephew of Urban VII. The history of this residence involved all the leading Roman architects of the day—Carlo Maderno, Gian Lorenzo Bernini, and Francesco Borromini.

Portrait of Urban VIII by Gian Lorenzo Bernini from about 1625. During Urban VIII's long pontificate, from 1623 to 1644, the face of Rome was dramatically altered.

Peter's. Their attraction for Bernini lay in the way they "mystified" the light from outside with the light within, thus transforming a structural requirement of the interior space into a feature.

Gian Lorenzo Bernini

Son of Pietro Bernini, a skilled Tuscan sculptor who worked on Santa Maria Maggiore in Rome, Gian Lorenzo Bernini was born in Naples on December 7, 1598. In terms of architecture, he and Borromini are the two leaders of Italian Baroque. Along with Pietro da Cortona, they formed a strong triumvirate in seventeenth-century Rome.

Bernini—architect, sculptor, painter, and theater designer—started out working alongside his father, but his professional career was molded by Carlo Maderno. Bernini took over from Maderno as architect on Palazzo Barberini and continued working there, assisted by Borromini, until 1632. It was he who built the side that runs along Via Barberini, the stairs, the antechambers, the great salon, and the broken bridge—a fake ruin constructed out of fragments of ancient buildings. As Franco Borsi commented, it is an excellent indicator of the new trend in taste, which aimed at astonishing and mystifying in order to gain recognition.

The young Bernini's first architectural commission was the restoration of the dilapidated church of Santa Bibiana. This he did between 1624 and 1626, installing an original facade which is memorable for its three-arch lower order, a true portico divided by Ionic columns, and an upper order which highlights the plastic power of the central loggia, terminating in a triangular tympanum. On the side are two bays that are crowned by a balustrade. The affected ways of the beginner and the reassuring link to the language of Roman Mannerism (Fontana's Scala Santa, for example) are still obvious, so much so that it hardly seems possible that this can be the work of the same sculptor, who in 1624 devised the Baldacchino for St. Peter's.

The enlargement of the cruciform St. Peter's, so determinedly pursued by Urban VIII, led Bernini—who became architect to St. Peter's in 1629—to win the commission to decorate the four pillars into which Urban wanted to set, like precious jewels, the relics of the sudarium of Veronica, the lance of Longinus (presented to Innocent VIII by Sultan Baiazet II at the end of the fifteenth century), the head of St. Andrew, and the largest fragment of the True Cross which, according to legend, had been found in Palestine by St. Helena, mother of Constantine.

"Living" sculpture at the bottom, at the top the pillars become architectural, with tabernacles formed from spiral "Salamonic" columns, which were believed to have come from the Temple in Jerusalem and to have been brought to Rome by Constantine.

Urban VIII and the Walls of Rome

The long rule of the Barberini pope, Urban VIII (1623–44), marked Rome profoundly, not least because of the numerous architectural projects he undertook, all recorded by Domenico Castelli. The epicenter of activity in Rome under Urban was the renewal at Castel Sant'Angelo. Urban gave Marcantonio de Rossi (1607–66) the task of renovating the fortifications, between 1626 and 1628.

Urban's interest in fortifications is one of the distinguishing features of his rule. He also gave De Rossi the task of erecting the impressive bastions on the Gianicolo. The pope's intention seemed to have been to build a new wall round the city, a smaller circuit than the late antique Aurelian Walls. In the end, the ambitious project resulted in walls only in the southwest corner of the city—Trastevere, Porta San Pancrazio (destroyed in 1849), and Porta Portese—all built by De Rossi.

The military feel of architecture in Rome became a characteristic feature even of the Quirinal Palace, papal residence from Clement

502

VIII (1592–1605) to Pius IX (1846–78). The piazza in front of the palace was developed to celebrate a jubilee year. But the introduction on the left of the piazza of a large rampart shoring up the facade of the palazzo (possibly by Bernini, who in 1635 built the balcony from which blessings were given) is doubtless connected to Urban's interest in military architecture. The architectural solution used here is one of the most impressive and enthralling of the seventeenth century.

A further commission connected to the Pamphili family—though received during the reign of Alexander VII—was the church of Sant'Andrea al Quirinale, considered by Bernini as his masterpiece. Work began in 1658, at the same time as that on the churches of the Assumption in Ariccia and San Tommaso da Villanova in Castel Gandolfo, both south of Rome. However, Sant'Andrea was not completed until 1670.

Its oval plan with the entrance on the longer side revived an idea already used by the archi-

Quirinal Palace, with the benediction loggia above the main entrance. The building was designed by Bernini for Urban VIII. The structure seen today is the result of successive alterations carried out by a number of popes from the end of the sixteenth century. Originally a papal summer residence, it was the home of the kings of Italy from 1870 to 1944. Since the end of the Second World War this extensive complex has been the residence of the Italian president.

Sant'Andrea al Quirinale

The low point of Bernini's career was in 1641, when the bell tower he was building on the facade of St. Peter's collapsed. As a result, he was sidelined by the new pope, Innocent X (1644–55), although this did not compromise his career as papal architect. Between 1645 and 1648 he was occupied with decorating the pillars in the nave of St. Peter's, inventing a motif of cherubs holding a shield containing a portrait of the pope. The effect was completed by another pair of cherubs displaying keys and a tiara (alluding to the papacy) or a book and a sword (alluding to St. Paul). At the bottom are the Pamphili doves, not just a heraldic emblem but also representing the Holy Ghost.

tect of the tiny church in Palazzo Propaganda Fide, who was later replaced by Borromini. Bernini applied the experience he had acquired in building family chapels, but on a much grander scale. The facade has curved lines with two low concave wings which counterpoint the turgid convex bulbous center, with Ionic columns. This is an allusion to the open tabernacle. Inside the church the curved lines are used once more for the altar, where the trabeation is topped by a split tympanum (recalling that on the bulbous entrance, which houses the statue of St. Andrew ascending heavenward on a cloud).

The interior, rich in polychrome marble, is encircled by a continuous trabeation, giving unity to a space throbbing with contrasts between the hollow chapels and the solid walls, decorated with pilaster strips. The ribbed and vaulted dome is inspired by the Pantheon and its gilt stucco swags repeat the motif Bernini used in Ariccia.

Pietro da Cortona and the Baroque Facade

Right in the middle of the city street network, in a corner that was choked by the coaches of

Sant'Andrea al Quirinale, built between 1658 and 1670 as the church of a Jesuit Novitiate founded in 1566. Its patron was Camillo Pamphili, nephew of Innocent X. Bernini's unusual architectural design, in which the shorter side of the building became the ceremonial axis, was the result of the restricted building space offered by the oval groundplan.

lawyers and magistrates working in the nearby courts, the fifteenth-century church of Santa Maria della Pace was a nightmare for town planners. The problem was eventually resolved by Alexander VII and Pietro Berrettini—better known as Pietro da Cortona—who created the present piazza in order to allow traffic to circulate more freely.

The changes they made in this part of town meant that the facade of the church had to be completely rebuilt. To accomplish this, Pietro da Cortona drew on his theatrical experience. Wittkower remarked that "the church looks like a stage, its piazza the auditorium, while the surrounding houses are the boxes." Pietro pushed

the architectural solutions he had already experimented with elsewhere to their limit. The upper register of the facade is directly inspired by the facade of Santi Luca e Martina, which Pietro built between 1635 and 1650.

The church of Santi Luca e Martina, on the edge of the archaeological area of the Forum, had previously been dedicated only to St. Luke, patron saint of the Accademia di San Luca, the artists' guild. It was totally refurbished and rededicated to include St. Martina, after her body was found during the excavations that Pietro da Cortona organized in the crypt as part of the construction of his own tomb. It had been the idea of Cardinal Francesco Barberini, patron of the Accademia, but was also funded by Pietro, who had recently been appointed head of the Academmia.

Another major innovation is found in the facade of Santi Luca e Martina. Here Pietro da Cortona confirmed the extraordinary architectural sensitivity apparent in his early work, such as the Villa del Pigneto (now destroyed), built for the Sacchetti family (1626–36), which mixed hints of the Vatican Belvedere, the Villa Aldobrandini, as well as the Temple of Fortune at Praeneste. The facade looks outwards with measured convexity, held in by the rigidity of the side piers, decorated with pilaster strips which block the forward thrust of the building and give rise to a surface seemingly as taut as a sail in the wind and broken only by the pilaster strips. The way in which the upper part perfectly matches the lower creates an organic unity which ironically foreshadows the powerful concavities of the inner apses. In this fashion, the facade is no longer a rigid barrier that separates the interior space from the space outside the building, but is rather a diaphragm based on the model of bringing opposing forces into harmony.

At Santa Maria della Pace this "magic" is repeated in the upper register, though using the lesser architectural elements available. These, however, are unified by the wide triangular tympanum binding it all together. At the bottom, the thrust cannot be contained and the bulbous center inflects in a circular fashion toward the outside, almost as if it is trying to take the piazza over by becoming a stage. The outward thrust is balanced by the church's two concave wings, which link the facade into the space in the piazza, while at the same time underlining the contrast between them.

By the time he designed the facade of Santa Maria in Via Lata, built between 1658 and 1662, Pietro da Cortona had refined his architectural vocabulary and reduced it to its essential components. Santa Maria in Via Lata is his definitive work. What takes center stage here is the way he

that the window hollows (which have no tympanum and are as tall as the drum itself) alternate with the full buttresses with their pillars and columns linked by a continuous trabeation. Above this, what in San Luca were conches in the curve of the cornice are here replaced by small ovoid windows set into a cornice that divides the stories, interrupted by a triangular tympanum. And thus it goes on with variations on the theme of Michelangelo's dome for St. Peter's.

Facade of Santa Maria in Via Lata by Pietro da Cortona, completed in 1662. The balanced proportions achieved between the two horizontal levels is determined by a similiarly harmonious group of complete columns bracketed into a single central bay.

Santi Luca e Martina, the church of the Accademia di San Luca, to which all Rome's artists belonged. Pietro da Cortona's important architectural achievement, is notable for its curvature, recessed central section, and sculptural effects which result from the interplay between pilasters and columns.

channels all the sculptural qualities of Santa Maria della Pace into one plane covered in columns.

The spatial problem that Pietro had to solve here was quite different, since the church did not overlook a piazza but stood on what is now Via del Corso. This means that the best view of the church is provided by a series of prospects running straight on from each other. This did not allow room for major alterations to the proportions of the facade. For this reason, the sculptural quality of the facade of Santa Maria in Via Lata is derived from the relationship between hollow and full spaces created by the presence of columns. Thus the upper register features a highly personal interpretation of the Serlian motif spread over twinned columns and setting up the importance of the triangular tympanum. On the other hand, in the lower register, the sides of the church recede slightly, just where the center is hollowed out of the volume of the facade. Inside the portico, the columns on the outside are repeated mirror-fashion, framing the main entrance in a transversal space which is terminated on either side by two small apses linked by a barrel vault. In this building, Pietro da Cortona brought together all the experience acquired from working on Santa Maria della Pace and Santi Luca e Martina.

The dome of Santi Ambrogio e Carlo in Via del Corso was destined to be Pietro's last project. Begun in 1668, it was completed only in 1672, three years after his death. Its evolution can be traced directly from Santi Luca e Martina. While its language is more peaceful, it lacks none of the earlier vigor. The drum stands out for the way

Alexander VII: The Town Planner

Amplificator urbis (the improver of Rome) was the term that Fabio Chigi, later Alexander VII (1655–67), used to describe himself. He dreamed of a Rome as splendid as ancient Rome, but built according to the style and taste of his own day. Alexander chose his papal name in memory of Alexander III (1159–81), a member of the Bandinelli family, since both popes were from Siena. Alexander III had proved a fierce opponent for Frederick Barbarossa, a theme felt appropriate for Chigi's time, rife with tensions between France and Spain. However, the choice of Alexander also suggested the pope's pride, in a thinly veiled allusion to Alexander the Great.

Richard Krautheimer's careful and exhaustive analysis of Alexander VII's papacy demonstrates that the pope was a town planner and a worthy heir to his great predecessor Sixtus V, to whom indeed Alexander looked for his criteria and aims. Alexander concentrated on the old street network, albeit with far less room to maneuver than Sixtus had enjoyed.

Rome's traffic problems had grown worse because of the ever more widespread use of carriages drawn by four, six, or sometimes even eight horses, replacing the traditional sedan chairs and other means of transport (such as traveling on horseback), which took up less space. One of Alexander's main concerns was therefore to try to eliminate anything that stuck out awkwardly into the street. It was with this in mind that he decided to demolish the ancient Arco di Portogallo, which dated from the age of Hadrian. For seventeenth-century Romans, however, the arch was simply a bottleneck which reduced the width of Via del Corso by half (the roadway here narrowed from thirty feet wide to just over sixteen) and snarled up the traffic. All that remains of the Arco di Portogallo today is a plaque commemorating where it once stood. All this was part of a much broader scheme. As Krautheimer remarked:

"Creating this type of perspective view down a long straight line was one of the main criteria which underlay Alexander VII's alterations to the street network. The only streets and piazzas that Alexander opened up and adorned with commemorative inscriptions were those used by high-ranking people who had come to visit Rome and have an audience with the Pope. The streets involved therefore led mainly toward the Quirinal Palace. They included Via della Dataria, which ran in from Via del Corso and the Trevi Fountain area, the streets giving access from Piazza Venezia through Piazza Santi Apostoli (where the Chigi family lived) and Piazza Magnanapoli, and, finally, the extension of Via del Babuino as far as the Quirinal…

Other areas affected by Alexander's plans were the main streets and piazzas on the way into the city center: Piazza del Popolo, the entire length of Via del Corso as far as the Gesù and, from there on across the Ponte Sant'Angelo to the Vatican Palace, Alexander's official residence, and the basilica built on the site of St. Peter's tomb.

There are even a number of street alterations that initially seem irrelevant but acquire new meaning in the context of a scheme which aimed at meeting the needs of important visitors to Rome. For instance, the road from Piazza Venezia and Piazza San Marco toward the Marcel de' Corvi district was widened, since the road continued towards the Forum and was thus used by every important visitor to the city. Similarly, in Trastevere the short Via di Santa Dorotea, running into Via della Lungara, was modified and widened in the summer of 1658, when it is possible that Queen Christina of Sweden was already negotiating a lease on Palazzo Riario-Corsini on Via della Lungara…

Clearly, none of this detracts from the fact that most of the building and town planning work that was executed by Alexander in the twelve years of his papacy was aimed above all at establishing his personal status and exalting his own family."

Via del Corso and the Trident

Alexander's building and town-planning activity affected every corner of the city. However, the area where it was concentrated was along and around the Corso, starting with the new layout of Piazza del Popolo.

The idea behind Bernini's redesign of the internal facade of Porta Flaminia (the gate from the north on to Piazza del Popolo) was as a welcome to Queen Christina of Sweden, newly converted to Roman Catholicism, who arrived in Rome in December 1655. Above the central support arch a plaque was installed with an inscription welcoming the queen. Although the inclusion of the date made this a message specifically for Christina, in reality it was intended for all visitors coming to the city.

If Alexander's intention had originally been to add a few such touches, the idea of completely rethinking the layout of the whole area soon took over. The street pattern that was known as the Trident was made up of three long straight streets: Via Lata (now Via del Corso) in the middle, with Via Paolina (now Via del Babuino) on the left, and Via Ripetta on the right. All three of these led into Piazza del Popolo, providing ideal material from which to shape an architectural theatrical set through which visitors and pilgrims would enter the heart of the city.

The two churches at the center of this project were commissioned from Carlo Rainaldi, who began work in 1661. Rainaldi's plans, however, were altered and held up by both Bernini and Carlo Fontana, who repeatedly interfered, nearly always to simplify the mature Baroque of the original. However, Rainaldi is deservedly credited with the success of this venture, as is demonstrated by the foundation plaque, which is dated 1662.

It is well known that Rainaldi was faced with a virtually insurmountable problem, which he overcame and resolved by what it is no exaggeration to describe as a stroke of genius. In order for the theatrical set to work, it was essential that the two churches be absolutely symmetrical. However, this was difficult because the sites on which they were to be constructed were neither the same shape nor size. Thus, even if Rainaldi had lined the two churches up exactly, they would still have looked unequal. The solution that he came up with was to use an elliptical design for the church on the smaller site. He then set the building as far back as he could, so that the smallest diameter of ellipse corresponded in width to that of the other building, which was circular in plan. This way, the two churches became "twins" and perfectly symmetrical.

The church of Santa Maria in Montesanto (that with the elliptical plan, tucked between Via del Babuino and the Corso) was already under construction by 1662. It was not finished, however, until 1675 when the other, Santa Maria de' Miracoli, got underway and was in turn completed in 1679. In Alexander VII's vision for the city plan, the street popularly known as the Corso (literally, the running track), where horseraces were held, was the main axis of the city. It was also the main route used by people coming into Rome from the Via Flaminia to the north and continuing to that other glory of Alexander's papacy, the Piazza of St. Peter.

Other Works by Bernini for Alexander VII

An anonymous painting from about 1640 shows what the open space in front of St. Peter's looked like before Alexander VII's measures were implemented. All in all, it was a rather squalid area. The painting also reveals the practical problems which resulted from the fact that the piazza had actually never been properly laid out. During important ceremonies temporary canopies were erected in order to protect visi- tors to St. Peter's or the Vatican Palace from either the rain or sun. As soon as he was elected pope, Alexander consulted Bernini about the best way to solve the problem. The solution eventually adopted came after intense discussions between Bernini, the pope, and the cardinals on St. Peter's congregation of buildings and works. Evidence relating to some of the criticisms which were leveled at Bernini survives in a collection of drawings now in the Brandegee Collection (Faulkner Farm, Massachusetts), but originally from congregation of buildings and works. Once thought to be by Bernini himself, their importance for the study of Bernini was revealed by Rudolf Wittkower, who argued that the unknown draftsman may have belonged to the school of Papiro Bartoli, who was an eccentric amateur and contemporary of Bernini. The drawings and designs incorporate all of the criticisms of Bernini that were undoubtedly made at the time. An understanding of the symbolic meaning underlying Bernini's project can be gathered from his own words.

Since the basilica of St. Peter's is in practice the matrix for all other churches, it must have a portico that truly demonstrates how it welcomes a whole range of people with open arms: Catholics, to confirm their belief, heretics, to reunite them with the Church, and infidels, to illuminate the true faith.

The anonymous draftsman also embraced this idea. However, what he was unconvinced by was its architectural expression. In the first drawing of the series, over Bernini's colonnade, he sketched a figure of St. Peter who grimaces as his arms contort in the effort to follow the line of the colonnade. What the draftsman proposed, on the other hand, was a completely circular portico linking right into the facade of the church. But the real motive underlying his implicit comment was the fact that the cupped colonnade, with its extended splayed jamb that pointed towards the pronaos of the basilica, would have meant that, when the pope appeared on the balcony to give a blessing, it would no longer be possible for him to see large sections of the crowd. This is highlighted in another drawing.

All the same, Alexander approved Bernini's plans and the first stone was laid on August 28, 1657. The commemorative medal struck for the occasion proves that this was meant to be the end of it. However, the plan was further modified. Indeed, Bernini had originally devised a portico made up of arches and twin columns, as can be seen in the medal as well as in an anonymous drawing in the Vatican Library. But five days after the foundation stone had been laid, Bernini replaced his first plan with another, which was dominated by a heavy Doric

The Scala Regia, begun under Urban VIII and completed by Bernini in 1666, during the pontificate of Alexander VII. Between St. Peter's and the papal palace, Bernini's imposing staircase succeeds in concealing the irregular topography on which it is built through an optical illusion. The impression of a long flight of stairs is created by a colonnade running beneath a coffered barrel vault, the distances between colonnade and side walls being carefully manipulated.

colonnade supporting a continuous architrave. It was this design that was constructed. The so-called third wing (which appears in the foreground of the medal) was never built, both due to Alexander's death and the escalating costs, which had already topped the million scudi mark.

The Scala Regia

Alexander VII put a great deal of time, effort, and imagination into planning a lengthy route through the city that would take important guests from Porta Flaminia in the north to St. Peter's in the west. Its conclusion was to be one of the most extraordinary theatrical setpieces Bernini's fertile mind ever dreamed up, the Scala Regia. Built between 1663 and 1666, the staircase was conceived as a link between St. Peter's and the neighboring papal apartments. Thus having crossed the whole of Rome and admired its architectural wonders, the pope's guests would find themselves before one last, unexpected, surprise—a majestic staircase leading them to Christ's representative on earth. Bernini could not come up with merely functional stairs, but had to fashion the link so that going up, them felt like ascending to heaven. It was not by accident, therefore, that on top of the entrance arch, he placed Alexander's Chigi arms, held aloft by two figures of Fame blowing silver trumpets, announcing the pope's glory.

Bernini's real triumph—which may have been inspired by Borromini's celebrated perspective corridor in Palazzo Spada—was to break the staircase up so that it appears far longer than it really is. A succession of lateral columns and the use of a barrel vault do the rest by emphasizing the perspective effect. In this staircase, the twin ideals of town planning and architecture that Alexander VII had dreamt of were made concrete.

Francesco Borromini

The other great protagonist and moving spirit of Roman Baroque was Francesco Castelli, who was born in Bissone on Lake Lugano in northern Italy in 1599. He is known to have been in Rome, where he took the name of Borromini, from 1619.

Like Bernini and Pietro da Cortona, Borromini worked on Palazzo Barberini for Carlo Maderno, a distant relative. It was Borromini's idea to have small square windows, inspired by Michelangelo's design for the attic in St. Peter's, on the top story. Here, however, there is a mixtilinear cornice which softly enfolds the central conch, then breaks into an oblique overhang that departs from the plane it was resting on. This establishes a kind of splayed elevation projecting the cornice into the space beyond. The two side consoles link the two stories together with coherent sculptural unity, just as the triglyph beneath the conch connects this to the inner cornice. All in all, this was a minor revolution in Renaissance principles, which held that the window, although sculptural, was nonetheless part of a plane running parallel to the wall. At the same time it was an early warning of Borromini's poetic independence.

San Carlo alle Quattro Fontane

After years of work with the chisel, Borromini was waiting for the chance to assert his architectural independence. That chance came in 1634 when the procurator general of the Trinitarian friars commissioned him to refurbish buildings purchased between 1611 and 1614. One of these was San Carlo (also known as San Carlino), a church that was dedicated to St. Charles Borromeo, who had been recently canonized by Paul V.

The lack of space imposed huge problems for Borromini which he resolved brilliantly. The cloister of the church, in a rectangular space, was brought to life using an octagonal oblong plan which makes the space convex on the shorter sides. The lower register is distinguished by a so-called Serlian arch, which Borromini had probably seen in the cloister of the Pellegrino Tibaldi's Collegio Borromeo in Pavia. The architecture of the upper register is changed by the introduction of a continuous trabeation, which is supported by columns with octagonal capitals. In this transition from the arch to the trabeation, Borromini cannot have been ignorant of the example of Bramante's courtyard in Santa Maria della Pace. The design is completed by a well, and highly original balustrades.

But the masterpiece is the church itself, one of the most important examples of Baroque architecture. Begun in 1638, San Carlo was designed to make the most of the restricted space available while at the same time providing a sacristy. In achieving this, Borromini spelled out his design method, which was based on developing geometric building blocks. Anthony Blunt saw a connection between this method and Galileo's thought, since Galileo had held that the book of nature "is written in the language of mathematics whose letters are triangles, circles, and other geometrical figures." But at this time Galileo was not widely read, and it seems more likely that Borromini's design, as Wittkower remarks, can be traced back to the way that medieval builders such as Villard de Honnecourt worked. It should also be noted that Galileo's concept is already explicit in the Bible, where in Ecclesiastes it is stated that God arranges everything by measure, number, and weight.

San Carlo alle Quattro Fontane, built by Borromini in several phases between 1638 and 1667 on a small and irregular plot. The two-story facade with its alternating convex-concave movement is considered the first building to use an architecture of curves.

Borromini succeeded in creating surprising optical effects in a compressed space in his cloister for the convent of San Carlo alle Quattro Fontane. The structure shows one of the characteristics of his work—the effort to avoid right angles.

The plan of San Carlo is based on the fusion of two equilateral triangles, overlapping on one side to form a lozenge. This becomes far more significant if it is remembered that the church belonged to the Trinitarian friars. The triangle, which symbolized the Trinity, is repeated on the lantern vault.

The impression on entering the church is of continuous enfolding space, which seems uninterrupted. Undoubtedly the columns are the main feature of the lower register. They are grouped into a series of four with wider spacing around the longitudinal and transverse axes in order to make room for access to the high altar as well as the two side altars. The columns are memorable for their capitals, which have reversed volutes of Roman inspiration (the model used for these was Hadrian's Villa at Tivoli). They give movement to a single space, and are held together by a continuous trabeation.

Looking up, the vault surprises. It has four large niches at the end of the drum linking the impost spandrels of the surrounding dome to the ornamental motif on the crown. The barrel-vaulted dome is decorated with interconnecting hexagons, octagons, and crosses inspired, via one of Serlio's etchings, by an ancient mosaic in Santa Costanza. Here, however, the pattern acquires added significance, since the cross is one of the Trinitarian friars' emblems.

Borromini continually turned to the use of symbols, unlike Bernini who was visually rhetorical in his style. Thus, it is no accident that the cross, the crown of eternal life, the palm, and cherubs, all of which allude to Solomon's Temple, recur on the facade. These decorations were executed only between 1655 and 1667, which was toward the end of Borromini's life. He was to commit suicide, tragically, in 1667.

The original drawings, now in the Albertina in Vienna, are ample proof that Borromini had planned a curved facade in a double S-shape right from the very beginning of the commission. The facade of the church, which has been imaginatively compared to a reliquary, places two orders of almost equal importance over each other—in itself a startling innovation—linking them by the central trabeation. But while in the lower order the concave/convex/concave succession is as a continuous surface, in the upper order it is broken into three concaves that are separated by the power of the columns. This is underlined by the sweep of the entablature that is surmounted by a balustrade. Such an arrangement has the effect that the convex aedicule and the oval medallion, both of which are supported by angels, can be isolated.

The Oratory of St. Philip Neri

As the same time as he was working on the commission for the Trinitarian Friars, Borromini was also building an oratory for the congregation of St. Philip Neri. An architectural competition for this commission had been won by Paolo Maruscelli, who had worked for the congregation, the Filippini, for some time. It is not entirely clear why in May 1637 Borromini was brought in to work alongside Maruscelli as co-architect, but shortly afterwards Maruscelli abandoned the commission.

The task facing Borromini after he took charge of the work was further complicated by the fact that the development had been put together without a unitary plan. Apart from the church of Santa Maria in Vallicella, other buildings already in existence on the site included a sacristy situated to the west of the left transept and two courtyards, a large one to the north and a small one to the south of the sacristy. The site where Maruscelli had planned to build the oratory faced the street to the west of the oratory facade.

Initially Borromini hunted around for different solutions but eventually he was forced to keep to the existing plan. Even the corner siting is due to Maruscelli. The truth is that when Borromini accepted the enforced position, he realized it gave rise to a whole series of structural headaches that Maruscelli had not been able to overcome.

The first problem was the unavoidable fact that the oratory facade looked askew when compared to the street. Next was the apparent impossibility of getting the inner windows of the oratory to line up with the openings of the small cloister where the corner pillar, which was larger than the rest, prevented a regular scansion. Borromini resolved the first problem by "sliding" the facade toward the body of the church, thus releasing it from the oratory entrance. The disadvantage of this was that it is a disappointment for visitors, who go through the central door expecting to find themselves entering the middle of the church but are instead diverted through a vestibule.

The other obstacle was brilliantly overcome by Borromini: he cleverly adjusted the interval between the pilasters which provide the frame for the lower order in the oratory chamber. In this way he did not attempt to conceal the irregularity of the wall but rather legitimized it by elevating it to the status of an ornamental motif. Essentially he turned it into the main architectural feature of the whole way space was used inside the building.

Other remarkable solutions that underscore Borromini's genius are the way he overcame the problem posed by the difference in height between the sacristy and the oratory, and his devising of corner pillars with convex profiles for the courtyards (part of the evolution of the device he used in the San Carlo refectory). It can also be observed in the attention he lavished on the fittings for the library, the fireplace in the parlor, and the washbasin in the refectory, which he envisaged as a place where people met and talked (as indeed was the custom), as well as where they took their meals. In all Borromini's work architecture was thought through, from the structure to the fittings. It was architecture with a craftsman-like quality that provided the true amalgam of the whole project.

The most important element of the Filippini complex is the southern facade of the monastery. The terms of the commission were adamant that this should 'be in brick and not marble, in order to emphasize its secondary position compared to the church with its marble facade. The monastery takes its lines from the church, but here they are interpreted in a highly original manner.

Conceived like a huge slab of soft clay, Borromini's facade moves toward the interior as if warmly welcoming all those entering. In this it is the forerunner—albeit in a subdued form—of the ecumenical feeling that was to be the inspiration behind the colonnade in the piazza of St. Peter's that Bernini was to build some twenty years later. For Borromini the full central body and the side wings corresponded to the body and arms of a man pouring out all his love.

The facade was built in special bricks, which were designed to diminish perception of the mortar to a minimum. The facade greets the eye as a continuous surface marked by the rhythmic succession of pilasters and topped by a mixtilinear tympanum reaching toward the sky. This was a totally new vocabulary in the new language of Baroque.

Sant'Ivo alla Sapienza

Borromini's love for symbols found fertile soil in another architectural masterpiece, Sant'Ivo alla Sapienza. He was tipped off about this commission by Bernini, although once again his scope for action was severely limited by the work already done by others. In 1642 Borromini finally started work on the chapel to the Palazzo della Sapienza, the seat of the pontifical university from Eugenius IV from the mid-fifteenth century until 1935. Both the main facade and the courtyard were complete, the work being done first by Pirro Ligorio and later by Giacomo della Porta, who had been commissioned to build the palazzo by Sixtus V.

Since the church had necessarily to be positioned at the eastern end of the courtyard, Borromini made use of the existing semicircle for the church facade. Because of this, from the outside there is no warning of the interior of the chapel, which is tucked behind its sober exterior. Undoubtedly Borromini wished for this contrast. Entering the church, space seems to explode in a continuous movement of systyles and diastyles, which are both reprised and calmed down in the serene curvature of the dome.

Rare in the Italian architectural lexicon, the hexagonal plan is in itself a novelty. Borromini's genius is revealed in the way he designed the chapel as a continuous space where the smaller areas do not seem like additions, but instead play a direct part in the unitary composition of the central space. He achieved this due to the inclusion of huge corner pillars that were strategically installed around the perimeter of the area, which widens out and narrows again like an enormous star.

The elevation is given a rhythmic scansion by Corinthian pilasters in the giant order. It is joined to the impost cornice which runs right round the walls of the church without interruption, echoing the design of the floor plan. Above the trabeation and progressively beveling toward the center, the dome joins up the corners, concaves, and convexes that form the star. On the outside, and coherent with the choices made for the lower order of the chapel, the dome is hidden by a multifoiled lantern marked by pilaster strips at the corners and sides of the windows. The stepped roof is modeled on the Pantheon, but the use of ribbing in a concave pattern engenders a tremendously powerful soaring sense which culminates in the helicoidal structure of the lantern.

Work dragged on for over eighteen years, not finishing until 1660. The passage of time was marked by Borromini in the building itself. The coats of arms of successive popes were incorporated into the structure. Thus, if the idea for the floor plan is really a stylized version of the Barberini bees, right down to the honeycomb decoration on the floor tiles, the Pamphili dove is enthroned in the metallic structure which finishes off the outside of the lantern, while the inside of the dome is decorated with the mountains and stars of Alexander VII.

However, the symbolism permeating the complex goes far deeper than this. The plan is like the Solomonic pentacle which is the symbol of wisdom. This is also alluded to in the inclusion of cherubs in the stucco of the dome and in the helicoidal structure of the lantern (really a crown) derived, as demonstrated by Fagiolo dell'Arco, from an image in Cesare Ripa's *Iconologia of Wisdom* wearing a distinctive dress with seven

University church of Sant'Ivo alla Sapienza, with its prominent spiral lantern. Constructed between 1642 and 1660, this building illustrates Borromini's ability to achieve monumental designs in a limited space.

Dome of Sant'Ivo alla Sapienza. The design of this part of the church is a good example of Borromini's technical mastery of unusual groundplans and his ability to combine them to harmonize with a customized décor. The unusual vault construction was regarded so skeptically by his contemporaries that Borromini had to offer a fifteen-year guarantee of stability.

flounces. Sant'Ivo is therefore revealed for what it is: a Solomonic Temple of Wisdom mixed with the symbolism of the apocalypse.

San Giovanni in Laterano and Sant'Agnese in Agone

The election of Innocent X heralded the most fortunate phase of Borromini's life, for it was Innocent who was to give him his major commissions. The restoration of the basilica of San Giovanni in Laterano, the cathedral of Rome, and the historic seat of the pope, bishop of Rome, can be compared only to similar work at St. Peter's.

The old basilica was in need of extensive repair and refurbishment. Innocent X, who wanted the work completed in time for the 1650 Jubilee, imposed the condition that the venerable basilica with its five aisles retain its original floor plan and, as far as possible, its structure. Thus Borromini had to abandon his idea of reworking the building on a grand scale and instead create a design that substantially met two requirements: consolidating the building and modernizing its interior. He was not even allowed to replace Daniele da Volterra's sumptuous ceiling with his own idea for a vault with wide flat ribs, along the lines of that in the chapel of the Magi at the church of Propaganda Fide. This revision would have joined up the clear-cut tops of the pilasters scanning the walls of the central nave. Had Borromini been given his way, the plan would have been transformed into an organically conceived, continuous space, splitting into side aisles from the central nave.

The constraints set by the pope did not make Borromini's job any easier. Essentially he was forced to update a five-aisle basilica full of columns which retained its medieval appearance. Borromini solved the problem by encasing each pair of columns in a pier, which he linked to the next by an arch, creating rectangular-section piers. In turn this allowed him to insert tabernacles lower than the arches on the long side, framed by pilasters over the entire height of the wall, like a giant order (similar to those in the St. Philip Neri cloister).

The decoration was completed by frames with stucco scenes from the Old and New Testaments as well as oval medallions flanking the windows. In this way Borromini gave the wall movement by a rhythm that is repeated on the counterface, which tightly links the whole scheme to the convex entrance doorway, offset in turn by the large concave west window. In contrast to this, the decoration of the side aisles is fairly simple, enlivened only by half-figures of cherubs.

It was not only in San Giovanni in Laterano that cherubs appear in Borromini's vocabulary. They can be found on the outer cornices of the lantern at Sant'Ivo, instead of the classic egg and dart motif, inside the dome and on the facade of San Carlo, and on the splendid bell tower of Sant'Andrea delle Fratte, where the clean lines of the chisel contrast with the fascinating but unintentional roughness (the final plaster was never applied) of the church lantern. Borromini waited for this to be done from 1653 to the day he died.

In 1653 Borromini was also given work at the church of Sant'Agnese on Piazza Navona and on the addition to Palazzo Pamphili, since the influential patrons were not satisfied with the work by Girolamo and Carlo Rainaldi commissioned less than a year earlier. In this short time the Rainaldi had forged ahead with the work,

with the result that Borromini was once more obliged to work within parameters partially set by someone else.

Innocent X, who had consulted Martino Longhi, was unhappy about how the steps leading to the church protruded into the piazza, the final element in a design which, by opting for a straight facade that was quite out of keeping with the stimulating sense of space in the piazza, essentially did little more than repeat the solutions that Maderno had proposed for St. Peter's. Here, however, the matter was made worse since there was no justification whatsoever for a result that seemed to detach the dome from the facade.

Borromini tore the facade down and built another which led gently toward the interior. Not only did this give the dome back its value but it also prevented the steps from getting in the way. Moreover, Borromini attempted to highlight the size of the dome by widening the facade with two convex avant-corps, which took up the theme of the facade of Santi Luca e Martina. For the same reason, above this Borromini planned a similar number of small bell towers, though their design was radically altered on construction. Like the bell tower at Sant'Andrea delle Fratte, they were to have cylindrical bases in order to echo the shape of the dome's drum, but in the end they were given oval bases. In this way, the architectural complex of the church established a dialectic

Between 1648 and 1649 Borromini redesigned the basilica of San Giovanni in Laterano for Innocent X. In contrast to St. Peter's, where the old building was completely replaced by a new structure, Borromini integrated the ancient remains of the church from the era of Constantine into his design. The walls of the nave from the old basilica were incorporated into the new walls as a kind of relic. The columns in the aisles were used—almost as emblems— as supports for the figures of apostles in the aedicules.

The unfinished church of Sant'Andrea della Fratte with its prominent campanile is a significant feature of the Roman cityscape. Borromini worked on the building from 1653 until his death in 1667.

513

Piazza Navona, built over the remains of the Stadium of Domitian at the instigation of Innocent X. In the foreground can be seen the Fountain of Neptune. Behind is the Four Rivers Fountain, built from a design by Gian Lorenzo Bernini in 1651 opposite the church of Sant'Agnese in Agone. The construction of Piazza Navona was one the main instruments the Pamphili family employed in order to aggrandize their achievements.

Salon of Palazzo Pamphili, built by Innocent X from designs by Carlo Rainaldi from 1646. The gallery and salon decoration are the work of Borromini. The painted ornamentation with scenes from the life of Aeneas, was executed by Pietro da Cortona.

relationship with the open piazza as well as with the Fountain of the Four Rivers already executed by Bernini. The "hollow" facade provides a brilliant point of synthesis for the whole of Piazza Navona.

Borromini was also responsible for the roof of the salon and gallery that linked Sant'Agnese to Palazzo Pamphili, decorated with scenes of Aeneas by Pietro da Cortona. Borromini's intention was to build an architecturally harmonious and coherent "wall" on the east of Piazza Navona, made up of the palazzo and the church. However, with the death of Innocent X Borromini's fortunes waned. Misunderstandings with Cardinal Camillo Pamphili, who was in charge of the work and had commissioned

Alessandro Algardi to build Villa San Pancrazio, reached breaking point and on July 2, 1657 Borromini was finally relieved of his duties and replaced by a panel of architects, which included Carlo Rainaldi.

Carlo Rainaldi

Carlo Rainaldi trained under his father Girolamo, who died in 1655 before his son was partially vindicated over the Borromini Sant'Agnese affair. Carlo's first assignment was assisting his father on construction of the Palazzo Senatorio on the Capitoline Hill, for the Capitoline Museum that had originally been designed by Michelangelo.

Carlo's first major commission, the high altar and canopy in Santa Maria della Scala, immediately reveals one of the recurrent themes in his artistic endeavor. This was the use of the column as an independent architectural feature that was given back a structural (loadbearing) purpose rather than being merely decorative. In this respect he was following in the footsteps of Pietro da Cortona's architectural poetry.

Most of the interior of Sant'Agnese bears this distinctive Rainaldi characteristic, despite the modifications made by Borromini. It was Carlo, rather than his then eighty-year-old father, who opted for the Byzantine cross and for other solutions such as pillars with large niches inspired by St. Peter's and the embedded column motif (changed by Borromini to highlight the columns by beveling the pillars). All of this again showed his indebtedness to Pietro da Cortona.

Rainaldi's most important work—apart from the splendid twin churches in Piazza del Popolo described earlier—is the completion of the facade of Sant'Andrea della Valle and Santa Maria in Campitelli, his masterpiece. The facade of Sant'Andrea della Valle was begun by Maderno but never completed. Rainaldi was given the commission in 1656 and work was completed by 1665. Working within Maderno's parameters, Rainaldi based the design on Santa Susanna. The front elevation, however, became less tight and more severe, partly due to the input of his pupil Carlo Fontana. It departs from Pietro da Cortona's model by repeating the columns in the upper order.

At the same time as he was finishing Sant'Andrea della Valle, Rainaldi was working on Santa Maria in Campitelli. Initially he had the idea of using a central plan along the lines of the ellipsoid layout in San Carlo, with a facade similar to that of Santa Maria della Pace. His final plan has divided critics. Some, like Argan, see it as a revolutionary attempt to break free of the typological barriers imposed by central and

longitudinal plans. Others, like Portoghesi, reject it as a compromise that worked purely by luck.

The plan for Santa Maria in Campitelli fuses a sort of sanctuary with a dome and an apse, with the earlier Byzantine cruciform floor plan. The result was not popular in Rome, where it had no precedent (if Santa Maria della Pace where, however, the two coexisting elements do not belong to a unitary plan is excluded), unlike Milan, where Riccino had built San Giuseppe in this way about 1607–16.

The impression gained on entering Santa Maria in Campitelli is a telescopic prospect, which draws the eye toward the votive chapel with its dome. The main feature of the internal decoration is the use of ribbed columns with Corinthian capitals linked by a wonderful continuous trabeation, almost identical to that in Sant'Agnese in Agone.

The high facade of the church also serves to conceal the low spherical vault of the dome. The main architectural feature on the facade is once again the use of columns, which are

Sant'Agnese in Agone, an important element in the Pamphili family's self-projection on Piazza Navona, probably originally intended to serve as the tomb of Innocent X. The form of the church today is the result of a complex construction process in which both Girolamo and Carlo Rainaldi were involved from 1652.

Sant'Andrea della Valle, the main Roman church of the Catholic Reformation order of the Theatines, begun by Carlo Maderno. From 1662 work on the facade was continued from a design by Carlo Rainaldi or, possibly, Carlo Fontana.

Santa Maria del Miracoli, built from 1658 for Pope Alexander VII by Carlo Rainaldi and the young Carlo Fontana. Its temple-like porch was unusual for this era. Together with the church of Santa Maria di Montesanto, built at the same time, it served as an important landmark at the start of the Corso.

repeated in the upper order. But the true significance of Rainaldi's work lies in the total coherence with which he arranged the various parts, beginning with the window motif in the upper register (reminiscent of the Serlian influence from Santa Maria in Via Lata), which expands, proliferates, and grows larger until it shapes the whole architectural surface.

Other Architects

Something similar had already been tried out by Martino Longhi the Younger (1602–60) on the splendid facade of Santi Vincenzo e Anastasio. This church stood out for a veritable forest of columns, giving rise to its nickname of "reed fen." Cardinal Mazarin wanted the medieval church refurbished after deciding to build two family tombs there. Longhi was from an artistic family: his grandfather was Martino the Elder, who designed San Girolamo degli Schiavoni and devised the basic plan for San Carlo on Via del Corso.

Longhi worked on Santi Vincenzo e Anastasio between 1644 and 1650. In the lower order, the columns, which come after an empty space, mark the sides of the facade and support a heavily abutted trabeation leading in the middle to two tympanums. In the upper order, the motif of the tympanum supported by columns is repeated and spreads until it covers the entire

surface in a truly sculptural manner. The side volutes, which terminate in two caryatids which are Mannerist in taste, are derived from Martino's facade of Sant'Antonio dei Portoghesi (1638), where the volutes terminate in bearded telamones that appear to support the capitals of the pilasters in the upper order.

It is clear, therefore, that seventeenth-century architectural vocabulary was varied by a whole series of personal terms, which sometimes gave rise to masterpieces such as Martino Longhi's Santi Vincenzo e Anastasio. At other times architects churned out conformist copies of tried-and-tested designs. An example is Algardi's Villa Bel Respiro (Borromini's favorite), which totally ignores the architectural problems posed by the Baroque villa. If indeed both Algardi and Borromini used Hadrian's Villa as their point of departure, the results they achieved do not stand comparison.

A very different architect was Giovanni Antonio de Rossi, who built Palazzo Altieri. He was influenced by Borromini's style of building using beveled corners, windows with curved and "pagoda" tympanums, first seen in the oratory of St. Philip Neri but by now part of a widespread language.

Flourishing Roman architecture came up with a whole range of ideas. G.B. Soria reinterpreted della Porta's San Luigi dei Francesi facade in his own work at San Gregorio Magno and Santa Caterina a Magnanapoli. Vincenzo della Greca managed a one-off achievement in the splendid steps he built for Santi Domenico e Sisto. Antonio Del Grande prosaically reused Rainaldi's facade for Palazzo Pamphili in Piazza Navona when between 1659 and 1661 he added the wing facing Piazza del Collegio Romano to Palazzo Doria-Pamphili.

Carlo Fontana

Carlo Fontana (1638–1714) seems to have been sent on purpose to lead architecture into the next century. Born in Brusata, near Como, he came to Rome when he was just seventeen and worked with all the great architects of Roman Baroque except Borromini. When only eighteen, he assisted Pietro da Cortona on Santa Maria della Pace and in 1655 he was working with Bernini on Palazzo Odescalchi in Piazza Santi Apostoli. At the same time he was helping out Carlo Rainaldi, whose pupil he was, on the facade of Sant'Andrea della Valle.

Thus it was that Fontana's malleable talent provided him with a unique opportunity of learning alongside the inventors of Baroque. Under their tutelage he mastered its vocabulary. In his hands, however, it tended to harden into academic rules. It was not by chance, therefore, that Fontana was elected head of the Accademia di San Luca, first in 1686 and then for eight consecutive years between 1692 and 1700, a measure of how much his architecture pleased his contemporaries.

In reality, within the context of seventeenth-century architecture Fontana's vocabulary was eclectic. He did not scorn even Borromini's ideas once he had freed them of their transgressive overtones. Although, as in San Carlo, the floor plan of Fontana's Santa Rita da Cascia derives from the geometry of the rhombus, the interior of the building itself deteriorates into flatness.

The facade of San Marcello on Via del Corso, perhaps Fontana's most famous work, dates from 1682–83. It is an example of his mature style, adopting Borromini's theme of a concave facade, but developing it in an entirely different manner. The entrance protrudes so much that it isolates the two wings of the facade, thus destroying the sense of continuity and connection that is then only partly recovered by introducing palm-leaf lateral volutes, which are avowedly symbolic in meaning.

Fontana's additions to Palazzo di Montecitorio are also pedantic. They cannot, however, dull Bernini's brilliance, which changed the very concept of a Baroque palazzo, taking the building from a hermetic block to a fluid organism which molds itself to fit the surrounding city scene. The work on Palazzo di Montecitorio was the high point of Fontana's career, not least because the permanent state of penury in which the Church found itself prevented Fontana from actually building his grandiose projects, these were doomed to remain on the drawing board.

Marco Bussagli

Carlo Rainaldi's facade for San Marcello al Corso. This frontage, framed by a continuous curve, was placed in front of an older structure in 1682 following designs by Jacopo Sansovino and Antonio da Sangallo the Younger.

Gardens of Rome

Compared with other Italian cities, or even with many other European cities, contemporary Rome is a green city, with large areas of parks and gardens. This is not surprising, since even in the days of ancient Rome the wealthy citizens had created *horti* (gardens) within their own domains. Gardens were thus an integral part of the urban landscape.

These Roman gardens, generally on different levels linked by flights of steps, often contained monumental fountains, whose refreshing play of water created a delightful atmosphere. Literary and archaeological evidence reveal details of famous properties such as the *horti Sallustiani*, named after their first owner, the historian Sallust (86–35 BC), author of the *Catiline Conspiracy*. The *horti Sallustiani*, which over the centuries became divided, were

Terraces in the Farnese gardens on the Palatine. Etching by Giovanni Battista Falda.

Ruins from Hadrian's Villa and surrounding gardens.

subsequently the site of the Villa Ludovisi and, eventually, of the Ludovisi quarter, the urban district that developed within the former boundaries of the gardens.

There are numerous other examples, such as the gardens created by Julius Caesar in Trastevere, by Lucullus on the Pincio, and by Maecenas on the Esquiline

Hill. Undoubtedly, however, the villa possessing the greatest area of green within its gardens was Nero's Golden House (*Domus Aurea*), the model without equal of an imperial villa. It was described—with scarcely concealed critical intent—by the historian Suetonius in his lives of the emperors (VI, 31). The property stretched

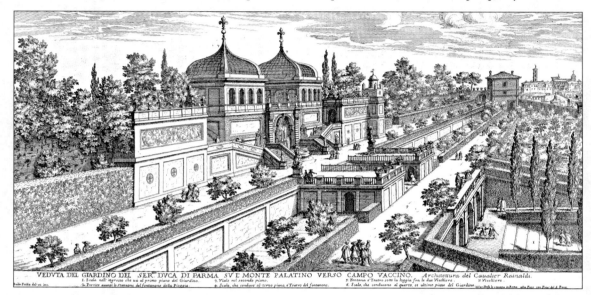

VEDVTA DEL GIARDINO DEL SER^mo DVCA DI PARMA SV'L MONTE PALATINO VERSO CAMPO VACCINO. *Architettura del Cavalier Rainaldi.*

Lake in the gardens of Villa Madama with a classicizing temple of Aesculapius.

Labyrinth in the gardens of Villa Madama with giants by Baccio Bandinelli.

vineyards from the later twelfth century onwards. Monasteries and other religious institutions played a special role, forming the core around which urban clusters developed. An example is the monastery of Santi Quattro Coronati near the Lateran Palace, and another that of the Dominicans at Santa Maria sopra Minerva, near the Pantheon. Each of these establishments had a cloister, an internal garden that symbolised the Earthly Paradise, the Heavenly Jerusalem, and Christ as the fount of life

from the Oppian to the Esquiline Hill and from the Palatine to the Celian Hill, covering a total area of more than 250 acres, mostly parkland and gardens. There were cultivated areas, woods, and vineyards, that were embellished with nymphaeums and panoramic terraces, and even a lake. A property on this scale was unique in the city's history, but the custom of having a large plot of land adjacent to an aristocratic residence continued to be a defining characteristic of Rome's urban layout.

Throughout the Middle Ages the built-up areas were concentrated in the northeast of the city. This left extensive uninhabited areas within the perimeter of the Aurelian Walls, which were used for cultivation and

The Palace Quirinal gardens, among the finest in Rome. This view is by Giovanni Battista Falda.

PROSPETTIVA DEL GIARDINO PONTIFICIO SVL QVIRINALE. *Architettura di Ottavio Mascarini.*

521

Coffee House and the Fontana di Caserta in the gardens of the Palace Quirinal.

Garden of Venus in the Villa Borghese park, with its geometrical flower beds and statues of classical heroes and gods.

(*fons vitae*). They also had plots of land, frequently fenced and protected, which provided subsistence for the monks. This was to become the model for aristocratic residences, where gardens were created within, or adjacent to, the buildings.

For example, the garden (*viridarium*) of Palazzo San Marco (now Venezia) recalls the function of many monastery cloisters, which was the cultivation of medicinal herbs. The Palazzo San Marco garden, created between 1455 and 1468, was, like the palace itself, made for the Venetian cardinal Pietro Barbo, later Paul II. Originally it lay on the east side of the present Piazza Venezia and was directly linked with the main building.

With the artistic and cultural revival of the Renaissance, there was a proliferation of new villas, both inside and outside the city walls and, consequently, extensive gardens. Some of these villas no longer exist, such as the villa of Cardinal du Bellay of Bordeaux, which stood in the area corresponding to the exedra of the Baths of Diocletian, or Villa Peretti-Montalto, whose gardens lay not far from the basilica of Santa Maria Maggiore. But others are still there to be admired, together with their gardens.

A typical example of the Renaissance urban villa is that known today as the Villa Farnesina, originally built for the Sienese banker Agostino Chigi. Full of greenery, situated on the banks of the Tiber, the villa's gardens were laid out in four parts in geometrical designs, following contemporary taste and ideas.

Hanging gardens are the striking feature of Villa Madama, built for Leo X under the supervision of Cardinal Giulio de' Medici, later Clement VII. Though Raphael's project for the villa was never completed, in its present form the villa still shows that it was inspired by knowledge of similar buildings

Water for the fountains in the gardens of Villa Medici comes from the Acqua Virgo, fed by a Roman aqueduct originally built under Agrippa.

Gardens of Villa Medici with the obelisk fountain.

in the Graeco-Roman style gained through a reading of Vitruvius. This influence can be seen in the elevated garden (*xystus*) above the fishpond, with a loggia at its edge; the Latin term that Raphael used for it is taken from Vitruvius. However, classical influence and the evocation of antiquity are demonstrated above all in the rustic garden, reached through a gateway flanked by two giants sculpted by Baccio Bandinelli. Fountains and running water enliven the atmosphere of the gardens. One of the most impressive of these fountains is Giovanni da Udine's Elephant Fountain, which immortalizes Annone, the white elephant from Ceylon given to Leo X by the king of Portugal, much loved by the Romans of that time.

Another fine example of a villa, and equally famous, is the Villa Borghese,

The gardens of Villa Medici decorated with statues and architectural elements in the antique style.

acres, the Botanic Gardens contain more than 8,000 plants from all over the world, from orchids to sequoias.

The gardens of the Quirinal Palace, some of the most beautiful in Rome, are of historical interest, as they represent the development of the Italianate garden. They were laid out in front of the early palace building designed by Ottaviano Mascherino in 1587, consisting then of geometrically arranged flowerbeds and paths, except for the farthest area, which was deliberately left to woodland and named *silva Estensium* (the wood of the Este: the Este family were the original owners before the land was bought by Sixtus V). The present appearance of the gardens is the result of complex restructuring begun by Clement VIII (1592–1605) and completed by Benedict XIV (1740–58). The Fountain of the Organ, attributed to Giovanni Fontana, dates from the earlier reorganization and was finished in 1596. The Coffee House, dating from the second phase and designed by Ferdinando Fuga, has a view of the Pincio. Today the gardens are part of the official residence of the President.

Villa Colonna, on the slopes of the Quirinal Hill, is also famous for its gardens. The annual celebration at which the kings of Naples paid homage to the pope's temporal and spiritual power, making a symbolic gift of a horse, took place here. The garden was made for Filippo Colonna at

whose public park, with a perimeter four miles long, is the largest in Rome. Originally on the city's northern boundary just outside the Aurelian Walls, Villa Borghese is today an integral part of the urban fabric. The artificial lake with its small temple in classical style, built by Antonio Asprucci in 1786, is particularly charming. It illustrates how taste in garden design in the eighteenth century was evolving towards the studied combination of architectural-type elements in classical style, such as fake ruins, with natural forms. This was the basis of the fashion for the picturesque, partly inspired by English landscape gardens.

The picturesque also had roots in the Arcadian concept of nature and art. The concept was nurtured by the Arcadian Academy at the Bosco del Parrasio on the Gianicolo Hill, and by the circle in Rome around Queen Christina of Sweden. The effect of the Bosco Parrasio architectural structure (designed by Antonio Canevari) is enhanced by the presence of laurels (an allusion to the crowning of poets), myrtle bushes, austere cypresses, pine trees, wisteria, oleanders, and ivy.

Also on the slopes of the Gianicolo are the university botanic gardens. These are on land that was formerly the gardens of the villa of Cardinal Corsini (now housing the Accademia dei Lincei). Covering thirty

the start of the seventeenth century, and in the nineteenth century it had monumental flights of steps added to link it to the villa at raised ground-floor level.

Other Roman gardens include the dramatically impressive garden of Villa Albani (inspired by the archaeological remains of Hadrian's Villa and—due to the architect Ottaviano Nelli—by the magnificence of Versailles), the garden of the Villa Medici, painted by Velázquez, who stayed there, and the garden of the Villa Doria Pamphili, known as "Belrespiro," with its secret garden, fountains, waterfalls, ornamental lakes, and sweeping stretches of green, all in the eighteenth-century English landscape style.

Marco Bussagli

Casino Belrespiro in the park of Villa Doria Pamphili. The Villa is surrounded by concealed gardens, fountains, lakes, and large geometrical open spaces.

Sculpture

Sculpture Before Bernini: the *St. Cecilia* of Stefano Maderno

If there is one sculpture among all those produced in Rome at the beginning of the seventeenth century which indicates the direction in which art would go, it is Stefano Maderno's (1576–1636) *St. Cecilia* in the church of Santa Cecilia in Trastevere. It was commissioned by Cardinal Paolo Emilio Sfondrato, who had the tomb of the saint opened in 1599.

Tradition has it that Maderno's finely polished statue represents the position in which St. Cecilia's body was found. Whether or not this is true—and critics have often questioned it—does not really matter. What is certain is that in this sculpture, executed in 1600, Maderno foreshadows many of the poetic impulses that would later flourish in the Baroque age. Maderno, originally from Ticino, aims straight at the beholder's emotions, directly engaging feeling and igniting emotions in a way that Bernini and Caravaggio were to perfect. The saint's body seems still warm, while on her neck can be seen the mark of the axe blow that ended her young life in the name of Christ.

The sculpture is a solid and truthful witness (the literal meaning of martyr is witness) of the saint's faith in God. At this time the theological meditations of Cardinal Bellarmine and St. Carlo Borromeo were moving toward a return to the simplicity of the religious practice of the early Christians. For this reason Maderno came up with the idea of a sculpture that gives the impression that the event has only just occurred, right under the eyes of the incredulous onlooker who, torn between pity and horror, cannot but be moved.

With the *St. Cecilia*, sculpture in Rome took a great leap forward, freeing itself from the formalist fetters of late Mannerism and leaving behind all artists who otherwise would have been able to offer their talents to the Borghese pope, Paul V. It is not that the work of these sculptors lacks quality, merely that as far as sculpture was concerned, artistic activity had become stale since the death of Michelangelo in 1564. Until Gian Lorenzo Bernini's extraordinary sculpture burst upon the scene, sculptors were only able to come up with timid innovations in what by now was a rigid code for form and subject-matter. It was not unusual for sculptors to produce affected work, such as Cristoforo Stati's *Venus and Adonis* in the Palazzo Comunale in Bracciano. Against this background, it is easy to see why Maderno's *St. Cecilia* had so explosive an effect, comparable to that produced in architecture by the facade of the church of Santa Susanna.

Nonetheless, Maderno cannot be called a Baroque sculptor. The inspiration of this work remained an isolated moment in his career; it is

Stefano Maderno, *St. Cecilia*, made in the Holy Year of 1600. The form of the work was influenced by the discovery that year of the martyr's well-preserved body. The realism of the sculpture works as an emotional appeal to the piety of the believer and is an impressive visualization of one of the central aspects of the Catholic Reformation, the cult of early Christian saints. Santa Cecilia in Trastevere.

of a different level from works commissioned for other churches in Rome (for instance, the angels in Santa Maria di Loreto and those in the transept of San Giovanni in Laterano) or the series of small terracottas, sometimes made into bronzes, depicting the Labors of Hercules (some now in the Hermitage in St. Petersburg), which reveal a return to the classical exploration of the theme.

Camillo Mariani and Francesco Mochi

Maderno belonged to the group of sculptors, active in the years around 1600, centered on Camillo Mariani (1556–1611), a sculptor born in Vicenza who made his debut in Rome in 1597 with work on the chapel of the Angeli in the church of the Gesù, where he made "a few little stucco putti," as Filippo Titi remarked in his A Study of Painting, Sculpture, and Architecture in the Churches of Rome (*Studio di Pittura, Scoltura, et Architettura nelle chiese di Roma*).

The work which assured Mariani's success in 1600 was a series of eight statues of saints in niches in the church of San Bernardo alle Terme, a church built in one of the four corner rotundas

of the Baths of Diocletian. The church had been refurbished at the end of the sixteenth century, thanks to the generosity of Caterina Sforza, countess of Santafiora. The brightness of Mariani's huge stucco figures melds with the background against which they are set, creating a luminous play that recalls Mariani's roots in Vicenza: he had learned his greatest lessons from the sculptor Alessandro Vittoria. Further proof of this can be seen in a comparison of Mariani's sculpture of St. Jerome in the Baths and the sculpture of St. Jerome which Vittoria had executed for Santa Maria dei Frari in Venice. Mariani, however, emphasized the sense of monumentality. This can even be noted in the closed figure of St. Catherine of Siena, also in San Bernardo alle Terme, reminiscent of the wide and geometric form found in Vittoria's *Our Lady of Sorrows* in Santi Giovannie Paolo in Venice.

It is clear then that the path leading to the new artistic language was by no means straight. Mariani was also given commissions for the Aldobrandini Chapel in Santa Maria sopra Minerva. Working alongside him there was Nicolas Cordier (1567–1612), a sculptor from Lorraine who was known as *il Franciosino*. The two sculptors had met when they, and other late Mannerist sculptors, were working in the Borghese Chapel (Cappella Paolina) in Santa Maria Maggiore. Cordier executed the recumbent statues of Salvestro Aldobrandini and Lesa Dati, Pope Clement VIII's parents. He designed prone figures with upright torsos which—though badly executed by Maso dal Bosco—recall the figure of Pope Julius II for Michelangelo's Julius II tomb in the church of San Pietro in Vincoli. Cordier also produced a static *St. Sebastian* and a *Charity*, flanked by somewhat affected putti, which completed the two tombs in the Borghese Chapel. Another somewhat affected work is Mariani's *Religion*, which was commissioned for the tomb of Lesa Dati, although here the painterly quality that was implicit in his Venetian training can also be seen.

In Mariani's favor, however, is the fact that he took into his studio the young Francesco Mochi (1580–1654), whose artistic career was destined to cross that of Gian Lorenzo Bernini. Mochi, born in Montevarchi, near Florence, studied under the painter Santi di Tito before discovering that his true vocation was sculpture. He moved to Rome, where he was employed by Mariani as an assistant on the commission in San Bernardo alle Terme. Mochi was a prominent figure during the first thirty years of the seventeenth century. His first major commission, for Orvieto Cathedral, was for an Annunciation, with the Virgin and Gabriel. He also made a statue of St. Philip for the cathedral.

Francesco Mochi, *St. Veronica*, made between 1635 and 1640. The agitated figure seems about to burst out of its niche in order to present the viewer with the miraculous imprint of Christ's countenance. The sculptures designed by Bernini for the piers in the crossing of St. Peter's to the most important of the relics in this area of the church: the sudarium of St. Veronica, the head of St. Andrew, fragments of the Cross, and the spear of Longinus. St. Peter's.

Francesco Mochi, *St. Martha*. His last work before his move to Piacenza and the court of Ranuccio Farnese. Made in 1612, the work is part of the sculptural decorations in the Barberini Chapel built in Sant'Andrea della Valle by Cardinal Matteo Barberini, later Urban VIII.

On the death of his master in 1611, Mochi took over the workshop and completed an unfinished statue of St. John the Evangelist for the Borghese Chapel in Santa Maria Maggiore, concluded in 1621. For the same chapel he also completed a relief depicting the recapture of Strigonia (Esztergom) in Hungary from the Ottoman Turks. Two little flying angels hold the symbols of the faith. Mochi's opportunity came when he was summoned to Piacenza to make the two celebrated equestrian monuments of Ranuccio and Alessandro Farnese.

Returning to Rome in 1629, he used the experience gained in Piacenza to fashion a small bronze statuette, *Carlo Barberini on Horseback*, which Jennifer Montagu has rightly called the most moving in Baroque art. The Barberini bronze is a scaled-down version of the monument to Alessandro Farnese. It returns to the motif of the advancing horseman, his cloak billowing in the wind. Garments bursting with dynamic power were Mochi's hallmark. They can be seen in his most famous work, the *St. Veronica* in St. Peter's.

Pietro Bernini

Pietro Bernini (1562–1629), the father of Gian Lorenzo, deserves special mention. After visiting Rome in his youth, he left Naples to return there some time in 1605–06. Pietro's reputation as a sculptor has suffered from the inevitable comparison with his son's work but it should not be forgotten that he was Gian Lorenzo's first teacher. Pietro was born in Sesto Fiorentino in Tuscany, where he became Sirigatti's pupil. Later he executed a number of commissions in the Naples area and for Amalfi Cathedral.

Pietro's first assignments in Rome were in the then hive of activity, the basilica of Santa Maria Maggiore. He sculpted a marble relief of the *Assumption* for the baptistery there and the *Coronation of Pope Clement VIII*, working on the *Assumption* between 1606 and 1611. The *Assumption* possesses an intense dynamism which is felt through the whole group. In the clouds at the top, the Virgin is borne aloft by cherubs singing praises. The cherubs are arranged in a circle that creates an ascending vortex, culminating with an angel playing a harp and another playing a portable organ. This contrasts with the vertical movement of the lower part of the scene, where powerfully molded figures stand in various attitudes around the Virgin's tomb, which is covered with flowers. The result is a composition imbued with an intensely pictorial feeling that to some extent foreshadows Gian Lorenzo's style.

In contrast to this, the *Coronation of Pope Clement VIII*, at the top of Clement's tomb on the right of the Borghese Chapel in Santa Maria Maggiore, is fairly static. Carved in 1611, the relief is above a statue of Clement by Silla Longhi, magnificently framed within the overall architectural structure by Flaminio Ponzio, who was in charge of the whole project. The aedicule containing Bernini's sculpture is flanked by two caryatids, also by Bernini. The spiral movement foreshadows the way in which in 1614–15 he was to sculpt the large *St. John the Baptist* for the Barberini Chapel in Sant'Andrea della Valle. Commissioned by Cardinal Maffeo Barberini, the future Urban VIII, the chapel was built by Matteo Castelli. It became a focal point for the artistic culture of the day, intent on moving on from the vocabulary of late Mannerism toward something more modern. Next to Ambrogio Buonvicino's static *St. John the Evangelist* and Cristoforo Stati's affected *St. Mary Magdalene* is Francesco Mochi's *St. Martha*, which stands out for its dynamism and the tension of the way the figure leans forward, reminiscent of the Angel Gabriel in the Orvieto *Annunciation*. This is further emphasized by the relief of the drapery folds, where jagged fringes help to reflect the light.

Pietro Bernini's work, on the other hand, does not seem so polished and the way in which the body twists is indebted to Michelangelo's *Christ Bearing the Cross* in Santa Maria sopra Minerva. It lacks power and seems hesitant. The right arm of the statue does not help: it is too small and limp so that instead of heightening the twisting movement it seems like a terrible loss of tone, made worse by the preciousness of the saint's curly hair, where the locks are overworked. The negative impact is completed by the animal skin worn by St. John the Baptist and the affected curly wool of the lamb.

Gian Lorenzo Bernini

By this time, Gian Lorenzo was already working with his father. Born in Naples on December 7, 1598 to Pietro Bernini and Angelica Galante, Gian Lorenzo Bernini's creative genius led contemporaries to think of him as being touched by divine power. It was "by divine will... in order to bring light to two centuries" that he had been born Italian (Baldinucci). Even Pope Urban VIII "would have liked to embalm Bernini and make him eternal." Not all agreed. Some who knew him found him "a sad and shrewd man," while others compared him to "the merciless dragon... vigilantly guarding the gardens of the Hesperides," as Valentino Martinelli reported.

What is certain, however, is that Gian Lorenzo was extremely good at self-promotion and tended to squeeze out other talented sculptors. There was often a clash of personalities between him and those who were not sufficiently malleable for his purposes. The classic example of this is the clash between Bernini and Borromini, though there were many more. According to Lione Pascoli, Bernini once tried to irritate Mochi by asking him where the wind ruffling his *St. Veronica* was blowing from. Mochi retorted with the acid comment: "From the cracks you made in the dome!"

Bernini's central position and the number of commissions he was awarded made him something of a sculptor-entrepreneur. Franco Borsi explains that Bernini farmed out some of his commissions to "artists, pupils, potential rivals, and older masters, all in a power game" that he constantly ratcheted up in proportion to the scale of the assignments he was giving out.

For this reason, Bernini became the fulcrum of a colossal machine, always ready to carry out the desires of the pope of the day. Apart from pupils and established artists, the machine also employed—under various guises, as the occasion demanded—people recommended by the pope. Among these were Giovan Maria Baratta (brother of the better-known Francesco), a favorite of the Pamphili family. There was also Gian Lorenzo's younger brother Luigi, whose tangles with the law gave his brother many a headache, and his son Paolo. All of these, like their colleagues, worked wherever they were needed and as the master directed. All of this helps to explain why Bernini's influence on the art of his time and that of the next century was so great. However, the basis of this complex structure, composed of money, power, jealousy, and diplomatic skill, was Gian Lorenzo's unarguable overwhelming virtuosity, as well as his exceptional technical ability.

Early Works

Bernini's ability as a sculptor—for this was his first vocation—emerged early, though the claims of some of his biographers that he produced his first work when still a child cannot be accepted. Nor can we agree with those critics who suggest that he worked for his father when they were still in Naples, or that he helped his father with the bust of Antonio Coppola in San Giovanni dei Fiorentini, sculpted in 1612. There is no doubt, however, that the two men did work together on the splendid *Faun Playing with Amoretti* (New York, Metropolitan Museum), sculpted around 1614. By now the young genius was able to pull together the experience he had acquired of still-lifes, which he had probably explored in sculptures of the four seasons for the Villa Aldobrandini in Frascati. In the same peri-

od, between 1614 and 1616, Gian Lorenzo produced works such as the *Young Jupiter with the Goat Amalthea* (begun in 1609 and completed before 1615). His more enthusiastic biographers claim that many mistook the sculpture for an antique sculpture. Whatever the truth, Cardinal Scipione Borghese, a discerning art collector, purchased it immediately.

In the same period Bernini produced some of his monumental sculptures such as *St. Sebastian*, commissioned by Maffeo Barberini and now in Lugano (Thyssen-Bornemisza Collection), and *St. Laurence on the Gridiron*, now in the Uffizi in Florence (the gift of Contini Bonacossi). At this time he gained his first private commissions: the gloomy bust of Bishop G.B. Santoni in the church of Santa Prassede and the monument to Giovanni Vigevano in Santa Maria sopra Minerva.

The Mythological Sculptures for Cardinal Borghese

Bernini's opportunity came when he was twenty, when Cardinal Scipione Borghese asked him to sculpt a group of Aeneas and Anchises, inspired by the celebrated passage in the *Aeneid* describing Aeneas' flight from the burning city of Troy. Aeneas leaves the city carrying his aged father on his shoulders, followed by his young son. The figurative solution that Bernini came up with, however, was still strongly influenced by his father and has much in common, as Baldinucci has pointed out, with Raphael's figure of a young man carrying an older in his *Fire in the Borgo* fresco in the Stanza dell'Incendio in the Vatican Palace. Critics disagree about whether father and son worked together on this sculpture (1618–19), which was made at the same time as they were working in the Barberini Chapel in Sant'Andrea della Valle. What is certain is that the position chosen for the aged Anchises is similar to Pietro's *St. John the Baptist*, but without the anatomical mistakes made there. Gian Lorenzo was already playing in virtuoso fashion with the spiral form of the three figures, which terminates with the statuettes of the household gods rescued by Anchises.

This spiral motif had its origins in late Mannerism. Bernini made it his own in a masterly fashion, using it in a number of different compositions to form the skeleton of the further three marble sculptures that Cardinal Borghese commissioned from him. All three, now in the Borghese Gallery in Rome, demonstrate how Bernini's style evolved between 1621 and 1625.

Bernini had already experimented with the potential offered by the spiral twist in *Neptune and Glaucus*, sculpted in 1520 for a fountain in

FOLLOWING PAGES:
Gian Lorenzo Bernini's *Rape of Proserpina*, made 1621–22. Galleria Borghese.

Detail from Gian Lorenzo Bernini's *Rape of Proserpina* showing the virtuosity of his treatment of the surfaces in depicting flesh tones. Galleria Borghese.

Fourth hall of the Galleria Borghese, the Sala degli Imperatori, dominated by Bernini's *Rape of Proserpina*. It takes its name from the porphyry busts of Roman emperors on display there.

Villa Montalto (now destroyed) belonging to Cardinal Alessandro Peretti. The sculpture, which now has its own room in the Victoria and Albert Museum in London, shows how the young sculptor was striving to make his material fluid and thus eliminate the concept of a best viewpoint. As in Bernini's other works from in this period, it is possible to walk around the *Neptune and Glaucus* and discover an infinity of equally valid viewpoints. There is no "front" or "back," as there had been for the *St. Sebastian*, where the spiral composition of the structure is concentrated in one plane, since the statue was made for a niche in the Barberini Chapel in Sant'Andrea della Valle. In concept, therefore, the sculpture was the equivalent of a relief.

The *Rape of Prosperina* (1621–22), on the contrary, is completely immersed in space. However, as for other sculptures commissioned by Cardinal Borghese, Gian Lorenzo had in mind a specific way of displaying his sculpture that would heighten the beholder's enjoyment of it if viewed from the best viewpoint. It is clear that the literary inspiration, Ovid's *Metamorphoses* was merely the pretext to set free a dynamism, immediately taken up by the marble, that is alive and throbs through the contrast between Prosperina's defenseless soft body and Pluto's powerful anatomy. Apart from anything else, the young Bernini here had a chance to recreate the virtuoso effect he had already experimented with in his *Aeneas and Anchises*, in which Anchises' flabby flesh falls in folds under the hands of his loving son who, in the effort to

keep hold of him, tightly grasps the old man's thigh and left leg. Now it is Prosperina's youthful flesh that reveals all its soft sensuality as she struggles in vain to break free of Pluto's rough arms. As she twists, she fills the lustful hands of the god of the underworld with the soft folds of flesh that are the joy of lovers. Thanks to his prodigious talent, Gian Lorenzo managed brilliantly to capture all this in marble.

David

When he tackled his *David* in 1623–24, Bernini knew that he was risking comparison with works in a sculptural tradition that included the great names of the artistic culture of the Italian Renaissance, from Donatello to Verrocchio and Michelangelo. He subverted the traditional way of representing David. Instead of depicting the static figure after killing Goliath (as had Donatello and Verrocchio) or the measured strain of the act itself (as had Michelangelo), Bernini once again countered with the dynamic charge of the spiral. It is well-known that he took his inspiration from the so-called *Borghese Gladiator*, now in the Louvre but at the time one of the prize pieces in Cardinal Borghese's collection. From the *Gladiator* derive the feet planted widely apart and the twisting torso. However, compared to its classical model, Bernini's figure has an upright torso (the original bends forward, on a level with his outstretched leg).

In comparison to the earlier celebrated David sculptures, Bernini paid particular attention to the biblical text and sought to follow it as closely as possible. Unlike the earlier sculptures, Gian Lorenzo's hero has a shepherd's pouch around his neck which already contains pebbles ready to use in the deadly sling which he will use against Goliath. The upper part of David's body is represented immediately after he has taken a stone from his pouch. This means that the torso twists and strains not just physically but psychologically. The *Borghese Gladiator* was represented in the moment in which the athlete fends off his enemy's blow with one arm while the other is about to strike a downward blow with his short sword (now lost). Bernini's *David*, however, is captured in the moment he is deciding where to aim while arming his weapon to make his stab mortally effective. His position corresponds to a moment of stillness between two equal and opposite movements. The hero is depicted when, having taken the stone from his pouch, he twists his body in the opposite direction, tensioning it spring-like, then stops to think for a split second before releasing the stone that will slay Goliath. All the strain that has been built up shows in David's

Gian Lorenzo Bernini's *Aeneas and Anchises* (1618–19), the first work he made for Cardinal Scipione Caffarelli Borghese. In contrast to Raphael's famous fresco of this motif in the Stanza of the Vatican Palace, Bernini's sculpture remains extraordinarily close to Virgil's text, apparent in the Phrygian headgear of Anchises, a reference to his eastern origins, as well as the fact that he is being carried on Aeneas' shoulders (Anchises had been made lame by an avenging bolt of lightning from Jupiter). Aeneas' exemplary conduct may be an allusion to the name of the work's patron, Scipione (staff, support). Galleria Borghese.

OPPOSITE:
Gian Lorenzo Bernini, *David*, made between 1623 and 1624. In contrast to the famous work of his predecessors Donatello and Michelangelo, Bernini chose to depict the moment of battle with the giant Goliath. The motif of the body's torsion may have been taken from the antique statue of the so-called *Borghese Gladiator*, now in the Louvre. Galleria Borghese.

face, a self-portrait that was executed with Cardinal Borghese's assistance, for he volunteered to hold a mirror up to enable the twenty-five-year-old Bernini to complete his work.

Apollo and Daphne

Without a doubt the work which, due to its unparalleled virtuosity, most astonished Bernini's contemporaries was the *Apollo and Daphne*, finished only in 1625. Work had been interrupted while Bernini sculpted the *David*. Because of a Latin couplet dictated by the Barberini pope, Urban VIII ("Whoever lusts after the joys of fleeting beauty fills his hands with leaves—or rather, tastes bitter berries"), this has been interpreted as a moralizing work. The episode, which like the *Rape of Prosperina* comes from Ovid's *Metamorphoses*, shows the frustrated love of the god Apollo for a nymph who preferred to turn into a laurel tree rather than give into his passion. Here again the classical model for the young Apollo can be seen. Both Apollo's figure and his position are directly derived from the celebrated *Belvedere Apollo*. Many critics think that the figure of Daphne, on the other hand, was literary in inspiration, based on poetry by Marino or Tasso.

The four sculptures commissioned by Cardinal Borghese not only highlight Bernini's astonishing technical and stylistic progress, but are also milestones in the development of Baroque poetics, mixing together spectacular effect, emotion, and truth.

St. Bibiana, St. Longinus, and the Baldacchino

It was not by chance that with the statue of *St. Bibiana*, executed in 1626 for the church of Santa Bibiana, Bernini—who was also a comic playwright and theater set designer—seized the opportunity to experiment with the theatrical potential of placing a statue in a niche emphasized with special lighting.

This is exactly what he was to do on a monumental scale with the crossing in St. Peter's and the rhetorical statue of *St. Longinus*. Here again, the whole area beneath the dome was arranged like a huge theatrical set in an attempt to diminish the embarrassing aesthetic imbalance that had been created when a longitudinal nave had been forced on Michelangelo's original central design. It is worth noting that long before Cardinal Maffeo Barberini became pope and took the name of Urban VIII, he had cursed Maderno's addition and even called for it to be ripped down altogether.

Apollo and Daphne (1622–25), the last sculpture created by Bernini for Cardinal Borghese. Bernini depicts the moment at which Daphne, pursued by Apollo, is transformed into a laurel tree. Galleria Borghese.

OPPOSITE:
Detail of the head of Daphe, showing the virtuoso treatment of the heroine's terror as she metamorphoses into a tree. Galleria Borghese.

Bernini started the *Baldacchino*, or bronze canopy, for St. Peter's in 1624. According to a contemporary satirical barb attached to the "speaking statue" Pasquino—"What the barbarians failed to do, the Barberini did" ("quod non fecerunt barbari, fecerunt Barberini")—the bronze for this came from the pronaos of the Pantheon. The central theatrical purpose of the *Baldacchino* was, at least as far as the eye was concerned, to bring the plan of the basilica back within the canons of centrality. Certainly, as far as the inner space of St. Peter's is concerned, the *Baldacchino* constitutes the key attraction that draws the attention of the faithful to precisely the most sacred point in the whole building. It is almost as if a huge processional canopy has just been put down by imaginary acolytes singing the praises of God. Thus Bernini's bronze canopy is the macroscopic marker of the place where St. Peter was buried. It was around this underlying concept, emerging from Bernini's experience of the ephemeral art which was so popular in Baroque Rome, that he fashioned a symbolic set, able at one and the same time to exalt the glory of the Church and the Barberini family.

Four marble bases hold the papal insignia and the sculptured allegory of the Church giving birth to Truth, traditionally attributed to Borromini. From these rise four Salamonic (spiral) columns which derive their shapes from the columns in Old Peter's, the ancient Constantinian basilica. Legend had it that these had come from Solomon's Temple in Jerusalem. Beyond the formal beauty of the supports, heightened by the contrast between the dark bronze and the gilded vine leaves, the *Baldacchino*, which uses the Salamonic column motif on a monumental scale, represents a macroscopic seal uniting the Old Testament wisdom of Solomon, the Christian tradition of Constantine, and the rebirth of a triumphal Church under the guidance of the Barberini family.

It is not by chance that the enormous columns support four false trabeations from which shines forth a golden sun, symbol of the Barberini, and from the cornice that joins them fall false pendants of a cloth with cherubs and bees, another Barberini symbol. The cherubs are repeated in the angels on the corners above and in the group of little angels bearing the papal insignia. The overall effect is reminiscent of the Ark of the Covenant.

The secret—and the fascination—of Bernini's invention, which is halfway between architecture and sculpture, lies in the fact that it provokes the same reactions that in a debate are caused by the use of rhetorical devices such as hyperbole and metonymy. If St. Peter's is the argument, then the *Baldacchino* is the hyperbole, in other words the rhetorical device consisting of exaggeration of

the whole story by choosing the climax of the tale and translating it into an image that yet again relates to a precise reference in classical sculpture. It is not hard to pick out features in Longinus' face that are taken from the *Laocoön*.

The other significant aspect apparent in the *St. Longinus* and the rearrangement of the crossing in St. Peter's, is Bernini's ability to arrange sculptural groups on the basis of the complexity of the tale they tell. In order to do this, he employed all the linguistic and technical devices he knew from architecture, sculpture, and painting. This was the start of what can be defined as the theory of *"bel composto,"* now called the

OPPOSITE AND LEFT:

The bronze *Baldacchino* in St. Peter's made from a design by Bernini between 1624 and 1633, assisted by Francesco Borromini. By raising the motif of the ancient Salamonic columns of the memorial to St. Peter onto a new level the sculptors not only created a visual link with tradition and magnified the importance of the sacrament, but were also able to provide a balance to the dominance of the dome.

Bernini's tomb for Urban VIII (1628–47), in which the polychrome design used by Guglielmo della Porta was developed still further. St. Peter's.

what the speaker wishes to say. It cannot be denied that the *Baldacchino* has exaggerated dimensions rather than being truly elegant. The work itself also plays upon the linguistic ambiguity of its own position. Bernini was well aware that in the center of any self-respecting church there had to be a ciborium. However, he wanted to place his *Baldacchino* there. He therefore used metonymy, that is to say, he used one word but gave it the meaning of another—by *baldacchino* Bernini meant *ciborium*. This is the fascination of his invention, the very soul of Baroque. It is this type of visual rhetoric that succeeds in persuading the faithful of the marvelous nature and importance of all they have come to see.

The *St. Longinus* in the crossing above the *Baldacchino* is the perfect example of this. Longinus' stance contains all the efficacy and theatricality of someone trying to convince the crowd. The statue of Longinus, named in the Gospels as the centurion who pierced the crucified Christ's side with his lance, is monumental. With arms spread wide, the sculpture captures the astonishment in the words attributed to Longinus in St. Matthew's Gospel, "Truly this man was the Son of God!" Here again, as he had for *David*, Bernini based his interpretation on the biblical text and, as he had succeeded in doing in the *David*, he managed to encapsulate

theory of the total work of art aimed at persuading and astonishing the beholder in general and the faithful in particular. The crossing in St. Peter's can be regarded as the starting-point of this path, which was to culminate in the masterpiece of the Cornaro Chapel in Santa Maria della Vittoria.

The Monument of Urban VIII

The monument of Urban VIII in St. Peter's, commissioned by the pope in 1628 but not completed until some time between 1637 and 1647, was the work that emphasized the pictorial aspects of *bel composto* by employing a broad range of materials. The luminous effect of the bronze used to cast the figure of the pope and the sarcophagus surmounted by the image of Death recall the virtuosity of the *Baldacchino* columns. The design and color of the gleaming marble surfaces that decorate the niches are reminiscent of those used in the crossing in St. Peter's. It is almost as if in designing the pope's tomb, Bernini was concerned to point out the main contributions that Urban had made to St. Peter's.

Fountains

The principal commissions that the Barberini family gave Bernini outside St. Peter's were for fountains. Here he departed completely from those typical of late Mannerism, frequently linked to architectural complexes. Instead he opted for natural features or unusual shapes, such as the *Fontana della Barcaccia* in Piazza di Spagna.

Inspired by the low, broad river craft (*barcace*) that carried wine along the quiet waters of the Tiber, the fountain, constructed in 1627–28 under the supervision of Pietro Bernini, stands out as one of Gian Lorenzo's most inspired inventions. Here once again he uses the rhetorical device of metonymy in a monument which is full of allusions, centered around the fact that water coming out of a boat designed to transport wine immediately evokes the feelings of plenty and joy. This is associated with Rome under Urban, which is identified as the Land of Plenty.

This idea is virtually repeated in the *Fontana delle Api* (Fountain of the Bees) constructed much later on, in 1644, but now almost entirely rebuilt by successive restorations. The Barberini heraldic bees spout water into a low trough from which animals and passers-by alike can drink. The fountain is finished off with a naturalistic touch—an open shell—which Bernini had used

Fontana della Barcaccia, the Boat Fountain, made by a young Gian Lorenzo Bernini in 1627–28 for Urban VIII. Its construction was part of efforts by the pope to incorporate the Acqua Vergina into the region between the Piazza di Spagna and the emerging Piazza del Popolo. The form of the fountain recalls the famous antique fountain shaped like a ship, which stood in front of the church of Santa Maria in Domnica. Piazza di Spagna.

four years earlier in the *Fontana del Tritone* (Triton Fountain), constructed on what had been the Barberini family's vineyard, but was now the site of their *palazzo* on the edge of town.

The Triton Fountain is composed of four dolphins whose tails mesh together to support an enormous open shell on which stands a muscular triton blowing for all he is worth into a conch. The intention behind the fountain was to create a water display that would provide an architectural reminder of the water supply provided by the Acqua Felice acqueduct commissioned by Urban VIII. What the pope needed was a water supply for his new residence and the surrounding area. Bernini invested this practicality with a symbolic dimension.

It is as though Neptune himself has taken the trouble to send his herald to announce that, thanks to the pope's generosity, even this area of Rome now enjoys the restorative benefits of water. The four dolphins emerge unexpectedly from the low broad pool, holding the shell with their tails. The shell opens and out of it comes a triton who makes the announcement. He blows into the conch, but instead of a stentorian blast that would engage everyone's attention, the much-desired water gushes forth, like a miracle. Thus Bernini unfailingly astonished both his patrons and the public alike, all captivated by the fascination of his creativity and imagination.

St. Teresa

Even those fiercely hostile to Bernini, such as the Pamphili pope Innocent X who succeeded Urban VIII, never tried to banish him from the artistic scene in Rome and by extension—no exaggeration in those days—the world. But it was no accident that during the early years of Innocent's papacy, Bernini concentrated on private commissions such as the Raimondi Chapel in San Pietro in Montorio and, above all, the Cornaro Chapel in Santa Maria della Vittoria.

Although the architectural side of the Cornaro Chapel has already been discussed, it is worth noting how closely the principal sculpture follows the description that St. Teresa left of her experience of mystical ecstasy. The sculpture also clearly demonstrates Bernini's desire to make a theatrical set of the altar, an eternal stage on which the great spectacle of faith and revelation is played out. The marble group that is the focus of the recently restored chapel is the scene of St. Teresa's ecstasy as it was depicted in contemporary prints. Lavin noted that the central niche and tabernacle which house the sculpture allude not just to the Eucharist, but also to the place where the mystical event occurred, traditionally identified—though St. Teresa herself said nothing on the subject—as the choir of the convent of the Incarnation at Ávila.

Bernini had to keep almost to the letter of the account that St. Teresa left in her *Life*.

"It pleased the Lord that sometimes I was able to contemplate the vision I here describe. I would see next to me, on my left, an angel in human form… He was not tall, but short and very beautiful. His face glowed so much that he seemed to belong to the highest angelic order… In his hands I saw a long gold lance with an iron tip from which I thought a tongue of flame issued. With this he appeared to pierce my heart several times and thus penetrate my innermost parts… The pain was so intense that I groaned a number of times. So overwhelming was the

For this Fontana del Tritone from 1640 on Piazza Barberini, Bernini created a fountain in which the architectural elements were greatly reduced in importance. The fountain is dominated by the figure of a triton in a shell borne by four dolphins.

sweetness provoked in me by that intense pain that I wished never to lose it…."

Only Bernini's genius could give physical form to the saint's figure and words.

The Fountain of the Four Rivers

After the unfortunate incident of the demolition of the campanile of St. Peter's, Bernini achieved rehabilitation in the eyes of Innocent X through his *Fontana dei Quattro Fiumi* (Fountain of the Four Rivers), made between 1648 and 1651 for an Egyptian obelisk unearthed in the Circus of Maxentius in 1647. Bernini had been categorically excluded from competing for this design long before he submitted any plans. It was only his stubbornness that led him, against all odds, to push ahead and complete his idea, casting a silver model which he submitted to the reluctant pope with the help of Prince Ludovisi and Donna Olimpia, the pope's sister-in-law and former lover.

The fountain recalls a huge table centerpiece, a form particularly suited to the evocative oval shape of Piazza Navona, which Palazzo Pamphili, built for the pope, overlooks. Using studies by Athanasius Kircher, Rivosecchi has demonstrated that the fountain is in fact an extraordinarily refined allegory of divine grace, which falls earthwards to sustain the four corners of the world known at the time. Thus the figure of the Nile, sculpted by Jacopo Antonio

Fountain of the Four Rivers on Piazza Navona made by Bernini between 1648 and 1651. This Baroque masterpiece combines sculptural and architectural elements with a complex iconography to create a unique synthesis that serves to preserve the memory of its patron, Innocent X.

re-establish him in the world's eyes was a monumental group, *Truth Unveiled by Time*. Bernini was able to sculpt only the figure of Truth himself. The iconography was lifted from the illustrations in one of the most popular books of the seventeenth century, Cesare Ripa's Iconology (*Iconologia*), published in 1603 and reprinted repeatedly, to the delight of artists and patrons alike. In Bernini's mind, the sun that the blossoming nude girl holds in her hand is an allusion not only to the brightness of daylight and the consequent lack of subterfuge, it also recalls the sun as emblem of the Barberini family, under whose protection Bernini had ample opportunity to demonstrate his ability and creativity.

The Chair of St. Peter

During the twelve years of the Chigi pope Alexander VII's papacy (1655–67) Bernini's major sculptural undertaking was the *Cathedra Petri*, the Chair of St. Peter, completed just a year before Alexander's death. The Chair was the result of a team effort involving Bernini's pupils and colleagues, principally Johannes Schor, a German sculptor responsible for the reliefs on the back of the throne. Here again the rhetorical device of metonymy came into play

One of the four masks which decorate the Fontana del Moro.

Fontana del Moro on the southern side of Piazza Navona. The sculpture from which the fountain derives its name is an Ethiopian fighting with a dolphin.

Fancelli, represents Africa; the Danube, by Antonio Raggi, Europe; the Ganges, by Claude Poussin, Asia; and the *Plate*, by Francesco Baratta, the Americas, discovered a century and a half earlier. The only elements made by Bernini himself are the lions drinking, symbolizing the sun and plenty, and the river horse—a literal representation of the then unknown hippopotamus—symbol of Typhon, god of destruction and darkness. Read as a whole, therefore, the fountain is an image of the universe illuminated by divine grace, capable of bringing the opposites of light and dark together into the harmonious balance of life.

All the same, the fountain is not merely the artistic transposition of the learned dissertations Athanasius Kircher expounded in his *Obelischus Pamphilijus* (The Pamphili Obelisk), but is rather a summation of all the aesthetic solutions that Bernini had proposed in his previous fountains. The work is based on the calculated contrast between the clear geometric form of the obelisk and the sharp rocks on which it rests. Bernini deliberately emphasized this contrast through naturalistic features such as the palm and the snake, whose irregular and sinuous shapes capture the multiform variety of God's creatures.

Truth Unveiled by Time

However, the work upon which Bernini pinned his hopes of a professional comeback that would

541

The Chair of St. Peter, made 1657–66, shows features typical of Bernini's late work. Sculpture and architecture combine with an ingenious use of light to form an evocative aesthetic whole. The concept, intended to illustrate the authority of papal teaching for the whole world, is represented by Sts. Augustine, Ambrose, Athanasius, and John Chrysostom. St. Peter's.

OPPOSITE:
Tomb of Alexander VII by Bernini's workshop, made from his designs 1676–1678. The upper level shows the deceased in an attitude of prayer while the pedestal is surrounded by allegorical figures of Charity, Justice, Prudence, and Truth.

Truth, from the tomb of Alexander VII. St. Peter's.

for the purpose of catching the eye of the faithful and keeping attention there.

A true theatrical set, the huge composition dominates the apse of St. Peter's, framed by two great pilasters. Its aim is to give the impression of nothing less than an explosion of the sacred within the architectural setting. In order to attain this purpose, Bernini used all the devices he had tried out elsewhere, for instance in the Cornaro Chapel. There as here, natural light is transformed into divine light and luminous grace. The artist was setting the scene for a true epiphany (the appearance of God). In the center is a halo of light (the window) containing the dove of the Holy Ghost, whose blinding splendor radiates all around, on the stuccowork and the gilded marble. This creates

a glory of clouds and angels who crown St. Peter's chair, which is supported by bronze and gilded bronze statues of the Four Fathers of the Church. The composition is also a reliquary. It even takes the shape of a reliquary in the truest sense of the word, as inside it houses the *Cathedra Petri*, a richly decorated wooden throne inlaid with ivory, dating from the time of Charlemagne and used by medieval popes. According to legend, this throne was no less than the chair of St. Peter himself. This is why the ensemble is a rhetorical metonymy: it applies the term that describes the content to either the content or the monument. Thus in calling it a *Cathedra*, Bernini meant "the Glory of the Church." He intended to suggest a whole series of allusions that range from the obvious reference to the *Etimasia* (the empty throne of God) through to the triumph of the holy sacrament, the subject of Raphael's fresco in the Stanza della Segnatura in the Vatican Palace.

The universal significance of the composition is demonstrated by the presence of the Four Fathers of the Church, two from the Roman tradition (Sts. Ambrose and Augustine in the foreground) and two from the Greek tradition (Sts. Athanasius and John Chrysostom). For them Bernini reused a sculptural motif from the Cornaro Chapel, heavily draped garments similar to those of the *St. Teresa* and *St. Longinus*. Nonetheless, a slightly different idea creeps in, the presence of a sudden breeze which lifts the folds—the breath of God.

The Ponte Castel Sant'Angelo *Angels*

Bernini was to use this idea again for his *Angels* in Sant'Andrea delle Fratte (1668–69), a trial run for the angels that his studio would make for the Ponte Sant'Angelo. It was during the short-lived rule of the Rospigliosi pope, Clement IX (1667–69), that the Ponte Sant'Angelo, the most spectacular enterprise of Roman Baroque, got underway. It was not completed, however, until 1672 by which time Clement X (1670–76) had succeeded Clement IX.

The idea of embellishing the bridge that crossed the Tiber at Castel Sant'Angelo with statues—even ephemeral ones—went back to the decorations prepared for Emperor Charles V's visit to Rome in April 1536, when temporary stucco statues were used. Domenico Bernini, Gian Lorenzo's son and biographer, tells us that it was Pope Clement, "as eager as his predecessors to increase the magnificence of St. Peter's basilica," who "instructed [Bernini] to invent some noble creation that would best adorn the

bridge next to the castle from which it takes its name." It is likely that Alexander VII had already thought of the idea, but had been unable to see it through.

The theme of the Ponte Sant'Angelo sculpture was the creation of a religious story in which, one by one, the angels exhibit all the instruments of the passion of Christ, demonstrating not only the reality of the Savior's sacrifice but also his human nature. The design Bernini drew up must have pleased Alexander, himself a playwright and man of the theater who had first met Bernini in 1634 when Bernini designed the set for *Sant'Alessio*, written by the future pope.

Walking across the bridge now took on the significance of following a great *Via Crucis* (stations of the cross), in which the angels, newly descended from heaven, allow the faithful to behold the unquestionable truth of the Gospels and the path to redemption that Christ desires. At the same time, however, the presence of the angels (of whom only the one with the *titulus crucis*—INRI superscription—is by Bernini himself) transforms the bridge to Castel Sant'Angelo into a paradisical road leading to the heavenly Jerusalem. It is easy to understand then, why the angels' robes are stirred by a non-existent breeze. It is the same breath that moves the feelings and touches the hearts of the faithful—the breath of God.

Last Works

Bernini produced a similar effect for the *Blessed Ludovica Albertoni*, which he executed around the same time, when work was already underway on the Ponte Sant'Angelo. Once again Bernini was able to capture the torment that the saint suffered during her mystical ecstasy. He shows this not just through the way she falls exhausted onto her bed but also in the way that the broad folds of her robe allude to the folding up of her soul, shaken by the unbearable divine vision.

Bernini's final monumental work—he was now nearly eighty—was the monument of Alexander VII in St. Peter's, built almost a decade after the pope's death. Though this too was produced by Bernini's workshop, it contains all of Bernini's inventive genius. He retained the triangular shape he had used for Urban VIII's monument but modernised it by introducing a spectacular new idea: an enormous drape of pink jasper borne aloft by the skeletal figure of Death, who also holds an hourglass, whose ebbing sands show the end of Alexander's time on earth.

This was almost an omen: two years after the completion of the tomb, Bernini died in Rome on November 28, 1680. He had set the mold for

over sixty years of artistic life, not just in Rome but throughout the world. His influence would last long into the following century: his work was the inheritance that future generations had to deal with.

Pupils and Followers: Bernini's Studio

There is no question that it was Bernini's genius that conditioned art in the seventeenth century. However, it is equally true that his artistic virtuosity could not have attained the strength it did, had he not worked with a host of sculptors

whose function was to enlarge its scope. In order to gain a clear picture of the artistic situation in Rome during the seventeenth century, it is therefore necessary to examine the people who worked in Bernini's workshop.

This is all the more pertinent in view of the fact that, while in the first half of the century Bernini worked alongside other major sculptors such as Francesco Mochi, Alessandro Algardi, and François Duquesnoy, from 1654, after their deaths (Duquesnoy had died earlier, in Livorno in 1643), Bernini totally dominated the scene. Indeed, following Alexander VII's election as pope, no one questioned this. In addition to this, Bernini's studio became the forcing ground where leading sculptors trained. It would be they who continued to spread Bernini's vision of art after his death, not just in Rome and throughout Italy, but in the rest of Europe too.

Within Bernini's circle there are a range of figures of varying importance. First, there are the minor figures of his younger brother Luigi (1612–81), who worked on the monument of the Countess Matilda of Tuscany in St. Peter's, and of his son, Paolo Valentino (1648–1728), whose *Infant Christ* is now in the Louvre. Since the studio offered a guaranteed income, it was hardly likely that Bernini would exclude his family, regardless of their artistic talent.

However, apart from the exceptions he made for his own family, Bernini was always careful to recruit the very best craftsmen. These included Girolamo Lucenti (1627–98), one of the best bronze-casters of the day, who cast artillery for the popes as well as striking medals, and Lazzaro Morelli (1608–90), who worked on the monument of Alexander VII, for which he sculpted the figure of Truth. Morelli was also responsible for the *Angel with the Scourge* on the Ponte Sant'Angelo, as well as exporting Bernini's influence to his native Ascoli Piceno.

To some extent it was possible to build an entire career in the master's shadow. Starting with small projects, sculptors worked their way up to ever more important assignments. This was the case with Francesco Baratta (1590–1666), who started off making pillars for the nave in St. Peter's and was later given the job of making the *Ecstasy of St. Francis* for the Raimondi Chapel in San Pietro in Montorio, in stucco. It was not by chance that Baratta was called in to work on the *Fountain of the Four Rivers*, for which he sculpted the powerful figure of the River Plate, whose ankle circlet demonstrates his wild nature, free from civilization, summing up the character of the new continent. In the same vein, Baratta produced the figure of the Moor for the *Fontana del Moro* (Fountain of the Moor), also in Piazza Navona. Apart from all of this, he also sculpted garden figures for the court of Saxony.

Giuliano Finelli and Andrea Bolgi

Bernini's studio also served as a platform from which sculptors could depart to work in the outside world—particularly as, all too often, the workshop proved a complex microcosm where jealousies and rivalries bred easily. This was the case with Giuliano Finelli (1601–53) and Andrea Bolgi (1606–56). Finelli entered Bernini's workshop while Pietro Bernini was still alive. It seems that his first assignment was two putti for the tomb of Ubaldino della Gherardesca in Santa Maria sopra Minerva. It is certain that he worked on *Apollo and Daphne*, *St. Bibiana*, and the *Baldacchino* in St. Peter's.

Finelli broke with Bernini when he felt he was being passed over in favor of Bolgi, who like him came from Carrara but had only recently arrived in Rome. Bolgi was immediately given a major assignment for the statue of St. Helena for St. Peter's. Finelli reacted by branching out on his own and went on to produce highly respected works such as the *St. Cecilia* in the church of Santa Maria di Loreto. This, although revealing the influence of Bernini's *St. Bibiana*, was also influenced by Pietro da Cortona.

Finelli's masterpiece is undoubtedly the bust of Michelangelo Buonarroti the Younger, a descendant of Michelangelo and a close friend of Pietro da Cortona. It may even have been at Pietro's suggestion that Finelli gained the commission while he was still in Rome (he moved to Naples in 1634). Apart from his unquestioned technical ability, Finelli used a wealth of detail as his answer to the solution put forward in portraits by Bernini. These were heroic portraits, fashioned to fill big spaces, such as the last one Bernini produced, *The Savior*, now in the Chrysler Museum in Norfolk, Virginia, in the United States, or his *Scipione Borghese*.

Finelli's work, on the other hand, vibrates with light and rippling surfaces. The planes continuously mutate to become folds of satin, threads of cotton, the hairs of a beard, or locks of hair. Although Finelli's bust had no commemorative purpose, it is one of the finest of the seventeenth century. It is, therefore, not surprising that when he returned to Rome in 1650 he pursued a career as a portraitist.

Bolgi, a quite different character, began by working in Livorno with Pietro Tacca. Once in Rome, Bernini gave him the opportunity to sculpt the statue of St. Helena for the crossing of St. Peter's. It is unquestionably the least successful of the four statues there: although well-balanced, it is cold and is marked by a contained piety which contrasts with the theatrical agitation of the other statues. Nonetheless, Bolgi gained a reputation as a portraitist. His skill lay in simplifying the planes of the faces and busts, reducing them to an almost geometrical candor. This can be seen best in his portrait of Laura Frangipani in the church of San Francesco di Ripa, where his simplification of the body contrasts with the delicacy of the brocade decoration and the stiff lightness of the collar.

Antonio Raggi and Leonardo Reti

Antonio Raggi (1624–86) was an original yet faithful interpreter of Bernini's style. He started out as an assistant on the decoration of the pillars in the nave of St. Peter's. Later, Bernini gave him the assignment of sculpting the composed figure of the River Danube for the Fountain of the Four Rivers in Piazza Navona. Raggi was also responsible for the decorative features on the organ in Santa Maria del Popolo and for one of the angels in the transept who hold aloft the beautiful cloth with the Visitation depicted on it. In addition, he was responsible for the stuccowork in Sant'Andrea al Quirinale and the *Angel with the Column* on Ponte Sant'Angelo.

However, Raggi's most striking artistic expression is the stucco decoration of the ceiling in the church of the Gesù, where he worked in perfect harmony with Giovan Battista Gaulli. During the long time it took to complete the commission (1669–83), Raggi always managed to combine the needs of the paintings with those of the sculpture, thus creating one of the most beautiful artistic works of the seventeenth century.

Raggi's path crossed that of the Lombard sculptor Leonardo Reti, who arrived in Rome in 1671, when he assisted with the stucco in the Gesù. At the same time, he worked with Ferrata, who also had commissions in the churches of San Giovanni dei Fiorentini and Sant'Agnese in Agone, for which Raggi had made, respectively, a *Baptism of Christ* and a *Death of St. Cecilia* relief.

Ercole Ferrata and Domenico Guidi

Ercole Ferrata (1610–86), who, like Raggi, was from Como, arrived in Rome in 1646 after a short time spent in the Abruzzi east of Rome. Unlike the sculptors mentioned above, Ferrata immediately set up his own studio. Its main business was working with other sculptors, from Bernini to Algardi. Indeed Ferrata's studio looked after nearly all the body of work—drawings, designs, and sketches—produced by Algardi, which meant that Algardi's style continued well into the second half of the century. It cleverly tempered with Bernini's style and gave

life to what was to become the artistic taste of the second half of the seventeenth century, and continued to condition taste many years into the next century.

Ferrata was commissioned by Bernini to make bronze crucifixes for the altars in St. Peter's, where he also worked on decorating the pillars. He produced the marble elephant for the obelisk outside Santa Maria sopra Minerva and the *Angel with the Cross* for Ponte Sant'Angelo. It is to Ferrata that the *St. Agnes* in Sant'Agnese in Agone is owed, a sculpture in the main influenced by Pietro da Cortona. For the church of San Giovanni dei Fiorentini, Ferrata produced the heroic *Faith*, who raises the chalice of the Eucharist as a symbol of the ostentation of belief. Finally, Ferrata sculpted *St. Andrew the Apostle*, *St. Andrew of Avellino*, and *Fame* in Bernini's style for the recently restored facade of the church of Sant'Andrea della Valle.

Another studio active in Rome, which alternately cooperated and competed with Ferrata's studio, belonged to Domenico Guidi (1625–1701), a Tuscan sculptor and nephew of the same Giuliano Finelli who had so suddenly departed from Bernini's workshop. It was for Bernini that Guidi produced the *Angel with a Lance* on Ponte Sant'Angelo. However, most of his collaborative work was with Algardi, though he managed to leave the stamp of his personal style on it. An example is the *Holy Family* relief for Sant'Agnese in Agone, inspired by Algardi's relief of Leo the Great and Attila, discussed below. Guidi also produced a portrait of Felicia Zacchia Rondanini, again modeled on Algardi (*Olimpia Maidalchini*). After this, much of his work was for foreign patrons, particularly from England and Poland.

Melchiorre Caffà

It is clear that the so-called "minor" Roman sculptors melded the various currents in taste which derived from the various studio masters. This did not mean that original talents did not emerge in their own right.

One such was the Maltese sculptor Melchiorre Gafà (1638–67), whose surname was Italianized to Caffà. He created some wonderfully evocative works, such as the *Ecstasy of St. Caterina* marble relief that was commissioned for the church of Santa Caterina a Magnanapoli, and which is unanimously acclaimed as his masterpiece. Set into the ornate high altar, the relief exploits the pictorial effect of the colored marble and offers a personal interpretation of Bernini's methods by deliberately containing the spectacular quality of the work within the conscious bounds of pretense.

Allessandro Algardi, *St. John the Evangelist*. This stucco statue from 1628 is from the Bandini Chapel in San Silvestro al Quirinale. The commission was conveyed to the sculptor by the painter Domenichino.

BOTTOM, RIGHT:
Alessandro Algardi, stucco statue of *St. Mary Magdalene* for the Bandini Chapel in San Silvestro al Quirinale. The influence of antique art is clear.

BELOW:
Alessandro Algardi, *Portrait of Olimpia Maldaichini*, a relative of Innocent X, which combines in a single image precise psychological observation with standard formulas of pathos such as the billowing widow's veil. Galleria Doria Pamphili.

Anti-Bernini Movement

"Sculpture still misses the sculptor, without whom it cannot reach the level of its sister, painting." So wrote Giovan Battista Bellori in his *Lives*, published in 1672 on the model of Vasari. In Bellori's view, in 1672 there was not a single sculptor who could be a worthy rival to his painter colleagues and their great art.

The virtual monopoly that Bernini held for three-quarters of the seventeenth century, from the mid-1620s onwards, gave rise to what amounted to an anti-Bernini movement. Reviled by the respected critic Giovan Battista Passeri as "the dragon of the Hesperides" which "spewed poison everywhere" so that no one could "steal the golden apples of papal favor," there is no doubt that Bernini left little room for competition. Nevertheless, his overpowering figure not only concealed the solid studio organization described above (while his workshop employed artists of true talent), but also indicates the artistic pulse of seventeenth-century sculpture.

Francesco Mochi

Francesco Mochi's early work has already been discussed, but the undoubted masterpiece of his later work is his *Baptism of Christ*, which manages to convey spiritual tension through physical tension. Originally commissioned for the church of San Giovanni dei Fiorentini, which turned it down, putting in its place a sculptural group of the same subject by Antonio Raggi, the *Baptism of Christ* ended up decorating the side of Ponte Milvio and was only recently moved to its present location in the entrance of Palazzo Braschi, the home of the Museo di Roma.

The Museo also houses Mochi's *Sts. Peter and Paul*, commissioned for San Paulo fuori le Mura. These too were turned down, but were purchased after Mochi's death by Alexander VII, who had them installed as decoration for Porta del Popolo, from where they have recently been moved. The *Baptism* dates from 1634–44, the *Sts. Peter and Paul* from between 1638 and 1652. They reveal a new direction in Mochi's creative vein: they endeavor to strip form bare and replace it with a dry and severe approach that does away with the theatricality of early Baroque. No one followed Mochi down this path.

Alessandro Algardi

The poetics of Alessandro Algardi (1598–1654) were quite different. Willing to highlight the pictorial effects of his art, he proved Bernini's only true rival in his attempt to guide sculpture toward a

ACCEPIT·ILLAM
DISCIPULUS·IN·SUA

MARIA
OPTIMAM·PARTEM·ELEGIT

strictly classical interpretation. On the other hand, in his native Bologna, Algardi had been a pupil of Ludovico Carracci, who was associated with the classicism of Guido Reni and Andrea del Sacchi, so it was unlikely that the young sculptor would take a different direction. To all of this was added the fact that, after arriving in Rome in 1625, he was employed by Cardinal Ludovisi as a "restorer" (rather than true restoration, the work involved adding to the antique sculpture). He was put in charge of the cardinal's extensive collection of Greek and Roman sculpture. There is little doubt, therefore, about how Algardi conceived art. The ancient masters played a dominating role in his conception, partly because between 1622 and 1625 he had been able to study the Gonzaga collection in Mantua before paying a short visit to Venice, where he was doubtless struck by the sculptural skills of Alessandro Vittoria.

Although he had had some commissions in Bologna, it was not until Algardi came to Rome that he received his first major commission. This was for stucco statues of Sts. John the Evangelist and Mary Magdalene for San Silvestro al Quirinale. These statues already show the influence of Bernini. This is especially noticeable in the *St. Mary Magdalene* (which may represent Mary of Bethany), which had some resemblance to Bernini's *St. Bibiana.* However, Algardi proves his originality in his interpretation of the drapery and in the balanced pose of the figure itself.

The difference between the two sculptors can be seen above all in their different conceptions of a portrait. A comparison of Bernini's bust of Pope Paul V of 1618 with Algardi's portrait of Cardinal Laudivio Zacchia less than a decade later reveals this. Bernini's bust looks as if it may move at any moment and the pope's sharp gaze seems to be studying the people who happen to be looking at it. Algardi's figure, clad in a fur mantel, seems immobile and absent, caught in a dimension almost outside time itself.

This dimension recalls one of Algardi's most beautiful portraits, that of Prince Camillo Pamphili, sculpted much later in 1644. By this time Algardi was a successful sculptor with a string of works to his credit, including *St. Filippo Neri with the Angel,* sculpted between 1635 and 1640, in the Chiesa Nuova (Santa Maria in Valicella) and the monument of Pope Leo XI, which took him ten years, from 1634 to 1644. These last two works have parallels with works by Bernini—the *St. Longinus* and the monument of Urban VIII—but Algardi was able to distance himself effectively.

If it is true that Algardi initiated his grand manner with the *St. Philip Neri,* it is equally true that he rejected Bernini's theatricality in favor of a muted style which is reflected in the geometry of the clothes as well as in the clear-cut linear features of the saint's face. The only concession he makes to pictorial effects is in the angel's robe with its unruly folds, though this is immediately quelled by the cold clarity of the marble. On the other hand, even Algardi's monument to Leo XI in St. Peter's, which reprised Bernini's triangle-based composition, conveys an overall cool effect by carefully avoiding the use of any material that might detract from the pale marble. In this way, Algardi staved off all pictorial effects reduced to the texturing of the surfaces attained by a skilful working of the marble. This does not mean that Algardi also shunned pow-

Alessandro Algardi's tomb for Leo XI. Built between 1634 and 1644, at the same time as Bernini's tomb for Urban VIII, it clearly borrows some of its concepts from Bernini's work. The figures of Liberty and Majesty at the sides were executed by Ercole Ferrata and Giuseppe Peroni. St. Peter's.

Alessandro Algardi, *Meeting between Pope Leo the Great and Attila.* The composition of this large relief is modeled on Raphael's representation of this crucial episode in the history of the papacy in the Stanza Eliodoro. Algardi's defining work, it is remarkable for the innovative forms of the layers in the relief: the foremost level, almost completely worked in the round, is set against a background which is graphic in nature. St. Peter's.

erful chiaroscuro effects. It is rather the manner in which he treated the marble surface, making it smooth and polished, that distinguishes him from Bernini. The result was that the monument of Leo XI became the model for papal funerary monuments through the end of the seventeenth century until the 1740s.

Something similar happened to what is perhaps Algardi's most famous work, the *Meeting between Pope Leo the Great and Attila,* sculpted between 1646 and 1653 for the Colonna Chapel in St. Peter's. Rightly considered as the prototype of Baroque reliefs, it has been called a painting by Carracci translated into marble. The huge relief reveals its debt to Raphael through Domenichino, who had also painted the same subject. Algardi's invention consists in the creation of the powerful illusion that the figures are coming out of the marble, by making the foreground figures almost fully rounded. The relief depicts the occasion in 425, when Pope Leo saw off Attila and the Huns with his standard in a sortie outside the gates of Rome. Behind the two figures are many levels to the relief, strengthening the sense of depth and the illusion of space.

François Duquesnoy

Another very different way of conceiving the relief was invented by François Duquesnoy (1597–1643). Also nicknamed Francesco il Fiammingo (the Fleming), because he came from Brussels, Duquesnoy did not live long enough to fully contest Bernini's cultural hegemony. Nonetheless his contribution to the Baroque aesthetic was considerable. He arrived in Rome in 1618 and was feted by the critics of the day who saw him as the champion of classical ideals. He became close friends with Nicolas Poussin, who influenced his early work, as can be seen in the *Bacchanalia of Putti* executed for Villa Pamphili and now in the Doria Pamphili Gallery, and the *Sacred and Profane Love* in the Galleria Spada.

The origin of Duquesnoy's sculpture can be traced back to Donatello's *schiacciato*, a type of low relief. The atmosphere generated by Duquesnoy's *Bacchanalia* relief, however, is the same as that created by Correggio and Rubens. The direct source of inspiration was the paintings of the same subject by Titian and Poussin. Duquesnoy sought to create a misty atmosphere that flatters the plump bodies of the little children and winged putti that so often appear in his work. An example is the monument to Adriano Uryburch in the church of Santa Maria dell'Anima, where the little angels holding up the central drape constitute the only human element in the whole composition.

When Duquesnoy was commissioned to carve the statue of St. Andrew for the crossing in St. Peter's (working from 1628 to 1640), comparisons to Bernini's *St. Longinus* were inevitable. It is obviously of the very highest quality (there is no comparison with Bolgi's *St. Helena*), all the same, it seems derivative from Bernini's *St. Longinus*, only managing to change Longinus' rhetorical gesture into a plea for help or pity.

As we have seen, Duquesnoy's best work was in his smaller sculpture, as can be seen from the wonderful *Bacchino* (which takes up Poussin's theme) in the Doria Pamphili Gallery and his *St. Susanna*, considered on a par with Bernini's *St. Bibiana*. Inspired by the classical model of

the *Capitoline Urania*, the statue has a balanced and self-contained dynamic which, as Bellori commented, expresses "a sweet air of the purest grace." In this work, the seventeenth-century classical ideal is truly given physical form. It was no accident, therefore, that the sculpture was repeatedly copied and became a source of inspiration for artists in the next century.

Marco Bussagli

ABOVE:
François Duquesnoy, *Victory of Sacred over Profane Love.* This marble relief from 1630 is notable for the painterly treatment of the surfaces and the subtly graduated layers of the relief. Galleria Doria Pamphili.

TOP:
François Duquesnoy, *Bacchanalia of Putti.* The theme of this relief from 1630 may be derived from Duquesnoy's admiration of Titian's depiction of the theme. The composition indicates the influence of Poussin, a friend of Duquesnoy. Galleria Doria Pamphili.

Seventeenth Century Painting and Caravaggio's Challenge

The Carracci and their School

The years around 1600 were fundamental to the development of Baroque painting in Rome. It was at this time that the masterpieces were produced which were to be the benchmarks for the best part of a century. During this time two main directions in painting emerged. One was associated with the figure of Michelangelo Merisi, known as Caravaggio, the other with the work of the three Carracci, two brothers and a cousin, who packed Rome with the best of their pupils from Bologna, including Domenichino, who set to work glorifying the city.

It is well known that the Carracci's Accademia dei Desiderosi (the Desirous) had become the best place to train, producing painters of the caliber of Guido Reni and Giovanni Lanfranco. Founded in 1583, the Academy—which changed its name to the Accademia degli Incamminati (the Progressives) in 1590—was based around drawing and studying anatomy from life. It therefore rid itself of the pictorial sophism held dear by the then famous Bolognese Mannerists such as Bartolomeo Passarotti, Sammacchini, and Ercole Procaccini. The difference between the Carracci Academy and similar institutions lay in the fact that the Carracci jettisoned what they regarded as the useless burden of aesthetic theories bound by fixed and repetitive models and formulas, to insist instead on personal commitment and effort in an attempt to discover, each and every time, new solutions to the problem of artistic representation through painting. In short, the secret that united first the Desiderosi then the Incamminati was the ceaseless practice of painting and decoration.

In this context, the eldest of the three Carracci, Ludovico (1555–1619), took on a role halfway between organizer and director of the Academy. Agostino (1557–1602), who was the elder of the two brothers, was given the task of teaching perspective and architecture. Annibale (1560–1609), the best-known and most enterprising of the three, was in charge of figure drawing, with particular emphasis on anatomy.

The Camerino and Galleria Farnese

It was Annibale whom the newly appointed Cardinal Odoardo Farnese called to Rome in the summer of 1595 to paint the gallery of the

Annibale Caracci, *Hercules at the Crossroads.* Originally in the Camerino of the Palazzo Farnese, the theme of the picture is the decision the hero had to make between virtue and vice. Naples, Museo Nazionale di Capodimonte.

OPPOSITE:
Annibale Caracci's ceiling paintings from the gallery in Palazzo Farnese, with mythological scenes of love stories from Ovid's *Metamorphoses.* Caracci succeeded in creating a new type of decoration by borrowing from the work of celebrated Roman models, such as Michelangelo's frescos in the Sistine Chapel, Raphael's frescos in the Villa Farnesina, and Caravaggio's panel paintings. The paintings are characterized by a combination of illusionistic elements with framed scenic images. so-called *quadi riportati.*

Palazzo Farnese. Nevertheless, the first task that Annibale completed for the cardinal was the decoration of a small room, the *Camerino*. This can be seen as a trial run for the fresco master-pieces that were to adorn the gallery.

The theme for the Camerino was devised by the learned humanist, Fulvio Orsini. It showed Virtue elevated over Vice, through scenes of Hercules and other mythological stories with this meaning, such as Ulysses and Circe, and Ulysses and the Sirens. It was not by chance that the central scene—the only one painted on canvas, now in the Museo di Capodimonte in Naples—showed Hercules at the crossroads, uncertain whether to follow the steep path of Virtue, which winds uphill, or to give in to the softness of Vice (which also signified the deceits of art).

From the formal point of view, this canvas points to the way in which, as soon as he finished the Camerino, Annibale Carracci was to use the same techniques on the ceiling of the gallery in Palazzo Farnese. The proximity of masterly frescos by Michelangelo and Raphael was to influence Annibale, pushing him into creating a grandiose style, but one which shied away from the courtly-heroic without being triumphal, dramatic without being theatrical.

Annibale Carracci's style set the pattern for much official painting over the following decades until the time of Pompeo Batoni. It is likely that the ever-present Fulvio Orsini had a hand in drawing up the iconography, while in the later stages Monsignor Giovanni Battista Agucchi, a close friend of Agostino, worked with him on it.

Initially the plan was to paint frescos commemorating the deeds of the military leader Alessandro Farnese, Cardinal Odoardo's father, who died in 1592. Later a decision was taken to revert to mythological and allegorical scenes, mainly taken from Ovid's *Metamorphoses*. If in the Camerino the theme had been the choice between Virtue and Vice, here the argument is the power of love which conquers all, even the feelings of the gods who, despite being eternal, cannot resist its pull. Thus the ceiling of the gallery, completed between 1587 and 1600, shows a succession of scenes, from the libidinous loves of Jupiter and Juno to the tender love of Diana and Endymion, even the monstrous love of Polyphemus for Galatea.

The center is dominated by the famous scene of the *Triumph of Bacchus and Ariadne*. Seated on chariots, they go in procession, like two classical rulers, amid the exultation and unbridled joy of a parade of satyrs and Sileni, maenads and nymphs. Drawing on both Renaissance and contemporary neoplatonic treatises, the frescos illustrated all aspects of love, from the feral Polyphemus and Acis through the sacred and profane.

The real invention of the ceiling frescos lies in their ability to arrange the scenes within settings that immediately reveal their nature as false or real paintings. They follow hard on each other's heels, in a succession of surprises and effects, not only completely renewing the tradition Michelangelo had begun with his Sistine Chapel ceiling, particularly in his *ignudi* and the figures in the medals, but also taking up Raphael's work in the Villa Farnesina frescos. A *trompe-l'oeil* effect is created that reveals a powerful architectural structure—an entablature supported by marble caryatids beneath a blue sky. Over the entablature the effect is completed by gilded and stuccoed framing devices. Compared to the large fresco cycles then being painted, the effect was astonishing.

San Giovanni in Laterano

It is revealing to recall that during the same period the transept of San Giovanni in Laterano was completed, commissioned by Clement VIII (1592–1605), who wanted to have the architecture and paintings refurbished in time for the jubilee in 1600. Clement's commission and that of the Palazzo Farnese gallery coincide precisely. They are thus yardsticks by which the trends in painting current at the time can be measured.

The theme of the San Giovanni in Laterano frescos was very different. They all depicted events that were connected to Constantine, who had consecrated the basilica and endowed it with its liturgical vessels and furnishing. The frescos are still in the late Mannerist style, as can be seen, for instance, in the *Baptism of Constantine* by Giuseppe Roncali (called Pomarancio) and in the *Ascension* by Giuseppe Cesari, better known as the Cavalier d'Arpino, which is indebted to Raphael's *Transfiguration*. Raphael's model was used as the basis for frescos, especially the way of connecting one scene to the next.

Annibale Carracci's approach, which was used here but had been tried out in the Sala di Costantino in the Vatican Stanze, was to set out the episodes as though they formed part of huge tapestries whose borders are scrolled up along the edge of the scenes. His work thus introduced a radical change into the vocabulary of painting at the start of the century. This was especially true compared to what can be considered the official style of painting approved by the pope's patronage.

The School of the Carracci

At more than sixty-five feet in length, twenty feet wide, and almost thirty-three feet high, the Palazzo Farnese gallery was much too large a project to be undertaken by one person, even an artist with Annibale Carracci's capacity for hard work. Thus, while the ceiling was almost entirely painted by Annibale, when it came to the walls, Annibale did not hesitate to bring in assistants such as Domenichino, Giovanni Lanfranco, Sisto Badalocchi, and, possibly, Antonio Carracci. The walls were frescoed in 1603–04 and the work gave the best pupils of the Carracci school a chance to gain the large public and private commissions then available in Rome.

Giovanni Lanfranco

It is not surprising therefore that during the first two decades of the seventeenth century—before and after his 1610–12 stay in Parma—Giovanni Lanfranco worked on most of the cycles of paintings commissioned in Rome. He also frequently assisted Guido Reni, as in the frescos for San Gregorio Magno (1608), the Borghese Chapel (Cappella Paolina) in Santa Maria Maggiore, and the chapel of the Annunciation in the Quirinal Palace (1609–10).

During his stay in Parma, Lanfranco learned from Correggio. By the time he came back to Rome he was ready to take on commissions in his own right. These include the ceiling decorations in Palazzo Mattei di Giove, executed about 1615. Inspired by the ceilings in Raphael's Loggias in the Vatican Palace, Lanfranco painted *Joseph Explaining the Prisoners' Dreams* and *Joseph Spurning Potiphar's Wife*, placing them in stucco frames reminiscent of paintings by Correggio and the Carracci.

Lanfranco's opportunity (apart from the frescos and canvases for Sant'Agostino) came with the commission to decorate the loggia ceiling in the Villa Borghese. This ceiling, completed 1624–25, was commissioned by Cardinal Scipione Borghese as a means of celebrating his family's return to favor following the election of the Barberini pope (Urban VIII, 1623–44). The architectural framework Lanfranco used in the decoration owes a clear debt to his experience of working under Annibale Carracci in the Palazzo Farnese gallery. Here too he uses an entablature supported by marble telamones through which the viewer glimpses blue sky scattered with white clouds. Looking up, at the center of the ceiling is a rectangular golden *quadratura* (illusionist decoration) inside which the viewer catches sight of a noble assembly of gods seated on soft cushions of vapor floating in the blue sky. The conception probably came from Ferrante Gianfattori, usually known as Ferrante Carlo, who from 1621 was secretary to Cardinal Scipione Borghese. The iconography of the huge fresco was an allusion to the supposed return to the golden age under the Borghese.

In the same years, Lanfranco was also working on another major cycle, which has now been broken up and divided between the United States (Paul Getty Museum, Los Angeles) and France (Musée des Beaux-Arts, Marseilles, Musée Sainte-Croix, Poitiers), as well as a number of private collections in Italy. The work consisted of huge canvases for the chapel of the Holy Sacrament in San Paolo fuori le Mura. It was probably commissioned by the abbot, Paolo Scotti, who may also have chosen the episodes from the Old Testament, whose common theme is that they were believed to point the way forward to the Eucharist. They include *Moses and the Messengers from Canaan* and *Elijah Receiving Bread from the Raven.*

The work which best reveals Lanfranco's debt to his contemporary, the great Correggio, is undoubtedly the dome of Sant'Andrea della Valle. Here, from 1625 until 1627, Lanfranco painted the *Glory of the Virgin*, in which the Virgin is enveloped in a luminous vortex of clouds and angels. With this work the vocabulary of painting is moved forward, becoming fully Baroque. From here onwards the sense of illusion and wonder that is provoked in the viewer were to be the hallmarks of the new art for the seventeenth century.

Domenichino

Annibale Carracci's circle produced another major player in Roman painting during the first thirty years of the century. This was Domenico Zampieri (1581–1641), better known as Domenichino, who moved to Rome from his native Bologna in 1602. He stayed there until 1630, when he retired to Naples.

It was immediately clearly apparent that Domenichino had a special relationship with Annibale Carracci. Once Annibale became aware of his pupil's talent, he did not hesitate to let him assist even on the most difficult projects of the Palazzo Farnese gallery, such as the *Lady with a Unicorn* and *Perseus and Andromeda*, although Domenichino still had to work from Annibale's own cartoons. Inside the palazzo Domenichino painted frescos (removed in 1820) for the so-called Casino della Morte, but once again working from Carracci's cartoons.

Thus it was that Domenichino—nicknamed "the Ox" because of his stubbornness and capacity for hard work—grew up in his master's shadow. However, he was able to make the most of his connections and he received the support of other painters from his native Bologna. One of his patrons was Cardinal Girolamo Agucchi, who in 1604 or 1605 commissioned paintings of the baptism, vision, and

Domenichino's large painting of the *Communion of St. Jerome* from 1614, showing a more logical order than the work by Agostino Caracci on which it is modeled. Along with his frescos, this painting established Domenichino's fame in Rome and is considered an example of early Baroque classicism. Vatican Museums, Pinacoteca.

Domenichino, *Diana the Huntress*. Painted in 1617 for Cardinal Pietro Aldobrandini, the picture is modeled on the description of the funeral games for Anchises, the father of Aeneas, in *Aeneid*. True to the text, Domenichino's picture portrays Diana as judge of the hunting competition, lavishing praise on the winner, who is shown in the upper right of the picture. Galleria Borghese.

temptation of St. Jerome for the lunettes in the cloister at Sant'Onofrio.

In these early works the attention that the young Domenichino paid to Raphael's pictorial vocabulary is already apparent, developed from studying the great Renaissance frescos at first hand. Thus the monumental quality and presence of the old men to the right in the *Baptism* recall the figures in Raphael's *School at Athens*. Similarly, the way that the figures are arranged in the *Vision of St. Jerome* owes a debt to Raphael's Sibyls in Santa Maria della Pace. This tendency was even more pronounced in the frescos Domenichino painted for the abbey at Grottaferrata south of Rome. This was his first major commission (1608–10), and was awarded to him as a consequence of his acquaintance with Annibale Carracci.

Half of the second decade of the century stands out for the sheer volume of masterpieces that were produced by Domenichino. These include the *Charity of St. Cecilia*, a fresco in the second chapel in the south aisle in San Luigi dei Francesi, which was dominated by Guido Reni's copy of Raphael's *St. Cecilia*. Domenichino's painting contains themes and figures that are familiar from Raphael's *Fire in the Borgo* in the Stanza dell'Incendio in the Vatican Palace, reinterpreted here in a devotional and popular key. Thus Raphael's representation of Aeneas carrying the aged Anchises to safety becomes a tender central scene in which a young man is carrying a beggar, while Raphael's hero hanging from the walls of the city in flames here becomes a young boy trying to clamber up

toward the saint, who is generously distributing goods and clothes.

It is easy to see why Domenichino was acclaimed as the Raphael of the seventeenth century and why his work is so important to the understanding of how the classical ideal was perceived in that century. The ideal did not shy away from allowing pathos as well as emotional turmoil to show in the subjects' faces. This is the other aspect of Baroque painting, which is best illustrated by looking at a work such as Domenichino's *Communion of St. Jerome* in the Picture Gallery (Pinacoteca) in the Vatican Museums, not only the high point of his career, but the benchmark for all painters of his day. This was to such an extent that a jealous Lanfranco distributed etchings of a work that Agostino Carracci had done on the same subject, and which Domenichino had studied in detail in his attempt to improve and modify the model in what was meant to be a tribute to his own Bolognese teachers. Lanfranco's attempt to discredit Domenichino failed utterly. Domenichino was fully absolved in the eyes of Poussin and Bellori, who wrote that "the movement, gesture, and actions of the figures are so different that, although there

Ceiling frescos by Domenichino in Sant'Andrea della Valle. Painted between 1623 and 1626, the paintings depict scenes from the life of St. Andrew and are in the choir of this Theatine church. The artist separated the individual episodes from each other by means of ornamental frames.

Part of Domenichino's ceiling decoration in Sant'Andrea della Valle showing the martyrdom of St. Andrew. In depicting this incident the artist created a harmonious link between the main action—preparations for the apostle's execution—and the landscape of the background, which features the Aurelian Walls of Rome.

are some ideas in common, it does not deserve to be branded as theft. Rather, it is a praise-worthy imitation."

As fate would have it, after this unpleasant-ness Lanfranco and Domenichino both ended up working on the same task in Sant'Andrea della Valle, albeit at different times. Between 1623 and 1626 Domenichino was commis-sioned by Cardinal Peretti Montalto to paint thirteen sections of the choir. The subject cho-sen was scenes from the life of St. Andrew. These included the *Calling of Andrew and Peter* and the *Flagellation, Martyrdom,* and *Glory* of St. Andrew.

By the time Domenichino was painting the frescos on the spandrels, it is possible that he was working with, perhaps even directly along-side, Lanfranco. Domenichino's frescos possess the courtly balance of a renewed form of clas-sicism, achieved due to the teachings of the Carracci, which breathed fresh life into Raphael's Renaissance ideal. Yet however surprising the pictorial invention may be, Domenichino never broke the magic of form.

than any of the other painters from Bologna. He was the only painter from the Bologna school to embrace Caravaggio's influence.

Among the works Reni produced in Rome is the renowned *Crucifixion of St. Peter*, painted in 1604–05, clearly inspired by Caravaggio's canvas of the same subject in Santa Maria del Popolo (discussed below). However, Reni's work does not possess the same dramatic dynamics as Caravaggio's. Unlike it, it is not composed along the diagonal but opts instead for the static composure of a triangle. Most of the height is filled with the upside-down cross on to which the saint is pinned. Reni's solution tends therefore to emphasize a classical and balanced beauty which cannot be disturbed even by the most tumultuous events, such as the martyrdom of a saint. His painting of the massacre of the Innocents, dating from about 1611, which was just after Reni had been back to Bologna for the first time, is similar. Yet it was this, the lesson Reni had learned from the Carracci, that made him great, to the point that he dominated the scene in Rome until 1614, when he withdrew and left the field open for Domenichino.

It is to Reni that we owe the large fresco of *St. Andrew Taken for Torture* in the small chapel of St. Andrew in San Gregorio Magno, which Cardinal Scipione Borghese commissioned in 1608. The work is constructed along a diagonal running from top left to bottom right, which frames the kneeling half-naked figure of the saint. This contrasts with the *Flagellation of St. Andrew* that Domenichino painted in the

Guido Reni's painting of St. Andrew led to execution. Completed in 1608, the picture is distinguished by its composition, the focus is the apostle praising the instrument of his martyrdom. Oratorio di San Gregorio Magno.

Guido Reni, ceiling fresco of Aurora. Painted in 1614, this fresco decorates the ceiling of the main hall in the Casino of the Palazzo Rospigliosi Pallavicini. It shows the rising sun, in the shape of Apollo's chariot surrounded by the hours of the day.

Guido Reni

Guido Reni (1575–1642) was the first of the great Bolognese artists to arrive in Rome, where he settled some time between 1599 and 1601. He was also the first to make a clean break with Rome, leaving in 1614 to return to Bologna. Although he trained at the Carracci Academy after a short time studying with the Flemish Mannerist Dionisio Calvaert, when in Rome Reni remained more independent of Annibale

same period when his master was called away to paint the lively *Angel Choir* in the apse of the chapel of St. Silvia, mother of St. Gregory, also in San Gregorio Magno.

Paul V's (1605–21) favor became apparent when he involved Reni in the painting of the Borghese Chapel in Santa Maria Maggiore, where he worked alongside others such as Lanfranco, Francesco Albani, Antonio Carracci, and Tommaso Campana. Leaving the spandrels to the Cavalier d'Arpino, Reni set about depicting the scenes of Narses and Heraclius as well as St. Francis and St. Dominic, two champions of Christian saintliness. Reni was also responsible for the paintings in the Room of the Aldobrandini Marriage in the Vatican Palace, as well as the Sala delle Dame (Ladies' Audience Chamber) there, which he completed in 1607–08.

In 1610 Reni painted the frescos for the chapel of the Annunciation in the Quirinal Palace. His most famous work—and the one which marks the pinnacle of his career in Rome—is the renowned *Aurora* ceiling which gave its name to the summer pavilion in the Palazzo Rospigliosi Pallavicini. What emerges here is Reni's Raphaelesque vein, characterized by terse, shrill color, bathed in the golden light of the sun and heightened by the intense blue of the sea.

The fresco shows Apollo driving the Sun's chariot, which is drawn by four horses symbolizing the four phases of the day (dawn, midday, twilight, and evening). Next to them stand the hours of the day. Leading the procession is Aurora (Dawn). The work became a landmark of Baroque painting. It was certainly this that Domenichino had in mind (albeit tempered with

Guercino's *Aurora*. Commissioned by Cardinal Ludovico Ludovisi, nephew of Gregory XV, this ceiling painting from 1621 depicts the same subject as Reni's fresco of seven years earlier. In contrast to Reni's picture, which took antique works as its model, Guercino's painting marks him out as an exponent of a dynamic early Baroque tendency in the School of Bologna.

Guercino's *Fame with Honor and Virtue*. The idea for this fresco painted for the Casino Ludovisi in 1621 probably derives from the Marchese Egidio Bentivoglio, and is a reference to the start of Gregory XV's pontificate.

classical references), when in about 1622, eight years afterwards, he painted the Sun's chariot at the center of the ceiling in Palazzo Costaguti, for which Agostino Tassi painted the *quadratura*.

Guercino

In 1621 Alessandro Ludovisi, from Bologna, was elected pope, ascending the papal throne under the name of Gregory XV (1621–23), the signal for painters from Bologna to flock to Rome. As far as Giovanni Francesco Barbieri (1591–1666), from Cento near Bologna—better known as Guercino—was concerned, this was the first chance he had had to break into the public and private commissions connected to the papal court. In February 1621 he moved to Rome, where he worked alongside Agostino Tassi, the *quadraturista*, who provided the imaginary architectural elements that framed Guercino's paintings. Guercino painted the *Sleeping Rinaldo Snatched by Armida*, commissioned for Palazzo Costaguti, which belonged to Costanzo Patrizi, a stunning début on the Roman scene.

Although he was loosely associated with the Carracci circle, Guercino was above all a natural talent who had learned his craft in provincial workshops such as those of the *quadraturista* Paolo Zagnoni and Benedetto Gennari, in whose studio he worked until Gennari's death in 1610. Guercino attained real importance when, working his way up from one commission to the next, he arrived at the court of Cardinal Ludovisi, soon to be Gregory XV, but at the time archbishop of Bologna.

It was no coincidence therefore that in 1621 Guercino was enlisted by Ludovico Ludovisi, nephew of the newly elected Gregory and immediately made a cardinal, to fresco the summer house of the villa he had purchased from Cardinal Del Monte near Porta Pinciana. The resulting work can be seen as a development of the theme already explored by Reni. However, the effect and intention were totally different since they aimed at what by now was unashamedly Baroque taste. The Sun's chariot and Aurora are no longer constrained within a composed and decorative framework but, on the contrary, the blue sky, clouds, and figures that make up the wonderful allegory spill out across all the available space. Even Agostino Tassi's peerless false architecture is scarcely sufficient to hold them in. Not only this, but what were termed the affections—that is, feelings in the broadest sense—ended up spilling out of the figures into the colors and the light, even the architecture. The group of the Sun and Aurora is alive with shrill and contrasting colors held within a clear frame.

The adjacent allegorical figure of Night, however, crouches in a den whose crumbling architecture grows dark as night falls and the shadows fill with weariness and dreams—or nightmares. The idea for the theme can probably be attributed to the Marquis Egidio Bentivoglio, ambassador of the Este in Rome. The cycle was completed with allegories of Day and of Fame with Honor and Virtue.

Guercino's magnificent fresco was not the first to fill the ceiling of a Roman palazzo with sky and architecture (the ceiling of the Sala Clementina in Palazzo Zuccari had been painted by Giovanni and Cherubino Alberti for Clement VIII some twenty years earlier). But in earlier examples the architecture had managed to contain the sky politely within the confines of the ceiling. Here, on the other hand, the sky ends up tearing the painted ceiling wide open, so that fantasy seems to invade the space of the frescoed room. In other words, Guercino foreshadowed those elements in Baroque painting which were to develop from the following decade until the theatrical climaxes by Baciccio and Andrea Pozzo at the end of the century. The problems involved here were addressed by Gian Lorenzo Bernini in his theory of *bel composto*.

It is clear therefore, that as far as painting is concerned, the first two decades of the seventeenth century were shaped by the presence in Rome of artists whose place of birth and cultural background was in Bologna. Even after Gregory XV's death in 1623 and Guercino's return to Bologna, Rome remained for some years to come in the thrall of painters such as Dominichino, Lanfranco, and Francesco Albani, all of whom were to leave only in the early 1630s.

Caravaggio

Unless the fundamental contribution that Caravaggio and his followers made to painting in Rome is taken into account the climate and outlook of painting in Rome in the early seventeenth century cannot be understood—nor form anything but a partial view of Baroque painting as a whole.

The conventional comparison is between Caravaggio as a revolutionary, and the Carracci and their followers as traditionalists. As has been seen, this is true only up to a point. Beyond this, the first and most important difference between the two currents lies—apart from stylistic difference—in the fact that Caravaggio was never the head of a school, as the Carracci were. Indeed, before he received his major commissions for altarpieces in Roman churches, it can be argued that Caravaggio's painting was only for the few, the initiated. Excluding the ceiling of the Ludovisi pavilion, painted around a theme dominated by astrological and alchemical symbolism, with foreshortened figures of Pluto, Jupiter, and Neptune, he never had the chance to master the technique of fresco. This meant that it was difficult for him to gain more or less official commissions. Despite this, Caravaggio's influence on Roman painting in particular, and on seventeenth-century painting in general, is astonishing, so much so that—as has been seen—it even managed to penetrate the opposing camp of the Carracci.

Born on September 29, 1571, to Fermo Merisi, superintendent of works for Francesco Sforza di Caravaggio, and Lucia Aratori, Caravaggio—as he was nicknamed after his birthplace near Milan—trained as a painter in the provinces. For four years, from 1584, he was pupil to Simone Peterzano, a painter from Bergamo, who falsely claimed to have been a pupil of Titian. In 1577 the Merisi family moved from their hometown to Milan escape the plague, which that year ravaged the town of Caravaggio.

Caravaggio's great artistic journey started when he moved to Rome, perhaps in 1593, to work in the studio of the Cavalier d'Arpino, where he specialized in fruit and still lifes, at this time considered a lesser genre. It was in this period that he painted the famous *Boy with Basket of Fruit* in the Borghese Gallery, in

Caravaggio, *Rest on the Flight to Egypt.* Painted between 1595 and 1599, the format and individual elements of this work are evidence of Caravaggio's northern Italian origins. The lyrical tone is unique in Caravaggio's work. The prominent view of the back of an angel playing an instrument is taken from a similar figure in Annibale Caracci's *Hercules at the Crossroads.* Galleria Doria Pamphili.

Detail of Caravaggio's *Calling of the Apostle Matthew* showing the heads of Christ and St. Peter. San Luigi dei Francesi.

Caravaggio, *Calling of St. Matthew*. This picture, from 1599–1600, is part of the decorative program of the Contarelli Chapel in San Luigi dei Francesi. Together with a depiction of the martyrdom of St. Matthew, the painting flanks the central altarpiece which shows the apostle writing his gospel in the presence of an angel. In his *Calling of St. Matthew* Caravaggio used his characteristic dramatic technique of depicting intense light for the first time, an effect which enables the figures to emerge from the depths of the painting. Caravaggio also sought to coordinate closely the effects of light in his painting with the actual lighting in the chapel.

which the exaggerated tension of the right shoulder shows that he had not yet mastered anatomy. He also painted the equally famous *Basket of Fruit* (Milan, Pinacoteca Ambrosiana), which may have been commissioned by Cardinal Federico Borromeo, whose vision of art—summed up in his Religious Painting (*De pictura sacra*, Milan 1624)—was to have extensive influence over painters in the first half of the seventeenth century.

This was, therefore, the environment in which Caravaggio, not yet thirty, was operating when from 1595 he benefitted from a good five years' patronage by Cardinal Del Monte. Bearing in mind the cardinal's passion for music, it is easy to see why Caravaggio should have produced so many works in which music plays a major role: the *Concert* (Metropolitan Museum, New York), the *Lute Player* (Hermitage, St. Petersburg), and, above all, the *Rest on the Flight to Egypt*, from 1595–99 (Doria Pamphili Gallery).

The lullaby that the angel plays to the sleeping Christ Child in the last is an actual piece of music by the Flemish musician Bauldewyn. The words of *How fair she is* (*Quam pulchra es*) for this piece come from the Song of Songs, which exegesis read as symbolizing the mystic marriage of Christ and the Virgin, that is of Christ and the Church. Far from being simple easel pieces, Caravaggio's early works thus conceal deep layers of meaning that reflect the cultural and theological interests of Cardinal Del Monte and his circle.

Studies of Caravaggio have revealed that the *Bacchus* in the Uffizi, given to Cardinal Del Monte by the Grand Duke of Tuscany, and the so-called *Ailing Bacchus* (Borghese Gallery) conceal allusions to Christ as the giver of spiritual life after the Resurrection. To some extent, a theme of spiritual intoxication emerges. This had been put forward by the Church Fathers but it is here reproposed in totally new figurative, almost revolutionary, terms.

Caravaggio's technique was quite different from that of his colleagues. He painted directly on to the canvas without making preparatory sketches (hardly any exist), even though this meant that he often had to rework version after version over the same ground.

What is astonishing, however, is his ability to attribute a highly personal interpretation to wellworn themes and iconography. A striking example of this is his *St. John the Baptist* in the Picture Gallery (Pinacoteca) in the Capitoline Museums. (It has recently been suggested that this may depict Isaac after the angel's intervention, which would explain why a ram is depicted rather than a lamb.) The canvas reveals a debt to Michelangelo's *ignudi* on the Sistine Chapel ceiling. Nonetheless, the composition, the use of light, and the choice of subject make the painting unique to Caravaggio. Painted in about 1600, it is one of the first works to indicate a darkening of Caravaggio's palette, though the seeds of this are already present in the *Rest on the Flight to Egypt*

Far from being something Caravaggio came up with in his studio, the new chromatic direction taken by his painting tended to identify light with divine grace and shade with guilt and sin. Proof of this is in the first large canvas Caravaggio painted for a major commission, the *Calling of St. Matthew* for the Contarelli Chapel (in which the Cavalier d'Arpino also worked) in San Luigi dei Francesi. The story is well known. Matthew, a tax collector for the Romans and a sinner, as the gospels describe him, responds to Christ's call.

Caravaggio synthesized the whole drama into one single scene. Matthew is seated at the tax collectors' table surrounded by dubious characters who are counting out money. He raises his eyes and puts his hand to his chest as if to ask, "You mean *me*?" Yet no one has spoken; Jesus makes a theatrical gesture similar to that of God the Creator in the Sistine Chapel. Immediately the future evangelist is plucked from the darkness of sin and taken into the light of true life.

It is not by chance that Christ makes the same gesture, with the same symbolic and luministic implications, as that made in the *Resurrection of Lazarus*. But in the *Calling*, the gesture has a dual meaning because it is echoed—though not so strongly—by St. Peter, who represents the Church. The work alludes to the conversion to Roman Catholicism of Henri IV, the king of France, when he abjured the Huguenots and Protestantism. The presence of St. Peter is therefore significant in that it is intended to show the need for personal choice in order to save one's soul, rejecting the Protestant belief that salvation is the result of predestination.

From this time on, therefore, Caravaggio's complex use of light—reduced to a mere stylis-

tic device by his followers—was affected by ever more complex symbolic meanings. An example of this is in the first version of the *Calling of St. Paul*, in which the value of light is clarified by the direct eruption of a young Christ held aloft in an angel's arms. In this, an elderly Saul, unable to bear the vision, falls to the ground, covering his eyes with his hands, while his terrified horse foams at the mouth and the confused elderly groom tries to defend himself with his shield and lance.

The definitive—and far less cumbersome—version is in the Cerasi Chapel in Santa Maria del Popolo. Nonetheless the symbolism of light remains the same: Saul, here a young man, lies on the ground bathed in a ray of light that

Caravaggio's *Martyrdom of St. Peter* was painted in 1601–02 as a counterpart to a scene showing the miraculous conversion of Saul in the Cerasi Chapel in Santa Maria del Popolo. The dramatic effect of the martyrdom is generated not only by Caravaggio's characteristic chiaroscuro but also by the strong emphasis evident in the composition on diagonals.

Federico Barocci, *Rest on the Flight to Egypt* (*Madonna delle ciliege*). Painted between 1570 and 1573, the picture modeled on a depiction of the Virgin by Correggio, is considered one of Barocci's mature works. Vatican Museums, Pinacoteca.

Federico Barocci, *Aeneas, Anchises, and Ascanius Fleeing Troy* (1596). This historical painting, faithful to Virgil's description in the *Aeneid*, is an example of the artistic ideals of the period which were revolutionized by Caravaggio. Galleria Borghese.

scarcely troubles his horse or groom; he is surrounded by the gloom of sin.

Caravaggio's poetry was enriched by other elements that appear in his paintings from time to time. The *Martyrdom of St. Matthew* and *St. Matthew and the Angel* complete the cycle in the Contarelli Chapel. The *Martyrdom* shows the saint in the robes of a Dominican friar, most probably as a way of contesting the fact that

Giordano Bruno had been condemned to burn at the stake in Campo dei Fiori in February 1600. Caravaggio took his cue from contemporary events and transformed them by adapting them to fit the theme in question. This meant that his work became alive with implications and hidden allusions.

Caravaggio used realism and scrupulously adhered to reality, however brutal it might be, as in the *Martyrdom of St. Peter* opposite the *Conversion of St. Paul* in Santa Maria del Popolo. This realism is the other major element in his poetry. In the *Martyrdom of St. Peter*, the protagonist of the composition is the diagonal movement of the upside-down cross, as though the saint is caught in some terrible slow-motion fall that he tries in vain to resist. The gaze of the beholder is captured by the straining muscularity of the executioners, their dirty feet, the saint's flabby flesh, the stones, and the metal spade used to dig a hole to fix the cross. In short, everything is intended to make the scene realistic and immediate, as if it is really occurring in front of the viewer.

This is the aim (or the main one of them) of Caravaggio's painting. He wants to grab his viewers' emotions and feelings and, in doing so, give them the chance to grow in faith. This is the case with the *Deposition* now in the Picture Gallery in the Vatican Museums, originally painted for the Oratorio of the Filippini (the man in the foreground has the features of St. Philip Neri, the founder of the order of the Oratorians). Caravaggio was seeking to elicit in his audience an enormous sense of pity. He consolidates this through the way that Christ's arm hangs limply down, clear homage to Michelangelo's *Pietà* in St. Peter's.

Caravaggio constantly sought to pull away from masking reality as, for instance, Federico Barocci (1525/35–1612) did in his work. Barocci managed to maintain a sense of decorum in the widest range of situations, from the *Institution of the Eucharist* in Santa Maria sopra Minerva to *Aeneas, Anchises, and Ascanius Fleeing Troy* in the Borghese Gallery. But Caravaggio's effort to depict grimy reality was fraught with difficulties as it could all too easily lead to a conflict with the ecclesiastical authorities and their preconceptions.

Caravaggio's manner of painting in no way conflicted with the convictions of the more enlightened minds of the time, such as Cardinal Bellarmine or St. Charles Borromeo, who desired a return to the Christian simplicity of early times. However, not everyone was able to understand this. Cardinal Bellarmine, for example, corresponded with Galileo, even though it was he who, in 1616, communicated the decisions of the Holy Office to Galileo.

Caravaggio did not have to try very hard before his work, imbued with Borromeo's emphasis on poverty and suffering, sparked a scandal. The dirty feet of the peasant paying devout homage to the *Madonna di Loreto* (the Loreto image was also known as the Pilgrims' Virgin) were taken as a lack of respect. Similarly the *Madonna of the Palafrenieri* was almost immediately withdrawn after being hung on the altar of the confraternity of the Palafrenieri in St. Peter's.

The least appreciated work was the *Death of the Virgin* now in the Louvre, originally painted for the Carmelites at Santa Maria della Scala. The Carmelites were offended by the figure of the Virgin and—with no evidence—accused Caravaggio of using the body of a prostitute who had drowned in the Tiber for his model. It was such professional difficulties that helped to create the myth—cut down to size by recent art history—of an accursed painter. On top of this came an incident that was to ruin Caravaggio's life and cause him to flee from Rome. On May 28, 1606 he became involved in a brawl over a game of racquets and killed his opponent. He took refuge in Naples, beginning what was to be a series of travels that only ended when he died on July 18, 1610 at Porto Ercole north of Rome, ironically just after the pope had granted him a pardon.

Caravaggio was never to return to Rome, although he did manage to get one of his last works to Cardinal Borghese. This was *David with the Head of Goliath*, which would appear to have been nothing short of an act of contrition on his part, since Goliath, who was slain by the future king of Israel, has Caravaggio's own features.

The School of Caravaggio

The fact that Caravaggio worked mainly in Rome during his extraordinary career (he was there from 1592 to 1606, after which he went to Naples, Malta, Palermo, back to Naples, and then to Porto Ercole) meant that Rome automatically became the capital of the Caravaggesque style, since his early followers worked there. They did not necessarily include painters who had actually known Caravaggio personally, such as Antiveduto Gramatica (1571–1626), who even employed him in his studio, although he did not allow himself to be influenced by the new style (he partly abandoned his own late Mannerist style, which he derived from Federico Barocci, in favor of naturalism, but only after 1610). Giovanni Baglione (1573–1644) also knew Caravaggio and thoroughly detested him, going as far as to sue him for defamation.

Caravaggio's followers came rather from painters such as Orazio Gentileschi (1563–1639) and Orazio Borgianni (1578?–1616). However, the main painter who continued his style was Bartolomeo Manfredi (1582?–1621), whose fame grew so great that contemporary critics coined the expression "in the genre of Manfredi," by which they meant painting in the Caravaggesque manner.

Nevertheless it should be emphasized that the relationship between master and followers

Caravaggio's *Madonna of the Palafrenieri* in St. Peter's, removed shortly after being placed in the basilica because of its uncompromising realism. The unusual composition resulted from extending the traditional depiction of St. Anne with the Virgin and Christ Child to include the triumph of the Virgin and Christ Child over Evil, which appears in the form of a snake. Galleria Borghese.

Orazio Gentileschi, *David after the Defeat of Goliath* (1610–12). Gentileschi, from Pisa, emphasizes the biblical hero's introspection after his triumph: Donatello had earlier adopted the same approach in his famous bronze *David*. The prototype of the biblical character as a man of action is thus extended to embrace a contemplative dimension. Galleria Borghese.

draughtsmanship, which emerges in works such as *David after the Defeat of Goliath*. Gentileschi's defense of Baglione is enlightening, as it reveals that the two painters were tied by bonds of friendship over and above their professional relationship. It was not by chance that Giovanni Baglione became Orazio Borgianni's first biographer, even remonstrating with the master because, he said, "he was wrong to describe him as great."

After a stay in Spain between 1598 and 1602, Borgianni fell under Caravaggio's influence, producing complex but beautiful works such as the *Sacra Conversazione* in the Galleria Nazionale d'Arte Antica in Palazzo Barberini. The fact that in 1610 Borgianni was elected to the Accademia dei Virtuosi—the academy of painters based in the Pantheon, being presented by Antiveduto Gramatica—can be read as official recognition of the Caravaggesque style.

What is certain, however, is that from this date Rome was quietly invaded by a host of Italian and foreign painters, all interested in learning the Caravaggesque way of painting and who were to spread it across Italy and Europe. The Italians (the foreigners will be discussed below) include Rutilio Manetti (1571–1639) from Siena, Orazio Riminaldi (1593–1630) from Pisa, Alessandro Turchi (1578–1650), better known as Orbetto, and Marcantonio Bassetti (1586–1630), both from Verona, as well as Giovan Battista Caracciolo (1570–1637), known as Battistello, from Naples, and Massimo Stanzione (1585?–1656) from Caserta. These painters—along with a host of others that it would take too long to mention— became the second-generation followers of Caravaggio. They had not known Caravaggio personally, but had seen his work in churches and private collections or had seen some of the many copies circulating. Many copyists tried to make ends meet by imitating the master's work with varying degrees of success. The most sought-after copies were by Angelo Caroselli, who usually signed them with his own name.

A number of the second-generation artists had also been brought up on the works of their contemporary Bartolomeo Manfredi. It was due to Manfredi that the Caravaggesque style was transformed into a true genre, able to exert its magic through shade and light—which was, however, stripped of all symbolic significance. Manfredi, protected by the Marquis Giustiniani, produced work that increasingly tended to use warm tones and colors. This can be seen in a comparison of his *Punishment of Cupid* (Chicago, Art Institute), painted between 1605 and 1610 and still dominated by cold terse colors, and a work such as his *Roman Charity* (Florence, Uffizi), which is imbued with golden light.

The same light recurs in the large canvas commissioned for Santa Maria dell'Anima from the

bears no resemblance to a conventional artistic school, with a pupil–master relationship. The idea of a school was made even more difficult by Caravaggio's personality which, as has been seen, had landed him in trouble with the law, especially when he slandered Baglione in 1603, accusing him of imitating his style.

In 1603 Caravaggio also broke with Orazio Gentileschi, the oldest of the first generation of his followers, and among the earliest to recognize his innovative impact. Gentileschi, trained in late Mannerist methods in his native Tuscany, had moved to Rome before Caravaggio (between 1576 and 1578), where he worked on the frescos in the Vatican Library commissioned by Sixtus V. Gentileschi retained the fairly light palette of late Mannerism as well as his typically Tuscan precise

Venetian painter Carlo Saraceni (1579–1619) a year before his death. The canvas, which depicts St. Benno taking back the keys to the city of Meissen, uses the radiant light purely to heighten the lines of the faces and the drapery folds.

By 1620 nearly all of Caravaggio's first-generation followers were dead. Nevertheless his style was by now an integral part of Roman painting: Antiveduto Gramatica had even been elected head of the Accademia di San Luca. In 1622 Artemisia Gentileschi (1593–1653), Orazio's daughter and pupil, came back to Rome. After the trial of Agostino Tassi, accused of raping her, she had gone to Florence, taking with her a painting style imbued with warm light and bloodthirsty subjects. Even diehard Carracci followers such as Lanfranco and Domenichino fell under the fascination of her work such as the *Cumaean Sibyl* in the Picture Gallery in the Capitoline Museums, from around 1622, which stands out for its Caravaggesque use of strong contrasts of light and shade.

The Bamboccianti and Foreign Painters

By the mid-1620s Rome was the painting capital of Europe, attracting both Italian and foreign artists alike. Among the foreign painters was a Dutch painter from Haarlem who settled in Via Margutta in about 1625. This was Pieter van Laer (1592?–1642), who was given the nickname of *Bamboccio* (clumsy) by the Romans because of his physique. Van Laer remained in Rome until 1638, gathering around him a group of painters who visited him in Via Margutta. The establishment painters of the academy dismissively dubbed them the Bamboccianti.

Their paintings, Caravaggesque in inspiration, depicted scenes of everyday life without concealed meanings. They endeavored to show life as it was, but nevertheless managed to convey extremes of poetry and pathos, as in the famous *Drinking Trough* by Michelangelo Cerquozzi (1602–60) or the *Brandy-Seller* by van Laer himself. In this way scenes of the Roman Campagna were no longer populated by the nymphs and goddesses of Francesco Albani's canvases, such as the *Toilet of Venus* in the Borghese Gallery. In their place were to be found peasants or picnicking gentry, as seen in so many landscapes with figures.

The new genre was disliked by the painting establishment, who saw it as dangerous competition. But without these foreigners, aspects of everyday Roman life would have been lost forever. Their contribution in this sense can be summed up by the *Market in Piazza del Popolo*

Francesco Albani, *The Fall* (1616–17). This tondo, along with three others, forms a cycle on the theme of love affairs during the different seasons. Francesco Albani is considered the most competent painter of mythological subjects in the Bologna School, and his pictures express a lively interest in landscapes. Galleria Borghese.

by Lighelbach (1622–74) (Vienna, Akademie der Bildenden Kunst).

The Bamboccianti started a revolution which spread through engravings of their paintings. These gave rise to genres such as that established by Antoine Le Nain (1588–1648) and, later on, by Pietro Longhi (1702–85).

However, the most famous Flemish artist in Rome was Rubens (1577–1640), who was attracted as much by the innovations of the Carracci as by Caravaggio himself. It is well known that Rubens made a copy of Caravaggio's *Deposition* in 1611–12, now in the National Gallery of

Pieter van Laer. *Horses Drinking.* This scene of an everyday event is characteristic of the influence of a small group of artists who modified Caravaggio's style of painting and spread it to northern Europe. They were known as the Bambocciati, from Laer's nickname *Bamboccio* (clumsy). Galleria Nazionale d'Arte Antica, Palazzo Barberini.

565

Canada in Ottawa. It is also known that Rubens played a major part in the duke of Mantua's decision to purchase Caravaggio's rejected *Death of the Virgin.*

During the 1610s other Flemish painters attracted by Caravaggio were in Rome. These include Gerrit van Honthorst (1590–1656), who was nicknamed Gherardo delle Notti (Gerard of the Night Scenes). His *Adoration of the Christ Child* is remarkable in that the source of the light is Christ himself, a device later adopted by many other painters. The canvas was probably selected by Giulio Mancini, Urban VIII's personal physician, which meant that before going to the Uffizi in Florence where it hangs today, the work must have been part of the papal collection.

The French painter Simon Vouet (1590–1649) was also in Rome, from late 1613 until 1627, when he returned to Paris. In 1624 he was elected head of the Accademia di San Luca. Attracted by the new Caravaggesque way of using light, Vouet left in Rome his *Birth of the Virgin*, a canvas with a slight view *di sotto in su*, still in San Francesco a Ripa.

Valentin de Boulogne (1594–1632) came to Rome about 1614 and continued to work for the most important families until his death.

Nicolas Poussin

The most important French painter in Rome from the 1620s to the 1660s was undoubtedly Nicolas Poussin (1594–1665). Invited to Rome by Giovan Battista Marino, who had met him in Paris and for whose work *L'Adone* he made pen and watercolor drawings, Poussin arrived there in 1624. Under the influence of Lanfranco and Pietro da Cortona, Poussin's Roman season opened in a grand manner, with masterpieces such as the *Martyrdom of St. Erasmus*, which was constructed along solid scenic lines and possessed an almost theatrical dramaticality, emphasized by wide fat brush strokes that prove he was paying close attention to Roman Baroque painting.

Initially Poussin's complex personality led him to embrace Raphael's classicism, sometimes much overdone as in the *Triumph of Neptune* in Philadelphia, modeled on Raphael's *Galatea*. At other times his classicism is filtered through the Carracci, as in the *Triumph of Bacchus*, painted for Cardinal Richelieu.

However, the most significant influence of Poussin's stay in Rome had, can be seen in the care he takes over landscapes. In this he was undoubtedly influenced by the beautiful Roman Campagna, in which he often walked. In his choice of this subject matter, which became prevalent after the 1640s, Poussin was influenced by Carracci models such as the *Flight into Egypt* as well as by the imaginary landscapes of Claude Lorraine, by now also in Rome (he arrived in about 1620 and remained there for the rest of his life).

In Poussin's landscapes the figures grow progressively smaller until they almost disappear amid the green of the trees. This is the case in *Agar and the Angel* in Palazzo Altieri or in the *Four Seasons*, his last masterpiece, begun in 1660, just before illness stopped him painting.

Velázquez

The other great painter in Rome toward the middle of the century—although he was there only briefly—is Velázquez (1599–1660). He arrived in Rome in February 1649 on an official mission to buy works of art, and marked his time in Rome by producing a masterpiece, the portrait of Innocent X, which was publicly exhibited by the Accademia dei Virtuosi in their Pantheon headquarters.

This was not the first time that Velázquez had been to Rome. He had made an earlier visit in 1629, when he produced two fine views of the gardens of the Villa Medici. Velázquez was profoundly influenced by Italian painting. It was in Rome that he painted his famous *Forge of Vulcan*, with the most beautiful rearview male nude of the whole seventeenth century, as well as his *Triumph of Bacchus*, which reminds one of its Caravaggesque lineage.

Pietro da Cortona

In Baroque architecture Pietro da Cortona (Pietro Berrettini, 1597–1669) is the third principal figure alongside Bernini and Borromini. In painting, as well, Pietro played a leading role in the artistic scene in Rome from the early 1630s right through until the end of the 1660s, except for the decade (1637–47) that he spent in Florence.

Settling in Rome in about 1611–12, Pietro fell into the sphere of influence of the Sacchetti family and of the scholar and collector Cassiano dal Pozzo, under whose protection he was able to deepen his studies of the classics, not merely to find out what had happened in the past and to discover a model, but also for visual inspiration. He studied anatomy, executing the drawings for Giovanni Maria Castellani's medical treatise. He was drawn to Raphael—his copy of the *Galatea* is still in the Accademia di San Luca—and Titian, but he was also interested in the Carracci and in Bernini's early sculpture.

OPPOSITE:
Nicolas Poussin. *Martyrdom of St. Erasmus.* This retable painted in 1629 for St. Peter's is the only painting by Poussin intended for a public building. The dramatic depiction of the agonies of the saint was made at the beginning of Poussin's stay in Rome and established his reputation in the city. Vatican Museums, Pinacoteca.

Simon Vouet, *Birth of the Virgin.* This painting, from 1621, is characteristic of the painter's Italian period, and illustrates the influence of the Caracci as well as Caravaggio. San Francesco alla Ripa.

Pietra da Corona, *Rape of the Sabine Women.* This pictorial rendering of a legendary event is animated by the dynamic movement of the composition, a trait which influenced later artists such as Luca Giordano. Pinacoteca Capitolina.

Carlo Maratta, *Nativity* (1655–57).
Rediscovered in the nineteenth century,
the fresco demonstrates the complex
compositions of Maratta, whose work
shows strong northern Italian traits as
well as the influences which followed a
study of the Carracci. Maratta's
classicizing tendencies were reinforced
by his friendship with the theoretician
Balori. Quirinal Palace.

Pietro's first major commission came when he
worked together with another artist from
Cortona, Pietro Paolo Bonzi, on the frescos for
the ceiling of Palazzo Mattei di Giove, a commission gained through Bonzi's connections.
Once in contact with the Mattei, Crescenzi, and
other prominent Roman families, Pietro found
that major commissions started coming to him
from a wide range of patrons including the
Barberini family and Marcello Sacchetti, who,
after the election of Urban VIII, gained high
office in the Apostolic Chamber.

Less than a year after his election, Urban gave
Pietro a commission for a fresco depicting St.
Bibiana refusing to sacrifice to idols. The work
was for the church of San Bibiana, which had
just been refurbished by Gian Lorenzo Bernini.
Pietro da Cortona's broad theatrical manner is
the obvious explanation of his success.

A little later Pietro produced the large canvas of
the *Adoration of the Shepherds* for San Salvatore in
Lauro. This was painted before 1626, the year in
which the church's patron, Cardinal Orsini, died.
The famous *Rape of the Sabine Women* dates
from either the late 1620s or early 1630s. It has
recently been suggested that it was commissioned
for the marriage of Giovan Francesco Sacchetti
to Beatrice Tassoni Este in February 1631.

The two works highlight different approaches
to pictorial representation. In the *Adoration*
Pietro uses only a few figures, but they are monumental in conception. In the *Rape of the Sabine
Women* however, he employs groups of figures
enabling him to show off his anatomical ability
in full. This combines well with his use of light
colors against elaborate theatrical backdrops.

It must have been these abilities that convinced Urban that he was right to choose Pietro

Pier Francesco Mola, *Joseph Recognized by his Brothers* (1655–57), considered Mola's best work. In spite of the dominant role played by the landscape whose individual components, such as the obelisk, serve to mark out the milieu in which the biblical hero moved, the organisation of the foreground is heavily indebted to Raphael and Pietro da Cortona. Quirinal Palace.

da Cortona, then thirty-six, to decorate the ceiling in his new palazzo just completed by Bernini, Palazzo Barberini. With regard to the theme, the pope probably held a competition which was won by the court poet Francesco Bracciolini, who came up with a complex allegorical framework that Pietro had to translate into painting. When the work was completed, in 1634–37, a leaflet was published to explain its meanings.

The theme was simple but unusual. Seated in the clouds above Time and Fate, Divine Providence commands Immortality, poised in flight, to place a crown of sparkling stars (symbols of immortality) over bees, symbols of the Barberini, which are themselves surrounded by a crown of laurel (also a symbol of immortality) that is in turn supported by the three theological Virtues. Higher up are the papal insignia.

Around are four mythological scenes (Athena slaying the giants, Silenus and the satyrs, Hercules defeating the Harpies, and Prudence closing the doors to the Temple of Janus) alluding to the pope's merits. Added to these was the pope's ability as a poet, celebrated by a small putto holding a laurel wreath above the papal tiara.

Leaving aside its cumbersome themes, the fresco is one of the masterpieces of Baroque, equal in importance only to the Palazzo Farnese gallery. Pietro reinvents space, making it almost throb as it opens out and closes up in front of the beholder. Indeed the beholder is aware of the contrast between the rigid structure of the imitation stucco architecture and the sky, which completely breaks through the wall. The figures, almost in frontal view, disappear giddily into the heavens.

Filippo Latri, *Gideon and the Fleece*. This episode from the Old Testament is one of the paintings in the gallery of the Quirinal Palace and made between 1655 and 1657. The night scene is notable for the distinctive use of light. Quirinal Palace.

Andrea Sacchi

To see how this is revolutionary, Pietro da Cortona's fresco need only be compared with the *Triumph of Divine Wisdom* painted by Andrea Sacchi (1599–1661) in Palazzo Barberini a few years earlier, in 1629–33. It not only uses much more subdued tones than that seen in Pietro da Cortona's work, but also opts for far more obvious solutions.

A pupil of Francesco Albani, Sacchi had been brought up on the same images by Raphael, Annibale Carracci, and Domenichino that Pietro da Cortona was familiar with. Sacchi became the leader of a current in painting that dominated the second half of the seventeenth century, and which was based on simplicity and the classical ideal. The Palazzo Barberini fresco, inspired by Raphael's *Parnassus*, reveals the differences between Sacchi and Pietro da Cortona, but their difference in approach was already clear.

To grasp this, two canvases that were painted at almost the same time need only be compared—Pietro da Cortona's *St. Damian Offering the Rule to the Virgin*, now in the Museum of Modern Art, Toledo (USA) and Sacchi's better-known *Vision of St. Romauld* in the Vatican Picture Gallery. Although there are fewer figures in Pietro's work (St. Damian and the Virgin), the

effect is more elaborate, because of the way Pietro uses the billowing clouds and more colors.

Sacchi, on the other hand, manages to convey the feeling of the vision merely by reducing the intensity of the color and the definition of the shade. In addition to this, he uses fewer colors and his composition is flatter in structure, divided as it is into two horizontal planes, whereas Pietro's work is dominated by the dynamism of the diagonal.

Sacchi's manner soon spread throughout Rome, influencing not only painters such as Sassoferrato (Gian Battista Salvi, 1605–85) and Giovanni Domenico Cerrini (1609–81) but also the immediate followers of Pietro da Cortona, such as Giacinto Gimignani (1611–81), who was involved in Sacchi's last great undertaking, the cycle of canvases he painted for the Baptistery of San Giovanni in Laterano. Sacchi was responsible for the scenes of St. John the Baptist while his pupils, including Carlo Maratta—who was to dominate painting in Rome until the end of the century—painted the scenes of Constantine.

Pietra da Cortona's Late Work

Pietro da Cortona's lengthy stay in Florence, though he maintained contact with Rome, left the field wide open for other artists, like Sacchi, to come in and substantially modify the painting scene. When he returned, Pietro undertook the most important religious painting commission he had been offered—the frescos in the Chiesa Nuova (Santa Maria in Vallicella). It took him over thirteen years to complete the cycle (including a break between 1651 and 1655). In the dome Pietro painted the *Glory of the Trinity* and in the apse the *Assumption of the Virgin*. The works are indebted to Giovanni Lanfranco, however the figures are far more fluid and the foreshortening much more incisive. The spandrels have images of four prophets (Isaiah, Jeremiah, Ezekiel, and Daniel), while amid Cosimo Fancelli's and Ercole Ferrata's gilded stuccowork the ceiling is opened up by the *Vision of St. Philip Neri during the Construction of the Church*.

During this period Pietro also worked on the ceiling of the gallery in Palazzo Pamphili (1651–54). The choice of the Virgilian theme of Aeneas gave Pietro the opportunity to highlight the ancestry of the new pope, Innocent X (1644–55), who claimed descent from Numa Pompilius, a descendant of Aeneas.

These are the principal images out of which the school of Pietro da Cortona grew, helped by Pietro himself when Alexander VII (1655–67) commissioned him to decorate the long gallery in the Quirinal Palace (the Gallery of Alexander

VII). With a true entrepreneurial spirit, Pietro placed young painters on to the job, which he himself supervised. Work commenced in 1655 and was completed two years later. The cycle was based on the theme of redemption, from the creation of Adam and Eve to the coming of Christ, in the *Nativity* by Carlo Maratta, which stands out for personality and style. Among the other painters who worked on the project, the following should be mentioned; Pier Francesco Mola (1612–66) who painted the grandiloquent *Joseph Recognized by his Brothers*, Giovanni Paolo Schor (1615–74), responsible for *Jacob and the Angel*, Filippo Lauri (1623–94), who painted *Gideon and the Fleece* where the dark

tones are reminiscent of Guercino, and Gaspar Dughet (1615–73), Poussin's cousin and teacher who, along with Filippo Lauri, was responsible for the landscapes.

The importance of the Gallery of Alexander VII cycle lies not so much in the quality or originality of the work, but rather in the fact that its creation meant that Pietro da Cortona molded the shape taken by painting in Rome during the second part of the century, clawing back much of his influence from Sacchi. It is no coincidence that of all the people who would rise to prominence in the second half of the century, it was Carlo Maratta who had worked for both masters.

Domenico Maria Canuti *Apotheosis of Romulus*. The artist, a native of Bologna, used the same illusionistic components in this ceiling fresco as he had shortly before in the vault of Santi Domenico e Sisto. As with his *Apotheosis of St. Dominic*, the *Apotheosis of Romulus* creates an illusion of architectural depth and was painted together with Enrico Haffner. Palazzo Altieri.

Francesco Cozza, *Birth of the Virgin.*
Palazzo Corona.

Late Baroque Fresco Cycles

Wittkower pointed out the paradox that none of the Baroque churches built by Bernini, Borromini, or—even stranger because he was also a painter—Pietro da Cortona made any allowance for interior space suitable for frescos.

This points to the conclusion that, despite many efforts, above all by Bernini, to achieve a unity of the arts, the goal was far from being achieved. Architecture, the most important of the arts, could be allied only with sculpture. All it allowed painting to do was to come up with colored surfaces, relegating it to the realms of pictorialism. It also meant that painting needed architectural surfaces as little defined as possible if it was to unfold the great creative fantasies that the painters were capable of. Even then, stuccowork and gilding crept back in when sculpture and architecture had gone out. In other words, great Baroque architecture was self-sufficient, while the great paintings of the day already possessed enough strength to do without either sculpture or architecture.

The result of this paradox was that many late Baroque cycles were executed in buildings that had been constructed decades earlier. Thus, for example, Ciro Ferri (1634–89), a trusted pupil of Pietro da Cortona who had completed several of Pietro's works, painted his *Glory of Paradise* fresco in the dome of Sant'Agnese in Agone, which had been finished thirteen years earlier (work began in 1670 and finished in 1693, after Ferri's death). In 1673 the ceiling of the library of Palazzo Pamphili in Piazza Navona was painted with a brilliant apotheosis of the Pamphili family by Francesco Cozza (1605–82), a pupil of Domenichino. In the same period Domenico Maria Canuti (1626–84), a Bolognese painter, arrived in Rome in 1672 and immediately found employment alongside his fellow citizen Enrico Haffner (1640–1702) painting architectural *quadrature* for the *Apotheosis of St. Dominic*, which followed an affected architectural conceit. The two painters used the same conceit in the *Apotheosis of Romulus* in Palazzo Altieri—confirmation, if it were needed, that Christian and secular themes were treated in exactly the same way.

In the same building is the *Triumph of Mercy*, painted after 1673 by a painter already mentioned several times, Carlo Maratta (1625–1713), originally from the Marches region. Advised by his friend and biographer Giovan Pietro Bellori, Maratta forged a highly successful compromise between the Cortonesque tendency and Sacchi's classical ideals. He held true to these ideals, reducing the number of figures and keeping to a minimum the interference caused by fictive architecture (the fresco is framed like a cameo). At the same time, however, he welcomed the inventions, surprise glimpses, and fluidity of figures whose virtues Pietro da Cortona had extolled over his long career. This compromise proved a winning formula, one which lasted well into the first decades of the next century, which was inevitably dominated by the shadow cast by Maratta, bolstered by the presence of his pupils.

To obtain an idea of the differences in intent, Maratta's fresco can be compared with the battle of Lepanto on the ceiling of the famous Galleria Colonna in Palazzo Colonna in Piazza Santi Apostoli, which was painted between 1675 and 1678 by Giovanni Coli (1636–81) and Filippo Gherardi (1634–1704), both from Lucca. It is clear that here, is a superficial interpretation of the influence of Pietro da Cortona that degenerates into a crowded, untidy composition poorly related to the architectural framework of the *quadratura*.

Jesuit Painting

A very different result can be found in a work that was carefully planned and perfectly executed, the *Triumph of the Name of Jesus* on the ceiling of the Gesù. It is clear that here close artistic collaboration existed between a talented painter such as Giovan Battista Gaulli, better known as Baciccio (1639–1709), who was born in Genoa but trained in Rome under Bernini, and the sculptor responsible for the stucco, Antonio Raggi, who had also trained with Bernini. Gaulli worked on the fresco from 1672 until 1679.

The result is a European masterpiece of Baroque. After he had finished, the ceiling was pierced by an invasion of light which once again possessed all the symbolic meanings that Caravaggio had given it. An exultation of angels illuminates the inner space of the church so brightly that the onlooker can hardly bear it.

Only the *Glory of St. Ignatius Loyola* by the Jesuit lay brother Andrea Pozzo (1642–1709) on the huge ceiling of the Jesuit church of Sant'Ignazio comes close to Gaulli's undertaking. Painted in 1691–94, Pozzo's enormous work brings the century to a close like a Bach crescendo. The astonished acolytes find their gaze catapulted into space. They see the architecture of the church stripped of its roof, jostling with saints and angels chasing out the impure spirits. Author of Perspective for Painters and Architects (*La Prospettiva de' Pittori e Architetti*) and an unrivaled *quadraturista* and master of perspective, Pozzo did nothing by halves, even making a porphyry star on the floor, to show people where to stand in order to enjoy the full effect of the Roman Baroque.

This chapter has endeavored to give as broad a panorama as possible of the artistic scene in Rome during the seventeenth century. It must be stressed that in the seventeenth century Rome was the artistic capital of Europe. This was not merely because it was a museum city and therefore a place that painters from all over Europe felt obliged to visit. Rather, Rome was where the new artistic language of Baroque was born. From here it spread all the way around the world, even to the far-off Americas and—due to the Portuguese—to India. Baroque was a global phenomenon that emerged from a for-tunate encounter between a handful of intelligent cardinals—many of whom were to become popes—and a stable of great artists, who knew how to interpret their era. It is this ability which is rightly considered one of the most important aspects of the human spirit.

Marco Bussagli

St. Ignatius Loyola cures victims of the plague, part of a decorative program by Andrea Pozzo which focused on the miracles of the founder of the Jesuit order. From 1680 the frescos of the vault were considered, both in Rome and beyond, an excellent example of the Baroque technique of creating the illusion of architectural depth in painting. Sant'Ignazio.

The Eighteenth Century

Architecture and Town Planning

The Beginning of the Century

The year 1700 for the city of Rome was agitated and teeming with activity. On September 27 of that year Innocent XII died, surrounded by an aura of sanctity as well as by the esteem and regret of the Romans, who remembered him above all as the pope who had decisively banned the politics of nepotism and had dedicated himself with impartiality to the social problems of the city and its people.

Slightly less than two months after Innocent's death, the new pope was elected. The awaited news (the great European powers looked on with great interest) of the death of Charles II of Spain made the college of cardinals quickly break the deadlock that they were in, since they did not want to find themselves unprepared when things started to happen. Thus it was that on November 29, Pietro Gianfrancesco Albani was elected to the papal throne, taking the name of Clement XI (1700–21).

Clement XI was certainly not lacking in love for and dedication to the arts. It is to him that the 1701 edict is owed, which attempted to limit the disquieting phenomenon of the export of antique works of art. In addition to this, it was he who enriched the Capitoline collection of sculpture that subsequently, because of the intervention of Clement XII, would become the first European museum open to the public. In reality, cultural conditions in general had changed some time earlier, so that grandiose programs could be carried out, even if large-scale architectural plans had to remain among the pope's aspirations.

A particular case in point is Carlo Fontana's project for the restructuring and conversion of the Colosseum into a church. The great mass of the Colosseum had been exploited for centuries as a travertine quarry for the building of works such as Palazzo San Marco (now Palazzo Venezia) and the Palazzo della Consulta. Indeed, during Clement's papacy the earthquake of February 1703 provided unexpected material for the building of Porto di Ripetta, since it caused three arches of the inner ring of the Colosseum to fall down. In the time of Innocent XI, Bernini had already been thinking of ways to organize the huge building. The idea was taken up by Fontana under Clement XI, as is shown by the dedication to Clement in *The Flavian Amphitheater or Colosseum Described and Delineated* that Fontana drew up in 1714 and which was published in 1725 in the Hague.

The project, like Bernini's, envisaged the realization in the northeastern zone of "a sanctuary worthy of veneration as the illustrious theater of martyrs and as the site in which infinite ranks of saints made their way to Heaven." It was to have a dome and be on a central plan with two radial chapels on the horizontal diameter,

Portico of Santa Maria in Trastevere, designed by Carlo Fontana from 1702. The church was remodeled in the nineteenth century, Fontana's project was part of a program undertaken by Clement XI to refurbish important early Christian churches.

closed at the back by loggias, which would link the church to the rest of the amphitheater.

Fontana's intervention reflected Clement's intentions to use the ancient pagan buildings of Rome to the glory of God, making novel witnesses to Christianity out of them. This attitude fitted perfectly with Clement's vision, which on the one hand tended towards the recovery of antique Christian remains (he also embraced the idea of an early Christian museum), and on the other satisfied the lively general interest in that period in archaeology. Finds such as the base of the Column of Antoninus Pius that came to light in 1703, now in the Cortile della Pigna in the Vatican Museums, served only to increase interest in antiquarian taste for the great ancient works of art. The chronic lack of papacy funds prevented the carrying out of Fontana's project, certainly a good thing as far as the safeguarding of the integrity of the Colosseum is concerned.

Carlo Fontana

The *Treatise of the Marvels of the Sacred City of Rome* by Pier Maria Felini, printed in 1610 and 1625, shows the original aspect of the venerable church of Santa Maria in Trastevere. In 1702 Clement XI commissioned the ubiquitous Carlo Fontana with the reconstruction of the facade in order to modernize its appearance, while respecting the existing portico and medieval structure. An etching by Vasi indirectly shows

Fontana's interventions. He substituted the three single-light windows with one square window (subsequently removed in Vespignani's restoration). Fontana made the forms softer, placing the columns crowned with Ionic capitals on the same number of pillars connected by arches. The roof jutting out over the portico was decorated with a balustrade. Fontana probably also designed the gates.

More or less at the same time, the restoration of the church of Santi Apostoli was undertaken, in part by Francesco Fontana (1668–1708), son of Carlo. Francesco died six years before his father, who never got over the loss. He was one of the group of Fontana's pupils operating in Rome in the first twenty years of the century,

Fountain of the Tritons in Piazza Santa Maria in Cosmedin by Francesco Bizzaccheri, with tritons by Francesco Moratti, 1717–19. Commissioned by Clement XI, the fountain shows the influence of Bernini's Fountain of the Triton in Piazza Barberini.

Santa Maria Maddalena near the Pantheon, completed in about 1735. With its imaginative Borromini-inspired design, it is one of the best examples of Roman Rococo. The attribution of the facade to Giuseppe Sardi, based on eighteenth-century travel guides, is now rejected because of stylistic features.

among whom Alessandro Specchi and Filippo Juvarra (whose work, however, was carried out mainly outside Rome) stood out. Much of the internal decoration of Santi Apostoli was carried out by Carlo, who directed it until 1714, after the death of Francesco.

The Odescalchi Chapel was created by Ludovico Sassi, another of Fontana's pupils. It features Innocent XI's arms in mosaic, which occupy the whole floor. To Francesco is also attributed the wooden ceiling of San Pietro in Vincoli that frames G.B. Parodi's great fresco in a deep transverse caisson. The restoration of San Clemente (1711–15) was entrusted to another of Fontana's sons and pupils, Carlo Stefano, who carried out the facade of Sant'Eusebio in 1711 as well.

Even though it left no trace of the earlier twelfth-century facade, the facade built by Carlo Stefano was an exact copy of the original and its candor and purity of line marry perfectly with the five regularly-spaced ancient columns in the portico. As at Santa Maria in Trastevere and San Pietro in Vincoli, the internal work focused on putting up the wooden caisson ceiling which recalls the Cosmatesque decoration of the floor. The rich great window with sinuous profiling stands out, similar to that at Santi Apostoli. Here, in contrast, the sobriety of the internal decoration (different from the proliferation at Santi Apostoli) gives character and vigor to the eighteenth-century addition that links instead to the polychrome of the ceiling, in the center of which is the *Glory of St. Clement*, painted shortly afterwards by Giuseppe Chiari.

In 1712 internal interventions took place in Santa Cecilia in Trastevere, under the direction of Antonio Paradisi, assisted by Berettoni. They set up a ceiling that featured low curving beams which make up the ribbing of the calotte, decorated in gold and stucco. The eighteenth-century restoration did, however, profoundly alter the overall effect.

The intervention in restructuring the area around Santa Maria in Cosmedin was much deeper. It was decided with a papal edict in 1715 to ensure the supply of water to the quarter. For this purpose the level of the piazza was lowered. At the same time Francesco Bizaccheri was entrusted with the creation of the basin of the fountain that already existed, completed in the middle by a sculpture by Francesco Moratti depicting tritons holding up a shell. At the center of the shell the mountains of Clement XI's arms stood out.

When, three years later, Clement's nephew, Cardinal Annibale Albani, became titular cardinal of Santa Maria in Cosmedin, he decided to modernize it. Of the picturesque facade by Giuseppe Sardi (1680–1753) nothing today remains, as the restoration that was carried out by Giovan Battista Giovenale between 1896 and 1899 returned it to its original early medieval appearance. However, it is possible to have a precise idea of Sardi's work not only through his design, which concentrates the idea in an almost definitive form, but also due to a nineteenth-century photograph by Cesare Vasari taken before the restoration (now in the Biblioteca Vallicelliana).

The artistic personality of Sardi is still debated. If scholars are in full agreement in attributing to him the restoration of Santa Maria in Cosmedin (if only because the canon, Giovanni Maria Crescimbeni, recorded the "judicious work of Giuseppe Sardi [who] without spoiling at all the ancient form" had made of it "one of the most beautiful churches in Rome"), the same cannot be said of another church traditionally attributed to Sardi, Santa Maria Maddalena near the Pantheon.

Rococo Poetics and Santa Maria Maddalena

The complex question of Santa Maria Maddalena, the building of which lasted more than three centuries (it was originally built at the beginning of the fifteenth century and was completely rebuilt in the seventeenth to Fontana's design, altered in turn by Giovanni Antonio de Rossi and by Carlo Giulio Quadri), was analyzed by Golzio in the 1930s. The positions taken by scholars on the problem of the facade are divided. Some, like Portoghesi, attribute it totally to Sardi, while others, like Wittkower, claim it for Quadri, who was active there from 1697 to 1699. However, Mallory has convincingly pointed out the difficulty of attributing the exuberant plaster decoration of the facade of about 1735 to Sardi.

What is certain is that the work stands out as an eloquent example of rococo poetics in Rome. The term Rococo, as is well known, is an Italianization of the French *rocaille*, literally "shell"; it began to be used from 1730 onwards.

A particularly French phenomenon, born in the last years of the reign of Louis XIV and subsequently developed in the whole of Europe, Rococo was adhered to in Italy in a discontinuous and very differentiated way. According to Matteuci Wishing to summarize its features, Rococo architecture means an architectonic architecture in which, "the structural elements, real or symbolic (rows, columns, pillars), are banned from the walls or hidden by ornamental elements, in which new singular fusions of field are reached, first bounded and differentiated among themselves and in negation of the massive and monumental values of the wall surface… Now that the strong full-bodied colors of the seventeenth century have been abandoned, everything is luminosity, diffused superficiality and nervousness, tension, and movement."

The difficulty of having the architectural poetics that developed in Italy, and Rome in particular, in the first years of the eighteenth century fully accepted as a similar definition, caused historians to coin the term *Barocchetto* (Little, or Derivative Baroque) which, however, because of the disparaging usage proved both inadequate and misleading. Contemporary critics debated the eternal question that placed the classicism of Bernini in opposition to the "Gothic" (as it was termed) of Borromini. In reality, the rancor towards Borromini was losing its force. People now spoke of "graceful irregularities," but it could not be accepted that "ridiculous imitators" (Lione Pascoli) should add fuel to that "delirious Borrominian faction," as Francesco Milizia (1725–98) called it.

The long shadow of Carlo Fontana and his pupils, even through the Accademia di San Luca (which had the monopoly), was opposed to the creative Borrominian freedom of the first half of the century, promoting a balanced, composed architecture which rarely stepped beyond the confines of monotonous conformity. It seems obvious, therefore, that in an atmosphere so heavily conditioned by its own past, the acceptance of the new style (as Rococo came to be called before 1730) was bound to be controversial. The effects of the controversy, this time in an anti-academic sense, are still found mid-century in the writings of Giovanni Gaetano Bottari, which this erudite writer affirmed, referring to the pupils of the Accademia, in his Dialogue on the arts of drawing (*Dialoghi sopra le arti del disegno*):

"After studying the principles of Vignola, and learning the ways of doing things of the ancient Greeks and of Michelangelo, they attempt to imitate them. But not knowing how to invent, instead of imitating, they copy, and they copy badly, because taking various good parts from here and there, they believe they are making something good by lumping them all together. They do not know that beautiful things lumped together badly make something ugly."

As can be seen, the situation of art, and of architecture in particular, risked becoming fossilized by rules and precepts which instead, in works like the Maddalena facade, were resolved by the inspiration and genius of those who were not afraid to dare. Recently the problem of Santa Maria Maddalena has been taken up again with plentiful documentation by Mortari, who reaches the conclusion that the final arrangement of the facade should be attributed to Sardi, but not the full paternity.

What it is interesting to emphasize here, however, is the dependence of the work on Borromini, in particular on San Carlo alle Quattro Fontane (San Carlino, to which, moreover, reference should be made with regard to the plan), from which was taken the subdivision of the facade surfaces, in two almost identical levels of height that were divided by a strongly jutting cornice.

The comparison between the two architectural realizations, a little less than eighty years apart, is useful to demonstrate the differences between the poetics of the mature Roman Baroque and those of Rococo, translated substantially in the abandonment of the strong plasticity that characterized the first, to the advantage of the lightness and delicacy of the second. The powerful columns, which vertically measure out the Borrominian facade, are transformed into slim pilasters that barely pucker the facade of the Maddalena, whose concavity gently welcomes the strong Roman light. The exuberance of the plaster decoration only enhances the overall effect.

Alessandro Specchi and the Porto di Ripetta

The most important work carried out during the papacy of Clement XI was the Porto di Ripetta, built in only two years, 1703–05, by Alessandro Specchi. Unfortunately, nothing remains of Specchi's work in Rome, which was a genuine intervention in the architectural fabric of the city, apart from the raising of the walls constituting the banks of the Tiber.

The actual appearance of the port can be reconstructed due to nineteenth-century photographs, engravings by Piranesi and Giuseppe Vasi, and the documentation supplied by Specchi himself. A fine etching in the Gabinetto Comunale delle Stampe in Rome shows not only the view of the finished work, but also the plan and the phases of the work undertaken. The area selected for the building of the port, which was needed for river activities, was—from the architectural point of view—a somewhat heterogenous entity, which was marked by the presence of the addition to Palazzo Borghese toward the river by Flaminio Ponzio, the opening of Via degli Aranci and Via Tomacelli, the facades of San Girolamo degli Schiavoni (Martino Longhi) and San Rocco, and small palazzi.

Specchi decided to take as his point of reference the church of San Girolamo, organizing the space around this median axis. The mixtilinear progress of the steps, which leaned towards the interior and then swelled again around the semi-elipse of the central raised square, constituted a connecting element to unify an otherwise insignificant and chaotic view. Not only this, but the flight of steps that descended to the waters of the river represented the gentle motif of a passage between the natural and the urban environment, almost as if the latter was born of the progressive geometricization of the river's current—both sinuous and continuous. In this way, from a structural point of view Specchi transported the curving movement of Borromini's San Carlino to an urban scale.

In other ways the work interpreted, perhaps unconsciously, another aspect of eighteenth-century culture that shall be returned to—that of Arcadia. This was meant as an osmosis between the human and the natural, so that nature was seen as a paradigm of comparison to incline towards in order to understand its marvelous and fascinating simplicity. However, it seems that Clement himself did not appreciate Specchi's intervention, as can be seen in his note of August 23, 1704.

Other Works by Specchi

The other works attributed to Specchi—whose career came to an unhappy end in 1725 because of the collapse of the arcade at San Paulo fuori le Mura, resulting in his expulsion from the Accademia di San Luca—were almost all carried out during the pontificate of Clement XI. To him

are owed Palazzo Pichini Roccagiovine on Piazza Farnese and the palazzo built for Livio de Carolis on the Corso. For the latter—now the head office of the Banco di Roma—Specchi took his inspiration from the Palazzo d'Aste Rinuccini Bonaparte by Giovanni Antonio de Rossi, adapting it to the urban context of the Corso and keeping the Borrominian solution of the corner pilasters.

In Palazzo Pichini Roccagiovine, on the other hand, a solution is found that is much more personal. Christian Norberg Schultz rightly compares the work to the most lively contemporary French architecture. Completed in 1710, the palazzo became the model from which minor bourgeois building work took inspiration. The palazzo is characterized by a facade where the median axis is marked vertically by colonnaded openings and horizontally by the sinuous profiles of the balconies.

If in Palazzo de Carolis, Specchi took up again the motif of Bernini's spiral staircase in Palazzo Barberini, here he adopted the more theatrical solution of the double-ramp open staircase—as Ferdinando Fuga would do later, in a different setting, again because of its greater availability of space, in Palazzo della Consulta.

What has been said is sufficient to demonstrate that, even if Spechi was not fortunate, and was disliked by the academic–conservative faction of the time, he must be considered an equal with the greatest figures of seventeenth-century Rome.

Open Competition under Clement XI

The years of the pontificate of Clement XI—despite serious political and economic difficulties—were lively from an architectural point of view. What was lacking was an overall urban planning view of the building activity, which was unraveling instead through episodes only slightly linked to each other, in the atmosphere of a general criterion of modernizing the face of the city—even if the idea Clement XI must have had of the Roman problem with urban planning found its point of reference in the model of Alexander VII.

Clement XI and Alexander VII had in common similar family arms and the awareness that they were heirs to the Roman imperial tradition. Thus, if the port with its staircase contributed to completing the space of the Trident, already defined by the interventions of Alexander VII, the construction of the new portico of Palazzo dei Conservatori on the Capitoline Hill had to celebrate the greatness of Rome, as well as that of Clement XI.

The Spanish Steps, showing the symmetry of the design, initiated by Innocent XIII. The complex combines town planning on a large scale with a richness of detail that can only be appreciated at close quarters.

Entrusted to Alessandro Specchi and carried out between 1719 and 1721, this work on the most important hill of Rome was to include the arrangement of the Egyptian statues and those purchased from the Cesi collection. The highly rhetorical intention was to celebrate Clement as the new Caesar who was giving back to the Capitoline Hill its role as the center of civic and political power of the city of which the Pope was prince, by decorating it with the vestiges of those antique civilizations that Rome had subjugated. This is what emerged from one of the many poetic components—in this case by Andrea Diotallevi—composed for a competition in 1716, announced to celebrate the victory against the Ottoman Turks by Prince Eugene of Savoy.

The open competitions held under Clement were one of the strong points of his papacy. It is to him that is owed the starting-up of the projects to settle the area that would later house the Spanish Steps on Piazza di Spagna, which were, however, built after his pontificate.

Innocent XIII and the Spanish Steps

On May 8, 1721 Michelangelo dei Conti, son of the duke of Poli, succeeded Clement as pope and took the name of Innocent XIII. Because of the brevity of his papacy—he died on March 7, 1724—Rome felt very little effect from his town planning and architectural policies. Nevertheless, Innocent had time to get work started (it was finished in 1726) on the Spanish Steps at Piazza di Spagna.

The final project approved by Innocent was designed by Francesco de Santis, who showed that he knew how to solve a complex town planning problem with rare sensitivity. Before the new construction was carried out, the green slope that descended from the church of Trinità dei Monti towards Bernini's Fontana della Barcaccia (the termination of Via Condotti) constituted an anomalous natural caesura in an area becoming ever more urbanized. It had not only become the privileged place for both tourists and pilgrims, but it had finished up by fulfilling a need of considerable political importance because of the presence of the Spanish embassy.

The spatial problems to be resolved were considerable. The area needed to fulfil the function of a link for views from different perspectives, the side view from Via del Babuino and the not perfectly centered-frontal view from Via Condotti. Various projects were presented in Clement's competition, including Alessandro Gauli and Sebastiano Cipriani, perhaps moreover by

Filippo Juvarra. Even Specchi presented a proposal which recalled the plan, already adopted, for the Porto di Ripetta. The presence of the two lateral ramps closely resembled those built in 1725, today no longer in existence, featured in the Scuderie Pontificie (papal stables) in Piazza del Quirinale, of which a record remains in a painting by Gian Paolo Parini (Quirinal Palace, Coffeehouse) dated 1733.

De Santis' project was very similar to that of Specchi, but with substantial modifications in the adoption of the flow of the steps, the convergence of the lateral ramps, and the adoption of a further central ramp, which in turn opens out like scissor blades, lining the last landing. In this way, the slope of the steps was gradual, allowing them to be ascended "with perfect ease and equal comfort," as was asserted by De Santis himself. In this way, the play of the steps became a powerful decorative element, emphasized by the fact that some were made with the central part convex, and others concave. Finally, with the threefold division of the fabric, explained De Santis, "it has been possible to allude to the name of the church overlooking it [Trinità, the Trinity]."

The Spanish Steps were one of the most important town planning projects of eighteenth-century Rome, begun because of the foresight and sensitivity of Clement XI and successively worked on until the reign of Benedict XIII, who commissioned Raguzzini to resolve the problems of statics that had gradually appeared, thus creating also the secondary ramp that starts in Piazza Mignanelli.

Filippo Raguzzini

The dominant personality of the papacy of the Orsini pope Benedict XIII (1724–30) was without doubt the Neapolitan Filippo Raguzzini, brought to Rome by Benedict with the group of the "Beneventani," whose artistic course ended with Benedict's death. Raguzzini's first works show the difficulty he had adapting to the architectural language of Rome. Thus the chapel of St. Dominic in Santa Maria della Minerva (1724–25), commissioned by Benedict to celebrate the founder of the order he himself belonged to, shows all the limits of redundancy and the lack of scope of the first years of Raguzzini's activity, bringing on to himself the criticism of Valesio and Ghezzi.

Raguzzini's stay in Rome, with all its opportunities to compare his own work directly with that of Pietro da Cortona and Borromini, indubitably positively influenced his architectural lexicon. If the solutions to modernize the facade of San Sisto Vecchio and its adjacent convent of Dominican nuns—also by papal commission—from 1724 to 1730 are rather flat and lifeless, Raguzzini proved that he had learnt his Borrominian lesson to the full in the construction of the long low facade of the hospital of San Gallicano, divided by the imposing entrance portal that separates the men's and women's wards.

Piazza Sant'Ignazio and the Bosco Parrasio

The most important and best-known work by Raguzzini is the rearrangement of Piazza San Ignazio, which showed his sensitivity to town planning. Raguzzini had to keep in mind the example of Pietro da Cortona (the urban setting of Santa Maria della Pace), even if in the case of Sant'Ignazio the setting of the church was unchangeable. For this reason, the viewpoint from which the piazza ideally should be viewed is precisely from the door of the church. This transforms the piazza into a theater proscenium, in which Raguzzini's new architecture acts as curtain and backdrop. Even from the diverging streets that separate the fabric of the new buildings, the great Baroque surface of the church facade is seen obliquely, so that it seems marginal compared with the whole complex of the piazza.

For the originality of the solution some commentators, including Norberg-Schultz, supported the idea that this resulted from the influence of Juvarra, appointed architect of St. Peter's in 1725. However, Juvarra's activity seems to be mainly unrelated to the Roman environment, as only his splendid Antinori Chapel in San Girolamo della Carità (1708) survives in Rome. In any case, Raguzzini's piazza—carried out from 1727 to 1728—was conceived as an open system, precisely because of the encumbering presence of the church. The palaces with concave facades on ellipsoid portions give movement to the rectangular complex of the urban space, like a kaleidoscopic surprise that opens unexpectedly before the spectator's eyes. It is one of the finest examples of Rococo architecture.

An important work that was carried out during Benedict's papacy, above all due to its aesthetic and literary implications, was the arrangement entrusted to Antonio Canevari, of the Bosco Parrasio on the slopes of the Gianiculo, the meeting place of the Arcadian academy. Completed on September 9, 1726, the work follows the tripartite regularity of the Spanish Steps and ends in the semi-circle of the theater where every year the Arcadians recited—and still recite today—their literary compositions. The ascent and successive ramps of diverging and converging steps towards the theatrical cavea, embellished by the marble lectern, confer the metaphorical sense of a journey towards a temple of art on the garden and building.

The enterprise was made possible due to the generosity of John V of Portugal, who was made a member of the Academy in 1721, and who donated funds for the purchase of the land and the construction of the building. He intended in this way to pay back the diplomatic help he had received from the Pope, and at the same time to strengthen the aesthetic and literary ideals of Arcadia, ideals that received concrete realization in Canevari's work. It was transformed into its present state by Giovanni Azzurri during the pontificate of Leo XIII at the end of the nineteenth century.

The activity of Canevari, a member of the academy from 1716, affected several Roman buildings, starting from the restoration work on Santi Giovanni e Paolo on the Caelian Hill, commissioned by Cardinal Paolucci and completed in 1718, as indicated on the inscription. Canevari's intervention concerned the interior above all and was explicated in a return to the Serlian motif, flanking the antique columns with pillars.

In the course of Benedict's brief reign, many initiatives of restoration work to ecclesiastical buildings must be numbered and a few of them mentioned. Thus, in ten years (1726–36) Filippo Barigioni remade the chapel of St. Francis of Paola in Sant'Andrea delle Fratte, making it luminous with colored marble and bronze. The French architect Antoine Dérizet practically rebuilt the whole of the church of Santi Andrea e Claudio in 1729. While from 1725 to 1731 Francesco Ferrari attended to the internal reconstruction of San Gregorio Magno, continuing the work of Giuseppe Soratini, who had also contributed to extending the monastery. To Ferrari the sober facade of Sant'Agata dei Goti, whose slightly concave profile between pairs of gigantic pilasters is lightly puckered by delicate plaster decoration is also attributed.

Ferdinando Fuga and the Quirinal Palace

Overcome by the scandal of Piazza Sant'Ignazio—maliciously christened "Piazza Guadagni" (Piazza Lucre) by the Romans—and, above all, deprived of the support of Benedict XIII, Raguzzini was arrested the day after the election of Clement XII (1730–40).

The protagonist of Roman architecture in the second quarter of the eighteenth century was Ferdinando Fuga (1699–1781). A Florentine like Clement XII, Fuga was named architect of the papal palaces by both Clement and his successor, Benedict XIV. He thus dominated the scene for almost thirty years, leaving no small influence on the appearance of the city.

Clement's urbanistic interests moved to the Quirinal. He appointed Fuga to complete the so-called "manica lunga" (long sleeve) along the northern side of Via Pia (now Via del Quirinale). Started by Bernini, who had built the wing of the palazzo and its facade on Via Pia for Alexander VII, and continued for nine windows beyond the main entrance by Alessandro Specchi, the Manica Lunga was finished between 1730 and 1732, thanks to Fuga, with the architectural event of the palace of the secretary of the cipher. It was this that was the real novelty, introduced by Fuga at the end of the long, low fabric of the construction, born with the eminently military purpose of acting as lodgings for the Swiss Guards.

No one, including Fuga himself, had dared to alter the architectural module invented by Bernini, made up—in the original plans, before the alterations of 1870—by the vertical succession of three rows of windows over which a fourth was superimposed, as evidenced by the presence of a stringcourse. The small palazzo was built, incorporating part of Palazzo Cantalmaggio, once the office of the captain of the Swiss Guards.

Considerably altered by Fuga, the old palazzo acted as the nucleus for the construction of the new building, which now had to accommodate the prelate in charge of the coding of the Pope's secret correspondence. Raising the height of the facade (subsequently radically altered in 1870) and emphasizing its plasticity, the building made a counterpoint, after the long pause of the Manica Lunga, to the massive body of the Quirinal Palace.

At the same time Fuga was commissioned with the completion of the papal stables. For these, however, he faithfully followed the design of Alessandro Specchi.

The most important work that was commissioned to Fuga by Clement XII in this part of Rome was the erection of the Palazzo della Consulta on the southeastern side of the piazza. Built between 1732 and 1735 to accommodate the Santa Consulta, the supreme court of the papal states, and two small garrisons with related logistical support (stables, lodgings, kitchens), the building faced problems related to the arrangement of space and the exploitation of the trapezoid area on which the palazzo was to rise. To this was added the need to organize the frontage on the piazza as a theater curtain, linking it with Via Pia. The arrangement of the space coincided with the sharing out of roles, placing the Santa Consulta on the piano nobile (first floor), while the military was relegated to the ground floor, the second mezzanine, and the attics.

Built around a comparatively small courtyard, the palazzo has the appearance of a compact entity that interprets well its dual military and reception role. The solution of the scissor-blade flight of steps opening on to the courtyard is felicitous. Here the reduction of the service structure to a theatrical wall, moved by the central barrel-vaults and the connections of the pilasters which widened the ascending and descending movement of the ramps (made more incisive by the filled base and the high cornice that compresses the whole), has precedents as much in Neapolitan architecture, with which Fuga was very familiar (for example Ferdinando Sanfelice's Palazzo Sanfelice and Palazzo Fernandes), as in the Rome of Alessandro Specchi (Palazzo Pichini Roccagiovine).

As for the facade of Palazzo della Consulta, it is decorated with statues and trophies sculpted by Filippo Valle. Fuga abandoned the original solution, which intended to use the rusticated ashlar of the first floor almost as a background on which the smooth panels of the windows lead off one after the other. The less bold, final design consisted of a simple second floor, marked by the discreet rhythm of the pilasters, and a ground floor featuring continuous smooth rusticated ashlar, compressed at the corners of the facade by rustic ashlar (corner pilasters), which also turn in correspondence with the central body. Here Tuscan tradition returns, with the use of the curving windows and the Michelangelesque balustrade ending the front of the building, even if the classical Bernini-

completely renewed by Valvassori, who let his imagination run riot in a series of unexpected solutions. If on the ground floor the wall marked with a delicate smooth rusticated ashlar is in direct contrast with the wide cornices of the windows (which lack molding of any sort and seem, as Portoghesi noted, to hang on the surface of the background), those of the first floor are surprising because of the presence of a second opening, which is framed in a strongly jutting

Palazzo della Consulta, designed by Ferdinando Fuga and built in 1732–35 by Clement XII for the congregation of the Santa Consulta. The rhythmic articulation of the first floor, with tall pilasters over a partly rusticated ground floor, points to the influence of Bernini's facade for Palazzo Chigi. The ornate sculptural decoration is by Filippo della Valle and Paolo Benaglia.

inspired orientation cannot be denied, embraced by Fuga in distinct contrast to what, in the same years, was being created by Gabriele Valvassori.

Gabriele Valvassori and Palazzo Doria Pamphili

The facade of Palazzo Doria Pamphili on the Corso can certainly be considered the most original contribution to the typology of aristocratic urban living. Built between 1731 and 1734, the work is impressive for both its elegance and the novelty of the solutions offered. Nevertheless it is not difficult to trace the point of reference of Valvassori's poetics in the architectural vocabulary of Borromini, creating movement on the long frontage of the facade of the palazzo with a jutting stringcourse cornice enriched by a balustrade, which is convex to match the profiles of the two lateral balconies and the balcony in the middle.

However, the protagonist—as has been noted universally—is the window. The typology was

cornice placed as a crown to the actual light of the window. The solution adopted in this latter case by Valvassori, from a merely formal point of view, has a direct precedent in the Borrominian windows of the facade of the Collegio di Propaganda Fide. The use of this singular device with the practical function—as at Palazzo Doria Pamphili—of increasing the light entering through the windows and illuminating the mezzanine, is echoed only in the almost contemporary facade of the bishop's palace in Würzburg and the internal facade of Palazzo Carignano in Turin. Grouped at intervals of three (rising to four on the central axis), the windows create a horizontal rhythm that crosses with the vertical movement of the smooth ashlar pilasters, giving the whole complex that organized lightness which makes this work one of the most important architectural events of the eighteenth century in Italy. Valvassori's Borrominian imagination drove itself to the extent of inventing capitals using the heraldic lily, although the whole work alludes to the classical form of the Corinthian.

As can be seen, the first five years of the papacy of Clement XII were characterized by

the birth of authentic works of art. If the facade of Santa Maria Maddalena (1735) is added, it can be affirmed that the architecture of this period offered the best of Roman Rococo. In this way it is possible to outline the complexity of the cultural environment of Rome, where opposite tendencies lived side by side. These included trends that were in some way linked to the current of European Rococo and others that instead saw academic rules in Bernini's classical principles, from which it was difficult to deviate. The unrealized project by Fuga at Palazzo della Consulta is evidence of this.

The first half of the eighteenth century in Rome was characterized by this dissidence, in which the tendency for Rococo did not emerge complete. Proof of this is that Valvassori's activities in Rome were considerably limited. Direct echoes of his poetics can be traced only in the facade of Palazzo Doria Pamphili on Via del Plebiscito, built by Paolo Ameli between 1741 and 1744.

Palazzo Doria Pamphili, detail of facade on the Corso. Designed by Gabriele Valvassori, the facade achieves its effect from the gentle wave-like movement created by the interplay of elegantly curved window pediments and balcony balustrades, making it one of the most innovative architectural creations of the eighteenth century in Rome.

Palazzo Doria Pamphili courtyard, designed by Gabriele Valvassori. In contrast to the dynamism of the facade, the courtyard expresses a serene formal language, the main feature is the classical arcade.

Alessandro Galilei and San Giovanni in Laterano

The result of the competition for the facade of San Giovanni in Laterano belongs to this same climate. In June 1732 a commission nominated by the Accademia di San Luca by order of the pope, of which the greatest names of the figurative culture of the period were members (including Sebastiano Conca, leader of the Accademia, Antoine Déruzet, the painter Giovanni Paolo Panini, and the sculptor Giuseppe Rusconi), judged the models and drawings that were shown to the public in the gallery of the Quirinal Palace.

The intrigues and cheating were such that Milizia commented: "And what a competition that was!" Nevertheless, only three architects reached the final—Alessandro Galilei, Ludovico Rusconi Sassi, and Luigi Vanvitelli. The final decision was to be made by the pope.

The victory of Galilei, a Florentine like Clement himself, has been regarded by historians on the one hand as an affirmation of retrograde and fossilized classicism (Portoghesi), and on the other, as an official affirmation regarding classical taste trapped by Rococo eccentricity (Wittkower). In reality, it seems that classicism of the gigantic order of the facade that framed the upper Serlian central part is revived in the theatricality of the statues that rise above the balustrade. Not that similar examples are lacking in late Baroque, but the total absence of the posterior mass of the dome confers on the sculpted figures standing out against the sky, an anti-classical vividness which cannot be found elsewhere.

It is enough to compare Galilei's solution with the close one by Vanvitelli, which survives in a drawing in the Raccolta Grafica Comunale. Vanvitelli's drawing is much milder than Galilei's, in part because of the lack of the raised level above the great central tympanum that in Galilei's design finished by offering a renewed vision, in which the personalities are alive and throbbing, with no classic composure at all. It can be imagined that Galilei's stay in Britain had an influence on his choice of the gigantic order of Palladian recollection, without realizing (as Wittkower rightly noted), however, that the facade proposed by Galilei was profoundly rooted in Roman architectural culture. This is documented in Maderno's St. Peter's facade and the Michelangelesque use of the balustrade that Fuga himself employed in Palazzo della Consulta.

Town Planning and Bourgeois Building

The development of a minor building program produced the birth of architectural typologies that in some way were new—the apartment block which, as Mario Bevilacqua noted, was considerably diversified "both with respect to the by now structured and coded typology of the noble palazzo and also with respect to public housing, whether for individual families or several families or as terrace houses." The apartment block, which was a novelty for this moment in history (it would become more widespread in this century and the next), was constituted by single-family residential units that

were placed vertically one above the other in a single building, and were completely independent of each other, although they were subject to common use of the communication spaces (which included entrance hall, stairs, courtyard) and of the services (courtyard, water and washing, stables, and coach-house). In this, the bourgeois house, while tending to reconstruct on the outside the architectural unity and dignity of the aristocratic palazzo, differed from it substantially, inasmuch as it lacked that indivisible unity that identifies the house with the family nucleus living there. This is the expression of an aristocratic ethical concept that precisely in the unity of the palazzo articulates a concept of unity, social dignity, and family reputation that cannot be ignored.

H.F. van Lint, *San Giovanni in Laterano, the Chapel of St. Lawrence* (*Sancta Sanctorum*), *and the Triclinium of Leo III.* Painted in the first half of the eighteenth century, this depicts the area shortly after the completion of Galilei's facade. Because of the lack of other reference points in the townscape, the building looms up like an enormous intruder. Rome, F. Megna Collection.

Facade of San Giovanni in Laterano, the winning entry in an architectural competition organised by Clement XII in 1732. Alessandro Galilei's design is notable for its use of elements from the work of celebrated architects such as Michelangelo and Palladio. The statues on the attic—Christ with the Apostles and the teachers of both Eastern and Western Catholic churches—assert the papacy's claim to ecclesiastical primacy.

587

However, note must be taken of the effort of the new architectural typology of the apartment block to have a connotation that differentiated between public housing with loan features and architecture for the aristocracy. In the first a criterion of exploitation of space was adopted, renouncing attempts at theatrical or monumental effects. Typical examples are Palazzo Del Cinque near Piazza di Montecitorio and Palazzo Giannini in Piazza Capranica, both in areas of Rome newly designated by the pope in terms of town planning.

Architectural Initiatives

When Nolli published the little map of Rome (*Pianta piccola di Roma*) in 1748, Piranesi illustrated it in the lower part under the key with an imaginary view of Rome that combined the two principal architectural achievements carried out in the papacy of Benedict XIV (1740–58): the facades of Santa Maria Maggiore and Santa Croce in Gerusalemme.

The external aspect of Santa Maria Maggiore after Paul V's interventions in 1605 is shown in an etching by Jacopo Lauro printed in 1618, in which the medieval mosaic of Filippo Rusati is visible on the upper part of the facade. In reality, Ferdinando Fuga had been working on the reconstruction of the facade of the church since 1735. Initially the intention had been to leave the ancient mosaics on view, as Carlo Fontana had done at Santa Maria in Trastevere. It was probably the influence of the solution adopted by Galilei at San Giovanni in Laterano that caused Fuga to opt for a facade with two superimposed rows. However, Fuga's invention consisted in creating, with the new facade, a screen that allowed the colored and translucent mosaic surfaces to be glimpsed, for which he took care to have light filter in through the skylights hidden behind the second balustrade. The base motif of the facade was constituted by the gable, whose alternate triangular and round tympana in the lower register created a horizontal rhythm, which successfully counterbalanced the upward thrust of the three-deep barrel vaults of the upper register. Doubling then on the right Flaminio Ponzio's sacristy, Fuga transformed the facade into a precious shrine, almost a casket.

The other great work that characterized the long rule of Benedict XIV (1740–58) was the remaking of the facade of Santa Croce in Gerusalemme, executed between 1742 and 1744 by Pietro Passalacqua and Domenico Gregorini. The two architects, who were of quite different backgrounds (Passalacque was Sicilian, Gregorini Roman), had already collaborated on the Teatro di Tor di Nona. It is difficult to work out who contributed what at Santa Croce, where a derivation from the Borrominian lexicon carried out on a profile of facade featuring an ample central convexity is obvious.

Passalacqua reused the design of the facade of Santa Croce on a reduced scale for that of the Santissima Annunziata (or the Annunziatina, 1744–46), moved to its present site on Borgo Santo Spirito in 1950 after the creation of Via della Conciliazione. Characterized by the gigantic order and the great oval central window, the facade of Santa Croce is placed between those of San Giovanni in Laterano and Santa Maria Maggiore as a third possible solution to the same problem, which is the osmotic relationship between the outside and inside space of the church.

Winckelmann and Neoclassicism

The great artistic revolution of the eighteenth century was represented by the Neoclassical current, born of a happy meeting between a Roman cardinal, his librarian, and the librarian's painter friend—a meeting that radically changed an era. Cardinal Alessandro Albani and Johann Joachim Winckelmann, who had become Albani's librarian in 1758, shared a passion for antiquity that Albani furthered with onerous but frequent excavations, whose finds helped his collections to grow ever larger.

Albani's villa on the Via Salaria was conceived less as a secluded residence than as a place for cultural meetings and for his private museum. It is not surprising that the large garden which crowns it derives, in its exedra conclusion, from Hadrian's Villa at Tivoli, or indeed that the statues decorating the building are of precise thematic arrangement: those of the emperors are in the Casino and those of poets and philosophers in the wings, while those of the gods are gathered in the exedra. For this reason, it was just in this such environment that the foundations were laid of that great international movement theorized by Winckelmann, which took the name of Neoclassicism.

Villa Albani was above all a cultural catalyst, a crucible in which were mixed together the interests of Albani—who probably took a large part in the project of the villa itself—the architectural sensitivity of Carlo Marchionni (to whom is owed, among other things, the building of the small temple set in the park, an early example of the picturesque), and the fundamental cultural contributions of figures such as Winckelmann and Raphael Mengs, who in 1761 painted on the vault of the gallery of the villa the celebrated *Parnassus*, the symbol of Neoclassical poetics.

Given that in the long history of Italian art it is not difficult to trace moments when classicism and the antique were temporarily returned to, starting from the art that flourished under Emperor Frederick II in the thirteenth century, what was the novelty of this movement? The confrontation between Neoclassicism and Baroque does not stand up to examination, since in the last analysis Baroque can be considered "yet another development of classical culture" (Argan). The caesura with respect to the past resides apparently in a marginal note, but is loaded with consequences. Rather, it is intrinsic to the fact that the Neoclassical movement removed the foundations from the general opinion that saw a substantial unity of culture between Greece and Rome-classical, precisely, according to what Vitruvius has passed down to us. In this way, the concept of classicism itself was profoundly modified.

Winckelmann's growing closeness to Greek artistic culture (even if it was only through approximate knowledge) brought about a situation where he identified in ancient Greece the place and period in which that rare flower of ideal beauty took root. In this way, Roman art became subordinated to Greek. Even if it depended on it, this constituted—compared with its matrix—regression. Indeed in his book, *History of the Art of Antiquity* (Dresden 1764), Winckelmann foresaw that the germ of decadence insinuated itself just in the achievement of perfection, explaining that "good is often lost in the artificial because we always want to do better."

Winckelmann indicated three phases of the artistic evolution of all periods, the first deriving from the necessity of representation, the second reaching the attainment of beauty, and the third falling into the superfluous. However, a vision of this type necessarily had to foresee a restoration of the original forms inasmuch, Winckelmann continued, "in this way it can happen, in the same way as the things of the world go around in a circle and return to the point they started from, that artists forced themselves to imitate the most antique style."

As Gombrich noted, this statement is as much inferred from an antique-style relief at Villa Albani as it is from the precepts of the rhetors of classical times (for whom the strict severity of the style "confers grandiosity on to the discourse," in the words of Winckelmann), but it can also be considered a declaration of intent. Winckelmann, who hoped for the recovery of "the noble simplicity and serene greatness of Greek statues," indicated that Raphael was one who had known "thanks to the imitation of the antique" how to grasp its essence. As can be seen, Winckelmann's vision moved from the analysis of Greek art to considering artistic phenomena that were considerably closer to him and which would subsequently become a part of the profound controversy about Baroque and Bernini. "The Cavalier d'Arpino, Bernini, and Borromini abandoned nature and antiquity in painting, sculpture, and architecture, in the same way as Marino and others had done in poetry."

In this way, with the recovery of ideal beauty from its distant origins, Neoclassicism cancelled that sense of cultural and historical continuity that in other periods (for example Baroque) had placed the ancient and the modern (Argan) into an osmotic relationship. It can be understood then, why Rome on one hand became a center of the natural application of Winckelmann's theories—which in some way were verified due to the analysis of the material of the great collections—and on the other hand, and indeed at the same time, it seemed like a pale reflection of the Greek model.

Giovan Battista Piranesi

The only important architectural event to occur during the papacy of Clement XIII (1758–69), isolated like a precious stone in its setting, was the church of Santa Maria del Priorato, created in 1765 by Giovan Battista Piranesi for the Knights of Malta. The restoration of the great complex on the Aventine Hill—the piazza, the villa with its entrance to the gardens, and the church—was commissioned by Cardinal Giovan Battista Rezzonico, grand master of the Knights and the pope's nephew.

Santa Maria del Priorato is the only concrete proof of architecture in which Piranesi, born in Maiano di Mestre near Venice in 1720 and reaching Rome at the age of twenty, had the opportunity to consolidate himself, given that his project for the apse of San Giovanni in Laterano was never carried out.

Piranesi's world was above all a world of paper, with fantastical architecture pictured on sheets of copper, engraved with a burin or through the magic of etching. But Piranesi was also a theorist who was often reproved for the alleged inconsistency between his formulation of maxims and their practical application. Santa Maria del Priorato tends to be viewed as a work of synthesis—perhaps because it was the only one realized—of Piranesi's theory. However, it should instead be considered not as the culmination of, but as a single application in, his artistic development.

A building such as Santa Maria del Priorato was created under the influence of its intended destination and, above all, had a character as a

589

Facade of Santa Croce in Gerusaleme, by Pietro Passalacqua and Domenico Gregorini, from 1742–44. This important late Baroque building, with its walls rhythmically articulated by four colossal stepped pilasters, is reminiscent of Borromini in its gentle concave-convex curves.

Facade of Santa Maria del Priorato, the only one of Giovan Battista Piranesi's architectural projects to be constructed (1765). The entrance to the priorate church of the Knights of Malta (rarely open to the public), framed by double pilasters ornamented with stucco military emblems, is considered an early example of neoclassical architecture in Rome.

place of both secular and religious sacredness at the same time, inasmuch as in ancient Rome the arms of victorious generals were purified on the Aventine Hill. The Knights of Malta were the heirs to chivalric knightly institutions such as the Knights of the Order of St. John, so that both the military and the religious were fused within it; it belonged, metaphorically, to the Christian figure of the Christian knight (*miles Christi*). It is not by chance then, that on the vault inside Santa Maria del Priorato the great central stucco unites a military theme with a Christian one of martyrdom, which is represented by palms twisted together—involving memories of Borromini—to announce the final victory.

If the decoration of the church and the low building that gives access to the garden, under the heroic image of the standards and military undertakings, conceal the feeling of death, this is made manifest in the arrangement of trophies on the piazza. The language of classicism used by Piranesi in the calligraphic decoration of the surfaces leaves space for monumentality that is classical but also derives from austere scenes of death, like those Piranesi worked on at Villa Corsini, where he drew and engraved urns, vases, and memorial stones.

Pius VI and the Resumption of Building

With the election as Pope of the fifty-eight-year-old Giannangelo Braschi with the name of Pius VI (1775–99), activity in Rome took new heart. Born into an aristocratic family from Cesena, Pius VI was not only a pope–patron, but took the trouble to improve the quality of life of his subjects by setting in motion public works such as the dredging of the Tiber, the reclamation of the marshes between Cisterna and Terracina outside Rome, and the improvement of transport, building roads between Velletri and Terracina and between Subiaco and Tivoli.

Pius' greatest fault was to renew the practice of nepotism, offering his nephew Luigi Onesti the possibility of taking over the properties that had belonged to the suppressed Jesuit order at Tivoli. The arrival of Onesti into the economic policies of the papacy had a negative effect on the management of the tax system. Yet Pius

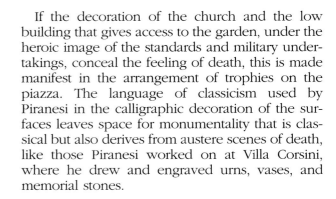

VI's papacy was full of splendor and magnificence. Rome become the desired destination of the greatest European artists and writers, including those such as Canova, Jacques-Louis David, and Goethe. Pius did a great deal to promote art and learning.

Pius' name is directly linked to two initiatives: the sacristy of St. Peter's and Palazzo Braschi, a final tangible statement of the temporal powers of the pope on the threshold of the nineteenth century. At various times, almost all popes, from Alexander VII to Clement XII, had concerned themselves with the sacristy, using the greatest architects of the seventeenth and eighteenth centuries but never succeeding in having the project completed, with the result that for centuries the church of Santa Maria della Febbre was used as the sacristy.

On April 6, 1776, Pius, together with his steward and the secretary of St. Peter's, started to examine the old projects and request new ones. Among these is worth remembering Cosimo Morelli's design. Taking his inspiration from a solution proposed by Carlo Fontana in his *Templum Vaticanum*, which was published in 1694, Morelli suggested opening up the spine of the Borgo, and thus creating a perspective cone that would then be linked to the sacristy. However, the Pope's choice fell instead on Carlo Marchionni, who reworked Filippo Juvarra's design.

The building had already attracted criticism from contemporaries ("from the best to the worst," commented Milizia acidly) and inevitably it suffered from the proximity of the works of Bramante and Michelangelo. Nevertheless, it must be pointed out that it is incomplete, as Ceccarelli has shown, since the southern side of the present sacristy should have been faced by a double exedra-fronted edifice, which would have brought the complex to a harmonious conclusion. It was the high costs that prevented its construction.

Completed in 1784, Marchionni's work was conditioned by a series of requirements, the first of which being that it was not to back on to St. Peter's, in order not to mar its profile. Then there had to be two entry points—one public,

Garden of the Priorate of the Knights of Malta, laid out in 1765 at the same time as the church of Santa Maria del Priorato from designs by Giovan Battista Piranesi.

the other private. Furthermore, service areas (wardrobe, room for the wax and candles, wine cellars) had to be included, plus accommodation for the canons as well as the sacristy proper (one communal, three separate). Thus the entire building rose around the communal sacristy, whose octagon ended in the great caisson dome, which recalled that by Bernini in Santa Maria dell'Assunzione in Ariccia. The two access corridors outlined the space of the courtyard, which distanced the new complex from the southern side of St. Peter's. However, if the different heights and the eminence of the dome make the building seem to flow on the exterior, the service wing weighs heavily on the complex. This is despite the fact that Marchionni had planned an airy space, which is very different from the cramped one which can be seen today.

Piazza del Popolo before Giuseppe Valadier's reorganization of the area in neoclassical style. The Baroque piazza is dominated by the twin churches of Santa Maria di Montesanto and Santa Maria dei Miracoli. Painting by an unknown artist in Weimar Castle.

View from the Pincio looking west over the elliptical Piazza del Popolo. The dome of St. Peter's is visible in the distance. Piazza del Popolo with Valadier's semicircular terraces at the foot of the Pincio, was laid out between 1811 and 1822.

Palazzo Braschi

Purchased in 1790 as a residence for the Pope's nephew Luigi Onesti Braschi, the battered Palazzo Santobono on Piazza Navona was completely rebuilt on the Pope's instructions. Architects of the standing of Giuseppe Valadier and Giuseppe Barbiere were summoned for this undertaking, but the Pope's choice fell on the solution proposed by Cosimo Morelli, from the Romagna (he was born in Imola in 1732), already designated papal architect for the Marches region. Indeed it could hardly have been otherwise, since Pius VI was under the illusion that the Renaissance splendors of Rome, and of Leo X in particular, could return to life during his papacy. Morelli's neo-sixteenth-century language was in perfect agreement with the cultural (and political) aspirations of the pope.

The formal repertory employed by Morelli in Palazzo Braschi does, in fact, belong to the Romanesque tradition, which, however, shrank to a sample of it without particular characteristics. Palazzo Braschi is on an irregular trapezoid plan. Its main facade, on the short side, shows the austerity of ashlarwork, contrasting with the two plain Doric columns supporting the continuous balcony on the facade. Inside is the most architecturally felicitous element of the building, the great staircase that majestically links the floors of the palazzo.

Giuseppe Valadier

Palazzo Braschi is important because it explains to some extent the reasons for the delay in Rome's ability to become accustomed to the new Neoclassical language, strange in a city which, as has been seen, was determining in the

formulation of the new poetics. It was only the genius of Giuseppe Valadier that enabled the city to return to its full claim as one of the great European capitals.

Born in Rome in 1762, Valadier had a career that progressed without interruption even before the historical cataclysms that shook the city. Architect for papal palaces from 1781, he lent his services both to Pius VI and to the French Napoleonic government (1809–14), as well as, immediately after his return to Rome from exile, to Pius VII (1800–23).

Valadier's activity extended over the whole area of town planning: he arranged Via Flaminia in 1805, supplied the general plan for the reorganization of Via dei Fori Imperiali in 1811, and restructured Piazza di San Giovanni in Laterano. His interests and abilities thus spread from town planning to architecture and the restoration of the great Roman buildings. Between 1819 and 1822 he was in charge of the renewal of the Colosseum and the Arch of Titus while, later, between 1829 and 1835, he restored the Temple of Fortuna Virilis. In this same period of time, he raised the single-order, Neoclassical facade of San Rocco, which knitted together with the complex of Giovanni Antonio de Rossi.

Detail from the base of the fountain in the center of Piazza del Popolo.

593

Giovanni Ceccari, *Neptune with Two Tritons* (1822–23), from the western exedra of Piazza del Popolo.

The most famous work, however, which brought together all of the diverse talents of Valadier as town planner, architect, and restorer, is indubitably Piazza del Popolo.

Piazza del Popolo

The first project for the organization of the area by Valadier (it had already been embellished by reiterated interventions by Alexander VII) dates from 1793–94, when the architect, responding to the public notice calling for tenders for a competition in 1773 for the Accademia di San Luca, designed the piazza on a trapezoidal plan with the shortest side on Porta Flaminia. As can be seen from Feoli's drawings and etchings, the longer sides would have been limited by the military buildings for the garrison (a requirement of the competition) and Valadier's invention of the superimposed rows of loggias, which would have been on the eastern and southern sides.

This initial choice, drawn up by Valadier in the first instance but never executed, depended heavily on the cultural roots as well as the aesthetic ideals pursued by Valadier, which largely coincided with those of Milizia. Even the option for a trapezium form reflected the recommendations of Milizia, who liked open areas in order to avoid the tedium of regularity. Valadier was probably the architect who more than any other reflected both the Neoclassical and Enlightenment architectural theories advocated by the pitiless Milizia, who addressed his barbed comments to the neo-sixteenth-century Rome contemplated lovingly by Pius VI.

Of the 1793 project almost no trace was left in the building worked on by Valadier between 1811 and 1822. The monotony of the long loggias disappeared completely and the entry into the piazza was widened panoramically into two broad exedras that linked the northern side, with the Porta del Popolo and the two low ashlar buildings designed by Valadier as a propylaeum, to the southern side, where the famous street pattern of the trident was opened, marked by twin churches. It is not difficult to read into this felicitous solution the influence of Bernini's Piazza San Pietro, here enriched and modified, due to the greenery and the tree-lined terraces of the Pincio Gardens, which enable a substantial height difference to be overcome.

The intervention of Luigi Martino Berthault, a garden specialist, influenced the arrangement of the greenery but this also followed the culture of the time, which was developing in terms of the picturesque and landscaped gardens. Here,

Sphinx from the sculptural group around the goddess Roma, designed as a counterpart to the Neptune Fountain. Piazza del Popolo.

as noted by Rosario Assunto, is the romantic sense of the eighteenth-century culture of an irregular nature that enclosed and benevolently besieged the architectural element. There is no doubt that Valadier's final solution for Piazza del Popolo was influenced by this.

With Valadier, the artistic period of the later eighteenth century draws to a close, even if one is by now well into the nineteenth century—Valadier died in 1839.

Marco Bussagli

Sculpture

The Birth of Rococo

Although it may seem paradoxical, much of what has passed into history as the "century of the Enlightenment," at least up to the latter end of the first half, was dominated by the continuing influence of Gian Lorenzo Bernini, made alive and vital by the massive presence of his pupils—or rather by the pupils of his pupils, such as Camillo Rusconi, trained in the workshop of Ercole Ferrata. The fact is that Bernini the sculptor, with all his genius, fixed models and typologies, which seemed so perfect in their interpretation of an era that had remained generally unchanged in the first half of the eighteenth century, that they themselves seemed unchangeable. If any alteration took place at all, it could be read in the political supremacy of France, which as a result had created a more intense relationship between Italian artists and northern European sculptors, with exchanges of courtesies that had already started in the previous century.

All this, however, does not mean that sculpture in Rome in the first half of the eighteenth century was a weary repetition of what had already been seen in late Baroque. The variations on the theme—if it can be defined in this way— led to a distancing from the seventeenth-century model of Bernini to the constitution of an artistic character of its own, which was invigorated by the presence of well-respected sculptors such as Le Gros, Maini, Bracci, and, in some respects, Cornacchini.

The eighteenth century in Rome did not suffer from having only a few patrons since they expressed themselves in works and sometimes even demanded sculpted cycles commissioned directly by the pope or by the most fashionable aristocratic families. However, the character that emerged, when looked at all together, is one of a certain detachment—and, sometimes, of a certain irony in the works carried out. The grandeur became more theatrical, the composition more rhythmic and musical, to the extent of being at times affected. In other words, what could be seen was what generally happens when a pre-constituted artistic vision, already packaged, is substituted for the natural model. Vigor is lost, although not necessarily charm.

The significant undertaking that inaugurated the century was the realization of the colossal statues of the Apostles in twelve monumental, green marble niches, decorated by the dove symbol of the Pamphili family, which Francesco Borromini built during the reconstruction of the interior of San Giovanni in Laterano. The statues, the completion of Borromini's project,

Francesco Moratti, *St. Simon* (1708–09). The balance of the sculpture is achieved by the apostle's attribute of a saw, the instrument of his martyrdom. San Giovanni in Laterano.

Pierre-Etienne Monnot, *St. Paul* (1708–18). The apostle's gesture of reaching out is balanced by his attributes of a book and a sword. San Giovanni in Laterano.

were executed before 1718 by the most important sculptors of the time from Rome and elsewhere. They include the *St. Simon* by Francesco Moratti from Padua (who died in 1719)—to whom is also owed the portrait of Carlo Maratta in Santa Maria degli Angeli, considered the prototype (of Berninian stamp) of the eighteenth-century court portrait—the *St. James the Less* by Angelo de Rossi of Genoa (1671–1715), and the *St. Philip* by Giuseppe Mazzuoli of Siena (1644–1725), who worked in the Rospigliosi Chapel in San Francesco in Ripa.

There are also magnificent works by French sculptors such as Pierre-Etienne Monnot (1657–1733), to whom are owed *St. Peter* and *St. Paul*, and, above all, Pierre Le Gros (1666–1719), the only one who effectively rivaled Camillo Rusconi, who was the most noted sculptor of the first half of the century. It is not without reason that the *St. Bartolomew* executed by Le Gros, without any indication on the part of Maratta—who had, however, given the drawings for most of the other statues—shows in the balance of the gesture a contained feeling of tragedy that dissolves into the virtuosity of the skin resting on the ample chest, which is created by the taut hem of the cloak. Executed between 1705 and 1712, together with *St. Thomas*, the figure of St. Bartolomew gave in to eighteenth-century affectation only through the ostentatiousness of the knife, the instrument

of his martyrdom by flaying. On the other hand, often in Maratta's works—which are nevertheless well-constructed—can be found a vein of affectation that is nothing other than the just interpretation of the taste of the period.

Influenced by Bernini, Ferrata, and also Duquesnoy, Le Gros worked intensely in Sant'Ignazio at the end of the seventeenth century, but his fortunes proper began in San Giovanni in Laterano, where he sculpted the tomb of Cardinal Gerolamo Casanate.

However, the first work of note by Le Gros is *St. Francis Saverio* in Sant'Apollinare. Sculpted in around 1702, this recounts the miraculous episode in which the saint threw a crucifix, given to him by St. Ignatius himself, into the sea in order to calm a violent storm. To his surprise, once the storm had dropped, the crucifix was brought back to him by an obliging crab. For this, Le Gros placed the figure of the saint on a rocky spur and, to give a greater emphasis to the episode, differentiated the material used for the crab, the crucifix (which is unfortunately no longer the original), and the halo, realizing them in gilded bronze. The technical ability of Le Gros is evident in his execution of the surcoat over the tunic, with the presence of fine lace puckering at the sleeves.

The work can be considered the prelude to Le Gros' masterpiece, the portrait of Cardinal Girolamo Casanate. This statue, which is of

Pierre Le Gros, *St. Bartholomew* (1708–18). The statue captures the beholder's attention through its intense use of images. The hunting knife, the instrument of the apostle's martyrdom, is ostentatiously displayed, as is his flayed skin. San Giovanni in Laterano.

Camillo Rusconi, *St. Matthew* (1708–18). The statue shows the apostle at a moment of psychological tension which is given visual expression by the juxtaposition of a book and the saint's head. St. Matthew is represented with his foot crushing a bag of money, a reference to his work as a tax-collector before being called to follow Christ. San Giovanni in Laterano.

considerable size, still today draws scholars to climb the stairs of the library founded by Casanate (the Biblioteca Casanatense) and enter the larger of the two reading rooms.

It is just this that is the sense of the pose that Le Gros attributed to Casanate—the gesture of the extended right arm is not intended to allude to anything but an informal welcome, implying also the desire to discuss culture, history, art, and religion. In his other hand, however, Casanate holds his cardinal's hat and, in an attempt to avoid dropping the papers concerning the legacy of the library founded in 1698, awkwardly pulls at his garment, a gesture that enabled Le Gros to display his virtuosity in the way he sculpted the folds and the lace, and confered on the figure an

even more familiar attitude that immediately is sublimated in the kind and intelligent flicker on his face. For all these reasons, the Casanate portrait can be considered the finest full-length portrait of the first half of the eighteenth century.

Giovan Battista Maini (1690–1752) certainly studied it when he was working on his monument to Cardinal Neri Corsini, in the Corsini Chapel in San Giovanni in Laterano. Placed between figures of Religion and a weeping angel, the Cardinal stands erect and elegant. Executed slightly less than thirty years later than that of Le Gros, Maini's work, however, far from finding a new solution, referred directly to what had probably been Le Gros' inspiration, the famous full-length portrait of Cardinal Richelieu by Philippe de Champaigne.

Camillo Rusconi (1658–1728) from Milan, not linked in any way to the figurative culture of France, came to Rome between 1684 and 1685 to execute four statues of the Apostles for San Giovanni in Laterano. In the monumentality and firmness of the figures, Rusconi shows that through his master, Ercole Ferrata, he had assimilated the teaching of Bernini and Algardi. Thus in *St. Matthew*, opening the ledger and crushing the bag of money he is no longer interested in, the echo of Raphael and Michelangelo's prophets can be felt, mediated, however, by the Baroque. The broad gesture recalls Algardi's *Attila* while the torment of the folds of the robe is reminiscent of Bernini.

Rusconi sculpted for wide solid surfaces that do not have much to do with the sophisticated chiaroscuro devices of the French. This is especially apparent in *St. James the Great*, where the theatrical though measured gesture creates a wide space under the arm, around which the whole figure is dynamically organized.

In order to fully realize the different way of conceiving work compared with French figurative culture, it is enough to look at the different way in which they deal with hair and beards. In Rusconi's Apostles, it is reduced to locks and is dealt with as highly plastic masses, while in Monnot's and Le Gros' work it is fragmented into curls and whorls which give a delicate chiaroscuro effect.

The work in which Camillo Rusconi's ability to mediate between the artistic ideals of Bernini and Algardi is most obvious, is the tomb of Gregory XIII (1572–85) in St. Peter's. Executed between 1719 and 1725, the tomb fuses the typologies of funerary monuments conceived by the two great sculptors of the preceding century. It is not difficult to confirm that the statue of the pope is derived from Bernini's bronze of Urban VIII for his tomb in St. Peter's. Rusconi took care to transform the raised arm into a convincing benediction, and in fact the head of the pope is turned towards the right, as if towards a cheering crowd. The compositional organization of the whole, however, with its celebratory relief of Gregory on the front of the sarcophagus, clearly took its inspiration from the tomb of Leo XI, as did the choice of executing the sculptural complex in white marble, avoiding the use of other materials such as bronze or colored marble.

In the same way, the shape of the urn is taken from Algardi, with the use of the section in the shape of an upturned trapeze. The large pall of cloth placed over the sepulchre, on the other hand, is clearly influenced by Bernini. Rusconi took his inspiration from the tomb of Alessandro VII, but instead of Death, who there pushes forward the cloth in a theatrical fold, he took the figure of Fortitude, who with a wide gesture raises the edge of the cloth to peep at the memorable gestures of Gregory XIII. In accordance with what is represented in the bas-relief of the tomb, he was responsible for the reformed calendar.

However, it should not be thought that the tomb of Gregory XIII is a mere mechanical mixture of Algardian and Berninian elements. It is a masterpiece, the high point of tomb architecture of the early eighteenth century. It is not the components that make up the work of art, but the ability to organize them in an original way.

In order to appreciate it completely, it is enough to compare Rusconi's work with the

Agostino Cornacchini, *Hope* (1725–26). The sculpture reveals Cornacchini's lack of compositional imagination, contrasting with the fluidity of Bernini's work. Monte di Pietà, chapel.

Agostino Cornacchini's equestrian statue of Charlemagne, completed 1725, considered a weak response to Bernini's Constantine on the far side of the vestibule of St. Peter's. In contrast to his celebrated model, Cornacchini sought to intensify the impact of the figure through a mosaic background. St. Peter's.

tomb of Innocent XI, executed, by Pierre Stephane Monnot between 1697 and 1704 on the basis of Maratta's drawing. It is not difficult to note the same sophisms encountered in the San Giovanni in Laterano statue. Exaggeratedly ornamented, even if it does reflect the outline of Bernini's tombs, it suffers from a too small figure of the pope and from the affectation which heralded the advent of Rococo.

The tomb of Alessandro Sobieski, sculpted by Camillo Rusconi at the end of a successful career, was of a completely different orientation. Here too, the elements of which it is composed do not constitute a novelty since they had been used previously by Carlo Fontana for his tomb of Christina of Sweden in St. Peter's. Renouncing polychromy and theatrical ostentation, Rusconi achieved a rigorous and elegant work that again reinvents Algardian forms, like the trapezoid sarcophagus, and Berninian forms, such as the medallion with the portrait of the deceased, used for the first time by Rusconi in his tomb of Maria Raggi in Santa Maria sopra Minerva, where he had worked at the beginning of the century.

This reflection on funerary typology concerned the most sculptors who, taking their inspiration from earlier work, created new solutions that were aesthetically equally valid. The allegory of *Charity* executed for the chapel of the Monte di Pietà also owes something to the tombs of Giovanni Andrea Muti and his wife, Maria Colomba Vicentini in San Marcello on the Corso, sculpted around 1725 by the Roman Bernardino Cametti (1669–1736). The Muti tombs are taken from Bernini's side "boxes" in the Cornaro Chapel in Santa Maria della Vittoria, but it is the accentuated diversification of the materials (including bronze) and the techniques (including mosaic for the bases) which constitutes the novelty. If to this is added the great ability of Cametti in working with embroidery and lace, it is not an exaggeration to speak of a masterpiece in their genre.

It was in this way, therefore, that—variant after variant—a new language was formed. A notable group of sculptors competed. Among them Giuseppe Rusconi (1687–1738) should not be overlooked. From Como, he was a pupil of and collaborator with, Camillo Rusconi (no relation). Giuseppe came to Rome in around 1705, inherited his master's workshop, and became a member in 1728 of the Accademia di San Luca. In the allegory of Fortitude for the Corsini Chapel in San Giovanni in Laterano, he experimented with Camillo Rusconi's broad plastic style, to whom, above all, he dedicated a fine portrait bust, now in the Capitoline Museums. The cherubs that accompany Fortitude are as graceful as those executed by Camillo Rusconi

for the Sobieski tomb, while the figure of Virtue enthroned in the niche of the Corsini Chapel recalls the Fortitude which the Camillo Rusconi sculpted for the tomb of Gregory XIII. Giuseppe, aware of changes in taste, made the figure more decorative and elegant so that it was in line with the canons of Rococo.

Close attention to chiaroscuro, rather than plasticity, can be found, alternatively, in the allegory of Faith that Francesco Moderati from Milan (1680–1729) executed for the chapel of the Monte di Pietà. The twist of the flexible body is emphasized by the tormented folds of the robe, which at times are arranged incongruously, as on the breast, but which nevertheless contribute toward characterizing the image. Finally, it should be noted that the little angel with the open book, holding it on his head, is the monumental transposition of Bernini's decoration of the columns of the nave of St. Peter's.

Making a match each side of the entrance with Moderati's statue is a figure of Hope, certainly the best work of Agostino Cornacchini (1686–after 1754), a sculptor from Pistoia who already gave rise to diverging opinions in his own period. Of Tuscan training and settled in Rome around 1712, Cornacchini is certainly an interpreter of Rococo who cannot be disregarded, if only for the importance of the work he had the opportunity to carry out. However, *Hope* already shows the limits of his art. While it is true that the figure is well-constructed and the two cherubs have all the softness of children (revealing considerable technical ability), it is equally true that incongruous solutions are present, such as the pedestal supporting the standing child behind the female figure and the hem of the skirt with which the woman tries to cover the other cherub. The taut and straight cloth splits the image awkwardly. The lowest point is the expression on the face of the woman, whose nose, while Greek, is too wide and imposing. Similarly, her mouth is gathered in a sort of smile that does not manage to be either benevolent or reassuring.

The work that most perplexed Cornacchini's contemporaries was the monumental equestrian statue of Charlemagne in the porch of St. Peter's. The statue, completed in 1725, had a precise political importance, in that it testified to the opening of relations with France, as desired by Benedict XIII, strengthening the ties of friendship. It is not difficult to see that Cornacchini's model was Bernini's *Constantine*. The choice was amply justified by the fact that Bernini's work would have made a match with Cornacchini's, since it is positioned on the right of the portico, beyond the door giving access to the Scala Regia.

It goes without saying that it would have been difficult to come out victorious from such a comparison, but the solution proposed by Cornacchini, no matter how much care was taken—it is almost at the limits of virtuosity, with a mosaic landscape in the background—did not satisfy even his contemporaries. What Cornacchini did not comprehend was that in Bernini's work, the function of the cloth was not to act as a theatrical curtain, as in the *Charlemagne*, but to amplify the rearing movement of the horse, whose diagonal articulation follows the flow of the folds. In Cornacchini's sculpture, the cloth need not be there at all strictly speaking. What worsens the situation is both the over-accentuated polychrome of the whole and the disproportion between horse and rider (the rider is too big).

All the same Cornacchini's work is important because it allows a focus to be placed on those elements that conditioned the change of taste at the end of the first quarter of the eighteenth century, determining the birth of Rococo—the predilection for fragmentary compositions, the inclination to the picturesque, and the love for working at the limits of virtuosity, as evident in the horse's tail and mane, which end up by being affected.

Confirmation of this is provided by the tomb of Gregorio Capponi in San Giovanni dei Fiorentini. Designed by Ferdinando Fuga, the tomb was sculpted in 1746 by René-Michel Slodtz (1705–64), who was called Michelangelo. While based on a pyramid, the composition is itself fragmentary because of the accentuated picturesque style brought about by an insistent use of white and colored marble. Its virtuosity is also accentuated by the rendering of the folds of the mantle on the female figure.

However, as occurs in all complex artistic phenomena, the eighteenth century in Rome does not offer unequivocal solutions. Nor do the sculptors themselves, since Slodtz, a Paris sculptor of Flemish origin, had two years earlier signed a work like the *St. Bruno* in St. Peter's, which was practically monochrome and constructed on wide, almost geometrical planes. It illustrates the moment in which St. Bruno declines the tiara and crozier offered to him by an angel. For the clarity of surface and purity of line, this work, which can be considered Slodtz's greatest work (he returned to France permanently), in some ways anticipates aspects of Neoclassicism.

The Trevi Fountain

The event that absorbed the best talents of the second quarter of the century and joined, as a bridge, the first half of the century to the second, was the realization of that great architectural and sculptural complex, the Trevi Fountain. Designed in 1732 by Nicola Salvi (1697–1751) from Rome after he won the competition organized by Clement XII, the fountain was formally opened—still incomplete—in 1744 and was finished, after the death of its creator, only in 1762.

In this manner, a longstanding town planning and architectural problem was solved in the most appropriate way, since a reorganization of the ancient fifteenth-century display had to been considered from at least 1625. Otherwise it would be incomprehensible why Maggi, in his seventeenth-century plan, should invent a Trevi Fountain similar in its architectural form to the Acqua Paola. It was Bernini who, in 1643, thought of moving the fountain to its present position, but the project was not pursued. From then onward, the problem of the new display passed from pope to pope until Benedict XIII in 1728, through Monsignor Sardini, the official in charge of the water supply, appointed the Neapolitan sculptor Paolo Benaglia to draw up free of charge a plan that was, however, never carried out.

Clement XII finally discarded Benaglia's plan definitively and made a decisive mark on the monumental development of the fountain when he decided to use, as a theatrical backdrop, the facade of the palazzo that the Duke of Poli had just had built, overriding the duke's protests. In this way, the fountain could extend over all sixty-five feet of the architectural prospect and all eighty-four of its height, occupying the entire long side of the small piazza. Thus, what might have been a secondary intervention of urban furnishing was transformed into one of the most important undertakings of the century.

Salvi's solution, with the steps descending towards the basin, perfectly interpreted the pope's expectations. The fountain was not simply accommodated by a piazza, but the space of the piazza became an integral part of the monument. It is not without reason that even the hypercritical Milizia, in 1785, could not help exclaiming, "No work more magnificent has been carried out in Rome this century!"

The fountain is one of those rare occasions in which sculpture and architecture are not only present on an equal footing, but complement each other, so that where sculpture imitates nature with its rocks and plants, horses and shells, it mediates between the natural world—represented by water—and the human world—represented by architecture. The flowing of water, rushing thunderously in a thousand streams, becomes a metaphor for existence and for the continuous evolution of nature in which humanity too takes part.

This is not a retrospective reading of Salvi's work: Salvi took care to collect the thoughts and intentions that had brought him to conceive of a fountain in such a manner in his Philosophical reasons (*Ragioni filosofiche*), now in the Vatican Library. He explained that Neptune, enthroned at the center of the central niche, represented water that "makes vivid the nutritive parts necessary for the production of forms and, mitigating the excessive heat that destroys it, can call itself the only perennial cause of their maintenance." In other words, the Trevi Fountain is none other than a hymn to life.

To understand that at the basis of the whole composition lay philosophical considerations, it suffices to note that the horses drawing a shell-

Nicola Salvi, Trevi Fountain. What is effectively a triumphal arch combines with the architecture of Palazzo Conti to create one of Rome's most impressive architectural setpieces. The most important sculptors of the age worked on this brilliant design from 1724 to 1736, creating the central group around Neptune, Abundance, and Health in the side niches, and the two reliefs depicting the history of the Acqua Vergine.

Pietro Bacci, *Neptune on a Chariot of Shells Drawn by Tritons.* This powerful central sculptural group from the Trevi Fountain, executed after 1759 by Bacci and probably borrowing heavily from a design by Bacci's predecessor Giovan Battista Maini, is the thematic and formal focus of the ensemble.

Filippo della Valle, *Annunciation* (1750). The sculptor was able to invest this relief with considerable dynamism by means of strong diagonals.

Pietro Bracci, tomb of Maria Clementina Sobieski (1744). The tomb was the result of collaboration between Bracci and the architect Filippo Barigioni. Its design indicates a shift away from the idea of the mystic union of the deceased with God towards a work which is purely commemorative. This is apparent in the use of the pyramid motif, a symbol of perpetual remembrance, as well as a painted portrait of Sobieski. St. Peter's.

shaped chariot through the water on which Neptune stands out have two different attitudes —one agitated, the other placid, an allusion to the dual nature of the sea, but recalling also Plato's myth of the charioteer, which filtered even into the illustrations of tarot cards.

The central group of Neptune and the tritons was commissioned from Giovan Battista Maini, sculptor of the monument to Cardinal Corsini, who made the plaster model. However, after Maini died in 1759 Pietro Bracci was appointed, who sculpted it in marble.

A pupil of Camillo Rusconi, the Roman Pietro Bracci (1700–73) attracted the attention of his contemporaries with his tomb of Benedict XIII in Santa Maria sopra Minerva, designed by Carlo Marchionni, and carried out in collaboration with Bartolomeo Pincellotti (who died in 1740), who was responsible for the figure of Humility. Executed between 1734 and 1737, the tomb, takes after the by now established Algardian model due to the ways Rusconi worked. Bracci sculpted the statue of Purity and, above all, the statue of the pope, clearly configured as an eighteenth-century reinterpretation of Bernini's figure of Alexander VII at prayer, realized for the funerary monument of the pontiff. Bracci's choice is, however, much more theatrical: Benedict XIII, seated on a throne, holds his hand to his breast in a gesture partly of Christian submission, and partly as an eternal promise of faith.

This work opened the doors of fame and success to Bracci, who in 1742 became a member of the Accademia di San Luca. Two years later he executed the sculptural groups for the tomb of Maria Clementina Sobieski in St. Peter's, conceived of by the architect Filippo Barigioni. The tomb can be considered to be one of the most beautiful works of its kind, with the use of a painted portrait, in accordance with a typology that, as has been seen, was gaining popularity in those years, and which Bracci himself reused in the tomb of Cardinal Leopoldo Calcagnini in Sant'Andrea delle Fratte (1746), returning to the motif of the pyramid, the symbol of eternity.

In the Clementina Sobieski tomb, what is most striking is the balance between the different materials (the great alabaster cloth, the white marble of the figures, and the gilded bronze of the crown and flame), which compete in forming the compositional unity held together by the Berninian type of invention of Barigioni. If to this is added the subtlety of Bracci, whose figure of Charity, even if inspired is not cloying, it is easy to understand why the Trevi Fountain could only benefit from Bracci's intervention. He knew how to restore substance and vigor in the Berninian style to the Neptune, which still suffers from the excessively long module, a characteristic of Maini. It is not difficult to observe that even the horses reveal their Berninian matrix (suffice it to think of the Fountain of the Four Rivers), while the tritons recall the late sixteenth-century examples of the Fountain of the Moor, even if the whole complex is reminiscent of the mythological atmosphere of Poussin.

Bracci was not the only sculptor to work on great enterprises. Over and beyond minor sculptors such as those already mentioned— Bartolomeo Pincellotti, Bernardo Ludovisi (1693–1749), Agostino Corsini (1688–1772), and Francesco Queirolo (1704–62) responsible for the *Seasons* that decorate the high plinth of the balustrade crowning the display—another great sculptor, Filippo Della Valle, worked on the undertaking. He was responsible for the allegories in the niches that flank the central large niche. On the left is *Abundance*, which reflects both the style and torsion of *Temperance* executed by Della Valle for the Corsini Chapel in San Giovanni in Laterano. However, here the figure has lost that Mannerist style of the Lateran statue and has become definitely late Baroque. On the right, on the other hand, compare *Health*, not too distant from *Justice*, sculpted for the tomb of Innocent XII in St. Peter's.

Born in Florence and arriving in Rome in 1725, Filippo della Valle (1698–1768), with respect to his colleagues had an international dimension, since he worked a great deal with British patrons, providing his admirers with copies of classical works or with modern work strongly influenced by classical sculpture. However, it was the tomb of Innocent XII, of which the compositional invention owed much to Fuga even if the design took its inspiration from Bernini's tomb of Urban VIII, that launched him in the circle of the great patrons. The statues, however, bear the characteristic Rococo stamp, strictly linked to the use of delicate chiaroscuro effects, that were emphasized by virtuosity. On the other hand, it is just these same chiaroscuro effects that can be found in a work such as the delicate marble relief decorating the lefthand altar with its scene of the Annunciation in Sant'Ignazio.

In other words, Bracci and Della Valle represent the two spirits of Rococo in Rome between the 1730s and the 1760s. In simple terms, the first is constructed and vigorous, and the second delicate and pictorial.

Midway through the century, Rome was a point of reference for visiting foreign artists. Among these, it is impossible not to recall the Flemish sculptor Piet Verschaffelt (1710–93), who created one of the symbols of the city, the Archangel Michael with widespread wings that was placed on the top of Castel Sant'Angelo to replace that by Raffaello da Montelupo, now in the courtyard "dell'Angelo." Verschaffelt sculpted the archangel in the act of sheathing his sword, thus bringing to an end the terrible plague of AD 590.

Among the foreigners in Rome it is important to recall Jean-Antoine Houdon (1741–1828), from Paris, a pupil of Slodtz, who created the *St. Bruno* for St. Peter's. Ironically, during his stay at the French Academy, the young Houdon—in Rome from 1764 to 1768—also had the opportunity to sculpt a *St. Bruno* for the Carthusians of Santa Maria degli Angeli, where the statue can still be admired today. The statue shows signs of the teaching of Houdon's master but the rigor of the lines and the purity of the volume demonstrates how the artistic climate was being altered.

These were slow and irregular changes: as late as 1771 Agostino Penna carried out such changes on the drawing of Posi and the tomb of Maria Flaminia Chigi Odescalchi, which are, indeed, not difficult to consider as the exact opposite of sobriety. The narrative mechanism underlying the composition is simple: two angels in flight are hanging, with great care, a cloth with the portrait of the deceased on the branches of an oak. A lion roars underneath and an eagle perches on the branches. Oak,

lion, and eagle are of course heraldic symbols of the two noble families Maria Flaminia belonged to. But what is of interest here is that the variety of materials used—bronze for the oak, yellow marble for the lion and rocks, porphyry for the cloth, white marble for the angels—exaggerated the Rococo taste for the picturesque just at a moment when artistic choices, driven by Neoclassicism, were heading towards linearity and simplicity.

Suffice it to think that in this period the texts of Winckelmann were already known, as they had been published seven years earlier. Only eight years later a guest of the Venetian ambassador would arrive in Rome, Antonio Canova (1757–1830) from Treviso, taking his first steps on a path to glory.

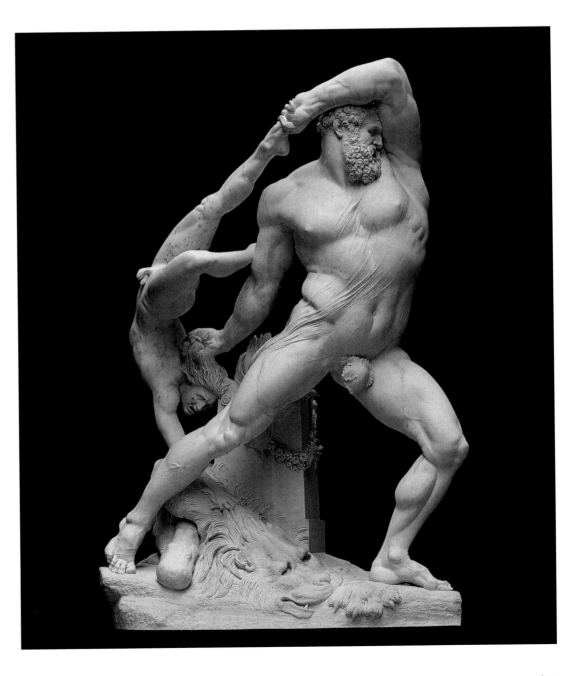

Antonio Canova, *Hercules and Licias* (1795–1815). Although the influence of antique sculpture such as the *Farnese Hercules* is clear, Canova transformed the antique type of figure into a dynamic composition by placing two semicircular fields of movement directly behind each other in the composition. Galleria d'Arte Moderna.

Antonio Canova

The young Canova only settled permanently in Rome in 1781. Barely two years later he obtained a commission for the tomb of Clement XIV in Santi Apostoli. Roman sculptors were not at all happy that the choice should fall to a young sculptor who was not yet well known and came from outside Rome. Nevertheless, when the monument was revealed to public admiration, the reaction was enthusiastic. Even the malicious Milizia could not help note in a letter that "even the ex-Jesuits bless Clement when he is made of marble," no small compliment in view of the fact that it had been Clement who had dissolved the Jesuit order in 1773.

The only feature reminiscent of funerary, monumental tradition is the triangular shape of the complex. For the rest, the work was an absolute innovation. Bare of any superfluous frills, the monument was designed on essential lines only, like those of the stylized papal throne. The sober difference of materials between white and red marble is transformed into a dynamic impulse due to the asymmetry of the position of the two figures of Meekness and Modesty.

Canova's genius revealed itself in the idea of integrating the entrance door of the sacristy into the composition of the monument. Since it was impossible to avoid the opening in view of the obligatory position of the tomb, Canova empha-

sized its presence, turning it into the symbolic value of a passage between the worlds of the living and the dead.

The solution was so successful that Canova used it once more in his tomb of Clement XIII in St. Peter's between 1784 and 1792. Here too, Berninian references are not lacking, as in the figure of the pope, but the overall setting places the whole amongst the finest works of Neoclassicism in general, not just in Rome. The asymmetrical figures of *Religion* and *Genius* generate a circular movement that pervades the entire composition. The movement is repeated in the embrace of *Cupid and Psyche*, a work almost contemporary with the monument to Clement XIII, which eventually ended up in the collection of Murat.

Canova's work spills over into the first thirty years of the nineteenth century. Strictly speaking, therefore, it lies beyond this discussion but two works cannot be silenced among those carried out in the new century: *Pauline Bonaparte Borghese as Venus*, which totally renewed the idea of a portrait in mythological guise, and *Hercules and Lichas*, both in Rome.

Hercules and Lichas, of twenty-year gestation (1795–1815), as much a masterpiece as the other, can be considered the mirror of an era. Commissioned by the queen of Naples on the model of the *Farnese Hercules*, the work remained unfinished despite the interpretations

Antonio Canova, *Pauline Borghese as Venus Victrix* (1805–08). Commissioned by Prince Camillo Borghese, the reclining figure of his wife, Napoleon's sister, represented a revolution in the genre of portraits based on mythological themes. Galleria Borghese.

Canova himself proposed in an attempt to finish it: the monarchy that threw liberty away once it was restored to power—or the opposite for the post-revolutionary French. It was finally bought by Prince Torlonia, who kept it in his palace until 1892, when he donated it to the Italian state.

Marco Bussagli

Detail of the head of *Pauline Borghese as Venus Victrix* by Antonio Canova. The symmetrical facial features are an indication that the sculpture was intended to idealize the subject. Galleria Borghese.

Detail of *Pauline Borghese as Venus Victrix*, showing the apple that Paris gave to Venus as a sign of her victory in the competition judged by Paris about which goddess was most beautiful. The allusion was intended as a glorification of Pauline Borghese's beauty. Galleria Borghese.

Painting

As with architecture and sculpture, painting in the eighteenth century is divided into two halves. With all its variations and modifications, it is not far from the truth to consider the new century as an ideal continuation of the seventeenth century, so much so that the first decades were dominated by the long shadow of Maratta and the notable presence of his pupils. In the 1770s, on the other hand, the Neoclassical revolution had taken hold and influenced art in the whole of Europe, as well as in the New World.

It was a last important moment for Rome, which found itself again at the center of the cultural interests of the period, an ideal heir to the figurative culture of classical Greece. It is not by chance that Napoleon thought of making Rome the second capital of his empire, even if by now the political and cultural focus had moved to Paris, a tendency that had already manifested itself in the first half of the eighteenth century, which had seen Venice flanking Paris, leaving Rome to its usual role as city-museum.

However, this is not the only variation that can be registered in Rome with regard to the seventeenth century. While maintaining the new century as a substantial continuity compared to the preceding one, be it in criticism (it would be Neoclassicism that would oppose Baroque, not Rococo) or choice of theme, it must be admitted that the forms and genres created in the course of the seventeenth century changed and lost their initial ideological content. Roman painting thus addressed virtuosity on the one hand, and the objective rendering of reality on the other.

However, a further important novelty that was a concern not only to Rome was works produced without commissions but intended generally for the art-loving public. In this way, if in Venice Canaletto painted narrow Venetian streets and porticos for the pleasure of his British admirers, in Rome the twenty-one-year-old Bernardo Bellotto, in around 1742, painted his caprices, destined to embellish aristocratic salons. The roots of what would become modern art can be identified here, in that the artist refused authority, and by painting affirmed his own creative genius, which had no need of a specific commission. In other words, painting was the affirmation of one's own expressive mode.

The corollary to this approach would be a distancing from religious and celebratory subjects (which would nevertheless continue to have champions worthy of respect such as Francesco Trevisani and Sebastiano Conca) and the entry into the scene of innovating personalities, such as Marco Benefial and Pier Leone Ghezzi. However, Rome had Maratta and his school as its reference point for the first three decades of the century.

Carlo Maratta

Even though he only lived through the initial thirteen years of the eighteenth century, Carlo Maratta (who was born near Ancona in 1625 and came to Rome at little more than twenty-five years of age), had great influence on painting in Rome. Trained in the studio of Andrea Sacchi, Carlo knew Poussin and, above all, was a close friend of Bellori, which explains his classicist choices.

The new century caught Maratta engaged in the realization of the *Baptism of Christ* for the Baptistery in St. Peter's, now—it was replaced by a mosaic reproduction—in Santa Maria degli Angeli, where Maratta's tomb is also to be found and was designed by the painter himself.

Moved for conservation reasons, the painting shows in its golden light a Christ of solid form, influenced by Pietro da Cortona, but with the head in the style of Giuseppe Cesari (better known as the Cavalier d'Arpino), betraying the influence of Raphael. Of a solid compositional plan, the *Baptism* is able to combine luminous seventeenth-century contrasts with the softness of pastel colors that anticipate subsequent chromatic tendencies.

OPPOSITE:
Carlo Maratta, *Baptism of Christ*. painted in about 1700 for the baptistery of St. Peter's. The influence of Raphael on Maratta, originally from Camerino, is clear. Santa Maria degli Angeli.

Carlo Maratta, *Rebecca at the Well*. The encounter of the Old Testament heroine with Jacob's servant was transformed by Maratta into a composition that is marked by strong classicizing elements. Galleria Corsini.

Between 1702 and 1703 Maratta executed two monochrome scenes in the Stanza di Eliodoro in the Vatican Palace which represented harvest and the grape-harvest; this was a great honor. A considerable part of his activity was dedicated to portrait-painting, which was in part due to its financial advantages. The theoretical arrangement was the one that Lomazzo derived from Raphael, according to which it was necessary to reconcile adherence to the physiognomy of the subject, with the ideal transposition of the features. It is, perhaps, sufficient to quote in this respect the portrait of Antonio Barberini situated in the Galleria Nazionale d'Arte Antica in Palazzo Barberini, which was painted in around 1660.

From 1706 until his death Maratta was ill and painted very little, although by now his influence on pictorial style was fully consolidated. Not without reason was he elected head of the Accademia di San Luca for life. Carlo Maratta constituted for the painters of the early eighteenth century a pole of attraction, sufficient to pull out of Gaulli's influence a painter such as Giovanni Odazzi (1663–1731), who, even though he had been Gaulli's pupil, found that he was adopting forms definitely in the style of Maratta.

This is clear in the large canvas at San Bernardo alle Terme representing Christ leaning from the cross to greet St. Bernard, painted around 1705. The colors and composition recall Maratta's *Baptism*, just like the use Odazzi made of the lighting effects. The source of light is Christ's halo, but the Caravaggesque shadows fade immediately on contact with the tranquil and sunny atmosphere that pervades the whole work.

Maratta had many followers. Giacinto Calandrucci (1646–1707) followed his master in the decoration of Villa Falconieri at Frascati. Andrea Procaccini (1671–1734) went permanently to Spain in 1720, taking with him his master's pictorial language. Finally, Giuseppe Passeri (1654–1714) modernized in eighteenth-century style Maratta's manner, while Pietro de Petri (1671–1716) in a sense anticipated aspects of Neoclassicism.

Maratta's most famous pupil was Giuseppe Chiari (1654–1727), born in Rome, as has recently been proved. Involved in the main pictorial cycles of the eighteenth century, Chiari was known above all for his *Glory of St. Clement*, painted on the ceiling of the church of San Clemente between 1715 and 1716. In this work Chiari put what he had learned from Gaulli to excellent use, but above all he took inspiration from Maratta's work at Palazzo Altieri, recalling the perspective *di sotto in su*, the dynamism of the figures, and the luminous beauty of the colors.

This influence is not surprising, since two years after Maratta's death in 1713, all painting in Rome was influenced by him. Not only did Pietro de Petri adapt his style to that of Chiari in San Clemente, but so did others who worked there, including Giovanni Odazzi.

Giuseppe Chiari, *Glory of St. Clement.* This ceiling painting, which was influenced by Maratta's work in Palazzo Altieri, aspires to similar theatrical effects. San Clemente.

Giuseppe Chiari, *Ceres, Venus, and Bacchus.* This mythological scene, painted about 1720, shows Bacchus pouring wine for Venus, who is accompanied by Ceres. Palazzo de Carolis, Banca di Roma collection.

The fame that was achieved by Chiari with San Clemente brought him involvement in another great Roman pictorial cycle, that of San Giovanni in Laterano, where Giovanni Paolo Melchiorri, Andrea Procaccini, Luigi Garzi, and Benedetto Luti all worked alongside him, and were all in one way or another connected to Maratta. Of the series of prophets, Giuseppe Chiari painted Abdia, which was dated in around 1718.

In the following year Chiari worked on the *Allegory of the Boat of St. Peter and the Theological Virtues*, in the Accademia di San Luca. In the middle, Chiari significantly placed *Faith*, blindfold, grasping a broken mast, as if he wanted to say that Providence was sailing the ship of the Church. It is not without reason that the Trinity appears high up in the clouds, with the dead Christ lying on the knees of the Father. The compositional scheme is still the one Chiari had used for the central group of the *Glory of St. Clement*, but reversed and made less dynamic.

This formula was used, particularly felicitously, by the other champion of the Roman classical school of Maratta's stamp, Luigi Garzi (1638–1721). Born in Rome of a family from Pistoia, Garzi completed his apprenticeship with Sacchi and became known in the circle of Maratta, while looking also to painters such as Lanfranco. His *Glory of St. Catherine* on the ceiling of Santa Caterina a Magnanapoli reoffers, with his own reinterpretation, Maratta's solution at Palazzo Altieri, which, as has been seen, was used several times by Chiari. At the apex of his career, Garzi found himself painting with Chiari in Palazzo De Carolis where, in the early 1720s, Chiari had painted a mythological scene with Ceres, Bacchus, and Venus. In around 1720 Garzi executed a hazy *Chariot of Apollo* which, while explicitly taking after Emilian models like Guido Reni and Guercino, diluted the effects of the light in an atmosphere that by now was typically eighteenth century.

The approach to the classicist concept of painting now had the flavor of intellectual reconstruction that passed through the studio of Guido Reni and Dosso Dossi, filtered by Poussin, as was revealed by two paintings in Palazzo De Carolis, *Venus and Adonis* and *Apollo and Daphne*. In this way a current of aesthetic research was outlined that viewed its point of reference in the ideals of both balance and composure, even if it was with nuances and variations.

In this sense, the panorama would not be complete without Benedetto Luti (1666–1724), a Florentine artist who came to Rome in around 1690. A shy intellectual who was disinclined to compete for the sake of his career, he did not seek public appointments, even while forming part of the academy of artists that were associated with the Pantheon and being nominated head of the Accademia di San Luca in 1720. Typical works were pastels of small size and Baroque style, showing heads of boys or girls. However, it must be noted that Luti showed a return to the style of Caravaggio, mediated through Guercino and with precise references to Raphael and Michelangelo, in his *Isaiah* in San Giovanni in Laterano. By contrast, his *Diana and the Nymphs* in Palazzo De Carolis is reminiscent of Sacchi's *Divine Wisdom* for its setting and colors, as well as its airiness. They are two extreme works that identify Luti as one of the outsiders of the beginning of the eighteenth century.

Benedetto Luti, *Diana and the Nymphs*. The painting, which identifies Diana with Night, is remarkable for its delicate recreation of moonlight. Palazzo de Carolis, Banca di Roma collection.

OPPOSITE, TOP:
Giuseppe Chiari, *Apollo and Daphne*. This depiction of an episode from Ovid's *Metamorphoses* shows the influence of seventeenth-century painting as well as the work of Maratta and Sacchi. Galleria Spada.

BOTTOM:
Benedetto Luti, *Allegory of Dawn* (*Chariot of Apollo*). This mythological scene, from 1720, draws on the paintings of Guido Reni and Guercino of the same subject in the previous century. Palazzo de Carolis, Banca di Roma collection.

Francesco Trevisani and Sebastiano Conca

Francesco Trevisani, *Banquet of Antony and Cleopatra*. For this theatrical composition, Trevisani combined the northern Italian and Venetian tradition of banqueting scenes, strong in the sixteenth century, with Roman classicizing tendencies. The detail shown here is the head of the court dwarf in the foreground. The dwarf's eastern dress is intended to create an exotic atmosphere. Galleria Spada.

Leading exponents of the classical current that was headed by Maratta, although with very different personalities compared to the pupils of Maratta recalled here, were two artists who must be considered the protagonists of the Roman scene in the first half of the eighteenth century, Francesco Trevisani (1656–1746) and Sebastiano Conca (1680–1764). Trevisani, from Capodistria, and Conca, from Gaeta, were painters who were able to deal with both compassionate religious themes and reassuring mythological scenes with lightness and harmony in equal measures.

Son of a Slovenian architect who was his first teacher, Francesco Trevisani was trained in Venice by the painter Antonio Zanchi d'Este, who introduced him to plays of light that were reminiscent of Caravaggio. Arriving in Rome in 1678, probably after a stay in Bologna that allowed him to become familiar with the style of the Caracci and Guido Reni, Francesco became the protegé of the Sienese Cardinal Flavio Chigi, nephew of the deceased Alexander

VII. His dependence on the Chigi family led Trevisani to work above all for Siena, where two large canvases were carried out in the cathedral before 1693, when this dependence was interrupted.

Trevisani had his opportunity when he was commissioned to do a series of large canvases for San Silvestro in Capite. Among these, his *Road to Calvary* is the one that best documents his Venetian origins, over which, however, was superimposed his knowledge of the painting of Domenichino and Poussin. Sestieri has correctly noted a trace of familiarity with the Bambloccianti, which was passionately collected by Cardinal Chigi. At the beginning of the eighteenth century, Trevisani found support of the economic and political nature that he desired in the person of Cardinal Pietro Ottoboni, living with him at Palazzo della Cancelleria with a monthly pension of fifty scudi.

Proof of this is the portrait in Barnard Castle (Bowes Museum), which has recently been dated to the first years of the eighteenth century. The work can be considered an example of how a portrait was conceived of at the beginning of the eighteenth century: a compromise between idealization, similarity, and dignity. Cardinal Ottoboni is represented standing and looking towards the spectator, as if he has interrupted the reading of the letter he holds in his hand because of the viewer's unexpected presence. In the bell on the desk can be heard the echo of Raphael's portrait of Leo X, evidently felt as a model even if the rather dark background and the meticulous care in the lace on the cassock clearly indicate that it belongs to work of his period.

Between 1708 and 1717 Trevisani carried out several pieces of work for the Prince of Schänborn, Lothar Franz, which are still in the Pommersfelden collection. Among these must be remembered *Apollo and Daphne*, a pictorial transposition of Bernini's celebrated sculpture. The canvas was part of a series of paintings on mythological subjects, such as the *Rape of Proserpine* and *Diana and Endymion*, which testify to the various directions taken by Trevisani, who was clearly attracted by the themes of Arcadia.

This aspect recurs also in works on religious subjects, such as *Sewing Virgin* on copper in the Uffizi. The love for simplicity and small things that stand out from the painting is an indication of a sensitivity close to that of Arcadia. Also, the radiant light in the style of Caravaggio and the workbasket in the foreground create an intimate atmosphere, which has its prototype in the fresco on the same subject by Guido Reni for the chapel at the Quirinal Palace.

Reni's influence on Trevisani returns in the *Lucretia* in the National Museum, Budapest, painted between 1708 and 1710, while the domestic and subdued atmosphere pervades the *Rest on the Flight to Egypt* in the Gemäldegalerie in Dresden. Despite the landscape setting, the work—painted around 1715—communicates a sense of family and happy serenity that derives from an observation of small things.

The theatrical and melodramatic aspect of Trevisani's work, on the other hand, is captured in the *Banquet of Antony and Cleopatra* in the Galleria Spada, dated between 1705 and 1717. This is a side of the poetics of the painter that had already emerged in the two large canvases for Sant'Ignazio in 1712, the *St. Joseph* and the *St. Luigi Gonzaga*, but which in the Galleria Spada canvas finds its perfect achievement. It has even been hypothesized that Trevisani was able to take inspiration from theatrical representations put on in his house on Via della Lungara.

Finally, among the important commissions received by Trevisani, the decoration of Palazzo De Carolis must not be overlooked, as well as the *Ecstasy of St. Francis* in Santa Maria in Aracoeli, which show his versatility.

The other protagonist of the first half of the eighteenth century, as has already been said, was Sebastiano Conca. He came to Rome in 1707 after a long apprenticeship with Francesco Solimena. A successful painter, he had a brilliant career and was head of the Accademia di San Luca several times. Like Trevisani, Conca was an exponent of the Maratta type of classicism that was current, and benefited in Rome from directly studying the works of Raphael, Michelangelo, and the Carracci. He also benefited from the political and economic support of Cardinal Ottoboni, who gave him lodgings in Palazzo De Cupis in Piazza Navona.

However, it was the patronage of Cardinal Tommaso Maria Ferrari and the fame that he won with his paintings, which induced the pope, Clement XI, to select Conca to paint the nave of San Clemente, where he did a fresco of the miracle of St. Clement showing the saint while he made water gush out for Christians forced to work in the marble quarries. The commission also brought him the *Jeremiah* for the nave of San Giovanni in Laterano, painted in 1718.

All this contributed to the increase in his fame. It was in 1718 that Conca was elected as a member of the Accademia di San Luca due to a canvas, still in the Accademia, the *Mystic Marriage of St. Catherine* in which the Virgin, the Christ Child, and St. Catherine are arranged in a triangular pattern, which is exalted by a radiant light that draws attention to the plastic effects of the cloth.

Sebastiano Conca, *Allegory of Music and Poetry*. The putto wrestling with a goose, lower left, is taken from the famous antique sculpture of the boy strangling a goose in the Capitoline Museums. The theme and individual features of the sculpture are expressions of a classicizing tendency. Galleria Spada.

Sebastiano Conca, *Allegory of Painting and Sculpture*. Galleria Spada.

On the other hand, works on mythological or historical subjects, such as *Antony and Cleopatra* in London, showing a wealth of figures and with a firm compositional plan, were also produced in these years. It is not by chance that Conca carried out an intense teaching programme, giving courses at his home on the drawing of the naked human figure. These were the years from 1710 to 1718.

However, the work that gave the definitive recognition to his fame was the ceiling *Glory of St. Cecilia* in Santa Cecilia in Trastevere, executed between 1721 and 1724. Commissioned by Cardinal Acquaviva, this work renewed the Maratta-type plan of Palazzo Altieri, limiting the sense of perspective and organizing the composition on that level so that it acquires a lightness and freshness unknown in similar Baroque painting. He too was involved in the enterprise of Palazzo De Carolis, for which he realized the *Triumph of the Virtues*, of complex iconography.

He lived his best years between 1730 and 1740. His fame brought him to work outside Rome as well, in Siena in particular, where he realized for the church of the hospital of Santa Maria della Scala a large fresco of which the outline is conserved at the Monte dei Paschi. The large canvas for the Chiesa Nuova (Santa Maria in Valicella) in Rome should be mentioned, the *Virgin and St. Philip Neri*, with its solid compositional plan influenced by Raphael but with warm, golden colors. More intimate, if chromatically similar, is the *St. Mary Magdalene* in the Galleria Doria Pamphili.

Pictorial research led Conca fondly to contemplate Neoclassical forms as in the *Allegory of Learning* in Palazzo Corsini. However, the change of taste caused by the election of Benedict XIV inclined towards an art that was yet more markedly classical and induced Conca to leave Rome for Naples.

Other Painters

The pictorial panorama of Rome in the first half of the eighteenth century was, of course, far more complex than can be represented in these pages, in part because the city, the pole of attraction for artists from all over Italy and Europe, attracted figures who, while living in the city in order to become up to date with the most recent pictorial trends, worked with patrons from outside Rome.

This was the case with the Milanese Francesco Fernandi (1679–1740), whose principal merit was to work with Pompeo Batoni, who frequently visited his residence in Via della Frezza in Rome. Fernandi obtained his important commissions from Turin.

By contrast, Giovan Domenico Piestrini (1678–1740) from Pistoia, after wandering around Italy arrived in Rome at the age of twenty-four and was accepted into Roman circles with the help of Cardinal Agostino Fabroni, his patron. It was not by chance that he took part in the great cycles at San Clemente, painting *St. Ignatius of Antioch Condemned to Death by Trajan* (since the stories of San Clemente were insufficient to complete the church, those of St. Ignatius and St. Servolus were included as well), and Palazzo De Carolis.

Placido Costanzi (1702–59) was born in Rome and spent his life there, active in the Quirinal Palace and the most important aristocratic palaces (Palazzi Pallavicini, Rondanini, and Ruspoli), as well as in the restoration of churches during the papacy of Benedict XIV.

The last representative of the Maratta current is Agostino Masucci (1690–1758), a pupil of Maratta, elected to the Accademia di San Luca in 1724. For this occasion, Masucci painted the *Martyrdom of St. Barbara*, which if on the one hand it anticipates the *Virgin with the Seven Founders of the Servite Order* (where the influence of Raphael is clearly evident) in the figure of the Virgin, on the other, in the figure of the centurion, it recalls the manner of Corrado Giaquinto (1703–65), in Rome in those years and a pupil with Sebastiano Conca, after a Neapolitan apprenticeship with Francesco Solimena.

Active not only in Rome, but also in Cesena, Pisa, and Naples, Giaquinto had a clear knowledge of how to create in his works an airiness and grace that were explicit in the iridescence of the colors, as in *Rest on the Flight to Egypt* in Stuttgart (Staatsgalerie).

As has been seen, over and beyond personal interpretations the artists that have been considered can all be brought into the classical current of Maratta's stamp, not seldom inclined to pictorial virtuosity and the idealization of the subject, but at the same time to the stereotyping of the pictorial formula, which in some way risked making the artistic language banal.

One artist reacted against these attitudes, who, because of his own positions, risked isolation within the artistic panorama. Marco Benefial (1684–1764) born in Rome (from a Gascon family), maintained stormy relationships with his protectors such as Prince Camillo Pamphili, who obtained his first important commission of *Jonah*, in San Giovanni in Laterano, and the Accademia di San Luca, who admitted Marco only in 1741 and expelled him in 1755.

Benefial tended to represent things for what they were, without using artifice or effort to make them more beautiful or to respect decorum. He carefully bore in mind, however, the lessons he had learned from Raphael and the Carracci, and above all absorbed the original value, that is to say, the precept of following the teaching of nature and the being at one with it.

For this reason he made no concessions when he painted the *Death of the Blessed Giacinta Marescotti* in San Lorenzo. Even if there are angels in glory, the figure of the woman was treated crudely and with a realism that spared the spectators nothing.

In the same way, the famous *Death of St. Margherita da Cortona* in Santa Maria in Aracoeli, painted between 1726 and 1733, simplifies the scene even more, placing an accent on the poverty of the environment and the simplicity of the clothes, which automatically became his means to underline the sanctity of the protagonist.

Just as isolated as Benefial was Pier Leone Ghezzi (1674–1765), son of Giuseppe, then a famous portrait painter. Pier Leone dedicated himself to caricature, caustically scratching at the society of his time with his pen.

Landscape Painting

If there is a pictorial theme that it is not possible to avoid discussing even in a rapid examination of the eighteenth century in Rome, it is landscape painting, *vedutismo*, different from landscapes pure and simple because it brings with it the germ of an alleged representative objectivity that does not appear in landscapes.

It was the Dutch painter Gaspar van Wittel (1653–1736) who introduced to Italy, and indeed to Rome in particular, the idea of the "real view," as is clearly seen in the splendid *Panoramic View of the Center of Rome with Sant'Andrea della Valle* in the Gabinetto Nazionale delle Stampe.

Of Flemish origin also was Jan Frans van Bloemen (1662–1749) who, arriving in Rome in 1688, revealed himself as one of the most valued specialists in the genre. His luminous landscapes are populated with small figures that may have been inspired by the world of classicism, the sacred world of the Bible, or by contemporary scenes.

Closer to the landscape taste of Poussin and, sometimes, the dramatic atmosphere of Salvator Rosa, was Andrea Locatelli (1693–1741), active above all in the decoration of palazzi, such as Palazzo Ruspoli on the Corso.

But the artist who best manifested the idea of eighteenth-century landscape painting in Rome was Gian Paolo Panini (1691–1765) from Piacenza. He settled in Rome in 1711 after a long apprenticeship with Bibbiena, who taught him the secrets of perspective and theatrical techniques. It is not by chance that his works, such as the famous view of Piazza del Quirinale and the equally well-known Santa Maria Maggiore, which magnified the recent intervention of Ferdinando Fuga (both in the Coffeehouse in the Quirinal Palace), are masterpieces of perspective. Populated with small contemporary figures (for which he had had lessons with Luti), these views are real instant photographs that throw light on the society of the period as well as its customs, as can be seen clearly on the canvas in the Louvre, the *Preparations to Celebrate the Birth of the Dauphin in Piazza Navona*.

The atmosphere created by contemplating Roman ruins led to a different way of interpreting landscape painting of the city, the *capriccio*, that is the assembling of significant views to create an imaginary landscape, rich with atmosphere.

A master of this type of work was the Venetian Bernardo Bellotto (1712–80), who was able to create a montage of glimpses of Rome and of his own city. Arriving in Rome in 1741 or 1742 for the customary instructive trip, Bellotto produced a series of Roman views and *capricci* that were destined to embellish the salons of Italian, as well as foreign, nobility.

Neoclassicism

In order to realize what position Rome occupied in the formulation of the new Neoclassical aesthetic from the pictorial point of view, it suffices to recall that Jacques-Louis David felt the need to return to Rome to paint what can be considered the manifesto of the new poetics, *The Oath of the Horatii*. However, this work, carried out in 1784, was simply the last act in a very much longer and more complex artistic process that had started out with the pictorial experiences of Pompeo Batoni and the innovatory events of Roman Jansenism, through which enlightened thought filtered even into the papal curia, and from which not even popes such as Benedict XIV and Clement XIV were immune.

Nonetheless, in Rome from 1747 until his death, was Anton Raphael Mengs (1728–79) who, together with his friend and companion Winckelmann, must be considered one of the two leading lights that led the way to the formulation of a Neoclassical aesthetic and painting. Formed under the guiding hand of his father Ismael, who had his studio under Conca and Benefial in Rome where he arrived in 1741, Mengs studied in depth Roman antiquities and the painting of Raphael.

Having become court painter at Dresden in 1744, he returned to Rome three years later, married, and took up teaching at the Capitoline

Gaspar van Wittel, called
Vanvittelli, *River Tiber from
Monte Sant'Angelo.* Van Wittel,
a Dutch painter, was one of the
founders of the *veduta* tradition
(paintings of townscapes,
sometimes imaginary). Apart
from *vedute* of Rome, which
was the largest part of his work,
de Wittel also painted views of
Naples and Venice, where he
settled in 1697. Florence,
Galleria Palatina.

Gian Paolo Panini, *Capriccio of
Ruins with Figures.* A capriccio
is an architectural montage of
buildings from a variety of
sources formed into a
harmonious whole. The
addition of figures animated the
composition and lent it an
idyllic quality. Galleria
Nazionale d'Arte Antica.

Bernardo Bellotto, View of the Tiber and Monte Sant'Angelo. Bellotto was a nephew of the most famous painter of vedute, the Venetian Canaletto. Painted in around 1769, this work shows Bellotto's characteristically radiant use of light, which endows the Roman architecture with a particular aura. Private collection.

Gian Paolo Panini, *Piazza and Basilica of Santa Maria Maggiore*. The broad perspective in this townscape reveals the influence of Panini's training in the workshop of the Bibbiena family, leading designers of theater sets. Quirinal Palace, Coffee House.

academy. With regard to these activities—cultural in the broadest sense—it must, however, be said that Mengs was not a great painter. If his self-portrait in the Uffizi is excepted for its spontaneity and freshness, works such as *Parnassus* (1761) and the *Allegory of the Clementine Museum* (1771–73), which should constitute the application of theoretical assumptions, in fact show all the limitations of cold and intellectualized painting.

Despite this, Mengs came to be considered a model of reference by an artist who can be defined as the greatest painter in Rome in the second half of the eighteenth century, Pompeo Batoni from Lucca, who was a pupil of Conca and Masucci. They helped him a great deal in his efforts to settle down in Rome. Batoni was a natural talent who was formed in the anti-Baroque tendencies of the century, presaging a Neoclassical orientation that brought him to closely study Rome's antiquities and the work of Raphael. It is not surprising that he had a predilection for mythological themes that often allowed him to place in evidence his rhetorical abilities, as in *Achilles at the Court of Lycomedes* and *The Education of Achilles by the Centaur Chiron*, both in the Uffizi.

From the 1740s onwards, his fame grew also in conjunction with an intense activity in painting portraits, in which he did not avoid underlining the programmatic intentions of a clear reference to classical culture. In this way, in his portrait of John Staples in the Museo di Roma, over and beyond the anonymous Roman ruins appears the so-called Ludovisi altar, recently restored by Bernini.

Pompeo Girolamo Batoni, *Achilles at the Court of Lycomedes* (1746). The picture depicts the unmasking of Achilles who had been living among the daughters of King Lycomedes disguised as a woman. Ulysses played a trick to reveal him as a man, presenting the court with gifts including a sword. The king's daughters were engrossed with the jewelry but Achilles seized the sword, revealing himself as a man. Batoni depicts this event in an animated Rococo style, with a number of classicizing elements. Florence, Uffizi.

That portrait painting was the principal way to ensure fame was well known by one of the best-known painters of the period, the Swiss Angelika Kauffmann (1741–1804), who was admitted to the Accademia di San Luca and received many compliments from Pompeo Batoni. Arriving in Rome in 1765, and settling there in the autumn of 1782, "the most cultured woman in Europe," as she was defined by her contemporaries, she held international contacts with Sir Joshua Reynolds and must be counted as one of the founder members of the Royal Academy, which was created as a temple to Neoclassical culture.

An admirer of Mengs, but gifted with a far more sensitive technique, Kaufmann drew inspiration as much from mythological themes (such as *Venus Showing Aeneas and Achates the Way to Carthage*, Feldrich, Chamber of Commerce of Vorarlberg), as from historical (for example *Coriolanus, Veturia, and Volumnia*, Wrotham Park) and biblical themes (*Nathan and David*, Bregenz, Vorarlberger Landesmuseum). All bore in mind the new dictates of Neoclassical aesthetics, which were purity and simplicity of form. It is, therefore, not surprising that the figure of Nathan is more that of an ancient Roman rather than that of a biblical personage.

In the same way, in certain paintings by Kauffmann, the Arcadian sentiment of nature blossoms, as in the *Female Bacchante* in Palazzo Barberini, where the nostalgia for an antiquity that all artists attempted to make perfectly real is palpable.

It is not by chance that from 1780 onward, under the direction of Antonio Asprucci (1723–1808), the ceiling of the rooms on the first floor of the Casino Borghese were covered with vivid dry temperas, which brought liveliness and vitality to the mythological themes of the statues of the Borghese collection. Thus, for example, inspired by the bronze statue of a dancing faun, Tommaso Conca and Giovan Battista Marchetti painted *Sacrifice to Silenus* on the ceiling of the room that contained the statue, while in the room with Bernini's *Apollo and Daphne*, Marchetti and Pietro Angeletti painted the *Metamorphosis of Daphne*. It was this, the massive pictorial undertaking of the end of the century, that placed the seal on a monumental scale on the novelties of Neoclassical culture. This, however, was an Arcadian and Pompeian, even perhaps Greek, Neoclassicism, which had involved not only Batoni, Mengs, and Kauffmann, but a whole range of painters that included Gavin Hamilton of Scotland, Cristoforo Unterberger of Trento, Domenico Corvi, Giuseppe Cades, Lapis, and Felice Giani (1758–1823), who had frescoed the *Triumph of Peace* in Palazzo di Spagna in this style, where the model of the Carracci was revisited in almost comic strip key.

Tommaso Maria Conca, *Sacrifice to Silenus*. This mythological scene, on the central ceiling panel in the eighth hall of the Casino Borghese, connects thematically with a bronze statue of a dancing silenus in the room.

Against this rampant manner appeared the painting of Vincenzo Camuccini (1771–1844), who was an insidious follower of Neoclassicism. A pupil of Corvi and Batoni, to whom he succeeded in both fame and honors, he modeled his pictorial language on that of David, with the express intention of giving a worthy image to the representation of civic and Romanesque virtues.

From his brush were born the *Death of Julius Caesar* and the *Death of Virginia* in the Museo di Capodimonte in Naples. The two enormous canvases (which stand just over twenty-three feet by thirteen) show an over-elaborate chiaroscuro painting, with which can be compared an attention to rhetorical gestures that at times did not disdain quotations from Raphael. The works were enormously successful. However they locked the creativity of Roman artists into the rigid form of a style that could no longer be changed.

Marco Bussagli

621

Roman Festivals

Roman carnivals were held. On Sunday, February 3 the Jews raced from Campo de' Fiori to Castel Sant'Angelo… On Monday, February 4… boys raced for a green silk banner… On Tuesday, February 5, after dinner, young men raced for a pink banner… On Wednesday, February 6, it was the turn of the older people… On Thursday, February 7, there was a festival at the arena, in the Roman manner, well organized… On Sunday, February 10, after dinner, in Testaccio there were the usual races of Barbary horses, Spanish jennets, and mares and heifers.

The list of races and competitions might have continued to include the donkey and bull races that enlivened Rome in 1499. It was in this year that Burckard, born in Strasbourg in about 1450 and master of ceremonies at the papal court during the reign of five popes, from 1483 until his

Anonymous, *Tournament on March 5, 1565 in the Belvedere of the Vatican*. Museo di Roma.

Gagliardi and Lauri, *Carousel at the celebrations for Queen Christina of Sweden in the Courtyard of the Palazzo Barberini* (1656). Museo di Roma.

Anon., *Charles III Riding towards St. Peter's* (1745).
Naples, Museo e Gallerie Nazionali di Capodimonte

death in 1506, wrote his diary for posterity with an account of these centuries-old entertainments.

The tradition of festivals had been deeply rooted in the city of Rome since antiquity, with religious ceremonies, circus games, and triumphs for victorious generals intermingled. In the early modern period the papacy of the Borgia pope Alexander VI (1492–1503) was an important period for these events. Alexander encouraged festivals and was responsible for revitalizing their most important features, following tradition but at the same time introducing innovation and formalizing ceremonial procedures. For the past two centuries or so, the most solemn of the religious festivals had been that which had evolved out of the

feast of indulgences introduced by Celestine V and instituted by Boniface VIII as the jubilee, or Holy Year. Originally it was held every fifty years, then every twenty-five.

Alexander VI invented the ceremony of opening the so-called "holy door" of St Peter's and the other principal basilicas of Rome for the jubilee. Burckard wrote that, at Christmas 1449, in preparation for the jubilee of 1500, "His Holiness walked up to the door which was to be opened. Tommaso Matarazzo, master mason and superintendent of St. Peter's, handed a mason's hammer to His Holiness, who then gave three blows to a prepared opening in the middle of the door, knocking the bricks to the ground." Since then all popes have repeated this ritual gesture, up to the present.

Roman festivals were not only religious in nature. In addition to the palio races and horseraces, Alexander VI wanted to revive

the tradition of triumphal processions, which dated back to the classical era. Naturally a large space was required for this. The obvious choice was Piazza Navona since 1477, which had been the site of Rome's most important market. In 1499 the triumph of Vespasian and Titus was reenacted, with one hundred citizens appearing as extras, dressed as ancient Romans. The following year, on the same site, the triumph of Caesar was presented, in honor of Cesare Borgia.

Alexander's projects had a decisive influence on Rome's urban development. Gradually, and especially during the seventeenth century, Rome effectively became an enormous theater with numerous special stages. Piazza Navona was the location for the festival of the Resurrection, a particularly sumptuous affair in the jubilee of 1625. In 1634 the *Giostra del Saracino* (tournament of the saracen), presented at

Gian Paolo Panini, *Preparations for a Festival in Piazza Navona* (1729). Paris, Louvre.

the behest of the Barberini family, was immortalized in a painting by Andrea Sacchi and Filippo Gagliardi. To put on an event such as this required the use of architects and scene-painters (in this case Francesco Guitti), and sometimes men of letters (in this case Guido Bentivoglio) to develop the theme, as well as a large band

of workmen capable of realizing the most fanciful contraptions.

One of the most important functions of Baroque festivals in Rome was—as has been pointed out by Marcello Fagiolo and Maurizio Fagiolo dell'Arco—that they represented an opportunity for putting into effect, at a relatively small cost, ideas that would otherwise have had to remain on paper. Thus there was a continual interchange of ideas between architecture and

ephemeral structures, between the styles used in regular architectural practice (which were of course in continuous evolution), and those that might be termed experimental, which were used in connection with ceremonies and special events (including the funerals of popes). In effect, these gave form to Baroque architecture. For example, Bernini could never have imagined his throne of St. Peter in the basilica of St. Peter's without having seen the

624

theatrical use of lighting in the temporary settings that were created for the religious ritual of the *Quarantaore* (Forty Hours' Devotion). Nor could he ever have had the idea for the Baldacchino in St. Peter's without having observed the use of baldachins in the canonization of saints, as in the case of St. Elizabeth of Portugal in 1625.

In Rome any occasion was regarded as suitable for a festivity. Given that Rome was important politically, major feasts often assumed much more serious implications. For example, the tournament held on March 5, 1565 in the courtyard of the Belvedere in the Vatican, known to us from Antonio Francesco Cirni's account and from an anonymous painting from the mid-seventeenth century, took on unexpected political significance because of the Ottoman Turk siege of Malta at the time. The festivities had been organized to celebrate the marriage of Annibale Altemps and Ortensia, who was the half-sister of Carlo Borromeo, but they ended by being viewed mainly in the light of events taking place on the international scene.

Similarly, the celebrations in honor of Queen Christina of Sweden, who arrived in Rome during the pontificate of Alexander VII, became an occasion for the celebration of the victory of Roman Catholicism over Protestantism. A visual record of the event remains in a large canvas painted by

Filippo Gagliardi and Filippo Lauri, depicting the tournaments in the courtyard of Palazzo Barberini in honor of Queen Christina on February 28, 1656. For this celebration there was no hesitation in knocking down a number of houses to make room for the spectators' stands and to create more space for the jousting. As well as the horsemen who were magnificently arrayed in the queen's heraldic colors (white and

Bartolomeo Pinelli, *Barbery Horses in Piazza del Popolo*. Museo di Roma.

blue) and others dressed in the papal colors (red and gold), floats bearing allegorical tableaux, such as a spectacular Hercules standing on the flame-breathing dragon, entered the great atrium, with Pietro da Cortona's ruined theatre as backdrop.

Other important occasions in Rome to be marked by festivals were those associated with strictly papal ceremonies, from the lavish procession winding from one focal point of the city to the next when a new pope "took possession" the day after his election, to the feast when the king of Naples (and later of the Two Sicilies) paid symbolic homage to the pope, acknowledging papal temporal and spiritual authority. The various events were documented in detailed accounts, engravings, and paintings, which provide an even better idea of

Giovanni Paolo Panini, *Charles of Bourbon Visiting Benedict XIV in the Coffee House, Palace Quirinal*. Naples, Museo e Gallerie Nazionali di Capodimonte.

their atmosphere and of the colors and rejoicing that these feasts generated.

Such festivals became one of the favorite subjects of artists. Gian Paolo Pannini, for example, has left a particularly attractive record of Charles III's procession to St. Peter's and of Charles de Bourbon's visit to the Quirinal Palace. The role of the painter was similar to that of a photographer in later times. For the *Preparations in Piazza Navona to Celebrate the Birth of the Dauphin*, for example, Pannini was commissioned by Cardinal de Polignac to immortalize the event on canvas. The painting, dated 1731 and just under ten feet long, depicts the festivities, which started on November 20, 1729 and went on for ten days.

But the festival that enjoyed greatest popularity among Roman citizens was undoubtedly the Carnival, which culminated in the Barbary horserace in Piazza del Popolo. This was demonstrated in a painting by Bartolomeo Pinelli, in which those moments can be relived when the wild riderless horses galloped between the spectators, who were yelling excitedly from the stands.

Marco Bussagli

627

The Nineteenth and Twentieth Centuries

Art Between 1900 and 1945

Before the Great War

When Rome became part of the kingdom of Italy in 1870, artistic activity in the city was deeply cosmopolitan. It included not only the highly active foreign academies, but also lively independent artistic communities such as those of French, German, Dutch, American, and British artists, who continued to draw inspiration from the idea of the Grand Tour, now at the height of its artistic influence. The sporadic nature of these visits and the frequent brevity of the artists' stay, however, meant that only rarely was it possible for Roman artists to exchange ideas with major figures resident in Rome such as Corot, Böcklin, Feuerbach, and Burne-Jones.

When Rome became part of the kingdom of Italy, a great Roman painter, Nino Costa, who had been in exile for political reasons, returned home, providing a focus for new artistic developments. As an important link with the principal artistic movements in Europe, from those in France (Costa was a friend of Corot) to those in Britain (he had links with the Pre-Raphaelites), Costa came to be seen as a model, even a moral one, by the younger Roman painters. Out of this emerged a movement of markedly Symbolist character, typified by a strong feeling for nature as well as by a social and political program—though the latter is not always obvious in the work produced.

In 1884 Costa had set up the "Scuola Etrusca" (Etruscan School), whose members included British and Italian painters (and pupils Pazzini and Cellini), and which was characterized by a sophisticated, archaizing aesthetic. In 1886 the young painters of the *In arte libertas* (Freedom through Art) society, including Morani, Ricci, Sartorio, Coleman, and Carlandi, invited Costa to join them and elected him as their leader. Art was moving away from the prevailing style influenced by Mariano Fortuny, the celebrated Spanish artist resident in Venice, whose brilliantly executed paintings, often of a commercial nature, were well known.

Giulio Aristide Sartorio, *The Gorgon and the Heroes* (1899). Sartorio, one of the leading painters in Rome at the turn of the century, was familiar with artistic developments in northern Europe. This painting is typical of his Symbolist style. Galleria Nazionale d'Arte Moderna.

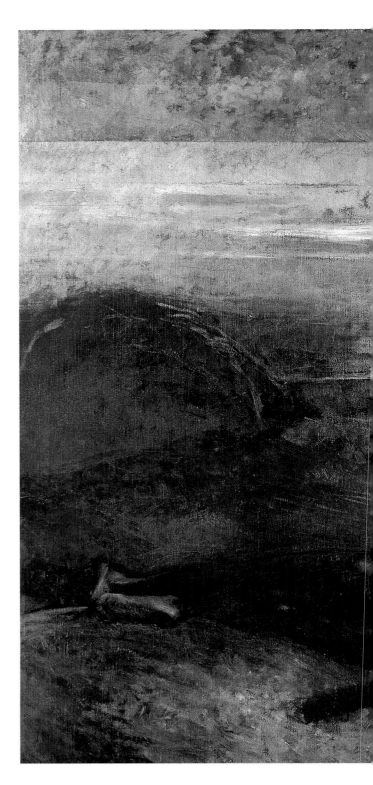

The most interesting work resulting from Costa's influence was that focused around the significant and influential figure of Gabriele d'Annunzio, who was at this time a young man interested in art criticism. The journal *La Cronaca Bizantina* (Byzantine Chronicle) was the ideological mouthpiece of the movement which, inspired by the decadent movement in Europe, and particularly in Britain, sought a mystical unity of the arts. The illustrations to

d'Annunzio's poem *Isotta Guttadauro* (1886) by the artists mentioned above, as well as by Marius de Maria and the senior in the group, Vincenzo Cabianca, are perhaps the most typical product to come from this movement.

A painter close to d'Annunzio, who nevertheless pursued his own course and appeared at intervals in Rome, was Francesco Paolo Michetti, a great painter, disliked by Costa because his work was dark, anti-classical, and crudely realistic, revealing

Francesco Paolo Michetti, *The Oath* (1883). This sober objective rendering of a religious ceremony is evidence of the realist tendency in Italian painting at the end of the nineteenth century. Galleria Nazionale d'Arte Moderna.

another aspect of decadent painting in Italy that was comparable with the anthropological and "popular" side of d'Annunzio.

Sartorio and Michetti were thus two sides of the same coin: Sartorio created aesthetic, refined Symbolist visions, Michetti realistic scenes that were transformed by his prodigious technique as well as, more importantly, by a febrile and morbid vision that lay beneath apparently popular scenes. The two sides of d'Annunzio came together in the work of these artists, the extremes of a single, decadent inspiration.

If Sartorio was to become the most important exponent of the Roman aesthetic current that looked towards central Europe (he had lived in Munich) and Britain, a younger artist, Felice Carena, was to be one of the most fascinating and important Italian Symbolists in the years before the First World War. Carena, who arrived in Rome from Turin in 1906, was to know great success. Inclined towards the French school (influenced by Carrière), he was also actively committed to an idealistic socialism, alongside Cena, an intellectual from Turin who organized schools for the peasants of the Roman Campagna, and Sibilla Aleramo, as well as some of the most innovative artists of the new century, such as Giacomo Balla and Cambellotti.

Also influenced by Costa's ethical stance was the group of Roman landscape artists known as the *XXV della Campagna Romana* (The Twenty-five of the Roman Campagna). Members of the *In arte libertas* group, in particular Sartorio, Coleman, and Carlandi, joined this new group. They painted the timeless landscape around Rome, taking inspiration from both the Pre-Raphaelites and Böcklin, creating a style that was to continue into the first decades of the new century.

In Search of the New: Divisionism in Rome

At the start of the century it was to be a painter from Turin, Giacomo Balla, who brought to Rome a mood of change that was to revive the debate between the academic painters and the Symbolists led by Costa. Inspired by his passion for photography, while in Rome Balla introduced Divisionism, an artistic technique which was based on the optical perception of light and color. As the first movement of the avant-garde, it shifted the problem of the representation of reality to the more abstract and fundamental question of how it is that reality is actually perceived.

Arriving in Rome in the last years of the nineteenth century, Balla began to question both the relationship between art and photography, and between science and representation. His students and followers included the younger Umberto Boccioni, Gino Severini, and Mario Sironi, who met Balla in 1903 and formed a close group around their master, who was nicknamed "Nocturne Giacomo" on account of his love of painting nocturnes, that is scenes illuminated by artificial light.

Balla's paintings were harsh, unforgiving examinations of tattered elements of a reality that he depicted as fragmented, through an eye which was as objective as the lens of a camera, in a brushstroke dividing up its colors. His favorite subjects were workers, the poor, and the insane, as well as landscapes from which he extracted the intimate and microscopic seething life. His interest in theosophy influenced the development of his view of nature as alive and pulsating. His socialism, influenced by the social

Giacomo Balla, *The Madwoman* (1905).
The unsparing realism is characteristic
of Balla's early work, which was greatly
influenced by his exposure to Post-
Impressionism in France and by his
interest in the still novel medium of
photography. Galleria Nazionale
d'Arte Moderna.

Umberto Boccioni, *Farmers* (1902). Boccioni, who moved to Rome in 1898 where he came into contact with Balla, was one of the central figures of Futurism. As with Balla, his early work is marked by realistic themes and the use of divisionism. Private collection.

idealism of Cena, influenced his choice of subjects to the marginalized and workers. He had an experimental interest in vision that led him to produce work of an extraordinary modernity and expressiveness. Using fragments, details, and parts in place of the whole, Balla contributed significantly to twentieth-century European art. His originality is still not fully appreciated. In the second half of the decade, he increased the spiritual aspect of his subjects and the content of the pictures, sometimes diluting the vigorous Divisionism in his search for an essentially luministic solution.

Umberto Boccioni began his artistic apprenticeship with Balla, developing his teacher's discoveries into a strong and dynamic style which was both passionate and highly personal. Gino Severini, who was likewise influenced by Balla, brought to his painting a meticulous Tuscan moderation, producing refined and concise work. Mario Sironi, who suffered the highs and lows of manic depressive illness, followed Boccioni's distortions, expanding his ideas expressionistically and imbuing the expressions of his figures with a sense of metaphysical unease.

Politically associated with the idealistic socialism of the period, the original group of painters separated during the first decade of the twentieth century. In 1906 Severini left for Paris, as did Boccioni. Sironi, suffering serious mental illness, produced less and less work, eventually ceasing to work altogether. Balla was left on his own in Rome to continue his rigorous and bewildering work.

However, at the beginning of the century other painters began to take up Balla's work on Divisionism, though they took it in a different direction. Attracted by the novelty of Divisionism, they tended to adopt a more graphic and decorative style, creating a modernism that was socially acceptable. The most important of these were Enrico Lionne, Antonio Discovolo, Aleardo Terzi, and, in particular, Camillo Innocenti and Antonio Noci.

Innocenti was the most successful of these painters. He depicted elegant scenes in a light sophisticated way, yet with an underlying mood of disquiet, with morbid shadows and an atmosphere of nostalgia and memory reminiscent of Bonnard or even Bergson, an expansive *luxe, calme, et volupté*. The mood is created not only by the subjects, but also by the color, which is glowing, passionate, inventive, and unnatural, and by the swirling decorative effect of the divided brushstrokes. Antonio Noci's work was more intimate but equally refined. Enrico Lionne was more eclectic, at times closer to Balla, at times to Innocenti. Like Antonio Discovolo and Aleardo Terzi, these painters came from the educated upper bourgeoisie, whose modern yearnings and aesthetic desires they sought to interpret.

Balla and Roman Futurism

Originating in 1910 in Milan, the home of Marinetti, Boccioni, and Carrà, Futurism in painting commenced in Rome with Balla. Until about 1930, when he departed from the movement, Balla was its mainstay. Encouraged by his former pupil Boccioni, he immediately became involved in the movement, contributing to the first *Manifesto of Futurist Painting* of February 2, 1910. Although he was excited by the innovative ideas, Balla struggled to find his own voice until 1912. Despite being bound to Boccioni by both affection and esteem, he was not willing to join in the younger man's work, which was developing along the lines of Picasso and the Cubists.

Balla wished to find his own, Italian, path, uncompromised by French influence. His investigations into movement and simultaneity followed an intricate journey of experimentation leading to his exclusion from the early group exhibitions of the movement. Using photography as a starting-point, he executed a number of studies that synthesized movement in a purely conceptual way—such as *Villa Borghese,* a polyptych made up of fifteen "simultaneous" views—or graphically, as in the paintings based on chronophotography and photodynamism, such as *Girl Running on a Balcony, Dog on a Leash,* and *Rhythm of a Violinist.* Only at the end of 1912 was he able to identify a truly new language, with *Abstract Speed, Iridescent Compenetration* (the titles are not contemporary with the works themselves), and *Swallows in Flight.* These forms of pure dynamism, representations of speed and lines of sound, mark the creation of a Futurist world that was entirely new and original, and the beginning of Balla's mature work within Futurism.

Futurism had previously consisted of occasional cultural events which were intended to provoke a reaction, but Rome at this time offered many opportunities to spread Futurist ideas. In February 1913 there was a Futurist exhibition at the Teatro Costanzi, and, at the end of the year, Giuseppe Sprovieri's Galleria Permanente Futurista opened. Though short-lived, the gallery was to organize exhibitions that presented Futurism as well as related international avant-garde movements.

he gave it renewed force with his investigations into popular art, together with Carrà.

Fortunato Depero, who had arrived in Rome from Rovereto near Lake Garda as a young man in late 1913, was to make a significant contribution to the Roman artistic world with his formal synthesis. Although he had already been moving in this direction under Balla's influence, his versatility led, in parallel with Balla, to his experimenting with "plastic complexes." He moved into interior design with the Cabaret del Diavolo in 1921–22 and worked in applied arts and theater design.

Enrico Prampolini, similarly attracted to Futurism in 1913 and 1914, was a versatile artist with an international outlook, maintaining close

Giacomo Balla, *Lines of Force in a Maiolica Landscape* (1917–18). The work illustrates Balla's attempt to represent synchronous dynamic movement pictorially. In doing so, he sought to elevate himself above the constraints of a specific genre. Oil and enamel on paper covered with canvas. Guidonia, Fondazione Bigiotti-Cigna.

Among the first of the young painters to join the Futurist movement was Mario Sironi. Having emerged from his periods of depression, from late 1913 he derived new energy from his association with the movement, initially in the wake of Boccioni. Although his dynamic work on form was already revealing its originality by the following year, it was in 1915 that, linking the Cubist and Futurist ideas of the Russian avant-garde of Malevich and Popova with his own Constructivist inclinations, he developed his own mechanical and synthetic vision. In 1916

relations with the principal avant-garde movements of Europe. He introduced the concept of the mechanical aspect of Futurism, which was later developed by Pannaggi. These painters were without doubt the most important interpreters of the developments taking place in Futurism, even though they were to leave Rome in the 1920s (Prampolini would return in the late 1930s).

From its beginning, Futurism was concerned with everyday life. It was Balla who succeeded in creating this connection, being aware that the aesthetic concept of Futurism could move from the painter's canvas to clothing, design, theater, cinema, and architecture, in a movement of total art that was to make even Boccioni exclaim that he had reached "a point it is difficult to find elsewhere in Europe today." This crucial realization—which was to influence every avant-garde movement in Europe—had its roots in the *Manifesto of the Futurist Reconstruction of the Universe* of 1915, signed with Depero (though the *Antineutral Garment* had already laid down the basis for this idea the year before), which marks the extension of the aesthetic of the traditional work of art to every aspect of daily life. "In Italy, Balla was the first to think of industrializing Futurism to applied arts, objects of everyday use" (G. Galli, 1919).

After the initial leadership of the movement by Boccioni, following his death during the war in 1916, Balla rapidly rose to have major influence within Futurism, precisely because of his versatility. In Rome he was seen as the leader of a school, to which were drawn a number of younger artists, in particular Fortunato Depero and Enrico Prampolini, but also Pannaggi, Dottori, Galli, De Pistoris, Benedetta, and Evola. Evola, an intellectual of great significance, painted for only a few years, leaving a series of abstract works with links to the most interesting experiments of the European avant-garde, from Dadaism to Kandinsky. Another eclectic and interesting painter is Vinicio Paladini, also close to German Dadaism and to Surrealism, whose Futurist work was particularly original.

Balla designed sets for Stravinsky's *Firebird*, produced by the Ballets Russes in 1917, using nothing more than space and flashing lights. He also decorated dance halls, for example the Bal Tik-tak (1921), always exploring new and original ways of applying Futurist artistic ideas. In painting, after the war, he extended his treatment of the spiritual and metaphysical areas of art, using his Futurism—which was now in a synthetic and geometrical phase—with cosmic passion and dynamism to produce an art of brilliant colors and forms which could be dramatic, playful, sentimental, or mechanical. His original themes and forms were used for both private and public space, which he decorated with an overflowing sense of joy. Thanks to Balla, Futurism in Rome in the 1920s enjoyed a period of great energy and the support of many young enthusiasts, who were experimenting with ideas of "mechanical art," characterized by an extraordinary liveliness of direction and creativity.

The last Futurist manifesto, *Aeropainting*, appeared in the 1930s, and was signed by Balla, Benedetta, Depero, Dottori, Fillia, Marinetti, Prampolini, Somenzi, and Tato. At the same time, new ideas for Futurism emerged, particularly from Balla and Prampolini, reinvigorating it right up to the eve of the Second World War. "Aeropainting," with its plastic forms and aerial and cosmic perspectives, took over from the mechanical and geometrical experiments of the 1920s, finding a resonance with other European movements such as the Bauhaus and Abstraction-Création.

This was to change in the 1930s, when the great Balla became isolated. Finally abandoning

Futurism in 1933, his painting now moved towards a photographic realism—which he had already experimented with in the 1920s—paying great attention to mass communication. Although he had always been fascinated by photography, in the 1930s he was to become involved with a particular style of presentation and effect. From fashion photography, thousands of copies of which appeared in magazines (as in the images of Roman photographers such as Ghergo and Luxardo, which emphasized the expressive use of viewpoint and light), Balla

Fortunato Depero, *Mechanics of a Ballet Dancer—The Ballet Idol*. Painted in 1917, the theme is a meditation on the phenomenon of movement, part of the program of the Manifesto of Futurist Painting. Trento, Museo d'Arte Moderna e Contemporanea.

Pasquarosa, *Still-Life* (1916–17). Oil on canvas. Private collection.

deduced formal and chromatic structures that deliberately suggested a fashionable icon of the collective imagination. He had an understanding of the value of the image that almost seems to anticipate pop art—just as it anticipated many other aspects of the late twentieth-century world, from pure abstraction to the spread of the language of art into everyday life. Though Balla's work at this time was isolated and individual, there is no doubt that something of his lucid vision for theater and photography, so rich in its chromatic effects, would recur in Melli's still-lifes of the late 1930s.

Rome 1913: the Roman Secessions

The artistic impasse in Rome in the years immediately before the First World War was of great significance. The cultural climate was uneasy and restless, particularly after the great international exhibition, the Cinquantenario of 1911. This had brought a stimulating breath of fresh European air to exhibitions in Rome, fostering lively debate and the participation of many Roman painters and critics optimistic about the future. After this, however, the cultural pattern in Rome returned, unchanged, to the status quo, to the academic and conservative exhibitions of the *Amatori e Cultori*, leaving a sense of dissatisfaction among the artists who had been

most involved in a significant revival in the development of art.

The outcome was a bitter split between the Establishment and young artists, culminating in the first Secession Exhibition in March 1913. Among much that was original, critical attention was directed particularly at the recent French style of the Fauves and the Nabis, as well as to the Post-Impressionists in general. The Secession exhibitions brought the works of Matisse, Gauguin, Cézanne, and Toulouse-Lautrec to Rome for the first time.

The Futurists, including Balla, had originally intended to take part in this but the exhibition committee, believing that the introduction of the avant-garde should be gradual, decided to restrict their contribution. As a result the Futurists disassociated themselves from the exhibition, organizing instead their own exhibition at the Teatro Costanzi that year. Balla, busy designing the cover of the Secession catalogue (with motifs of iridescent compenetration), did not exhibit with them.

A group of young Roman artists was drawn to the new French painting, producing work that was characterized by violent, sometimes strident, and highly expressive color. The most interesting of these artists were Cipriano Efisio Oppo, the newly converted Felice Carena, Pasquarosa, Ferruccio Ferrazzi, Edita Broglio, Roberto Melli, and Armando Spadini. The new styles also attracted others such as Nino Bertoletti, Deiva De Angelis, and Carlo Socrate, as well as a particularly interesting group of sculptors—D'Antino, Selva, Drei, Biagini, and Cambellotti—who were to be important in the following decade. Also associating themselves with the Secession—and thus to some extent setting themselves up as the more moderate wing of the Divisionists—were Innocenti, Lionne, Noci, and Terzi who, although involved in these avant-garde developments, were producing more elegant and accessible work.

Oppo, the most thorough and enthusiastic ideologue, worked as an art critic as well. His compact paintings, with acid colors and Expressionist distortions, are among the most interesting of the period. Ferrazzi and Melli were also proceeding in the same direction, although retaining links with the Futurists, as was Edita Broglio, who was inspired by the mystical leanings of the *Blauer Reiter* movement. Carena produced work of great elegance and expressiveness which was influenced by Fauvism and Gauguin, as did the more isolated Spadini and Pasquarosa. Pasquarosa, a fine Post-Impressionist who had only recently appeared on the scene, painted still-lifes of great freshness and intensity. Spadini, whose work has the soft tones of the Impressionists,

particularly of Renoir, was, with Carena, a painter of modern and psychological elegance who was to be influential in the so-called "return to order," which was a rejection of the avant-garde, of the next decade.

Along with these Roman artists, the Secession exhibitions included some of the most important artists of the new international avant-garde, who interpreted modernity as an expressive distortion rather than a drastic break with the past. Among the foreign artists shown were Klimt, Schiele, Munch, Mestrovic, Pecstein, Liebermann, and Rodin, as well as French painters—Matisse, Renoir, Bonnard, and Denis. Italians exhibiting included Viani, Casorati, Arturo Martini, Gino Rossi, Andreotti, Boldini, Chini, Nomellini, Zecchin, Morandi, and Tosi.

Postwar Rome

Between 1918 and 1919, after the First World War, Rome saw a return to its lively cultural life, enlivened by much artistic debate. After the fourth Secession Exhibition, a muted affair that opened at the end of 1916 and finished at the beginning of 1917, art in Rome fell into a state of suspended animation as a result of the war, although the art world was somewhat enlivened by the return of a number of artists, with Carena, Ferrazzi, and Sironi returning from the war, Socrate from France and Spain, and Oppo convalescing from injuries, as well as the arrival of new faces. Notable among these new arrivals

was Giorgio de Chirico, who as a soldier spent his leave in Rome, moving there for good in the autumn of 1918.

In the late spring of 1918, two almost simultaneous exhibitions were indicative of a changing situation, towards a reform of the work of the Secessionists and Futurists—which by now seemed dated and lacking in energy—and towards a renewal that remained avant-garde but now looked towards a formal tradition of classical composition. In May, a group exhibition opened at the Galleria dell'Epoca, the First Independent Exhibition. Exhibitors included de Chirico, with his Metaphysical paintings being shown in Rome for the first time, Carrà, who was pursuing a new, more metaphysical path as

Felice Carena, *Gualfarda* (1914). Oil on canvas. Private collection.

Cipriano Effisio Opo, *Carena* (1914). Oil on canvas. Private collection.

well, Ferrazzi, Soffici, and Prampolini. In the following month, an exhibition of art by young painters opened at the Casina del Pincio, organized by Piacentini and Tridenti, with Oppo, Spadini, Pasquarosa, Socrate, Selva, Biagini, Ferrazzi, and others.

Towards the end of the year such events became even more frequent. Rome was firmly on the map as one of the European capitals involved in the intense debate between supporters of the avant-garde and those who desired a "return to order." The journal *Valori Plastici* (Plastic Values) was launched at the end of 1918, and in October that year, Bragaglia opened his famous gallery, the Casa d'Arte Bragaglia, with an exhibition devoted to Balla. This was followed in 1919 and 1920 by exhibitions of work by de Chirico—still Metaphysical in style—Sironi, Depero, De Pisis, Zadkine, Itten, and the Dadaists.

Valori Plastici and the Return to Order

During 1919, ideas on the return to order were becoming more precise. As has been said, at the beginning of the year de Chirico and Carrà had not yet rejected the avant-garde ideas that they were later to depart from as a result of their rediscovery of Old Masters. Perhaps only Mario Broglio, the great entrepreneur and editor of *Valori Plastici*, had a clear idea about the direction he wanted his supporters to take. This can be seen from his articles in *Valori Plastici*. From the very first issue he took up a critical position—though still indirectly, so as not to alienate his friends with his too radical (and precocious) position—towards the latest manifestations of the avant-garde: De Chirico was still mourning the death of his memorable friend Apollinaire, the prophet of the French avant-garde, and even Carrà, already closer to Broglio in his thinking, still had his years as a militant Futurist to put behind him.

One event in particular helps to explain the change in atmosphere in Rome in the middle of 1919. In July, Mario Sironi held his first one-man exhibition at Bragaglia's gallery. Sironi was a Roman artist, a Futurist facing a crisis of confidence. The works he showed were intended to create a synthesis between Futurism and a new vision of a Metaphysical reality, without abandoning the syntheses of the avant-garde, but instead relating them to a mute, contemporary reality, which took Old Masters as a moral, rather than formal, model. It was a position that attempted to retain the formulae of the avant-garde while producing a distillation that was a

Giorgio de Chirico, *The Argonauts' Greeting* (1920). The picture shows the disturbing composition characteristic of de Chirico's pittura metafisica (metaphysical painting), with isolated, classicizing figures silently inhabiting an otherwise empty city, seen as a stageset. Tempera on canvas. Private collection.

Felice Carena, *Quiet* (1921). The idyllic landscape of this picture has parallels with the art of Giorgione and Titian, an example of the influence of Renaissance painting on Carena. Galleria d'Arte Moderna Ricci Oddi.

dialectic fusion of Futurism and Classicism. Mario Broglia was damning in his condemnation of Sironi, taking it upon himself to criticize the exhibition in the June–October edition of *Valori Plastici.*

To try to revive the old order now seemed heresy to the Roman painters. If there was to be a return, it should be total, a *ritorno al mestiere* (return to the craft) of the Old Masters, a negation of every aspect of the modern and of the analytic and synthetic formulae of the avantgarde. The return to the Old Masters, to tradition and classicism, left no room for regret for the modern.

De Chirico was the most radical. Between 1919 and 1921 he produced very few paintings, being engrossed in experiments with traditional painting techniques, for example making his

own emulsions—alchemical inventions which often meant that the work deteriorated (as had been the case with some of Leonardo da Vinci's paintings). His main influences were the early work of Raphael and the art of the Italian Renaissance, painters such as Perugino and Carpaccio with their evocation of a classicism that de Chirico called "Olympian."

By the autumn and winter of 1919, the direction of the new movement appeared clearly defined. It now uncompromisingly sought its inspiration directly from the Old Masters. The *valori plastici* (plastic values) selected were to be those of the Italian fifteenth-century Renaissance (for de Chirico) or the fourteenth century (for Carrà). In the November–December issue of *Valori Plastici*, Carrà published his *Lot's Daughters*, the first picture to move definitively away from Metaphysical painting to enunciate the principles of "The Renewal of Painting in Italy," which was also the title of an article by Carrà in the same issue of the journal ("*Il rinovimento della pittura in Italia*"), which discussed the sculptural qualities of the painting of Giotto and the Italian primitives. The same issue reproduced one of Morandi's still-lifes, still Metaphysical in style (through Carrà's syntheticism),

combined with the inheritance of the avant-garde to go beyond it (in Italy, with Sironi, or earlier in France, with Severini and Picasso), *Valori Plastici* rejected the very recent past in order to recapture days gone by, which were perceived as a dream, a cultural transference, an absolute and timeless ideal.

Valori Plastici's innovative program immediately attracted followers. One artist drawn into

Francesco Tromabadori, *Still-Life with Fruit and Game* (c. 1935). Oil on canvas. Private collection.

and another in which the order of objective reality already placed the objects in a spatial dimension, inspired by the Renaissance.

In July–August 1920, de Chirico published his first Renaissance-inspired paintings (*Self-Portrait, Signorina Amata, The Virgin of Time*, and *The Prodigal Son*). He had already, in 1919, published his programmatic *Self-Portrait with Mother* (a synthesis of his idea of classicism which appeared in *Valori Plastici*), *alongside still Metaphysical* works from 1918–19.

The die was cast. In Rome the return to order suggested an atmosphere of timeless art, long perceived by Broglio. This new style found its position within a strand of Italian tradition, in which the Old Masters and the Platonic ideal of classicism took the place of history and the contemporary. While the return to order frequently

Carrà's orbit was Arturo Martini, who as early as 1920 was echoing the Giotto-inspired forms of his friend Carrà. Martini officially joined the group between the end of 1920 and January 1921, spending long periods in Rome and Anticoli Corrado, a hilltop village in the mountains east of Rome, until 1929. His sculpture has a solid and synthetic sense of volume which is in harmony with Broglio's formal neo-Platonism, and with an Apollonian ideal of the purity of Classicism.

Edita Broglio appears to freeze her incandescent forms, not as yet in painting, however, but in drawing. The perspectives are Metaphysical, or "primitive," with a clear structural sign, as invoked by de Chirico: "To repeat once again, the spirit of Classicism is the spirit of the sign and of the line... By a strange coincidence, the linear spirit of Hellenistic classicism reappears in the work of our great fifteenth-century artists. These painters experienced the same emotions of line and sign as the Greeks" ("Classicismo pittorico" in *La Ronda*, July 1920).

Among the earliest Roman artists to be associated with *Valori Plastici* were Roberto Melli and Francalancia. Melli, who worked as a sculptor (only one of his sculptures, from 1913, was reproduced in *Valori Plastici*), critic, and painter, enclosed the blinding colors of his Secessionist canvases within geometrical forms, with metallic planes. Drawings by Francalancia

Virgilio Guidi, *The Airship* (c. 1922). Oil on canvas. Private collection.

were included in the 1921 exhibition taking place in Germany. Unlike Melli, Francalancia did not take part in the debates in *Valori Plastici,* but his drawings of 1920 demonstate a popular primitivism, in the style of Henri Rousseau, which was to briefly evolve into a refined and magical Giotto-inspired art.

At the same time, between 1919 and 1920, a different but parallel version of the return to order was emerging in Rome, which was to lead to a passionate debate in *Valori Plastici* at the beginning of 1921. While initially challenging this new style, *Valori Plastici* finally absorbed it—or rather, was taken over by it—since the opposition's ideas were, for a variety of reasons, to prove victorious in the Roman context.

Returning to Rome from the war, Felice Carena was to make a significant contribution to the artistic debate there. Working on his own, he elaborated an idiosyncratic "return to order" that was based on his own aesthetic reflections. The results were different from, but in some ways also complementary to, the painting of de Chirico and Carrà.

Carena's return to order, expressed in sinuous forms without harsh angles, combined explicit references to Old Masters, which he interpreted in an individual way compared to the position taken up by *Valori Plastici*. He picked up on sixteenth- and seventeenth-century painting (regarding Courbet and Cézanne as its heirs), with its solid impasto and exaggerated luminosity. Carena's work suggests a modern Caravaggio; his effects of projected and radiating light seem to have been obtained from the artificial light of an electric lamp. Although conceptually parallel with the central group of *Valori Plastici*, with their attempts to recover the forms and crystalline purity of the fourteenth century and the Renaissance, Carena's artistic inspiration places him in quite another tradition.

The dividing-line between the group that supported *Valori Plastici* and Carena, who was apparently more isolated, was eventually to inspire lively debate, though their intentions were essentially identical. *Valori Plastici*'s publication of de Chirico's famous bitingly contemptuous "polemic on the seventeenth century" in March–April 1921 effectively placed the two tendencies in the return to Roman order—"purist" and "seventeenth-century"—in opposition, the latter being more broadly and eclectically oriented towards the idea of tradition. Immediately after this, however, Broglio, who was faced with the apparent spread of enthusiasm for the seventeenth century among the Roman artists, decided to soften his approach and even embraced artists who sided explicitly with this tendency, such as Spadini, Socrate, and Oppo, including them in the 1922 *Valori Plastici* group exhibition in Florence (the Fiorentina Primaverile).

Yet while the purist attitude of the *Valori Plastici* group was to dominate the minority on the Roman scene (Francalancia, Ceracchini, and Di Cocco, as well as, of course, Edita and Mario Broglio, who had started to paint again after a long period of inactivity in the 1920s), it was the vision being perfected by Carena that was to attract the majority—and the most important —of followers. From Socrate to Trombadori, from Oppo to Donghi and Guìdi, in Rome the return to order took on a more softly modeled appearance, with a seventeenth-century luminosity and stillness. The key player in 1919–20 was Carena. When Roberto Longhi, analysing this common inspiration, wrote of Socrate as being Caravaggio-like, of Donghi as being like Orazio Gentileschi, or of Trombadori as Flemish-inspired, he was merely emphasizing the tradition of neo-seventeenth-century painting which characterized the "magic realism" of Roman art.

It is significant that de Chirico, who in 1921 had been the primary theoretical opponent of the seventeenth-century tendency (in painting moving towards a broader historical eclecticism), was by the time of the closure of *Valori Plastici* in 1922, reconsidering his purist position. He now embraced a more romantic and eclectic lyricism, with echoes of Courbet and Böcklin, seventeenth-century still-lifes, and a reinvented and picturesque Baroque Rome, with masterpieces of lofty and evocative poetry.

With de Chirico's change of direction, the era of *Valori Plastici* came to an end. At the same time, an eclectic return to the Old Masters pervaded Rome and became the dominant style. Characterized by a clear and calculated structure of images, this offered a sense of the expectation and lyrical suspension within objects, imbued with a sense of the Old Masters and the classical, the legacy of the radical return to order which had been promoted by *Valori Plastici*. The Old Masters became the term of reference: history in its totality became the inspiration. In Rome the return to order—from as early as 1922 and the *Valori Plastici* exhibition in Florence—no longer suffered from arguments over Renaissance and Baroque, or between purists and historicists. Painting advanced along a broad traditional path, in which Expressionism united with a lyrically purified magic realism, in an atmosphere of suspense created by the search for metaphysical links between image and painting.

The 1920s

When a group of young Roman painters at their artistic peak exhibited in the Rome Biennale in 1923, a number of critics dismissed their work as neoclassical. The painters were Bertoletti, Socrate, Oppo, Trombadori, and Ferrazzi, as well as Donghi and de Chirico. Carena had been, as has been previously discussed, crucial for the development of many of these artists. In his manifesto-painting *La quiete* (Quiet) of 1921, he directly quoted Giorgione and Titian, creating a model that was to inspire Socrate and Bertoletti in two paintings shown at the Biennale, which derived their subject-matter from the Dresden *Venus*.

In the early 1920s, the question of classical or Neoclassical roused strong passions in the Roman art world. Setting aside the question of the quality of the varied works painstakingly produced, the principal object of debate was the use of Old Masters. Oppo rejected the definition of neoclassical in connection with himself and his friends at the Rome Biennale. More conventional criticism was directed towards the almost literal re-use by these painters of works by Giorgione, Manet, Böcklin, Courbet, Hayez, the Flemish school, Caravaggio, Tintoretto, and Jacopo da Bassano.

Carena and de Chirico were to depart from Rome in 1924, leaving behind a number of masterpieces and the dual idea of tradition and total

Ferruccio Ferrazzi, *Young Woman* (1922). The painting is influenced by Giorgione's *Sleeping Venus*, an example of the ideas inspiring Carena's circle. Private collection.

originality. It should not be forgotten, however, that what is conventionally called the "return to order," that is to say, a rejection of the avant-garde, occurred in Rome only in an attenuated form. Only de Chirico, Carrà, Morandi, Sironi, and, to some extent, Melli, had had direct contacts with avant-garde movements (Futurism and Metaphysical painting). The others, who were

Antonio Donghi, *Lauro de Bosis* (1924). Oil on canvas. Private collection.

almost all younger, had emerged from a climate of Secessionist modernity which considered the fragmented forms of Futurism excessive, preferring vivid *fauve* color and expressionistically distorted forms. This stance—an alternative, deliberately less radical, Modernism—left space for a "return" that favored a quiet and mysterious climate to the initially more influential positions of the true "returners" of the avant-garde. This movement might perhaps be called "magic realism," a term coined in Germany by Franz Roh but already used by Bontempelli. The Roman group in the end became part of the great national Italian movement—although not without opposition—organized by Margherita Sarfatti under the title of *Novecento Italiano* (1926).

As for the purist group which remained true to the first primitivist formulations, Mario Broglio and Edita Broglio were obviously the leaders of the school. Although both began to paint again in the mid-1920s, after the demands of editing *Valori Plastici*, it was due to Mario's almost abstract vision, inspired by Piero della

Francesca, that this path was opened up. Edita resolved the difficult intellectual problems set by her husband in a practical way, in canvases that have a crystalline simplicity. Demonstrating that the Platonic ideal is single and absolute, Mario Broglio painted in a way that was practically indistinguishable from his wife Edita's work. It was not a matter of priority of invention between the two, rather an ideal and timeless symbiosis, which is transposed into a painting in which matter is canceled out in enamel-like surfaces and tranquil geometric forms.

Francalancia's work was grounded upon this theoretical basis. In the 1920s he painted landscapes that combined the Piero della Francesca-inspired purity of fifteenth-century predellas with the naiveté of a Rousseau. Ceracchini, after an initial foray into an almost brutal naive primitivism, followed in the steps of Carrà, particularly in works such as *Lot's Daughters*, developing a stiff and archaizing primitivism, in compositions that were influenced by fourteenth- and fifteenth-century religious painting. Ceracchini's Renaissance spatiality was in turn the inspiration for the young Francesco Di Cocco, who added perspectival distortions of an almost Mannerist kind and disproportions which seem to take the return to order in a direction more disturbing than classical, anticipating the developments that would take place in the 1930s among the new generation.

Amongst the artists of the "seventeenth-century" tendency, which with its familiarity with the Old Masters was ready to embrace a multitude of influences, from the purist de Chirico and Broglio, perhaps the most influential figures were Ferrazzi, Guidi, and Donghi. Ferrazzi's work is characterized by its originality, leaving the artist isolated on the European level. From 1921 he derived a more restrained classicism from Spadini, with figures and brushwork on to which he did not hesitate to impose his own visionary and fantastic style, which blended Metaphysical and sixteenth-century painting in a style that seems also influenced by the Expressionist films of directors such as Fritz Lang (*Metropolis*).

Guidi was immediately attracted to the idea of the Old Masters, in 1921 copying Correggio's *Danaë* in the Borghese Gallery in Rome. De Chirico had already worked there in the early days of *Valori Plastici*. After 1920 Guidi moved away from a Spadini-influenced style, instead developing an original synthesis of Piero della Francesca's fifteenth-century art and the luminism of Caravaggio. The similarity of what Guidi was trying to do with Casorati's work is clear, but he had his own, very Roman, lyrical, and magical style, in particular a warm and physical feel for paint.

Donghi, whose early works had been of a banal Impressionist realism, emerged strongly in 1922–23. The 1922 Biennale, at which Casorati, Guidi, and Carena exhibited, had a decisive role in defining Donghi's version of magic realism, with its "Old Master" abstract immobility, reminiscent, as Longhi noted, of Gentileschi. The painting is carefully and highly finished, and the

which between 1918 and 1920 revealed hints of the angular planes of Cubism. The references to the art of the seventeenth to nineteenth centuries are derived from Carena and Soffici and resulted in an almost perfect imitation of traditional painting techniques. Socrate exhibited in 1922 with the *Valori Plastici* group in Florence, thus setting the seal on the relationship between

Riccardo Francalancia, *The Tescio Valley* (1927). Oil on canvas. Private collection.

figures seem to be transfixed under a microscope, their outlines standing out from a glowing background, adding to the sensation of unreality. Donghi was the true poet of imperturbable silence, a distinctive mark of the Roman artistic style.

Carlo Socrate, influenced by Caravaggio and, particularly, by Courbet (one of the painters most closely studied by de Chirico between 1922 and 1924), focused on a static reality,

seventeenth-century painting and an ordered purism, with a magic realism style that was pervaded by Old Master influence.

Oppo developed in a similar way, exploring as early as 1920 in his *Portrait of the Artist's Fiancée*, the solid forms of the Old Masters, following Spadini and the historicizing influence of Carena. Like others, he took inspiration from Manet, Rubens, and Ghirlandaio in his search for a historical reality, a modern dialogue with

Antonietta Raphaël, *Still-Life with Guitar* (1928–29). This composition, by a self-taught painter, shows the influence of Derain. Private collection.

The New Generation: Rome 1927

Towards the end of the 1920s, as the initial creative impetus of the *Novecento Italiano* group began to flag, a small group of young artists was already putting forward arguments for a radical reform of art in Rome. Once again the innovative Carena, who was popular with the younger generation of Roman artists in the early 1920s, took the lead. In March 1922 Carena and the sculptor Attilio Selva had opened an art school, attracting younger painters who were to go on to make a significant contribution to the artistic debate. Fausto Pirandello and Emanuele Cavalli applied to the school in 1922, and Giuseppe Capogrossi in 1923. Freed of the restrictions of rigid academic art training, the students were encouraged by Carena to discover their feelings and develop their expressive and poetic sides.

Pirandello chose as subjects peasant and rural scenes, as did Carena, but he infused them with a deeply-felt realistic and disturbing sensuality, distorted and twisted. Capogrossi and Cavalli remained respectful of the silent magic of their master's work while producing a softer kind of painting of subjects that seem suffused with ancient primitive mystery.

In May 1927, an exhibition was held at the Pensione Dinesen in Rome of the work of three young artists, Capogrossi, Cavalli, and Di Cocco, who shared a studio in Via Marianna Dionigi. The critics commented on their originality, noting "a highly modern temperament, despite the close study of the masters" (W. Arslan). The modernity lay in some of the distortions—more lyrical than formalist—in their dark and thickly painted canvases: portraits crushed under undulating lines, landscapes twisted as if racked by a disturbing wind. De Libero later wrote that it was an exhibition that revealed "artists worth keeping an eye on." It was certainly true that there was an eager small group of young artists who were keen to do something new, including Gino Scipione, Mafai, and Mazzacurati, who signed their names in the visitors' book the on the first day of the exhibition.

At the time of the exhibition, the embryonic group, now joined by Antonietta Raphaël, had not yet found its own style. Scipione and Mafai were painting small works reminiscent of Guidi's landscapes as well as shop signs and advertisements, without any clear artistic focus. They found inspiration for renewal in the 1927 exhibition, which offered a new, free, and lyrical way of interpreting reality, more expressive than Expressionist, and outside the current preoccupation with Old Masters. The version of the past that attracted them instead—Cavalli, Capogrossi, Di Cocco, like Mafai and Scipione, spent much

the past, a painted order that was both sculptural and pictorially dazzling.

Trombadori learned how to focus on detailed reality from Flemish art, fixing it as if in a photographic laboratory, producing vitrified still-lifes and landscapes that are stripped of all context and offer a silent and total appearance of reality, in a confluence of seventeenth-century art and the abstraction of Broglio.

Bertoletti, a devotee and scholar of the Old Masters and close friend of de Chirico, was another who put forward a purified version of the Old Masters, concealing Cézanne's method beneath simplified forms, as can be seen in the explicit brushstrokes of his sketches.

Finally, Bartoli, who exhibited with *Valori Plastici* in 1922, was to give concrete shape to the forms inherited from Cézanne, with an intellectual refinement that perhaps limits his originality.

Arriving in Rome from Ferrara, Filippo De Pisis, the poetic artist of nostalgic and autobiographical paintings, was to go beyond a delicate Dadaism and the dreamlike style of his Metaphysical sketches towards an exploration of an Impressionist reality that recalls Bonnard. In the first half of the 1920s, which he spent in Rome, De Pisis' admiration for Spadini's light touch was crucial in helping him to achieve the freedom of a mature style that would characterize his work for the rest of his life.

time in the art library in Palazzo Venezia—was that formulated by the eccentric Di Cocco, a primitivism that was derived from Caracchini's rural and peasant-inspired work but rendered more complex by "cerebral" distortions.

The proof of this collaboration is not only the early work of Scipione and Mazzacurati (1927–28), who were drawing on typologies and styles typical of Di Cocco until 1923, but also in the fact that Ceraccchini was the first to invite them (with Di Cocco) to an exhibition at the Circolo di Roma in 1929. Mafai, on the other hand, was more interested in the distorted faces of Capogrossi and Cavalli's dark portraits and the distorting luminosity of their landscapes.

This sparked off new developments in the work of the two groups of friends, Capogrossi and Cavalli on the one hand (Pirandello remained in touch with their work from Paris, where he exhibited in 1928 with Cavalli and Di Cocco and on his return in 1931), and Mafai, Scipione, and Raphaël on the other. Di Cocco moved between the two groups, pursuing his own individual and solitary path. From 1927 the work produced by the two groups, which had only slightly overlapped, began to diverge. Paradoxically, Scipione and Mafai became more interested in the work presented at the Pensione Dinesen by Cavalli and Capogrossi while Capogrossi, going to Paris in 1928, abandoned this path and, together with Pirandello, moved in a new direction.

Contact between them was reinstated after Scipione's death. Mafai developed his own tonalism, following the style that had been launched by Cavalli, Capogrossi, and Pirandello's group, which had been joined by Melli and Cagli.

The Via Cavour School

The association between Scipione and Mafai began in 1924. Early the next year they were joined by Antonietta Raphaël. The presence of this unorthodox Lithuanian, a passionate musician who had lived in London and Paris, was certainly the inspiration for the two young aspiring artists in their anticonformist quest for a new art. Raphaël's proud and stormy character and her bohemian life in these two cities, so different from the bourgeois upbringing of the two young men—and so shocking—opened up new horizons of freedom and an eclectic international culture.

Nevertheless, the strictly artistic training of the group did not come about at the *Scuola Libera del Nudo* (Free Life School) from 1924, nor from any suggestions directly from Raphaël, who had taken no interest in painting prior to their

meeting, but rather from Scipione and Mafai's own studies of art history, along with Cavalli and Capogrossi, as they devoured the books in the Palazzo Venezia library. El Greco and Goya, along with Bosch, Breughel, and Parmigianino, were some of their eccentric choice of Old Master painters, at a time when attention was focused for the most part on Piero della Francesca, Masaccio, and Raphael. It was not until 1927–28, at the beginning of their mature period, that Scipione and Mafai discovered

Mario Mafai, *Girl* (1931). Oil on canvas. Private collection.

648

Rousseau and Derain, Chagall and Kokoschka, who were to have a lasting influence on their visual universe, concerned with the fantastic and dreamlike—to use Mafai's word, with the *favoloso* (like a fairy story or legend).

In 1928 Mafai exhibited his first pictures, establishing his own style, even if it still had its roots in the Paris school, in painters such as Dufy and Vlaminck. The distorted faces were now executed with conviction, while the primitivism aimed at by Raphaël, reminiscent of a Pasquarosa steeped in Chagall's Jewishness, is transposed in a gentler form into Mafai's dreamlike landscapes and figures. Scipione was still pursuing forms of the Ceracchini type. It was not until the following year that, with an almost inconceivable leap of imagination, he burst out with a new style of painting—red, overheated, and visionary.

It was left to Roberto Longhi to give a name to this new Roman style. After reviewing the first exhibition at the Sindacato Laziale in March 1929, he picked out the new work by Scipione, Mafai, and Raphaël, stressing the Expressionist and French influence. It was from here that the celebrated name of *Scuola di Via Cavour* (Via Cavour School) first appeared. Subsequently, in the 1930s, it was to be known as the École de Rome. Longhi wrote of "explosive mixtures," "dark and devastated landscapes where a decaying Impressionism changes into expressive hallucination," and "bacillary virulence." Longhi also noted the influence of Dufy in Mafai's work and of Chagall in Raphaël's. That he barely mentioned Scipione is indicative of the fact that Scipione's work was not yet fully mature at this time.

It was in fact to be Mafai who first achieved a mature and original voice, in his visionary and lyrical "overheated" landscapes. This maturity was to serve as an inspiration and example for Scipione. After a summer spent on his own, burying himself in hermetic and visionary texts from Gongora to Ungaretti and the Bible, Scipione began to produce his own version of visionary lyricism. His paintings flow over into surreal images, with a new and freer technique, highly expressive, with much use of red. They go beyond the encounter with the real physical object to give a dreamlike interpretation of his fantasies, he was obsessed with death (he had tuberculosis) and giving rise to a nocturnal neo-Baroque style of great intensity. From the end of 1929 to 1930, Scipione produced a series of masterpieces which recorded the dramatic decline in his health. From 1931 to 1933, the year he died, his illness prevented him from painting more than some ten canvases.

The unexpected energy of Scipione's work, which combined Surrealism with Expressionism to produce an alchemy beyond any reference to physical reality, was of such novelty and originality that it led Mafai to reconsider his own work. He left for Paris with Raphaël at the beginning of 1930 in search of inspiration. For Mafai, who was a lyrical painter of reality, Scipione's visionary works had reached a point he perhaps felt was too extreme, excluding the possibility of poetic abandon. In Paris Mafai lightened his palate, making his painting "simpler and more immediate," as Scipione wrote to his friend Mazzacurati. De Pisis and Dufy influenced his work, which found a poetic balance that was criticized by Scipione as "weak and insipid." Nevertheless, the triumph of the two painters occurred in P. M. Bardi's Galleria di Roma in November 1930, where they were hailed by the most sophisticated and modern critics, who could see in their dual version of surreal visions and lyrical and transfigured reality a new, original voice.

From 1932, by which time Scipione had more or less stopped painting, Mafai was pursuing a new path. He had finally detached himself from the "heroic" period of the association, exploring a reality strongly influenced by psychology. He now used paint more thickly, with a thoughtfulness that was to develop into a theory of color that eventually became the other major artistic innovation of the 1930s.

The École de Rome: a Platonic Association

The years between the Pensione Dinesen exhibition in 1927 and 1930 saw Pirandello moving to Paris in 1927, followed immediately by his friends Cavalli and Capogrossi and by Di Cocco. At this time Paris was witnessing the emergence of the *Italiens de Paris*, as the group of Italians, which included de Chirico, Severini, Savinio, Campigli, De Pisis, and Paresce, came to be known. Organized by Tozzi, the group sought to offer an independent response to Surrealism, claiming that they had been responsible for the movement through de Chirico, and hence for the correct interpretation of its metaphysical meaning and its development in an Italian direction, countering André Breton's arrogant claims. The young painters sought to become part of this movement and find their own role in it, as can be established from a postcard sent by Pirandello to Cavalli in 1929. It is clear that the climate at the time, partly Metaphysical, partly Surrealist, was what chiefly interested them, along with the work of Picasso and Braque. The young painters spent much time contemplating and analyzing Campigli and Tozzi's frescos and de Chirico and Savinio's canvases, with their

Emanuele Cavalli, *Summer* (1938). Oil on canvas. Private collection.

OPPOSITE:
Corrado Cagli, *View of Rome* (1937). Encaustic tempera on panel. Private collection.

sense of mystery and an inexplicable presence, as well as Picasso's monumental figures and the thick paint of Braque's Cubism.

France supplied influences of a different type. In France Cavalli was initiated into an esoteric society inspired by theosophy and magic, and his friends must have been influenced by him. This would explain the mysterious auras and ectoplasm found in many enigmatic drawings by Pirandello from this time, as well as in paintings such as *Interno di Mattina* (Morning Interior). It would also explain the magical concept of color and form that was to invigorate tonalism in the early 1930s, developed by Cavalli, as well as the mysterious subject-matter of his paintings, as with many by Capogrossi.

Between the years 1931 and 1932, Cavalli and Capogrossi shared a studio in the Prati district of Rome, working side by side and developing their ideas about tonalism: "To identify the essence of painting with the nature of the spiritual energies that influence us, to grasp the relationship between the meaning of the form and the essence of painting, to go beyond color as an expression of nature, to extract from it an order, in its infinite variety, identical with the substance of modern spirituality," as Capogrossi, Cavalli, and Melli wrote in the *Manifesto of Plastic Primordialism* in October 1933. Cavalli continued, writing of "painting that cannot be seen, profoundly harmonic even in its innermost structure... always true to itself,

like a crystal which, though broken into many parts, retains its form."

Melli came to join them, as did the young Corrado Cagli, Bontempelli's nephew. Melli had gone through a period in the 1920s when he had stopped painting in order to devote himself entirely to the cinema, producing set designs. Resuming painting, he had found among the younger painters a newness of subject-matter to which he was able to contribute with his bright detached planes of color. Cagli brought with him a sense of modern mythology acquired from Bontempelli, which was to be important to the group as a whole. They found their muses in Cavalli's wife, Vera Haberfeld, a niece of Weiss, the psychoanalyst who translated Freud into Italian, and the celebrated writer Elsa Morante. Together with these women, the painters frequented the floating Tofini on the river Tiber, a meeting-place that, with its mixture of athletes, poets, and philosophers, must have suggested the rarefied atmosphere of a Platonic academy.

In May 1932, the first exhibition that brought together Cagli, Capogrossi, Cavalli, Pirandello, and Paladini (an ex-Futurist with a love of Surrealism) was held at Bardi's Galleria di Roma, which eighteen months previously had discovered Scipione and Mafai. In the paintings exhibited, the tonalism is influenced by Pirandello's use of the palette-knife. By December, however, in a second exhibition of just Cagli, Capogrossi, and Cavalli that was organized by Bardi, the development towards a smoother surface, like that of a fresco, is clear. A year later in December 1933, the three friends had their launch in Paris with an exhibition at the Bernheim-Jeune Gallery, where Waldemar George, the Italophile critic of the *Italiens de Paris*, was to coin the famous label *École de Rome* (School of Rome), mimicking the *École di Paris* (School of Paris).

The paintings exhibited were modern versions of classical subjects: immobile athletes, poets, and other figures. The subjects seem to allude to hermetic initiations, scenes of religious mysteries, rituals performed in a timeless abstraction. The colors are bright, as in early Renaissance frescos, without shadows, with a tonalism that is now cool, now warm, based on symbolic harmonies. Balthus was struck by their work, altering his style after the Paris exhibition to move in a similar direction.

The distance between the two groups of young artists, who had originally set out together following similar aims in 1927 at the Pensione Dinesen, was now characterized by almost diametrically reversed oppositions. Mafai was the interpreter of reality (Raphaël had moved away from painting to dedicate herself to sculpture), while Cavalli, Capogrossi, and Cagli attempted to give form to the invisible, to the primitive myth.

The École de Rome: Tonalism, Expressionism, and the Neo-Baroque

In the mid-1930s Rome was regarded as the most progressive and dynamic center of art in Italy. After an attempt to infuse new life into the *Novecento Italiano* group with *Muralismo*, it was Sironi, the movement's champion, who in February 1935 recognized that the honor of upholding the most lively and brilliant developments in Italian art fell now to the group— which has come to be called Roman—of Cagli, Capogrossi, Cavalli, the late Scipione, Mafai, and, among sculptors, Fazzini and Crocetti. "The Roman group brings together in this Quadriennale a harvest worthy of notice, keeping burning, and infusing with energy, the flame of belief in a modern art that is much more than yesterday's reheated dish, or a pious fiction. Rome is the mainstay of the art of today."

By this period, the tonalism of the École de Rome had become the accepted modern style, just as the term École de Rome was now used of all the youthful tendencies, however diverse, which had made it their own, each bringing its own expressive contribution, and making it the dominant style. In the later 1930s, Mafai, for example, used a delicate version of Expressionist and intimate tonalism that he formed into visions that vibrate with heat, the colors almost seeming to shimmer under the sinuous and expressive brushstrokes.

Ziveri and Katy Castellucci, who developed along closely similar lines, due in part to their intense relationship, embarked on their tonal period in 1933, with a lyrical sense reminiscent of Mafai's painting. Diaphanous isolated figures emerge from the restrained but vibrant tonal harmony of the painting. Castellucci's work is delicate and poetic, recalling that of Sandro Penna. Ziveri's work is more dramatic and constructed, putting forward articulated and architectural compositions similar to those of Cagli, Capogrossi, and Cavalli.

Janni (from 1933), Franco Gentilini (from 1934), and Monti (from 1933) were to pursue until about 1937–39 a path closely related to the hieratic and immobile work of Capogrossi and Cavalli, using tonalism in an almost musical way, with light colors.

As of 1935 the group that made up the École de Rome split. Cavalli and Capogrossi continued with their investigations into tonal and magic abstraction, producing some extraordinary work of a disturbing mysteriousness, allegories of a world dominated by a hermetic melancholy. Melli too used reality to create an abstract chessboard of form and color, in a vision which, like that of his fellow artists, reveals the anxieties of a tragic decade through enigmatic forms, sealed up like chrysalises. Cagli, on the other hand, moved more towards a Baroque style, recalling that of Scipione but achieved through the use of strictly tonal methods. His style became looser, in a technique that imitates encaustic painting. In intention and subject-matter it does derive from the Old Masters but it demonstrates a swift, almost eighteenth-century virtuosity, combining Imperial Rome with the Baroque city without a break. It influenced the work of the Basaldella brothers, Afro and Mirko. While Mirko translated Cagli's Baroque Expressionism into sculpture, Afro brought to his paintings his own contribution of a Venetian, Tiepolo-inspired Rococo, harking back to his origins in Friuli, near Venice.

This introduction of a more explicit Baroque style that was linked to tonalism, was to lead many painters to a reconsideration of the expressive possibilities of the art of the seventeenth century, though in a very different manner from the way in which it had been taken up in the early 1920s. Now the seventeenth century fascinated, not as the continuation of an Italian tradition, but as marking an Expressionist break away from the classical canons of painting. A climate was emerging that anticipated the end of an epoch and was to find in the tragedy of war the confirmation of a dramatic presentiment.

Pirandello, a major—and perhaps still insufficiently recognized—figure in Italian painting, continued in his exploration of the reality of bodies and objects, producing work that creates a sense of alarm and disquiet. Rejecting a psychological approach, as did his friends, he did not seek to create the reality of a dream, but rather to expose a condition suspended between

Alberto Ziveri, *The Brawl* (1937–38). Oil on canvas. Galleria Nazionale d'Arte Moderna.

pure form and harsh reality. Within this paradox, he laid bare the insoluble dialectic between suffering matter and the sublimating spirit, which was held in check by the inevitability of existence. Pirandello's raw vision of reality was to anticipate that of the end of the decade.

The Late 1930s: the Turn to Realism

Around 1937, just as tonalism had become the dominant style, a group of young artists was strongly drawn by the need to find a less abstract form of expression, more suited to the dramatic time they were living through—and, more importantly, towards which they were inexorably moving. Demands for a new art began to emerge clearly—for an art that could render with communicative and expressive urgency, not only the stoic attitude of a Cavalli or a Capogrossi, but also a physical and carnal reality, one whose wounds were red with blood (blood which was already being shed in Spain and would soon be shed throughout Europe and the world).

Guzzi, a perceptive and intelligent critic as well as a painter, was perhaps the first to move away from the by now fossilized tonalist painting. As early as 1936 he began to study seventeenth-century painting (the most dramatic work of Caravaggio) and nineteenth-century realism (Courbet and, in particular, Goya), endowing his figures with a solid chiaroscuro, seeking in the thickness of the impasto a new and expressive density. As always with Italian art, the great national artistic legacy was turned into a tool to enable the development of new stylistic forms.

Guzzi was joined by Ziveri, who found a direction for his passionate work; in 1937 he traveled in the Netherlands and France, studying Rembrandt, Courbet, and Delacroix and acquired a taste for a solid and dramatic style of painting that was both Romantic and Expressionist. In 1938 Ziveri showed his first paintings in this new style at the Biennale. Dramatic and Expressionist yet with a sense of the seventeenth century and tempering a raw simplicity with a classic refinement free of affectation, these works were an original voice.

At the same time, Renato Guttuso, the rising star of Italian painting, was moving away from the tonal influence of Cagli to work in a distinctly Expressionist style, producing violent pictures whose vigorously carnal nudes and subject-matter stripped of all elegance anticipate the angularity of Picasso. The violence of his painting and his explicit anti-fascist stance immediately placed him at the forefront of the new generation.

This group came to public notice in 1940 in an exhibition at the Galleria di Roma, under the aegis of Guzzi, who wrote the introduction to the exhibition catalogue. Works by Ziveri, Guttuso, Montanarini, Tamburi, Guzzi, and the sculptor Pericle Fazzini were exhibited. Guzzi's introduction set out clearly the move away from tonalism and the search for a new, realistic impetus:

"A desire to draw nearer and penetrate reality, it will attempt at all costs to represent reality in a new balance in which the sense of the style can, so to speak, plunge into the objective existence of things. No more dreamlike reality, but a dream of reality. To go further, since we are not afraid of words—a new realism."

Guttuso was soon to detach himself from this romantic, backward-looking group, from the climate of realism of Ziveri and Guzzi, both banal and refined, and, to a lesser extent, from that of Montanarini and Tamburi, to move towards an art of a more explicit socially engaged nature which went beyond the morally charged denunciation of his friends to an overt political denunciation. He took his inspiration from Picasso's

Renato Guttuso, *Crucifixion* (1941). Oil on canvas. This unusual depiction of the central event of the Gospels was awarded a prize in 1942 in Bergamo but was condemned by both Fascist and Church circles. Oil on canvas. Galleria Nazionale d'Arte Moderna.

Guernica, with all its disturbing and explosive elements that had made such a work significant for Italy at this time. Passion and political commitment, realism and expressionism came together in paintings of pure and lyrical color, with broken and syncopated lines, determining the incisive substratum of an art representing resistance—eventually to be one of the platforms for the revival of Italian art after the Second World War.

Mafai too was to develop a harsher Expressionism after 1939, producing paintings that are deliberately dirty and confused, almost like graffiti against the regime, whose hands were now stained with blood.

Pirandello remained faithful to tonalism but continued to experiment with the material of painting, lacerating it as he lacerated the bodies of his bathers, whose contorted figures seem to belong to Dante's *Inferno*, or throwing both objects and landscapes into an incomprehensible confusion with a calm fury and a lucid understanding of the drama.

Toti Scialoja and Stradone, the last in an era that was coming to its tragic end, continued to pursue a path leading from Scipione, seen through the lens of Soutine, an emaciated Baroque Expressionism, nocturnal and feverish. In contrast to the provocative choice of realism by painters such as Guttuso, already influenced by Picasso, these painters chose a different path and different style of painting, which in 1947 Brandi was to call *fuori strada* (off the beaten track), as it retained an introspection still faithful to an existential and subjective passion. Leoncillo did the same, though he was shortly afterwards to move towards neo-Cubism.

In 1943, when the Rome Quadriennale was still taking place, Allied troops entered Rome. It was the end of an era, one which had produced a wealth of intellectual and aesthetic solutions while always maintaining a close dialogue with the rest of Europe. It was also the conclusion of one of the most complex, profound, and tormented periods in Italian art. But it was also the beginning of new developments which understandably, in the passionate years of anti-fascism, sought to overthrow and forget a politically contradictory period that had ended in a terrible war. All too often, although it is perhaps understandable, the art produced at the time is confused with the period itself.

Fabio Benzi

CONTENTS

Acknowledgments

Without the help and generous collaboration of many individuals and institutions it would have been impossible to carry out a publishing project of the size and complexity of *Rome, Art and Architecture*.

I am particularly grateful to Professor Adriano La Regina, Superintendent of Archaeology in Rome and to Professor Claudio Strinati, Superintendent of the Artistic and Historical Heritage of Rome, for their generous and courteous assistance. I was greatly aided by the Archaeological Office for Southern Etruria, the Office for the Artistic and Historical Heritage of Parma and Piacenza, the Galleria Nazionale d'Arte Moderna, the Galleria Borghese, the Galleria Spada, the Galleria Nazionale d'Arte Antica in Palazzo Barberini, and the Galleria Nazionale d'Arte Antica in Palazzo Corsini.

I would also like to thank His Excellency Cardinal Virgilio Noè, President of the Fabric of St Peter's, the Pontifical Council for Social Communication, Dr Marjorie Weeke, the Pontifical Commission of Sacred Archaeology, and Dr Francesco Buranelli, Regent of the Office of the Pontifical Monuments, Museums, and Galleries. I am indebted to Monsignor D. J. David Lewis, Capitular Vicar of the Basilica of Santa Maria Maggiore, Monsignor Alfonso Porta, Canon Camerlengo of San Giovanni in Laterano, and the Very Reverend Don Raffaele Farina, Prefect of the Biblioteca Apostolica Vaticana.

The interiors of a number of Roman churches were photographed for the first time: this would not have been possible without the cooperation of the Ministry of the Interior and of the Vicariate of the Dioceses of Rome.

Thanks are due also to all those parish priests who helped to make the photographers' task easier, and in particular I should like to mention the parishes of Santa Maria in Campitelli, Santi Martiri Marcellino e Pietro al Laterano, and San Lorenzo in Lucina.

I should like to acknowledge the help given by the General Secretariat of the Office of the President of the Republic, by the Commune of Rome, and by Banca di Roma.

I received unfailing cooperation from the Compagnia di Belle Arti in the person of Dr Marco Varucca, the Museo Diocesano of Orte, the Museo di Arte Moderna e Contemporanea of Trento and Rovereto, the Accademia Nazionale dei Lincei, the Biblioteca Nazionale Centrale, the Istituto Poligrafico e Zecca dello Stato, the Associazione Culturale Arco Farnese, the Gabinetto Numismatico of the Castello Sforzesco in Milan, and the Istituto Archeologico Germanico of Rome.

Several owners of private *palazzi* welcomed us into their homes and we found them to be as friendly as they were cultured. It is a pleasure to thank Princess Maria Camilla Pallavicini and Don Piergiorgio Caracciolo, Prince Prospero Colonna, Prince Don Nicolò Boncompagni Ludovisi, Marchesa Giovanna Sacchetti, and the architect Ernesto Azzalin. Dr Elio Biaggi, author of the fundamental study *Le preziose patine dei sesterzi di Roma imperiale*, and the publishers Priuli e Verluca Editori have kindly allowed a number of illustrations in their book to be reproduced here.

Many other people have played a part in this very long and complex work. It is impossible to mention them all, but our sincere thanks go to every one of them.

Antonio Stella
Chairman, Magnus Edizioni SpA

Bibliography

ANCIENT ROME

Anon., *Case e palazzi d'Etruria*, catalogo della mostra, Milan 1985.
Anon., *I luoghi del consenso imperiale. Il Foro di Augusto. Il Foro di Traiano*, catalogo della mostra, Rome 1995.
Anon., *Kaiser Augustus und die verlorene Republik*, catalogo della mostra, Mainz 1988.
Anon., *La colonna di Marc'Aurelio*, Rome 1955.
Anon., *La peinture de Pompéi. Témoignages de l'art romain dans la zone ensevelie par Vésuve en 79 ap. J.-Chr.*, I–II, Paris 1991–1993 (trad. it. del I volume: *La pittura di Pompei*, Milan 1991).
Anon., *Le tranquille dimore degli dèi*, Venice 1986.
Anon., *Memoria dell'antico nell'arte italiana*, I: *L'uso dei classici*, Turin 1984, fig. 185.
Anon., *Roma e l'Italia fra i Gracchi e Silla* (Incontro di Studio, Pontignano, 18–21 settembre 1969), Dialoghi di Archeologia, IV–V, 2–3, 1970–1971.
Anon., *Studi sull'arco onorario romano*, a cura di G. A. Mansuelli, Rome 1978.
Aberson M., *Temples votifs et butin de guerre dans la Rome républicaine*, Rome 1994.
Andreae B., *L'art de l'ancienne Rome*, Paris 1973.
Andreae B., *L'arte nell'età imperiale*, in Anon., *Princeps Urbium. Cultura e vita sociale dell'Italia romana*, Milan 1991, pp. 3–144.
Andreae B., *La Rome antique*, Paris 1989.
Andrén A., *Architectural Terracottas from Etrusco-Italic Temples*, Lund-Leipzig 1940.
Baldassarre I. (coordinamento di), *Pompei. Pitture e Mosaici*, Istituto dell'Enciclopedia Italiana, Rome 1990.
Barbet A., *La peinture murale romaine. Les styles décoratifs pompéiens*, Paris 1985.
Becatti G., *Arte e gusto negli scrittori latini*, Florence 1951.
Becatti G., *L'arte romana*, Milan 1962.
Becatti G., *La colonna coclide istoriata. Problemi storici, iconografici, stilistici*, Rome 1960.
Bejor G., *L'arte romana: centro e periferia, arte colta e arti plebee*, in Anon., *Civiltà dei Romani, IV: Un linguaggio comune*, Milan 1993, pp. 161–178.
Bertman S., *Art and the Romans. A Study of Roman Art as a dynamic Expression of Roman Character*, Lawrence (Kansas) 1975.
Bianchi Bandinelli R., *Archeologia e cultura*, Milano-Napoli 1961, Rome 1979.
Bianchi Bandinelli R., *Dall'Ellenismo al Medioevo*, Rome 1978.
Bianchi Bandinelli R., *La pittura antica*, Rome 1980.
Bianchi Bandinelli R., *Ritratto*, in *Enciclopedia dell'arte antica classica e orientale*, VI, Rome, 1965, pp. 695–798, ristampato in *L'arte classica*, Rome 1984, pp. 223–282.
Bianchi Bandinelli R., *Roma. L'arte romana nel centro del potere*, Milan Rome 1969.
Bianchi Bandinelli R., *Roma. La fine dell'arte antica*, Milan 1970.
Bianchi Bandinelli R., *Romana Arte* (voce enciclopedica), in *Enciclopedia dell'arte antica classica e orientale*, VI, Roma 1965, pp. 939–999.
Bianchi Bandinelli R., *Storicità dell'arte classica*, Florence 1943, Bari 1973.
Bianchi Bandinelli R., *Sulla formazione del ritratto romano* (1957), in *Archeologia e cultura*, Rome 1979, pp. 164–180.
Bianchi Bandinelli R., Torelli M., Coarelli F., Giuliano A., *Il monumento teatino di C. Lusius Storax al Museo di Chieti*, in *Studi Miscellanei 10*, Rome 1966, pp. 57 sgg.
Bianchi Bandinelli R., Torelli M., *L'arte dell'antichità classica. Etruria-Roma*, Turin 1976.
Blake M. E., *The pavements of the Roman Buildings of the Republic and Early Empire*, Memoirs of the American Academy of Rome, 8, 1930.
Bloch H., *I bolli laterizi e la storia edilizia romana*, Rome 1947, 1982.
Boethius A., Ward Perkins J. B., *Etruscan and Roman Architecture*, Harmondsworth 1970.
Borda M., *La pittura romana*, Milan 1958.
Brendel J. O., *Introduzione all'arte romana*, Turin 1982.
Brilliant R., *Roman Art from the Republic to Constantine*, London 1974.
Carandini A., *La villa romana e la piantagione schiavistica*, in A. Momigliano, A. Schiavone (direzione di), *Storia di Roma. IV. Caratteri e morfologie*, Turin 1989, pp. 101–200.
Castagnoli F., *Topografia e urbanistica di Roma antica*, Bologna 1969.

Chevallier R., *L'artiste, le collectionneur & le faussaire. Pour une sociologie de l'art romaine*, Paris 1991.
Città e architettura nella Roma imperiale, Atti del 27 ottobre 1981 nel 25° anniversario dell'Accademia di Danimarca, Odense 1983.
Clarke J.R., *The Houses of Roman Italy, 100 B.C.–A.D. 250. Ritual, Space and Decoration*, Berkley-Los Angeles-Oxford 1991.
Coarelli F., *Architettura sacra e architettura privata nella tarda-repubblica*, in *Architecture et société de l'archaisme grec à la fin de la République romaine*, Atti del Convegno (Roma 1980), Paris-Rome 1983, pp. 193–217.
Coarelli F., *Cultura artistica e società*, in A. Momigliano, A. Schiavone (direzione di), *Storia di Roma. II. L'Impero mediterraneo*, Turin 1990, pp. 159–188.
Coarelli F., *Il Campo Marzio. Dalle origini alla fine della Repubblica*, Rome 1997.
Coarelli F., *Il Foro Boario*, Rome 1988.
Coarelli F., *Il Foro Romano. Periodo arcaico*, Rome 1983.
Coarelli F., *Il Foro Romano. Periodo repubblicano e augusteo*, Rome 1985.
Coarelli F., *Il sepolcro degli Scipioni*, Dialoghi di Archeologia, VI, 1972, pp. 36 sgg..
Coarelli F., Kajanto I., Nyberg U., *L'area sacra di Largo Argentina*, I, Rome 1981.
Coarelli F., *L' «ara di Domizio Enobarbo» e la cultura artistica in Roma nel II secolo a.C.*, in «Dialoghi di Archeologia» III, 1969.
Coarelli F., *La cultura artistica*, in A. Schiavone (direzione di), *Storia di Roma. II, 3. L'Impero mediterraneo. La cultura e l'Impero*, Turin 1992, pp. 631–652.
Coarelli F., *La cultura figurativa*, in A. Momigliano, A. Schiavone (direzione di), *Storia di Roma II. L'Impero mediterraneo*, Turin 1990, pp. 631670.
Coarelli F., *La riscoperta del sepolcro degli Haterii. Una base con dedica a Silvano*, in *Studies in Classical Art and Archaeology. A Tribute to P.H. v. Blanckenhagen*, New York 1979, pp. 255–269.
Coarelli F., *Polycles*, Studi Miscellanei, 15, Rome 1970, pp. 77 sgg.
Coarelli F., *Revixit Ars. Arte e ideologia a Roma. Dai modelli ellenistici alla tradizione repubblicana*, Rome 1996.
Coarelli F., *Roma, Guide archeologiche Laterza*, Rome – Bari 1980.
Coarelli F., *Roma, Guide archeologiche Laterza*, Rome – Bari 1952.
Colini A. M., Cozza L., *Ludus Magnus*, Rome 1962.
Colonna G., *I Latini e gli altri popoli del Lazio*, in *Italia omnium terrarum alumna*, Milan 1988, pp. 411–530.
Colonna G., *La produzione artigianale*, in A. Momigliano, A. Schiavone (direzione di), *Storia di Roma I. Roma in Italia*, Turin 1988, pp. 292–316.
Comella A. M., *Complessi votivi in Italia in epoca medio e tardo repubblicana*, Mélanges de l'École Française de Rome, 93, 1981, pp. 717–803.
Cozza L., *Mura di Roma dalla Porta Nomentana alla Tiburtina*, Rome 1998.
Cozza L., *Osservazioni sulle mura aureliane a Roma*, Rome 1987.
Crawford M., *Roman Republican Coinage*, Cambridge 1974.
Crema L., *L'architettura romana*, Turin 1959.
Cristofani M., a cura di, *La grande Roma dei Tarquini*, catalogo della mostra, Rome 1990.
Dacos N., *Fabullus et l'autre peintre de la Domus Aurea*, Dialoghi di Archeologia, II, 2, 1968, pp. 210–226.
De Albentiis E., *La casa dei Romani*, Milan 1990.
De Maria S., *Gli archi onorari di Roma e dell'Italia romana*, Rome 1988.
De Vos A. M., *Pompei, Guide archeologiche Laterza*, Rome – Bari 1982.
Donati A., a cura di, *Romana Pictura. La pittura romana dalle origini all'età bizantina*, catalogo della mostra (Rimini 28 marzo-30 agosto 1998), Milan 1998.
Dorigo W., *Pittura tardo-romana*, Milan 1966.
Dudley D. R., *Urbs Roma, a source book of classical texts on the city*, Aberdeen 1967.
Enciclopedia dell'Arte Antica (EAA), Suppl. 1970–1994, Roma 1997: *Dalle origini fino all'età medio-repubblicana* (M. Cristofani), pp. 1–6. *Età tardo-repubblicana e imperiale fino alla Tetrarchia* (P. Zanker), pp. 6–22.
Felletti Maj B. M., *La tradizione italica nell'arte romana*, Rome 1977.
Ferrary J.-L., *Philhellénisme et impérialisme. Aspects idéologiques de la conquête romaine du monde hellénistique*, Rome 1988.
Fittschen K., Zanker P., *Katalog der römischen Porträts in den capitolinischen Sammlungen*, 1985, vol. I.
Franchi L., *Ricerche sull'arte di età severiana in Roma*, Rome 1964.

Frova A., *L'arte di Roma e del mondo romano*, Turin 1961.
Gabba A., *L'imperialismo romano*, in A. Momigliano, A. Schiavone (direzione di), *Storia di Roma II. L'Impero mediterraneo*, Turin 1990, pp. 189–233.
Gatti G., *Topografia ed edilizia di Roma antica*, Rome 1989 (il volume, postumo, raccoglie la ristampa anastatica di studi compresi fra il 1934 e il 1979).
Ghedini F., *Arte romana: generi e gesti*, in Anon., *Civiltà dei Romani, IV: Un linguaggio comune*, Milan 1993, pp. 161–178.
Giuliano A., *Arco di Costantino*, Milan 1955.
Giuliano A., *Documenti per servire allo studio del monumento degli Haterii*, Memorie dell'Accademia dei Lincei, ser. VIII, XIII 1968, 6, pp. 449–482.
Gjerstad E., *Early Rome, I–VI*, Acta Instituti Romani Regni Sueciae, Lund 1953–1973.
Grimal P., *Les jardins romains*, Paris 19692.
Gros P., *Architettura e società nell'Italia romana*, Rome 1987.
Gros P., *Aurea Templa. Recherches sur l'architecture religieuse de Rome à l'époque d'Auguste*, Rome 1976.
Gros P., *L'architettura romana dagli inizi del III sec. a.C alla fine dell'Alto Impero I. I monumenti pubblici*, Milan 1998.
Gros P., *Les premières générations d'architectes hellénistiques à Rome*, in *Mélanges J. Heurgon*, Rome 1976, pp. 387–409.
Gros P., Torelli M., *Storia dell'urbanistica. Il mondo romano*, Rome – Bari 1988.
Guilhembet J. P., *Habitavi in oculis* (Cicéron, *Planc.*, 66). *Recherches sur la résidence urbaine des classes dirigeantes romaines des Gracques à Auguste. La maison dans la ville*, in corso di stampa.
Gullini G., *L'architettura e l'urbanistica*, in Anon., *Princeps Urbium. Cultura e vita sociale dell'Italia romana*, Milan 1991, pp. 419–735.
Hamberg P. G., *Studies in Roman Imperial Art with special reference to the State Reliefs of the second century*, Rome 1968 (I ed. svedese, Uppsala 1945).
Hanestad N., *Roman Art and Imperial Policy*, Åarhus 1986.
Hanestad N., *The Roman World*, London 1987.
Hanfmann G. M. A., *Arte romana*, Milan 1965 (I ed. tedesca, Wiesbaden 1964).
Hellenismus in Mittelitalien (herausg. von P. Zanker), Kolloquium in Göttingen vom 5. bis 9 Juni 1974, Göttingen 1976.
Hölscher T., *Il linguaggio dell'arte romana. Un sistema semantico*, Turin 1993 (I ed. tedesca, Heidelberg 1987).
Hölscher T., *Monumenti statali e pubblico*, Rome 1994 (I ed. tedesca, Heidelberg 1988).
Homo L., *Roma imperiale e l'urbanesimo nell'antichità*, Milan 1976 (I ed. francese, Paris 1951).
Jordan H., Hülsen C., *Topographie der Stadt Rom im Alterthum, I–II*, Berlin 1878–1907.
Kähler H., *Roma e l'arte imperiale*, Milan 1963 (I ed. tedesca, Baden Baden 1962).
Kraus T., *Das römische Weltreich*, Berlin 1967.
L'art décoratif à Rome à la fin de la République et au début du Principat, Table ronde organisée par l'École Française de Rome (Rome 10–11 mai 1979), Rome 1981.
L'Orange H. P., Von Gerkan A., *Der spätantike Bildschmuck des Konstantinbogens*, Berlin 1939.
La Penna A., *La legittimazione del lusso privato da Ennio a Vitruvio. Momenti, elementi e personaggi*, Maia, n.s. 41, 1987, pp. 3–34.
La Rocca E., Farinella V., *La Colonna Traiana*, Rome 1996.
La Rocca E., *La riva a mezzaluna. Culti, agoni, monumenti funerari presso il Tevere nel Campo Marzio*, Rome 1984.
La Rocca E., *Linguaggio artistico e ideologia politica in età repubblicana*, in *Roma e l'Italia. Radices imperii*, Milan 1990, pp. 289–495.
Lanciani R., *Rovine e scavi di Roma antica*, Rome 1985 (I ed. inglese, London 1897).
Lanciani R., *Storia degli scavi di Roma*, I–IV, Rome 1902–1904.
Lugli G., *Fontes ad topographiam veteris urbis Romae pertinentes, I–VII*, Rome 1952–1969.
Lugli G., *I monumenti antichi di Roma e suburbio, I–III e Supplemento*, Rome 1931–1940.
Lugli G., *Roma antica. Il centro monumentale*, Rome 1946.
Mac Donald W. L., *The Architecture of the Roman Empire, I: An Introductory Study*, New Haven-London 1965.
Magi F., *I rilievi flavi del Palazzo della Cancelleria*, Rome 1945.

Mansuelli G. A., *Roma e il mondo romano, I–II*, Turin 1981.
Massa Pairault F.-H., *Iconologia e politica nell'Italia antica*. Roma, Lazio, Etruria dal VII al I secolo a.C., Milan 1992.
Meneghini R., *Il Foro di Nerva*, Rome 1991.
Menichetti M., *Archeologia del potere. Re, immagini e miti a Roma e in Etruria in età arcaica*, Milan 1994.
Mielsch H., *La villa romana*, Florence 1990.
Morel J.-P., *L'artigianato e gli artigiani*, in A. Momigliano, A. Schiavone (direzione di), *Storia di Roma II. L'Impero mediterraneo*, Turin 1990, pp. 143–158.
Morricone Matini M.L., in *Enciclopedia dell'Arte Antica*, Supplemento 1970, Rome 1970, s.v. «Mosaico».
Morricone Matini M.L., *Palatium (Mosaici Antichi d'Italia)*, Rome 1967.
Morricone Matini M.L., *Pavimenti di signino repubblicani di Roma e dintorni (Mosaici Antichi d'Italia)*, Rome 1971.
Nash E., *Bildlexicon zur Topographie des antiken Rom, I–II*, Tübingen 1961–1962.
Nash E., *Pictorial Dictionary of Ancient Rome*, London 19682.
Nash E., *Pictorial Dictionary of Ancient Rome*, New York 19682.
Packer E. J., *The Forum of Trajan in Rome. A Study of the Monuments, I–III*, California University 1997.
Pearson J., Il *Colosseo*, Milan 1975.
Pensabene P., Panella C., *Arco di Costantino. Tra archeologia e archeometria*, Rome 1999.
Pérez Chr., *Monnaie du pouvoir. Pouvoir des monnaies. Une pratique discoursive originale: le discours figuratif monétaire* (Ier siècle av. J.-Chr.-14 ap. J.-Chr.), Paris 1986.
Peroni R., *Comunità e insediamento in Italia fra Età del bronzo e prima Età del ferro*, in A. Momigliano, A. Schiavone (direzione di), *Storia di Roma. I. Roma in Italia*, Turin 1988, pp. 7–37.
Pesando F., *"Domus". Edilizia privata e società pompeiana fra III e I sec. a.C.*, Rome 1997.
Pesando F., L. *Cornelio Scipione Barbato fortis vir sapiensque, Bollettino di Archeologia, I*, 1990, pp. 23 sgg.
Pfanner M., *Der Titusbogen*, Mainz 1983.
Picard G. C., *Roman Painting*, London 1970.
Picard G. Ch., *Roma e l'arte imperiale*, Milan 1963 (I ed. francese, Paris 1962).
Pietilä-Castren L., *Magnificentia publica. The Victory Monuments of the Roman Generals in the Era of Punic Wars*, Commentationes humanarum litterarum, 84, Helsinki 1987.
Platner S. B., Ashby T., *A Topographical Dictionary of Ancient Rome*, Oxford-London 1929.
Pollitt J. J., *The Art of Rome (753 B.C.–A.D. 337)*, Englewood Cliffs (New York) 1966.
Pollitt J. J., *The Art of Rome (753 B.C.–A.D. 337). Sources and Documents*, Cambridge 19832.
Poulsen V. H., *Les portraits romains. I. République et dynastie julienne*, Copenhagen 1962.
Riegl A., *Arte tardoromana*, Turin 1959 (I ed. tedesca, Vienna 1901).
Roma medio-repubblicana, catalogo della mostra, Rome 1973.
Romano E., Dal *De officiis a Vitruvio, da Vitruvio a Orazio: il dibattito sul lusso edilizio*, in *Le project de Vitruve. Object, destinataires et reception du De architectura*, Actes du Colloque International Rome 26–27 mars 1993, Rome 1994, pp. 63–73.
Sauron G., *Quis deum? L'expression plastique des idéologies politiques et religieuses à Rome à la fin de la République et au début du Principat*, Rome 1994.
Settis S., *"Ineguaglianze" e continuità: un'immagine dell'arte romana* in O. J. Brendel, *Introduzione all'arte romana*, Turin 1982, pp. 161–200.
Settis S., La Regina A., Agosti G., Farinella V., *La Colonna Traiana*, Turin 1988.
Settis S., *Un'arte al plurale. L'impero romano, i Greci e i posteri*, in A. Momigliano, A. Schiavone (direzione di), *Storia di Roma. IV. Caratteri e morfologie*, Turin 1989, pp. 827–878.
Steinby E. M., *a cura di, Lexicon Topographicum Urbis Romae*, Rome 1991.
Strazzulla M. J., *Principato di Apollo. Mito e propaganda nelle lastre "Campana" dal tempio di Apollo Palatino*, Rome 1990.
Strong E., *L'arte di Roma antica*, Bergamo 1929.
Strong E., *La scultura romana da Augusto a Costantino, I–II*, Florence 1923–1926.
Tamm B., *Auditorium and Palatium*, Lund 1963.
Torelli M., *Culto imperiale e spazi urbani in età flavia. Dai rilievi Hartwig all'Arco di Tito*, in L'Urbs. *Éspace urbain et histoire*, Rome 1987, pp. 563–582.
Torelli M., *L'arte degli Etruschi*, Rome – Bari 1985.
Torelli M., *Polis e "palazzo". Architettura, ideologia e artigianato greco in Etruria tra VII e VI secolo a.C.*, in *Architecture et société de l'archaïsme grec à la fin de la République romaine, Atti del Convegno* (Rome 1980), Paris-Rome 1983, pp. 471 sgg.
Torelli M., *Typology and Structure of Roman Historical Reliefs*, Ann Arbor 1976, 1982.
Toynbee J. M. C., *The Art of the Romans*, London 1963.
Vacca F., *Memorie di varie antichità trovate in diversi luoghi della città di Roma*, a cura di B. Brizzi, Rome 1988.
Valentini R., Zucchetti G., *Codice topografico della città di Roma, I–IV*, Rome 1940–1953.
Vessberg O., *Studien zur Kunstgeschichte der Römischen Republik*, Lund 1941.
Voisin J. L., *Exoriente sole, in L'Urbs. Éspace urbain et histoire*, Rome 1987, pp. 509–543.
Von Blanckenhagen P.H., *Flavische Architektur und ihre Dekoration*, Berlin 1940.
Von Heinze H., *Römische Kunst*, Stuttgart 1969.
Von Kaschnitz-Weinberg G., *Römische Kunst, I–IV*, Hamburg 1961–1963.
Ward Perkins J. B., *Architettura romana*, Milan 1974.
Wataghin Cantino G., *La Domus Augustana*, Turin 1966.
Wheeler M., *Arte e architettura romana*, Milan 1990 (I English ed., London 1976).
Wickhoff F., *Arte romana*, Padova 1947.
Wickhoff F., *Römische Kunst*, Berlin 1912 (trad. it. L'arte romana, Padova 1947).
Winkes R., a cura di, *The Age of Augustus*, Interdisciplinary Conference held at Brown University (April 30–May 2 1982), Providence 1985.
Zaccaria Ruggiu A. P., *Spazio privato e spazio pubblico nella città romana*, Rome 1995.
Zanker P., *Augusto e il potere delle immagini*, Turin 1989 (trad. it. dell'edizione originale del 1987).
Zanker P., *Das Trajansforum als Monument imperialer Selbstdarstellung*, Archäologischer Anzeiger, 1970, pp. 499 sgg..
Zanker P., *Immagini e valori collettivi*, in A. Momigliano, A. Schiavone (direzione di), *Storia di Roma. II, 2. I Principi e il mondo*, Turin 1991, pp. 193–220.
Zanker P., *Klassizistische Statuen. Studien zur Veränderung des Kunstgeschmacks in der römischen Kaiserzeit*, Magonza 1974.
Zanker P., *Pompei. Società, immagini urbane e forme dell'abitare*, Turin 1993.
Zehnacker H., *Moneta. Recherches sur les emissions et l'art del emissions monétaires de la République romaine* (289–31 av. J.-Ch.), Rome 1973.
Ziolkowski A., *The Temples of Mid-Republican Rome and their Historical and Topographical Context*, Rome 1992.

PALEO-CHRISTIAN ROME

Anon., *Il palazzo apostolico lateranense, a cura di C. Pietrangeli*, Florence 1992.
Anon., *San Giovanni in Laterano, a cura di C. Pietrangeli*, Florence 1991.
Anon., *San Paolo fuori le mura, a cura di C. Pietrangeli*, Florence 1989.
Anon., *San Pietro, a cura di C. Pietrangeli*, Florence 1990.
Anon., *Santa Maria Maggiore a Roma, a cura di C. Pietrangeli*, Florence1988.
Age of Spirituality. *Late Antique and Early Christian Art, Third to Seventh Century*, Catalogue of the Exhibition at the Metropolitan Museum of Art (November 19, 1977–February 12, 1978), New York 1979.
Age of Spirituality: a Symposium, New York 1980.
Alexander S. S., *Studies in Constantinian Church Architecture, Rivista di Archeologia Cristiana, XLIX*, 1973, pp. 33–44.
Apollonj Ghetti B. M., *Problemi relativi alle origini dell'architettura paleocristiana*, Atti del IX Congresso internazionale di Archeologia Cristiana, Rome 1975, I, Vatican City 1978.
Apollonj Ghetti B. M., *S. Crisogono (Le chiese di Roma illustrate, 92)*, Rome 1966.
Armellini M., Cecchelli C., *Le chiese di Roma*, Rome 1942.
Arnaldi G., *Le origini dello Stato della Chiesa*, Turin 1987.
Bertelli G. et alii, *Strutture murarie degli edifici religiosi di Roma dal IV al IX secolo*, Rivista dell'Istituto nazionale di Archeologia e Storia dell'Arte, 23–24, 1976–1977, pp. 95–172.
Bertolini O., *Le origini del potere temporale e del dominio temporale dei papi*, XX Settimana di Studio del Centro italiano di Studi sull'Alto Medioevo, Spoleto 6–12 aprile 1972, I, Spoleto 1973, pp. 231–255.
Bertolini O., *Per la storia delle diaconie romane nell'Alto Medioevo sino alla fine del sec. VIII*, in Scritti scelti, a cura di O. Banti, Livorno 1967, pp. 311–460.
Bisconti F., *Genesi e primi sviluppi dell'arte cristiana: i luoghi, i modi, i temi*, in *Dalla terra alle genti. La diffusione del Cristianesimo nei primi secoli*, Milan 1996, pp. 71–93.
Bisconti F., *La pittura paleocristiana*, in *Romana Pictura. La pittura romana dalle origini all'arte bizantina*, Milan 1998, pp. 33–53.
Bisconti F., *L'arte delle catacombe*, in *Dalla terra alle genti. La diffusione del Cristianesimo nei primi secoli*, Milan 1996, pp. 94–106.
Bovini G., *La proprietà ecclesiastica e la condizione giuridica della Chiesa in età paleocristiana*, Milan 1949.
Brandenburg H., *La chiesa di S. Stefano Rotondo a Roma. Nuove ricerche e risultati*, Rivista di Archeologia Cristiana, 68, 1992, pp. 201–232.
Brown P., Il *mondo tardoantico*, Turin 1974.
Cameron A., *The Date and the Owners of the Esquiline Treasure*, American Journal of Archeology, 89, 1985, pp. 135–145.
Carletti C., *Iscrizioni cristiane a Roma. Testimonianze di vita cristiana (secoli III–IV)*, Florence 1986.
Carletti S., *Le antiche chiese dei martiri romani (Le chiese di Roma illustrate, 122–123)*, Rome 1972.
Cecchelli C. et alii, *S. Agata dei Goti*, Rome 1923.
Cecchelli C. *Vita di Roma nel Medioevo*, Rome 1951–1960.
Cecchelli C., *Roma medievale*, in F. Castagnoli, C. Cecchelli, G. Giovannoni, M. Zocca, *Topografia e urbanistica di Roma: Storia di Roma, XXII, a cura dell'Istituto di Studi romani*, Rome 1957, pp. 189–341.
Cecchelli M., *Intorno ai complessi battesimali di San Pietro in Vaticano e di S. Agnese sulla Via Nomentana*, Quaderni dell'Istituto di Archeologia e Storia antica dell'Università di Chieti, 3, 1982–1983, pp. 181–199.
Cecchelli M., *La chiesa di S. Agata in fundo lardario e il cimitero dei Ss. Processo e Martiniano. Note sulla topografia delle due Aurelie*, Quaderni dell'Istituto di Archeologia e Storia antica dell'Università di Chieti, 1, 1980, pp. 112.
Cecchelli M., *Note sui titoli romani*, Archeologia Classica, 37, 1985, pp. 293–305.
Cecchelli M., *Scavi e ricerche di archeologia cristiana a Roma, 1983–1993*, Atti del VII Congresso Nazionale di Archeologia cristiana, Cassino, settembre 1993.
Chastagnol A., *Le snat romain sous le regne d'Odoacre*, Bonn 1966.
Christe Y., *Victoria-Imperium-Judicium. Un scheme antique du pouvoir dans l'art paléochrétien et médieval*, Rivista di Archeologia Cristiana, XLIX, 1973, pp. 87–110.
Davis Weyer C., *S. Stefano Rotondo in Rome and oratory of the Theodore I*, in *Italian church decoration of the Middle Ages and Early Renaissance*, a cura di W. Tronzo, Bologna 1989, pp. 71–80.
De Bruyne L., *La peinture cemeteriale constantinienne*, Akten des VII Internationalen Kongresses Christliche Archeologie, Trier 1965, Città del Vaticano-Berlin 1969, pp. 159–214.
De Rossi G.B., *La Roma sotterranea Cristiana, I–III*, Rome 1864–1877.
De Wit J., *De la ville antique à la ville byzantine. Le probleme des subsistances*, Rome 1990.
Deckers J. G., Fasola U. M., Seeliger H. R., Guyon J., Schumacher W. N., *Die Katakombe "Santi Marcellino e Pietro". Repertorium der Malereien. La catacomba dei Santi Marcellino e Pietro. Repertorio delle pitture*, Città del Vaticano-Mnster 1991.
Deichmann F. W., Bovini G., Brandenburg H., *Repertorium der christlich-antiken Sarkophage. Erster Band. Roma und Ostia*, Wiesbaden 1967.
Deichmann F. W., *Archeologia Cristiana*, Rome 1993.
Duval N., *Problematique d'une architecture chrétienne au IVe siecle*, in Revue des études augustiniennes, 35, 1989, pp. 308–313.
Episcopo S., *L'Ecclesia baptisimalis nel suburbio di Roma*, Atti del VI Congresso Nazionale di Archeologia cristiana, Pesaro-Ancona 12–23 settembre 1983, Ancona 1985, pp. 297–308.
Faedo L., *Per una classificazione preliminare dei vetri dorati tardoromani*, Annali della Scuola Normale Superiore di Pisa, VIII, 3, 1978, pp. 1025–1043.
Falesiedi U., *Le diaconie. I servizi assistenziali nella Chiesa antica*, Annali della Scuola Normale Superiore di Pisa, VIII, 3, 1978.
Ferrari G., *Early roman monasteries*, Vatican City 1957.
Ferrua A., Carletti C., *Damaso e i martiri di Roma*, Vatican City 1985.
Ferrua A., Epigrammata damasiana, Vatican City 1942.
Ferrua A., Le pitture della nuova catacomba di Via Latina, II ed., Vatican City 1974.
Fiocchi Nicolai V., Bisconti F., Mazzoleni D., *Le catacombe cristiane di Roma. Origini, sviluppo, apparati decorativi, documentazione epigrafica*, Regensburg 1998.
Fiocchi Nicolai V., *Strutture funerarie ed edifici di culto paleocristiani di Roma dal III al VI secolo*, in *Le iscrizioni dei cristiani in Vaticano. Materiali e contributi scientifici per una mostra epigrafica*, a cura di I. Di Stefano Manzella, Vatican City 1997, pp. 121–141.
Fraschetti A., *Spazi del sacro e spazi della politica*, in *Storia di Roma*, 3, 1. L'età tardoantica: crisi e trasformazioni, Turin 1993, pp. 675–696.
Fraschetti A., *Costantino e l'abbandono del Campidoglio, in Società romana e impero tardoantico, II*, Rome – Bari 1986, pp. 59–98.
Geertman N., *Forze centripete e centrifughe nella Roma cristiana: il Laterano, la basilica Iulia e la basilica Liberiana*, Rendiconti della nd, 59, 1990, pp. 53–91.
Geertman N., *More Veterum*, Groningen 1975.
Giardina A., *Carità eversiva: le donazioni di Melania la Giovane e gli equilibri della società tardoromana*, Studi Tardoantichi, 2, 1986, pp. 77–102.
Grabar A., *L'arte paleocristiana (200–395)*, Milan 1980.
Gregoire R., *Monaci e monasteri a Roma nei secoli VI–VII*, Archivio della Società Romana di Storia Patria, 104, 1981, pp. 5–24.
Grisar H., *Roma alla fine del mondo antico, I–II*, Rome 1943.
Grossi V., *Chiesa e poveri nei primi secoli*, in Anon., *Poveri e povertà nella storia della Chiesa*, Modena 1988, pp. 9–27.
Grossi V., Siniscalco P., La vita cristiana nei primi secoli, Rome 1988.
Guidobaldi F., Guiglia Guidobaldi, *Pavimenti marmorei di Roma dal IV al IX secolo*, Vatican City1983.
Guidobaldi F., *San Clemente. Gli edifici romani, la basilica paleocristiana e le fasi altomedievali*, Rome 1992.
Heres Th. L., *Paries*, Amsterdam 1982.
Huelsen Ch., *Le chiese di Roma nel Medioevo*, Florence 1927.
I Goti, catalogo della mostra, Milan 1994.
Jastrzebowska E., *La basilique des apôtres Rome. Fondation de Constantin ou de Maxence?*, in *Mosaique. Recueil d'hommages Henri Stern*, Paris 1983, pp. 223–229.
Jones A. H. M., Martindale J. R., Morris J., *The Prosopography of the Later Roman Empire, I*, Cambridge 1971.
Kinney D., *S. Maria in Trastevere from its founding to 1215*, New York University, Ph. D. 1975.

Kitzinger E., *L'arte bizantina*, Milan 1989.
Kollwitz J., *Die Malerei der konstantinischen Zeit, Akten des VII Internationalen Kongresses Christliche Archeologie*, Trier 1965, Città del Vaticano-Berlin 1969, pp. 29–158.
Krautheimer R. et alii, *Corpus basilicarum christianarum Romae, I–V*, Vatican City1937–1980.
Krautheimer R., *Architettura paleocristiana e bizantina*, Turin 1986.
Krautheimer R., *Corpus Basilicarum christianarum Romae. Le basiliche paleocristine di Roma (secc. IV–IX)*, Vatican City 1937–1980.
Krautheimer R., Roma. *Profilo di una città 312–1308*, Rome 1981.
Krautheimer R., *Tre capitali cristiane*, Turin 1987.
Le Goff J., Morawski P., *Età Medievale*, Casale Monferrato 1988.
Lestocquoy J., *L'administration de Rome et les diaconies du VI au IX siecle*, Rivista di Archeologia Cristiana, VII, 1930, pp. 261–298.
Llewellyn P., *Roma nei secoli oscuri*, Rome – Bari 1975.
Lotti L., *S. Agata dei Goti, Alma Roma*, 16, 1975, 3–4, pp. 91–96.
Mara M. G., *Monachesimo di lingua greca e latina, in Il monachesimo del primo millennio*, Atti del Convegno Internazionale di Studi, Roma-Casamari 1989, Rome 1989, pp. 113–130.
Mara M. G., *Ricchezza e povertà del Cristianesimo primitivo*, Rome 1991.
Marazzi F., *L'insediamento nel suburbio di Roma fra IV e VIII secolo*, Bullettino dell'Istituto Storico Italiano per il Medio Evo, 94, 1988, pp. 251–313.
Marrou H. I., *L'origine orientale des diaconies romaines*, Melanges d'archeologie et d'histoire, LVII, Paris 1940, pp. 95–142.
Matthiae G., Andaloro M., *Pittura romana del Medioevo. Secoli IV–X*, Rome 1989.
Matthiae G., *Mosaici medievali di Roma*, Rome 1967.
Mazzarino S., *L'impero romano*, Rome – Bari 1990.
Meneghini R., Santangeli Valenzani R., *Sepolture intramuranee e paesaggio urbano a Roma tra V e VII secolo*, in *La storia economica di Roma nell'Alto Medioevo alla luce dei recenti scavi archeologici*, Florence 1993, pp. 89–112.
Momigliano A. (a cura di), *Il conflitto tra paganesimo e cristianesimo nel secolo IV*, Turin 1975.
Moreau J., *La persecuzione del Cristianesimo nell'impero romano*, Brescia 1977.
Ortolani G., *Le torri pentagonali del Castro Pretorio*, Analecta Romana, 19, 1990, pp. 239–252.
Pani Ermini L., *Testimonianze archeologiche di monasteri a Roma nell'Alto Medioevo*, Archivio della Società Romana di Storia Patria, 104, 1981, pp. 25–45.
Pietri Ch., *Regions ecclesiastiques et paroisses romaines, Actes du XIe Congres International d'Archeologie chrétienne*, Lyon-Vienne-Grenoble-Geneve-Aoste (21–28 septembre 1986), Vatican City 1989, pp. 1035–1062.
Pietri Ch., *Roma Christiana*, Rome 1976.
Recchia V., Gregorio Magno e la società agricola, Rome 1978.
Reekmans L., *L'implantation monumental chrétienne dans la zone suburbaine de Rome du IVe au IXe siecle*, Rivista di Archeologia Cristiana, XLIV, 1968 (pubbl. 1969), pp. 173–208.
Reekmans L., *L'implantation monumental chrétienne dans le paisage urbain de Rome de 300–850*, Actes du Congres d'Archeologie Chritienne, Lyon-Geneva-Aoste-Turin, 1986, Vatican City1989, pp. 861–915, XLIV, 1968 (pubbl. 1969), pp. 173–208.
Reekmans L., *La chronologie de la peinture paléochrétienne. Notes et réflexions*, Rivista di Archeologia Cristiana, XLIX, 1973, pp. 271–291.
Sansterre J. M., *Les moines grecs et orientaux Rome aux epoques byzantine et carolingienne*, Bruselles 1980.
Saxer V., *L'utilisation par la liturgie de l'espace urbain et suburbain: l'exemple de Rome dans l'Antiquité et le Haut Moyen Age*, Actes du XIe Congres International d'Archeologie chritienne, Lyon-Vienna-Grenoble-Geneva-Aoste (21–28 septembre 1986), Vatican City 1989, pp. 917–1032.
Testini P., *L'oratorio scoperto al "Monte di Giustizia" presso la Porta Viminale a Roma*, Rivista di Archeologia Cristiana, 44, 1968, pp. 105–130.
Testini P., *Le catacombe e gli antichi cimiteri cristiani in Roma*, Bologna 1966.
Testini P., *Osservazioni sull'iconografia del Cristo in trono fra gli Apostoli*, Rivista dell'Istituto di Archeologia e Storia dell'Arte, XI–XII, 1963, pp. 230–300.
Tolotti F., *Il cimitero di Priscilla*, Vatican City 1970.
Tolotti F., *Le basiliche cimiteriali con deambulatorio del suburbio romano: questione ancora aperta*, Roemische Mitteilungen, 89, 1982, pp. 154–211.
Valentini R., Zucchetti G., *Codice topografico della città di Roma*, I–IV, Rome 1940–1953.
Verrando G. N., *L'attività edilizia di papa Giulio I e la basilica al III miglio della Via Aurelia ad Callistum*, Melanges de l'Ecole francaise de Rome, Antiquit, 97, 1985, 2, pp. 1021–1061.
Vielliard R., *Recherches sur les origines de la Rome chrétienne*, Rome 1959.
Volbach W. F., *Elfenbeinarbeiten der Spaetantike und des fruehen Mittelalters, II* ed., Mainz 1976.
Wilpert J., I *sarcofagi cristiani antichi, I–III*, Rome 1929–1936.
Wilpert J., *Le pitture delle catacombe romane*, Rome 1903.
Wirth F., *Roemische Wandmalerei vom Untergang Pompeijs bis ans Ende des dritten Jahrhunderts, II* ed., Darmstadt 1968.
Zanchi Roppo F., *Vetri paleocristiani a figure d'oro conservati in Italia*, Bologna 1969.
Zanchi Roppo F., *Vetri paleocristiani a figure d'oro*, Ravenna 1967.

THE MIDDLE AGES

Amadei E., *Le Torri di Roma*, Rome 1969.
Andaloro M., Gandolfo F., *Aggiornamento scientifico a G. Matthiae, Pittura romana del Medioevo*. Secoli XI–XIV, Rome 1988.
Andaloro M., *La datazione della tavola di Santa Maria in Trastevere, Rivista dell'Istituto Nazionale di Archeologia e Storia dell'Arte*, n.s., 19–20, (1972–1973), pp. 85–153.
Armellini M., *Le chiese di Roma*, a cura di C. Cecchelli, Rome 1942.
Belli Barsali I., *L'oreficeria medievale*, Milan 1966.
Bertelli C., *La pittura medievale a Roma e nel Lazio, in La pittura in Italia*. L'Altomedioevo, Milano 1994, pp. 206–242.
Bianchi L., *Case e torri medievali a Roma*, Rome 1998.
Brandi C., *Giotto*, Milan 1983.
Brentano R., *Rome before Avignon*, New York 1974.
Buchowiecki W., *Handbuch der Kirchen Roms*, 3 vol., Vienna 1967–1974.
Buchowiecki W., *Handbuch der Kirchen Roms*, IV vol., a cura di B. Kuhn-Forte, Vienna 1998.
Buono R., *Il Museo di San Giovanni in Laterano*, Rome 1986.
Cecchelli C., *Vita di Roma nel Medio Evo*, Rome 1951–1952.
Claussen P. C., *Magistri Doctissimi Romani. Die römischen Marmorkünstler des Mittelalters*, (Corpus Cosmatorum, I), Stuttgart 1987.
Claussen P. C., *Marmi antichi nel Medioevo romano. L'arte dei Cosmati*, in *Marmi antichi*, a cura di G. Borghini, Rome 1989, pp. 65–79.
D'Onofrio M., *Le committenze ed il "mecenatismo" di papa Niccolò III*, in *Roma anno 1300*, a cura di A. M. Romanini, Rome 1983, pp. 553–562.
D'Onofrio M., Leonardis V., *La città nel Medioevo, in Roma. L'Urbe nei secoli*, Florence 1994, pp. 101–149.
De Blaauw S., *"Cultus et decor". Liturgia e architettura nella Roma tardoantica e medievale*, 2 vol., Vatican City1994.
De Rossi G. B., *Musaici cristiani e saggi dei pavimenti delle chiese di Roma anteriori al secolo XV*, Rome 1872–1892.
Demus O., *Pittura murale romanica*, Milan 1969.
Die mittelalterlichen Grabmäler in *Rom und in Latium vom 13.* bis zum 15. Jahrhundert, II, Die Monumentalgräber, a cura di J. Garms, A. Sommerlechner, W. Telesko, Vienna 1994.
Duchesne L., *Le Liber Pontificalis. Texte, introduction et commentaire*, 2 vol., Paris 1886–1892; *Additions et corrections*, a cura di C. Vogel, Paris 1957 (ristampa 3 vol., Paris 1981).
Enciclopedia dell'arte medievale, a cura di A. M. Romanini, Istituto dell'Enciclopedia Italiana, Rome 1991–1998 (volumi finora pubblicati I–IX).
Federico II e l'arte del Duecento italiano, Atti della III Settimana di Studi di Storia dell'Arte medievale dell'Università di Roma (15–20 maggio 1978), a cura di A. M. Romanini, Galatina 1980.
Ferrari G., *Early Roman Monasteries*, Vatican City 1957.
Fragmenta Picta. *Affreschi e mosaici staccati del Medioevo* romano, catalogo della mostra, (Rome, Castel Sant'Angelo 15 dicembre 1989–18 febbraio 1990), Rome 1989.
Fratini C., *Considerazioni e ipotesi sulla "Cornice di Sant'Apollinare" nelle Grotte Vaticane*, in *San Pietro. Arte e storia nella basilica vaticana*, a cura di G. Rocchi Coopmans de Yoldi, s.l. 1996, pp. 51–68.
Gandolfo F., *Reimpiego di sculture antiche nei troni papali del XII secolo*, Atti della Pontificia Accademia Romana di Archeologia, Rendiconti, III s., 47 (1974–1975), pp. 203–218.
Gandolfo F., Simbolismo antiquario e potere papale, Studi romani, 29 (1981), pp. 9–28.
Gardner J., T*he Tomb and the Tiara. Curial Tomb Sculpture in Rome and Avignon in the Later Middle Ages*, Oxford 1992.
Garrison E. B., *Studies in the history of medieval Italian painting*, 4 vol., Florence 1953–1962.
Geertman H., More Veterum. *Il Liber Pontificalis e gli edifici ecclesiastici di Roma nella tarda antichità e nell'alto Medioevo*, Groningen 1975.
Gnoli U., *Topografia e toponomastica di Roma medievale e moderna*, Rome 1939.
Golzio V., Zander G., *Le chiese di Roma dall'XI al XIV secolo*, Bologna 1963.
Gregorovius F., *Storia della città di Roma nel Medio Evo*, 4 vol., Rome 1910.
Grisar H., *Geschichte Roms und der Päpste im Mittelalter*, Freiburg 1901.
Guide rionali di Roma, a cura di C. Pietrangeli e altri.
Guidobaldi F., Guiglia Guidobaldi A., *Pavimenti marmorei di Roma dal IV al IX secolo*, Vatican City1983.
Guidobaldi F., S. Clemente. *Gli edifici romani, la basilica paleocristiana e le fasi altomedievali*, Rome 1992, vol. I (S. Clemente Miscellany IV.I).
Herklotz I., *"Sepulcra" e "Monumenta" del Medioevo*. Studi sull'arte sepolcrale in Italia, Rome 1985.
Hermanin F., *L'arte di Roma dal secolo VIII al XIV*, Bologna 1945.
Huelsen C., *Le chiese di Roma nel Medio Evo*, Florence 1967 (ristampa Hildesheim 1975).
Il Palazzo Apostolico lateranense, a cura di C. Pietrangeli, Florence 1991.
Jewellyn P. I., *Rome in the Dark Ages*, London 1971 (ed. italiana, Roma nei secoli oscuri, Bari 1976).
Kirsch J. P., *Die Stationkirchen des Missale Romanum*, Freiburg 1927.
Kitzinger E., *The art of Byzantium and the Medieval West*, Bloomington (Indiana), 1976.
Krautheimer R., Corbett S., Frankl W., Frazer A. K., *Corpus Basilicarum Christianarum Romae*, 5 vol., Città del Vaticano–Rome-New York 1937–1977.
Krautheimer R., *Early Christian and Byzantine Architecture*, II ed., Harmondsworth 1975 (ed. italiana, Architettura paleocristiana e bizantina, Turin 1986).
Krautheimer R., *Roma. Profilo di una città, 312–1308*, Rome 1981.
La basilica di San Pietro, a cura di C. Pietrangeli, Florence 1989.
La basilica romana di Santa Maria Maggiore, a cura di C. Pietrangeli, Florence 1987.
La Diocesi di Roma (Corpus della scultura altomedievale, 7), 6 vol., Spoleto 1974–1995.
Le chiese di Roma illustrate, collana di monografie fondata da C. Galassi Paluzzi.
Matthiae G., *Le chiese di Roma dal IV al X secolo*, Rome 1962.
Matthiae G., *Mosaici medievali delle chiese di Roma*, 2 vol., Rome 1967.
Matthiae G., *Pietro Cavallini*, Rome 1972.
Matthiae G., *Pittura romana del Medioevo*, 2 vol., Rome s.d. [1965–1966].
Oakeshott W., *The Mosaics of Rome from the third to the fourteenth Centuries*, London 1967.
Pace V., *«Nihil innovetur nisi quod traditum est». Sulla scultura romana del Medioevo, in Studien zur Geschichte der Europaitschen Skulptur im 12./13. Jahrhundert*, Acten der Colloquia (Frankfurt a. M. Liebeghauses 1991–1992) a cura di H. Beck und K. Hengevoss-Durkop, I, Frankfurt a. M. 1994, pp. 587–603.
Paravicini Bagliani A., *Le chiavi e la tiara*, Rome 1998.
Parlato E., Romano S., *Roma e il Lazio*, (Italia Romanica, 13), Milan 1992.
Pensabene P., *Il reimpiego dei marmi antichi nelle chiese altomedievali a Roma*, in *Marmi antichi*, a cura di G. Borghini, Rome 1989, pp. 55–64.
Restauri della Soprintendenza alle Gallerie e alle opere d'arte medievali e moderne per il Lazio (1970–1971), Rome 1972.
Roma anno 1300, Atti della IV Settimana di Studi di Storia dell'Arte medievale dell'Università di Roma "La Sapienza", a cura di A. M. Romanini (19–24 maggio 1980), Rome 1983.
Roma e l'età carolingia, Atti delle giornate di studio a cura dell'Istituto di Storia dell'Arte dell'Università di Roma (3–8 maggio 1976), Rome 1976.
Roma nel Duecento. L'arte nella città dei papi da Innocenzo III a Bonifacio VIII, a cura di A. M. Romanini, Turin 1991.
Roma, Napoli, Avignone. Arte di curia, arte di corte 1300–1377, a cura di A. Tomei, Turin 1996.
Romanini A. M., *Arnolfo di Cambio e lo "stil novo" del gotico italiano*, Milan 1969.
Romano S., *Eclissi di Roma. Pittura murale a Roma e nel Lazio da Bonifacio VIII a Martino V (1295–1431)*, Rome 1992.
San Giovanni in Laterano, a cura di C. Pietrangeli, Florence 1990.
San Paolo fuori le mura a Roma, a cura di C. Pietrangeli, Florence 1988.
Sancta Sanctorum, Milan s.d. [1995].
Serafini A., *Torri campanarie di Roma e del Lazio nel Medioevo*, 2 vol., Rome 1927.
Skulptur und Grabmal des Spätmittelalters in Rom und Italien, Akten des Kongresses "Scultura e monumento sepolcrale del Tardo Medioevo a Roma e in Italia" (Rom 4.-6. Juli 1985), a cura di J. Garms e A. M. Romanini, Vienna 1990.
Tesori d'arte sacra di Roma e del Lazio dal Medioevo all'Ottocento, catalogo della mostra, (Roma, Palazzo delle Esposizioni, novembre-dicembre 1975), Rome 1975.
Toesca P., *Il Medioevo*, vol. I, II, Turin 1965.
Tomei A., *Iacobus Torriti pictor. Una vicenda figurativa del tardo Duecento romano*, Rome 1990.
Toubert H., *Un art dirigé*, Paris 1990.
Valentini R., Zucchetti G., *Codice topografico della città di Roma*, Rome 1940–1953.
Van Marle R., *La peinture romaine au Moyen Age, son dévelopment du 6me jusquà la fin de 13me siècle*, Strasbourg 1921.
Waetzold S., *Die Kopien des 17. Jahrhunderts nach Mosaiken und Wandmalereien in Rom*, Vienna 1964.
Wilpert J., *Die römischen Mosaiken und Malereien der kirchlichen Bauten von IV. bis XIII. Jahrhundert*, 4 vol., Freiburg i.B. 1917.

THE FIFTEENTH CENTURY

Acidini Luchinat C., *0*, Florence 1994.
Aurigemma M. G., *Il palazzo cardinalizio di Domenico della Rovere in Borgo*, in S. Danesi Squarzina, a cura di, *Roma, centro ideale dell'Antico nei secoli XV e XVI*, Milan 1989.
Benzi F., *Sisto IV Renovator Urbis*. Architettura a Roma 1471–1484, RomE 1990.
Berti L., Baldini U., *Filippino Lippi*, Florence 1991.
Bonsanti G., *Beato Angelico*. Catalogo completo, Florence 1998.
Borsi F., Borsi S., *Alberti, Art e dossier*, n. 93, settembre 1994.
Borsi F., *Leon Battista Alberti*, Milan 1980.
Borsi S., *Masaccio, Art e Dossier*, n. 116, ottobre 1996.
Bussagli M., *Benozzo Gozzoli, Art e Dossier*, n. 143, marzo 1999.
Calvesi M., Il *gaio classicismo. Pinturicchio e Francesco Colonna nella Roma di Alessandro VI*, in *S. Danesi Squarzina*, a cura di, Roma, centro ideale dell'Antico nei secoli XV e XVI, Milan 1989.

Calvesi M., *La Cappella Sistina nel Quattrocento*, Rome 1979.
Cannatà R., Cavallaro A., *Strinati C.*, a cura di, Umanesimo e primo Rinascimento in S. Maria del Popolo, catalogo della mostra (Roma 1981), Rome 1981.
Casanova M. L., *Palazzo Venezia*, Rome 1992.
Cavallaro A., *Antoniazzo Romano e gli antoniazzeschi. Una generazione di pittori nella Roma del Quattrocento*, Udine 1992.
Cavallaro A., *Aspetti e protagonisti della pittura del Quattrocento romano in coincidenza dei giubilei*, in M. Fagiolo, M. L. Madonna, a cura di, *Roma 1300–1875. La città degli anni santi*, Milan 1985.
Cavallaro A., *Draghi, mostri e semidei, una rivisitazione fiabesca dell'Antico nel soffitto pinturicchiesco del palazzo di Domenico della Rovere*, in S. Danesi Squarzina, a cura di, *Roma, centro ideale dell'Antico nei secoli XV e XVI*, Milan 1989.
Cavallaro A., *Studio e gusto dell'antico nel Pisanello, in Anon., Da Pisanello alla nascita dei musei capitolini. L'Antico a Roma alla vigilia del Rinascimento*, catalogo della mostra (Roma 1988), Milan – Rome 1988.
Christiansen K., *Gentile da Fabriano*, London 1982.
Cieri Via C., *"Sacrae effigies" e "signa arcana": la decorazione di Pinturicchio e scuola nell'appartamento Borgia* in Vaticano, in S. Danesi Squarzina, a cura di, *Roma, centro ideale dell'Antico nei secoli XV e XVI*, Milan 1989.
Cole Ahl D., *Benozzo Gozzoli (1996)*, Cinisello Balsamo 1997.
Corbo A. M., *Artisti ed artigiani in Roma al tempo di Martino V e di Eugenio IV*, Rome 1969.
Cornini G., De Strobel A., Serlupi Crescenzi M., *La Sala Vecchia degli Svizzeri e la Sala dei Chiaroscuri*, in Anon.., *Raffaello nell'appartamento di Giulio II e Leone X*, Milan 1993.
Dacos N., *La découverte de la Domus Aurea et la formation des grotesques à la Renaissance*, London 1969.
Danesi Squarzina S., *Eclisse del gusto cortese e nascita della cultura antiquaria: Ciriaco, Feliciano, Marcanova, Alberti*, in Anon., *Da Pisanello alla nascita dei musei capitolini. L'Antico a Roma alla vigilia del Rinascimento*, catalogo della mostra (Rome 1988), Milan – Rome 1988.
Danesi Squarzina S., *La Casa dei Cavalieri di Rodi: architettura e decorazione*, in S. Danesi Squarzina, a cura di, *Roma, centro ideale dell'Antico nei secoli XV e XVI*, Milan 1989.
Danesi Squarzina S., *Note sulla cultura architettonica a Roma durante il papato di Alessandro VI*, in M. Calvesi, a cura di, *Le arti a Roma sotto Alessandro VI*, Rome 1981.
De Marchi A., *Gentile da Fabriano, Art e Dossier*, n. 136, luglio-agosto 1998.
De Marchi A., *Gentile da Fabriano. Un viaggio nella pittura italiana alla fine del gotico*, Milan 1992.
Ettlinger I. D., *The Sistine Chapel before Michelangelo. Religious imagery and Papal primacy*, Oxford 1965.
Farinella V., *Archeologia e pittura a Roma tra Quattrocento e Cinquecento*, Turin 1992.
Fremantle R., *Masaccio. Catalogo completo*, Florence 1998.
Frugoni C., *L'Antichità dai Mirabilia alla propaganda politica, in Memoria dell'antico nell'arte italiana*, a cura di S. Settis, I, Turin 1984.
Golzio V., Zander G., *L'arte in Roma nel secolo XV*, Bologna 1968.
Joannides P., *Masaccio and Masolino. A complete catalogue*, London 1993.
Kennedy R. W., *The contribution of Martin V to the Rebuilding of Rome 1420–1431*, in *The Renaissance reconsidered*, Northampton (Mass.) 1964.
Maddalo S., *Roma nelle immagini miniate del primo Quattrocento: realtà, simbolo e rappresentazione fantastica*, in Anon., *Da Pisanello alla nascita dei musei capitolini. L'Antico a Roma alla vigilia del Rinascimento*, catalogo della mostra (Roma 1988), Milan-Rome 1988.
Madonna M. L., *Una operazione urbanistica di Alessandro VI: la via alessandrina in Borgo*, in M. Calvesi, a cura di, *Le arti a Roma sotto Alessandro VI*, Rome 1981.
Marconi P., *La città come forma simbolica*, Rome 1973.
Marini P., a cura di, *Pisanello, catalogo della mostra* (Verona 1996), Milan 1996.
Müntz E., *Les Arts à la Cour des papes pendant le XVe et le XVIe siècle*, Parigi 1878–1882.
Negri Arnoldi F., *La scultura del Quattrocento*, Turin 1994.
Padoa Rizzo A., *Benozzo Gozzoli. Catalogo completo*, Florence 1992.
Paolucci A., *Antoniazzo Romano*, Florence 1992.
Parlato E., *Il gusto all'antica di Filarete scultore*, in Anon., *Da Pisanello alla nascita dei musei capitolini. L'Antico a Roma alla vigilia del Rinascimento*, catalogo della mostra (Rome 1988), Milan-Rome 1988.
Parlato E., *La decorazione della cappella Carafa: allegoria ed emblematica negli affreschi di Filippino Lippi alla Minerva*, in S. Danesi Squarzina, a cura di, *Roma, centro ideale dell'Antico nei secoli XV e XVI*, Milan 1989.
Pasti S., Nicolò V, *l'Angelico e le antichità di Roma di Benozzo Gozzoli*, in Anon., *Da Pisanello alla nascita dei musei capitolini. L'Antico a Roma alla vigilia del Rinascimento*, catalogo della mostra (Roma 1988), Milan-Rome 1988.
Pinelli A., *La pittura a Roma e nel Lazio nel Quattrocento*, in *La Pittura in Italia. Il Quattrocento*, Milan 1987, II.
Platina B., *Historici liber de vita Christi ac omnium pontificum*, in L. Muratori, *Rerum italicarum scriptores*, Città di Castello 1913–1932.
Pope-Hennessy J., *Donatello*, Turin 1994.
Pope-Hennessy J., *Italian Renaissance Sculpture*, London 1963.
Puppi L., a cura di, *Pisanello. Una poetica dell'inatteso*, Cinisello Balsamo 1996.
Righetti Tosti-Croce M., *Pisanello a S. Giovanni in Laterano*, in Anon., *Da Pisanello alla nascita dei musei capitolini. L'Antico a Roma alla vigilia del Rinascimento*, catalogo della mostra (Roma 1988), Milan-Rome 1988.
Romano S., *Eclissi di Roma. Pittura murale a Roma e nel Lazio da Bonifacio VIII a Martino V (1295–1431)*, Rome 1992.
Rykwert J., Engel A., *Leon Battista Alberti*, catalogo della mostra (Mantova 1994), Milan 1994.
Saxl F., *L'appartamento Borgia, in Storia delle immagini*, Bari 1982.
Scalabroni L., *Masolino a Montegiordano: un ciclo perduto di "uomini illustri"*, in Anon., *Da Pisanello alla nascita dei musei capitolini. L'Antico a Roma alla vigilia del Rinascimento*, catalogo della mostra (Roma 1988), Milan -Rome 1988.
Schulz J., *Pinturicchio and the revival of antiquity, Journal of the Warburg and Courtauld Institutes*, XXV, 1962.
Tafuri M., *"Cives esse non licere". Nicolò V e Leon Battista Alberti*, in *Ricerca del Rinascimento*. Principi, città, architetti, Turin 1992.
Tafuri M., *L'architettura dell'Umanesimo*, Bari 1969.
Ventura L., *Pisanello, Art e Dossier*, n.113, giugno 1996.
Westfall C. W., *L'invenzione della città. La strategia urbana di Nicolò V e Alberti nella Roma del Quattrocento*, Rome 1984.
Wittkower R., *Principi architettonici nell'età dell'Umanesimo*, Turin 1962.

THE SIXTEENTH CENTURY

Anon., *Antonio da Sangallo il Giovane. La vita e l'opera*, a cura di G. F. Spagnesi, Rome 1986.
Anon., *Aspetti dell'arte a Roma prima e dopo Raffaello*, catalogo della mostra (Rome 1984), Rome 1984.
Anon., *Caravaggio*, CdRom Arte n. 4, novembre 1996.
Anon., *Giulio Romano*, catalogo della mostra (Mantova 1989), Milan 1989.
Anon., *I luoghi di Raffaello a Roma*, catalogo della mostra (Rome 1983), Rome 1983.
Anon., *Il Rosso e Volterra*, catalogo della mostra (Volterra 1994), Venice 1994.
Anon., *L'architettura a Roma e in Italia (1580–1621)*, a cura di G. F. Spagnesi, Rome 1989.
Anon., *La Cappella Sistina. La volta restaurata, il trionfo del colore*, Novara 1992.
Anon., *La Galleria delle carte geografiche in Vaticano. Storia e iconografia*, Modena 1994.
Anon., *La pittura del Cinquecento a Roma e nel Lazio, in La pittura in Italia. Il Cinquecento*, a cura di G. Briganti, Milan 1987.
Anon., *La regola e la fama. San Filippo Neri e l'arte*, catalogo della mostra (Roma 1995), Milan 1995.
Anon., *La storia dei Giubilei, 1450–1575*, vol. II, Florence 1998.
Anon., *Le Palais Farnèse*, Rome 1981.
Anon., *Lineamenti di storia dell'architettura*, a cura di A. White, Rome 1974.
Anon., *Michelangelo e la Sistina. La tecnica il restauro il mito, catalogo della mostra* (Vatican City1990), Rome 1990 .
Anon., *Oltre Raffaello. Aspetti della cultura figurativa del Cinquecento romano*, catalogo della mostra (Rome 1984), Rome 1984.
Anon., *Raffaello in Vaticano*, catalogo della mostra (Vatican City1984–1985), Milan 1984.
Anon., *Raffaello nell'Appartamento di Giulio II e di Leone X*, con introduzione di C. Pietrangeli, Milan 1993.
Anon., *Raffaello: l'architettura ›picta‹ percezione e realtà*, catalogo della mostra (Roma 1984), Rome 1984.
Anon., *Sisto IV e Giulio II mecenati e promotori di cultura*, Savona 1989.
Abromson M.C., *Clement VIII's patronage of the brothers Alberti*, The Art Bulletin, 60, 1978.
Ackerman J., *L'architettura di Michelangelo*, Turin 1968.
Aliberti Gaudioso F.M., Aliberti Gaudioso E., *Gli affreschi di Paolo III a Castel Sant'Angelo 1543–1548*, 2 vol., catalogo della mostra (Roma 1981–1982), Rome 1981.
Argan G.C., Contardi B., *Michelangelo, Art e Dossier*, n. 9, gennaio 1987.
Baglione G., *Le Vite de' pittori, scultori et architetti dal pontificato di Gregorio XIII del 1572 in fino a' tempi di Papa Urbano Ottavo nel 1642*, Rome 1642.
Baldini U., *Michelangelo scultore*, Milan 1973.
Barocchi P., *Il Rosso Fiorentino*, Rome 1950.
Barolsky P., *A fresco decoration by Pellegrino Tibaldi*, Paragone, n. 237, 1969.
Barolsky P., *Daniele da Volterra. A catalogue raisonnè*, New York 1979.
Battisti E., *Il significato simbolico della Cappella Sistina*, Commentari, 1957.
Battisti E., *L'antirinascimento (1962)*, Milan 1989.
Benedetti S., *Giacomo Del Duca e l'architettura del Cinquecento*, Rome 1972–1973.
Benedetti S., *Letture di architettura. Saggi sul Cinquecento romano*, Rome 1987.
Benedetti S., Zander G., *L'arte in Roma nel secolo XVI*, 1, L'architettura, Bologna 1990.
Benzi F.,Vincenti Montanaro C., *Palazzi di Roma*, Venice 1997.
Bonelli R., *Da Bramante a Michelangelo*, Venice 1960.
Borea E., *Grazia e furia in Marco Pino*, Paragone, 13, 1962.
Borsi F., Borsi S., *Bramante*, Milan 1989.
Briganti G., *Il manierismo e Pellegrino Tibaldi*, Rome 1945.
Briganti G., *La maniera italiana (1961)*, Florence 1986.
Brugnoli M.V., *Baldassarre Peruzzi nella chiesa di S. Maria della Pace e nell'"Uccelleria" di Giulio II*, Bollettino d'Arte, 1973.
Brugnoli M.V., *Gli affreschi di Perin del Vaga nella Cappella Pucci. Note sulla prima attività romana del pittore*, Bollettino d'Arte, 47, 1962.
Bruschi A., *Bramante architetto*, Bari 1969.
Bussagli M., in Anon., *Raffaello*, CdRom Arte n. 9, settembre 1997.
Calì M., *Da Michelangelo all'Escorial. Momenti del dibattito religioso nell'arte del Cinquecento*, Turin 1980.
Calvesi M., *Caravaggio, Art e Dossier*, n. 1, aprile 1986.
Calvesi M., *Le arti in Vaticano (1965)*, Milan 1980.
Calvesi M., *Le realtà del Caravaggio*, Turin 1990.
Calvesi M., *Raffaello. La Trasfigurazione*, in Anon., *Oltre Raffaello. Aspetti della cultura figurativa del Cinquecento romano*, catalogo della mostra (Roma 1984), Rome 1984.
Camesasca E., *Tutta l'opera del Cellini*, Milan 1955.
Cannatà R., a cura di, *Palazzo Spada. Le decorazioni restaurate*, Milan 1995.
Carloni P., Cassanelli L., Grasso M., *Giorgio Vasari. Palazzo della Cancelleria*, in Anon., *Oltre Raffaello. Aspetti della cultura figurativa del Cinquecento romano*, catalogo della mostra (Rome 1984), Rome 1984.
Chastel A., *Il Sacco di Roma*, Turin 1983.
Chastel A., *La grottesca (1988)*, Turin 1989.
Chiappini di Sorio I., *Cristoforo Roncalli detto il Pomarancio*, Bergamo 1983.
Cleri B., a cura di, *Federico Zuccari. Le idee, gli scritti, Atti del convegno* (Sant'Angelo in Vado), Milan 1997.
Coliva A., *Parmigianino, Art e Dossier*, n. 82, settembre 1993.
Cox-Rearick, a cura di, *Francesco Salviati o la Bella Maniera*, catalogo della mostra (Roma 1998), Milan 1998.
Dacos N., *Le Logge di Raffaello (1976)*, Rome 1986.
Darragou E., *Le Studiolo du Cardinal Ferdinand à la Villa Medicis*, Revue de l'Art, 19, 1973.
Davis C., *Per l'attività di Vasari nel 1553: incisioni degli affreschi di Villa e la Fontanalia di Villa Giulia*, Mitteilungen des Kunsthistorischen Institutes in Florenz, XXIII, 1979.
De Maio R., *Michelangelo e la Controriforma*, Bari 1978.
De Maio R., *Pittura e Controriforma*, Rome – Bari 1983.
De Tolnay C., *Michelangelo*, Princeton 1945.
De Tolnay C., *Morte e Resurrezione* in *Michelangelo*, Commentari, 1964.
Di Teodoro F. P., *Raffaello, Baldassar Castiglione e la "Lettera a Leone X"*, Bologna 1994.
Dumont C., *Francesco Salviati au Palais Sacchetti de Rome et la décoration murale italienne (1520–1560)*, Rome 1973.
Fagiolo M., Madonna M. L., a cura di, *Roma 1300–1875. La città degli anni santi*, Milan 1985.
Farinella V., *Archeologia e pittura a Roma tra Quattrocento e Cinquecento*, Turin 1992.
Freedberg S. J., *Parmigianino. His Work on Painting*, Cambridge 1950.
Frommel C. L., *Baldassare Peruzzi als Maler und Zeichner*, Monaco 1967–1968.
Frommel C. L., *Der römische Palastbau der Hochrenaissance*, Tübingen 1973.
Frommel C. L., Ferino Pagden S., Oberhuber K., *Giulio Romano, Art e Dossier*, n. 40, novembre 1989.
Frommel C. L., Ray S., Tafuri M., *Raffaello architetto*, Milan 1984.
Gentili A., in Anon., *Tiziano*, CdRom Arte n. 12, marzo 1998.
Gentili A., *Tiziano, Art e Dossier*, n. 47, giugno 1990.
Gere J., a cura di, *Taddeo Zuccari*, catalogo della mostra (San Severino Marche 1992), San Severino Marche 1992.
Gere J., *Two late fresco cycles by Perin del Vaga: The Massimi chapel and the Sala Paolina*, The Burlington Magazine, CII, 1960.
Gould C., Parmigianino, Milan 1994.
Gramberg W., *Die Düsseldorfer Skizzenbücher des Guglielmo della Porta*, Berlin 1964.
Hartt F., *Lignum Vitae in Medio Paradisi: The Stanza d'Eliodoro and the Sistine Ceiling*, The Art Bulletin, XXXII, 1950.
Heikamp D., *Die Entwurfszeichnungen für die Grabmäler der Medicer Päpste Leo X und Clemens VII*, Albertina Studien, IV, 1966, pp. 134–154.
Hennemberg J., *L'oratorio dell'Arciconfraternita del Santissimo Crocifisso di San Marcello*, Rome 1974.
Hirst M., *Sebastiano del Piombo*, Oxford 1981.
Hochmann M., *La Stanza delle Muse. Il restauro delle tele e del soffitto di Jacopo Zucchi*, catalogo della mostra (Roma 1995), Rome 1995.
Hunter J., G. *Seciolante da Sermoneta, committenti e committenza, Quaderni della Fondazione Camillo Caetani*, Rome 1983.
Huntley G. H., *Andrea Sansovino*, Cambridge 1935.
Lee Rubin P., *Giorgio Vasari. Art and History*, New Haven-London 1995.
Lombardi F., *Roma. Chiese, conventi, chiostri. Progetto per un inventario 313–1925*, Rome 1993.
Madonna M. L., a cura di, *Roma di Sisto V. Le arti e la cultura*, Rome 1993.
Mancinelli F., Colalucci G., Gabrielli N., *Michelangelo. Il Giudizio Universale, Art e Dossier*, n. 88, marzo 1994.
Mancini P., Scarfone G., *L'oratorio del Santissimo Crocifisso*, Rome 1975.
Monbeig Goguel C., a cura di, *Raffaello e i suoi, catalogo della*

mostra (Romae 1992), Rome 1992.
Morello G., a cura di, *Raffaello e la Roma dei Papi*, catalogo della mostra, Rome 1985.
Mori G., *Arte e astrologia, Art e Dossier*, n. 10, febbraio 1987.
Mori G., *Baldassarre Peruzzi. Oroscopo di Agostino Chigi*, in Anon., *I luoghi di Raffaello a Roma*, catalogo della mostra (Rome 1983), Rome 1983.
Mori G., *Prospero Fontana. Palazzo Firenze*, in Anon., *Oltre Raffaello. Aspetti della cultura figurativa del Cinquecento romano*, catalogo della mostra (Rome 1984), Rome 1984.
Mori G., *Sebastiano del Piombo. La Farnesina, le lunette*, in Anon.., *I luoghi di Raffaello a Roma*, catalogo della mostra (Roma 1983), Rome 1983.
Mortari F., *Francesco Salviati*, Rome 1992.
Neppi L., *Palazzo Spada*, Rome 1985.
Nova A., *B. Ammannati e P. Fontana a Palazzo Firenze*, Ricerche di Storia dell'Arte, 1983.
Nova A., *"Occasio pars virtutis". Considerazioni sugli affreschi di Francesco Salviati per il cardinale Ricci*, Paragone, 365, 1980.
Oberhuber K., *Raffaello*, Milan 1982.
Oberhuber K., *Raffaello. L'opera pittorica*, Milan 1999.
Panofsky E., *Tiziano. Problemi di iconografia (1969)*, a cura di A. Gentili, Venice 1992.
Parma Armani E., *Perin del Vaga. L'anello mancante*, Genova 1986.
Pietrangeli C., a cura di, *Il Palazzo Apostolico Vaticano*, Florence 1992.
Pillsbury D. E., *Jacopo Zucchi in S. Spirito in Sassia*, The Burlington Magazine, 857, 1974.
Pinelli A., *La Bella Maniera. Artisti del Cinquecento tra regola e licenza*, Turin 1993.
Pinelli A., *Pittura e Controriforma. "Convenienze" e misticismo in Giovanni de' Vecchi*, Ricerche di Storia dell'Arte, 6, 1977.
Pittoni G., *Jacopo Sansovino scultore*, Venice 1909.
Pope Hennessy J., *Italian High Renaissance and Baroque Sculpture*, London 1963 and 1970.
Pope-Hennessy J., *Raffaello (1970)*, Turin 1983.
Portoghesi P., *Architettura del Rinascimento a Roma*, Milan 1979.
Pugliatti T., *Giulio Mazzoni e la decorazione a Roma nella cerchia di Daniele da Volterra*, Rome 1984.
Pugliatti T., *Un fregio di Pellegrino Tibaldi nel Palazzo Ricci-Sacchetti a Roma*, in *Scritti di storia dell'arte in onore di F. Zeri*, Milan 1984, I.
Roli R., *Giovanni de' Vecchi, Arte antica e moderna*, 1965.
Röttgen H., *Il Cavalier d'Arpino*, Rome 1973.
Russo L., *Pier Marcello Venusti, pittore lombardo*, Bollettino d'Arte, n. 64, 1990.
Saxl F., *La fede astrologica di Agostino Chigi*, Rome 1934.
Scalabroni L., *Jacopo Zucchi. Palazzo Firenze*, in Anon, *Oltre Raffaello. Aspetti della cultura figurativa del Cinquecento romano*, catalogo della mostra (Rome 1984), Rome 1984.
Shearman J., *Funzione e illusione (1971)*, Milan 1983.
Shearman J., *The Chigi Chapel in Santa Maria del Popolo*, Journal of the Warburg and Courtauld Institutes, XXIV, 1961.
Shearman J., *The "Dead Christ"* by Rosso Fiorentino, Bulletin of the Museum of Fine Arts, Boston, 64,1966.
Smith G., *The Casino of Pius IV*, Princeton University Press 1977.
Spezzaferro L., *Il Recupero del Rinascimento*, in *Storia dell'arte italiana*, Turin 1981, VI.
Steinmann E., *Das Grabmal Pauls III in St. Peter in Rom*, Rome 1912.
Strinati C., *Gli anni difficili di Federico Zuccari, Storia dell'Arte*, n. 21, 1974.
Strinati C., *Raffaello, Art e Dossier*, n. 97, gennaio 1995.
Strinati C., *Roma nell'anno 1600. Studio di pittura*, Ricerche di Storia dell'Arte, 10, 1980.
Volpe C., Lucco M., *L'opera completa di Sebastiano del Piombo*, Milan 1980.
Weisz J., *Pittura e misericordia: the oratory of S. Giovanni Decollato in Rome*, Ann Arbor 1982.
Wilde J., *The Decoration of the Sistine Ceiling, Proceedings of the British Academy*, 94, 1958.
Zapperi R., *Tiziano, Paolo III e i suoi nipoti*, Turin 1990.
Zeri F., *Intorno a Girolamo Siciolante*, Bollettino d'Arte, 1951.
Zeri F., *Pittura e Controriforma. L'«arte senza tempo» di Scipione da Gaeta (1957)*, Turin 1970.
Zuccari A., *Aggiornamenti sulla decorazione cinquecentesca di alcune cappelle del Gesù*, Storia dell'Arte, 50, 1984.
Zuccari A., *Raffaello e le dimore del Rinascimento*, Art e Dossier, n. 7, novembre 1986.
Zuccari A., Sebastiano del Piombo. *S. Pietro in Montorio, Cappella Borgherini*, in Anon., *Oltre Raffaello. Aspetti della cultura figurativa del Cinquecento romano*, catalogo della mostra (Roma 1984), Rome 1984.

THE SEVENTEENTH CENTURY

Anon., Barocco, in *Enciclopedia Universale dell'Arte, II*, Venice – Rome 1958, coll. 345–468.
Anon., *Bernini in Vaticano*, catalogo della mostra, maggio-luglio 1981, Rome 1981.
Anon., *Bernini scultore. La nascita del Barocco in casa Borghese*, catalogo della mostra, a cura di A. Coliva, S. Schütze, maggio-settembre 1998, Rome 1998.
Anon., *Caravaggio e la collezione Mattei*, catalogo della mostra, aprile-maggio 1995, Milan 1995.
Anon., *Caravaggisti*, Dossier Art, 109, Florence 1996.
Anon., *Da Caravaggio a Ceruti. La scena di genere e l'immagine dei pitocchi nella pittura italiana*, catalogo della mostra, Milan 1998.
Anon., *Domenichino 1581–1641*, catalogo della mostra, ottobre 1996-gennaio 1997, Milan 1996.
Anon., *Il Seicento. Documenti e interpretazioni*, B.S.A./ Ricerche di Storia dell'Arte, 1–2 1976, Rome 1976.
Anon., *La via degli Angeli. Il restauro della decorazione di Ponte Sant'Angelo*, a cura di L. C. Alloisi, M. G. Tolomeo, Rome 1988.
Anon., *Mattia Preti tra Roma, Napoli e Malta*, catalogo della mostra, Naples 1999.
Anon., *Pietro da Cortona 1597–1669*, catalogo della mostra a cura di A. Lo Bianco, ottobre 1997-febbraio 1998, Milan 1997.
Anon., *Pietro da Cortona per la sua terra. Da allievo a maestro*, catalogo della mostra, a cura di R. Contini, febbraio-maggio 1997, Milan 1997.
Anon., *Rubens e il suo secolo*, catalogo della mostra, Ferrara 1999.
Antonazzi G., *Il Palazzo di Propaganda*, Rome 1979.
Argan G. C., *Borromini*, Verona 1952.
Argan G. C., *L'architettura barocca in Italia*, Milan 1957.
Argan G. C., *L'arte barocca*, Geneva 1989.
Aronberg Lavin M., *Barberini inventories*, Princeton 1980.
Bagione G., *Le vite dei pittori, scultori e architetti*, Rome 1942.
Baldinucci F., *Notizie dei professori del disegno da Cimabue in qua, Firenze 1681–1728*, ed. anast. Florence 1847, con nota di P. Barocchi, Florence 1974.
Bassani R., Bellini F., *Caravaggio assassino*, Rome 1994.
Bellori G. P., *Le vite de' pittori, scultori e architetti moderni, Roma 1672*, a cura di G. Previtali, Turin 1976.
Bellori G. P., *Nota delli musei, librerie e gallerie et ornamenti di statue e pitture ne' palazzi, nelle case e Giardini di Roma*, Roma 1664, a cura di E. Zocca, Rome 1976.
Bernardini M. G., *Fagiolo dell'Arco M.*, a cura di, *Bernini regista del Barocco*, catalogo della mostra, Milano 1999.
Bernini D., *Vita del Cavalier Gio Lorenzo Bernino*, Rome 1713.
Bernini G. L., *Fontana di Trevi, commedia inedita* a cura di C. D'Onofrio, Rome 1963.
Blunt A., *The Palazzo Barberini. The contributions of Maderno, Bernini and Pietro da Cortona*, Journal of Warburg and Courtauld Institutes, 20–21, 1958, pp. 258 ss..
Blunt A., *Vita e opere di Borromini*, Bari 1983.
Bodart D., *Les peintres des Pays–bas meridionaux et de la principauté de Liège à Rome au XVIIIème siècle*, Bruselles –Rome 1970.
Bodart D., Rubens, Dossier Art, 44, Florence 1990.
Borromeo F., *De pictura sacra, Milan 1624*, a cura di C. Castiglioni, Sora 1932.
Borromini F., *Opera del Caval. F. Borromini, cavata dai suoi originali, cioè la chiesa e la fabbrica della Sapienza a Roma*, Rome 1720.
Borromini F., *Opus Architectonicum*. Opra del Caval. F. *Borromini cavata dao suoi originali, cioè l'oratorio e la fabbrica per l'abitazione dei PP. dell'oratorio di S. Filippo Neri in Roma*, Rome 1725.
Borsi F., a cura di, *Il Palazzo del Quirinale*, Rome 1972.
Borsi F., *Bernini Architetto. L'Opera completa*, Milan 1980.
Borsi F., *Bernini. La straordinaria avventura umana del genio che trasformò l'architettura in scultura, donando a Roma i capolavori del seducente universo barocco*, Rome 1986.
Borsi F., *La chiesa di S. Andrea al Quirinale*, Rome 1967.
Borsi F., *Roma di Urbano VIII. La pianta di Giovanni Maggi*, 1625, Rome 1990.
Briganti G., *Il Palazzo del Quirinale*, Rome 1962.
Briganti G., *Pietro da Cortona o della pittura barocca*, Florence 1962.
Bussagli M., *Il nudo nell'arte*, Florence 1998.
Bussagli M., *Storia degli Angeli. Racconto di immagini e di idee*, Milan 1992.
Calvesi M., *Caravaggio o la ricerca della salvazione*, Storia dell'Arte, 9–10, 1971, pp. 93–142.
Calvesi M., *Caravaggio*, Dossier Art, 1, 1986.
Calvesi M., *La realtà del Caravaggio*, Turin 1990.
Cappelletti F., Testa L., *Il trattenimento di Virtuosi. Le collezioni secentesche di quadri nei Palazzi Mattei di Roma*, Rome 1994.
Coffin D. R., *Gardens and Gardening in Papal Roma*, Princeton 1991.
Contardi B., *La retorica e l'architettura del Barocco*, Rome 1978.
Corradini S., *Caravaggio. Materiali per un processo*, Rome 1993.
Croce B., *Storia dell'età barocca in Italia*, Bari 1929.
D'Onofrio C., *Acque e fontane di Roma*, Pomezia 1977.
D'Onofrio C., *Gian Lorenzo Bernini e gli angeli di Ponte Sant'Angelo. Storia di un ponte*, Rome 1981.
D'Onofrio C., *Roma nel Seicento*, Rome 1969.
D'Ors E., *Del Barocco*, Milan 1945.
Dacos N., *Les peintres belges à Rome au XVI siècle*, Bruselles – Rome 1964.
De Benedictis C., *Per la storia del collezionismo italiano. Fonti e documenti*, Florence 1991.
Dorati M. C., *Il Bernini e gli angeli di Ponte sant'Angelo nel diario di un contemporaneo*, Commentari, 17,1966, pp. 349–352.
Emiliani A., *Guido Reni*, Dossier Art, 27, 1988.
Fagiolo dell'Arco M., Carandini S., *L'effimero Barocco. Strutture della festa nella Roma del Seicento, I–II*, Rome 1978.
Fagiolo M., a cura di, *La città effimera e l'universo artificiale del giardino*, Rome 1980.
Fagiolo M., Fagiolo dell'Arco M., *Bernini. Una introduzione al "gran teatro del Barocco"*, Rome 1966.
Fagiolo M., Spagnesi G., a cura di, *Immagini del Barocco. Bernini e la cultura del Seicento*, Atti del convegno presso l'Enciclopedia Italiana, Rome 1981.
Fasolo F., *L'opera di Hieronimo e Carlo Rainaldi*, Rome 1960.
Ferrari O., *Bernini*, Dossier Art, 57, 1991.
Ficacci L., *Guercino*, Dossier Art, 61, 1991.
Fokker T. H., *Roma* Baroque Art, Oxford 1933.
Galassi-Paluzzi C., *Storia segreta dello stile dei Gesuiti*, Rome 1951.
Gallo M., *Orazio Borgianni pittore romano (1574–1616) e Francisco de Castro conte di Castro*, Rome 1997.
Ghelfi B., a cura di, *Il libro dei conti del Guercino. 1629–1666*, Bologna 1997.
Gigli G., *Diario Romano (1608–1670)*, a cura di G. Ricciotti, Rome 1959.
Griseri A., *La metamorfosi del Barocco*, Turin 1967.
Hager W., *Barockarchitektur*, Baden-Baden 1968.
Hauser A., *Sozialgeschichte der Kunst und Literatur*, München 1955, tr. it., Storia sociale dell'Arte, I, Turin 1986/16.
Hempel E., *Carlo Rainaldi*, Munich 1919.
Joscelin G., *Athanasius Kircher. A Renaissance man and the Quest for Lost Knowledge*, London 1979.
Kircher A., *Obeliscus Pamphilius, hoc est interpretatio nova et hucsque intentata obelisci hieroglyphici quem non ita pridem ex veteri hippodromo Antonini Caracallae Caesari*, in *Agonale forum transtulit, integritate restituit et in urbis aeternae ornamentum erexit Innocentius X Pont Max*, Rome 1950.
Krautheimer R., *Roma di Alessandro VII. 1655–1667*, Rome 1987.
Lavin I., *Bernini and the Crossing of St. Peter's*, New York 1968.
Lavin I., *Bernini e l'unità delle arti visive*, Rome 1980.
Macioce S., *Undique splendent. Aspetti della pittura sacra nella Roma di Clemente VIII Aldobrandini (1592–1605)*, Rome 1990.
Marini M., *Caravaggio*, Rome 1987.
Marini M., Io, *Michelangelo da Caravaggio*, Rome 1974.
Martinelli V., *Bernini*, Milan 1979.
Martinelli V., *Manierismo, Barocco, Rococò nella scultura italiana*, Milan 1979.
Moir A., *The Italian Followers of Caravaggio*, Cambridge (U.S.A.) 1967.
Montagu J., *A Model by Francesco Mochi for the "Saint Veronica"*, Burlington Magazine, CXXIV, 1982, pp. 430–437.
Montagu J., *Alessandro Algardi*, New Haven-London 1985.
Montagu J., *Roman Baroque Sculpture. The Industry of Art*, New Haven-London 1989, tr. it., La scultura barocca romana. Un'industria dell'arte, Milan 1991.
Morselli R., *Guido Reni: i collezionisti, gli allievi, le copie*, in *La Scuola di Guido Reni*, Modena 1992, pp. 19–25.
Munoz A., Roma barocca, Milan 1928.
Nava Cellini A., *La scultura del Seicento*, Turin 1982.
Negri A., *Fontana di Trevi, Rione Trevi*, Guide Rionali di Roma, Rome 1992.
Negri A., *Guida del Quirinale, Rione Trevi*, Guide di Roma, 1985.
Norberg-Schultz Ch., *Architettura barocca*, Milan 1971.
Pacciarottti G., *La pittura del Seicento*, Turin 1997.
Pascoli L., *Vite de' pittori, scultori e architetti moderni*, Rome 1730–1736.
Passeri G. B., *Vite de' pittori, scultori et architetti che hanno lavorato in Roma morti dall'anno 1641 all'anno 1673*, Roma 1672, a cura di J. Hess, Leipzig – Vienna 1934.
Pericoli Ridolfini C., a cura di, *Guide rionali di Roma. Rione IV Parione, I–II*, Rome 1973–1974.
Petrocchi M., *Roma nel Seicento*, Bologna 1970.
Petrucci C. A., *Catalogo generale delle Stampe tratte dai rami incisi posseduti dalla Calcografia Nazionale*, Rome 1953.
Pietrangeli C., a cura di, *Guide Rionali. Rione V Ponte, I–IV*, Rome 1978–1981.
Pietrangeli C., *Guide rionali di Roma. Rione IX Pigna, I–III*, Rome 1977–1980.
Portoghesi P., *Borromini*, Milan 1984.
Portoghesi P., *Roma barocca*, Bari 1992.
Ripa C., *Iconologia, Siena 1613, rist. anast.* a cura di P. Buscaroli, Milan 1992.
Rivosecchi V., *Esotismo in Roma barocca*. Studi su padre Kircher, Rome 1982.
Salerno L., *Pittori di paesaggio nel Seicento a Roma*, 3 vol., Rome 1977–1980.
Sestrieri G., *Repertorio della pittura romana della fine del Seicento e del Settecento*, 3 vol., Turin 1994.
Strinati C., Vodret R., a cura di, *Caravaggio e i suoi. Percorsi caravaggeschi in Palazzo Barberini*, Naples 1999.
Titi F., *Studio di pittura, scoltura et architettura, nelle chiese di Roma (1674–1763)*, ed. comparata a cura di B. Contardi e S. Romano, 2 vol., 1987.
Verdone M., *Feste e spettacoli a Roma*, Rome 1993.
Wittkower R., *A counter-project to Bernini's "Piazza di San Pietro"*, Journal of the Warbourg and Courtauld Institute, 1–2, 1939–1940, pp. 88–106.
Wittkower R., *Art and Architecture in Italy: 1600 to 1750*, Harmondesworth 1958, tr. it., *Arte e architettura in Italia. 1600–1750*, Turin 1993.
Wittkower R., Jaffe I. B., *Baroque Art: The Jasuit Contribution*, tr. it., *Architettura e arte dei Gesuiti*, Milan 1992.
Wöllflin H., *Renaissance und Barock*, Munich 1888.

THE EIGHTEENTH CENTURY

Anon., *Architettura del Settecento a Roma. Nei disegni della raccolta grafica comunale, catalogo della mostra*, Rome 1991.
Anon., *Baroque and Rococo. Architecture and decoration*, New York 1978.
Anon., *Il Settecento a Roma*, catalogo della mostra, Rome 1959.
Anon., *L'Angelo e la città*, catalogo della mostra, Rome 1987.
Anon., *L'arte per i papi e per i principi nella campagna romana. Grande pittura del '600 e del '700*, catalogo della mostra, Rome 1990 (2 vol.).
Anon., *La problematica del Neoclassicismo, Bollettino del Centro di Studi di Architettura Andrea Palladio, XIII*, 1971.
Anon., *Manierismo, Barocco e Rococò, concetti e termini*, Rome 1962.
Anon., *Piranese et les Français 1740–1790*, catalogo della mostra, Rome 1976.
Anon., *Piranesi nei luoghi di Piranesi*, Rome 1979.
Anon., *Roma splendidissima e magnifica. Luoghi di spettacolo a Roma dall'Umanesimo a oggi*, catalogo della mostra, Milan 1997.
Anon., *Sebastiano Conca*, catalogo della mostra, Gaeta 1981.
Acquaro Graziosi M. T., *L'Arcadia. Trecento anni di storia*, Rome 1991.
Algarotti F., *Saggio sopra la pittura*, Livorno 1763.
Apolloni M. F., *Canova*, Dossier Art, 68, 1992.
Argan G. C., *Antonio Canova*, Rome 1969.
Argan G. C., *Il Neoclassicismo*, a cura di M. Fagiolo dell'Arco, Rome 1968.
Argan G. C., *L'Europa delle capitali*, Geneva-Milan 1965.
Arisi F., *Gian Paolo Panini e i fasti della Roma del '700*, Rome 1986.
Arisi F., *Gian Paolo Panini*, Cremona 1992.
Assunta R., *Infinita contemplazione*, Naples 1979.
Assunta R., *Specchio vivente del mondo (Artisti stranieri a Roma 1600–1800)*, Rome 1980.
Bandini C., *Roma nel Settecento*, Rome 1930 (2 vol.).
Barroero L., a cura di, *Guide rionali di Roma*. Rione I, Monti I–IV, Rome 1978–1984.
Bartoccini F., *Roma nell'Ottocento. Il tramonto della "città santa". Nascita di una capitale*, Bologna 1985.
Battisti E., *Lione Pascoli scrittore d'arte, Rendiconti dell'Accademia dei Lincei. Classe di scienze morali, VIII*, 1953, pp. 122–150.
Baumgarte S., *Les oeuvres de Camillo Rusconi à Rome, Revue de l'art ancien et moderne*, 70, 1936, pp. 233–238.
Belli Barsali I., a cura di, *Pompeo Batoni, catalogo della mostra*, Lucca 1967.
Belli Barsali I., *Ville di Roma*, Milan 19832.
Benisovich N. M., *Ghezzi and the French Artists in Rome*, Apollo, n.s., 63, 1967, pp. 340–347.
Bentivoglio E., *Palazzo Marucelli a Roma. Architettura di Sebastiano Cipriani*, in *L'architettura da Clemente XI a Benedetto XIV. Pluralità di tendenze*, a cura di E. Debenedetti, Rome 1989, pp. 15–32.
Berliner R., *Zeichnungen von Carlo und Filippo Marchionni*, München Jahrbuch der Bildenden Kunst, 1958–1959, pp. 267–396.
Bernardini B., *Descrizione del nuovo ripartimento de' rioni di Roma fatto per ordine di N.S. Papa Benedetto XIV*, Rome 1744.
Bevilacqua M., *Casa Giannini a piazza Capranica e la tipologia del palazzo ad appartamenti nella Roma di metà 1700*, in *L'architettura da Clemente XI a Benedetto XIV. Pluralità di tendenze*, a cura di E. Debenedetti, Rome 1989, pp. 205–220.
Bodart D., *Disegni giovanili inediti di P. L. Ghezzi nella Biblioteca Vaticana*, Palatino, XI, 1967, pp. 141–154.
Borsi F., a cura di, *Arte a Roma dal Neoclassicismo al Romanticismo*, Rome 1979.
Bottari G. G., *Dialoghi sopra le arti del disegno*, Lucca 1750.
Bottari G. G., *Raccolte di lettere sulla pittura, scultura e architettura*, Roma 1754–1773, ed. a cura di S. Ticozzi, Milan 1822–1825 (7 vol.).
Braham A., Hager H., Carlo Fontana. *The Drawing at Windsor Castle*, London 1977.
Briganti G., a cura di, *La pittura in Italia. Il Settecento, I–II*, Milan 1990.
Busiri vici A., *Andrea Locatelli e il paesaggio romano del Settecento*, Rome 1976.
Cagiano de Azvedo M., *Il gusto del restauro delle opere d'arte antiche*, Rome 1948.
Camesasca E., *L'opera completa del Bellotto*, Milan 1974.
Cavazzi L., *Piranesi e la veduta di Roma del Settecento a Roma, Bollettino dei Musei Comunali di Roma*, Rome 1990, pp. 143–147.
Ceccarelli S., *Carlo Marchionno e la Sagrestia Vaticana*, in *Carlo Marchionni. Architettura, decorazione e scenografia contemporanea*, a cura di E. Debenedetti, Rome 1988, pp. 57–134.
Ceschi C., *Le chiese di Roma dagli inizi del Neoclassicismo al 1961*, Bologna 1963.
Chyurlia R., *Pompeo Batoni o del classicismo settecentesco*, Emporium, 117, 1953, pp. 56–67.
Ciucci G., *Piazza del Popolo, storia, architettura, urbanistica*, Rome 1973.
Clark A. M., *Batoni's Professional Career and Style*, in *Studies in Italia Art and Architecture. Fifteenth through Eighteenth Centuries*, a cura di H. A. Milton, Cambridge (U.S.A.) – London 1980, pp. 323–337.
Clark A. M., *Sebastiano Conca and the Roman Rococo*, Apollo, n.s., 63, 1967, pp. 328–335.
Clark A., *Pompeo Batoni*, a cura di E. P. Brown, Oxford 1985.
Cocchetti L., *Pompeo Batoni e il neoclassicismo a Roma*, Commentari, 4, 1952, pp. 274–289.
Contardi B., Curcio G., a cura di, In *Urbe architectus. La professione dell'architetto.* Roma 1680–1750, catalogo della mostra, Rome 1991.
Crescimbeni G. M., *Stato della basilica di S.Maria in Cosmedin di Roma nel presente anno MDCCXIX*, Rome 1719.
Cretoni A., Roma giacobina. *Storia della Repubblica Romana 1798–1799*, Rome 1971.
Croce B., *L'Arcadia e la poesia del Settecento, in B. Croce, La letteratura italiana nel Settecento*, Bari 1949, pp. 1–18.
Curcio G., *L'area di Montecitorio. La città pubblica e la città privata nella Roma della prima metà del Settecento*, in E. Debenedetti, a cura di, *Studi sul Settecento romano e l'architettura da Clemente XI a Benedetto XIV*. Pluralità di tendenze, 5, 1989, pp. 157–204.
D'Avossa A., *Andrea Sacchi*, Rome 1985.
D'Onofrio C., *Acque e fontane di Roma*, Pomezia 1977.
D'Onofrio C., *Il Tevere a Roma*, Rome 1970.
D'Onofrio C., *Scalinate di Roma*, Rome 1973.
Damming E., *Il movimento giansenista a Roma nella seconda metà del secolo XVIII*, Vatican city 1945.
De Rossi G., *Studio di architettura civile*, Rome 1702–1722, 3 vol.
Debenedetti E., a cura di, *Carlo Marchionni. Architettura, decorazione e scenografia contemporanea*, Studi sul Settecento romano, 4, 1988.
Debenedetti E., a cura di, *Committenza Albani. Note sulla Villa Albani-Torlonia, Studi sul Settecento romano, 1–2*, 1985–1986.
Debenedetti E., a cura di, *L'architettura da Clemente XI a Benedetto XIV. Pluralità di tendenze*, Studi sul Settecento romano, 5, 1989.
Debenedetti E., a cura di, *Valadier segno e architettura*, catalogo della mostra, Rome 1985.
Debenedetti E., a cura di, *Ville e palazzi, illusione scenica e miti archeologici, Studi sul Settecento romano, 3*, 1987.
Debenedetti E., *La pittura del Settecento a Roma. Da Clemente XI a Benedetto XIV*, Rome 1991.
Delli S., *Le strade di Roma*, Rome 1975.
Di Federico F., *Francesco Trevisani and the Decoration of the Crucifixion Chapel in San Silvestro in Capite*, The Art Bulletin, LIII, 1971, pp. 52–67.
Di Federico F., *Francesco Trevisani*, Washington 1977.
Engass R., *Early Eighteenth-Century Sculpture in Roma*, London 1976, 2 vol.
Faccioli C., *Giovan Battista Nelli e la sua gran "Piante di Roma" del 1748*, Studi Romani, 14, 1966, pp. 415–422.
Fagiolo M., a cura di, *Festa a Roma. Dal Rinascimento al 1870*, catalogo della mostra, Milan 1997.
Falcidia G., *Per una definizione del "caso" Benefial*, Paragone, XXIX, 1978, pp. 24–51.
Faldi I., *Gli inizi del Neoclassicismo in pittura nella prima metà del Settecento*, in Anon., *Nuove idee e nuova arte nel Settecento italiano, Atti dei Convegni Lincei*, Rome 1977, pp. 495–523.
Fontana C., *L'Anfiteatro Flavio o Colosseo descritto e delineato*, L'Aja 1725.
Fruntaz A. P., a cura di, *Le piante di Roma*, Rome 1962, 3 vol..
Giovannoni G., *Il Settecento*, in F. Castagnoli, C. Cecchelli, G. Giovannoni, M. Zocca, a cura di, *Topografia urbanistica di Roma*, Bologna 1958, pp. 455–470.
Giuntella V. E., *Roma nel Settecento*, Rome 1971.
Golzio V., *Palazzi romani dalla rinascita al Neoclassicismo*, Bologna 1971.
Golzio V., *Seicenti e Settecenti*, Turin 1950.
Gombrich E. M., *Arte e progresso. Storia e influenza di un'idea*, Bari 1985.
Gradara C., *Pietro Bracci, scultore romano, 1700–1773*, Milan 1920.
Gross H., *Rome in the Age of Enlightement. The post-Tridentine syndrome and the ancien regime*, Cambridge 1990, tr. it., Roma nel Settecento, Bari 1990.
Hugh H., *Filippo della Valle, The Connoisseur, 1959*, pp. 172–179.
Hugh H., *Neoclassicism*, Harmondsworth 1968.
Kieven E., a cura di, *Ferdinando Fuga e l'architettura romana del Settecento. I disegni di architettura delle collezioni del Gabinetto Nazionale delle Stampe: il Settecento*, catalogo della mostra, Rome 1988.
Lavagnino E., *Roma nel Settecento*, in Anon., *Il Settecento a Roma*, catalogo della mostra, Rome 1959, pp. 17–23.
Lefevre R., *Palazzo Chigi*, Roma 1973.
Loret M., *Attività ignota di Filippo Juvarra a Roma*, Critica d'Arte, 1936, pp. 198–201.
Loret M., *I pittori napoletani a Roma nel Settecento*, Capitolium, 1934, pp. 541–555.
Mallory N. A., *Notizie sulla pittura romana del XVIII secolo (1718–1760)*, Bollettino d'Arte, LXI, 1976, pp. 102–113.
Mallory N. A., *Roman Rococo Architecture from Clement XI to Bendict XIV*, New York 1977.
Mancini C. M., *Le "Memorie del Cav. Leone Ghezzi scritte da sé medesimo da gennaio 1731 al lugluio 1734"*, Palatino, XII, 1968, pp. 480–487.
Martinelli V., *Un modello di Francesco Trevisani per il profeta Baruch nella basilica lateranense*, Arte Veneta, XXXII, 1978, pp. 376–382.
Matteucci E., *L'architettura nel Settecento*, Turin 1988.
Milizia F., *Principi di architettura civile*, Bassano 17482.
Mortari L., *S. Maria Maddalena*, Rome 1987.
Moschini V., *Filippo della Valle*, L'Arte, 1925, pp. 177–190.
Moschini V., *Giaquinto artista rappresentativo della pittura barocca tarda a Roma*, L'Arte, 1924, pp. 104–123.
Munoz A., *Antonio Canova. Le opere*, Rome 1957.
Nava Cellini A., *La scultura del Settecento*, Turin 1982.
Negro A., a cura di, *Fontana di Trevi, Guide rionali di Roma. Rione II* Trevi, Rome 1992.
Norbrg-Schultz Ch., *Architettura tardobarocca*, Milan 19893.
Pane R., Ferdinando Fuga, Naples 1956.
Pascoli L., *Vite de' Pittori, Scultori et Architetti moderni, I–II*, Roma 1730–1736, a cura di V. Martinelli, Perugia 1993.
Portoghesi R., *Roma barocca*, Bari-Rome 1992.
Pozzo A., *Prospettiva di Pittori e Architetti di Andrea Pozzo della Compagnia di Gesù a Roma, I–II*, Rome 1693–1700.
Sander O., a cura di, *Angelika Kauffmann e Roma*, catalogo della mostra, Rome 1998.
Sassoli M. G., *Apparati architettonici per fuochi d'artificio a Roma nel Settecento*, Milan 1994.
Sestieri G., *La pittura nel Settecento*, Turin 1988.
Titi F., *Studio di pittura, scoltura et architettura, nelle chiese di Roma (1674–1763)*, edizione comparata a cura di B. Contardi e S. Romano, Rome 1987, 2 vol..
Winckelmann J. J., *Geschichte der Kunst des Aterthums*, Dresden 1764.
Wittkower R., *Art and Architecture in Italy: 1600 to 1750*, Harmondesworth 1958, tr. it., *Arte e architettura in Italia. 1600–1750*, Turin 1993.

FROM THE NINETEENTH TO THE TWENTIETH CENTURY

Arte moderna in Italia 1915–1935, catalogo della mostra a cura di C. L. Ragghianti, Florence 1967.
Artisti Collezionisti Mostre negli anni di Primato. 1940–1943, catalogo della mostra a cura di A. Masi e P. Vivarelli, Rome 1996.
Aspetti dell'arte a Roma, 1870–1914, catalogo della mostra a cura di D. Durbé, Rome 1972.
Benzi F., *Carena 1919–1924: dal "ritorno all'ordine" alla Scuola degli Orti Sallustiani*, in *Le Capitali d'Italia*. Turin-Rome 1911–1946, catalogo della mostra a cura di M. Vescovo e N. Vespignani, Turin 1997.
Benzi F., *Materiali inediti dall'archivio di Cipriano Efisio Oppo*, Bollettino d'Arte, nn. 37–38, maggio-agosto 1986.
Benzi F., *Scuole e tendenze nell'arte romana degli anni Trenta*, in *Le Scuole Romane, sviluppi e continuità*, catalogo della mostra a cura di F. Benzi, R. Lambarelli, E. Mascelloni, Verona 1988.
Bossaglia R., *Il "Novecento Italiano"*, Milan 1979.
Calvesi M., *La metafisica schiarita*, Milan 1982.
Damigella A. M., *La pittura simbolista in Italia, 1885–1900*, Turin 1981.
De Libero L., *Un po' di prefazione e un po' di storia*, Letteratura, n. 89, 1954.
Divisionismo romano, catalogo della mostra a cura di L. Stefanelli Torossi, Rome 1989.
E'42. *L'Esposizione universale di Roma. Utopia e scenario del regime*, catalogo della mostra a cura di M. Calvesi, E. Guidoni, S. Lux, Rome 1987.
Fagiolo M., *Scuola Romana*, Rome 1986.
Fossati P., *"Valori Plastici" 1918–1922*, Turin 1981.
Gli anni del Premio Bergamo. Arte in Italia intorno agli anni Trenta, catalogo della mostra a cura di M. Argentieri e P. Vivarelli, Bergamo 1993.
Gli artisti di Villa Strohl-Fern, catalogo della mostra a cura di L. Stefanelli Torossi, Rome 1983.
Guttuso Pirandello Ziveri. *Realismo a Roma, 1938–1943*, catalogo della mostra a cura di F. D'Amico, Rome 1995.
Il Novecento Italiano 1923/1933, catalogo della mostra a cura di R. Bossaglia, Milan 1983.
La Metafisica: gli anni Venti, catalogo della mostra a cura di R. Barilli e F. Solmi, Bologna 1980.
Les Réalismes 1919–1939, catalogo della mostra a cura di J. Clair, Parigi 1981.
Miti del '900. Letteratura-Arte, catalogo della mostra a cura di Z. Birolli, Milan 1979.
Pacini P., *Intorno al numero cubista di "Valori Plastici"*, Critica d'Arte, nn. 175-177, 1981.
Pirani F., *Le Biennali Romane*, in *Il Palazzo delle Esposizioni*, catalogo della mostra a cura di R. Siligato e M. E. Tittoni, Rome 1991.
Realismo Magico, catalogo della mostra a cura di M. Fagiolo, Verona 1988.
Roma 1911, catalogo della mostra a cura di G. Piantoni, Rome 1980.
Roma 1918–1943, catalogo della mostra a cura di F. Benzi, Rome 1998.
Roma 1934, catalogo della mostra a cura di G. Appella e F. D'Amico, Modena e Rome 1986.
Secessione Romana 1913–1916, catalogo della mostra a cura di R. Bossaglia, P. Spadini, M. *Quesada*, Rome 1987.
Siligato R., *Le due anime del Palazzo: il Museo Artistico Industriale e la Società degli Amatori e Cultori di Belle Arti*, in *Il Palazzo delle Esposizioni*, catalogo della mostra a cura di R. Siligato e M. E. Tittoni, Rome 1991.
Verdone M., Pagnotta F., Bidetti M., *La Casa d'Arte Bragaglia 1918–1930*, Rome 1992.
Zambrotta T., *Le esposizioni del Sindacato Laziale Fascista degli artisti 1929-1942*, in *Il Palazzo delle Esposizioni*, catalogo della mostra a cura di R. Siligato e M. E. Tittoni, Rome 1991.

Index of Names

669

Index of Work

Photographic Credits

Accademia Nazionale dei Lincei: 464–465
Archivi Alinari – Florence: 132, 133
Archivio Arco Farnese: 632, 633, 634, 636, 637 (left and right), 640, 641, 642, 643, 644, 645, 646, 647, 650, 651, 652
Archivio Fotografico Monumenti, Musei e Gallerie Pontificie: 26, 36, 48, 59, 64 (top), 73, 82–83, 96, 97, 124, 125, 143 (right and left), 145, 164, 168–169, 182 (bottom), 190–191, 232, 237, 238, 239, 244–245, 266–267, 270–271, 272–273, 281, 322, 327, 338–339, 340, 341, 376–377, 378–379, 380, 382, 383, 384–385, 386, 387, 388–389, 390 (top and bottom), 391, 393 (top and bottom), 394–395, 416, 422 (left), 424, 440 (left and right), 441, 442–443, 444–445, 446, 447, 448, 449 (top and bottom), 450, 451, 452 (right), 453, 454–455, 456–457, 459, 460, 461, 462 (top and bottom), 463, 466, 468, 470, 471, 472–473, 475, 479 (top), 508, 554 (top), 562 (top), 566
Archivio Fotografico SAR: 15, 19 (top), 28 (right), 74, 75 (top and bottom), 98, 99, 100 (top), 101 (right), 154, 155 (bottom)
Archivio G.N.A.M.: 631, 648, 654
Archivio Magnus: 29 (bottom–Marton), 33 (top–Marton), 38 (bottom–Vasari), 39 (Vasari), 58 (Listri), 62 (Marton), 38 (bottom–Vasari), 39 (Vasari), 58 (Listri), 62 (Marton), 92 (Vannini), 93 (Vannini), 100 (bottom–Scopel), 138 (bottom–Listri), SESTINO 144–145 (Listri), 156 (Magliani), 162–163 (Magliani), 166 (Magliani), 167 (Magliani), 176 (Marton), 194 (Magliani), 195 (bottom–Magliani), 205 (Magliani), 206 (Magliani), 211 (Magliani), 212 (Magliani), 213 (Magliani), 215 (Magliani), 216 (Magliani), 219 (Magliani), 220 (top–Magliani), 221 (Magliani), 224 (Magliani), 226 (Magliani), 227 (top and bottom–Magliani), 228 (Magliani), 229 (Magliani), 230–231 (Magliani), 233 (Magliani), 234 (top–Magliani), 234 (bottom–Listri), 235 (Magliani), 240 (Magliani), 242 (Magliani), 243 (Magliani), 247 (Magliani), 248 (Magliani), 250 (Magliani), 251 (Magliani), 252 (Magliani), 253 (Magliani), 256 (Magliani), 257 (Magliani), 258–259 (Magliani), 260 (Magliani), 261 (Magliani), 262 (left and right–Magliani), 263 (Magliani), 264 (Magliani), 265 (Magliani), 268 (Magliani), 269 (Magliani), 274 (Magliani), 275 (Magliani), 276 (Magliani), 277 (Magliani), 278 (Magliani), 286 (Magliani), 287 (Magliani), 288 (Magliani), 290 (Magliani), 291 (Magliani), 292–293 (Magliani), 294 (Magliani), 295 (Magliani), 296–397 (Magliani), 301 (left and right–Magliani), 302 (left–Magliani), 303 (left–Magliani), 304 (Magliani), 305 (Magliani), 307 (top and bottom–Magliani), 309 (Magliani), 312–313 (Magliani), 315 (Magliani), 316 (Magliani), 317 (Magliani), 318 (top and bottom–Magliani), 319 (Magliani), 320–321 (Magliani), 323 (Magliani), 342–343 (Magliani), 344 (Vasari), 349 (top–Listri), 350 (Listri), 351 (Magliani), 356 (bottom–Listri), 357 (Listri), 358 (Magliani), 359 (left–Magliani), 361 (Magliani), 363 (Magliani), 367 (Magliani), 268 (Magliani), 369 (left–Magliani), 373 (Magliani), 375 (Magliani), 381 (Magliani), 392 (Magliani), 396

(Magliani), 397 (Magliani), 398 (Magliani), 399 (Magliani), 400 (Magliani), 401 (Magliani), 403 (Magliani), 404 (bottom–Magliani), 405 (Listri), 406 (top–Listri), 406 (bottom–Magliani), 407 (left–Listri), 410–411 (Listri), 411 (Listri), 412 (bottom–Magliani), 413 (Magliani), 417 (top and bottom–Listri), 418 (top and bottom–Magliani), 419 (Magliani), 420 (top–Listri), 420 (bottom–Magliani), 421 (Magliani), 422 (right–Magliani), 423 (left–Magliani), 425 (Magliani), 426 (left and right–Magliani), 428 (Magliani), 429 (Magliani), 430 (Magliani), 431 (Magliani), 433 (Magliani), 434 (right–Magliani), 435 (Listri), 436 (Magliani), 437 (Magliani), 438 (Listri), 439 (Magliani), 452 (left–Magliani), 458 (Listri), 469 (Magliani), 474 (Magliani), 477 (top and bottom–Listri), 478 (top and bottom–Listri), 479 (top–Magliani), 480 (Magliani), 481 (Magliani), 486–487 (Listri), 492 (Listri), 493 (Listri), 495 (bottom–Magliani), 496 (top and bottom–Magliani), 497 (top–Magliani), 497 (bottom–Listri), 501 (Listri), 502 (top and bottom–Listri), 503 (Marton), 504 (Magliani), 505 (top and bottom–Magliani), 513 (top–Magliani), 516 (Listri), 518 (top– Magliani), 518 (bottom–Listri), 519 (Magliani), 520 (top–Listri), 520 (bottom–Marton), 521 (top and bottom–Listri), 522 (top and bottom–Listri), 523 (top and bottom–Listri), 524 (top and bottom–Listri), 525 (top and bottom–Listri), 526 (Magliani), 527 (right–Magliani), 530 (right–Listri), 531 (Listri), 532 (Listri), 533 (Listri), 534 (Listri), 535 (Listri), 537 (left–Mastrorillo), 539 (Listri), 540 (Listri), 541 (top–Listri), 546 (top–Listri), 546 (bottom–Magliani), 549 (bottom–Listri), 551, 555 (top and bottom–Magliani), 556 (top–Magliani), 556 (bottom–Listri), 557 (Listri), 558 (Listri), 561 (Magliani), 563 (Listri), 565 (top and bottom–Listri), 567 (Magliani), 571 (Listri), 573 (Magliani), 574 (Magliani), 575 (left and right–Magliani), 578 (Listri), 579 (Listri), 580 (Marton), 584 (Magliani), 585 (top and bottom–Listri), 586–587 (Magliani), 590 (left–Magliani), 590 (right–Morselli), 591 (Morselli), 592 (bottom–Marton), 593 (top–Magliani), 593 (bottom–Listri), 594 (top and bottom–Listri), 595 (Listri), 596 (left and right–Magliani), 597 (left and right–Magliani), 599 (right–Listri), 603 (Listri), 604 (top–Magliani), 605 (Vasari), 606 (Listri), 608 (Listri), 609 (top left–Magliani), 609 (top right–Listri),609 (bottom right–Listri), 610 (top and bottom–Listri), 611 (Listri), 612 (top and bottom–Listri), 613 (top and bottom–Listri), 621 (Listri)
Arte Fotografica: 572
Arti Doria Pamphilj: 549 (top)
Biblioteca Apostolica Vaticana: 171 (bottom), 177, 298, 300 (left), 407 (right), 494 (top and bottom)
Biblioteca Nazionale Centrale di Roma: 495 (top)
British Museum, London: 171 (top)
Bruno, Giuseppe: 29 (top), 31 (left top and bottom), 32 (top and bottom), 141 (top and bottom)
Collezioni private: 619 (top), 638–639
Dagli Orti, Giovanni: 127

De Luca, Araldo: 17, 18, 19 (bottom), 27, 30, 34, 43, 44, 47, 50 (top and bottom), 51, 52, 53, 54, 56–57, 60–61, 63, 66, 68–69, 71, 72, 87, 113, 116, 123 (top and bottom), 134, 136, 137 (top), 138 (top), 139, 144, 225, 283, 488, 559, 567 (bottom)
De Masi, Lorenzo: 49, 128–129
École Nationale Supérieur des Beaux–Arts, Paris,: 14, 37, 117 (top), 120–121, 142
Foto Archivio Fabbrica di San Pietro in Vaticano: 178, 192–193, 279 (top and bottom), 359 (right), 360, 408–409, 432 (left), 527 (left), 536, 537 (right), 542, 543 (top and bottom), 547, 548, 598 (left and right), 599 (left), 604 (bottom)
Foto Massimo Borchi/Archivio Fotografico SIE: 348–349
I.C.C.D.: 106, 107, 110
Istituto Archeologico Germanico – Roma: 112, 130, 137 (bottom)
Istituto Fotografico Editoriale Scala: 40, 41, 45, 140, 180 (top and bottom), 184, 185, 195 (top), 199 (top and bottom), 202 (top), 218, 249, 282, 289, 299, 302 (right), 306, 314, 324–325, 326, 330, 335, 370, 371, 372 (top and bottom), 402, 404 (top), 427, 509 (top), 530 (left), 550, 560, 564, 616–617, 618, 620, 622 (top and bottom), 623, 624–625, 626, 627
Kunsthistorisches Museum, Vienna: 81
Listri, Massimo: 11, 38 (top), 79, 170 (bottom), 355, 364–365, 366, 414, 592 (top), 607 (top and bottom)
Magliani, Mauro: 432 (right), 434 (left), 467, 489, 490–491, 509 (bottom), 517, 554 (bottom), 562 (bottom)
Martin, Joseph /Archivio L.A.R.A.: 108–109
Museo d'Arte Moderna e Contemporanea di Trento e Rovereto: 635
Ny Carlsberg Glyptotek, Copenhagen,: 65
Parrocchia di Santa Maria in Campitelli: 300 (right)
Pedicini, Luciano: 67, 70, 101 (left), 102, 432 (right), 476
Pontificia Commissione di Archeologia Sacra: 155 (top), 157, 158, 165, 170 (top), 179, 181, 182 (top), 183, 186 (top and bottom), 188, 189, 196, 197, 198, 200, 202 (bottom), 203, 204
Renzoni, Valentino: 64 (bottom)
Sciandrone, Franco: 303 (right)
Simeone, Giovanni /Archivio Sime: 11 (bottom), 12, 13, 16, 21, 22, 23, 24–25, 28 (left), 33 (bottom), 34–35, 84, 88–89, 90–91, 94, 95, 104, 105, 111, 117 (bottom), 118–119, 122 (top and bottom), 131, 146, 147, 148, 149, 150, 151, 152, 153, 214, 236, 412 (top), 414–415, 498–499, 500, 513 (bottom), 514–515, 538, 541 (bottom), 580–581, 602–603
Vasari, Archivio: 20, 78–79, 85, 88, 159, 173, 174, 175, 207 (top and bottom), 208, 209, 217, 220 (bottom), 241, 246, 308, 331, 332–333, 345 (top), 346–347, 354, 355 (bottom), 356 (top), 369 (right), 482, 483, 484, 485, 512 (left and right), 568, 569, 570, 619 (bottom), 628–629, 630, 655
Veggi, Giulio /Archivio White Star: 31 (right)